UNIVERSITY CASEBOOK SERIES®

LAW AND RELIGION

CASES AND MATERIALS

FOURTH EDITION

LESLIE C. GRIFFIN
William S. Boyd Professor of Law
University of Nevada, Las Vegas, William S. Boyd School of Law

FOUNDATION
PRESS

University Casebook Series is a trademark registered in the U.S. Patent and Trademark Office.

© 2007, 2010 THOMSON REUTERS/FOUNDATION PRESS
© 2013 LEG, Inc. d/b/a West Academic Publishing
© 2017 LEG, Inc. d/b/a West Academic
    444 Cedar Street, Suite 700
    St. Paul, MN 55101
    1-877-888-1330

Printed in the United States of America

ISBN: 978-1-63460-523-6

For William S. Boyd

and

*My Students and Colleagues at
UNLV Boyd School of Law*

ACKNOWLEDGMENTS

The law of law and religion has changed considerably since the first edition of this book was published in 2007. This fourth edition has been restructured to reflect these developments. The Court has issued significant opinions interpreting both RFRA (the Religious Freedom Restoration Act) and RLUIPA (the Religious Land Use and Institutionalized Persons Act). Both Establishment and Free Exercise jurisprudence have been transformed by the Court's prayer decision in *Town of Greece v. Galloway* and its ministerial-exception decision in *Hosanna-Tabor v. E.E.O.C.* Thus the first seven chapters address constitutional and statutory protection of religious freedom and establishment jurisprudence as they are interpreted in 2016. Later chapters include specialty topics—comparative religious freedom, religion and politics, and science and religion—that can be assigned according to student and professor interest.

I learned from teaching different subjects from numerous casebooks that constant ellipses and brackets are distracting to readers. Hence in this edition I use ellipses only where necessary to avoid confusion and brackets to indicate where I have added text to the original.

I am grateful to Tessa Boury at Foundation Press for her encouragement and sponsorship of this new edition. UNLV law students Katherine Frank, Paige Foley, Gabriel Czop, and Kelsey Stegall contributed numerous suggestions and edits. Jennifer Gross, Head of Collections at UNLV's law library, was invaluable in assisting with research and finding sources. Mayara Cueto-Diaz worked her technical magic on the manuscript. Contributors to the earlier editions are remembered in the following paragraphs.

Many generous people helped me to produce this casebook. For excellent research assistance, I thank Billy C. Allen, David N. Chang, Kang Chen, Bryan P. Dahlberg, Yvonne Ho, Ana Lee Sanchez Jacobs, Jeremy L. Moore, Sabrina A. Neff, Keri L. Tonn, and Lloyd Van Oostenrijk for their work on the first edition. Subsequent supplements and the second edition were enhanced by the hard work of Craig Conway, Heather Cook, Brett Covington, Laura Cox, Walter Cubberly, Sarah Nealis Furbee, Donna Haynes, Meredith Johnson, Amanda Mitchell, Misty Morales, Nick Oweyssi, Rebekah Reed, Michael Schakow, Charlotte Simon, William Taylor, Claudia Trevino, Faisal Vellani, and Brian Winegar. David McClure, Head of Research and Curriculum Services at UNLV, devoted enormous time and energy to researching, proofreading, and cite-checking the third edition.

I have also profited from the insights of students who took my seminar in law and religion at the University of Nevada, Las Vegas, Boyd School of Law; the University of Houston Law Center; the University of Alabama School of Law; and Santa Clara University

School of Law. The University of Houston Law Center supported the first two editions with a research grant. Mon Yin Lung, Ellen B. Koch, Coby C. Nathanson, Nicole Brothers, and Peter Egler assisted with the detailed assistance that only a library staff can give. My colleagues at the University of Houston, especially David Crump, Victor Flatt, Doug Moll, Craig Joyce, Joan Krause, Gerry Moore, Michael Olivas, Irene Merker Rosenberg, Richard Saver, Stacey Tovino, Jacqueline Weaver, and Steve Zamora provided helpful advice about the text and their own areas of expertise. Miriam Cherry, Margaret Imber, Mark Strasser, Chip Phinney, Alison Tucher, Dinah Shelton, Anita Bernstein and Jeff Kahn also helped by reading drafts. Good advice about publishing a casebook came from Steve Errick, Barbara Babcock, Robert Drinan, Tom Grey, Robert Rabin, and Kathleen Sullivan. Sandra Hoffpauir, Nadia Mosqueda, Michelle Ozuna, April Moreno, Chivonne Trigo, Edina Dervisefendic, Ana Aguirre, Mary Chapa, and Lucy Duran provided invaluable assistance with the production of the manuscript. I thank them all for their generosity in working so hard on my behalf.

I would like to thank the authors and copyright holders of the following works, who permitted their inclusion in this book:

Bellah, Robert, "Civil Religion in America," Daedalus, 96:1 (Winter, 1967) pp. 1–21, copyright ©1967 by the American Academy of Arts and Sciences. Reprinted with the permission of the author and Daedalus;

Blitt, Robert C., Should New Bills of Rights Address Emerging International Rights Norms? The Challenge of "Defamation of Religion," 9 Northwestern University Journal of International Human Rights 1, 10–11, 17–25 (2010), copyright © 2010. Reprinted with permission of Robert C. Blitt and the Northwestern University Journal of International Human Rights;

Bray, Zachary, "RLUIPA and the Limits of Religious Institutionalism," 2016 Utah L. Rev. 41, copyright © 2016. Reprinted with permission of the author;

Brunson, Samuel, "Stuck in the Middle With . . . the IRS?, The Surley Subgroup Blog, copyright © 2016. Reprinted with permission of the author;

Deutsch, Elizabeth. "Expanding Conscience, Shrinking Care," 124 Yale L.J. 2470, 2477–83 (2015), copyright © 2015. Reprinted with the permission of the author and the Yale Law Journal;

Griffin, Leslie, "We Do Not Preach. We Teach.": Religion Professors and the First Amendment, 19 Quinnipiac Law Review 1, 9–26, copyright © 2000. Reprinted with the permission of the author and Quinnipiac Law Review Association;

Kuo, David, Appleism is a New Religion, copyright © 2007, available at http://blog.beliefnet.com/jwalking/2007/06/appleism-kuo.html, June 25, 2007. Reprinted with permission from Beliefnet;

Oxford University Press. The Scripture quotations contained herein are from the New Revised Standard Version Bible, copyright © 1989 by the Division of Christian Education of the National Council of the Churches of Christ in the U.S.A., and are used by permission. All rights reserved;

Pew Research Center on Religion & Public Life, "America's Changing Religious Landscape," http://www.pewforum.org/2015/05/12/americas-changing-religious-landscape/, copyright © 2015. Reprinted with permission of the Pew Research Center;

Rawls, John, The Idea of Public Reason Revisited, 64 University of Chicago Law Review 765, 765–68, 773–76, 784–86, 797–99, 805–06, copyright © 1997. Reprinted with permission of the Estate of John Rawls through Margaret Fox Rawls and the University of Chicago Law Review;

Smart, Ninian, The World's Religions (2nd edition), pp. 11–12, 13–22, copyright © 1989, 1998 Ninian Smart. Reprinted with the permission of Cambridge University Press and the Estate of Ninian Smart.

SUMMARY OF CONTENTS

TABLE OF CONTENTS

TABLE OF CASES

The principal cases are in bold type.

TABLE OF AUTHORITIES

LAW AND RELIGION

CASES AND MATERIALS

FOURTH EDITION

CHAPTER 1

FREE EXERCISE OF "RELIGION"

The First Amendment to the United States Constitution states that Congress shall "make no law respecting an establishment of religion or prohibiting the free exercise thereof." As you read the following cases, ask yourself what groups, organizations, or beliefs qualify as "religious." Then consider whether and in what circumstances the U.S. Constitution allows Congress or the states to restrict the free exercise of religion.

A. WHAT IS FREE EXERCISE?

Reynolds v. United States*
Supreme Court of the United States, 1878.
98 U.S. 145, 8 Otto 145, 25 L.Ed. 244.

■ MR. CHIEF JUSTICE WAITE delivered the opinion of the court.

. . .

5. Should the accused have been acquitted if he married the second time, because he believed it to be his religious duty? . . .

On the trial, the plaintiff in error, the accused, proved that at the time of his alleged second marriage he was, and for many years before had been, a member of the Church of Jesus Christ of Latter-Day Saints, commonly called the Mormon Church, and a believer in its doctrines; that it was an accepted doctrine of that church "that it was the duty of male members of said church, circumstances permitting, to practise polygamy; . . . that this duty was enjoined by different books which the members of said church believed to be of divine origin, and among others the Holy Bible, and also that the members of the church believed that the practice of polygamy was directly enjoined upon the male members thereof by the Almighty God, in a revelation to Joseph Smith, the founder and prophet of said church; that the failing or refusing to practise polygamy by such male members of said church, when circumstances would admit, would be punished, and that the penalty for such failure and refusal would be damnation in the life to come." He also proved "that he had received permission from the recognized authorities in said church to enter into polygamous marriage; . . . that Daniel H. Wells, one having authority in said church to perform the

---

* Text omissions are indicated by three dots. Editor's added information is indicated by [ ]. There is no indication when footnotes are omitted. When they do appear, footnotes are numbered as in the material quoted.—Eds.

marriage ceremony, married the said defendant on or about the time the crime is alleged to have been committed, to some woman by the name of Schofield, and that such marriage ceremony was performed under and pursuant to the doctrines of said church."

Upon this proof he asked the court to instruct the jury that if they found from the evidence that he "was married as charged—if he was married—in pursuance of and in conformity with what he believed at the time to be a religious duty, that the verdict must be 'not guilty.' " This request was refused, and the court did charge "that there must have been a criminal intent, but that if the defendant, under the influence of a religious belief that it was right,—under an inspiration, if you please, that it was right,—deliberately married a second time, having a first wife living, the want of consciousness of evil intent—the want of understanding on his part that he was committing a crime—did not excuse him; but the law inexorably in such case implies the criminal intent."

Upon this charge and refusal to charge the question is raised, whether religious belief can be accepted as a justification of an overt act made criminal by the law of the land. The inquiry is not as to the power of Congress to prescribe criminal laws for the Territories, but as to the guilt of one who knowingly violates a law which has been properly enacted, if he entertains a religious belief that the law is wrong.

Congress cannot pass a law for the government of the Territories which shall prohibit the free exercise of religion. The first amendment to the Constitution expressly forbids such legislation. Religious freedom is guaranteed everywhere throughout the United States, so far as congressional interference is concerned. The question to be determined is, whether the law now under consideration comes within this prohibition.

The word "religion" is not defined in the Constitution. We must go elsewhere, therefore, to ascertain its meaning, and nowhere more appropriately, we think, than to the history of the times in the midst of which the provision was adopted. The precise point of the inquiry is, what is the religious freedom which has been guaranteed.

Before the adoption of the Constitution, attempts were made in some of the colonies and States to legislate not only in respect to the establishment of religion, but in respect to its doctrines and precepts as well. The people were taxed, against their will, for the support of religion, and sometimes for the support of particular sects to whose tenets they could not and did not subscribe. Punishments were prescribed for a failure to attend upon public worship, and sometimes for entertaining heretical opinions. The controversy upon this general subject was animated in many of the States, but seemed at last to culminate in Virginia. In 1784, the House of Delegates of that State having under consideration "a bill establishing provision for teachers of the Christian religion," postponed it until the next session, and directed that the bill should be published and distributed, and that the people be requested "to signify their opinion respecting the adoption of such a bill at the next session of assembly."

This brought out a determined opposition. Amongst others, Mr. Madison prepared a "Memorial and Remonstrance," which was widely circulated and signed, and in which he demonstrated "that religion, or the duty we owe the Creator," was not within the cognizance of civil government. At the next session the proposed bill was not only defeated, but another, "for establishing religious freedom," drafted by Mr. Jefferson, was passed. In the preamble of this act, religious freedom is defined; and after a recital "that to suffer the civil magistrate to intrude his powers into the field of opinion, and to restrain the profession or propagation of principles on supposition of their ill tendency, is a dangerous fallacy which at once destroys all religious liberty," it is declared "that it is time enough for the rightful purposes of civil government for its officers to interfere when principles break out into overt acts against peace and good order." In these two sentences is found the true distinction between what properly belongs to the church and what to the State.

In a little more than a year after the passage of this statute the convention met which prepared the Constitution of the United States. Of this convention Mr. Jefferson was not a member, he being then absent as minister to France. As soon as he saw the draft of the Constitution proposed for adoption, he, in a letter to a friend, expressed his disappointment at the absence of an express declaration insuring the freedom of religion, but was willing to accept it as it was, trusting that the good sense and honest intentions of the people would bring about the necessary alterations. Five of the States, while adopting the Constitution, proposed amendments. Three—New Hampshire, New York, and Virginia—included in one form or another a declaration of religious freedom in the changes they desired to have made, as did also North Carolina, where the convention at first declined to ratify the Constitution until the proposed amendments were acted upon. Accordingly, at the first session of the first Congress the amendment now under consideration was proposed with others by Mr. Madison. It met the views of the advocates of religious freedom, and was adopted. Mr. Jefferson afterwards, in reply to an address to him by a committee of the Danbury Baptist Association, took occasion to say: "Believing with you that religion is a matter which lies solely between man and his god; that he owes account to none other for his faith or his worship; that the legislative powers of the government reach actions only, and not opinions,—I contemplate with sovereign reverence that act of the whole American people which declared that their legislature should 'make no law respecting an establishment of religion or prohibiting the free exercise thereof,' thus building a wall of separation between church and

State. Adhering to this expression of the supreme will of the nation in behalf of the rights of conscience, I shall see with sincere satisfaction the progress of those sentiments which tend to restore man to all his natural rights, convinced he has no natural right in opposition to his social duties." Coming as this does from an acknowledged leader of the advocates of the measure, it may be accepted almost as an authoritative declaration of the scope and effect of the amendment thus secured. Congress was deprived of all legislative power over mere opinion, but was left free to reach actions which were in violation of social duties or subversive of good order.

Polygamy has always been odious among the northern and western nations of Europe, and, until the establishment of the Mormon Church, was almost exclusively a feature of the life of Asiatic and of African people. At common law, the second marriage was always void, and from the earliest history of England polygamy has been treated as an offence against society. After the establishment of the ecclesiastical courts, and until the time of James I., it was punished through the instrumentality of those tribunals, not merely because ecclesiastical rights had been violated, but because upon the separation of the ecclesiastical courts from the civil the ecclesiastical were supposed to be the most appropriate for the trial of matrimonial causes and offences against the rights of marriage, just as they were for testamentary causes and the settlement of the estate of Deceased persons.

By the statute of 1 James I. (c. 11), the offence, if committed in England or Wales, was made punishable in the civil courts, and the penalty was death. As this statute was limited in its operation to England and Wales, it was at a very early period re-enacted, generally with some modifications, in all the colonies. In connection with the case we are now considering, it is a significant fact that on the 8th of December, 1788, after the passage of the act establishing religious freedom, and after the convention of Virginia had recommended as an amendment to the Constitution of the United States the declaration in a bill of rights that "all men have an equal, natural, and unalienable right to the free exercise of religion, according to the dictates of conscience," the legislature of that State substantially enacted the statute of James I., death penalty included, because, as recited in the preamble, "it hath been doubted whether bigamy or poligamy be punishable by the laws of this Commonwealth." From that day to this we think it may safely be said there never has been a time in any State of the Union when polygamy has not been an offence against society, cognizable by the civil courts and punishable with more or less severity. In the face of all this evidence, it is impossible to believe that the constitutional guaranty of religious freedom was intended to prohibit legislation in respect to this most important feature of social life. Marriage, while from its very nature a sacred obligation, is nevertheless, in most civilized nations, a civil contract, and usually regulated by law. Upon it society may be said to be built, and out of its fruits spring social relations and social obligations and duties, with which government is necessarily required to deal. . . . An exceptional colony of polygamists under an exceptional leadership may sometimes exist for a time without appearing to disturb the social condition of the people who surround it; but there cannot be a doubt that, unless restricted by some form of constitution, it is within the legitimate scope of the power of every civil government to determine whether polygamy or monogamy shall be the law of social life under its dominion.

In our opinion, the statute immediately under consideration is within the legislative power of Congress. It is constitutional and valid as prescribing a rule of action for all those residing in the Territories, and in places over which the United States have exclusive control. This being so, the only question which remains is, whether those who make polygamy a part of their religion are excepted from the operation of the statute. If they are, then those who do not make polygamy a part of their religious belief may be found guilty and punished, while those who do, must be acquitted and go free. This would be introducing a new element into criminal law. Laws are made for the government of actions, and while they cannot interfere with mere religious belief and opinions, they may with practices. Suppose one believed that human sacrifices were a necessary part of religious worship, would it be seriously contended that the civil government under which he lived could not interfere to prevent a sacrifice? Or if a wife religiously believed it was her duty to burn herself upon the funeral pile of her dead husband, would it be beyond the power of the civil government to prevent her carrying her belief into practice?

So here, as a law of the organization of society under the exclusive dominion of the United States, it is provided that plural marriages shall not be allowed. Can a man excuse his practices to the contrary because of his religious belief? To permit this would be to make the professed doctrines of religious belief superior to the law of the land, and in effect to permit every citizen to become a law unto himself. Government could exist only in name under such circumstances.

NOTES AND QUESTIONS

1.   Why did the United States Constitution need an amendment to protect the free exercise of religion? According to the opinion, does the First Amendment prohibit state and federal governments from taxing individuals in order to support religion? Is it the Free Exercise Clause or the Establishment Clause that would bar taxation?

2.   If the First Amendment builds a wall of separation between church and state, how can the government criminalize marriage conducted according to a religious ceremony? Is the opinion's distinction between belief and conduct persuasive?

3. Do you agree that legalizing polygamy would have disrupted the social order in 1879? Was the Court correct to consider this factor in reaching its decision? Would polygamy disrupt the social order today? Do you think that polygamy should be legal today? Or should polygamy be illegal, and Mormons exempt from that law because of their sincere religious belief? Would such an exemption make every citizen a law unto himself?

Is your reasoning about polygamy influenced by the Supreme Court's decision in Obergefell v. Hodges, 135 S.Ct. 2584 (2015), that the Equal Protection and Due Process Clauses of the Fourteenth Amendment prohibit state bans on same-sex marriage?

Rodney Hans Holm married Suzie Stubbs in a legal marriage ceremony and then participated in a religious marriage ceremony with Suzie's sister Ruth when Ruth was 16 years old. By the age of 18, Ruth was the mother of two of Holm's children. Holm was convicted of unlawful sexual conduct with a minor and bigamy. He unsuccessfully appealed his convictions on free exercise grounds under the Utah and U.S. Constitutions, arguing that *Reynolds* was "nothing more than a hollow relic of bygone days of fear, prejudice, and Victorian morality." Do you agree with Holm or the court that upheld his conviction? See State v. Holm, 137 P.3d 726, 742 (Utah 2006). Would his conviction be invalidated today due to *Obergefell*?

4. In Davis v. Beason, 133 U.S. 333 (1890), the Court upheld the conviction of Mormons in the territory of Idaho for falsely swearing the following oath when they registered to vote:

> I do further swear that I am not a bigamist or polygamist; that I am not a member of any order, organization, or association which teaches, advises, counsels, or encourages its members, devotees, or any other person, to commit the crime of bigamy or polygamy, or any other crime defined by law, as a duty arising or resulting from membership in such order, organization, or association, or which practices bigamy, polygamy, or plural or celestial marriage as a doctrinal rite of such organization; that I do not and will not, publicly or privately, or in any manner whatever, teach, advise, counsel, or encourage any person to commit the crime of bigamy or polygamy, or any other crime defined by law, either as a religious duty or otherwise.

Were the convictions defensible under *Reynolds'* reasoning? Do you think the convictions would be upheld today? See Romer v. Evans, 517 U.S. 620, 634 (1996) ("To the extent *Davis* held that persons advocating a certain practice may be denied the right to vote, it is no longer good law.").

5. According to Professor Robert Gordon, "From 1860 to 1890, the federal government was mobilized to deploy an extraordinary arsenal of legal resources against Mormon families, churches, economic institutions, and political arrangements. In just a few years, the government disenfranchised polygamists and even those who merely advocated polygamy, repealed women's suffrage in the Utah territory, disqualified polygamists from jury duty, criminalized plural marriage and brought 2,500 prosecutions against polygamists, including 200 against pregnant women for 'fornication.'" Robert W. Gordon, The Constitution of Liberal Order at the Troubled Beginnings of the Modern State, 58 U. Miami L. Rev. 373, 382 (2003) (citing Sarah Barringer Gordon, The Mormon Question: Polygamy and Constitutional Conflict in Nineteenth Century America (2002)). Under such pressure, the church officially ended the practice of polygamy in 1890, although some Mormon groups such as the Fundamentalist Church of Jesus Christ of Latter-day Saints (FLDS) continue to practice it. Is the First Amendment violated when religious groups change their teachings under pressure from the state?

Did the *Reynolds* Court need to "sav[e] women and children from polygamy"? Were women victimized by the Court's holding and language? Are women victimized by polygamy? Is your answer affected by the fact that Mormons extended the right to vote to women in Utah in 1870, fifty years before the passage of the Nineteenth Amendment? See Marie Ashe, Women's Wrongs, Religions' Rights: Women, Free Exercise, and Establishment in American Law, 21 Temple Pol. & Civ. Rts. L. Rev. 163, 166, 172, 173 (2011).

After receiving a telephone tip that a 16-year-old girl was sexually abused at the Yearning for Zion Ranch, an FLDS community in El Dorado, Texas, the Texas Department of Family and Protective Services took possession of all 468 children at the ranch, removing them to foster care across the state in order to protect them from the ranch's culture of polygamy, which encouraged spiritual marriages of girls under age 18. The Supreme Court of Texas ruled that the state should have pursued less drastic measures than removing all the children from their families. See In re Texas Dept. of Family and Protective Services, 255 S.W.3d 613 (Tex. 2008). A state report later concluded that 12 girls at the ranch were married between the ages of 12 and 15. The state prosecuted the husbands of those girls for sexual assault. Does the seizure of the children indicate that Mormons face discrimination because of their religious beliefs? Does it persuade you that polygamy should be legal? Raymond Jessop was convicted of sexual assault of a child and sentenced to ten years in prison in the first trial arising from the raid. See Michelle Roberts, AG Sits in on Child Sex Assault Trial, Houston Chron., Dec. 9, 2009, at A03.

   6. Does the following case adhere to the rule of *Reynolds*, as Justice Scalia argues?

Employment Div., Dept. of Human Resources of Oregon v. Smith

Supreme Court of the United States, 1990.
494 U.S. 872, 110 S.Ct. 1595, 108 L.Ed.2d 876.

■ JUSTICE SCALIA delivered the opinion of the Court, in which REHNQUIST, C.J., and WHITE, STEVENS and KENNEDY, joined.

This case requires us to decide whether the Free Exercise Clause of the First Amendment permits the State of Oregon to include religiously inspired peyote use within the reach of its general criminal prohibition on use of that drug, and thus permits the State to deny unemployment benefits to persons dismissed from their jobs because of such religiously inspired use.

I

Oregon law prohibits the knowing or intentional possession of a "controlled substance" unless the substance has been prescribed by a medical practitioner. The law defines "controlled substance" as a drug classified in Schedules I through V of the Federal Controlled Substances Act, as modified by the State Board of Pharmacy. Persons who violate this provision by possessing a controlled substance listed on Schedule I are "guilty of a Class B felony." As compiled by the State Board of Pharmacy under its statutory authority, Schedule I contains the drug peyote, a hallucinogen derived from the plant *Lophophora williamsii Lemaire.*

Respondents Alfred Smith and Galen Black (hereinafter respondents) were fired from their jobs with a private drug rehabilitation organization because they ingested peyote for sacramental purposes at a ceremony of the Native American Church, of which both are members. When respondents applied to petitioner Employment Division (hereinafter petitioner) for unemployment compensation, they were determined to be ineligible for benefits because they had been discharged for work-related "misconduct."

Citing our decisions in *Sherbert v. Verner*, 374 U.S. 398 (1963), and *Thomas v. Review Bd. of Indiana Employment Sec. Division*, 450 U.S. 707 (1981), the Oregon Supreme Court concluded that respondents were entitled to payment of unemployment benefits.

II

A

The Free Exercise Clause of the First Amendment, which has been made applicable to the States by incorporation into the Fourteenth Amendment, see *Cantwell v. Connecticut*, 310 U.S. 296, 303, 60 S.Ct. 900, 903, 84 L.Ed. 1213 (1940), provides that "Congress shall make no law respecting an establishment of religion, or *prohibiting the free exercise thereof....*" U.S. Const., Amdt. 1 (emphasis added.) The free exercise of religion means, first and foremost, the right to believe and profess whatever religious doctrine one desires. Thus, the First Amendment obviously excludes all "governmental regulation of religious *beliefs* as such." *Sherbert v. Verner, supra,* 374 U.S., at 402, 83 S.Ct., at 1793. The government may not compel affirmation of religious belief, see *Torcaso v. Watkins,* 367 U.S. 488, 81 S.Ct. 1680, 6 L.Ed.2d 982 (1961), punish the expression of religious doctrines it believes to be false, *United States v. Ballard,* 322 U.S. 78, 86–88, 64 S.Ct. 882, 886–87, 88 L.Ed. 1148 (1944), impose special disabilities on the basis of religious views or religious status, see *McDaniel v. Paty,* 435 U.S. 618, 98 S.Ct. 1322, 55 L.Ed.2d 593 (1978); *Fowler v. Rhode Island,* 345 U.S. 67, 69, 73 S.Ct. 526, 527, 97 L.Ed. 828 (1953); cf. *Larson v. Valente,* 456 U.S. 228, 245, 102 S.Ct. 1673, 1683–84, 72 L.Ed.2d 33 (1982), or lend its power to one or the other side in controversies over religious authority or dogma, see *Presbyterian Church in U.S. v. Mary Elizabeth Blue Hull Memorial Presbyterian Church,* 393 U.S. 440, 445 452, 89 S.Ct. 601, 604–608, 21 L.Ed.2d 658 (1969); *Kedroff v. St. Nicholas Cathedral,* 344 U.S. 94, 95–119, 73 S.Ct. 143, 143–56, 97 L.Ed. 120 (1952); *Serbian Eastern Orthodox Diocese v. Milivojevich,* 426 U.S. 696, 708–725, 96 S.Ct. 2372, 2380–2388, 49 L.Ed.2d 151 (1976).

But the "exercise of religion" often involves not only belief and profession but the performance of (or abstention from) physical acts: assembling with others for a worship service, participating in sacramental use of bread and wine, proselytizing, abstaining from certain foods or certain modes of transportation. It would be true, we think (though no case of ours has involved the point), that a State would be "prohibiting the free exercise [of religion]" if it sought to ban such acts or abstentions only when they are engaged in for religious reasons, or only because of the religious belief that they display. It would doubtless be unconstitutional, for example, to ban the casting of "statues that are to be used for worship purposes," or to prohibit bowing down before a golden calf.

Respondents in the present case, however, seek to carry the meaning of "prohibiting the free exercise [of religion]" one large step further. They contend that their religious motivation for using peyote places them beyond the reach of a criminal law that is not specifically directed at their religious practice, and that is concededly constitutional as applied to those who use the drug for other reasons. They assert, in other words, that "prohibiting the free exercise [of religion]" includes requiring any individual to observe a generally applicable law that requires (or forbids) the performance of an act that his religious belief forbids (or requires). As a textual matter, we do not think the words must be given that meaning. It is no more necessary to regard the collection of a general tax, for example, as "prohibiting the free exercise [of religion]" by those citizens who believe support of organized government to be sinful, than it is to regard the same tax as "abridging the freedom . . . of the press" of those publishing companies that must pay the tax as a condition of staying in business. It is a permissible reading of the text, in the one case as in the other, to say that if prohibiting the exercise of religion (or burdening the activity of printing) is not the object of the tax but merely the incidental effect of a generally applicable and otherwise valid provision, the First Amendment has not been offended.

Our decisions reveal that the latter reading is the correct one. We have never held that an individual's religious beliefs excuse him from compliance with an otherwise valid law prohibiting conduct that the State is free to regulate. On the contrary, the record of more than a century of our free exercise jurisprudence contradicts that proposition. As described succinctly by Justice Frankfurter in *Minersville School Dist. v. Gobitis*, 310 U.S. 586, 594–595 (1940): "Conscientious scruples have not, in the course of the long struggle for religious toleration, relieved the individual from obedience to a general law not aimed at the promotion or restriction of religious beliefs. The mere possession of religious convictions which contradict the relevant concerns of a political society does not relieve the citizen from the discharge of political responsibilities." We first had occasion to assert that principle in *Reynolds v. United States*, 98 U.S. 145 (1879), where we rejected the claim that criminal laws against polygamy could not be constitutionally applied to those whose religion commanded the practice.

Subsequent decisions have consistently held that the right of free exercise does not relieve an individual of the obligation to comply with a "valid and neutral law of general applicability on the ground that the law proscribes (or prescribes) conduct that his religion prescribes (or proscribes)."

The only decisions in which we have held that the First Amendment bars application of a neutral, generally applicable law to religiously motivated action have involved not the Free Exercise Clause alone, but the Free Exercise Clause in conjunction with other constitutional protections, such as freedom of speech and of the press, see *Cantwell v. Connecticut*, 310 U.S., at 304–307, 60 S.Ct., at 903–905 (invalidating a licensing system for religious and charitable solicitations under which the administrator had discretion to deny a license to any cause he deemed nonreligious); *Murdock v. Commonwealth of Pennsylvania*, 319 U.S. 105, 63 S.Ct. 870, 87 L.Ed. 1292 (1943) (invalidating a flat tax on solicitation as applied to the dissemination of religious ideas); *Follett v. McCormick*, 321 U.S. 573, 64 S.Ct. 717, 88 L.Ed. 938 (1944) (same), or the right of parents, acknowledged in *Pierce v. Society of the Sisters of the Holy Names of Jesus and Mary*, 268 U.S. 510, 45 S.Ct. 571, 69 L.Ed. 1070 (1925), to direct the education of their children, see *Wisconsin v. Yoder*, 406 U.S. 205, 92 S.Ct. 1526, 32 L.Ed.2d 15 (1972) (invalidating compulsory school-attendance laws as applied to Amish parents who refused on religious grounds to send their children to school). Some of our cases prohibiting compelled expression, decided exclusively upon free speech grounds, have also involved freedom of religion, cf. *Wooley v. Maynard*, 430 U.S. 705, 97 S.Ct. 1428, 51 L.Ed.2d 752 (1977) (invalidating compelled display of a license plate slogan that offended individual religious beliefs); *West Virginia Bd. of Education v. Barnette*, 319 U.S. 624, 63 S.Ct. 1178, 87 L.Ed. 1628 (1943) (invalidating compulsory flag salute statute challenged by religious objectors). And it is easy to envision a case in which a challenge on freedom of association grounds would likewise be reinforced by Free Exercise Clause concerns. Cf. *Roberts v. United States Jaycees*, 468 U.S. 609, 622, 104 S.Ct. 3244, 3251–52, 82 L.Ed.2d 462 (1984) ("An individual's freedom to speak, to worship, and to petition the government for the redress of grievances could not be vigorously protected from interference by the State [if] a correlative freedom to engage in group effort toward those ends were not also guaranteed").

The present case does not present such a hybrid situation, but a free exercise claim unconnected with any communicative activity or parental right. Respondents urge us to hold, quite simply, that when otherwise prohibitable conduct is accompanied by religious convictions, not only the convictions but the conduct itself must be free from governmental regulation. We have never held that, and decline to do so now. There being no contention that Oregon's drug law represents an attempt to regulate religious beliefs, the communication of religious beliefs, or the raising of one's children in those beliefs, the rule to which we have adhered ever since *Reynolds* plainly controls.

■ JUSTICE BLACKMUN, with whom JUSTICE BRENNAN and JUSTICE MARSHALL join, dissenting.

This Court over the years painstakingly has developed a consistent and exacting standard to test the constitutionality of a state statute that burdens the free exercise of religion. Such a statute may stand only if the law in general, and the State's refusal to allow a religious exemption in particular, are justified by a compelling interest that cannot be served by less restrictive means.

Until today, I thought this was a settled and inviolate principle of this Court's First Amendment jurisprudence. . . .

The carefully circumscribed ritual context in which respondents used peyote is far removed from the irresponsible and unrestricted recreational use of unlawful drugs.[6] The Native American Church's

---

[6]   In this respect, respondents' use of peyote seems closely analogous to the sacramental use of wine by the Roman Catholic Church. During Prohibition, the Federal Government exempted such use of wine from its general ban on possession and use of alcohol. However compelling the Government's then general interest in prohibiting the use of alcohol may have been, it could not plausibly have asserted an interest sufficiently compelling to outweigh Catholics' right to take communion.

internal restrictions on, and supervision of, its members' use of peyote substantially obviate the State's health and safety concerns.[7]

II

Respondents believe, and their sincerity has *never* been at issue, that the peyote plant embodies their deity, and eating it is an act of worship and communion. Without peyote, they could not enact the essential ritual of their religion.

If Oregon can constitutionally prosecute them for this act of worship, they, like the Amish, may be "forced to migrate to some other and more tolerant region." This potentially devastating impact must be viewed in light of the federal policy—reached in reaction to many years of religious persecution and intolerance—of protecting the religious freedom of Native Americans.

NOTES AND QUESTIONS

1.   Distinguish *Smith* from *Reynolds*. Is Justice Scalia correct that *Smith* follows the rule enunciated in *Reynolds*? Did both decisions protect religious freedom?

A Muslim wife complained that her husband had beaten her and forced her to have sexual intercourse against her will due to his dissatisfaction with her inability to cook acceptable meals for his houseguests. The trial judge ruled that criminal restraint, sexual assault and criminal sexual contact were not established under New Jersey's domestic violence laws. The husband had not met the requirements of criminal intent, the judge ruled, because "he was operating under his [Muslim] belief that it is, as the husband, his desire to have sex when and whether he wanted to, was something that was consistent with his practices and it was something that was not prohibited." Because of the husband's religious beliefs, therefore, the judge "found that defendant did not act with a criminal intent when he repeatedly insisted upon intercourse, despite plaintiff's contrary wishes." Is this ruling consistent with *Reynolds* and *Smith*? See S.D. v. M.J.R., 2 A.3d 412 (N.J.Super.A.D. 2010) (*Reynolds* and *Smith* hold that husband must be held to the standards of the criminal law even if his religious beliefs contradict it; judge was in error not to enforce domestic violence law).

2.   Does the sacramental wine exception to Prohibition mentioned in footnote 6 of Justice Blackmun's dissent suggest that the legislatures and the courts may be more willing to protect majority or mainstream religions than minority or unusual religions? Do you agree with the suggestion in

---

[7]   The use of peyote is, to some degree, self-limiting. The peyote plant is extremely bitter, and eating it is an unpleasant experience, which would tend to discourage casual or recreational use. Not only does the church's doctrine forbid nonreligious use of peyote; it also generally advocates self-reliance, familial responsibility, and abstinence from alcohol. There is considerable evidence that the spiritual and social support provided by the church has been effective in combating the tragic effects of alcoholism on the Native American population. Far from promoting the lawless and irresponsible use of drugs, Native American Church members' spiritual code exemplifies values that Oregon's drug laws are presumably intended to foster.

footnote 7 and accompanying text that the Native American Church's own restrictions on the use of peyote should override the State's health concerns?

3. How different is the dissent's "compelling interest" test from Justice Scalia's "neutral laws of general applicability" standard? Can you think of a scenario in which these two tests would yield widely different results? What about similar outcomes? We examine the application of these tests in Chapter 3.

4. What are some criticisms of the *Smith* case? How can these be countered? See Nelson Tebbe, Free Exercise and the Problem of Symmetry, 56 Hastings L.J. 699, 700 (2005) (Asserting that the two main criticisms of *Smith* were: 1) it could lead to too much government regulation and 2) "religious minorities . . . can suffer disproportionately from laws that enact majoritarian mores."). For a comprehensive discussion of how Congress responded after the *Smith* decision, see City of Boerne v. Flores, 521 U.S. 507 (1997). The casebook examines *Smith* and free exercise in more detail in Chapter 3.

5. As you read the following case, consider why the Court found a free exercise violation. What distinguishes *Lukumi* from *Reynolds* and *Smith*?

Church of the Lukumi Babalu Aye, Inc. v. City of Hialeah

Supreme Court of the United States, 1993.
508 U.S. 520, 113 S.Ct. 2217, 124 L.Ed.2d 472.

■ JUSTICE KENNEDY delivered the opinion of the Court.

The principle that government may not enact laws that suppress religious belief or practice is so well understood that few violations are recorded in our opinions. Cf. *McDaniel v. Paty*, 435 U.S. 618 (1978); *Fowler v. Rhode Island*, 345 U.S. 67 (1953). Concerned that this fundamental nonpersecution principle of the First Amendment was implicated here, however, we granted certiorari.

I

A

This case involves practices of the Santeria religion, which originated in the 19th century. When hundreds of thousands of members of the Yoruba people were brought as slaves from western Africa to Cuba, their traditional African religion absorbed significant elements of Roman Catholicism. The resulting syncretion, or fusion, is Santeria, "the way of the saints." The Cuban Yoruba express their devotion to spirits, called *orishas*, through the iconography of Catholic saints, Catholic symbols are often present at Santeria rites, and Santeria devotees attend the Catholic sacraments.

The Santeria faith teaches that every individual has a destiny from God, a destiny fulfilled with the aid and energy of the *orishas*. The basis of the Santeria religion is the nurture of a personal relation with the *orishas*, and one of the principal forms of devotion is an animal sacrifice. The sacrifice of animals as part of religious rituals has ancient roots. Animal sacrifice is mentioned throughout the Old Testament, and it played an important role in the practice of Judaism before destruction of the second Temple in Jerusalem. In modern Islam, there is an annual sacrifice commemorating Abraham's sacrifice of a ram in the stead of his son.

According to Santeria teaching, the *orishas* are powerful but not immortal. They depend for survival on the sacrifice. Sacrifices are performed at birth, marriage, and death rites, for the cure of the sick, for the initiation of new members and priests, and during an annual celebration. Animals sacrificed in Santeria rituals include chickens, pigeons, doves, ducks, guinea pigs, goats, sheep, and turtles. The animals are killed by the cutting of the carotid arteries in the neck. The sacrificed animal is cooked and eaten, except after healing and death rituals.

Santeria adherents faced widespread persecution in Cuba, so the religion and its rituals were practiced in secret. The open practice of Santeria and its rites remains infrequent. The religion was brought to this Nation most often by exiles from the Cuban revolution. The District Court estimated that there are at least 50,000 practitioners in South Florida today.

B

Petitioner Church of the Lukumi Babalu Aye, Inc. (Church) and its congregants practice the Santeria religion. The president of the Church is petitioner Ernesto Pichardo, who is also the Church's priest and holds the religious title of *Italero*, the second highest in the Santeria faith. In April 1987, the Church leased land in the city of Hialeah, Florida, and announced plans to establish a house of worship as well as a school, cultural center, and museum.

The prospect of a Santeria church in their midst was distressing to many members of the Hialeah community, and prompted the city council to hold an emergency public session on June 9, 1987.

[At that meeting], the city council adopted Resolution 87–66, which noted the "concern" expressed by residents of the city "that certain religions may propose to engage in practices which are inconsistent with public morals, peace or safety," and declared that "the City reiterates its commitment to a prohibition against any and all acts of any and all religious groups which are inconsistent with public morals, peace or safety." Next, the council approved an emergency ordinance, Ordinance 87–40, which incorporated in full, except as to penalty, Florida's animal cruelty laws. Among other things, the incorporated state law subjected to criminal punishment "whoever . . . unnecessarily or cruelly . . . kills any animal."

In September 1987, the city council adopted three substantive ordinances addressing the issue of religious animal sacrifice. Ordinance 87–52 defined "sacrifice" as "to unnecessarily kill, torment, torture, or mutilate an animal in a public or private ritual or ceremony not for the primary purpose of food consumption," and prohibited owning or possessing an animal "intending to use such animal for food purposes." It restricted application of this prohibition, however, to any individual or group that "kills, slaughters or sacrifices animals for any type of ritual, regardless of whether or not the flesh or blood of the animal is to be consumed." The ordinance contained an exemption for slaughtering by "licensed establishment[s]" of animals "specifically raised for food purposes." . . . [Ordinance 87–71] provided that "it shall be unlawful for any person, persons, corporations or associations to sacrifice any animal within the corporate limits of the City of Hialeah, Florida." The final Ordinance, 87–72, defined "slaughter" as "the killing of animals for food" and prohibited slaughter outside of areas zoned for slaughterhouse use. The ordinance provided an exemption, however, for the slaughter or processing for sale of "small numbers of hogs and/or cattle per week in accordance with an exemption provided by state law." All ordinances and resolutions passed by unanimous vote. Violations of each of the four ordinances were punishable by fines not exceeding $500 or imprisonment not exceeding 60 days, or both.

Following enactment of these ordinances, the Church and Pichardo filed this action pursuant to 42 U.S.C. § 1983 in the United States District Court for the Southern District of Florida. Named as defendants were the city of Hialeah and its mayor and members of its city council in their individual capacities. . . . The District Court granted summary judgment to the individual defendants, finding that they had absolute immunity for their legislative acts and that the ordinances and resolutions adopted by the council did not constitute an official policy of harassment, as alleged by petitioners.

After a 9-day bench trial on the remaining claims, the District Court ruled for the city, finding no violation of petitioners' rights under the Free Exercise Clause. The Court of Appeals for the Eleventh Circuit affirmed in a one-paragraph *per curiam* opinion, stat[ing] simply that it concluded the ordinances were consistent with the Constitution.

II

The Free Exercise Clause of the First Amendment, which has been applied to the States through the Fourteenth Amendment, provides that "Congress shall make no law respecting an establishment of religion, or *prohibiting the free exercise thereof . . .* " (Emphasis added.) The city does not argue that Santeria is not a "religion" within the meaning of the First Amendment. Nor could it. Although the practice of animal sacrifice may seem abhorrent to some, "religious beliefs need not be acceptable, logical, consistent, or comprehensible to others in order to merit First Amendment protection." Given the historical association between animal sacrifice and religious worship, petitioners' assertion that animal sacrifice is an integral part of their religion "cannot be deemed bizarre or incredible." Neither the city nor the courts below have questioned the sincerity of petitioners' professed desire to conduct animal sacrifices for religious reasons.

The record in this case compels the conclusion that suppression of the central element of the Santeria worship service was the object of the ordinances. First, though use of the words "sacrifice" and "ritual" does not compel a finding of improper targeting of the Santeria religion, the choice of these words is support for our conclusion. There are further respects in which the text of the city council's enactments discloses the improper attempt to target Santeria. Resolution 87–66 recited that "residents and citizens of the City of Hialeah have expressed their concern that certain religions may propose to engage in practices which are inconsistent with public morals, peace or safety," and "reiterate[d]" the city's commitment to prohibit "any and all [such] acts of any and all religious groups." No one suggests, and on this record it cannot be maintained, that city officials had in mind a religion other than Santeria.

It becomes evident that these ordinances target Santeria sacrifice when the ordinances' operation is considered. Apart from the text, the effect of a law in its real operation is strong evidence of its object. To be sure, adverse impact will not always lead to a finding of impermissible targeting. For example, a social harm may have been a legitimate concern of government for reasons quite apart from discrimination. The subject at hand does implicate, of course, multiple concerns unrelated to religious animosity, for example, the suffering or mistreatment visited upon the sacrificed animals and health hazards from improper disposal. But the ordinances when considered together disclose an object remote from these legitimate concerns. The design of these laws accomplishes instead a "religious gerrymander," an impermissible attempt to target petitioners and their religious practices.

IV

The Free Exercise Clause commits government itself to religious tolerance, and upon even slight suspicion that proposals for state intervention stem from animosity to religion or distrust of its practices, all officials must pause to remember their own high duty to the Constitution and to the rights it secures. Those in office must be resolute in resisting importunate demands and must ensure that the sole reasons for imposing the burdens of law and regulation are secular. Legislators may not devise mechanisms, overt or disguised, designed to persecute or oppress a religion or its practices. The laws here in question were enacted contrary to these constitutional principles, and they are void.

Reversed.

NOTES AND QUESTIONS

1.   *Lukumi* holds that the government may not improperly target a religion. Is that the *only* limitation that the Free Exercise Clause places on the government? Does *Lukumi* follow the rule of *Smith* or add a new rule to Free Exercise jurisprudence?

2.   Why should animal sacrifice deserve constitutional protection while peyote use and polygamy do not? Does that practice seem less abhorrent or disruptive of the social order than polygamy or peyote use? Is animal sacrifice respected because of its ancient roots in Judaism and Islam? Is animal sacrifice comparable to the use of wine in communion?

Jose Merced is a Santerian Oba Oriate (priest) from Euless, Texas. His religion's priestly initiation rituals require the sacrifice of four-legged animals. Merced usually sacrifices goats during those ceremonies. A city law prohibits the domestic slaughter of animals (except chickens and turkeys) and allows four-legged animals to be kept only on properties that are much larger than Merced's home, where he conducts the rituals. Home shrines are the norm for the Santeria religion. Should Merced win or lose his lawsuit against Euless for violations of his religious freedom? See *Merced v. Kasson*, 577 F.3d 578 (5th Cir. 2009) (upholding Merced's claim). Why isn't public health a sufficiently compelling government interest to override Merced's claim?

3.   Most states, including Kentucky, restrict the possession of venomous snakes in their health laws. Kentucky also has a law prohibiting use of "any kind of reptile in connection with any religious service." Jamie Coots, a Kentucky Pentecostal pastor and co-star of the *Snake Salvation* reality television program, wrote an op-ed in *The Wall Street Journal* complaining about his prosecutions for possessing snakes. He and his congregants handled snakes during their church services. They cited biblical texts that Jesus tells disciples to "take up serpents" without fear and gives them the power to "tread on serpents." Their handling of venomous snakes is part of their religious ritual. See Jamie Coots, The Constitution Protects My Snake-Handling, Wall St. J., Oct. 3, 2013, at A21. Is Coots' religious freedom violated by prosecutions for possessing and transporting snakes? What outcome for a Kentucky prosecution under *Smith* and *Lukumi*? See Calvin Massey, Venomous Snakes, Religious Services and the Constitution, The Faculty Lounge, Oct. 4, 2013, at http://www.thefacultylounge.org/2013/10/venomous-snakes-religious-services-and-the-constitution.html (health law is constitutional under *Smith*, but religious service law is unconstitutional under *Lukumi*).

4.   Does *Lukumi* prove that the courts, not the legislatures, are best equipped to protect unpopular minority religions? See Thomas C. Berg, Minority Religions and the Religion Clauses, 82 Wash. U. L.Q. 919, 965

(2004) (asserting that because "laws tend to reflect the majority's values, rules that on their face treat all faiths equally, and reflect no intent to discriminate, will nevertheless have an unequal impact on different faiths"); Gregory C. Sisk, How Traditional and Minority Religions Fare in the Courts: Empirical Evidence from Religious Liberty Cases, 76 U. Colo. L. Rev. 1021 (2005) (arguing that mainstream faiths face more difficulty in the courts than minority religions do).

5.   Before Japanese forces bombed Pearl Harbor on December 7, 1941, the FBI investigated Japanese-American Buddhists to verify their loyalty to the United States. They compiled a list of Buddhist priests who were arrested immediately after the Pearl Harbor attacks, before the later internment of non-priest individuals of Japanese ancestry. The FBI had concluded that Japanese Christians were more likely to be loyal American citizens than Japanese Buddhists. Was *Lukumi* violated by these actions? Did banning Shinto and Buddhist practice in the internment camps violate free exercise? See Duncan Ryûken Williams, Camp Dharma: Japanese-American Buddhist Identity and the Internment Experience of World War II, in Charles Prebish and Martin Baumann, eds., Westward Dharma: Buddhism Beyond Asia 191–200 (2002).

B. WHAT IS RELIGION?

In *Reynolds*, *Smith*, and *Lukumi* the Court agreed that the cases involved individuals' *religious* beliefs that were protected by the First Amendment. The following notes identify different rituals, practices, and belief systems. As you read each note, decide whether the beliefs and conduct described qualify as a religion and deserve First Amendment protection.

1.   THE CHURCHES OF MARIJUANA

Does any one of these marijuana churches deserve more First Amendment protection than the others? How do you compare the claims of the marijuana users with the Native American peyote rituals in *Smith*? Does the legalization of recreational marijuana use in four states affect your answer?

a.   According to the district court, "David Meyers stated that he began worshipping marijuana because it brought peace into his life. Meyers founded the 'Church of Marijuana' in 1973. The church allegedly has 800 members and one designated meeting spot. The church's 'religion' is to grow, possess, and distribute marijuana. The church's 'bible' is a ponderously titled book: *Hemp & the Marijuana Conspiracy: The Emperor Wears No Clothes—The Authoritative Historical Record of the Cannabis Plant, Marijuana Prohibition, & How Hemp Can Still Save the World* ('Hemp'). The church does not have a formal clergy, but does have approximately 20 'teachers.' Meyers did not explain what the teachers do. Although there are teachers, the church has no hierarchy or governing body. The church does not attempt to propagate its beliefs in any way, and does not assert that everyone should smoke marijuana. Nonetheless, part of the 'religion' is to work towards the legalization of marijuana. Meyers testified that he (and presumably other church members) pray to the marijuana plant. The church's only ceremony revolves around one act: the smoking and passing of joints. Joint smoking apparently results in a sort of 'peaceful awareness.' Meyers did not assert that this 'peaceful awareness' is a religious state. While 'peacefully aware' (vulgarly known as being 'high'), church members 'talk to one another.' Meyers did not divulge the nature of their discussions. There are no formal church services." United States v. Meyers, 906 F.Supp. 1494, 1504 (D. Wyo. 1995); see also United States v. Meyers, 95 F.3d 1475 (10th Cir. 1996). Is the court's description of the Church of Marijuana too sarcastic, suggesting the animosity prohibited by *Lukumi*?

b.   The McBrides are members of the Rastafarian faith, which began in Jamaica in the 1930s and regards the Ethiopian Emperor Haile Selassie as a god. Rastafarians believe that marijuana, or "ganja," is a sacrament and that when one inhales and smokes it, he achieves a spiritual self-consciousness that cannot be achieved without the use of marijuana. One religious studies expert testified that Rastafarians cannot practice their religion without the use of marijuana. See Kansas v. McBride, 24 Kan.App.2d 909, 955 P.2d 133 (1998).

c.   The First Church of Cannabis, Inc.'s mission statement, according to its website, is: "Cannabis, 'The Healing Plant' is our sacrament. It brings us closer to ourselves and others. It is our fountain of health, our love, curing us from illness and depression. We embrace it with our whole heart and spirit, individually and as a group." When "Cannaterians" take their sacrament, they recite the following prayer: "Be nice to as many people as you can. It's Absolutely Free. I'll be nice to you and you'll be nice to me. Just like Tag. If we start tonight, Tomorrow will be a better world." First Church of Cannabis, http://www.cannaterian.org/.

2. VEGANISM

Should the Free Exercise Clause protect the animal sacrifice of Santeria but not Veganism's commitment to animal rights, or should Vegan Jerold Friedman succeed on the following religious freedom claim:

> As a strict Vegan, [Friedman] fervently believes that all living beings must be valued equally and that it is immoral and unethical for humans to kill and exploit animals, even for food, clothing and the testing of product safety for humans, and that such use is a violation of natural law and the personal religious tenets on which [he] bases his foundational creeds. He lives each aspect of his life in accordance with this system of spiritual beliefs. As a Vegan, . . . [he] cannot eat meat, dairy, eggs, honey or any other food which contains ingredients derived from animals. Additionally, [he] cannot wear leather, silk or any other material which comes from animals, and cannot use any products such as household cleansers, soap or toothpaste which have been tested for human safety on animals or derive any of their ingredients from animals. . . . [he] has even been arrested for civil disobedience at animal rights demonstrations.

Friedman was required to get a mumps vaccine at his workplace. The mumps vaccine was grown in chicken embryos and Friedman argued vaccination would violate his religious beliefs. See Friedman v. Southern California Permanente Medical Group, 102 Cal.App.4th 39, 44, 125 Cal.Rptr.2d 663 (2002).

3. MOVE

Is MOVE any different from Veganism?

John Africa founded MOVE, "a 'revolutionary' organization 'absolutely opposed to all that is wrong.' " MOVE has no hierarchy. MOVE's goals are "to bring about absolute peace, . . . to stop violence altogether, to put a stop to all that is corrupt." Toward that end, Africa and other MOVE adherents are committed to a "natural," "moving," "active," and "generating" way of life. By contrast, what they alternatively refer to as "this system" or "civilization" is "degenerating": its air and water are "perverted"; its food, education, and governments are "artificial"; its words are "gibberish."

Central to this conception of an unadulterated existence is MOVE's religious diet. "That diet is comprised largely of raw vegetables and fruits; MOVE members who fully adhere to the diet decline to eat any foods that have been processed or cooked. . . . Failure to follow the diet constitutes deviation from the 'direct, straight, and true' and results in 'confusion and disease.' . . . Africa contends that the diet, in conjunction with 'our founder's wisdom,' transformed him from a weak, timid, and ailing being to a strong, confident, and healthy individual. 'Our religious diet is work, hard work, simple consistent unmechanized unscientific self-dependent work,' he concludes; 'our religious diet is family, unity, consistency, (and) uncompromising togetherness.'" Africa v. Pennsylvania, 662 F.2d 1025, 1027–28 (3d Cir. 1981).

4. KOZY KITTEN CAT FOOD

Stanley Oscar Brown has a "personal religious creed" that "Kozy Kitten People/Cat Food . . . is contributing significantly to [his] state of well being . . . (and therefore) to (his) overall work performance by increasing his energy." Brown filed a religious discrimination claim with the E.E.O.C. Should his "belief in pet food" qualify as a religion? Brown v. Pena, 441 F.Supp. 1382, 1384 (S.D. Fla. 1977).

5. HUMANISM

"The Center for Inquiry is a nonprofit corporation that describes itself as a humanist group that promotes ethical living without belief in a deity. The Center seeks to show, among other things, that it is possible to have strong ethical values based on critical reason and scientific inquiry rather than theism and faith. The Center maintains that its methods and values play the same role in its members' lives as religious methods and values play in the lives of adherents." Center members, however, refuse to call their Center for Inquiry a religion because "they are unwilling to pretend to be something they are not, or pretend to believe something they do not." Ctr. for Inquiry, Inc. v. Marion Circuit Court Clerk, 758 F.3d 869, 871–72 (7th Cir. Ind. 2014). Is the Humanism of the Center for Inquiry a religion for First Amendment purposes even though the members do not call it a religion?

6. CREATIVE INTELLIGENCE AND TRANSCENDENTAL MEDITATION

The Science of Creative Intelligence was founded by Maharishi Mahesh Yogi. "It teaches that 'pure creative intelligence' is the basis of life, and that through the process of Transcendental Meditation students can perceive the full potential of their lives. Essential to the practice of Transcendental Meditation is the 'mantra'; a mantra is the sound aid used while meditating. Each meditator has his own personal mantra which is never to be revealed to any other person. It is by concentrating on the mantra that one receives the beneficial effects said to result from Transcendental Meditation." See Malnak v. Yogi, 592 F.2d 197, 198 (3d Cir. 1979).

"To acquire his mantra, a meditator must attend a ceremony called a 'puja.' . . . During the puja the student [stands or sits] in front of a table while the teacher [sings] a chant and ma[kes] offerings to a deified 'Guru Dev.' The chanter . . . makes fifteen offerings to Guru Dev and fourteen obeisances to Guru Dev. The chant then describes Guru Dev as a personification of 'kindness' and of 'the creative impulse of cosmic life,' and the personification of 'the essence of creation,' . . . The chanter then makes three more offerings to Guru Dev and three additional obeisances to Guru Dev. The chant then moves to a passage in which a string of divine epithets are applied to Guru Dev. Guru Dev is called 'The Unbounded,' 'the omnipresent in all creation,' 'bliss of the Absolute,' 'transcendental joy,' 'the Self-Sufficient,' 'the embodiment of pure knowledge which is beyond and above the universe like the sky,' 'the One,' 'the Eternal,' 'the Pure,' 'the Immovable,' 'the Witness of all intellects, whose status transcends thought,' 'the Transcendent along with the three gunas,' and 'the true preceptor.' " Id.

A Hindu monk directs the puja, but the teachers "unwaveringly insist that the Puja chant has no religious meaning whatsoever and is, in fact, a 'secular Puja,' quite common in Eastern cultures." They also insist "Transcendental Meditation is primarily a relaxation or concentration technique with no 'ultimate' significance." Id. at 203, 213.

Why would the teachers dispute the claim that their rituals are religious? Would it violate free exercise if a court ruled that they are a religion? Are the teachers atheists?

7. THE RELIGIOUSLY-UNAFFILIATED NONES

The "Nones" refers to the growing group of Americans who self-identify as atheist, agnostic, or "nothing in particular," and are not affiliated with any specific religion. A Pew Forum report found that nearly one of four Americans, and more than one-third of adults under 30, are "Nones." There are more than 56 million religiously-unaffiliated persons in the United States. Two-thirds of the religiously-unaffiliated Nones say they believe in God, more than half say they often feel a deep connection with nature and the earth, more than a third classify themselves as "spiritual" but not "religious," and one-fifth say they pray every day. See The Pew Forum on Religion & Public Life, America's Changing Religious Landscape, May 12, 2015, http://www.pewforum.org/2015/05/12/americas-changing-religious-landscape/.

8. SUN WORSHIPPING ATHEISM

Marshel Copple was a corrections officer at Ironwood State Prison who created a website and then posted on it about his religion, Sun Worshipping Atheism. A Sun Worshipping Atheist "does not believe in god, but believes that the demands of nature are like a higher power that must be answered to avoid disease and unhappiness and to be morally responsible. The name point of [Sun Worshipping Atheism] is rational worship of the sun. As beings that evolved in the sunlight there are many benefits to our health and well-being that come from sunlight and so we honor it." Copple told his employer that he couldn't work overtime or longer than 12-hour shifts because it violated his religious beliefs. Copple v. California Dep't of Corr. & Rehab., No. G050690, 2015 WL 1383578, at *1 (Cal. Ct. App. Mar. 24, 2015), reh'g denied (Apr. 10, 2015), review denied (June 10, 2015).

Sun Worshipping Atheism's beliefs are: "Identifying a scientific reality of the existence of the universe and that human needs are evolved, that the mind, body and soul, they're all one thing. They're the body, so taking care of the body is the way to take care of the soul. And then specific things from there, sunlight, rest, stimulation, rest, [sic] the things that humans evolved to need and that have a significant effect on mood and brain function." Sun Worshiping Atheism's practices, done to "maintain mind-body well-being," are: "(1) Pray in the sun." "(2) Take natural fresh air daily." "(3) Sleep eight hours or more." "(4) Eat and drink when you need to." "(5) Exercise frequently." "(6) Rest each day." "(7) Have a job." "(8) Be social frequently." "(9) Respect the integrity of the independent mind." "(10) Be skeptical in all things."

Sun Worshipping Atheism's "structure is very loose and grass roots," without any hierarchy. It has no church, temple, synagogue, or any other physical structure for practice of its beliefs. There are no rituals for birth, death, or marriage, nor are there holidays, religious days, or days of rest. Sun Worshipping Atheism has no required ceremonies or services, although meditating in the sun may be "helpful." Copple is the only Sun Worshipping Atheist.

9. SCIENTOLOGY

The Church of Scientology was founded in 1954 by L. Ron Hubbard. According to Hubbard's system of Dianetics, humans possess both an analytical mind and a reactive mind. The reactive mind stores emotions in the form of engrams. The analytical mind is freed to act more fully when humans release their engrams and reach the state of "clear." Scientology counselors use electrical e-meters to audit the reactive mind and to help believers attain the state of clear. See J. Gordon Melton, Scientology, in Catharine Cookson, ed., Encyclopedia of Religious Freedom 430–33 (2003). In 1963, the Food and Drug Administration seized some of the church's e-meters, alleging "false and misleading labeling" under the Food, Drug and Cosmetic Act as well as false healing. See Founding Church of Scientology v. United States (D.C. Cir.), cert. denied, Founding Church of Scientology of Washington, D.C. v. United States. Is Scientology a religion? Does the government violate free exercise when it pursues Scientology for false labeling and false healing for these religious activities?

France has an anti-sect law that allows the state to take action against sects or cults that practice mental manipulation, false claims of healing or fraud. Sects are distinguished from traditional religions like Catholicism or Islam. According to French law, Scientology is a sect. French judges fined Scientology 600,000 euros for fraud after a woman complained that she paid 20,000 euros for an e-meter and other equipment under pressure from Scientologist officials. French prosecutors were unsuccessful in their efforts to have Scientology banned in France. See Gordon H. Smith, Religious Freedom and the Challenge of Terrorism, 2002 B.Y.U. L. Rev. 205; N.A., Scientology Fraud Case, Townsville Bulletin (Australia), Oct. 29, 2009. Should the government be allowed to define groups as sects rather than religions and to monitor the sects' behavior more strictly?

10. UTILITARIANISM

Utilitarianism is "the moral theory that an action is morally right if and only if it produces at least as much good (utility) for all people affected by the action as any alternative action the person could do instead. Its best-known proponent is John Stuart Mill, who formulated the greatest happiness principle: always act so as to produce the greatest happiness." Utilitarians debate "whether the utilitarian principle should be applied to individual actions or to some form of moral rule. According to *act utilitarianism*, each action's rightness or wrongness depends on the utility *it* produces in comparison with possible alternatives. Even act utilitarians agree, however, that rules of thumb like 'keep your promises' can be used for the most part in practice because following them tends to maximize utility. According to *rule utilitarianism*, on the other hand, individual actions are evaluated, in theory not just in practice, by whether they conform to a justified moral rule, and the utilitarian standard is applied only to general rules." Dan W. Brock, Utilitarianism, in R. Audi, ed., The Cambridge Dictionary of Philosophy 824 (1995).

11. CHURCH OF THE NEW SONG

The Church of the New Song, the Eclatarian faith, was founded by Harry Theriault and Jerry M. Dorrough at a federal penitentiary in Atlanta. The Church of the New Song can be found only at three federal penitentiaries. The Eclatarians worship a divine spirit known as Eclat. The Church of the New Song does not promote a particular philosophy of life, but rather encourages free-form philosophy. The group's attempt to hold a paschal-type feast included a request for prison officials to provide steak and wine. See Theriault v. Silber, 391 F.Supp. 578 (D.C. Tex. 1975), vacated by Theriault v. Silber, 547 F.2d 1279 (5th Cir. 1977).

12. WICCA

Wiccans are sometimes called Witches. "The Wiccan faith is a matriarchal religion which originated in Europe. In this faith, there is a belief in a deity, but not in the sense of an anthropomorphic God. Rather, the Wiccan belief is that there is a primordial, supernatural force which is the creator of the world and universe and which permeates everything therein. . . . [T]here is a deification of this force, and all individuals are seen as divine sparks from this divinity with a concomitant moral and ethical responsibility to themselves and to everything in nature. This responsibility arises from the fact that each individual is connected to all things in the universe in what is known as the 'karmic circle,' and each individual both causes the events occurring within the circle and is affected thereby.

"The Wiccan church is not Christian, but it does believe in the teachings of Christ. It does not believe in the devil. In the Wiccan faith, there are eight Sabbaths per year, which are major festivals celebrating changes of seasons. . . . The sacraments and ceremonies of the Wiccan doctrinal theology include: honoring the deity through reverence and homage, communion, marriages (referred to as 'hand fastings'), funeral ceremonies, and ceremonies for naming babies." See Roberts v. Ravenwood Church of Wicca, 249 Ga. 348, 292 S.E.2d 657, 658 (1982).

13. KU KLUX KLAN

At a hearing, a state chaplain for the area Ku Klux Klan testified "that the cross-lighting ceremony is a necessary and integral part of the religious rituals of the Ku Klux Klan" because Christ was the light of the world. He also stated,

> It is the belief of the Klan that the cross as a burning fire be lifted upon a hill where all people can see it as a light unto the world pursuant to the religious traditions of the Klan as a Christian organization.

He described the cross burning as representing

> the circle, the inner and outer circle of people that gather around the cross and, as you mentioned, were around the cross to protect it from the fire . . . from spreading, also represent the inner and outer circle which is representative of the white race, whose invention was the wheel, and it's further stated in the book of Ezekiel of the wheel within a wheel that represented the race of God.

He also testified to the KKK's reliance on the Bible as their "religious charter," and stated the group did not have "ordained ministers but everyone is ordained by God to speak the word of God." See Commonwealth v. Lower, 2 Pa. D. & C. 4th 107 (1989).

14. PAGANS

Bertram Dahl is a self-described high priest of Paganism, which he says is dedicated to seeking "the truth of what came before the idea of monotheism." When Dahl moved to Beebe, Indiana, he introduced himself to the mayor and announced his plan to open a Pagan house of worship on his property. Dahl and his wife had previously operated their "Seekers Temple" out of a trailer in El Paso, Arkansas, teaching that gods are not omnipresent but rather "must be approached and called upon if one is to have a working relationship with them." Seekers Temple taught that "the very definition of 'god,' among other words, has been changed by the Church and we simply do not accept this false definition. Rather we choose the definition of the old days when a god was simply someone who came from the heavens." Richard Fausset, Pagan High Priest Finds Few Believers Inside an Arkansas City Hall, N.Y. Times, Jul. 28, 2014, at A11.

15. THE CHURCH OF THE FLYING SPAGHETTI MONSTER

Members of the Church of the Flying Spaghetti Monster, known as Pastafarians, believe that the Spaghetti Monster created the universe. Church members across the country have fought to be pictured in their drivers' license photos wearing a spaghetti strainer on their heads. Wisconsin resident Michael Schumacher, who won the right to be pictured wearing a colander, said that "the only dogma we believe is that there is no dogma. [We] worship the Flying Spaghetti Monster who was boiled alive for our sins." Samara Kalk Derby, DMV Honors Pasta Church, Wisconsin State Journal, Feb. 29, 2016, at A3. Can a spoof be a religion?

FSM's catechism reads:

Can I get a "Ramen" from the congregation?!

Behold the Church of the Flying Spaghetti Monster (FSM), today's fastest-growing carbohydrate-based religion. According to church founder Bobby Henderson, the universe and all life within it were created by a mystical and divine being: the Flying Spaghetti Monster. What drives the FSM's devout followers, aka Pastafarians? Some say it's the assuring touch from the FSM's Noodly Appendage. There are those who love the worship service, which is conducted in Pirate-Speak and attended by congregants in dashing buccaneer garb. Still others are drawn to the Church's flimsy moral standards, religious holidays every Friday, and the fact that Pastafarian Heaven is way cooler. Does your Heaven have a Stripper Factory and a Beer Volcano? Intelligent Design has finally met its match—and it has nothing to do with apes or the Olive Garden of Eden.

Can FSM be both a parody and a religion? See Cavanaugh v. Bartelt, No. 4:14-CV-3183, 2016 WL 1446447 (D. Neb., April 12, 2016).

16. RELIGION OR PHILOSOPHY?

Are the beliefs labeled or summarized below in notes a–g religions that deserve First Amendment protection, or personal or philosophical beliefs that fall outside the protection of the First Amendment?

a. What about "Judaism, Christianity, Islam, Hinduism, Buddhism, Shintoism, Confucianism, and Taoism. . . . Hare Krishnas, Bantus, Mormons, Seventh Day Adventists, Christian Scientists, Scientologists, Branch Davidians, Unification Church Members, and Native American Church Members (whether Shamanists or Ghost Dancers). . . . Paganism, Zoroastrianism, Pantheism, Animism, Wicca, Druidism, Satanism, and Santeria. . . . [w]hat we now call 'mythology': Greek religion, Norse religion, and Roman religion. . . . Nihilism, anarchism, pacifism, utopianism, socialism, libertarianism, Marxism, vegetism, and humanism." United States v. Meyers, 906 F.Supp. 1494, 1503–04 (D.Wyo. 1995).

b. This group "has no carefully articulated system of doctrine and ethics; rather it participates in traditional rites and festivals in the shrine setting and, by extension, in the household. The typical setting for the practice is the shrine *(jinja)* precinct, which is an enclosed sacred area with a gate, ablution area, and sacred buildings including the main sanctuary which houses the symbol of the kami and a worship area. The natural surroundings are also regarded as permeated with the kami presence; in fact, occasionally a mountain or sacred forest may take the place of the sanctuary. Important in worship at the shrine are rituals which bring about purification from defilements and which foster an integration of human life with the life-bearing power of the kami. Other rituals center around rites of dedication such as offerings of sprigs of the sacred sasaki tree or offerings of foods to the kami. Priests chant special prayers for the worshippers expressing gratitude to the kami." P.E. Nosco, in John Bowker, ed., The Oxford Dictionary of World Religions 892–93 (1997).

c. "There are four classes of people: priests, nobles, commoners, serfs. These are ranked relative to one another, depending on their perceived proximity to ultimate reality. The priests, who are considered especially close to ultimate reality, are on the top of society, followed by the nobles, the commoners and the serfs. Thus, at birth one is given an identity that specifies his or her relationship to ultimate reality. One is either close to it or far from it, meaning that one's existence is more or less meaningful—more or less real—in comparison with others. Depending on class, an individual is assigned a set of duties that must be performed in order to maintain his or her status relative to others and relative to ultimate reality." Will Deming, Rethinking Religion: A Concise Introduction 25–26 (2004).

d.   " 'Avoiding the two extremes (of self-denial and self-indulgence) . . . has realized the Middle Path: it gives vision, it gives knowledge, and it leads to calm, to insight, to awakening, to nirvana.' . . . This teaching presents a path for living—a path that is balanced and oriented toward the cessation of suffering. The Path often is divided into eight categories: right views, right thoughts, right speech, right action, right livelihood, right effort, right mindfulness, and right concentration. . . . The five 'moral precepts' are not to kill, not to steal, not to lie, not to abuse sex, and not to take intoxicants. 'Concentration' has to do with the practice of mental discipline that is commonly called 'meditation.' . . . To practice this form of discipline, one sits down in a stable posture and concentrates on the movement of the breath. As thoughts arise in the mind, one observes them and lets them flow away, returning to concentration on the movement of the breath. Wisdom constitutes the insight that finally frees a person from suffering and from the cycle of death and rebirth." Malcolm David Eckel, in Jonathan Z. Smith, ed., The HarperCollins Dictionary of Religion 140–41 (1995).

e.   "But I say to you, 'Love your enemies and pray for those who persecute you, so that you may be children of your Father in heaven; for he makes his sun rise on the evil and on the good, and sends rain on the righteous and on the unrighteous. For if you love those who love you, what reward do you have? Do not even the tax collectors do the same?' " Matthew 5:44–46.

f.   "The name of the faith means 'submission to God,' the adherent being therefore 'one who submits himself to God,' i.e. surrenders himself unconditionally to the divine will." Edmund Bosworth, in John R. Hinnells, ed., A New Dictionary of Religions 238 (1995).

g.   This system "is made up of (1) a worldview, which by reference to Torah sets forth the intersection of the supernatural and the natural worlds, accounts for how things are, and puts them together into a cogent and harmonious picture; (2) a way of life explained by that worldview that carries out the concrete laws of the Torah and so expresses the worldview in concrete actions; and (3) a social group . . . for which the worldview accounts and which is defined as an entity and in concrete terms by the way of life." Jacob Neusner, in Jonathan Z. Smith, ed., The HarperCollins Dictionary of Religion 598 (1995).

C. HOW SHALL COURTS DEFINE RELIGION?

Following are two extensive definitions of religion, the first by a prominent scholar of religious studies, and the second by the Supreme Court of the United States in *United States v. Seeger*. *Seeger* is the only case in which the Court has defined religion, and the definition occurred in a case of statutory, not constitutional, interpretation. Do these definitions of "religion" help you to decide what is and is not a religion in the materials above?

Ninian Smart, The World's Religions
11–12, 13–22 (2d ed. 1998).

THE NATURE OF A RELIGION

In thinking about religion, it is easy to be confused about what it is. Is there some essence which is common to all religions? And cannot a person be religious without belonging to any of the religions? The search for an essence ends up in vagueness—for instance in the statement that religion is some system of worship or other practice recognizing a transcendent Being or goal. Our problems break out again in trying to define the key term "transcendent." And in answer to the second question, why yes: there are plenty of people with deep spiritual concerns who do not ally themselves to any formal religious movement, and who may not themselves recognize anything as transcendent. They may see ultimate spiritual meaning in unity with nature or in relationships to other persons.

It is more practical to come to terms first of all not with what religion is in general but with what *a* religion is. Can we find some scheme of ideas which will help us to think about and to appreciate the nature of the religions? . . . One approach is to look at the different aspects or dimensions of religion.

The Practical and Ritual Dimension

Every tradition has some practices to which it adheres—for instance regular worship, preaching, prayers, and so on. They are often known as rituals (though they may well be more informal than this word implies). This *practical* and *ritual* dimension is especially important with faiths of a strongly sacramental kind, such as eastern Orthodox Christianity with its long and elaborate service known as the Liturgy. The ancient Jewish tradition of the Temple, before it was destroyed in 70 C.E., was preoccupied with the rituals of the sacrifice, and thereafter with the study of such rites seen as equivalent to their performance, so that study itself becomes almost a ritual activity. Again, sacrificial rituals are important among Brahmin forms of the Hindu tradition.

Also important are other patterns of behavior which, while they may not strictly count as rituals, fulfill a function in developing spiritual awareness or ethical insight: practices such as yoga in the Buddhist and Hindu traditions, methods of stilling the self in Eastern Orthodox mysticism, meditations which can help to increase compassion and love, and so on. Such practices can be combined with rituals of worship, where meditation is directed toward union with God. They can count as a form of prayer. In such ways they overlap with more formal or explicit rites of religion.

The Experiential and Emotional Dimension

We only have to glance at religious history to see the enormous vitality and significance of experience in the formation and development of religious traditions. Consider the visions of the Prophet Muhammad, the conversion of Paul, the enlightenment of the Buddha. These were seminal events in human history. And it is obvious that the *emotions* and *experiences* of men and women are the food on which the other dimensions of religion feed: ritual without feeling is cold, doctrines without awe or compassion are dry, and myths which do not move hearers are feeble. So it is important in understanding a tradition to try to enter into the feelings which it generates—to feel the sacred awe, the calm peace, the rousing inner dynamism, the perception of a brilliant emptiness within, the outpouring of love, the sensations of hope, the gratitude for favors which have been received. One of the main reasons why music is so potent in religion is that it has mysterious powers to express and engender emotions . . .

The Narrative or Mythic Dimension

Often experience is channeled and expressed not only by the ritual but also by sacred narrative or myth. This is the third dimension—the mythic or narrative. It is the story side of religion. It is typical of all faiths to hand down vital stories: some historical; some about that mysterious primordial time when the world was in its timeless dawn; some about things to come at the end of time; some about great heroes and saints; some about great founders, such as Moses, the Buddha, Jesus, and Muhammad; some about assaults by the Evil One; some parables and edifying tales; some about the adventures of the gods; and so on. These stories often are called myths. This term may be a bit misleading, for in the modern study of religion there is no implication that a myth is false.

The seminal stories of a religion may be rooted in history or they may not. Stories of creation are before history, as are myths which indicate how death and suffering came into the world. Others are about historical events—for instance the life of the Prophet Muhammad, or the execution of Jesus, and the enlightenment of the Buddha. Historians have sometimes cast doubt on some aspects of these historical stories, but from the standpoint of the student of religion this question is secondary to the meaning and function of the myth; and to the believer, very often, these narratives *are* history . . .

The Doctrinal and Philosophical Dimension

Underpinning the narrative dimension is the *doctrinal* dimension. Thus, in the Christian tradition, the story of Jesus' life and the ritual of the communion service led to attempts to provide an analysis of the nature of the Divine Being which would preserve both the idea of the Incarnation (Jesus as God) and the belief in one God. The result was the doctrine of the Trinity, which sees God as three persons in one substance. Similarly, with the meeting between early Christianity and the great Graeco-Roman philosophical and intellectual heritage it became necessary to face questions about the ultimate meaning of creation, the inner nature of God, the notion of grace, the analysis of how Christ could be both God and human being, and so on. These concerns led to the elaboration of Christian doctrine. In the case of Buddhism, to take another example, doctrinal ideas were more crucial right from the start, for the Buddha presented a philosophical vision of the world which itself was an aid to salvation.

In any event, doctrines come to play a significant part in all the major religions, partly because sooner or later a faith has to adapt to social reality and so to the fact that much of the leadership is well educated and seeks some kinds of intellectual statement of the basis of the faith. . . .

The Ethical and Legal Dimension

Both narrative and doctrine affect the values of a tradition by laying out the shape of a worldview and addressing the question of ultimate liberation or salvation. The law which a tradition or subtradition incorporates into its fabric can be called the *ethical* dimension of religion. In Buddhism, for instance, there are certain universally binding precepts, known as the five precepts or virtues, together with a set of further regulations controlling the lives of monks and nuns and monastic communities. In Judaism we have not merely the Ten Commandments but a complex of over six hundred rules imposed upon the community by the Divine Being. All this Law or Torah is a framework for living for the Orthodox Jew. It is also a part of the ritual dimension, because, for instance, the injunction to keep the Sabbath as day of rest is also the injunction to perform certain sacred practices and rituals, such as attending the synagogue and maintaining purity.

Similarly, Islamic life has traditionally been controlled by the Law or *shar'a*, which shapes society as both a religious and a political society, as well as shaping the moral life of the individual—prescribing that he should pray daily, give alms to the poor, and so on, and that society should have various institutions, such as marriage, modes of banking, etc.

Other traditions can be less tied to a system of law, but still display an ethic which is influenced and indeed controlled by the myth and doctrine of the faith. For instance, the central ethical attitude in the Christian faith is love. This springs not just from Jesus' injunction to his followers to love God and their neighbors: it flows too from the story of Christ himself who gave his life out of love for his fellow human beings. It is also rooted in the very idea of the Trinity, for God from all eternity is a society of three persons, Father, Son, and Holy Spirit, kept together by the bond of love. The Christian joins a community which reflects, it is hoped at any rate, the life of the Divine Being, both as Trinity and as suffering servant of the human race and indeed of all creation.

The Social and Institutional Dimension

The dimensions outlined so far—the experiential, the ritual, the mythic, the doctrinal, and the ethical—can be considered in abstract terms without being embodied in external form. The last two dimensions have to do with the incarnation of religion. First, every religious movement is embodied in a group of people, and that is very often rather formally organized—as Church, or Sangha, or *umma*. The sixth dimension therefore is what may be called the *social* or *institutional* aspect of religion. To understand a faith we need to see how it works among people. This is one reason why such an important tool of the investigator of religion is that subdiscipline which is known as the sociology of religion. Sometimes the social aspect of a worldview is simply identical with society itself, as in small-scale groups such as tribes. But there is a variety of relations between organized religions and a society at large: a faith may be the official religion, or it may just be one denomination among many, or it may be somewhat cut off from social life, as a sect. Within the organization of one religion, moreover, there are many models—from the relative democratic governance of a radical Protestant congregation, to the hierarchal and monarchical system of the Church of Rome. . . .

The Material Dimension

This social or institutional dimension of religion almost inevitably becomes incarnate in a different way, in *material* form, as buildings, works of art, and other creations. Some movements—such as Calvinist Christianity, especially in the time before the present century—eschew external symbols as being potentially idolatrous; their buildings are often beautiful in their simplicity, but their intention is to be without artistic or other images which might seduce people from the thought that God is a spirit who transcends all representations. However, the material expressions of religion are more often elaborate, moving, and highly important for believers in their approach to the divine. How indeed could we understand Eastern Orthodox Christianity without seeing what ikons are like and knowing that they are regarded as windows onto heaven? How could we get inside the feel of Hinduism without attending to the varied statues of God and the gods?

Also important material expressions of a religion are those natural features of the world which are singled out as being of special sacredness and meaning—the river Ganges, the Jordan, the sacred mountains of China, Mount Fuji in Japan, Ayers Rock in Australia, the Mount of Olives, Mount Sinai, and so forth. Sometimes of course these sacred landmarks combine with more direct human creations, such as the holy city of Jerusalem, the sacred shrines of Banaras, or the temple at Bodh Gaya which commemorates the Buddha's Enlightenment.

Uses of the Seven Dimensions

To sum up: we have surveyed briefly the seven dimensions of religion which help to characterize religions as they exist in the world. The point of the list is so that we can give a balanced description of the movements which have animated the human spirit and taken a place in the shaping of society, without neglecting either ideas or practices.

Naturally, there are religious movements or manifestations where one or other of the dimensions is so weak as to be virtually absent: nonliterate small-scale societies do not have much means of expressing the doctrinal dimension; Buddhist modernists, concentrating on meditation, ethics, and philosophy, pay scant regard to the narrative dimension of Buddhism; some newly formed groups may not have evolved anything much in the way of the material dimension. Also there are so many people who are not formally part of any social religious grouping, but have their own particular worldviews and practices, that we can observe in society atoms of religion which do not possess any well-formed social dimension. But of course in forming a phenomenon within society they reflect certain trends which in a sense form a shadow of the social dimension (just as those who have not yet got themselves a material dimension are nevertheless implicitly storing one up, for with success come buildings and with rituals ikons, most likely).

NOTES AND QUESTIONS

1.   Do you think that Professor Smart's framework applies to secular ideologies? Are "scientific humanism, Marxism, Existentialism, nationalism, and so on" religions?

2. The anthropologist Clifford Geertz defined religion as "(1) a system of symbols which acts to (2) establish powerful, pervasive, and long-lasting moods and motivations in men by (3) formulating conceptions of a general order of existence and (4) clothing these conceptions with such an aura of factuality that (5) the moods and motivations seem uniquely realistic." Do you prefer this concise definition to Smart's?

3. The Supreme Court provided its most extensive definition of religion in a statutory case involving the draft, not in a free exercise case. In the following case, the Court addressed the constitutionality of Section 6(j) of the Universal Military Training and Service Act, which read as follows:

> Nothing in this title shall be construed to require any person to be subject to combatant training and service in the armed forces of the United States who, by reason of religious training and belief, is conscientiously opposed to participation in war in any form. Religious training and belief in this connection means an individual's belief in relation to a Supreme Being involving duties superior to those arising from any human relation, but does not include essentially political, sociological, or philosophic views or a merely person[al] moral code. [Universal Military Training and Service Act, 50 U.S.C. App. § 456(j), § 6(j) (1958 ed.)].

According to the statute, only individuals who were conscientiously opposed to war "by reason of religious training and belief" were entitled to conscientious objector status. The statute defined religious training and belief to mean "an individual's belief in relation to a Supreme Being involving duties superior to those arising from any human relation, but does not include essentially political, sociological, or philosophic views or a merely person[al] moral code." Did the Court do a good job defining religion in the following opinion?

United States v. Seeger

Supreme Court of the United States, 1965.
380 U.S. 163, 85 S.Ct. 850, 13 L.Ed.2d 733.

■ MR. JUSTICE CLARK delivered the opinion of the Court.

The constitutional attack [on § 6(j), above] is launched under the First Amendment's Establishment and Free Exercise Clauses and is twofold: (1) The section does not exempt nonreligious conscientious objectors; and (2) it discriminates between different forms of religious expression in violation of the Due Process Clause of the Fifth Amendment.

We have concluded that Congress, in using the expression "Supreme Being" rather than the designation "God," was merely clarifying the meaning of religious training and belief so as to embrace all religions and to exclude essentially political, sociological, or philosophical views. We believe that under this construction, the test of belief "in a relation to a Supreme Being" is whether a given belief that is sincere and meaningful occupies a place in the life of its possessor parallel to that filled by the orthodox belief in God of one who clearly qualifies for the exemption. Where such beliefs have parallel positions in the lives of their respective holders we cannot say that one is "in a relation to a Supreme Being" and the other is not. We have concluded that the beliefs of the objectors in these cases meet these criteria, and, accordingly, we affirm the judgments in Nos. 50 and 51 and reverse the judgment in No. 29.

THE FACTS IN THE CASES.

No. 50: Seeger was convicted in the District Court for the Southern District of New York of having refused to submit to induction in the armed forces. He was originally classified 1–A in 1953 by his local board, but this classification was changed in 1955 to 2–S (student) and he remained in this status until 1958 when he was reclassified 1–A. He first claimed exemption as a conscientious objector in 1957 after successive annual renewals of his student classification. Although he did not adopt verbatim the printed Selective Service System form, he declared that he was conscientiously opposed to participation in war in any form by reason of his "religious" belief; that he preferred to leave the question as to his belief in a Supreme Being open, "rather than answer 'yes' or 'no' "; that his "skepticism or disbelief in the existence of God" did "not necessarily mean lack of faith in anything whatsoever"; that his was a "belief in and devotion to goodness and virtue for their own sakes, and a religious faith in a purely ethical creed." He cited such personages as Plato, Aristotle and Spinoza for support of his ethical belief in intellectual and moral integrity "without belief in God, except in the remotest sense." His belief was found to be sincere, honest, and made in good faith; and his conscientious objection to be based upon individual training and belief, both of which included research in religious and cultural fields. Seeger's claim, however, was denied solely because it was not based upon a "belief in a relation to a Supreme Being" as required by § 6(j) of the Act. At trial Seeger's counsel admitted that Seeger's belief was not in relation to a Supreme Being as commonly understood, but contended that he was entitled to the exemption because "under the present law Mr. Seeger's position would also include definitions of religion which have been stated more recently," and could be "accommodated" under the definition of religious training and belief in the Act. He was convicted.

No. 51: Jakobson was also convicted in the Southern District of New York on a charge of refusing to submit to induction.

Jakobson was originally classified 1–A in 1953 and intermittently enjoyed a student classification until 1956. It was not until April 1958 that he made claim to noncombatant classification (1–A–O) as a conscientious objector. He stated on the Selective Service System form that he believed in a "Supreme Being" who was "Creator of Man" in the sense of being "ultimately responsible for the existence of" man and who was "the Supreme Reality" of which "the existence of man is the *result*." He explained that his religious and social thinking had developed after much meditation and thought. He had concluded that man must be "partly spiritual" and, therefore, "partly akin to the Supreme Reality"; and that his "most important religious law" was that "no man ought ever to wilfully sacrifice another man's life as a means to any other end. . . . " In December 1958 he requested a 1–O classification since he felt that participation in any form of military service would involve him in "too many situations and relationships that would be a strain on [his] conscience that [he felt he] must avoid." He submitted a long memorandum of "notes on religion" in which he defined religion as the "*sum and essence of one's basic attitudes to the fundamental problems of human existence*"; he said that he believed in "Godness" which was "the Ultimate Cause for the fact of the Being of the Universe"; that to deny its existence would but deny the existence of the universe because "anything that Is, has an Ultimate Cause for its Being." There was a relationship to Godness, he stated, in two directions, i.e., "vertically, towards Godness directly," and "horizontally, towards Godness through Mankind and the World." He accepted the latter one. . . .

No. 29: Forest Britt Peter was convicted in the Northern District of California on a charge of refusing to submit to induction. In his Selective Service System form he stated that he was not a member of a religious sect or organization; he failed to execute section VII of the questionnaire but attached to it a quotation expressing opposition to war, in which he stated that he concurred. In a later form he hedged the question as to his belief in a Supreme Being by saying that it depended on the definition and he appended a statement that he felt it a violation of his moral code to take human life and that he considered this belief superior to his obligation to the state. As to whether his conviction was religious, he quoted with approval Reverend John Haynes Holmes' definition of religion as "the consciousness of some power manifest in nature which helps man in the ordering of his life in harmony with its demands . . . [; it] is the supreme expression of human nature; it is man thinking his highest, feeling his deepest, and living his best." The source of his conviction he attributed to reading and meditation "in our democratic American culture, with its values derived from the western religious and philosophical tradition." As to his belief in a Supreme Being, Peter stated that he supposed "you could call that a belief in the Supreme Being or God. These just do not happen to be the words I use."

INTERPRETATION OF § 6(j).

1.   The crux of the problem lies in the phrase "religious training and belief" which Congress has defined as "belief in a relation to a Supreme Being involving duties superior to those arising from any

human relation." In assigning meaning to this statutory language we may narrow the inquiry by noting briefly those scruples expressly excepted from the definition. The section excludes those persons who, disavowing religious belief, decide on the basis of essentially political, sociological or economic considerations that war is wrong and that they will have no part of it. These judgments have historically been reserved for the Government, and in matters which can be said to fall within these areas the conviction of the individual has never been permitted to override that of the state. The statute further excludes those whose opposition to war stems from a "merely personal moral code," a phrase to which we shall have occasion to turn later in discussing the application of § 6(j) to these cases. We also pause to take note of what is not involved in this litigation. No party claims to be an atheist or attacks the statute on this ground. The question is not, therefore, one between theistic and atheistic beliefs. We do not deal with or intimate any decision on that situation in these cases. Nor do the parties claim the monotheistic belief that there is but one God; what they claim (with the possible exception of Seeger who bases his position here not on factual but on purely constitutional grounds) is that they adhere to theism, which is the "Belief in the existence of a god or gods; * * * Belief in superhuman powers or spiritual agencies in one or many gods," as opposed to atheism. Our question, therefore, is the narrow one: Does the term "Supreme Being" as used in § 6(j) mean the orthodox God or the broader concept of a power or being, or a faith, "to which all else is subordinate or upon which all else is ultimately dependent"? Webster's New International Dictionary (2d ed.) In considering this question we resolve it solely in relation to the language of § 6(j) and not otherwise.

2. . . . Over 250 sects inhabit our land. Some believe in a purely personal God, some in a supernatural deity; others think of religion as a way of life envisioning as its ultimate goal the day when all men can live together in perfect understanding and peace. There are those who think of God as the depth of our being; others, such as the Buddhists, strive for a state of lasting rest through self-denial and inner purification; in Hindu philosophy, the Supreme Being is the transcendental reality which is truth, knowledge and bliss. Even those religious groups which have traditionally opposed war in every form have splintered into various denominations: from 1940 to 1947 there were four denominations using the name "Friends,"; the "Church of the Brethren" was the official name of the oldest and largest church body of four denominations composed of those commonly called Brethren; and the "Mennonite Church" was the largest of 17 denominations, including the Amish and Hutterites, grouped as "Mennonite bodies" in the 1936 report on the Census of Religious Bodies. This vast panoply of beliefs reveals the magnitude of the problem which faced the Congress when it set about providing an exemption from armed service. It also emphasizes the care that Congress realized was necessary in the

fashioning of an exemption which would be in keeping with its long-established policy of not picking and choosing among religious beliefs.

In spite of the elusive nature of the inquiry, we are not without certain guidelines. In amending the 1940 Act, Congress adopted almost intact the language of Chief Justice Hughes in United States v. Macintosh, supra:

> "The essence of religion is belief in a relation to *God* involving duties superior to those arising from any human relation." At 633–634. (Emphasis supplied.)

By comparing the statutory definition with those words, however, it becomes readily apparent that the Congress deliberately broadened them by substituting the phrase "Supreme Being" for the appellation "God."

Under the 1940 Act it was necessary only to have a conviction based upon religious training and belief; we believe that is all that is required here. Within that phrase would come all sincere religious beliefs which are based upon a power or being, or upon a faith, to which all else is subordinate or upon which all else is ultimately dependent. The test might be stated in these words: A sincere and meaningful belief which occupies in the life of its possessor a place parallel to that filled by the God of those admittedly qualifying for the exemption comes within the statutory definition. This construction avoids imputing to Congress an intent to classify different religious beliefs, exempting some and excluding others, and is in accord with the well-established congressional policy of equal treatment for those whose opposition to service is grounded in their religious tenets.

3.   Section 6(j), then, is no more than a clarification of the 1940 provision involving only certain "technical amendments," to use the words of Senator Gurney. As such it continues the congressional policy of providing exemption from military service for those whose opposition is based on grounds that can fairly be said to be "religious." To hold otherwise would not only fly in the face of Congress' entire action in the past; it would ignore the historic position of our country on this issue since its founding.

4.   Moreover, we believe this construction embraces the ever-broadening understanding of the modern religious community. The eminent Protestant theologian, Dr. Paul Tillich, whose views the Government concedes would come within the statute, identifies God not as a projection "out there" or beyond the skies but as the ground of our very being. The Court of Appeals stated in No. 51 that Jakobson's views "parallel [those of] this eminent theologian rather strikingly." In his book, Systematic Theology, Dr. Tillich says:

> "I have written of the God above the God of theism. . . . In such a state [of self-affirmation] the God of both religious and

theological language disappears. But something remains, namely, the seriousness of that doubt in which meaning within meaninglessness is affirmed. The source of this affirmation of meaning within meaninglessness, of certitude within doubt, is not the God of traditional theism but the 'God above God.' the power of being, which works through those who have no name for it, not even the name God." II Systematic Theology 12 (1957).

Another eminent cleric, the Bishop of Woolwich, John A. T. Robinson, in his book, Honest To God (1963), states:

"The Bible speaks of a God 'up there.' No doubt its picture of a three-decker universe, of 'the heaven above, the earth beneath and the waters under the earth,' was once taken quite literally * * *"

"[Later] *in place of a God who is literally or physically 'up there' we have accepted, as part of our mental furniture, a God who is spiritually or metaphysically 'out there.' . . .*"

The Schema of the recent Ecumenical Council included a most significant declaration on religion:[4]

"The community of all peoples is one. One is their origin, for God made the entire human race live on all the face of the earth. One, too, is their ultimate end, God. Men expect from the various religions answers to the riddles of the human condition: What is man? What is the meaning and purpose of our lives? What is the moral good and what is sin? What are death, judgment, and retribution after death? . . . The Church regards with sincere reverence those ways of action and of life, precepts and teachings which, although they differ from the ones she sets forth, reflect nonetheless a ray of that Truth which enlightens all men." . . .

Dr. David Saville Muzzey, a leader in the Ethical Culture Movement, states in his book, Ethics As a Religion (1951), that "[e]verybody except the avowed atheists (and they are comparatively few) believes in some kind of God," and that "The proper question to ask, therefore, is not the futile one, Do you believe in God? but rather, What *kind* of God do you believe in?"

These are but a few of the views that comprise the broad spectrum of religious beliefs found among us. But they demonstrate very clearly the diverse manners in which beliefs, equally paramount in the lives of their possessors, may be articulated. They further reveal the difficulties inherent in placing too narrow a construction on the provisions of § 6(j)

---

[4]   Draft declaration on the Church's relations with non-Christians, Council Daybook, Vatican II, 3d Sess., p. 282, N.C.W.C., Washington, D.C., 1965.

and thereby lend conclusive support to the construction which we today find that Congress intended.

5.   We recognize the difficulties that have always faced the trier of fact in these cases. We hope that the test that we lay down proves less onerous. The examiner is furnished a standard that permits consideration of criteria with which he has had considerable experience. While the applicant's words may differ, the test is simple of application. It is essentially an objective one, namely, does the claimed belief occupy the same place in the life of the objector as an orthodox belief in God holds in the life of one clearly qualified for exemption?

Moreover, it must be remembered that in resolving these exemption problems one deals with the beliefs of different individuals who will articulate them in a multitude of ways. In such an intensely personal area, of course, the claim of the registrant that his belief is an essential part of a religious faith must be given great weight. . . . The validity of what he believes cannot be questioned. Some theologians, and indeed some examiners, might be tempted to question the existence of the registrant's "Supreme Being" or the truth of his concepts. But these are inquiries foreclosed to Government. As Mr. Justice Douglas stated in United States v. Ballard, 322 U.S. 78, 86, 64 S.Ct. 882, 886, 88 L.Ed. 1148 (1944): "Men may believe what they cannot prove. They may not be put to the proof of their religious doctrines or beliefs. Religious experiences which are as real as life to some may be incomprehensible to others." Local boards and courts in this sense are not free to reject beliefs because they consider them "incomprehensible." Their task is to decide whether the beliefs professed by a registrant are sincerely held and whether they are, in his own scheme of things, religious.

But we hasten to emphasize that while the "truth" of a belief is not open to question, there remains the significant question whether it is "truly held." This is the threshold question of sincerity which must be resolved in every case. It is, of course, a question of fact—a prime consideration to the validity of every claim for exemption as a conscientious objector.

NOTES AND QUESTIONS

1.   The Court concluded: "We believe that under this construction, the test of belief 'in a relation to a Supreme Being' is whether a given belief that is sincere and meaningful occupies a place in the life of its possessor parallel to that filled by the orthodox belief in God of one who clearly qualifies for the exemption." Do you agree with the Court that the test is of "simple application" and is "objective"? Is there an alternative test that you think the Court should have used? Is there a definition of religion that would be more appropriate today?

In an important concurrence in *Malnak v. Yogi*, Judge Arlin Adams analyzed *Seeger* as favoring a broad definition of religion, and proposed instead a "modern" definition of religion that would look to familiar religions as models and then analogize to other candidates for religion. In making the analogy, Adams identified three main "indicia" of a genuine religion. First, the ideas and questions that underlie the religion are the most important—the "ultimate" questions that face humans, including "the meaning of life and death, man's role in the Universe, the proper moral code of right and wrong." Second, the answers to such questions must be comprehensive, "embedded in a system of ideas that connects overarching concerns with deep commitments about the nature of reality." Third, an organizational structure, including any services, rituals, clergy, and so on, would be additional, although not determinative, evidence of religion. See Sarah Barringer Gordon, Malnak v. Yogi: Transcendental Meditation and the Definition of Religion, in L. Griffin, ed., Law and Religion: Cases in Context (Aspen 2010); Malnak v. Yogi, 592 F.2d 197, 207–210 (3d Cir. 1979). Using that standard, Adams concluded that the Science of Creative Intelligence and Transcendental Meditation (infra Section B) was a religion even though its adherents said it was secular. Is the Adams test better than *Seeger* in resolving the questions in Section B about what qualifies as a religion?

2. Did the Court's use of the theologians' views add anything important to the definition of religion? Why were so many of the theologians selected Christian? Did the addition of Dr. Muzzey mean that the Court considered a full range of religious views? What theologians would or should the Court rely on today to figure out a definition of religion? Justice Douglas' concurrence included descriptions of Hinduism and Buddhism. Should Justice Clark have included such materials in his opinion?

3. In the omitted section of the decision, the Court ruled that Seeger, Jakobson and Peter qualified as C.O.s. Do you agree?

4. Now, applying everything you learned in this chapter, is Appleism a religion?

David Kuo, Appleism is a New Religion . . .

http://blog.beliefnet.com/jwalking/2007/06/appleism-kuo.html, June 25, 2007.

Welcome to Appleism—the religion that is Apple.

For decades we have heard of the "Cult of Apple" and the "Mac Cult"—the relatively small group of slavishly devoted technology fanatics obsessed with Apple and its pontiff, Steve Jobs. These "cultists" were typically artsy, creative types, who sneered at anything Microsoft and "Windows" because Windows was a shamelessly pathetic rip off of Mac's operating system and because Microsoft "had no taste"—as Jobs once sermonized. And so people bought into this idea of the Apple cult.

Apple isn't a cult anymore, it has become a full blown religion with scores of millions of followers. The frenzy around the iPhone brings to mind the clamoring throngs that greeted Jesus at the height of his ministry.

There are many, many different tests for what makes something a religion. They range from belief in a higher power to sacred rituals to moral codes to sacred places. In every instance Appleism passes the test.

Religions are based on some belief in a higher or supernatural power. Meet Steve Jobs whose story is supernatural. He started Apple with a friend in his parent's garage and by the time he was 30 was running a multibillion company that had revolutionized computing. Then he was tossed aside, sent to the desert abandoned and despised. Apple slowly sank. At a moment when the company, er, faith, was near its end Jobs returned—the Second Coming—and brought salvation (also known as the iMac, iBook, and iPod). With the introduction of iPhone, however, Appleism may be outgrowing even Jobs with a belief in the power of Apple in and of itself. Apple has become its own deity.

Sacred v. profane objects, places, and times. This one is easy. Sacred: Apple. Profane: Microsoft. Sacred times? MacWorld, Appleism's equivalent of the annual return to Mecca. Then there is this coming Friday where millions will be standing in line to pay homage to the most sacred Apple of all—the iPhone. However, it is unclear whether some will one day move to make June 29th, the date of iPhone's introduction, a national holiday.

Ritual acts focused on sacred objects, places, times. Every time someone with an iPod uses its ubiquitous "click wheel" and every time someone sits before a Mac, or opens a Macbook Pro (like the one I am currently using) they are performing a ritual act of worship, sacred in its own way. The same is true when using iTunes to manage music or iPhoto to manage pictures or iMovie to create films—these are all ritual acts both devoted to Appleism and made possible by the Apple deity.

Characteristically religious feelings (awe, wonder, gratitude, guilt, adoration, etc.). Appleism's followers know of guilt and they experience it every time they use a Windows computer. I have a friend who is a loyal Mac guy but recently finished a big project on an IBM. He emailed me and talked about his guilt. (I'm not joking). More than guilt though, they know of awe, wonder, and gratitude. Every new Apple invention, every time Steve Jobs take a stage to announce something beautiful and wonderful all Appleists tingle with joy and anticipation.

A worldview and morality based on the faith. Appleism espouses a liberal worldview that challenges conventional morality and norms and encourages creativity. It was clearly seen in the famed "Think Different" ad campaign that highlighted everyone from John Lennon and Gandhi to two lesbians kissing in bed. It is, however, most clearly seen in the new "Get a Mac" ads where the casual kid who represents the Mac is constantly poking fun at the tie-wearing guy—the symbol of stodgy conservatism. These ads don't just poke fun at Microsoft but at the kind of boring, humdrum, life that Microsoft empowers. They are jabs at the conventional; jabs at the orthodox and tried and true. They are ads that strike at the heart of older religions while evangelizing Appleism.

Oh, and one more thing.

I am an Appleist. I have a MacBook and an iMac. My wife and I have more than 7,000 photos on iPhoto and more than 15,000 songs (all legal—ok, there may be a few from the old Napster days) on iTunes. We have at least four iPods in the house. I own Apple stock. I have watched every iPhone ad repeatedly. Since my own faith in Jesus requires that I have no God before my God it is clear that something in my life must change. And things will change. Right after I get that iPhone.

British neuroscientists concluded that trips to the Apple Store trigger the same brain reaction as images of a deity for religious people. See Mark Millan, Apple Triggers "Religious" Reaction in Fans' Brains, Report Says, CNN Tech, May 19, 2011, at http://www.cnn.com/2011/TECH/gaming.gadgets/05/19/apple.religion/. Does this confirm Apple is a religion?

In the next chapter, we examine the second Religion Clause of the First Amendment—the Establishment Clause. Do you think the courts should use the same definition of religion for Establishment that they do for Free Exercise? Harvard Law Professor Laurence Tribe once proposed a simple formula: when an activity or belief was *arguably religious*, it should be protected under the Free Exercise Clause; when such activity or belief is *arguably not religious*, government support or encouragement would not violate the Establishment Clause. See Laurence H. Tribe, American Constitutional Law 826–29 (1978). Is that a good idea, or should there be one definition of religion for both clauses?

CHAPTER 2

INTRODUCTION TO ESTABLISHMENT

The First Amendment states Congress shall "make no law respecting an establishment of religion or prohibiting the free exercise thereof." This chapter introduces the Establishment Clause, and Chapter 3 examines its case law in more detail. The Supreme Court has not developed a coherent Establishment Clause jurisprudence; instead, individual justices have developed different tests to determine when an establishment of religion occurs. Section A explores cases in which the Court explains why a "fusion of governmental and religious functions" constitutes a core violation of the Establishment Clause.

Section B introduces the *Lemon*, endorsement, and coercion tests. The controversial three-part *Lemon* test was taken from the 1971 opinion Lemon v. Kurtzman, 403 U.S. 602, 612–13 (1971), which identifies how a statute may survive Establishment Clause scrutiny:

> First, the statute must have a secular legislative purpose; second, its principal or primary effect must be one that neither advances nor inhibits religion, finally, the statute must not foster an excessive government entanglement with religion.

Although Justice Antonin Scalia and other members of the Court repeatedly called for *Lemon*'s overruling, the Court continues to rely on the three prongs of this test—in brief, secular purpose, primary effect and excessive entanglement—to decide the constitutionality of government actions that involve religion. Over the years, however, some Court opinions modified the *Lemon* test. In particular, Justice Sandra Day O'Connor combined the prongs of the *Lemon* test to develop an *endorsement* test that holds the government violates the Establishment Clause whenever it endorses religion. In contrast, Justice Anthony Kennedy argued the government violates the Establishment Clause whenever it *coerces* religious belief or practice. Justices Scalia and Thomas offered a much more restrictive coercion analysis than Justice Kennedy. Because Justice Samuel Alito replaced Justice O'Connor on the Court, it is uncertain whether the Court will continue to employ the endorsement test. Section B includes the *Lemon*, *endorsement*, and *coercion* tests.

Section C explores the topic of the government's relationship to prayer. The Court's older prayer cases took a strict separationist approach to the relationship of the government and prayer. The Court's most recent prayer case, *Town of Greece v. Galloway*, however, calls into question all the Court's establishment standards. No justice in *Greece* voted for a separationist approach to government and prayer, and neither the endorsement nor the coercion approach commanded a majority of the Court.

A. FUSION OF GOVERNMENTAL AND RELIGIOUS FUNCTIONS

According to the following opinion, the religion clauses serve two purposes: "to foreclose state interference with the practice of religious faiths, and to foreclose the establishment of a state religion familiar in other Eighteenth Century systems." As you read *Larkin*, ask yourself why there was enough "fusion" of church and state to violate the Establishment Clause. Did the State of Massachusetts interfere with the practice of religion? Did the State of Massachusetts establish the Armenian Catholic Church? Did the church exercise government authority?

Larkin v. Grendel's Den, Inc.
Supreme Court of the United States, 1982.
459 U.S. 116, 103 S.Ct. 505, 74 L.Ed.2d 297.

■ CHIEF JUSTICE BURGER delivered the opinion of the Court.

The question presented by this appeal is whether a Massachusetts statute, which vests in the governing bodies of churches and schools the power effectively to veto applications for liquor licenses within a five hundred foot radius of the church or school, violates the Establishment Clause of the First Amendment or the Due Process Clause of the Fourteenth Amendment.

I

A

Appellee [Grendel's Den] operates a restaurant located in the Harvard Square area of Cambridge, Mass. The Holy Cross Armenian Catholic Parish is located adjacent to the restaurant; the back walls of the two buildings are 10 feet apart. In 1977, appellee applied to the Cambridge License Commission for approval of an alcoholic beverages license for the restaurant.

Section 16C of Chapter 138 of the Massachusetts General Laws provides: "Premises . . . located within a radius of five hundred feet of a church or school shall not be licensed for the sale of alcoholic beverages if the governing body of such church or school files written objection thereto."[1]

---

[1]   Section 16C defines "church" as "a church or synagogue building dedicated to divine worship and in regular use for that purpose, but not a chapel occupying a minor portion of a building primarily de voted to other uses." "School" is defined as "an elementary or secondary school, public or private, giving not less than the minimum instruction and training required by [state law] to children of compulsory school age." Mass.G.L. ch. 138, § 16C.

Holy Cross Church objected to appellee's application, expressing concern over "having so many licenses *so* near." The License Commission voted to deny the application, citing only the objection of Holy Cross Church and noting that the church "is within 10 feet of the proposed location."[2]

II

[The Court rejected appellants' argument that zoning laws like the Massachusetts statute are necessary to protect schools and churches from stores that sell liquor. The Court agreed that courts should usually defer to zoning decisions, but noted that § 16C was not an ordinary zoning law because it gave a veto to private, nongovernmental entities.]

B

The purposes of the First Amendment guarantees relating to religion were twofold: to foreclose state interference with the practice of religious faiths, and to foreclose the establishment of a state religion familiar in other Eighteenth Century systems. Religion and government, each insulated from the other, could then coexist. Jefferson's idea of a "wall," see *Reynolds*, was a useful figurative illustration to emphasize the concept of separateness. Some limited and incidental entanglement between church and state authority is inevitable in a complex modern society, but the concept of a "wall" of separation is a useful signpost. Here that "wall" is substantially breached by vesting discretionary governmental powers in religious bodies.

[Applying the *Lemon* test, the Court concluded that the statute had a secular purpose, to protect schools and churches from liquor sellers, and that it had a primary and principal effect of advancing religion.]

Turning to the third phase of the inquiry called for by *Lemon v. Kurtzman*, we see that we have not previously had occasion to consider the entanglement implications of a statute vesting significant governmental authority in churches. This statute enmeshes churches in the exercise of substantial governmental powers contrary to our consistent interpretation of the Establishment Clause; "[the] objective is to prevent, as far as possible, the intrusion of either [Church or State] into the precincts of the other." [In *Lemon*, we stated:]

> Under our system the choice has been made that government is to be entirely excluded from the area of religious instruction

---

Section 16C originally was enacted in 1954 as an absolute ban on liquor licenses within 500 feet of a church or school, 1954 Mass.Acts, ch. 569, § 1. A 1968 amendment modified the absolute prohibition, permitting licenses within the 500-foot radius "if the governing body of such church assents in writing," 1968 Mass.Acts, ch. 435. In 1970, the statute was amended to its present form, 1970 Mass.Acts, ch. 192.

[2] In 1979, there were 26 liquor licensees in Harvard Square and within a 500-foot radius of Holy Cross Church; 25 of these were in existence at the time Holy Cross Church objected to appellee's application.

and churches excluded from the affairs of government. The Constitution decrees that religion must be a private matter for the individual, the family, and the institutions of private choice, and that while some involvement and entanglement are inevitable, lines must be drawn.

Our contemporary views do no more than reflect views approved by the Court more than a century ago:

The structure of our government has, for the preservation of civil liberty, rescued the temporal institutions from religious interference. On the other hand, it has secured religious liberty from the invasion of the civil authority. *Watson v. Jones*, 80 U.S. (13 Wall.) 679, 730, 20 L.Ed. 666 (1872).

As these and other cases make clear, the core rationale underlying the Establishment Clause is preventing "a fusion of governmental and religious functions."[10] The Framers did not set up a system of government in which important, discretionary governmental powers would be delegated to or shared with religious institutions.

Section 16C substitutes the unilateral and absolute power of a church for the reasoned decisionmaking of a public legislative body acting on evidence and guided by standards, on issues with significant economic and political implications. The challenged statute thus enmeshes churches in the processes of government and creates the danger of "[p]olitical fragmentation and divisiveness on religious lines," [*Lemon*]. Ordinary human experience and a long line of cases teach that few entanglements could be more offensive to the spirit of the Constitution.

■ JUSTICE REHNQUIST, dissenting.

Dissenting opinions in previous cases have commented that "great" cases, like "hard" cases, make bad law. Today's opinion suggests that a third class of cases—silly cases—also make bad law. The aim of this effort is to prove that a quite sensible Massachusetts liquor zoning law is apparently some sort of sinister religious attack on secular government reminiscent of St. Bartholemew's Night. Being unpersuaded, I dissent.

In its original form, § 16C imposed a flat ban on the grant of an alcoholic beverages license to any establishment located within 500 feet of a church or a school. Over time, the legislature found that it could meet its goal of protecting people engaged in religious activities from liquor-related disruption with a less absolute prohibition. Rather than set out elaborate formulae or require an administrative agency to make

---

[10] At the time of the Revolution, Americans feared not only a denial of religious freedom, but also the danger of political oppression through a union of civil and ecclesiastical control. In 18th-century England, such a union of civil and ecclesiastical power was reflected in legal arrangements granting church officials substantial control over various occupations, including the liquor trade.

findings of fact, the legislature settled on the simple expedient of asking churches to object if a proposed liquor outlet would disturb them. Thus, under the present version of § 16C, a liquor outlet within 500 feet of a church or school can be licensed unless the affected institution objects. The flat ban, which the majority concedes is valid, is more protective of churches and more restrictive of liquor sales than the present § 16C.

The evolving treatment of the grant of liquor licenses to outlets located within 500 feet of a church or a school seems to me to be the sort of legislative refinement that we should encourage, not forbid in the name of the First Amendment. If a particular church or a particular school located within the 500–foot radius chooses not to object, the State has quite sensibly concluded that there is no reason to prohibit the issuance of the license. Nothing in the Court's opinion persuades me why the more rigid prohibition would be constitutional, but the more flexible not. . . . The state does not, in my opinion, "advance" religion by making provision for those who wish to engage in religious activities, as well as those who wish to engage in educational activities, to be unmolested by activities at a neighboring bar or tavern that have historically been thought incompatible.

NOTES AND QUESTIONS

1. Is the fusion of governmental and religious functions unconstitutional because it harms the church? Because it harms the state? Or for both reasons?

2. Do you think it would be appropriate for a church to provide input into the decision about liquor licenses but not to exercise veto power? Is it constitutional for a state to include a church on a list of entities whose advice must be sought before a license is granted? If the list includes schools, libraries, hospitals, playgrounds, and parks, is it constitutional to include a church along with those other groups? Is it constitutional to exclude churches from the list? See Jacob J. Waldman, That's What I Like About Utah: *Larkin v. Grendel's Den* and the Alcoholic Beverage Control Act, 37 Colum. J.L. & Soc. Probs. 239, 273 (2003).

3. An 1897 New York law prohibits bars within 200 feet of a school or religious institution. After a new owner purchased and renovated a bar, some neighbors discovered the old law on the Internet and decided to challenge the bar's owners under the statute. The bars are within 200 feet of a mosque that is difficult to see. The gold lettering on the mosque's front door does not say mosque, and a representative of the mosque said, "We don't have a dispute with any of the neighbors. We are here to support them. Our main thing is to be neutral. . . . We don't want anyone to lose their jobs." See David Lombino, N.Y. State Tries To Close TriBeCa Bars For Being Too Close to a Mosque, N.Y. Sun, Mar. 7, 2006, at 1. Is the New York law constitutional under *Larkin*? Why or why not? At another new bar across the street from a mosque, after Muslims complained about the bar's presence, the bar owner volunteered to put curtains at the bar window so that Muslims could not see customers drinking. Is this a good resolution to the problem? See Pamela Geller, Shariah in Chi Manhattan: Muslims Threaten Fashionable Bar Owner After He Laughs Off Bar Demand, Atlas Shrugs, Oct. 30, 2009.

Developers planned to build an 8,000–seat, $64 million amphitheater in a park on Coney Island. Members of an Orthodox Jewish synagogue across the street from the park challenged the building under a state law that "bans permits for amplified sound within 500 feet of religious institutions, schools, courthouses and other gathering places when they are in session." Is this the kind of neutral law allowed by *Larkin*? The synagogue holds its largest services on Friday and Saturday nights when schools and courthouses are likely to be closed. If the synagogue is the only institution challenging the building, should its objections be denied under *Larkin*? See Elizabeth Hays, Coney Island Synagogue to Use City Noise Law to Foil Markowitz's Concert Hall, N.Y. Daily News, May 17, 2009.

4.   Do you think that § 16C was a wise accommodation of religion that should have been permitted by the Court, as Justice Rehnquist suggests?

5.   Would the Founders of our nation be surprised to discover that Holy Cross Armenian Catholic Church violated the Establishment Clause by its veto of the liquor license?

6.   As background to the following case, *Kiryas Joel*, note that in 1985 the Supreme Court decided that a program giving federal funds to New York City to pay the salaries of public school teachers who taught remedial courses in or near religious schools violated the Establishment Clause. The Court concluded that this arrangement provided excessive entanglement between church and state. See Aguilar v. Felton, 473 U.S. 402 (1985). *Aguilar* was later overruled by Agostini v. Felton, 521 U.S. 203 (1997), after the Court decided that *Aguilar* was too hostile to religion.

Board of Education of Kiryas Joel Village School District v. Grumet

Supreme Court of the United States, 1994.
512 U.S. 687, 114 S.Ct. 2481, 129 L.Ed.2d 546.

■ JUSTICE SOUTER delivered the opinion of the Court.

The village of Kiryas Joel in Orange County, New York, is a religious enclave of Satmar Hasidim, practitioners of a strict form of Judaism. The village fell within the Monroe-Woodbury Central School District until a special state statute passed in 1989 carved out a separate district, following village lines, to serve this distinctive population. 1989 N.Y. Laws, ch. 748. The question is whether the Act creating the separate school district violates the Establishment Clause of the First Amendment, binding on the States through the Fourteenth Amendment. Because this unusual Act is tantamount to an allocation of political power on a religious criterion and neither presupposes nor requires governmental impartiality toward religion, we hold that it violates the prohibition against establishment.

I

The Satmar Hasidic sect takes its name from the town near the Hungarian and Romanian border where, in the early years of this century, Grand Rebbe Joel Teitelbaum molded the group into a distinct community. After World War II and the destruction of much of European Jewry, the Grand Rebbe and most of his surviving followers moved to the Williamsburg section of Brooklyn, New York. Then, 20 years ago, the Satmars purchased an approved but undeveloped subdivision in the town of Monroe and began assembling the community that has since become the village of Kiryas Joel. When a zoning dispute arose in the course of settlement, the Satmars presented the Town Board of Monroe with a petition to form a new village within the town, a right that New York's Village Law gives almost any group of residents who satisfy certain procedural niceties. Neighbors who did not wish to secede with the Satmars objected strenuously, and after arduous negotiations the proposed boundaries of the village of Kiryas Joel were drawn to include just the 320 acres owned and inhabited entirely by Satmars. The village, incorporated in 1977, has a population of about 8,500 today. Rabbi Aaron Teitelbaum, eldest son of the current Grand Rebbe, serves as the village rov (chief rabbi) and rosh yeshivah (chief authority in the parochial schools).

The residents of Kiryas Joel are vigorously religious people who make few concessions to the modern world and go to great lengths to avoid assimilation into it. They interpret the Torah strictly; segregate the sexes outside the home; speak Yiddish as their primary language; eschew television, radio, and English-language publications; and dress in distinctive ways that include headcoverings and special garments for boys and modest dresses for girls. Children are educated in private religious schools, most boys at the United Talmudic Academy where they receive a thorough grounding in the Torah and limited exposure to secular subjects, and most girls at Bais Rochel, an affiliated school with a curriculum designed to prepare girls for their roles as wives and mothers.

These schools do not, however, offer any distinctive services to handicapped children, who are entitled under state and federal law to special education services even when enrolled in private schools. Starting in 1984 the Monroe-Woodbury Central School District provided such services for the children of Kiryas Joel at an annex to Bais Rochel, but a year later ended that arrangement in response to our decisions in *Aguilar v. Felton*, 473 U.S. 402, 105 S.Ct. 3232, 87 L.Ed.2d 290 (1985), and *School Dist. of Grand Rapids v. Ball*, 473 U.S. 373, 105 S.Ct. 3216, 87 L.Ed.2d 267 (1985). Children from Kiryas Joel who needed special education (including the deaf, the mentally retarded, and others suffering from a range of physical, mental, or emotional disorders) were then forced to attend public schools outside the village, which their families found highly unsatisfactory. Parents of most of these children withdrew them from the Monroe-Woodbury secular schools, citing "the panic, fear and trauma [the children] suffered in leaving their own community and being with people whose ways were so different."

By 1989, only one child from Kiryas Joel was attending Monroe-Woodbury's public schools; the village's other handicapped children received privately funded special services or went without. It was then that the New York Legislature passed the statute at issue in this litigation, which provided that the village of Kiryas Joel "is constituted a separate school district, . . . and shall have and enjoy all the powers and duties of a union free school district."

Although it enjoys plenary legal authority over the elementary and secondary education of all school-aged children in the village, the Kiryas Joel Village School District currently runs only a special education program for handicapped children. The other village children have stayed in their parochial schools, relying on the new school district only for transportation, remedial education, and health and welfare services. If any child without a handicap in Kiryas Joel were to seek a public-school education, the district would pay tuition to send the child into Monroe-Woodbury or another school district nearby. Under like arrangements, several of the neighboring districts send their handicapped Hasidic children into Kiryas Joel, so that two thirds of the full-time students in the village's public school come from outside. In all, the new district serves just over 40 full-time students, and two or three times that many parochial school students on a part-time basis.

II

Larkin presented an example of united civic and religious authority, an establishment rarely found in such straightforward form in modern America, and a violation of "the core rationale underlying the Establishment Clause." The Establishment Clause problem presented by Chapter 748 is more subtle, but it resembles the issue raised in *Larkin* to the extent that the earlier case teaches that a State may not delegate its civic authority to a group chosen according to a religious criterion. Authority over public schools belongs to the State, and cannot be delegated to a local school district defined by the State in order to grant political control to a religious group. What makes this litigation different from *Larkin* is the delegation here of civic power to the "qualified voters of the village of Kiryas Joel," 1989 N.Y. Laws, ch. 748, as distinct from a religious leader such as the village rov, or an institution of religious government like the formally constituted parish council in *Larkin*. In light of the circumstances of these cases, however, this distinction turns out to lack constitutional significance.

It is, first, not dispositive that the recipients of state power in these cases are a group of religious individuals united by common doctrine, not the group's leaders or officers. In the circumstances of these cases, the difference between thus vesting state power in the members of a religious group as such instead of the officers of its sectarian organization is one of form, not substance. That individuals who happen to be religious may hold public office does not mean that a State may deliberately delegate discretionary power to an individual, institution, or community on the ground of religious identity. If New York were to delegate civic authority to "the Grand Rebbe," *Larkin* would obviously require invalidation (even though under *McDaniel* the Grand Rebbe may run for, and serve on, his local school board), and the same is true if New York delegates political authority by reference to religious belief. Where "fusion" is an issue, the difference lies in the distinction between a government's purposeful delegation on the basis of religion and a delegation on principles neutral to religion, to individuals whose religious identities are incidental to their receipt of civic authority.

Of course, Chapter 748 delegates power not by express reference to the religious belief of the Satmar community, but to residents of the "territory of the village of Kiryas Joel." 1989 N.Y. Laws, ch. 748. Thus the second (and arguably more important) distinction between these cases and *Larkin* is the identification here of the group to exercise civil authority in terms not expressly religious. But our analysis does not end with the text of the statute at issue, and the context here persuades us that Chapter 748 effectively identifies these recipients of governmental authority by reference to doctrinal adherence, even though it does not do so expressly. We find this to be the better view of the facts because of the way the boundary lines of the school district divide residents according to religious affiliation, under the terms of an unusual and special legislative Act.

It is undisputed that those who negotiated the village boundaries when applying the general village incorporation statute drew them so as to exclude all but Satmars, and that the New York Legislature was well aware that the village remained exclusively Satmar in 1989 when it adopted Chapter 748.

Because the district's creation ran uniquely counter to state practice, following the lines of a religious community where the customary and neutral principles would not have dictated the same result, we have good reasons to treat this district as the reflection of a religious criterion for identifying the recipients of civil authority. Not even the special needs of the children in this community can explain the legislature's unusual Act, for the State could have responded to the concerns of the Satmar parents without implicating the Establishment Clause, as we explain in some detail further on. We therefore find the legislature's Act to be substantially equivalent to defining a political subdivision and hence the qualification for its franchise by a religious test, resulting in a purposeful and forbidden "fusion of governmental and religious functions." *Larkin v. Grendel's Den, Inc.,* 459 U.S. at 126.

C

[W]e do not deny that the Constitution allows the State to accommodate religious needs by alleviating special burdens. . . . Just as the Court in *Larkin* observed that the State's interest in protecting religious meeting places could be "readily accomplished by other means," *Larkin v. Grendel's Den, Inc.,* 459 U.S. at 124, there are several alternatives here for providing bilingual and bicultural special education to Satmar children. Such services can perfectly well be offered to village children through the Monroe-Woodbury Central School District. Since the Satmars do not claim that separatism is religiously mandated, their children may receive bilingual and bicultural instruction at a public school already run by the Monroe-Woodbury district. Or if the educationally appropriate offering by Monroe-Woodbury should turn out to be a separate program of bilingual and bicultural education at a neutral site near one of the village's parochial schools, this Court has already made it clear that no Establishment Clause difficulty would inhere in such a scheme, administered in accordance with neutral principles that would not necessarily confine special treatment to Satmars.

III

Justice Cardozo once cast the dissenter as "the gladiator making a last stand against the lions." B. Cardozo, Law and Literature 34 (1931). Justice SCALIA's dissent is certainly the work of a gladiator, but he thrusts at lions of his own imagining. We do not disable a religiously homogeneous group from exercising political power conferred on it without regard to religion. Unlike the States of Utah and New Mexico (which were laid out according to traditional political methodologies taking account of lines of latitude and longitude and topographical features), the reference line chosen for the Kiryas Joel Village School District was one purposely drawn to separate Satmars from non-Satmars.

[A concurrence by JUSTICE BLACKMUN is omitted.]

■ JUSTICE STEVENS, with whom JUSTICE BLACKMUN and JUSTICE GINSBURG join, concurring.

New York created a special school district for the members of the Satmar religious sect in response to parental concern that children suffered "panic, fear and trauma" when "leaving their own community and being with people whose ways were so different." To meet those concerns, the State could have taken steps to alleviate the children's fear by teaching their schoolmates to be tolerant and respectful of Satmar customs. Action of that kind would raise no constitutional concerns and would further the strong public interest in promoting diversity and understanding in the public schools.

Instead, the State responded with a solution that affirmatively supports a religious sect's interest in segregating itself and preventing its children from associating with their neighbors. The isolation of these children, while it may protect them from "panic, fear and trauma," also unquestionably increased the likelihood that they would remain within the fold, faithful adherents of their parents' religious faith. By creating a school district that is specifically intended to shield children from contact with others who have "different ways," the State provided official support to cement the attachment of young adherents to a particular faith. It is telling, in this regard, that two-thirds of the school's full-time students are Hasidic handicapped children from *outside* the village; the Kiryas Joel school thus serves a population far wider than the village—one defined less by geography than by religion.

Affirmative state action in aid of segregation of this character is unlike the evenhanded distribution of a public benefit or service, a "release time" program for public school students involving no public premises or funds, or a decision to grant an exemption from a burdensome general rule. It is, I believe, fairly characterized as establishing, rather than merely accommodating, religion.

■ JUSTICE O'CONNOR, concurring in part and concurring in the judgment.

III

I think this law, rather than being a general accommodation, singles out a particular religious group for favorable treatment. The Court's analysis of the history of this law and of the surrounding statutory scheme persuades me of this.

Our invalidation of this statute in no way means that the Satmars' needs cannot be accommodated. There is nothing improper about a legislative intention to accommodate a religious group, so long as it is implemented through generally applicable legislation. New York may, for instance, allow all villages to operate their own school districts. If it does not want to act so broadly, it may set forth neutral criteria that a village must meet to have a school district of its own; these criteria can then be applied by a state agency, and the decision would then be reviewable by the judiciary. A district created under a generally applicable scheme would be acceptable even though it coincides with a village that was consciously created by its voters as an enclave for their religious group. I do not think the Court's opinion holds the contrary.

I also think there is one other accommodation that would be entirely permissible: the 1984 scheme, which was discontinued because of our decision in *Aguilar*. The Religion Clauses prohibit the government from favoring religion, but they provide no warrant for discriminating *against* religion. All handicapped children are entitled by law to government-funded special education. If the government provides this education on-site at public schools and at nonsectarian private schools, it is only fair that it provide it on-site at sectarian schools as well.

I thought this to be true in *Aguilar*, and I still believe it today. The Establishment Clause does not demand hostility to religion, religious ideas, religious people, or religious schools. It is the Court's insistence on disfavoring religion in *Aguilar* that led New York to favor it here. The Court should, in a proper case, be prepared to reconsider *Aguilar*, in order to bring our Establishment Clause jurisprudence back to what I think is the proper track—government impartiality, not animosity, toward religion.

■ JUSTICE KENNEDY, concurring in the judgment.

II

"The principle that government may accommodate the free exercise of religion does not supersede the fundamental limitations imposed by the Establishment Clause," *Lee v. Weisman*, 505 U.S. 577, 587, 112 S.Ct. 2649, 2655, 120 L.Ed.2d 467 (1992), and in my view one such fundamental limitation is that government may not use religion as a criterion to draw political or electoral lines. Whether or not the purpose is accommodation and whether or not the government provides similar gerrymanders to people of all religious faiths, the Establishment Clause forbids the government to use religion as a line-drawing criterion. There is no serious question that the legislature configured the school district, with purpose and precision, along a religious line. This explicit religious gerrymandering violates the First Amendment Establishment Clause.

As the plurality indicates, the Establishment Clause does not invalidate a town or a State "whose boundaries are derived according to neutral historical and geographic criteria, but whose population happens to comprise coreligionists." People who share a common religious belief or lifestyle may live together without sacrificing the basic rights of self-governance that all American citizens enjoy, so long as they do not use those rights to establish their religious faith. Religion flourishes in community, and the Establishment Clause must not be construed as some sort of homogenizing solvent that forces unconventional religious groups to choose between assimilating to mainstream American culture or losing their political rights. There is more than a fine line, however, between the voluntary association that leads to a political community comprised of people who share a common religious faith, and the forced separation that occurs when the government draws explicit political boundaries on the basis of peoples' faith. In creating the Kiryas Joel Village School District, New York crossed that line, and so we must hold the district invalid.

■ JUSTICE SCALIA, with whom THE CHIEF JUSTICE and JUSTICE THOMAS join, dissenting.

The Court today finds that the Powers That Be, up in Albany, have conspired to effect an establishment of the Satmar Hasidim. I do not know who would be more surprised at this discovery: the Founders of our Nation or Grand Rebbe Joel Teitelbaum, founder of the Satmar. The Grand Rebbe would be astounded to learn that after escaping brutal persecution and coming to America with the modest hope of religious toleration for their ascetic form of Judaism, the Satmar had become so powerful, so closely allied with Mammon, as to have become an "establishment" of the Empire State. And the Founding Fathers would be astonished to find that the Establishment Clause—which they designed "to insure that no one powerful sect or combination of sects could use political or governmental power to punish dissenters," has been employed to prohibit characteristically and admirably American accommodation of the religious practices (or more precisely, cultural peculiarities) of a tiny minority sect. *I*, however, am *not* surprised. Once this Court has abandoned text and history as guides, nothing prevents it from calling religious toleration the establishment of religion.

II

For his thesis that New York has unconstitutionally conferred governmental authority upon the Satmar sect, Justice SOUTER relies extensively, and virtually exclusively, upon *Larkin*. Justice SOUTER believes that the present litigation "resembles" *Grendel's Den* because that case "teaches that a State may not delegate its civic authority *to a group chosen according to a religious criterion*," (emphasis added). That misdescribes both what that case taught (which is that a State may not delegate its civil authority *to a church*), and what these cases involve (which is a group chosen according to cultural characteristics). The statute at issue there gave churches veto power over the State's authority to grant a liquor license to establishments in the vicinity of the church. The Court had little difficulty finding the statute unconstitutional.

Justice SOUTER concedes that *Grendel's Den* "presented an example of united civic and religious authority, an establishment rarely found in such straightforward form in modern America." The uniqueness of the case stemmed from the grant of governmental power directly to a religious institution, and the Court's opinion focused on that fact, remarking that the transfer of authority was to "churches" (10 times), the "governing body of churches" (twice), "religious institutions" (twice), and "religious bodies" (once). Astonishingly, however, Justice SOUTER dismisses the difference between a transfer of government power to citizens who share a common religion as opposed to "the officers of its sectarian organization"—the critical factor that made *Grendel's Den* unique and "rare"—as being "one of form, not substance."

Justice SOUTER's steamrolling of the difference between civil authority held by a church and civil authority held by members of a church is breathtaking. To accept it, one must believe that large portions of the civil authority exercised during most of our history were unconstitutional, and that much more of it than merely the Kiryas Joel school district is unconstitutional today. The history of the populating of North America is in no small measure the story of groups of people sharing a common religious and cultural heritage striking out to form their own communities. It is preposterous to suggest that the civil institutions of these communities, separate from their churches, were constitutionally suspect. And if they were, surely Justice SOUTER cannot mean that the inclusion of one or two nonbelievers in the community would have been enough to eliminate the constitutional vice. If the conferral of governmental power upon a religious institution *as such* (rather than upon American citizens who belong to the religious institution) is not the test of *Grendel's Den* invalidity, there is no reason why giving power to a body that is overwhelmingly dominated by the members of one sect would not suffice to invoke the Establishment Clause. That might have made the entire States of Utah and New Mexico unconstitutional at the time of their admission to the Union, and would undoubtedly make many units of local government unconstitutional today.

III

I have little doubt that Justice SOUTER would laud this humanitarian legislation if all of the distinctiveness of the students of Kiryas Joel were attributable to the fact that their parents were nonreligious commune dwellers, or American Indians, or gypsies. The creation of a special, one-culture school district for the benefit of those children would pose no problem. The neutrality demanded by the Religion Clauses requires the same indulgence towards cultural characteristics that *are* accompanied by religious belief.

NOTES AND QUESTIONS

1.   Which opinion is most persuasive, the one written by Justice Souter, Stevens, O'Connor, Kennedy, or Scalia? Why?

2.   Why does Justice Souter conclude the "allocation of political power on a religious criterion" is unconstitutional? Was the power in Kiryas Joel really allocated on a religious criterion, or was a cultural characteristic employed instead, as Justice Scalia suggests in his dissent? Is Justice Scalia correct that Justice Souter's theory of the Establishment Clause allows a special district for American Indians and gypsies but not for the Satmar Hasidim?

3.   What are the alternatives to the Kiryas Joel school district that Justice Souter identifies in his opinion? How do you assess their adequacy and their constitutionality?

4. Justice O'Connor frequently argued for the accommodation of religion in other Establishment Clause cases. Why did she believe that this accommodation of Kiryas Joel is unconstitutional? Do you agree with Justice O'Connor that the government should be allowed to provide remedial education on-site at sectarian schools, the arrangement that was prohibited by *Aguilar*? Or should the Hasidim forfeit any claim to remedial education from the government when they enroll in private schools? For a discussion of how much the Hasidim should be accommodated, see Abner S. Greene, Kiryas Joel and Two Mistakes About Equality, 96 Colum. L. Rev. 1 (1996) and Ira C. Lupu, Uncovering the Village of Kiryas Joel, 96 Colum. L. Rev. 104 (1996).

5. How could the state teach other students to be tolerant of the Satmar customs without violating the Constitution? If the state implemented such a program, would this program in and of itself violate the Establishment Clause?

6. What is the difference between a religious gerrymander and the accommodation of religion?

7. Compare the Rehnquist dissent in *Larkin* to Justice Scalia's dissent in *Kiryas Joel*. Did the Court go too far in both cases in finding an Establishment Clause violation? Were the majority opinions hostile to religion?

8. After the Supreme Court decided *Kiryas Joel* (*Kiryas Joel I*), the New York legislature made three attempts to pass legislation broad and neutral enough to allow any local community to found its own school district. See Chapter 241, N.Y. Educ. Law § 1504 (McKinney 1994); Chapter 390, N.Y. Educ. Law § 1504 (McKinney 1997); Chapter 405, N.Y. Educ. Law § 83 (McKinney 1999). Twice the New York courts found Establishment Clause violations on the theory that the purpose of the legislation remained religion-based aid to the Satmars. The challengers did not appeal a third ruling that the Kiryas Joel school district was valid. The newest law gives any municipality that has 10,000 to 125,000 residents and is contained within a larger school district the right to petition for its own separate school district, financed by state education aid. The law's terms are broad enough to cover more than two dozen municipalities. The Kiryas Joel School District is open for business and is now a member of the New York State Association of School Boards, which had joined the constitutional challenges to Kiryas Joel's existence. See Tamar Lewin, Controversy Over, Enclave Joins School Board Group, N.Y. Times, Apr. 20, 2002; Nomi Stolzenberg, Board of Education of Kiryas Joel Village School District v. Grumet: A Religious Group's Quest For Its Own Public School, in L. Griffin, ed., Law and Religion: Cases in Context (Aspen 2010).

9. *Churches in Public Schools.* How do you assess the constitutionality of holding church in a public high school? Years of litigation followed attempts by the Bronx Household of Faith, an evangelical Christian church, to hold Sunday services at the Anne Cross Mersereau Middle School in New York. An initial Second Circuit ruling allowed the church services to be held in the school. See Bronx Household of Faith v. Board of Educ. of City of New York, 226 F.Supp.2d 401 (S.D.N.Y. 2002), aff'd by Bronx Household of Faith v. Board of Educ. of City of New York, 331 F.3d 342 (2d Cir. 2003) (*"Bronx Household II"*) (ruling that schools' policy of excluding churches from the rental market violated the First Amendment).

The question of holding church services in public schools returned to the Second Circuit in Bronx Household of Faith v. Board of Educ. of City of New York, 492 F.3d 89 (2d Cir. 2007) (*"Bronx Household III"*). The court returned a fractured decision. In *"Bronx Household II,"* 331 F.3d 342 (2003), the court had ruled that the schools' policy of excluding churches from the rental market violated the First Amendment. In response to that ruling, the Board of Education passed a new policy stating: "No permit shall be granted for the purpose of *holding religious worship services, or otherwise using a school as a house of worship,*" but allowing permits for religious clubs. In *Bronx Household III*, Judge Calabresi wrote that the dispute was ripe and that the new standard was viewpoint-neutral and therefore constitutional. Judge Walker wrote that the dispute was ripe and that the new standard was viewpoint-discriminatory and unconstitutional. Judge Leval concluded the dispute was not ripe.

In *Bronx Household IV*, the Second Circuit ruled 2–1 that the school district could bar the use of public school facilities for after-hours religious worship services. On the Establishment Clause issue, Judge Leval concluded that the churches' use of school facilities and utilities could entangle the government with religion and that the presence of religious worship services in the public schools could be seen as an endorsement of religion. In his words, "[d]uring these Sunday services, the schools are dominated by church use … and some schools effectively become churches." Do you agree this is an Establishment Clause problem? The opinion then added that the schools are used primarily on Sunday, thus showing a bias toward Christian churches, and that the church services are not open to the general public. Are these factors relevant to the Establishment Clause analysis? See The Bronx Household of Faith v. Board of Educ. of City of New York, 650 F.3d 30 (2d Cir. 2011), cert. denied, 132 S.Ct. 816 (2011). Judge Walker dissented from Judge Leval's Establishment Clause analysis. What arguments do you think he gave? See id.

Post-*Bronx Household IV*, the district court ruled that the Supreme Court's decision in *Hosanna-Tabor Evangelical Lutheran Church and School v. EEOC*, 132 S.Ct. 694 (2012), meant Bronx Household's lawsuit should succeed. Because *Hosanna-Tabor* recognized a right for churches to conduct their own religious affairs without government interference, the court ruled, it followed that churches must be free to choose the best location for their worship without government interference. Thus, if Bronx Household wanted to worship on public property because it was cheaper than comparable commercial space, the government could not stand in its way. The district judge then asserted that even the city's determination that Bronx Household wanted to engage in religious worship violated the

Establishment Clause and *Hosanna-Tabor*. Bronx Household of Faith v. Board of Educ. of City of New York, 876 F.Supp.2d 419 (S.D.N.Y. June 29, 2012).

In Bronx Household of Faith v. Board of Educ. of City of New York, 750 F.3d 184 (2d Cir. 2014), cert. denied, 135 S.Ct. 1730 (2015) (*Bronx Household V*), the Second Circuit rejected the district court's reasoning. First, it ruled, in enforcing the religious worship rule, the city had not made any assessment of what worship means to Bronx Household; in fact, the city had relied exclusively on Bronx's application, which stated the church wanted to use the school's facilities for "religious worship." And, the Second Circuit observed, even if the government had reviewed Bronx's application to learn if it was involved in religious worship, *Hosanna-Tabor* was not violated "because in *Hosanna-Tabor* the Supreme Court itself did precisely what the District Court found a governmental entity prohibited from doing." Id. at 204. In other words, in *Hosanna-Tabor* the Court decided who was a minister before granting the exception. Under the Court's precedent, therefore, the courts may decide not only who is a minister, but also what constitutes religious worship.

Do *Larkin* and *Kiryas Joel* shed any light on this question, or are they irrelevant to the issue of holding worship services in public schools?

10. *Government Operating "As an Arm" of a Religious Group.* In an unusual lawsuit, the United States Department of Justice filed a complaint against the Town of Colorado City, Arizona, and the City of Hildale, Utah, alleging the city governments "operated as an arm" of the Fundamentalist Church of Jesus Christ of Latter-day Saints (FLDS) to discriminate against non-FLDS members. According to the complaint,

> The Cities' public officials, the Colorado City/Hildale Marshal's Office ("the Marshal's Office"), and utility entities have acted in concert with FLDS leadership to deny non-FLDS individuals housing, police protection, and access to public space and services. Furthermore, the Defendants have denied non-FLDS members access to housing in the Cities, and they have coerced, intimidated, threatened, and interfered with the housing rights of non-FLDS members. The Marshal's Office has inappropriately used its state-granted law enforcement authority to enforce the edicts of the FLDS, to the detriment of non-FLDS members. In addition, the Cities' officials have misdirected and misused public resources in the service of the FLDS.

United States v. Town of Colorado City, Plaintiff's Complaint, No. 3_12CV08123, 2012 WL 2354466 (D. Ariz. Jun. 21, 2012). The Marshal's Office was accused of selectively prosecuting non-FLDS individuals for trespass and traffic violations. Marshal's Deputies were also dispatched in official vehicles "to confront persons about their alleged disobedience to FLDS rules and instructing such persons to report to FLDS leadership." The government alleged that Warren Jeffs, leader of the FLDS church, directed the local governments from prison. For example, city officials allegedly shot and killed local dogs in order to enforce a Jeffs edict banning all domestic dogs from the cities. The Cities also denied public services to non-FLDS residents by threatening to arrest FLDS children if they played in the local park and delaying or denying water and utilities services to non-FLDS residents.

Is the following section of the complaint accurate in describing an Establishment Clause violation?

> The actions and omissions of the Marshal's Office constitute an impermissible delegation of decision-making and authority to the FLDS, an entanglement of religious and civil functions, a fusion of government power and religious authority, and have the purpose and effect of the Cities impermissibly advancing religion. Because of these actions and omissions, there is no effective means of guaranteeing that the Cities' governmental power is neutrally employed.

Id. What cases should be referenced with that language?

In response to the complaint, Hildale, Utah argued (among other defenses) that the conduct alleged, if true, "was caused, in whole or in part, by the acts or omissions of third parties over whom Hildale Defendants had no control" and "was completed by individuals acting outside their official capacities with Hildale Defendants, not within the course or scope of their employment with Hildale Defendants, and/or without the authority of Hildale Defendants." Colorado City, Arizona raised similar defenses. Hildale Defendants' Answer and Jury Demand, United States v. Town of Colorado City, No. CV-12-8123-PCT-HRH, 2012 WL 6709516 (D. Ariz., Dec. 13, 2012); Town of Colorado City, Arizona's Answer to Complaint, United States v. Town of Colorado City, No. CV-12-8123-PCT-HRH, 2012 WL 6709491 (D. Ariz., Dec. 13, 2012). Were these appropriate defenses to an Establishment Clause violation?

The Arizona and Utah cities took the position that the Department of Justice's lawsuit was an attack on their religious freedom. During closing arguments, the attorney for Colorado City told the jury: "You're the only ones who can tell the federal government no, it's not okay in these United States of America to prosecute individuals because of their religious beliefs." See Fernanda Santos, Towns Run By Polygamist Sect Violated Rights of Others, Jury Finds, N.Y. Times, Mar. 8, 2016, at A18. What, if any, free exercise protections do city and state governments have against the federal government? What about individuals in government roles? Were the government officials in this case merely acting in accordance with their religious beliefs? How do you think the *Kiryas Joel* court justices would have analyzed the prosecution?

On March 7, 2016, the jury in Town of Colorado City decided in the Department of Justice's favor, finding that the two towns operated as arms of FLDS. If you worked for the Justice Department, what would you recommend that the cities do to fix the violations? Should an entire city become the subject of federal oversight and management? Should police and other government services in the cities be put into a federal receivership? See Nigel Duara, Sect Loses to U.S. Officials, L.A. Times,

Mar. 8, 2016, at A5. Do you agree with the cities' attorneys that "the towns were victims of a deep-seated desire by the U.S. government to extinguish the religion and its way of life"? Id.

How do you react to the following allegation in the complaint? Was the Marshal's conduct really unconstitutional in this instance?

> Non-FLDS individuals experience the hardship and mental and physical stress resulting from the knowledge that the Marshal's Office will not come to their aid in time of need. For example, in January 2012, a woman who was, in effect, excommunicated by the FLDS, fled her home in the Cities with her six young daughters after learning that FLDS leaders demanded that she sever all contact with five of her six children. This woman believed, based on its policies and previous actions, that the Marshal's Office would not come to her assistance to protect her parental rights if she complained about the FLDS edict separating mothers from their children. She decided, as many other non-FLDS members have done, to flee with her children under cover of darkness to safety outside of the Cities. The failure and refusal of the Marshal's Office to protect all citizens without regard to religion has given rise to an "underground railroad," composed of non-FLDS members who provide safe havens and a means of egress for individuals abandoned by law enforcement.

See Complaint, infra.

11. Larkin *and* Lemon. Recall that the *Larkin* standard developed as an attempt to flesh out the meaning of the third part of the *Lemon* test, the excessive entanglement prong. If *Lemon* were discredited or overruled, could the Court still maintain the anti-fusion principle as a valid interpretation of the First Amendment? We study *Lemon* in the next section.

B. THE *LEMON* TEST, ENDORSEMENT, AND COERCION

Many of the Supreme Court's cases about the Establishment Clause involve government financial aid to religious institutions. *Lemon* is one of a modern series of cases about the constitutionality of aid to church-related elementary and secondary schools. The funding cases are examined in more detail in Chapter 3. In this section, the readings focus on the three-part test (in brief, secular purpose, primary effect, and excessive entanglement) that the Court has employed to determine if a range of governmental actions violates the Establishment Clause. It then introduces the *endorsement* and *coercion* tests as alternatives to *Lemon*.

Throughout these readings, you should learn to identify the various tests and to apply them to different sets of facts. As you do so, ask why the test has been so controversial and whether the test has the same implications for government conduct that it did in 1971.

Lemon v. Kurtzman

Supreme Court of the United States, 1971.
403 U.S. 602, 91 S.Ct. 2105, 29 L.Ed.2d 745.

■ MR. CHIEF JUSTICE BURGER delivered the opinion of the Court.

These two appeals raise questions as to Pennsylvania and Rhode Island statutes providing state aid to church-related elementary and secondary schools. Pennsylvania has adopted a statutory program that provides financial support to nonpublic elementary and secondary schools by way of reimbursement for the cost of teachers' salaries, textbooks, and instructional materials in specified secular subjects. Rhode Island has adopted a statute under which the State pays directly to teachers in nonpublic elementary schools a supplement of 15% of their annual salary. Under each statute state aid has been given to church-related educational institutions. We hold that both statutes are unconstitutional.

II

The language of the Religion Clauses of the First Amendment is at best opaque, particularly when compared with other portions of the Amendment. Its authors did not simply prohibit the establishment of a state church or a state religion, an area history shows they regarded as very important and fraught with great dangers. Instead they commanded that there should be "no law *respecting* an establishment of religion." A law may be one "respecting" the forbidden objective while falling short of its total realization. A law "respecting" the proscribed result, that is, the establishment of religion, is not always easily identifiable as one violative of the Clause. A given law might not *establish* a state religion but nevertheless be one "respecting" that end in the sense of being a step that could lead to such establishment and hence offend the First Amendment.

In the absence of precisely stated constitutional prohibitions, we must draw lines with reference to the three main evils against which the Establishment Clause was intended to afford protection: "sponsorship, financial support, and active involvement of the sovereign in religious activity."

Every analysis in this area must begin with consideration of the cumulative criteria developed by the Court over many years. Three such tests may be gleaned from our cases. First, the statute must have a secular legislative purpose; second, its principal or primary effect must be one that neither advances nor inhibits religion, finally, the statute must not foster "an excessive government entanglement with religion."

[The Court concluded the acts had a secular purpose (to "enhance the quality of the secular education in all schools") and did not decide the primary effect prong, because] "the cumulative impact of the entire relationship arising under the statutes in each State involves excessive entanglement between government and religion."

III

... The State must be certain, given the Religion Clauses, that subsidized teachers do not inculcate religion—indeed the State here has undertaken to do so. To ensure that no trespass occurs, the State has therefore carefully conditioned its aid with pervasive restrictions. An eligible recipient must teach only those courses that are offered in the public schools and use only those texts and materials that are found in the public schools. In addition the teacher must not engage in teaching any course in religion.

A comprehensive, discriminating, and continuing state surveillance will inevitably be required to ensure that these restrictions are obeyed and the First Amendment otherwise respected. Unlike a book, a teacher cannot be inspected once so as to determine the extent and intent of his or her personal beliefs and subjective acceptance of the limitations imposed by the First Amendment. These prophylactic contacts will involve excessive and enduring entanglement between state and church.

IV

A broader base of entanglement of yet a different character is presented by the divisive political potential of these state programs. In a community where such a large number of pupils are served by church-related schools, it can be assumed that state assistance will entail considerable political activity. Partisans of parochial schools, understandably concerned with rising costs and sincerely dedicated to both the religious and secular educational missions of their schools, will inevitably champion this cause and promote political action to achieve their goals. Those who oppose state aid, whether for constitutional, religious, or fiscal reasons, will inevitably respond and employ all of the usual political campaign techniques to prevail. Candidates will be forced to declare and voters to choose. It would be unrealistic to ignore the fact that many people confronted with issues of this kind will find their votes aligned with their faith.

Ordinarily political debate and division, however vigorous or even partisan, are normal and healthy manifestations of our democratic system of government, but political division along religious lines was one of the principal evils against which the First Amendment was intended to protect. The potential divisiveness of such conflict is a threat to the normal political process. To have States or communities divide on the issues presented by state aid to parochial schools would tend to confuse and obscure other issues of great urgency. We have an expanding array of vexing issues, local and national, domestic and international, to debate and divide on. It conflicts with our whole history and tradition to permit questions of the Religion Clauses to assume such importance in our legislatures and in our elections that they could divert attention from the myriad issues and problems that confront every level of government. The highways of church and state relationships are not likely to be one-way streets, and the Constitution's authors sought to protect religious worship from the pervasive power of government. The history of many countries attests to the hazards of religion's intruding into the political arena or of political power intruding into the legitimate and free exercise of religious belief.

V

In *Walz* it was argued that a tax exemption for places of religious worship would prove to be the first step in an inevitable progression leading to the establishment of state churches and state religion. That claim could not stand up against more than 200 years of virtually universal practice imbedded in our colonial experience and continuing into the present.

The progression argument, however, is more persuasive here. We have no long history of state aid to church-related educational institutions comparable to 200 years of tax exemption for churches. Indeed, the state programs before us today represent something of an innovation. We have already noted that modern governmental programs have self-perpetuating and self-expanding propensities. These internal pressures are only enhanced when the schemes involve institutions whose legitimate needs are growing and whose interests have substantial political support. Nor can we fail to see that in constitutional adjudication some steps, which when taken were thought to approach "the verge," have become the platform for yet further steps. A certain momentum develops in constitutional theory and it can be a "downhill thrust" easily set in motion but difficult to retard or stop. Development by momentum is not invariably bad; indeed, it is the way the common law has grown, but it is a force to be recognized and reckoned with. The dangers are increased by the difficulty of perceiving in advance exactly where the "verge" of the precipice lies. As well as constituting an independent evil against which the Religion Clauses were intended to protect, involvement or entanglement between government and religion serves as a warning signal.

Finally, nothing we have said can be construed to disparage the role of church-related elementary and secondary schools in our national life. Their contribution has been and is enormous. Nor do we ignore their economic plight in a period of rising costs and expanding need. Taxpayers generally have been spared vast sums by the maintenance of these educational institutions by religious organizations, largely by the gifts of faithful adherents.

The merit and benefits of these schools, however, are not the issue before us in these cases. The sole question is whether state aid to these schools can be squared with the dictates of the Religion Clauses. Under our system the choice has been made that government is to be entirely excluded from the area of religious instruction and churches excluded from the affairs of government. The Constitution decrees that religion must be a private matter for the individual, the family, and the institutions of private choice, and that while some involvement and entanglement are inevitable, lines must be drawn.

NOTES AND QUESTIONS

1.   Assess Chief Justice Burger's argument about the political divisiveness of government programs aiding religion. Is the possibility of political divisiveness a reason not to give aid to religious institutions?

2.   Assess Justice Rehnquist's later criticism that the entanglement prong of *Lemon* is the Court's "Catch-22 paradox of its own creation . . . whereby aid must be supervised to ensure no entanglement but the supervision itself is held to cause an entanglement." See Aguilar v. Felton, supra, at 420–21 (Rehnquist, J., dissenting).

3.   *Endorsement and Coercion.* In Estate of Thornton v. Caldor, 472 U.S. 703 (1985), the Court invalidated a Connecticut statute that required employers to grant employees a day off for their Sabbath. Thornton, a Presbyterian, refused to work on Sundays, and rejected Caldor's offer of a transfer to a Massachusetts store that was closed on Sundays, or to a different position with a lower salary. He was then transferred from his management position to a clerical position. In declaring the law unconstitutional, Chief Justice Burger wrote that the statute, which included no exceptions for special circumstances, "arms Sabbath observers with an absolute and unqualified right not to work on whatever day they designate as their Sabbath" and "imposes on employers and employees an absolute duty to conform their business practices to the particular religious practices of the employee." Id. at 709. Burger concluded:

> This unyielding weighting in favor of Sabbath observers over all other interests contravenes a fundamental principle of the Religion Clauses, so well articulated by Judge Learned Hand:
>
>> "The First Amendment . . . gives no one the right to insist that in pursuit of their own interests others must conform their conduct to his own religious necessities."
>
> As such, the statute goes beyond having an incidental or remote effect of advancing religion. The statute has a primary effect that impermissibly advances a particular religious practice [and thus fails the *Lemon* test].

Justice O'Connor concurred in the judgment, but relied on her interpretation of *Lemon*, namely, the endorsement test, to invalidate the Connecticut statute:

> In my view, the Connecticut Sabbath law has an impermissible effect because it conveys a message of endorsement of the Sabbath observance. There can be little doubt that an objective observer or

the public at large would perceive this statutory scheme precisely as the Court does today. The message conveyed is one of endorsement of a particular religious belief, to the detriment of those who do not share it. As such, the Connecticut statute has the effect of advancing religion, and cannot withstand Establishment Clause scrutiny. Id. at 711.

How do you assess the Connecticut statute from *Caldor*? Was it an accommodation of religion that the Court should have permitted? How would it work in the workplace?

Justice O'Connor had relied on the endorsement test a year earlier, in Lynch v. Donnelly, 465 U.S. 668 (1984), when she concurred in another Burger opinion. Chief Justice Burger wrote that the public display of a crèche in a holiday display that also included "a Santa Claus house, reindeer pulling Santa's sleigh, candy-striped poles, a Christmas tree, carolers, cutout figures representing such characters as a clown, an elephant, and a teddy bear, hundreds of colored lights, [and] a large banner that reads 'SEASONS GREETINGS' " did not violate the Establishment Clause. Justice O'Connor relied on an endorsement test that she thought captured the first two prongs of the *Lemon* test: "The purpose prong of the Lemon test asks whether [the] government's actual purpose is to endorse or disapprove of religion. The effect prong asks whether, irrespective of [the] government's actual purpose, the practice under review in fact conveys a message of endorsement or disapproval. An affirmative answer to either question should render the challenged practice invalid." Id. at 690. *Lynch* also explained the constitutional problem with government endorsement of religion in the following lapidary statement: it "sends a message to nonadherents that they are outsiders, not full members of the political community, and an accompanying message to adherents that they are insiders, favored members of the political community." Id. at 688.

In a later crèche case, County of Allegheny v. ACLU, 492 U.S. 573 (1989), Justice O'Connor concurred in a decision that a Christian Nativity scene on the Grand Staircase of the Allegheny County Courthouse violated the Establishment Clause, but an eighteen-foot Chanukah menorah or candelabrum, located outside the City-County Building and next to the city's forty-five-foot decorated Christmas tree and a "salute to liberty" sign, did not. O'Connor again relied upon the endorsement standard, concluding that the crèche conveyed a message of exclusion to non-Christians, while the combined display of menorah and Christmas tree did not send a message of endorsement of Judaism and/or Christianity.

Justice Kennedy argued that both the crèche and the menorah were constitutional, and criticized the endorsement test as a "recent, and in my view, most unwelcome addition to our tangled Establishment Clause jurisprudence." Id. at 668. According to Kennedy, "the endorsement test is flawed in its fundamentals and unworkable in practice. The uncritical adoption of this standard is every bit as troubling as the bizarre result it produces in the cases before us." Kennedy believed that the endorsement test invalidated historical and traditional practices and rituals—such as displaying the nativity scene—that were appropriate accommodations of religion under the Establishment Clause. He proposed in its place a coercion test: "government may not coerce anyone to support or participate in any religion or its exercise." The crèche and the menorah withstood the coercion analysis. In her concurring opinion in *Allegheny*, Justice O'Connor directly addressed Justice Kennedy's arguments when she wrote: "An Establishment Clause standard that prohibits only 'coercive' practices or overt efforts at government proselytization, but fails to take account of the numerous more subtle ways that government can show favoritism to particular beliefs or convey a message of disapproval to others, would not, in my view, adequately protect the religious liberty or respect the religious diversity of the members of our pluralistic political community. Thus, this Court has never relied on coercion alone as the touchstone of Establishment Clause analysis." Id. at 627–28.

Is Justice O'Connor's endorsement test clearer and easier to apply than the *Lemon* test? From whose perspective does one employ the endorsement test: the reasonable person, the objective observer, the ideal observer, the public at large, the average citizen, a religious believer, an atheist, Justice O'Connor, or an "'ultra-reasonable observer' who understands the vagaries of [the Supreme Court's] First Amendment jurisprudence"? See Capitol Square Review and Advisory Bd. v. Pinette, 515 U.S. 753, 781 (1995). Is Justice O'Connor correct that the coercion test insufficiently protects religious liberty?

Three years after *Allegheny*, Justice Kennedy relied on the coercion test to invalidate nonsectarian prayers by a rabbi at a high school graduation. See Lee v. Weisman, 505 U.S. 577 (1992). Kennedy declined the invitation of the petitioners and the United States to reconsider *Lemon*, arguing that doing so was unnecessary to find a constitutional violation in this case. "It is beyond dispute that, at a minimum, the Constitution guarantees that government may not coerce anyone to support or participate in religion or its exercise, or otherwise act in a way which 'establishes a [state] religion or religious faith, or tends to do so.'" Id. at 587. In dissent, however, Justice Scalia, a constant critic of *Lemon*, dismissed the coercion test for ending an important American tradition of graduation prayer: "As its instrument of destruction, the bulldozer of its social engineering, the Court invents a boundless, and boundlessly manipulable, test of psychological coercion, which promises to do for the Establishment Clause what the *Durham* rule did for the insanity defense." Id. at 632. Justice Scalia ridiculed the idea that the high school students were coerced into participation in the prayers.

The following term, Justice Scalia bemoaned the Court's refusal to abandon *Lemon*: "Like some ghoul in a late-night horror movie that repeatedly sits up in its grave and shuffles abroad, after being repeatedly killed and buried, *Lemon* stalks our Establishment Clause jurisprudence once again, frightening the little children and school attorneys of Center Moriches Union Free School District. Its most recent burial, only last Term, was, to be sure, not fully six feet under: Our decision in *Lee v. Weisman* conspicuously avoided using the supposed 'test' but also declined the invitation to repudiate it. Over the years, however, no fewer than five of the currently sitting Justices have, in their own opinions, personally driven pencils through the creature's heart (the author of today's opinion repeatedly), and a sixth has joined an opinion doing so." See Lamb's Chapel v. Center Moriches Union Free Sch. Dist., 508 U.S. 384, 398 (1993) (Scalia, J., concurring in judgment).

The Supreme Court later decided two cases about the Ten Commandments. In McCreary County, Ky. v. American Civil Liberties Union of Ky., 545 U.S. 844, 859 (2005), Justice Souter's opinion invalidated displays of the commandments in county courthouses because they did not have a secular purpose. Souter observed, "[t]hough we have found government action motivated by an illegitimate purpose only four times since *Lemon*,* and 'the secular purpose requirement alone may rarely be determinative . . . , it nevertheless serves an important function.' " In contrast, while upholding the display of a Ten Commandments monument on state capitol grounds, Chief Justice Rehnquist wrote that *Lemon* was "not useful" to the analysis. "Instead, our analysis is driven both by the nature of the monument and by our Nation's history." See Van Orden v. Perry, 545 U.S. 677 (2005).

We study the constitutionality of public displays of religious symbols in Chapter 3.

4. *Buddhism.* Could Buddhism become an established religion within the United States? In Brooks v. City of Oak Ridge, 222 F.3d 259 (6th Cir. 2000), cert. denied, 531 U.S. 1152 (2001), the court rejected a citizen's allegation that Oak Ridge, Tennessee's "Friendship Bell" endorsed the Buddhist religion in violation of the Establishment Clause. The bell celebrated fifty years of friendship between Oak Ridge and Japan and was similar to bells used in Buddhist temples. "On the exterior of the bell are 108 knobs and two large panels bearing images associated with Japan and Tennessee, including the official flowers, birds, and trees of each. The surface of the bell is inscribed with the following words: 'International Friendship,' 'Peace,' 'Pearl Harbor, December 7, 1941, VJ Day, September 2, 1945,' and 'Hiroshima, August 6, 1945, Nagasaki, August 9, 1945.' "

Buddhist monasteries in Japan, India, and China usually contain these bells, which announce times for prayer and meals. The bell shape is used to indicate the location of monasteries on maps. Buddhists ring the bells 108 times on New Year's Eve "to atone for the 108 sins or shortcomings of mankind." "[T]he sound of the bell is a kind of mantra or a chant, which has the kind of sound quality that conveys the unity of the Cosmos, or in this case, the oneness of the Buddha."

---

*   Justice Souter cited *Stone v. Graham*, 449 U.S. 39, 41 (1980); *Wallace v. Jaffree*, 472 U.S. 38, 56–61 (1985); *Edwards v. Aguillard*, 482 U.S. 578, 586–93 (1987); and *Santa Fe Independent School District v. Doe*, 530 U.S. at 308–309. These cases invalidated a Ten Commandments display, a moment of silence, the teaching of creationism, and prayer at football games.

The Sixth Circuit concluded the fiftieth anniversary and the commitment to peace met the secular purpose requirement; that a reasonable observer would believe that Oak Ridge was endorsing peace and friendship with Japan, not Buddhism; and that there was no entanglement because the city did not interact with any religious group in owning or maintaining the bell. A concurrence by Judge Norris concluded that the bell was not a religious symbol.

Is it constitutionally significant that the citizens who designed the bell were not Buddhist and that no Buddhist groups were involved in commissioning or maintaining the bell? Would it make a difference if the majority of the town's population were practicing Buddhists? What if they frequently visited the bell and performed religious rituals there? Would such Buddhist participation make this case more analogous to *Kiryas Joel*?

On December 8, 1941, the day after the Japanese attacks on Pearl Harbor, Hawaii, the Salinas, California police ordered a Buddhist priest to remove the temple bell because its ringing might guide the Japanese Navy onto American territory. "He said if we did not take our gong down, he would burn the tower containing it." Was the Establishment Clause violated? Free Exercise? Does this event influence your interpretation of the Friendship Bell? See Duncan Ryûken Williams, Complex Loyalties: Issei Buddhist Ministers during the Wartime Incarceration, Pacific World: Journal of the Institute of Buddhist Studies (Third Series, Vol. 5, 2004): 255–274.

5. *"Nor inhibits religion."* An interesting twist on *Lemon* arose in Los Angeles County, where the county's *removal* of a cross from its seal was challenged as a violation of the Establishment Clause. In ruling that no Establishment Clause violation had occurred, the Ninth Circuit observed there is little law deciding what *inhibits* (not advances) religion under prong two of the *Lemon* test. The court concluded that the county's decision, which was undertaken in order to avoid litigation, had a secular purpose and did not inhibit religion. See Vasquez v. Los Angeles County, 487 F.3d 1246 (9th Cir. 2007), cert. denied, 552 U.S. 1062 (2007).

In 2014, Los Angeles County supervisors voted 3–2 to return the cross to the county seal. The cross is attached to the San Gabriel Mission, which is pictured in the seal. Cross supporters argue that when the cross was removed from the seal in 2004, the cross was also absent from the mission due to earthquake repairs. Now, however, Mission San Gabriel's building includes the cross. Supporters argue that the seal with cross is therefore historically accurate. Opponents argue that the cross favors one religion. Did adding the cross to the seal violate the Establishment Clause according to *Lemon*? In April 2016, a California federal district court granted a permanent injunction against the display of the cross because it violated both the federal and California constitutions. On the Establishment Clause issue, the court applied *Lemon* even though *Lemon* "has been 'much criticized both inside and outside the Court,' and 'sometimes ignored by the Court altogether,'" and ruled that adding the cross to the seal violated both the purpose and effect prongs of *Lemon*. Reverend Father Ian Elliott Davies et al. v. Los Angeles County Board of Supervisors, No. 214CV00907CASFFM, 2016 WL 1383458, at *15 (C.D. Cal. Apr. 6, 2016). What reasoning do you think the court employed to reach this conclusion? Do you agree with the district court's interpretation of *Lemon*?

The Ninth Circuit cited *Vasquez* and analyzed prong two of *Lemon* in ruling that a school district did not violate the Establishment Clause when it prevented a student from playing *Ave Maria* at the high school's graduation. After the preceding year's graduation, the school district received complaints about a song that mentioned God, heaven, and angels, and in response the school required "purely secular" songs. According to the court, the attempt to comply with the Establishment Clause kept the school district's decision from being hostile to religion. See Nurre v. Whitehead, 580 F.3d 1087 (9th Cir. 2009).

6. *History and Tradition.* In Marsh v. Chambers, 463 U.S. 783 (1983), the Court upheld the constitutionality of the Nebraska legislature's practice of opening each day with a chaplain's prayer. The chaplain was paid by state funds. The Court emphasized that the practice of opening sessions of Congress with prayer had continued without interruption for almost 200 years. Is it constitutionally significant that the First Congress paid a chaplain to open its sessions with a prayer? See id. at 787–88 ("It can hardly be thought that in the same week Members of the First Congress voted to appoint and to pay a chaplain for each House and also voted to approve the draft of the First Amendment for submission to the states, they intended the Establishment Clause of the Amendment to forbid what they had just declared acceptable."). As a member of the House of Representatives, James Madison created rules and authorized payment for chaplains. On the other hand, after he left the presidency he wrote letters stating that the chaplaincy violated the Establishment Clause. If "Madison is best understood as having consistently opposed legislative chaplaincies throughout his life," should *Marsh* and its progeny be overruled? See Andy G. Olree, James Madison and Legislative Chaplains, 102 Nw.U. L. Rev. 145, 155 (2008). Does *Marsh* prove that there is a historical practice exception to the Establishment Clause that overrides the other Establishment Clause tests—*Lemon*, endorsement, and coercion?

The circuit courts interpreted and applied *Marsh* for 31 years. The Fourth Circuit, for example, ruled that a Forsyth County, North Carolina Board of Commissioners prayer policy violated *Marsh* because Christian prayers were given at the meetings. The court stated that the "exception created by *Marsh* is limited to the sort of nonsectarian legislative prayer that solemnizes the proceedings of legislative bodies without advancing or disparaging a particular faith.'" Joyner v. Forsyth County, N.C., 653 F.3d 341, 349 (4th Cir. 2011).

The Second Circuit, employing the endorsement test, ruled that prayers at Town Board meetings in the Town of Greece, New York, violated the Establishment Clause because "the prayer practice impermissibly affiliated the town with a single creed, Christianity." Galloway v. Town of Greece, 681 F.3d 20, 22 (2d Cir. 2012). Instead of examining individual prayers, the court asked "whether the town's practice, viewed *in its totality* by an ordinary, reasonable observer, conveyed the view that the town favored or disfavored certain religious beliefs." Id. at 29 (emphasis added). What combination of facts do you think would support such a ruling? See id. (Clergy were exclusively Christian between 1999 and 2007; clergy selection process was restricted to town's limits, thereby ensuring only Christian participation; town did not solicit volunteers; content of prayers was almost exclusively Christian; most prayer-givers gave the impression that they were speaking on behalf of the town rather than themselves by saying "we" and "our"; Town Board members participated in the prayer; audience members were asked to participate).

The Supreme Court granted certiorari in *Town of Greece* and reversed the Second Circuit. In the next section, we examine the Court's rulings on prayer and ask if the reasoning of *Town of Greece* signals a new approach to the Establishment Clause by the Court.

C. PRAYER AND GOVERNMENT

In 1992, Justice Kennedy applied the coercion test to invalidate a Providence, Rhode Island school policy that invited a local rabbi to offer prayers at a high school graduation. Justices Blackmun and Souter wrote separate concurrences (which were joined by Justice O'Connor), while Justice Scalia dissented. What approach does each opinion, concurrence, and dissent take toward the Establishment Clause?

Lee v. Weisman

Supreme Court of the United States, 1992.
505 U.S. 577, 112 S.Ct. 2649, 120 L.Ed.2d 467.

■ KENNEDY, J., delivered the opinion of the Court, in which BLACKMUN, STEVENS, O'CONNOR, and SOUTER, JJ., joined. BLACKMUN, J., and SOUTER, J., filed concurring opinions, in which STEVENS and O'CONNOR, JJ., joined. SCALIA, J., filed a dissenting opinion, in which REHNQUIST, C.J., and WHITE and THOMAS, JJ., joined.

■ JUSTICE KENNEDY delivered the opinion of the Court.

I

A

Deborah Weisman graduated from Nathan Bishop Middle School, a public school in Providence, at a formal ceremony in June 1989. She was about 14 years old. For many years it has been the policy of the Providence School Committee and the Superintendent of Schools to permit principals to invite members of the clergy to give invocations and benedictions at middle school and high school graduations. Many, but not all, of the principals elected to include prayers as part of the graduation ceremonies. Acting for himself and his daughter, Deborah's father, Daniel Weisman, objected to any prayers at Deborah's middle school graduation, but to no avail. The school principal, petitioner Robert E. Lee, invited a rabbi to deliver prayers at the graduation exercises for Deborah's class. Rabbi Leslie Gutterman, of the Temple Beth El in Providence, accepted.

It has been the custom of Providence school officials to provide invited clergy with a pamphlet entitled "Guidelines for Civic Occasions," prepared by the National Conference of Christians and Jews. The Guidelines recommend that public prayers at nonsectarian civic ceremonies be composed with "inclusiveness and sensitivity," though they acknowledge that "prayer of any kind may be inappropriate on some civic occasions." The principal gave Rabbi Gutterman the pamphlet before the graduation and advised him the invocation and benediction should be nonsectarian.

Rabbi Gutterman's prayers were as follows:

"INVOCATION

"God of the Free, Hope of the Brave:

"For the legacy of America where diversity is celebrated and the rights of minorities are protected, we thank You. May these young men and women grow up to enrich it.

"For the liberty of America, we thank You. May these new graduates grow up to guard it.

"For the political process of America in which all its citizens may participate, for its court system where all may seek justice we thank You. May those we honor this morning always turn to it in trust.

"For the destiny of America we thank You. May the graduates of Nathan Bishop Middle School so live that they might help to share it.

"May our aspirations for our country and for these young people, who are our hope for the future, be richly fulfilled.

AMEN"

"BENEDICTION

"O God, we are grateful to You for having endowed us with the capacity for learning which we have celebrated on this joyous commencement.

"Happy families give thanks for seeing their children achieve an important milestone. Send Your blessings upon the teachers and administrators who helped prepare them.

"The graduates now need strength and guidance for the future, help them to understand that we are not complete with academic knowledge alone. We must each strive to fulfill what

You require of us all: To do justly, to love mercy, to walk humbly.

"We give thanks to You, Lord, for keeping us alive, sustaining us and allowing us to reach this special, happy occasion.

AMEN"

The school board (and the United States, which supports it as *amicus curiae*) argued that these short prayers and others like them at graduation exercises are of profound meaning to many students and parents throughout this country who consider that due respect and acknowledgment for divine guidance and for the deepest spiritual aspirations of our people ought to be expressed at an event as important in life as a graduation. We assume this to be so in addressing the difficult case now before us, for the significance of the prayers lies also at the heart of Daniel and Deborah Weisman's case.

II

It is beyond dispute that, at a minimum, the Constitution guarantees that government may not coerce anyone to support or participate in religion or its exercise, or otherwise act in a way which "establishes a [state] religion or religious faith, or tends to do so." The State's involvement in the school prayers challenged today violates these central principles.

That involvement is as troubling as it is undenied. A school official, the principal, decided that an invocation and a benediction should be given; this is a choice attributable to the State, and from a constitutional perspective it is as if a state statute decreed that the prayers must occur. The principal chose the religious participant, here a rabbi, and that choice is also attributable to the State.

The State's role did not end with the decision to include a prayer and with the choice of a clergyman. Principal Lee provided Rabbi Gutterman with a copy of the "Guidelines for Civic Occasions," and advised him that his prayers should be nonsectarian. Through these means the principal directed and controlled the content of the prayers. Even if the only sanction for ignoring the instructions were that the rabbi would not be invited back, we think no religious representative who valued his or her continued reputation and effectiveness in the community would incur the State's displeasure in this regard. It is a cornerstone principle of our Establishment Clause jurisprudence that "it is no part of the business of government to compose official prayers for any group of the American people to recite as a part of a religious program carried on by government," and that is what the school officials attempted to do.

Petitioners argue, and we find nothing in the case to refute it, that the directions for the content of the prayers were a good-faith attempt by the school to ensure that the sectarianism which is so often the flashpoint for religious animosity be removed from the graduation ceremony. The concern is understandable, as a prayer which uses ideas or images identified with a particular religion may foster a different sort of sectarian rivalry than an invocation or benediction in terms more neutral. The school's explanation, however, does not resolve the dilemma caused by its participation. The question is not the good faith of the school in attempting to make the prayer acceptable to most persons, but the legitimacy of its undertaking that enterprise at all when the object is to produce a prayer to be used in a formal religious exercise which students, for all practical purposes, are obliged to attend.

We are asked to recognize the existence of a practice of nonsectarian prayer, prayer within the embrace of what is known as the Judeo-Christian tradition, prayer which is more acceptable than one which, for example, makes explicit references to the God of Israel, or to Jesus Christ, or to a patron saint. There may be some support, as an empirical observation, to the statement of the Court of Appeals for the Sixth Circuit, picked up by Judge Campbell's dissent in the Court of Appeals in this case, that there has emerged in this country a civic religion, one which is tolerated when sectarian exercises are not. If common ground can be defined which permits once conflicting faiths to express the shared conviction that there is an ethic and a morality which transcend human invention, the sense of community and purpose sought by all decent societies might be advanced. But though the First Amendment does not allow the government to stifle prayers which aspire to these ends, neither does it permit the government to undertake that task for itself.

[Our] precedents caution us to measure the idea of a civic religion against the central meaning of the Religion Clauses of the First Amendment, which is that all creeds must be tolerated and none favored. The suggestion that government may establish an official or civic religion as a means of avoiding the establishment of a religion with more specific creeds strikes us as a contradiction that cannot be accepted.

As we have observed before, there are heightened concerns with protecting freedom of conscience from subtle coercive pressure in the elementary and secondary public schools.

We need not look beyond the circumstances of this case to see the phenomenon at work. The undeniable fact is that the school district's supervision and control of a high school graduation ceremony places public pressure, as well as peer pressure, on attending students to stand as a group or, at least, maintain respectful silence during the invocation and benediction. This pressure, though subtle and indirect, can be as real as any overt compulsion. Of course, in our culture standing or remaining silent can signify adherence to a view or simple respect for the views of others. And no doubt some persons who have no desire to join a prayer have little objection to standing as a sign of respect for those who do. But for the dissenter of high school age, who has a reasonable perception that she is being forced by the State to pray in a manner her conscience will not allow, the injury is no less real. There can be no doubt that for many, if not most, of the students at the graduation, the act of standing or remaining silent was an expression of participation in the rabbi's prayer. That was the very point of the religious exercise. It is of little comfort to a dissenter, then, to be told that for her the act of standing or remaining in silence signifies mere respect, rather than participation. What matters is that, given our social conventions, a reasonable dissenter in this milieu could believe that the group exercise signified her own participation or approval of it.

There was a stipulation in the District Court that attendance at graduation and promotional ceremonies is voluntary. Petitioners and the United States, as *amicus*, made this a center point of the case, arguing that the option of not attending the graduation excuses any inducement or coercion in the ceremony itself. The argument lacks all persuasion. Law reaches past formalism. And to say a teenage student has a real choice not to attend her high school graduation is formalistic in the extreme. True, Deborah could elect not to attend commencement without renouncing her diploma; but we shall not allow the case to turn on this point. Everyone knows that in our society and in our culture high school graduation is one of life's most significant occasions.

For the reasons we have stated, the judgment of the Court of Appeals is

Affirmed.

■ JUSTICE BLACKMUN, with whom JUSTICE STEVENS and JUSTICE O'CONNOR join, concurring.

I join the Court's opinion today because I find nothing in it inconsistent with the essential precepts of the Establishment Clause developed in our precedents. The Court holds that the graduation prayer is unconstitutional because the State "in effect required participation in a religious exercise." Although our precedents make clear that proof of government coercion is not necessary to prove an Establishment Clause violation, it is sufficient. Government pressure to participate in a religious activity is an obvious indication that the government is endorsing or promoting religion.

But it is not enough that the government restrain from compelling religious practices: It must not engage in them either. The Court repeatedly has recognized that a violation of the Establishment Clause is not predicated on coercion. The Establishment Clause proscribes public schools from "conveying or attempting to convey a message that religion or a particular religious belief is *favored* or *preferred*," even if the schools do not actually "impos[e] pressure upon a student to participate in a religious activity."

■ JUSTICE SOUTER, with whom JUSTICE STEVENS and JUSTICE O'CONNOR join, concurring.

I join the whole of the Court's opinion, and fully agree that prayers at public school graduation ceremonies indirectly coerce religious observance. I write separately nonetheless on two issues of Establishment Clause analysis that underlie my independent resolution of this case: whether the Clause applies to governmental practices that do not favor one religion or denomination over others, and whether state coercion of religious conformity, over and above state endorsement of religious exercise or belief, is a necessary element of an Establishment Clause violation.

I

Forty-five years ago, this Court announced a basic principle of constitutional law from which it has not strayed: the Establishment Clause forbids not only state practices that "aid one religion . . . or prefer one religion over another," but also those that "aid all religions." *Everson v. Board of Education of Ewing Township*, 330 U.S. 1, 15, 67 S.Ct. 504, 511, 91 L.Ed. 711 (1947). Today we reaffirm that principle, holding that the Establishment Clause forbids state-sponsored prayers in public school settings no matter how nondenominational the prayers may be. In barring the State from sponsoring generically theistic prayers where it could not sponsor sectarian ones, we hold true to a line of precedent from which there is no adequate historical case to depart. Such is the settled law. Here, as elsewhere, we should stick to it absent some compelling reason to discard it.

B

Some have challenged this precedent by reading the Establishment Clause to permit "nonpreferential" state promotion of religion. The challengers argue that, as originally understood by the Framers, "[t]he Establishment Clause did not require government neutrality between religion and irreligion nor did it prohibit the Federal Government from providing nondiscriminatory aid to religion." While a case has been made for this position, it is not so convincing as to warrant reconsideration of our settled law; indeed, I find in the history of the Clause's textual development a more powerful argument supporting the Court's jurisprudence following *Everson*.

What we thus know of the Framers' experience underscores the observation of one prominent commentator, that confining the Establishment Clause to a prohibition on preferential aid "requires a premise that the Framers were extraordinarily bad drafters—that they believed one thing but adopted language that said something substantially different, and that they did so after repeatedly attending to the choice of language." [Laycock, "Nonpreferential" Aid to Religion: A False Claim About Original Intent, 27 Wm. & Mary L.Rev. 875, 882–883 (1986)]. We must presume, since there is no conclusive evidence to the contrary, that the Framers embraced the significance of their textual judgment. Thus, on balance, history neither contradicts nor warrants reconsideration of the settled principle that the Establishment Clause forbids support for religion in general no less than support for one religion or some.

C

While these considerations are, for me, sufficient to reject the nonpreferentialist position, one further concern animates my judgment. In many contexts, including this one, nonpreferentialism requires some distinction between "sectarian" religious practices and those that would be, by some measure, ecumenical enough to pass Establishment Clause muster. Simply by requiring the enquiry, nonpreferentialists invite the courts to engage in comparative theology. I can hardly imagine a subject less amenable to the competence of the federal judiciary, or more deliberately to be avoided where possible

Nor does it solve the problem to say that the State should promote a "diversity" of religious views; that position would necessarily compel the government and, inevitably, the courts to make wholly inappropriate judgments about the number of religions the State should sponsor and the relative frequency with which it should sponsor each. In fact, the prospect would be even worse than that. As Madison observed in criticizing religious Presidential proclamations, the practice of sponsoring religious messages tends, over time, "to narrow the recommendation to the standard of the predominant sect." We have not changed much since the days of Madison, and the judiciary should not willingly enter the political arena to battle the centripetal force leading from religious pluralism to official preference for the faith with the most votes.

[JUSTICE SOUTER also concluded that under settled precedent coercion was not required for an Establishment Clause violation.]

■ JUSTICE SCALIA, with whom THE CHIEF JUSTICE, JUSTICE WHITE, and JUSTICE THOMAS join, dissenting.

I

A

I may add, moreover, that maintaining respect for the religious observances of others is a fundamental civic virtue that government (including the public schools) can and should cultivate—so that even if it were the case that the displaying of such respect might be mistaken for taking part in the prayer, I would deny that the dissenter's interest in avoiding *even the false appearance of participation* constitutionally trumps the government's interest in fostering respect for religion generally.

III

The deeper flaw in the Court's opinion does not lie in its wrong answer to the question whether there was state-induced "peer-pressure" coercion; it lies, rather, in the Court's making violation of the Establishment Clause hinge on such a precious question. The coercion that was a hallmark of historical establishments of religion was coercion of religious orthodoxy and of financial support *by force of law and threat of penalty*. Typically, attendance at the state church was required; only clergy of the official church could lawfully perform sacraments; and dissenters, if tolerated, faced an array of civil disabilities. Thus, for example, in the Colony of Virginia, where the Church of England had been established, ministers were required by law to conform to the doctrine and rites of the Church of England; and all persons were required to attend church and observe the Sabbath, were tithed for the public support of Anglican ministers, and were taxed for the costs of building and repairing churches. But there is simply no support for the proposition that the officially sponsored nondenominational invocation and benediction read by Rabbi Gutterman—with no one legally coerced to recite them—violated the Constitution of the United States. To the contrary, they are so characteristically American they could have come from the pen of George Washington or Abraham Lincoln himself.

IV

Another happy aspect of the case is that it is only a jurisprudential disaster and not a practical one. Given the odd basis for the Court's decision, invocations and benedictions will be able to be given at public school graduations next June, as they have for the past century and a half, so long as school authorities make clear that anyone who abstains from screaming in protest does not necessarily participate in the prayers. All that is seemingly needed is an announcement, or perhaps a written insertion at the beginning of the graduation program, to the effect that, while all are asked to rise for the invocation and benediction, none is compelled to join in them, nor will be assumed, by rising, to have done so. That obvious fact recited, the graduates and their parents may proceed to thank God, as Americans have always done, for the blessings He has generously bestowed on them and on their country.

* * *

The reader has been told much in this case about the personal interest of Mr. Weisman and his daughter, and very little about the personal interests on the other side. They are not inconsequential. Church and state would not be such a difficult subject if religion were, as the Court apparently thinks it to be, some purely personal avocation that can be indulged entirely in secret, like pornography, in the privacy of one's room. For most believers it is *not* that, and has never been. Religious men and women of almost all denominations have felt it necessary to acknowledge and beseech the blessing of God as a people, and not just as individuals, because they believe in the "protection of divine Providence," as the Declaration of Independence put it, not just for individuals but for societies; because they believe God to be, as Washington's first Thanksgiving Proclamation put it, the "Great Lord and Ruler of Nations." One can believe in the effectiveness of such public worship, or one can deprecate and deride it. But the longstanding American tradition of prayer at official ceremonies displays with unmistakable clarity that the Establishment Clause does not forbid the government to accommodate it. . . .

I must add one final observation: The Founders of our Republic knew the fearsome potential of sectarian religious belief to generate civil dissension and civil strife. And they also knew that nothing, absolutely nothing, is so inclined to foster among religious believers of various faiths a toleration—no, an affection—for one another than voluntarily joining in prayer together, to the God whom they all worship and seek. Needless to say, no one should be compelled to do that, but it is a shame to deprive our public culture of the opportunity, and indeed the encouragement, for people to do it voluntarily. The Baptist or Catholic who heard and joined in the simple and inspiring prayers of Rabbi Gutterman on this official and patriotic occasion was inoculated from religious bigotry and prejudice in a manner that cannot be replicated. To deprive our society of that important unifying mechanism, in order to spare the nonbeliever what seems to me the minimal inconvenience of standing or even sitting in respectful nonparticipation, is as senseless in policy as it is unsupported in law.

For the foregoing reasons, I dissent.

NOTES AND QUESTIONS

1. *The Opinion.* Of the four opinions you just read by Justices Kennedy, Blackmun, Souter, and Scalia, whose is most compelling? Why did Justice Souter think a concurrence was necessary? According to Justice Blackmun's papers, Justice Kennedy was originally assigned to write the majority opinion upholding the prayers (with Justices Scalia, Rehnquist, White, and Thomas), but then changed his vote. Blackmun then assigned Kennedy the majority opinion. "Kennedy's first draft, however, was based on a legal rationale far narrower than those favored by the others in the majority—Justices O'Connor, Stevens, Souter, and Blackmun—and they were anxious that his opinion not be too narrow. Kennedy's argument was that even voluntary school-sponsored prayer is coercive for the non-believer, but the other justices in the majority felt that school-sponsored prayer did more; that it, in effect, established a kind of state religion in violation of the Constitution." See Nina Totenberg, Weekend Edition

Sunday: Papers of Former Supreme Court Justice Harry Blackmun (NPR radio broadcast, Mar. 7, 2004).

According to Totenberg, the justices repeatedly asked Kennedy to make changes in his draft. "For example, Kennedy's first draft contained this sentence: 'This is not a case in which the graduating student could avert her eyes or otherwise avoid with ease a religious display to which she objects. After all, at graduation,' Kennedy observed, 'the state has in every practical effect compelled attendance.' Several justices wanted the sentence deleted; Blackmun wanted the whole paragraph out because, quote, 'I am afraid that this paragraph will suggest that outside the school setting, subtle government pressure on religion would be permissible.' " Id. Why is the sentence about students averting their eyes so troubling? Justice Souter was concerned Kennedy's draft "create[d] the impression that prayers at graduation ceremonies might be permissible so long as the state instructs students to sit during them, thus avoiding the problem of a non-believer being singled out when he or she fails to stand." Id. Does Kennedy's opinion address Souter's concern?

2. *Prayer at Football Games*. Should *Weisman* apply to high school football games? In Texas, the Santa Fe Independent School District adopted a policy permitting student-led prayer at football games. Students voted whether to have an invocation and, if the vote succeeded, to elect the speaker. The District Court entered an order modifying that policy to permit only nonsectarian, nonproselytizing prayer. The Court of Appeals held that, even as modified by the District Court, the football prayer policy was invalid. Governor George Bush filed amicus briefs on behalf of the school district in the Fifth Circuit and in the U.S. Supreme Court because he "support[ed] the rights of students to participate in the free exercise of religion, a right that is guaranteed by the Constitution, and he believes the government should not dictate or censor the content of student-led prayer." Brief of Amici Curiae State of Texas et al., Santa Fe Indep. Sch. Dist. v. Doe, 1999 WL 1272942.

The Supreme Court, however, rejected the state's argument that the policy did not involve state action and barred the prayers, noting that the school district sponsored the election and the football game, and that the policy *encouraged* prayer. See Santa Fe Independent School District v. Doe, 530 U.S. 290 (2000). Following *Lemon*, the majority detected a "sham secular purpose" in the school district's argument that the policy solemnized events in a secular manner. The majority also emphasized the facts that supported state action, namely, that school officials were involved in the election process and that school resources were being used to support the prayers:

> The actual or perceived endorsement of the message, moreover, is established by factors beyond just the text of the policy. Once the student speaker is selected and the message composed, the invocation is then delivered to a large audience assembled as part of a regularly scheduled, school-sponsored function conducted on school property. The message is broadcast over the school's public

address system, which remains subject to the control of school officials. It is fair to assume that the pregame ceremony is clothed in the traditional indicia of school sporting events, which generally include not just the team, but also cheerleaders and band members dressed in uniforms sporting the school name and mascot. The school's name is likely written in large print across the field and on banners and flags. The crowd will certainly include many who display the school colors and insignia on their school T-shirts, jackets, or hats and who may also be waving signs displaying the school name. It is in a setting such as this that "the board has chosen to permit" the elected student to rise and give the "statement or invocation."

In this context the members of the listening audience must perceive the pregame message as a public expression of the views of the majority of the student body delivered with the approval of the school administration. In cases involving state participation in a religious activity, one of the relevant questions is "whether an objective observer, acquainted with the text, legislative history, and implementation of the statute, would perceive it as a state endorsement of prayer in public schools." Regardless of the listener's support for, or objection to, the message, an objective Santa Fe High School student will unquestionably perceive the inevitable pregame prayer as stamped with her school's seal of approval.

Chief Justice Rehnquist's dissent complained that the majority was hostile to "*all things* religious[.]" Id. at 318 (emphasis added). Was the Chief Justice correct in his criticism? After all, unlike *Lee v. Weisman*, the prayer was chosen *by the students* and spoken *by a student*, rather than school officials. Rehnquist wrote:

> The Court also relies on our decision in *Lee v. Weisman*, to support its conclusion. In *Lee*, we concluded that the content of the speech at issue, a graduation prayer given by a rabbi, was "directed and controlled" by a school official. In other words, at issue in *Lee* was *government* speech. Here, by contrast, the potential speech at issue, if the policy had been allowed to proceed, would be a message or invocation selected or created by a student. That is, if there were speech at issue here, it would be *private* speech. The "crucial difference between *government* speech endorsing religion, which the Establishment Clause forbids, and *private* speech endorsing religion, which the Free Speech and Free Exercise Clauses protect," applies with particular force to the question of endorsement. Id. at 324 (emphasis in the original).

Do you agree?

3. *Town of Greece*. Which Establishment Clause tests did the Court employ in *Town of Greece*? Was the Court's reasoning consistent with earlier precedents?

Town of Greece, New York v. Galloway

Supreme Court of the United States, 2014.
134 S.Ct. 1811, 82 USWL 4334.

■ JUSTICE KENNEDY delivered the opinion of the Court, except as to Part II-B. THE CHIEF JUSTICE and JUSTICE ALITO join this opinion in full. JUSTICE SCALIA and JUSTICE THOMAS join this opinion except as to Part II-B.

The Court must decide whether the town of Greece, New York, imposes an impermissible establishment of religion by opening its monthly board meetings with a prayer. It must be concluded, consistent with the Court's opinion in *Marsh v. Chambers,* 463 U.S. 783, 103 S.Ct. 3330, 77 L.Ed.2d 1019 (1983), that no violation of the Constitution has been shown.

I

Greece, a town with a population of 94,000, is in upstate New York. For some years, it began its monthly town board meetings with a moment of silence. In 1999, the newly elected town supervisor, John Auberger, decided to replicate the prayer practice he had found meaningful while serving in the county legislature. Following the roll call and recitation of the Pledge of Allegiance, Auberger would invite a local clergyman to the front of the room to deliver an invocation. After the prayer, Auberger would thank the minister for serving as the board's "chaplain for the month" and present him with a commemorative plaque. The prayer was intended to place town board members in a solemn and deliberative frame of mind, invoke divine guidance in town affairs, and follow a tradition practiced by Congress and dozens of state legislatures.

The town followed an informal method for selecting prayer givers, all of whom were unpaid volunteers. A town employee would call the congregations listed in a local directory until she found a minister available for that month's meeting. The town eventually compiled a list of willing "board chaplains" who had accepted invitations and agreed to return in the future. The town at no point excluded or denied an opportunity to a would-be prayer giver. Its leaders maintained that a minister or layperson of any persuasion, including an atheist, could give the invocation. But nearly all of the congregations in town were Christian; and from 1999 to 2007, all of the participating ministers were too.

Greece neither reviewed the prayers in advance of the meetings nor provided guidance as to their tone or content, in the belief that exercising any degree of control over the prayers would infringe both the free exercise and speech rights of the ministers. The town instead left the guest clergy free to compose their own devotions. The resulting prayers often sounded both civic and religious themes. Typical were invocations that asked the divinity to abide at the meeting and bestow blessings on the community:

> "Lord we ask you to send your spirit of servanthood upon all of us gathered here this evening to do your work for the benefit of all in our community. We ask you to bless our elected and appointed officials so they may deliberate with wisdom and act with courage. Bless the members of our community who come here to speak before the board so they may state their cause with honesty and humility. . . . Lord we ask you to bless us all, that everything we do here tonight will move you to welcome us one day into your kingdom as good and faithful servants. We ask this in the name of our brother Jesus. Amen."

Some of the ministers spoke in a distinctly Christian idiom; and a minority invoked religious holidays, scripture, or doctrine, as in the following prayer:

> "Lord, God of all creation, we give you thanks and praise for your presence and action in the world. We look with anticipation to the celebration of Holy Week and Easter. It is in the solemn events of next week that we find the very heart and center of our Christian faith. We acknowledge the saving sacrifice of Jesus Christ on the cross. We draw strength, vitality, and confidence from his resurrection at Easter. . . . We pray for peace in the world, an end to terrorism, violence, conflict, and war. We pray for stability, democracy, and good government in those countries in which our armed forces are now serving, especially in Iraq and Afghanistan. . . . Praise and glory be yours, O Lord, now and forever more. Amen."

Respondents Susan Galloway and Linda Stephens attended town board meetings to speak about issues of local concern, and they objected that the prayers violated their religious or philosophical views. At one meeting, Galloway admonished board members that she found the prayers "offensive," "intolerable," and an affront to a "diverse community." After respondents complained that Christian themes pervaded the prayers, to the exclusion of citizens who did not share those beliefs, the town invited a Jewish layman and the chairman of the local Baha'i temple to deliver prayers. A Wiccan priestess who had read press reports about the prayer controversy requested, and was granted, an opportunity to give the invocation.

The District Court on summary judgment upheld the prayer practice as consistent with the First Amendment. The Court of Appeals for the Second Circuit reversed. It held that some aspects of the prayer program, viewed in their totality by a reasonable observer, conveyed the message that Greece was endorsing Christianity. Having granted certiorari to decide whether the town's prayer practice violates the

Establishment Clause, the Court now reverses the judgment of the Court of Appeals.

II

In *Marsh v. Chambers,* 463 U.S. 783, 103 S.Ct. 3330, the Court found no First Amendment violation in the Nebraska Legislature's practice of opening its sessions with a prayer delivered by a chaplain paid from state funds. The decision concluded that legislative prayer, while religious in nature, has long been understood as compatible with the Establishment Clause. As practiced by Congress since the framing of the Constitution, legislative prayer lends gravity to public business, reminds lawmakers to transcend petty differences in pursuit of a higher purpose, and expresses a common aspiration to a just and peaceful society.

The Court's inquiry, then, must be to determine whether the prayer practice in the town of Greece fits within the tradition long followed in Congress and the state legislatures. Respondents assert that the town's prayer exercise falls outside that tradition and transgresses the Establishment Clause for two independent but mutually reinforcing reasons. First, they argue that *Marsh* did not approve prayers containing sectarian language or themes, such as the prayers offered in Greece that referred to the "death, resurrection, and ascension of the Savior Jesus Christ," and the "saving sacrifice of Jesus Christ on the cross." Second, they argue that the setting and conduct of the town board meetings create social pressures that force nonadherents to remain in the room or even feign participation in order to avoid offending the representatives who sponsor the prayer and will vote on matters citizens bring before the board. The sectarian content of the prayers compounds the subtle coercive pressures, they argue, because the nonbeliever who might tolerate ecumenical prayer is forced to do the same for prayer that might be inimical to his or her beliefs.

A

An insistence on nonsectarian or ecumenical prayer as a single, fixed standard is not consistent with the tradition of legislative prayer outlined in the Court's cases.

To hold that invocations must be nonsectarian would force the legislatures that sponsor prayers and the courts that are asked to decide these cases to act as supervisors and censors of religious speech, a rule that would involve government in religious matters to a far greater degree than is the case under the town's current practice of neither editing or approving prayers in advance nor criticizing their content after the fact. It would be but a few steps removed from that prohibition for legislatures to require chaplains to redact the religious content from their message in order to make it acceptable for the public sphere. Government may not mandate a civic religion that stifles any but the most generic reference to the sacred any more than it may prescribe a religious orthodoxy. See *Lee v. Weisman,* 505 U.S. 577, 590, 112 S.Ct. 2649, 120 L.Ed.2d 467 (1992) ("The suggestion that government may establish an official or civic religion as a means of avoiding the establishment of a religion with more specific creeds strikes us as a contradiction that cannot be accepted").

Respondents argue, in effect, that legislative prayer may be addressed only to a generic God. The law and the Court could not draw this line for each specific prayer or seek to require ministers to set aside their nuanced and deeply personal beliefs for vague and artificial ones. There is doubt, in any event, that consensus might be reached as to what qualifies as generic or nonsectarian. Honorifics like "Lord of Lords" or "King of Kings" might strike a Christian audience as ecumenical, yet these titles may have no place in the vocabulary of other faith traditions. The difficulty, indeed the futility, of sifting sectarian from nonsectarian speech is illustrated by a letter that a lawyer for the respondents sent the town in the early stages of this litigation. The letter opined that references to "Father, God, Lord God, and the Almighty" would be acceptable in public prayer, but that references to "Jesus Christ, the Holy Spirit, and the Holy Trinity" would not. Perhaps the writer believed the former grouping would be acceptable to monotheists. Yet even seemingly general references to God or the Father might alienate nonbelievers or polytheists.

In rejecting the suggestion that legislative prayer must be nonsectarian, the Court does not imply that no constraints remain on its content. The relevant constraint derives from its place at the opening of legislative sessions, where it is meant to lend gravity to the occasion and reflect values long part of the Nation's heritage. Prayer that is solemn and respectful in tone, that invites lawmakers to reflect upon shared ideals and common ends before they embark on the fractious business of governing, serves that legitimate function. If the course and practice over time shows that the invocations denigrate nonbelievers or religious minorities, threaten damnation, or preach conversion, many present may consider the prayer to fall short of the desire to elevate the purpose of the occasion and to unite lawmakers in their common effort. That circumstance would present a different case than the one presently before the Court.

The tradition reflected in *Marsh* permits chaplains to ask their own God for blessings of peace, justice, and freedom that find appreciation among people of all faiths. That a prayer is given in the name of Jesus, Allah, or Jehovah, or that it makes passing reference to religious doctrines, does not remove it from that tradition. These religious themes provide particular means to universal ends. Prayer that reflects beliefs specific to only some creeds can still serve to solemnize the occasion, so long as the practice over time is not "exploited to proselytize or advance any one, or to disparage any other, faith or belief."

Finally, the Court disagrees with the view taken by the Court of Appeals that the town of Greece contravened the Establishment Clause by inviting a predominantly Christian set of ministers to lead the prayer. The town made reasonable efforts to identify all of the congregations located within its borders and represented that it would welcome a prayer by any minister or layman who wished to give one. That nearly all of the congregations in town turned out to be Christian does not reflect an aversion or bias on the part of town leaders against minority faiths. So long as the town maintains a policy of nondiscrimination, the Constitution does not require it to search beyond its borders for non-Christian prayer givers in an effort to achieve religious balancing. The quest to promote "a 'diversity' of religious views" would require the town "to make wholly inappropriate judgments about the number of religions [it] should sponsor and the relative frequency with which it should sponsor each," *Lee,* a form of government entanglement with religion that is far more troublesome than the current approach.

B

It is an elemental First Amendment principle that government may not coerce its citizens "to support or participate in any religion or its exercise." *County of Allegheny,* 492 U.S., at 659, 109 S.Ct. 3086 (KENNEDY, J., concurring in judgment in part and dissenting in part). On the record in this case the Court is not persuaded that the town of Greece, through the act of offering a brief, solemn, and respectful prayer to open its monthly meetings, compelled its citizens to engage in a religious observance. The inquiry remains a fact-sensitive one that considers both the setting in which the prayer arises and the audience to whom it is directed.

The analysis would be different if town board members directed the public to participate in the prayers, singled out dissidents for opprobrium, or indicated that their decisions might be influenced by a person's acquiescence in the prayer opportunity. No such thing occurred in the town of Greece. Although board members themselves stood, bowed their heads, or made the sign of the cross during the prayer, they at no point solicited similar gestures by the public. Respondents point to several occasions where audience members were asked to rise for the prayer. These requests, however, came not from town leaders but from the guest ministers, who presumably are accustomed to directing their congregations in this way and might have done so thinking the action was inclusive, not coercive. Respondents suggest that constituents might feel pressure to join the prayers to avoid irritating the officials who would be ruling on their petitions, but this argument has no evidentiary support. Nothing in the record indicates that town leaders allocated benefits and burdens based on participation in the prayer, or that citizens were received differently depending on whether they joined the invocation or quietly declined. In no instance did town leaders signal disfavor toward nonparticipants or suggest that their stature in the community was in any way diminished. A practice that classified citizens based on their religious views would violate the Constitution, but that is not the case before this Court.

In their declarations in the trial court, respondents stated that the prayers gave them offense and made them feel excluded and disrespected. Offense, however, does not equate to coercion. Adults often encounter speech they find disagreeable; and an Establishment Clause violation is not made out any time a person experiences a sense of affront from the expression of contrary religious views in a legislative forum, especially where, as here, any member of the public is welcome in turn to offer an invocation reflecting his or her own convictions.

In the town of Greece, the prayer is delivered during the ceremonial portion of the town's meeting. Board members are not engaged in policymaking at this time, but in more general functions, such as swearing in new police officers, inducting high school athletes into the town hall of fame, and presenting proclamations to volunteers, civic groups, and senior citizens. It is a moment for town leaders to recognize the achievements of their constituents and the aspects of community life that are worth celebrating. By inviting ministers to serve as chaplain for the month, and welcoming them to the front of the room alongside civic leaders, the town is acknowledging the central place that religion, and religious institutions, hold in the lives of those present. Indeed, some congregations are not simply spiritual homes for town residents but also the provider of social services for citizens regardless of their beliefs. The inclusion of a brief, ceremonial prayer as part of a larger exercise in civic recognition suggests that its purpose and effect are to acknowledge religious leaders and the institutions they represent rather than to exclude or coerce nonbelievers.

* * *

The town of Greece does not violate the First Amendment by opening its meetings with prayer that comports with our tradition and does not coerce participation by nonadherents. The judgment of the U.S. Court of Appeals for the Second Circuit is reversed.

■ JUSTICE ALITO, with whom JUSTICE SCALIA joins, concurring.

I

[S]ince the principal dissent accuses the Court of being blind to the facts of this case, I recount facts that I find particularly salient.

For the first four years of the practice, a clerical employee in the office would randomly call religious organizations listed in the Greece "Community Guide," a local directory published by the Greece Chamber of Commerce, until she was able to find somebody willing to give the invocation. This employee eventually began keeping a list of individuals who had agreed to give the invocation, and when a second clerical employee took over the task of finding prayer-givers, the first employee gave that list to the second. The second employee then randomly called organizations on that list—and possibly others in the Community Guide—until she found someone who agreed to provide the prayer.

Apparently, all the houses of worship listed in the local Community Guide were Christian churches. That is unsurprising given the small number of non-Christians in the area.

II

I turn now to the narrow aspect of the principal dissent, and what we find here is that the principal dissent's objection, in the end, is really quite niggling.

B

If, as the principal dissent appears to concede, such a rotating system would obviate any constitutional problems, then despite all its high rhetoric, the principal dissent's quarrel with the town of Greece really boils down to this: The town's clerical employees did a bad job in compiling the list of potential guest chaplains. For that is really the only difference between what the town did and what the principal dissent is willing to accept.

The informal, imprecise way in which the town lined up guest chaplains is typical of the way in which many things are done in small and medium-sized units of local government. In such places, the members of the governing body almost always have day jobs that occupy much of their time. The town almost never has a legal office and instead relies for legal advice on a local attorney whose practice is likely to center on such things as land-use regulation, contracts, and torts. When a municipality like the town of Greece seeks in good faith to emulate the congressional practice on which our holding in *Marsh* was largely based, that municipality should not be held to have violated the Constitution simply because its method of recruiting guest chaplains lacks the demographic exactitude that might be regarded as optimal.

IV

There can be little doubt that the decision in *Marsh* reflected the original understanding of the First Amendment. It is virtually inconceivable that the First Congress, having appointed chaplains whose responsibilities prominently included the delivery of prayers at the beginning of each daily session, thought that this practice was inconsistent with the Establishment Clause.

V

This brings me to my final point. I am troubled by the message that some readers may take from the principal dissent's rhetoric and its highly imaginative hypotheticals. . . . I am concerned that at least some readers will take these hypotheticals as a warning that this is where today's decision leads—to a country in which religious minorities are denied the equal benefits of citizenship.

Nothing could be further from the truth. All that the Court does today is to allow a town to follow a practice that we have previously held is permissible for Congress and state legislatures. In seeming to suggest otherwise, the principal dissent goes far astray.

■ JUSTICE THOMAS, with whom JUSTICE SCALIA joins as to Part II, concurring in part and concurring in the judgment.

Except for Part II-B, I join the opinion of the Court, which faithfully applies *Marsh*. I write separately to reiterate my view that the Establishment Clause is "best understood as a federalism provision," *Elk Grove Unified School Dist. v. Newdow*, 542 U.S. 1, 50, 124 S.Ct. 2301, 159 L.Ed.2d 98 (2004) (THOMAS, J., concurring in judgment), and to state my understanding of the proper "coercion" analysis.

II

Even if the Establishment Clause were properly incorporated against the States, the municipal prayers at issue in this case bear no resemblance to the coercive state establishments that existed at the founding. "The coercion that was a hallmark of historical establishments of religion was coercion of religious orthodoxy and of financial support *by force of law and threat of penalty*." In a typical case, attendance at the established church was mandatory, and taxes were levied to generate church revenue. Dissenting ministers were barred from preaching, and political participation was limited to members of the established church. . . . They exercised government power in order to exact financial support of the church, compel religious observance, or control religious doctrine. . . .

Thus, to the extent coercion is relevant to the Establishment Clause analysis, it is actual legal coercion that counts—not the "subtle coercive pressures" allegedly felt by respondents in this case. The majority properly concludes that "[o]ffense . . . does not equate to coercion," since "[a]dults often encounter speech they find disagreeable[,] and an Establishment Clause violation is not made out any time a person experiences a sense of affront from the expression of contrary religious views in a legislative forum." I would simply add, in light of the foregoing history of the Establishment Clause, that "[p]eer pressure, unpleasant as it may be, is not coercion" either.

■ JUSTICE BREYER, dissenting.

As we all recognize, this is a "fact-sensitive" case. . . . I also here emphasize several factors that I believe underlie the conclusion that, on the particular facts of this case, the town's prayer practice violated the Establishment Clause.

First, Greece is a predominantly Christian town, but it is not exclusively so. A map of the town's houses of worship introduced in the District Court shows many Christian churches within the town's limits. It also shows a Buddhist temple within the town and several Jewish synagogues just outside its borders, in the adjacent city of Rochester, New York. Yet during the more than 120 monthly meetings at which prayers were delivered during the record period (from 1999 to 2010), only four prayers were delivered by non-Christians. And all of these occurred in 2008, shortly after the plaintiffs began complaining about the town's Christian prayer practice and nearly a decade after that practice had commenced.

Second, the town made no significant effort to inform the area's non-Christian houses of worship about the possibility of delivering an opening prayer. Third, in this context, the fact that nearly all of the prayers given reflected a single denomination takes on significance. That significance would have been the same had all the prayers been Jewish, or Hindu, or Buddhist, or of any other denomination. The significance is that, in a context where religious minorities exist and where more could easily have been done to include their participation, the town chose to do nothing. Fourth, the fact that the board meeting audience included citizens with business to conduct also contributes to the importance of making more of an effort to include members of other denominations. Fifth, neither does the Constitution forbid efforts to explain to those who give the prayers the nature of the occasion and the audience.

■ JUSTICE KAGAN, with whom JUSTICE GINSBURG, JUSTICE BREYER, and JUSTICE SOTOMAYOR join, dissenting.

For centuries now, people have come to this country from every corner of the world to share in the blessing of religious freedom. Our Constitution promises that they may worship in their own way, without fear of penalty or danger, and that in itself is a momentous offering. Yet our Constitution makes a commitment still more remarkable—that however those individuals worship, they will count as full and equal American citizens. A Christian, a Jew, a Muslim (and so forth)—each stands in the same relationship with her country, with her state and local communities, and with every level and body of government. So that when each person performs the duties or seeks the benefits of citizenship, she does so not as an adherent to one or another religion, but simply as an American.

I respectfully dissent from the Court's opinion because I think the Town of Greece's prayer practices violate that norm of religious equality—the breathtakingly generous constitutional idea that our public institutions belong no less to the Buddhist or Hindu than to the Methodist or Episcopalian. I do not contend that principle translates here into a bright separationist line. To the contrary, I agree with the

Court's decision in *Marsh* upholding the Nebraska Legislature's tradition of beginning each session with a chaplain's prayer. And I believe that pluralism and inclusion in a town hall can satisfy the constitutional requirement of neutrality; such a forum need not become a religion-free zone. But still, the Town of Greece should lose this case. The practice at issue here differs from the one sustained in *Marsh* because Greece's town meetings involve participation by ordinary citizens, and the invocations given—directly to those citizens—were predominantly sectarian in content. Still more, Greece's Board did nothing to recognize religious diversity: In arranging for clergy members to open each meeting, the Town never sought (except briefly when this suit was filed) to involve, accommodate, or in any way reach out to adherents of non-Christian religions. So month in and month out for over a decade, prayers steeped in only one faith, addressed toward members of the public, commenced meetings to discuss local affairs and distribute government benefits. In my view, that practice does not square with the First Amendment's promise that every citizen, irrespective of her religion, owns an equal share in her government.

I

To begin to see what has gone wrong in the Town of Greece, consider several hypothetical scenarios in which sectarian prayer—taken straight from this case's record—infuses governmental activities:

- You are a party in a case going to trial; let's say you have filed suit against the government for violating one of your legal rights. The judge bangs his gavel to call the court to order, asks a minister to come to the front of the room, and instructs the 10 or so individuals present to rise for an opening prayer. The clergyman faces those in attendance and says: "Lord, God of all creation, ... We acknowledge the saving sacrifice of Jesus Christ on the cross. We draw strength . . . from his resurrection at Easter. Jesus Christ, who took away the sins of the world, destroyed our death, through his dying and in his rising, he has restored our life. Blessed are you, who has raised up the Lord Jesus, you who will raise us, in our turn, and put us by His side. . . . Amen." The judge then asks your lawyer to begin the trial.

- It's election day, and you head over to your local polling place to vote. As you and others wait to give your names and receive your ballots, an election official asks everyone there to join him in prayer. He says: "We pray this [day] for the guidance of the Holy Spirit as [we vote]. . . . Let's just say the Our Father together. 'Our Father, who art in Heaven, hallowed be thy name; thy Kingdom come, thy will be done, on earth as it is in Heaven. . . .'" And after he concludes, he makes the sign of the cross, and appears to wait expectantly for you and the other prospective voters to do so too.

- You are an immigrant attending a naturalization ceremony to finally become a citizen. The presiding official tells you and your fellow applicants that before administering the oath of allegiance, he would like a minister to pray for you and with you. The pastor steps to the front of the room, asks everyone to bow their heads, and recites: "[F]ather, son, and Holy Spirit—it is with a due sense of reverence and awe that we come before you [today] seeking your blessing. . . . You are . . . a wise God, oh Lord, . . . as evidenced even in the plan of redemption that is fulfilled in Jesus Christ. We ask that you would give freely and abundantly wisdom to one and to all . . . in the name of the Lord and Savior Jesus Christ, who lives with you and the Holy Spirit, one God for ever and ever. Amen."

I would hold that the government officials responsible for the above practices—that is, for prayer repeatedly invoking a single religion's beliefs in these settings—crossed a constitutional line. . . . One glaring problem is that the government in all these hypotheticals has aligned itself with, and placed its imprimatur on, a particular religious creed. "The clearest command of the Establishment Clause," this Court has held, "is that one religious denomination cannot be officially preferred over another." By authorizing and overseeing prayers associated with a single religion—to the exclusion of all others—the government officials in my hypothetical cases (whether federal, state, or local does not matter) have violated that foundational principle. They have embarked on a course of religious favoritism anathema to the First Amendment.

And making matters still worse: They have done so in a place where individuals come to interact with, and participate in, the institutions and processes of their government.

II

C

To recap: *Marsh* upheld prayer addressed to legislators alone, in a proceeding in which citizens had no role—and even then, only when it did not "proselytize or advance" any single religion. It was that legislative prayer practice (not every prayer in a body exercising any legislative function) that the Court found constitutional given its "unambiguous and unbroken history." But that approved practice, as I have shown, is not Greece's. None of the history *Marsh* cited—and none the majority details today—supports calling on citizens to pray, in a manner consonant with only a single religion's beliefs, at a participatory public proceeding, having both legislative and adjudicative components. Or to use the majority's phrase, no "history shows that th[is] specific practice is permitted." And so, contra the majority, Greece's prayers cannot simply ride on the constitutional coattails of the legislative tradition *Marsh* described. The Board's practice must, in its own particulars, meet constitutional requirements.

And the guideposts for addressing that inquiry include the principles of religious neutrality I discussed earlier. The government (whether federal, state, or local) may not favor, or align itself with, any particular creed. And that is nowhere more true than when officials and citizens come face to face in their shared institutions of governance. In performing civic functions and seeking civic benefits, each person of this nation must experience a government that belongs to one and all, irrespective of belief. And for its part, each government must ensure that its participatory processes will not classify those citizens by faith, or make relevant their religious differences.

None of this means that Greece's town hall must be religion- or prayer-free. "[W]e are a religious people," *Marsh* observed, and prayer draws some warrant from tradition in a town hall, as well as in Congress or a state legislature. What the circumstances here demand is the recognition that we are a pluralistic people too. When citizens of all faiths come to speak to each other and their elected representatives in a legislative session, the government must take especial care to ensure that the prayers they hear will seek to include, rather than serve to divide. No more is required—but that much is crucial—to treat every citizen, of whatever religion, as an equal participant in her government.

And contrary to the majority's (and Justice ALITO's) view, that is not difficult to do. If the Town Board had let its chaplains know that they should speak in nonsectarian terms, common to diverse religious groups, then no one would have valid grounds for complaint. Or if the Board preferred, it might have invited clergy of many faiths to serve as chaplains, as the majority notes that Congress does. When one month a clergy member refers to Jesus, and the next to Allah or Jehovah—as the majority hopefully though counterfactually suggests happened here, the government does not identify itself with one religion or align itself with that faith's citizens, and the effect of even sectarian prayer is transformed.

IV

When the citizens of this country approach their government, they do so only as Americans, not as members of one faith or another. And that means that even in a partly legislative body, they should not confront government-sponsored worship that divides them along religious lines. I believe, for all the reasons I have given, that the Town of Greece betrayed that promise. I therefore respectfully dissent from the Court's decision.

NOTES AND QUESTIONS

1. *Earlier Cases.* Would Chief Justice Burger, the author of *Larkin*, have concluded that the legislative prayer examined in *Galloway* created an impermissible fusion of governmental and religious functions? Following their opinions in *Weisman*, how do you think Justices Stevens and Souter would have voted in this case?

2. *Justice Kennedy.* How do you assess Justice Kennedy's opinion of the Court? Why did Justice Kennedy favor the coercion test? Which Establishment Clause argument is more important to the case, the historical analysis or the coercion test? What would have happened in this case if an endorsement analysis had been applied to the facts instead of Justice Kennedy's standards? Do you agree "For those made uncomfortable, for those who might have felt excluded, Kennedy's advice boiled down to: *Suck it up.*"? See Ruth Marcus, The Insensible Justice of Majority Rule, Washington Post, May 11, 2014, at A19.

3. *Justice Kagan.* How do you assess Justice Kagan's dissent? Do you think its reasoning is original? Is she more inclusive than the justices in the majority? Do you agree religious invocations are acceptable before government meetings as long as all religions are represented? Or should Justice Kagan have stood for a strict separationist approach to government prayer and religion? Do you agree with Professor Feldman that Justice Kagan's approach is politically correct but legally unadministrable:

> [C]orrect as a political and ethical matter—religious pluralism reduces religious conflict, sectarianism increases it. But making it a constitutional principle is exceedingly risky. Who decides just how much religious pluralism is enough, and which denominations need to be included? Kagan's rule wouldn't be administrable as a majority opinion. It would put the courts in the position of refereeing religious pluralism. If the town of Greece wants to open its council meetings with prayers, it really should be inclusive. But Kennedy's plurality opinion got it right. So long as no one is coerced, inclusiveness is a political virtue—but not a constitutional requirement.

See Noah Feldman, Say a Prayer for Justice Kennedy, Bloomberg View, May 5, 2014, at http://www.bloombergview.com/articles/2014-05-05/say-a-prayer-for-justice-kennedy.

4. *Justice Breyer.* Do you agree with Justice Breyer that the town should have done the following things in order to make its prayers inclusive?

> It could, for example, have posted its policy of permitting anyone to give an invocation on its website, greeceny.gov, which provides dates and times of upcoming town board meetings along with minutes of prior meetings. It could have announced inclusive policies at the beginning of its board meetings, just before introducing the month's prayer giver. It could have provided information to those houses of worship of all faiths that lie just

outside its borders and include citizens of Greece among their members. Given that the town could easily have made these or similar efforts but chose not to, the fact that all of the prayers (aside from the 2008 outliers) were given by adherents of a single religion reflects a lack of effort to include others.

5. *Justices Scalia and Thomas.* Why did these two Justices refuse to join Part II-B of Justice Kennedy's opinion? Why did Justice Scalia refuse to join Part I of Justice Thomas's opinion? Would these two Justices invalidate any government prayers? According to Justice Thomas, "The coercion that was a hallmark of historical establishments of religion was coercion of religious orthodoxy and of financial support *by force of law and threat of penalty.*" How is that standard different from Justice Kennedy's coercion standard?

6. *Justice Alito.* Are you surprised Justice Alito wrote that Justice Kagan's dissent was "really quite niggling"? How would Justice Alito analyze Justice Kagan's three hypotheticals? How do you think those hypotheticals should come out?

7. *Fact-Intensive.* Do you agree this decision was based on the specific facts of the case? If so, which facts were most important? To the majority? To the dissent? Is a fact-intensive decision good or bad for the Establishment Clause? See Christopher C. Lund, Leaving Disestablishment to the Political Process, 10 Duke J. Const. L. & Pub. Pol'y 45, 53 (2014) ("The predictable result is that no one has any idea where the line is. And this may be an intended result too. The Court wants to set the bar high enough to discourage plaintiffs from bringing these suits, but the absence of any bar whatsoever would only encourage abuses by defendants. When the goal is to paralyze both sides, it is best to have an unclear test.").

8. *Commentary.* Do you agree with Professor Brownstein that *Town of Greece* is "misguided and unpersuasive"? That the Town "discriminated in favor of established religious congregations and against three groups of residents: religious minorities with too few adherents to organize a congregation in the Town; nonaffiliated, spiritual individuals who as a matter of religious choice decline to join any of the organized congregations in the community; and non-religious residents"? Alan Brownstein, Constitutional Myopia: The Supreme Court's Blindness to Religious Liberty and Religious Equality Values in Town of Greece v. Galloway, 48 Loy. L.A. L. Rev. 371, 386 (2014).

9. *What Should Happen Next?* If you were an atheist or a humanist, what would you do now? Would you sign up to pray before your local town board meetings? What wording would you use for your prayer?

If you were a devout Christian, would you now push to include more Christian prayers at your town meetings? If you were on the town board, would you let people of other faiths give prayers? Would you seek out persons of other and no faiths to give prayers, or would you figure the Supreme Court told you you didn't have to? See William P. Marshall, Town of Greece v. Galloway: No Surprises, No Solutions, May 7, 2014, ACSblog, https://www.acslaw.org/acsblog/town-of-greece-v-galloway-no-surprises-no-solutions ("In the end, the real problem with the *Galloway* decision may not be that it upheld the particular prayer protocol of the Town of Greece but rather that it will only encourage communities to further push the envelope towards increasingly sectarian practices. After all, telling religious leaders that the words they chose to use in their public prayers should be bound only by their own consciences is not an invitation for ecumenicalism (although it might be an invitation for them to bring a first amendment lawsuit if their particular sectarian message is deemed out of bounds by their legislative body).").

10. *The Meaning of* Greece. Before *Greece* was decided, a Virginia district court issued an injunction against the Board of Supervisors of Pittsylvania County, enjoining the Board "from repeatedly opening its meetings with prayers associated with any one religion." Hudson v. Pittsylvania Cnty., Va., 774 F.3d 231, 233 (4th Cir. 2014). Should the injunction be dissolved post-*Greece*? The district court distinguished *Greece* and modified, but did not dissolve, the injunction:

> There are several critical points of distinction between the facts of *Town of Greece* and the prayer practice of the Board of Supervisors of Pittsylvania County. First and foremost, unlike in *Town of Greece,* where invited clergy and laypersons offered the invocations, the Board members themselves led the prayers in Pittsylvania County. Thus, unlike in *Town of Greece,* where the government had no role in determining the content of the opening invocations at its board meetings, the government of Pittsylvania County itself, embodied in its elected Board members, dictated the content of the prayers opening official Board meetings. Established as it was by the Pittsylvania County government, that content was consistently grounded in the tenets of one faith—Christianity. . . . Not only did the Pittsylvania County Board members determine the content of the opening prayers at Board meetings, the members often directed the public to participate in the prayers by asking them to stand. Further, as the Board members themselves served as exclusive prayer providers, persons of other faith traditions had no opportunity to offer invocations.

Hudson v. Pittsylvania Cnty., Va., 107 F. Supp. 3d 524, 525 (W.D. Va. 2015). The court modified the injunction to "exclude any suggestion that opening prayers offered at the start of Pittsylvania County Board of Supervisors meetings must be generic or nonsectarian." Id.

How many justices on the Court would agree with the district court judge's reasoning? See also Lund v. Rowan Cnty., 103 F. Supp. 3d 712 (M.D.N.C. 2015) ("The crucial question in comparing the present case with *Town of Greece* is the significance of the identity of the prayer-giver, either as a member of the legislative body or a non-member of the legislative body. In the present matter, the Commissioners themselves—and only the Commissioners—delivered the prayers at the Board's meetings. In contrast, the Town of Greece invited volunteers from a variety of religious faiths to provide the prayers. After careful consideration, this Court concludes that this distinction matters under the Establishment Clause."); but see Bormuth v. Cty. of Jackson, 116 F. Supp. 3d 850, 859 (E.D. Mich. 2015) ("it is not clear that the direction to 'Please rise' carries more coercive weight when voiced by the Commissioners themselves than by a guest chaplain selected by the Board of Commissioners.").

Are these district courts interpreting *Greece* properly?

11. *The End of Endorsement and Coercion?* Does it violate *Weisman* to hold a high school graduation at a Christian church rented for the occasion? Would it affect your analysis to learn the church had banners asking children to join school ministries and staffed information desks with religious literature? That a 15-to-20 foot cross in the sanctuary towered over the graduation? See Doe ex rel. Doe v. Elmbrook School Dist., 687 F.3d 840 (7th Cir. 2012) (school district's decision to use church for graduation violated *Weisman*). Were other Establishment Clause rules violated by the ceremony? See id. at 856 ("We conclude that the practice of holding high school graduation ceremonies in the Elmbrook Church sanctuary conveys an impermissible message of endorsement. Under the circumstances here, the message of endorsement carried an impermissible aspect of coercion, and the practice has had the unfortunate side effect of fostering the very divisiveness that the Establishment Clause was designed to prevent.")

The Court denied cert. in *Elmbrook* over a dissent from Justices Scalia and Thomas. Scalia argued the Court's recent decision in *Town of Greece* conflicted with *Elmbrook*'s holding, and that the Court needed to say so one way or another. According to the dissenters: "First, *Town of Greece* abandoned the antiquated 'endorsement test,' which formed the basis for the decision below. . . . Second, *Town of Greece* made categorically clear that mere '[o]ffense . . . does not equate to coercion' in any manner relevant to the proper Establishment Clause analysis. . . . Last but by no means least, *Town of Greece* left no doubt that 'the Establishment Clause must be interpreted "by reference to historical practices and understandings." ' " Elmbrook Sch. Dist. v. Doe, 134 S. Ct. 2283, 2284–85 (2014).

Was Scalia correct in interpreting *Town of Greece*? Or was this merely another opportunity for him to criticize Justice Kennedy's coercion test, which was employed in both *Weisman* and *Town of Greece*? What would Justice Scalia say to Professor Chemerinsky, who argued the town's prayers were unconstitutional under *any* Establishment Clause standard:

> Under any theory of the Establishment Clause, the Town of Greece acted unconstitutionally. Under the more relaxed approach to the Establishment Clause, which finds a violation only when there is government endorsement of religion, the Town of Greece acted unconstitutionally in so clearly linking itself to Christianity by inviting only Christian clergy to deliver explicitly Christian prayers. And the town also acted unconstitutionally under the view that the Establishment Clause is violated only if there is "coercion." The prayers were delivered to an audience of local children and adults, who attended meetings at the Town

Board's invitation or direction. Children's athletic teams were invited to be publicly honored; police officers and their families attended to participate in oath-of-office ceremonies; people came to speak about local issues of great personal importance; and business owners came to request zoning permits. All of these people—Christians and non-Christians—were asked to stand and bow their heads and participate in many of these prayers. But Muslims, Jews, and nonbelievers cannot in good conscience participate in a prayer to Jesus Christ, and doing so should not be the price of civic participation.

Erwin Chemerinsky, Appearances Can Be Deceiving; October Term 2013 Moved the Law to the Right, 17 Green Bag 2d 389, 394–95 (2014).

In Chapter 3, we examine the older Establishment Clause precedents to determine if *Greece* has really upended establishment jurisprudence.

CHAPTER 3

WHAT IS AN ESTABLISHMENT OF RELIGION?

In Chapter 2, Introduction to Establishment, we explored cases in which the Court explained why a "fusion of governmental and religious functions" constitutes a core violation of the Establishment Clause. You were also introduced to the controversial three-part *Lemon* test, taken from the 1971 opinion Lemon v. Kurtzman, 403 U.S. 602 (1971), and the endorsement and coercion tests developed by Justices O'Connor and Kennedy in response to *Lemon*. We also asked if those Establishment Clause tests survive the Court's decision in *Town of Greece v. Galloway*. In this chapter we examine other aspects of the Establishment Clause in more detail.

In Section A, we focus on public, government-sponsored displays of religious symbols and monuments. Section A examines the constitutionality of displays of the Ten Commandments and crosses at war memorials. An open question remains how the Court's symbols and monuments jurisprudence will be affected by the replacement of Justice O'Connor by Justice Alito on the Court and by the reasoning of *Town of Greece*.

Section B examines public funding of religion, an area significantly affected by *Lemon*, from Everson v. Board of Education of Ewing Township, 330 U.S. 1 (1947), to Zelman v. Simmons-Harris, 536 U.S. 639 (2002) and beyond. *Everson* was the Court's first modern statement on the Establishment Clause; it incorporated the clause and applied it to a state government. *Everson* upheld a program that reimbursed parents of religious school children for bus fare while identifying a no-aid, strict-separationist interpretation of establishment. *Zelman* held that a Cleveland vouchers program constitutionally included payments to religious school parents. Many commentators thought *Zelman* marked a breach in *Everson*'s wall of separation between church and state. In 2016, we must ask if the Court will abandon restrictions on government aid to religion in favor of a general theory of pro-funding neutrality.

Section C examines the connections between *Everson* and the equal access line of cases, which hold that free speech requires religious viewpoints to be treated equally whenever the government creates a public forum. After *Lemon* provided a no-aid interpretation of the Establishment Clause, many public schools and universities relied upon that clause to deny student and community groups access to school facilities. Those policies were challenged under the Free Speech Clause of the First Amendment, which holds "Congress shall make no law . . .

abridging the freedom of speech." Beginning with *Widmar v. Vincent*, 454 U.S. 263 (1981), in which the Court ruled that the University of Missouri may not bar evangelical Christian student groups from using university buildings for extracurricular religious worship and religious teaching, the Court developed an "equal access" line of cases holding that the Establishment Clause does not require schools to deny equal access to religious groups.

Under free speech law, if the government opens a designated or limited public forum for private speakers, it must be viewpoint-neutral. The equal access cases hold that the schools may not discriminate against religious viewpoints by excluding religious groups from the use of school facilities. See Erwin Chemerinsky, Constitutional Law: Principles and Policies 1177–81 (4th ed. 2011). At the end of Section C, we study the implications of the equal access principle for government speech in another Ten Commandments monument case, Pleasant Grove City v. Summum, 555 U.S. 460 (2009).

Don't forget that, as we saw in Chapter 2, the Court's Establishment Clause case law over this seventy-year period has not been simple or straightforward. Indeed, numerous commentators have complained about the inconsistency and confusion within First Amendment jurisprudence.

A. RELIGIOUS SYMBOLS AND MONUMENTS

As we learned in Chapter 2, in 1984 the Court ruled in Lynch v. Donnelly, 465 U.S. 668 (1984), that a Pawtucket, Rhode Island Christmas display did not violate the Establishment Clause. The display included "a Santa Claus house, reindeer pulling Santa's sleigh, candy-striped poles, a Christmas tree, carolers, cutout figures representing such characters as a clown, an elephant, and a teddy bear, hundreds of colored lights, a large banner that reads "SEASONS GREETINGS," as well as a crèche. The crèche included figures of the Infant Jesus, Mary and Joseph, angels, shepherds, kings, and animals. Chief Justice Burger's opinion of the Court upheld the display by relying on the *Lemon* test and finding the city had a secular purpose, did not impermissibly advance religion, and did not create excessive entanglement between church and state.

Justice O'Connor's concurrence relied on the endorsement test, concluding "Pawtucket did not intend to convey any message of endorsement of Christianity or disapproval of non-Christian religions. The evident purpose of including the crèche in the larger display was not promotion of the religious content of the crèche but celebration of the public holiday through its traditional symbols." Id. at 691.

The four dissenting Justices Brennan, Marshall, Blackmun, and Stevens, argued instead that the crèche has "clear religious import" and "specifically Christian religious meaning" and therefore should not be sponsored by the City. Id. at 705. "To be so excluded on religious grounds by one's elected government is an insult and an injury that, until today, could not be countenanced by the Establishment Clause." Id. at 709. Justices Blackmun and Stevens also argued the Court's ruling encouraged the "misuse of a sacred symbol" in a commercial setting. Id. at 727.

Five years later, the Court addressed a new display case from Pittsburgh. In County of Allegheny v. American Civil Liberties Union, 492 U.S. 573 (1989), a crèche was placed on the Grand Staircase of the Allegheny County Courthouse. In a second setting, a Chanukah menorah was placed next to a Christmas tree and a sign saluting liberty outside the City-County Building. The Court ruled the crèche was unconstitutional and the menorah constitutional. In *Allegheny*, Justice O'Connor joined the dissenters in *Lynch*—Justices Blackmun, Brennan, Marshall, and Stevens—to form a majority, and Justice Blackmun adopted O'Connor's *Lynch* endorsement test for the majority. Since *Lynch*, Chief Justice Burger had retired from the Court and was replaced by William Rehnquist as Chief Justice. Rehnquist's seat was filled by Antonin Scalia. Rehnquist, Scalia and White joined Kennedy's *Allegheny* dissent from the crèche ruling, which strongly criticized O'Connor's endorsement test and introduced Kennedy's coercion test, which we studied in detail in Chapter 2 in *Lee v. Weisman*.

According to Blackmun's analysis, the crèche, which "includes figures of the infant Jesus, Mary, Joseph, farm animals, shepherds, and wise men, all placed in or before a wooden representation of a manger, which has at its crest an angel bearing a banner that proclaims 'Gloria in Excelsis Deo!' [Glory to God in the highest]" and was surrounded by poinsettias and trees, conveyed a message of endorsement of Christianity because it was "indisputably religious—indeed sectarian." Id. at 598. Blackmun's menorah analysis was more complex. "Menorah" is Hebrew for candelabrum, and is used in connection with the holiday of Chanukah, which commemorates the rededication of the Temple in 164 B.C.E. According to the opinion:

> The Temple housed a seven-branch menorah, which was to be kept burning continuously. When the Maccabees rededicated the Temple, they had only enough oil to last for one day. But, according to the Talmud, the oil miraculously lasted for eight days (the length of time it took to obtain additional oil). To celebrate and publicly proclaim this miracle, the Talmud prescribes that it is a mitzvah (*i.e.*, a religious deed or commandment), for Jews to place a lamp with eight lights just outside the entrance to their homes or in a front window during the eight days of Chanukah. Where practicality or safety from persecution so requires, the lamp may be placed in a window or inside the home. The Talmud also ordains certain

blessings to be recited each night of Chanukah before lighting the lamp. One such benediction has been translated into English as "We are blessing God who has sanctified us and commanded us with mitzvot and has told us to light the candles of Hanukkah."

Id. at 583. Blackmun decided the menorah is a religious symbol, but its message is not "exclusively religious," and that Chanukah is both a religious and a cultural holiday. Id. at 613. The placement of the eighteen-foot menorah next to the forty-five-foot Christmas tree and the liberty sign reinforced the cultural aspect and kept the display secular. "[T]he combination of the tree and the menorah communicates, not a simultaneous endorsement of both the Christian and Jewish faiths, but instead, a secular celebration of Christmas coupled with an acknowledgment of Chanukah as a contemporaneous alternative tradition." Id. at 617–18. Blackmun even observed that a secular symbol for Chanukah may not exist: "[a]n 18-foot dreidel would look out of place and might be interpreted by some as mocking the celebration of Chanukah." Id. at 618.

Justice O'Connor agreed with Blackmun that the Christmas tree was not a religious symbol, that the crèche and the menorah were religious symbols, and then disagreed with him about Chanukah, concluding that Chanukah is a religious holiday. She wrote separately to argue that the display did not endorse religion not because the menorah and the holiday had become secular but because the display conveyed a message of pluralism and freedom to the reasonable observer. The sign accompanying the menorah and tree stated "During this holiday season, the city of Pittsburgh salutes liberty. Let these festive lights remind us that we are the keepers of the flame of liberty and our legacy of freedom," which supported the message of pluralism. Id. at 634.

Justice Brennan voted that both displays were unconstitutional. He challenged the idea that the Christmas tree is secular, and argued that the juxtaposition of the tree with the menorah reinforced the religious meaning of the Christmas tree rather than undermining the religious message of the menorah. Do you agree that the Christmas tree is religious? What about Christmas lights?

Justice Kennedy thought both displays were constitutional because neither coerced religious belief, the test that Kennedy also employed in his majority opinion in *Lee v. Weisman*, supra. According to Kennedy,

No one was compelled to observe or participate in any religious ceremony or activity. Neither the city nor the county contributed significant amounts of tax money to serve the cause of one religious faith. The crèche and the menorah are purely passive symbols of religious holidays. Passersby who disagree with the message conveyed by these displays are free to ignore them, or even to turn their backs, just as they are free to do when they disagree with any other form of government speech.

There is no realistic risk that the crèche and the menorah represent an effort to proselytize or are otherwise the first step down the road to an establishment of religion.

Id. at 664. Justice Kennedy also observed that he had not known the history of the menorah recounted by Justice Blackmun, and warned that the Court was "ill-equipped to sit as a national theology board" by use of the endorsement test.

In 2004, the Supreme Court decided two cases about the constitutionality of Ten Commandments displays, ruling in the following cases that a courthouse Ten Commandments display violated the Establishment Clause while a Ten Commandments monument on Texas capitol grounds did not. In Stone v. Graham, 449 U.S. 39 (1980), the Court had invalidated a Kentucky statute requiring that the Ten Commandments be posted on the wall of each public classroom in the state. The Court concluded that the statute had no secular purpose under *Lemon*. It rejected the state's argument that the posting was secular because the Ten Commandments were the fundamental legal code of Western Civilization. Are the following cases consistent with *Stone v. Graham?*

Ten Commandments Display at McCreary County Courthouse,
McCreary County, Kentucky.
Reprinted with permission of the Liberty Counsel.

In County of Allegheny v. American Civil Liberties Union, 492 U.S. 573 (1989), a crèche was placed on the Grand Staircase of the Allegheny County Courthouse. In a second setting, a Chanukah menorah was placed next to a Christmas tree and a sign saluting liberty outside the City–County Building.

McCreary County, Kentucky v. American Civil Liberties Union of Kentucky

Supreme Court of the United States, 2005.
545 U.S. 844, 125 S.Ct. 2722, 162 L.Ed.2d 729.

■ JUSTICE SOUTER delivered the opinion of the Court.

Executives of two counties posted a version of the Ten Commandments on the walls of their courthouses. After suits were filed charging violations of the Establishment Clause, the legislative body of each county adopted a resolution calling for a more extensive exhibit meant to show that the Commandments are Kentucky's "precedent legal code" The result in each instance was a modified display of the Commandments surrounded by texts containing religious references as their sole common element. After changing counsel, the counties revised the exhibits again by eliminating some documents, expanding the text set out in another, and adding some new ones.

The issues are whether a determination of the counties' purpose is a sound basis for ruling on the Establishment Clause complaints, and whether evaluation of the counties' claim of secular purpose for the ultimate displays may take their evolution into account. We hold that the counties' manifest objective may be dispositive of the constitutional enquiry, and that the development of the presentation should be considered when determining its purpose.

I

In the summer of 1999, petitioners McCreary County and Pulaski County, Kentucky (hereinafter Counties), put up in their respective courthouses large, gold-framed copies of an abridged text of the King James version of the Ten Commandments, including a citation to the Book of Exodus. In McCreary County, the placement of the Commandments responded to an order of the county legislative body requiring "the display [to] be posted in 'a very high traffic area' of the courthouse." In Pulaski County, amidst reported controversy over the propriety of the display, the Commandments were hung in a ceremony presided over by the county Judge-Executive, who called them "good rules to live by" and who recounted the story of an astronaut who became convinced "there must be a divine God" after viewing the Earth from the moon. The Judge-Executive was accompanied by the pastor of his church, who called the Commandments "a creed of ethics" and told the press after the ceremony that displaying the Commandments was "one of the greatest things the judge could have done to close out the millennium." In both counties, this was the version of the Commandments posted:

"Thou shalt have no other gods before me.

"Thou shalt not make unto thee any graven images.

"Thou shalt not take the name of the Lord thy God in vain.

"Remember the sabbath day, to keep it holy.

"Honor thy father and thy mother.

"Thou shalt not kill.

"Thou shalt not commit adultery.

"Thou shalt not steal.

"Thou shalt not bear false witness.

"Thou shalt not covet.

"Exodus 20:3–17."

In each county, the hallway display was "readily visible to . . . county citizens who use the courthouse to conduct their civic business, to obtain or renew driver's licenses and permits, to register cars, to pay local taxes, and to register to vote."

Within a month [of an ACLU legal challenge], and before the District Court had responded to the request for injunction, the legislative body of each County authorized a second, expanded display, by nearly identical resolutions reciting that the Ten Commandments are "the precedent legal code upon which the civil and criminal codes of . . . Kentucky are founded," and stating several grounds for taking that position: that "the Ten Commandments are codified in Kentucky's civil and criminal laws"; that the Kentucky House of Representatives had in 1993 "voted unanimously . . . to adjourn . . . 'in remembrance and honor of Jesus Christ, the Prince of Ethics' "; that the "County Judge and . . . magistrates agree with the arguments set out by Judge [Roy] Moore" in defense of his "display [of] the Ten Commandments in his courtroom"; and that the "Founding Father[s] [had an] explicit understanding of the duty of elected officials to publicly acknowledge God as the source of America's strength and direction."

As directed by the resolutions, the Counties expanded the displays of the Ten Commandments in their locations, presumably along with copies of the resolution, which instructed that it, too, be posted. In addition to the first display's large framed copy of the edited King James version of the Commandments, the second included eight other documents in smaller frames, each either having a religious theme or excerpted to highlight a religious element. The documents were the "endowed by their Creator" passage from the Declaration of Independence; the Preamble to the Constitution of Kentucky; the national motto, "In God We Trust"; a page from the Congressional Record of February 2, 1983, proclaiming the Year of the Bible and including a statement of the Ten Commandments; a proclamation by President Abraham Lincoln designating April 30, 1863, a National Day of Prayer and Humiliation; an excerpt from President Lincoln's "Reply to Loyal Colored People of Baltimore upon Presentation of a Bible," reading that "[t]he Bible is the best gift God has ever given to man"; a proclamation by President Reagan marking 1983 the Year of the Bible; and the Mayflower Compact.

[After the district court enjoined the second display, the Counties] then installed another display in each courthouse, the third within a year. No new resolution authorized this one, nor did the Counties repeal the resolutions that preceded the second. The posting consists of nine framed documents of equal size, one of them setting out the Ten Commandments explicitly identified as the "King James Version" at Exodus 20:3–17, and quoted at greater length than before:

"Thou shalt have no other gods before me.

"Thou shalt not make unto thee any graven image, or any likeness of any thing that is in heaven above, or that is in the earth beneath, or that is in the water underneath the earth: Thou shalt not bow down thyself to them, nor serve them: for I the LORD thy God am a jealous God, visiting the iniquity of the fathers upon the children unto the third and fourth generation of them that hate me.

"Thou shalt not take the name of the LORD thy God in vain: for the LORD will not hold him guiltless that taketh his name in vain.

"Remember the sabbath day, to keep it holy.

"Honour thy father and thy mother: that thy days may be long upon the land which the LORD thy God giveth thee.

"Thou shalt not kill.

"Thou shalt not commit adultery.

"Thou shalt not steal.

"Thou shalt not bear false witness against thy neighbour.

"Thou shalt not covet thy neighbour's house, thou shalt not covet th[y] neighbor's wife, nor his manservant, nor his maidservant, nor his ox, nor his ass, nor anything that is th[y] neighbour's."

Assembled with the Commandments are framed copies of the Magna Carta, the Declaration of Independence, the Bill of Rights, the lyrics of the Star Spangled Banner, the Mayflower Compact, the National Motto, the Preamble to the Kentucky Constitution, and a picture of Lady Justice. The collection is entitled "The Foundations of American Law and Government Display" and each document comes with a statement about its historical and legal significance. The comment on the Ten Commandments reads:

"The Ten Commandments have profoundly influenced the formation of Western legal thought and the formation of our country. That influence is clearly seen in the Declaration of

Independence, which declared that 'We hold these truths to be self-evident, that all men are created equal, that they are endowed by their Creator with certain unalienable Rights, that among these are Life, Liberty, and the pursuit of Happiness.' The Ten Commandments provide the moral background of the Declaration of Independence and the foundation of our legal tradition."

II

C

1

Lemon said that government action must have "a secular purpose," and after a host of cases it is fair to add that although a legislature's stated reasons will generally get deference, the secular purpose required has to be genuine, not a sham, and not merely secondary to a religious objective.... As we said, the Court often does accept governmental statements of purpose, in keeping with the respect owed in the first instance to such official claims. But in those unusual cases where the claim was an apparent sham, or the secular purpose secondary, the unsurprising results have been findings of no adequate secular object, as against a predominantly religious one.[13]

2

The Counties' second proffered limitation can be dispatched quickly. They argue that purpose in a case like this one should be inferred, if at all, only from the latest news about the last in a series of governmental actions, however close they may all be in time and subject. But the world is not made brand new every morning, and the Counties are simply asking us to ignore perfectly probative evidence; they want an absentminded objective observer, not one presumed to be familiar with the history of the government's actions and competent to learn what history has to show. The Counties' position just bucks common sense: reasonable observers have reasonable memories, and our precedents sensibly forbid an observer "to turn a blind eye to the context in which [the] policy arose."

IV

The importance of neutrality as an interpretive guide is no less true now than it was when the Court broached the principle in *Everson v. Board of Education of Ewing Township*, 330 U.S. 1, 67 S.Ct. 504, 91

---

[13] The dissent nonetheless maintains that the purpose test is satisfied so long as any secular purpose for the government action is apparent. *Post*, at 2757–2758 (opinion of SCALIA, J.). Leaving aside the fact that this position is inconsistent with the language of the cases just discussed, it would leave the purpose test with no real bite, given the ease of finding some secular purpose for almost any government action. While heightened deference to legislatures is appropriate for the review of economic legislation, an approach that credits any valid purpose, no matter how trivial, has not been the way the Court has approached government action that implicates establishment.

L.Ed. 711 (1947), and a word needs to be said about the different view taken in today's dissent. Given the variety of interpretative problems, the principle of neutrality has provided a good sense of direction: the government may not favor one religion over another, or religion over irreligion, religious choice being the prerogative of individuals under the Free Exercise Clause. . . . The dissent, however, puts forward a limitation on the application of the neutrality principle, with citations to historical evidence said to show that the Framers understood the ban on establishment of religion as sufficiently narrow to allow the government to espouse submission to the divine will. The dissent identifies God as the God of monotheism, all of whose three principal strains (Jewish, Christian, and Muslim) acknowledge the religious importance of the Ten Commandments. On the dissent's view, it apparently follows that even rigorous espousal of a common element of this common monotheism, is consistent with the establishment ban.

But the dissent's argument for the original understanding is flawed from the outset by its failure to consider the full range of evidence showing what the Framers believed. The dissent is certainly correct in putting forward evidence that some of the Framers thought some endorsement of religion was compatible with the establishment ban; . . . . But the fact is that we do have more to go on, for there is also evidence supporting the proposition that the Framers intended the Establishment Clause to require governmental neutrality in matters of religion, including neutrality in statements acknowledging religion. The very language of the Establishment Clause represented a significant departure from early drafts that merely prohibited a single national religion, and, the final language instead "extended [the] prohibition to state support for 'religion' in general."

V

Given the ample support for the District Court's finding of a predominantly religious purpose behind the Counties' third display, we affirm the Sixth Circuit in upholding the preliminary injunction.

It is so ordered.

■ JUSTICE O'CONNOR, concurring.

Reasonable minds can disagree about how to apply the Religion Clauses in a given case. But the goal of the Clauses is clear: to carry out the Founders' plan of preserving religious liberty to the fullest extent possible in a pluralistic society. By enforcing the Clauses, we have kept religion a matter for the individual conscience, not for the prosecutor or bureaucrat. At a time when we see around the world the violent consequences of the assumption of religious authority by government, Americans may count themselves fortunate: Our regard for constitutional boundaries has protected us from similar travails, while allowing private religious exercise to flourish. The well-known statement that "[w]e are a religious people," has proved true. Americans attend their places of worship more often than do citizens of other developed nations, and describe religion as playing an especially important role in their lives. Those who would renegotiate the boundaries between church and state must therefore answer a difficult question: Why would we trade a system that has served us so well for one that has served others so poorly?

It is true that many Americans find the Commandments in accord with their personal beliefs. But we do not count heads before enforcing the First Amendment. Nor can we accept the theory that Americans who do not accept the Commandments' validity are outside the First Amendment's protections. There is no list of approved and disapproved beliefs appended to the First Amendment—and the Amendment's broad terms ("free exercise," "establishment," "religion") do not admit of such a cramped reading. It is true that the Framers lived at a time when our national religious diversity was neither as robust nor as well recognized as it is now. They may not have foreseen the variety of religions for which this Nation would eventually provide a home. They surely could not have predicted new religions, some of them born in this country. But they did know that line-drawing between religions is an enterprise that, once begun, has no logical stopping point. They worried that "the same authority which can establish Christianity, in exclusion of all other Religions, may establish with the same ease any particular sect of Christians, in exclusion of all other Sects." Memorial 186. The Religion Clauses, as a result, protect adherents of all religions, as well as those who believe in no religion at all.

■ JUSTICE SCALIA, with whom THE CHIEF JUSTICE and JUSTICE THOMAS join, and with whom JUSTICE KENNEDY joins as to Parts II and III, dissenting.

I

A

On September 11, 2001 I was attending in Rome, Italy an international conference of judges and lawyers, principally from Europe and the United States. That night and the next morning virtually all of the participants watched, in their hotel rooms, the address to the Nation by the President of the United States concerning the murderous attacks upon the Twin Towers and the Pentagon, in which thousands of Americans had been killed. The address ended, as Presidential addresses often do, with the prayer "God bless America." The next afternoon I was approached by one of the judges from a European country, who, after extending his profound condolences for my country's loss, sadly observed "How I wish that the Head of State of my country, at a similar time of national tragedy and distress, could conclude his address 'God bless _____.' It is of course absolutely forbidden."

That is one model of the relationship between church and state—a model spread across Europe by the armies of Napoleon, and reflected in the Constitution of France, which begins "France is [a] ... secular ... Republic." Religion is to be strictly excluded from the public forum. This is not, and never was, the model adopted by America. George Washington added to the form of Presidential oath prescribed by Art. II, § 1, cl. 8, of the Constitution, the concluding words "so help me God." The Supreme Court under John Marshall opened its sessions with the prayer, "God save the United States and this Honorable Court." The First Congress instituted the practice of beginning its legislative sessions with a prayer. The same week that Congress submitted the Establishment Clause as part of the Bill of Rights for ratification by the States, it enacted legislation providing for paid chaplains in the House and Senate. The day after the First Amendment was proposed, the same Congress that had proposed it requested the President to proclaim "a day of public thanksgiving and prayer, to be observed, by acknowledging, with grateful hearts, the many and signal favours of Almighty God." President Washington offered the first Thanksgiving Proclamation shortly thereafter, devoting November 26, 1789 on behalf of the American people "to the service of that great and glorious Being who is the beneficent author of all the good that is, that was, or that will be." The same Congress also reenacted the Northwest Territory Ordinance of 1787, 1 Stat. 50, Article III of which provided: "Religion, morality, and knowledge, being necessary to good government and the happiness of mankind, schools and the means of education shall forever be encouraged." And of course the First Amendment itself accords religion (and no other manner of belief) special constitutional protection.

These actions of our First President and Congress and the Marshall Court were not idiosyncratic; they reflected the beliefs of the period. Those who wrote the Constitution believed that morality was essential to the well-being of society and that encouragement of religion was the best way to foster morality.... With all of this reality (and much more) staring it in the face, how can the Court *possibly* assert that "the First Amendment mandates governmental neutrality between ... religion and nonreligion," and that "[m]anifesting a purpose to favor ... adherence to religion generally," is unconstitutional? Who says so? Surely not the words of the Constitution. Surely not the history and traditions that reflect our society's constant understanding of those words.

Historical practices thus demonstrate that there is a distance between the acknowledgment of a single Creator and the establishment of a religion. The former is, as *Marsh v. Chambers* put it, "a tolerable acknowledgment of beliefs widely held among the people of this country." The three most popular religions in the United States, Christianity, Judaism, and Islam—which combined account for 97.7% of all believers—are monotheistic. All of them, moreover (Islam included), believe that the Ten Commandments were given by God to Moses, and are divine prescriptions for a virtuous life. Publicly honoring the Ten Commandments is thus indistinguishable, insofar as discriminating against other religions is concerned, from publicly honoring God. Both practices are recognized across such a broad and diverse range of the population—from Christians to Muslims—that they cannot be reasonably understood as a government endorsement of a particular religious viewpoint.[4]

III

C

Nor is it the case that a solo display of the Ten Commandments advances any one faith. They are assuredly a religious symbol, but they are not so closely associated with a single religious belief that their display can reasonably be understood as preferring one religious sect over another. The Ten Commandments are recognized by Judaism, Christianity, and Islam alike as divinely given.[12]

In sum: The first displays did not necessarily evidence an intent to further religious practice; nor did the second displays, or the resolutions authorizing them; and there is in any event no basis for attributing whatever intent motivated the first and second displays to the third. Given the presumption of regularity that always accompanies our review of official action, the Court has identified no evidence of a purpose to advance religion in a way that is inconsistent with our cases. The Court may well be correct in identifying the third displays as the fruit of a desire to display the Ten Commandments, but neither our cases nor our history support its assertion that such a desire renders the fruit poisonous.

For the foregoing reasons, I would reverse the judgment of the Court of Appeals.

---

[4]   This is not to say that a display of the Ten Commandments could never constitute an impermissible endorsement of a particular religious view. The Establishment Clause would prohibit, for example, governmental endorsement of a particular version of the Decalogue as authoritative. Here the display of the Ten Commandments alongside eight secular documents, and the plaque's explanation for their inclusion, make clear that they were not posted to take sides in a theological dispute.

[12]   Because there are interpretational differences between faiths and within faiths concerning the meaning and perhaps even the text of the Commandments, Justice STEVENS maintains that *any* display of the text of the Ten Commandments is impermissible because it "invariably places the [government] at the center of a serious sectarian dispute." *Van Orden, post,* 545 U.S., at 718–19, 125 S.Ct., at 2880 (dissenting opinion). I think not. The sectarian dispute regarding text, if serious, is not widely known. I doubt that most religious adherents are even aware that there are competing versions with doctrinal consequences (I certainly was not). In any event, the context of the display here could not conceivably cause the viewer to believe that the government was taking sides in a doctrinal controversy.

A controversial tablet displaying the Ten Commandments,
located on the grounds of the Texas State Capitol in Austin, Texas, USA.
Photograph taken by the Office of the Attorney General of Texas.

Van Orden v. Perry

Supreme Court of the United States, 2005.
545 U.S. 677, 125 S.Ct. 2854, 162 L.Ed.2d 607.

■ CHIEF JUSTICE REHNQUIST announced the judgment of the court and
delivered an opinion, in which JUSTICE SCALIA, JUSTICE KENNEDY, and
JUSTICE THOMAS join.

The question here is whether the Establishment Clause of the First
Amendment allows the display of a monument inscribed with the Ten
Commandments on the Texas State Capitol grounds. We hold that it
does.

The 22 acres surrounding the Texas State Capitol contain 17
monuments and 21 historical markers commemorating the "people,
ideals, and events that compose Texan identity."[1] The monolith
challenged here stands 6-feet high and 3 1/2-feet wide. It is located to
the north of the Capitol building, between the Capitol and the Supreme
Court building. Its primary content is the text of the Ten
Commandments. An eagle grasping the American flag, an eye inside of
a pyramid, and two small tablets with what appears to be an ancient
script are carved above the text of the Ten Commandments. Below the
text are two Stars of David and the superimposed Greek letters Chi and

---

[1] The monuments are: Heroes of the Alamo, Hood's Brigade, Confederate Soldiers,
Volunteer Fireman, Terry's Texas Rangers, Texas Cowboy, Spanish-American War, Texas
National Guard, Ten Commandments, Tribute to Texas School Children, Texas Pioneer
Woman, The Boy Scouts' Statue of Liberty Replica, Pearl Harbor Veterans, Korean War
Veterans, Soldiers of World War I, Disabled Veterans, and Texas Peace Officers.

Rho, which represent Christ. The bottom of the monument bears the inscription "PRESENTED TO THE PEOPLE AND YOUTH OF TEXAS BY THE FRATERNAL ORDER OF EAGLES OF TEXAS 1961."

The legislative record surrounding the State's acceptance of the monument from the Eagles—a national social, civic, and patriotic organization—is limited to legislative journal entries. After the monument was accepted, the State selected a site for the monument based on the recommendation of the state organization responsible for maintaining the Capitol grounds. The Eagles paid the cost of erecting the monument, the dedication of which was presided over by two state legislators.

Petitioner Thomas Van Orden is a native Texan and a resident of Austin. At one time he was a licensed lawyer, having graduated from Southern Methodist Law School. Van Orden testified that, since 1995, he has encountered the Ten Commandments monument during his frequent visits to the Capitol grounds. His visits are typically for the purpose of using the law library in the Supreme Court building, which is located just northwest of the Capitol building.

Forty years after the monument's erection and six years after Van Orden began to encounter the monument frequently, he sued numerous state officials in their official capacities under Rev. Stat. § 1979, 42 U.S.C. § 1983, seeking both a declaration that the monument's placement violates the Establishment Clause and an injunction requiring its removal. [The district court ruled the monument constitutional because it had a secular purpose and did not endorse religion.]

Our cases, Januslike, point in two directions in applying the Establishment Clause. One face looks toward the strong role played by religion and religious traditions throughout our Nation's history. The other face looks toward the principle that governmental intervention in religious matters can itself endanger religious freedom.

Whatever may be the fate of the *Lemon* test in the larger scheme of Establishment Clause jurisprudence, we think it not useful in dealing with the sort of passive monument that Texas has erected on its Capitol grounds. Instead, our analysis is driven both by the nature of the monument and by our Nation's history.

In this case we are faced with a display of the Ten Commandments on government property outside the Texas State Capitol. Such acknowledgments of the role played by the Ten Commandments in our Nation's heritage are common throughout America. We need only look within our own Courtroom. Since 1935, Moses has stood, holding two tablets that reveal portions of the Ten Commandments written in Hebrew, among other lawgivers in the south frieze. Representations of the Ten Commandments adorn the metal gates lining the north and south sides of the Courtroom as well as the doors leading into the

Courtroom. Moses also sits on the exterior east facade of the building holding the Ten Commandments tablets.

Similar acknowledgments can be seen throughout a visitor's tour of our Nation's Capital. For example, a large statue of Moses holding the Ten Commandments, alongside a statue of the Apostle Paul, has overlooked the rotunda of the Library of Congress' Jefferson Building since 1897. And the Jefferson Building's Great Reading Room contains a sculpture of a woman beside the Ten Commandments with a quote above her from the Old Testament (Micah 6:8). A medallion with two tablets depicting the Ten Commandments decorates the floor of the National Archives. Inside the Department of Justice, a statue entitled "The Spirit of Law" has two tablets representing the Ten Commandments lying at its feet. In front of the Ronald Reagan Building is another sculpture that includes a depiction of the Ten Commandments. So too a 24-foot-tall sculpture, depicting, among other things, the Ten Commandments and a cross, stands outside the federal courthouse that houses both the Court of Appeals and the District Court for the District of Columbia. Moses is also prominently featured in the Chamber of the United States House of Representatives.

Our opinions, like our building, have recognized the role the Decalogue plays in America's heritage. These displays and recognitions of the Ten Commandments bespeak the rich American tradition of religious acknowledgments.

The placement of the Ten Commandments monument on the Texas State Capitol grounds is a far more passive use of those texts than was the case in *Stone*, where the text confronted elementary school students every day. Indeed, Van Orden, the petitioner here, apparently walked by the monument for a number of years before bringing this lawsuit. The monument is therefore also quite different from the prayers involved in *Schempp* and *Lee v. Weisman*. Texas has treated her Capitol grounds monuments as representing the several strands in the State's political and legal history. The inclusion of the Ten Commandments monument in this group has a dual significance, partaking of both religion and government. We cannot say that Texas' display of this monument violates the Establishment Clause of the First Amendment.

The judgment of the Court of Appeals is affirmed.

It is so ordered.

■ JUSTICE THOMAS, concurring.

This case would be easy if the Court were willing to abandon the inconsistent guideposts it has adopted for addressing Establishment Clause challenges, and return to the original meaning of the Clause. I have previously suggested that the Clause's text and history "resis[t] incorporation" against the States. If the Establishment Clause does not restrain the States, then it has no application here, where only state action is at issue.

Even if the Clause is incorporated, or if the Free Exercise Clause limits the power of States to establish religions, our task would be far simpler if we returned to the original meaning of the word "establishment" than it is under the various approaches this Court now uses. The Framers understood an establishment "necessarily [to] involve actual legal coercion."

There is no question that, based on the original meaning of the Establishment Clause, the Ten Commandments display at issue here is constitutional. In no sense does Texas compel petitioner Van Orden to do anything. The only injury to him is that he takes offense at seeing the monument as he passes it on his way to the Texas Supreme Court Library. He need not stop to read it or even to look at it, let alone to express support for it or adopt the Commandments as guides for his life. The mere presence of the monument along his path involves no coercion and thus does not violate the Establishment Clause.

■ JUSTICE BREYER, concurring in the judgment.

The case before us is a borderline case.

Here the tablets have been used as part of a display that communicates not simply a religious message, but a secular message as well. The circumstances surrounding the display's placement on the capitol grounds and its physical setting suggest that the State itself intended the latter, nonreligious aspects of the tablets' message to predominate. And the monument's 40-year history on the Texas state grounds indicates that that has been its effect.

As far as I can tell, 40 years passed in which the presence of this monument, legally speaking, went unchallenged (until the single legal objection raised by petitioner). And I am not aware of any evidence suggesting that this was due to a climate of intimidation. Hence, those 40 years suggest more strongly than can any set of formulaic tests that few individuals, whatever their system of beliefs, are likely to have understood the monument as amounting, in any significantly detrimental way, to a government effort to favor a particular religious sect, primarily to promote religion over nonreligion, to "engage in" any "religious practic[e]," to "compel" any "religious practic[e]," or to "work deterrence" of any "religious belief." Those 40 years suggest that the public visiting the capitol grounds has considered the religious aspect of the tablets' message as part of what is a broader moral and historical message reflective of a cultural heritage.

I rely less upon a literal application of any particular test than upon consideration of the basic purposes of the First Amendment's Religion Clauses themselves. This display has stood apparently uncontested for nearly two generations. That experience helps us understand that as a practical matter of *degree* this display is unlikely to prove divisive. And this matter of degree is, I believe, critical in a borderline case such as this one.

At the same time, to reach a contrary conclusion here, based primarily upon on the religious nature of the tablets' text would, I fear, lead the law to exhibit a hostility toward religion that has no place in our Establishment Clause traditions. Such a holding might well encourage disputes concerning the removal of longstanding depictions of the Ten Commandments from public buildings across the Nation. And it could thereby create the very kind of religiously based divisiveness that the Establishment Clause seeks to avoid.

■ JUSTICE STEVENS, with whom JUSTICE GINSBURG joins, dissenting.

The sole function of the monument on the grounds of Texas' State Capitol is to display the full text of one version of the Ten Commandments. The monument is not a work of art and does not refer to any event in the history of the State. It is significant because, and only because, it communicates the following message:

"I AM the LORD thy God.

"Thou shalt have no other gods before me.

"Thou shalt not make to thyself any graven images.

"Thou shalt not take the Name of the Lord thy God in vain.

"Remember the Sabbath day, to keep it holy.

"Honor thy father and thy mother, that thy days may be long upon the land which the Lord thy God giveth thee.

"Thou shalt not kill.

"Thou shalt not commit adultery.

"Thou shalt not steal.

"Thou shalt not bear false witness against thy neighbor.

"Thou shalt not covet thy neighbor's house.

"Thou shalt not covet thy neighbor's wife, nor his manservant, nor his maidservant, nor his cattle, nor anything that is thy neighbor's."[1]

II

Moreover, despite the Eagles' best efforts to choose a benign nondenominational text,[15] the Ten Commandments display projects not

---

[1] At the bottom of the message, the observer learns that the display was "[p]resented to the people and youth of Texas by the Fraternal Order of Eagles of Texas" in 1961.

[15] See *ante*, at 2869 (BREYER, J., concurring in judgment). Despite the Eagles' efforts, not all of the monuments they donated in fact conform to a "universally-accepted" text. Compare, *e.g.*, Appendix, *infra* (including the command that "Thou shalt not make to thyself any graven images"), and *Adland v. Russ*, 307 F.3d 471, 475 (C.A.6 2002) (same), with *Freedom From Religion Foundation*, 898 P.2d, at 1016 (omitting that command altogether). The distinction represents a critical divide between the Protestant and Catholic faiths. During

just a religious, but an inherently sectarian message. There are many distinctive versions of the Decalogue, ascribed to by different religions and even different denominations within a particular faith; to a pious and learned observer, these differences may be of enormous religious significance.[16] In choosing to display this version of the Commandments, Texas tells the observer that the State supports this side of the doctrinal religious debate. The reasonable observer, after all, has no way of knowing that this text was the product of a compromise, or that there is a rationale of any kind for the text's selection.[17]

Even if, however, the message of the monument, despite the inscribed text, fairly could be said to represent the belief system of all Judeo-Christians, it would still run afoul of the Establishment Clause by prescribing a compelled code of conduct from one God, namely a Judeo-Christian God, that is rejected by prominent polytheistic sects, such as Hinduism, as well as nontheistic religions, such as Buddhism. And, at the very least, the text of the Ten Commandments impermissibly commands a preference for religion over irreligion. Any of those bases, in my judgment, would be sufficient to conclude that the message should not be proclaimed by the State of Texas on a permanent monument at the seat of its government.

■ [JUSTICE O'CONNOR dissented based on her concurrence in *McCreary*. A dissent by JUSTICE SOUTER is omitted.]

NOTES AND QUESTIONS

1.   The monument in Austin contained the text commonly thought to be the Ten Commandments. According to Hebrew Bible scholar John J. Collins, however, multiple versions exist:

---

the Reformation, Protestants destroyed images of the Virgin Mary and of Jesus Christ that were venerated in Catholic churches. Even today there is a notable difference between the imagery in different churches, a difference that may in part be attributable to differing understandings of the meaning of what is the Second Commandment in the King James Bible translation and a portion of the First Commandment in the Catholic translation. See Finkelman, The Ten Commandments on the Courthouse Lawn and Elsewhere, 73 Ford. L.Rev. 1477, 1493–1494 (2005).

[16] For example, in the Jewish version of the Sixth Commandment God commands: "You shall not murder"; whereas, the King James interpretation of the same command is: "Thou shalt not kill." Compare W. Plaut, The Torah: A Modern Commentary 534 (1981), with Appendix, *infra*. The difference between the two versions is not merely semantic; rather, it is but one example of a deep theological dispute. See Finkelman, *supra*, at 1481–1500; P. Maier, Enumerating the Decalogue; Do We Number the Ten Commandments Correctly? 16 Concordia J. 18, 18–26 (1990). Varying interpretations of this Commandment explain the actions of vegetarians who refuse to eat meat, pacifists who refuse to work for munitions makers, prison officials who refuse to administer lethal injections to death row inmates, and pharmacists who refuse to sell morning-after pills to women. Although the command is ambiguous, its power to motivate like-minded interpreters of its message cannot be denied.

[17] Justice SCALIA's willingness to dismiss the distinct textual versions adhered to by different faiths in the name of generic "monotheism" based on mere speculation regarding their significance, *McCreary County*, is not only somewhat ironic, see A. Scalia, A Matter of Interpretation 23–25 (1997), but also serves to reinforce the concern that interjecting government into the religious sphere will offend "adherents who consider the particular advertisement disrespectful."

The Ten Commandments as found in Exodus 20 are usually attributed to the E source of the Pentateuch. Another series of laws in Exod 34:11 is called "the Yahwist Decalogue," although it is clearly not a decalogue. The closest parallel to Exodus 20 is found in Deut 5:6–21. Other lists of commandments that partially overlap the Decalogue are found in Lev 19:1–18 and Deut 27:15–26. The requirements of the covenant are said to be "ten words" in Exod 34:28; Deut 4:13; 10:4. In fact, there is some variation in the way that the commandments are counted. Jewish tradition distinguishes five positive commandments (down to honoring parents) and five negative. Christians generally distinguish between obligations to God and obligations to one's neighbor. In some Christian traditions (Catholic, Anglican, Lutheran) the obligations to God are counted as three. (The prohibition of idolatry is subsumed under the first commandment.) A distinction is made between coveting one's neighbor's wife and coveting other property. The Reformed tradition groups the commandments as four and six, distinguishing the prohibition of idolatry and regarding the prohibition of coveting as a single commandment. This division of the commandments seems to be most in line with the text of Exodus.

See John J. Collins, Introduction to the Hebrew Bible 126–27 (2004).

Is the existence of different versions of the Ten Commandments relevant to the holding? According to Justice Scalia:

> Because there are interpretational differences between faiths and within faiths concerning the meaning and perhaps even the text of the Commandments, Justice STEVENS maintains that *any* display of the text of the Ten Commandments is impermissible because it "invariably places the [government] at the center of a serious sectarian dispute." Van Orden, 125 S.Ct., at 2880 (dissenting opinion). I think not. The sectarian dispute regarding text, if serious, is not widely known. I doubt that most religious adherents are even aware that there are competing versions with doctrinal consequences (I certainly was not). In any event, the context of the display here could not conceivably cause the viewer to believe that the government was taking sides in a doctrinal controversy.

Is Justice Scalia correct that the "sectarian dispute regarding text is not widely known?" If there are different sets of commandments, why should it matter if they are widely known or not? Is Justice Scalia correct that the Ten Commandments are constitutional because the monotheistic faiths accept them? Justice Stevens responds:

> Even if, however, the message of the monument, despite the inscribed text, fairly could be said to represent the belief system of all Judeo-Christians, it would still run afoul of the Establishment Clause by prescribing a compelled code of conduct from one God, namely a Judeo-Christian God, that is rejected by prominent

polytheistic sects, such as Hinduism, as well as nontheistic religions, such as Buddhism.

Is Justice Stevens implying that all Ten Commandments displays are unconstitutional? Is this statement consistent with Justice Souter's claim in *McCreary*—that the Establishment Clause does not preclude all "sacred text[s] [from being] integrated constitutionally into a governmental display on the subject of law, or American history?"

2.   According to theologians Stanley M. Hauerwas and William H. Willimon, the Ten Commandments cannot be understood as secular texts; they "teach us how to worship God, not how to build democracy." "Placing the commandments on the wall of a U.S. courtroom implies that somehow these commandments can be abstracted from the worship of God and is a clear violation of the third commandment." See The Truth About God (1999). Does that mean the commandments can never serve a secular purpose? Do the theologians' comments support Justice Stevens' argument that the Ten Commandments monument in Texas was religious and not secular? Is religion trivialized by the argument that the Ten Commandments are really a secular source of law? In his book about "bleached faith," Professor Steven Goldberg tellingly reports that for many years the American people and the Supreme Court rejected Jehovah's Witnesses' attempts to *obey* the commandments (by refusing to recite the pledge of allegiance), while honoring attempts to *display* empty symbols of them across the country. Do you agree? See Steven Goldberg, Bleached Faith: The Tragic Cost When Religion is Forced into the Public Square (2008).

3.   If the Ten Commandments are an important source of law, could the first four commandments be incorporated into secular law without violating the Establishment Clause? Are the Fifth and Seventh Commandments sources of secular law or simply moral obligations? Could the Tenth Commandment be a source of criminal law? Does the Eighth Commandment require that all lying be against the law? See Marci Hamilton, The Ten Commandments and American Law: Why Some Christians' Claims to Legal Hegemony Are Not Consistent with the Historical Record, Writ, Sept. 11, 2003, http://writ.news.findlaw.com/hamilton/20030911.html. If countries that were not influenced by the Ten Commandments have laws against theft, murder and perjury, is it an indication that the Ten Commandments are not the source of the law?

If the first four commandments are about one's relationship with God and the next six are specific responsibilities toward the neighbor, should only the last six be posted because only those six are legitimate sources of law? See Nancy J. Duff, Should the Ten Commandments Be Posted in the Public Realm? Why the Bible and the Constitution Say, "No," 159, 167 in William P. Brown, ed., The Ten Commandments: The Reciprocity of Faithfulness (2004).

4.   Is it significant that the words "I AM the LORD thy GOD" on the monument are large, or that the "prohibitions on murder, adultery, and theft are smaller than the text which identifies God as the source of the

commandments"? See Erwin Chemerinsky, Why Justice Breyer Was Wrong in *Van Orden v. Perry*, 14 Wm. & Mary Bill Rts. J. 1, 5–6 (2005).

5. *Justice Breyer—The Swing Vote.* Was Justice Breyer's decision to dissent in *McCreary* and to join the majority in *Van Orden* wise, candid and pragmatic, the mark of a good judge who is able to decide each case on the merits? Or was it "a regrettable sign of a failed judge"? See William Van Alstyne, Ten Commandments, Nine Judges, and Five Versions of One Amendment—The First. ("Now What?"), 14 Wm. & Mary Bill Rts. J. 17, 25 (2005). Is Justice Thomas correct that Breyer's opinion illustrates the inappropriate basing of court decisions on the personal preference of judges? How do Breyer's opinions in these cases compare with his dissent in *Zelman*? What constitutional principle seems to be governing his decisions?

Was it wrong for Justice Breyer to take into account the possible consequences of the destruction of the Texas monument? If Breyer believed that the Texas monument passed the *Lemon* test, should he have simply "said so and have left it at that"? See id. ("[H]is public breast-baring—of 'concerns' over possible new rounds of lawsuits and adverse reaction to a decision if it went against Texas—was unseemly at best.").

In 2001, Taliban leaders ordered the destruction of Buddha statues carved into sandstone cliffs in Bamiyan, Afghanistan. Work on the Buddhas began in the second century, when Bamiyan, which was along the Silk Road, was the westernmost outpost of Buddhism. The statues, which were 175, 125 and 26 feet high, and decorated with blue, red and gilt coloring, took centuries to build. Because the Taliban's Islamic leaders believed it was sacrilegious to picture humans in art, they forced local residents to attach explosives to the statues and blow them up. Artists and historians around the world bemoaned the loss of the Buddhas. See John Otis, Buddha Rebirth? Experts Weigh the Possibility of Reconstructing the Giant Statues the Taliban Demolished, San Antonio Express-News (Texas), Jan. 7, 2002, at 1A. Similar Buddhist statues survived in neighboring Turkmenistan, like Afghanistan a Muslim-majority country. See A Foil to Taliban, The Statesman (India), Mar. 14, 2001. Does the world's criticism of the destruction of the Buddhas confirm Justice Breyer's point that it is politically divisive to destroy religious displays such as the Ten Commandments? If Buddhist missionaries had built giant Buddha statues in American cities, how would the First Amendment require that they be treated? Could a statue of the Buddha be added to the Texas State Capitol Park without violating the First Amendment?

Debate continues about whether to reconstruct the Bamian Buddhas or to leave the empty holes in the cliff. Some Afghans want the statues rebuilt while Westerners refuse to finance any restoration. Apparently some Afghanis think restoring the statues would be a symbolic victory over the Taliban while some Western restorationists argue there is not enough original material left to *restore* the Buddhas; they would have to be *replaced*. Rod Nordland, Countries Divided on Future of Ancient Buddhas, N.Y. Times, Mar. 22, 2014.

6. *Justice O'Connor—Not the Swing Vote.* According to Professor Erwin Chemerinsky, one of the biggest surprises in the two Ten Commandments cases was the swing vote—or rather, who was *not* the swing vote. As co-counsel to the plaintiff, Van Orden, Chemerinsky, like many, predicted that Justice O'Connor would be the swing vote. He describes the pre-decision playing field as follows:

> I saw little chance of getting the votes of Chief Justice Rehnquist or Justices Scalia, Kennedy, or Thomas. They consistently had expressed a view of the Establishment Clause that left little chance that they would find a religious symbol on government property to be unconstitutional. Justice Kennedy, for example, wrote an opinion in *County of Allegheny v. American Civil Liberties Union, Greater Pittsburgh Chapter* arguing for allowing religious symbols on government property and contending that the government violates the Establishment Clause only if it literally establishes a church or coerces religious participation. Rehnquist and Scalia joined this opinion. I could not think of a way under this test to argue that the Ten Commandments display between the Texas State Capitol and the Texas Supreme Court is unconstitutional.

> Justice Thomas has argued repeatedly that he does not believe that the Establishment Clause applies to state and local governments at all. . . . On the other hand, Justices Stevens, Souter, Ginsburg, and Breyer have been much more willing to enforce the Establishment Clause. They dissented in *Zelman v. Simmons-Harris*, where the Court held that vouchers from the government may be used for parochial schools. They also dissented in *Agostini v. Felton*, which allowed more aid to parochial schools, and *Rosenberger v. Rectors and Visitors of the University of Virginia*, which held that the government cannot deny funding to religious student groups when money is available to secular groups.

Erwin Chemerinsky, Why Justice Breyer Was Wrong in *Van Orden v. Perry*, 14 Wm. & Mary Bill Rts. J. 1 (2005).

It is a Supreme Court litigator's job to anticipate how the justices will vote. Why did so many predict the wrong swing vote in 2005? What about these Ten Commandment displays would persuade Justice Breyer but not Justice O'Connor?

7. *Update on* McCreary County. After the Supreme Court decided *McCreary County*, the Sixth Circuit affirmed the district court's permanent injunction prohibiting the Ten Commandments displays. According to the circuit court, "on remand, the 'objective observer' who has reasonable memories would have seen the same Foundations Displays posted in the courthouses with the same set of resolutions authorizing the displays, and would have instantly recognized the same religious purpose that [the county] articulated during the previous round of litigation." Although the county had passed new resolutions about the purpose of the commandments in 2007, Judge Clary ruled that those attempts violated the Establishment Clause because they were "adopted only as a litigating position" and did not display any change in the officials' actual purpose. See American Civil Liberties Union of Kentucky v. McCreary County, Kentucky, 607 F.3d 439 (6th Cir. 2010), cert. denied, 131 S.Ct. 1474 (2011).

In ACLU of Ky. v. Grayson County, Ky., 591 F.3d 837 (6th Cir. 2010), however, the court upheld an identical Foundations of American Law and Government Display in the county courthouse because there was no evidence of religious purpose. A private citizen, the Reverend Chester Shartzer, had approached county officials with the desire to post the display, and the county had no public ceremony when it opened the exhibit. Would Justice Souter conclude that the county had acted with a sham secular purpose? The court thought there was no evidence that the reverend had acted with a religious purpose. Is that ruling credible? Can all Establishment Clause violations now be solved by linking public displays to private citizens? The following case addresses the question whether the government may cure an Establishment Clause violation by transferring ownership of a religious monument to private owners.

8. *The Mojave Desert Cross.* Is the cross involved in the following case, *Salazar v. Buono,* a religious symbol? Is there a secular purpose for its presence at a war memorial?

Consider the following background to *Salazar v. Buono.* In 1934, the Veterans of Foreign Wars (VFW) built a Latin cross atop a prominent outcropping called Sunrise Rock in a Mojave Desert federal preserve. Although originally wooden, the cross now stands between five and eight feet tall and is constructed out of metal pipes painted white and bolted into the rock. The cross is visible from a distance of about 100 yards to vehicles traveling on a service road. The cross was erected in memory of WWI veterans, but no plaque or sign indicates it was intended as a memorial.

The legal controversy about the cross initially began in 1999, when a retired National Park Service (NPS) employee requested permission to build a "stupa" (a dome-shaped Buddhist shrine) near the cross. The NPS denied the request and Frank Buono, another former NPS employee, filed suit in 2001. Buono is a practicing Roman Catholic and does not find the cross itself offensive, but he objects to the government's favoritism of the cross over other symbols. The Government argued that Buono lacked standing to bring suit because he did not suffer any injury. The California district court disagreed, pointing out that "religious display cases are a particularized subclass of Establishment Clause standing jurisprudence. The injury that gives standing to plaintiffs in these cases is that caused by unwelcome direct contact with a religious display that appears to be endorsed by the state." Buono v. Norton, 212 F.Supp.2d 1202, 1211 (C.D. Cal. 2002). The court wrote that any viewing of an unconstitutional religious symbol is significant, no matter how brief, and rejected the government's argument that the cross was not a violation of the Establishment Clause because Buono was still free to enjoy "nearly all" of the preserve. Turning to the *Lemon* test, the Court found that because "the primary effect of the presence of the cross" was to "advance religion," the cross failed the effects prong of the test. The district court granted a permanent injunction, prohibiting the display of the cross on Sunrise Rock.

As litigation continued, the Department of the Interior covered the cross with a tarpaulin secured by a lock, but after it blew away, a plywood box was constructed around the cross. On appeal, the Ninth Circuit affirmed the Establishment Clause violation, writing that "even if the shorter height of the Sunrise Rock cross means that it is visible to fewer people . . . this makes it no less likely that the Sunrise Rock cross will project a message of government endorsement . . . Nor does the remote location of Sunrise Rock make a difference." Buono v. Norton, 371 F.3d 543, 549 (9th Cir. 2004). However, the Ninth Circuit stayed the permanent injunction but allowed for "alternative methods" of compliance with the district court order.

Immediately prior to the Ninth Circuit's decision, Congress passed legislation directing the Department of the Interior to transfer the one acre of land on which the cross sits to VFW, in exchange for a parcel of equal value located elsewhere. The Ninth Circuit did not rule on whether such a transfer would remedy the Establishment Clause violation, and the case ended up back in the California district court. The district court examined the land transfer agreement and found that it allowed the government to maintain significant property rights, including the right to repossess the property at any time if VFW was not adequately maintaining the cross. The court thus concluded that VFW was nothing more than a "straw purchaser" and the government impermissibly "engaged in herculean efforts to preserve the Latin Cross on federal land and . . . the proposed transfer of the subject property [could] only be viewed as an attempt to keep the Latin cross atop Sunrise Rock without actually curing the continuing Establishment Clause violation." Buono v. Norton, 364 F.Supp.2d 1175, 1178, 1182 (C.D. Cal. 2005). The court declared the land transfer invalid, and the Ninth Circuit subsequently affirmed the decision, writing that "carving out a tiny parcel of property in the midst of this vast Preserve—like a donut hole with the cross atop it—will do nothing to minimize the impermissible governmental endorsement" of the religious symbol. Buono v. Kempthorne, 502 F.3d 1069, 1086 (9th Cir. 2007).

On February 23, 2009, the U.S. Supreme Court granted certiorari to hear the following issues: (1) whether an individual has standing to bring an Establishment Clause suit challenging a religious display situated on federally owned land and (2) whether Congressional legislation ordering the transfer of land containing a religious symbol to a private entity is a permissible remedy to an Establishment Clause violation. Salazar v. Buono, 129 S.Ct. 1313 (2009). The Supreme Court remanded the case to the district court on procedural grounds in the following opinion. What do the justices' separate opinions on the case tell you about their views of the Establishment Clause and the state of Establishment Clause jurisprudence? Do you think *Town of Greece* suggests the Court would view this case differently today?

The Mojave Desert Cross.
The Cross was covered during litigation.
Courtesy of courtzero.org

Salazar v. Buono

Supreme Court of the United States, 2010.
1559 U.S. 700, 130 S.Ct. 1803, 176 L.Ed.2d 634.

■ JUSTICE KENNEDY announced the judgment of the Court and delivered an opinion, in which THE CHIEF JUSTICE joins and JUSTICE ALITO joins in part.

III

The question now before the Court is whether the District Court properly enjoined the Government from implementing the land-transfer statute. The District Court did not consider whether the statute, in isolation, would have violated the Establishment Clause, and it did not forbid the land transfer as an independent constitutional violation. Rather, the court enjoined compliance with the statute on the premise that the relief was necessary to protect the rights Buono had secured through the 2002 injunction.

Here, the District Court did not engage in the appropriate inquiry. The land-transfer statute was a substantial change in circumstances bearing on the propriety of the requested relief. The court, however, did not acknowledge the statute's significance. It examined the events that led to the statute's enactment and found an intent to prevent removal of the cross. Deeming this intent illegitimate, the court concluded that nothing of moment had changed. This was error. Even assuming that the land-transfer statute was an attempt to prevent removal of the cross, it does not follow that an injunction against its implementation was appropriate.

By dismissing Congress's motives as illicit, the District Court took insufficient account of the context in which the statute was enacted and the reasons for its passage. Private citizens put the cross on Sunrise

Rock to commemorate American servicemen who had died in World War I. Although certainly a Christian symbol, the cross was not emplaced on Sunrise Rock to promote a Christian message. Placement of the cross on Government-owned land was not an attempt to set the *imprimatur* of the state on a particular creed. Rather, those who erected the cross intended simply to honor our Nation's fallen soldiers.

Time also has played its role. The cross had stood on Sunrise Rock for nearly seven decades before the statute was enacted. By then, the cross and the cause it commemorated had become entwined in the public consciousness. Members of the public gathered regularly at Sunrise Rock to pay their respects. Rather than let the cross deteriorate, community members repeatedly took it upon themselves to replace it. Congress ultimately designated the cross as a national memorial, ranking it among those monuments honoring the noble sacrifices that constitute our national heritage. It is reasonable to interpret the congressional designation as giving recognition to the historical meaning that the cross had attained.

In belittling the Government's efforts as an attempt to "evade" the injunction, the District Court had things backwards. Congress's prerogative to balance opposing interests and its institutional competence to do so provide one of the principal reasons for deference to its policy determinations. Here, Congress adopted a policy with respect to land it now owns in order to resolve a specific controversy. Congress, the Executive, and the Judiciary all have a duty to support and defend the Constitution. The land-transfer statute embodies Congress's legislative judgment that this dispute is best resolved through a framework and policy of accommodation for a symbol that, while challenged under the Establishment Clause, has complex meaning beyond the expression of religious views. That judgment should not have been dismissed as an evasion, for the statute brought about a change of law and a congressional statement of policy applicable to the case.

Respect for a coordinate branch of Government forbids striking down an Act of Congress except upon a clear showing of unconstitutionality. The same respect requires that a congressional command be given effect unless no legal alternative exists. Even if, contrary to the congressional judgment, the land transfer were thought an insufficient accommodation in light of the earlier finding of religious endorsement, it was incumbent upon the District Court to consider less drastic relief than complete invalidation of the land-transfer statute. For instance, if there is to be a conveyance, the question might arise regarding the necessity of further action, such as signs to indicate the VFW's ownership of the land. As we have noted, Congress directed the Secretary of the Interior to install near the cross a replica of its original memorial plaque. One of the signs that appears in early photographs of the cross specifically identifies the VFW as the group that erected it.

* * *

The judgment of the Court of Appeals is reversed, and the case is remanded for further proceedings.

It is so ordered.

■ CHIEF JUSTICE ROBERTS, concurring.

At oral argument, respondent's counsel stated that it "likely would be consistent with the injunction" for the Government to tear down the cross, sell the land to the Veterans of Foreign Wars, and return the cross to them, with the VFW immediately raising the cross again. I do not see how it can make a difference for the Government to skip that empty ritual and do what Congress told it to do—sell the land with the cross on it. "The Constitution deals with substance, not shadows."

■ JUSTICE ALITO, concurring in part and concurring in the judgment.

I join Justice KENNEDY's opinion in all respects but one: I would not remand this case for the lower courts to decide whether implementation of the land-transfer statute enacted by Congress in 2003, Department of Defense Appropriations Act, 2004, § 8121, would violate the District Court's injunction or the Establishment Clause. The factual record has been sufficiently developed to permit resolution of these questions, and I would therefore decide them and hold that the statute may be implemented.

The singular circumstances surrounding the monument on Sunrise Rock presented Congress with a delicate problem, and the solution that Congress devised is true to the spirit of practical accommodation that has made the United States a Nation of unparalleled pluralism and religious tolerance.

One possible solution would have been to supplement the monument on Sunrise Rock so that it appropriately recognized the religious diversity of the American soldiers who gave their lives in the First World War. In American military cemeteries overseas, the graves of soldiers who perished in that war were marked with either a white cross or a white Star of David. More than 3,500 Jewish soldiers gave their lives for the United States in World War I, and Congress might have chosen to place a Star of David on Sunrise Rock so that the monument would duplicate those two types of headstones. But Congress may well have thought—not without reason—that the addition of yet another religious symbol would have been unlikely to satisfy the plaintiff, his attorneys, or the lower courts that had found the existing monument to be unconstitutional on the ground that it impermissibly endorsed religion. Congress chose an alternative approach that was designed to eliminate any perception of religious sponsorship stemming from the location of the cross on federally owned land, while at the same time avoiding the disturbing symbolism associated with the destruction of the historic monument. Although Justice Stevens characterizes this land exchange as one that endorses "a particular religious view," it is noteworthy that Congress, in which our country's religious diversity is well represented, passed this law by overwhelming majorities: 95–0 in the Senate and 407–15 in the House. In my view, there is no legal ground for blocking the implementation of this law.

■ JUSTICE STEVENS, with whom JUSTICE GINSBURG and JUSTICE SOTOMAYOR join, dissenting.

IV

Congressional action, taken after due deliberation, that honors our fallen soldiers merits our highest respect. As far as I can tell, however, it is unprecedented in the Nation's history to designate a bare, unadorned cross as the national war memorial for a particular group of veterans. Neither the Korean War Memorial, the Vietnam War Memorial, nor the World War II Memorial commemorates our veterans' sacrifice in sectarian or predominantly religious ways. Each of these impressive structures pays equal respect to all members of the Armed Forces who perished in the service of our Country in those conflicts. In this case, by contrast, a sectarian symbol *is* the memorial. And because Congress has established no other national monument to the veterans of the Great War, this solitary cross in the middle of the desert is *the* national World War I memorial. The sequence of legislative decisions made to designate and preserve a solitary Latin cross at an isolated location in the desert as a memorial for those who fought and died in World War I not only failed to cure the Establishment Clause violation but also, in my view, resulted in a dramatically inadequate and inappropriate tribute.

I believe that most judges would find it to be a clear Establishment Clause violation if Congress had simply directed that a solitary Latin cross be erected on the Mall in the Nation's Capital to serve as a World War I Memorial. Congress did not erect this cross, but it commanded that the cross remain in place, and it gave the cross the imprimatur of Government. Transferring the land pursuant to § 8121 would perpetuate rather than cure that unambiguous endorsement of a sectarian message.

The Mojave Desert is a remote location, far from the seat of our Government. But the Government's interest in honoring all those who have rendered heroic public service regardless of creed, as well as its constitutional responsibility to avoid endorsement of a particular religious view, should control wherever national memorials speak on behalf of our entire country.

NOTES AND QUESTIONS

1. *Oral Argument.* How would you answer Chief Justice Roberts' question to the Solicitor General: "What if the government sold simply one square foot, or whatever the area that the base of the cross is—is resting on the ground? Would your argument be the same?" Transcript of Oral Argument, Salazar v. Buono, 2009 WL 3197881 at *19 (No. 08–472). In another exchange, the Chief Justice asked Buono's lawyer, "if the government sold this land to a private party, no cross in the picture at all, and they go to settlement and at settlement the private landowner who is going to buy it says, you know, I'm going to put a big cross up on this property once I get it, can the government still sell it to him?" The lawyer responded "Yes, absolutely." Id. at *34. Is that answer correct under the law? Does that exchange resolve the constitutional question in the actual case?

Justice Ginsburg posed another hypothetical: "What about the government's argument that suppose the government took down the cross, gave it back to the Veterans of Foreign Wars, sold them the land in exchange for land of equal value, and then the Veterans said, fine, the cross was ours to begin with. Now the land is ours, so we just put it back. If that would be consistent with the injunction?" Id. at *43. Buono's lawyer responded: "I believe that that—obviously not the facts presented by our case, Justice Ginsburg, but that likely would be consistent with the injunction, that's correct. But it is not the scenario we have here." Id. at *43. Was that a good response? Does Justice Ginsburg's question pose the best solution to the case?

Justice Ginsburg also raised questions about the Arlington National Cemetery with Buono's lawyer, Mr. Eliasberg:

> JUSTICE GINSBURG: . . . what happens in Arlington Cemetery, where there's the Argonne Cross Memorial and the Canadian Cross of Sacrifice, both right here in Arlington, what happens to them?
>
> MR. ELIASBERG: . . . , I believe that the Argonne Cross in the national—in memorial cemetery is extremely different. There are, in the national cemeteries, the—the VA offers, to veterans and their family, a choice of putting up 39 different emblems and beliefs on their tombstones. In Arlington, there is a cross that is surrounded by a sea of tombstones with symbols of the faith of all of the different service members.
>
> In that context, I don't think anyone would perceive that the government was favoring one particular religion because of the variety of choices and religious symbols expressed there. That's very different from a stand-alone cross of one religious symbol that is not surrounded by any other context, . . .

Id. at *49–50. Is Mr. Eliasberg correct?

What is your reaction to the following exchange between Justice Antonin Scalia and Buono's lawyer, Mr. Eliasberg? Are Scalia's comments consistent with his opinions in the Ten Commandments cases?

JUSTICE SCALIA: The cross doesn't honor non-Christians who fought in the war? Is that—is that—

MR. ELIASBERG: I believe that's actually correct.

JUSTICE SCALIA: Where does it say that?

MR. ELIASBERG: It doesn't say that, but a cross is the predominant symbol of Christianity and it signifies that Jesus is the son of God and died to redeem mankind for our sins, and I believe that's why the Jewish war veterans—

JUSTICE SCALIA: It's erected as a war memorial. I assume it is erected in honor of all of the war dead. It's the—the cross is the—is the most common symbol of—of—of the resting place of the dead, and it doesn't seem to me—what would you have them erect? A cross—some conglomerate of a cross, a Star of David, and you know, a Moslem half moon and star?

MR. ELIASBERG: Well, Justice Scalia, if I may go to your first point. The cross is the most common symbol of the resting place of Christians. I have been in Jewish cemeteries. There is never a cross on a tombstone of a Jew.

(Laughter.)

MR. ELIASBERG: So it is the most common symbol to honor Christians.

JUSTICE SCALIA: I don't think you can leap from that to the conclusion that the only war dead that that cross honors are the Christian war dead. I think that's an outrageous conclusion.

MR. ELIASBERG: Well, my—the point of my—point here is to say that there is a reason the Jewish war veterans came in and said we don't feel honored by this cross. This cross can't honor us because it is a religious symbol of another religion.

Id. at *38–39.

2.   In Chapter 2, you learned that Justice Kennedy strongly criticized the endorsement test in *Allegheny County* as a "most unwelcome addition to our tangled Establishment Clause jurisprudence." Do Justice Kennedy's and Justice Alito's reactions to this case convince you the Court may abandon the endorsement test? In Chapter 2, you also read *Town of Greece v. Galloway*, which was decided post-*Salazar*. Would the reasoning in *Greece* have affected the outcome in *Buono*?

3.   What should the district court decide in response to Justice Kennedy's ruling? The district court approved a settlement in which the government conveyed the land under the cross to the Veterans of Foreign Wars (VFW) in exchange for other property. A sign will indicate that the land is private property. See Settlement Agreement, Buono v. Salazar, No.

5:01–CV–00216–RT–SGL, Apr. 16, 2012, at http://www.scribd.com/doc/9112 4039/Sunrise-Rock-Settlement-Agreement.

The original cross was stolen during the litigation. A replacement cross was installed in its place after the settlement agreement took effect. In November 2012 the original cross was found attached to a fence post in Half Moon Bay, California, with a note to alert authorities. See Jaxon Van Derbeken, Mojave Cross Stolen Two Years Ago Hung on Post With Note, San Fran. Chron., Nov. 6, 2012, at C1; David Olson, Mojave Desert: Cross Stands Again, The Press-Enterprise (Riverside), Nov. 11, 2012.

4.   *Oklahoma Ten Commandments.* Oklahoma legislators thought they were on safe constitutional ground when they funded a Ten Commandments monument, avoiding an establishment violation because "(1) the text was the same as the text displayed on the Ten Commandments monument on the grounds of the Texas State Capitol, and (2) a non-religious historic purpose was given for the placement of the monument." Do you agree?

The Oklahoma Supreme Court, however, ruled that the monument violated the Oklahoma Constitution, which prohibits public money or property being spent for the use, benefit, or support of a sect or system of religion. The court also concluded "the Ten Commandments are obviously religious in nature and are an integral part of the Jewish and Christian faiths." Prescott v. Oklahoma Capitol Preservation Commission, 2015 OK 54. We study whether such state constitution no-funding provisions are unconstitutional in Section B.

5.   *Big Mountain Jesus.* The Knights of Columbus, a Catholic religious organization, first received a Special Use Permit from the United States Forest Service in 1953 to place the statue of Big Mountain Jesus (who is 6 feet tall and has a 6-foot base) on federal land leased to the Whitefish Mountain Resort in Whitefish, Montana. Should the renewal of the permit violate the Establishment Clause? What else would you need to know in order to decide the question? See Freedom from Religion Foundation v. Weber, 951 F.Supp.2d 1123 (D. Mont. 2013).

The original application stated the Knights erected the statue "for the purpose of erecting a shrine over the Big Mountain Ski run." Some World War II veterans remembered shrines in the mountains of Italy and France and wanted to replicate them and honor their fellow veterans in the shrine. The statue is obscured by trees and not immediately visible to all skiers. Visitors frequently leave ski goggles, hats, and poles with Jesus. Sometimes skiers meet at the statue. Which of these facts do you think was most significant to the court's decision to uphold the renewal of the permit? Which Establishment Clause analysis best fits these facts? See id. (ruling that the permit renewal satisfied both the *Lemon* and *Van Orden* tests). Do you agree with the district court that for the government, the permit's renewal was a secular purpose distinct from the religious purpose of the Knights? The district court also ruled that the statue's presence at a private ski resort meant that the government could not be perceived as endorsing religion. Do you agree? Why would the court think that all the *Van Orden* factors were satisfied by Big Mountain Jesus?

In a 2–1 decision, the Ninth Circuit ruled Big Mountain Jesus was constitutional. The opinion by Judge Owens held that the statue had secular purposes ("the statue's cultural and historical significance for veterans, Montanans and tourists; the statue's inclusion in the National Register of Historic Places; and the government's intent to preserve the site 'as a historic part of the resort.' ") and did not endorse religion. Do you agree with Judge Owens that the location—a resort used for skiing, hiking and berry-picking—"suggests a secular context"? Or with dissenting Judge Pregerson that a twelve-foot statue of Jesus cannot be secular? Judge Smith's concurrence argued that the statue was private, not government, speech. See Freedom from Religion Foundation, Inc. v. Weber, 628 Fed.Appx. 952 (2015). What do you think the Supreme Court would rule about Big Mountain Jesus?

As you learned in Chapter 2, in *Lemon*, government funding of religion has long been restricted due to Establishment Clause precedents. We examine the evolving understandings of government aid to religious institutions in the following section.

B. PUBLIC FUNDING OF RELIGION

There are three distinct areas of public funding of religion, and each era pushes at the boundaries of separationist ideals. The first era began with the Court's landmark ruling in *Everson v. Board of Education of Ewing Township*. Justice Black's *Everson* opinion built the wall of separation between church and state as the proper metaphor for the Establishment Clause, yet upheld a New Jersey program providing busing to parochial school students. Section B1 examines *Everson* and the dominant no-aid-to-religion cases that followed from 1947 to 2002. Starting in the 1990s, the Court began questioning the wall of separation, with some justices arguing the no-aid doctrine was permeated with bigotry. Section B2 starts with the Court's 2002 decision upholding vouchers to private and religious schools in *Zelman v. Simmons-Harris*, in which the wall appeared to crumble. Finally, Section B3 asks if the Court will abolish the wall between separation of church and state by requiring that religious and non-religious organizations be funded in the name of neutrality and equality.

1. THE WALL OF SEPARATION: NO AID TO RELIGION

Everson v. Board of Education of Ewing Township

Supreme Court of the United States, 1947.
330 U.S. 1, 67 S.Ct. 504, 91 L.Ed. 711.

■ MR. JUSTICE BLACK delivered the opinion of the Court.

A New Jersey statute authorizes its local school districts to make rules and contracts for the transportation of children to and from schools.[1] The appellee, a township board of education, acting pursuant to this statute, authorized reimbursement to parents of money expended by them for the bus transportation of their children on regular busses operated by the public transportation system. Part of this money was for the payment of transportation of some children in the community to Catholic parochial schools. These church schools give their students, in addition to secular education, regular religious instruction conforming to the religious tenets and modes of worship of the Catholic Faith. The superintendent of these schools is a Catholic priest.

The New Jersey statute is challenged as a "law respecting an establishment of religion." The First Amendment, as made applicable to the states by the Fourteenth, Murdock v. Commonwealth of Pennsylvania, 319 U.S. 105, 63 S.Ct. 870, 872, 87 L.Ed. 1292, 146 A.L.R. 81, commands that a state "shall make no law respecting an establishment of religion, or prohibiting the free exercise thereof." These words of the First Amendment reflected in the minds of early Americans a vivid mental picture of conditions and practices which they fervently wished to stamp out in order to preserve liberty for themselves and for their posterity. Doubtless their goal has not been entirely reached; but so far has the Nation moved toward it that the expression "law respecting an establishment of religion," probably does not so vividly remind present-day Americans of the evils, fears, and political problems that caused that expression to be written into our Bill of Rights. Whether this New Jersey law is one respecting the "establishment of religion" requires an understanding of the meaning of that language, particularly with respect to the imposition of taxes. Once again, therefore, it is not inappropriate briefly to review the background

---

[1] "Whenever in any district there are children living remote from any schoolhouse, the board of education of the district may make rules and contracts for the transportation of such children to and from school, including the transportation of school children to and from school other than a public school, except such school as is operated for profit in whole or in part.

"When any school district provides any transportation for public school children to and from school, transportation from any point in such established school route to any other point in such established school route shall be supplied to school children residing in such school district in going to and from school other than a public school, except such school as is operated for profit in whole or in part." New Jersey Laws, 1941, c. 191, p. 581; N. J. R. S. Cum. Supp., tit. 18, c. 14, ß 8.

and environment of the period in which that constitutional language was fashioned and adopted.

A large proportion of the early settlers of this country came here from Europe to escape the bondage of laws which compelled them to support and attend government favored churches. The centuries immediately before and contemporaneous with the colonization of America had been filled with turmoil, civil strife, and persecutions, generated in large part by established sects determined to maintain their absolute political and religious supremacy. With the power of government supporting them, at various times and places, Catholics had persecuted Protestants, Protestants had persecuted Catholics, Protestant sects had persecuted other Protestant sects, Catholics of one shade of belief had persecuted Catholics of another shade of belief, and all of these had from time to time persecuted Jews. In efforts to force loyalty to whatever religious group happened to be on top and in league with the government of a particular time and place, men and women had been fined, cast in jail, cruelly tortured, and killed. Among the offenses for which these punishments had been inflicted were such things as speaking disrespectfully of the views of ministers of government-established churches, nonattendance at those churches, expressions of non-belief in their doctrines, and failure to pay taxes and tithes to support them.

These practices of the old world were transplanted to and began to thrive in the soil of the new America. The very charters granted by the English Crown to the individuals and companies designated to make the laws which would control the destinies of the colonials authorized these individuals and companies to erect religious establishments which all, whether believers or non-believers, would be required to support and attend. An exercise of this authority was accompanied by a repetition of many of the old world practices and persecutions. Catholics found themselves hounded and proscribed because of their faith; Quakers who followed their conscience went to jail; Baptists were peculiarly obnoxious to certain dominant Protestant sects; men and women of varied faiths who happened to be in a minority in a particular locality were persecuted because they steadfastly persisted in worshipping God only as their own consciences dictated. And all of these dissenters were compelled to pay tithes and taxes[8] to support government-sponsored churches whose ministers preached inflammatory sermons designed to strengthen and consolidate the established faith by generating a burning hatred against dissenters.

These practices became so commonplace as to shock the freedom-loving colonials into a feeling of abhorrence. The imposition of taxes to

---

[8] Almost every colony exacted some kind of tax for church support. See e.g. 110 (Virginia); 131 (North Carolina); 169 (Massachusetts); 270 (Connecticut); 304, 310, 339 (New York); 386 (Maryland); 295 (New Hampshire).

pay ministers' salaries and to build and maintain churches and church property aroused their indignation. It was these feelings which found expression in the First Amendment. No one locality and no one group throughout the Colonies can rightly be given entire credit for having aroused the sentiment that culminated in adoption of the Bill of Rights' provisions embracing religious liberty. But Virginia, where the established church had achieved a dominant influence in political affairs and where many excesses attracted wide public attention, provided a great stimulus and able leadership for the movement. The people there, as elsewhere, reached the conviction that individual religious liberty could be achieved best under a government which was stripped of all power to tax, to support, or otherwise to assist any or all religions, or to interfere with the beliefs of any religious individual or group.

The movement toward this end reached its dramatic climax in Virginia in 1785–86 when the Virginia legislative body was about to renew Virginia's tax levy for the support of the established church. Thomas Jefferson and James Madison led the fight against this tax. Madison wrote his great Memorial and Remonstrance against the law. In it, he eloquently argued that a true religion did not need the support of law; that no person, either believer or non-believer, should be taxed to support a religious institution of any kind; that the best interest of a society required that the minds of men always be wholly free; and that cruel persecutions were the inevitable result of government-established religions. Madison's Remonstrance received strong support throughout Virginia, and the Assembly postponed consideration of the proposed tax measure until its next session. When the proposal came up for consideration at that session, it not only died in committee, but the Assembly enacted the famous "Virginia Bill for Religious Liberty" originally written by Thomas Jefferson. The preamble to that Bill stated among other things that

> "Almighty God hath created the mind free; that all attempts to influence it by temporal punishments, or burthens, or by civil incapacitations, tend only to beget habits of hypocrisy and meanness, and are a departure from the plan of the Holy author of our religion who being Lord both of body and mind, yet chose not to propagate it by coercions on either ... ; that to compel a man to furnish contributions of money for the propagation of opinions which he disbelieves, is sinful and tyrannical; that even the forcing him to support this or that teacher of his own religious persuasion, is depriving him of the comfortable liberty of giving his contributions to the particular pastor, whose morals he would make his pattern. * * * "

And the statute itself enacted

"That no man shall be compelled to frequent or support any religious worship, place, or ministry whatsoever, nor shall be enforced, restrained, molested, or burthened, in his body or goods, nor shall otherwise suffer on account of his religious opinions or belief. . . . "

This Court has previously recognized that the provisions of the First Amendment, in the drafting and adoption of which Madison and Jefferson played such leading roles, had the same objective and were intended to provide the same protection against governmental intrusion on religious liberty as the Virginia statute. The state courts, in the main, have remained faithful to the language of their own constitutional provisions designed to protect religious freedom and to separate religions and governments. Their decisions, however, show the difficulty in drawing the line between tax legislation which provides funds for the welfare of the general public and that which is designed to support institutions which teach religion.

The "establishment of religion" clause of the First Amendment means at least this: Neither a state nor the Federal Government can set up a church. Neither can pass laws which aid one religion, aid all religions, or prefer one religion over another. Neither can force nor influence a person to go to or to remain away from church against his will or force him to profess a belief or disbelief in any religion. No person can be punished for entertaining or professing religious beliefs or disbeliefs, for church attendance or non-attendance. No tax in any amount, large or small, can be levied to support any religious activities or institutions, whatever they may be called, or whatever from they may adopt to teach or practice religion. Neither a state nor the Federal Government can, openly or secretly, participate in the affairs of any religious organizations or groups and vice versa. In the words of Jefferson, the clause against establishment of religion by law was intended to erect "a wall of separation between Church and State."

New Jersey cannot consistently with the "establishment of religion" clause of the First Amendment contribute tax-raised funds to the support of an institution which teaches the tenets and faith of any church. On the other hand, other language of the amendment commands that New Jersey cannot hamper its citizens in the free exercise of their own religion. Consequently, it cannot exclude individual Catholics, Lutherans, Mohammedans, Baptists, Jews, Methodists, Non-believers, Presbyterians, or the members of any other faith, *because of their faith, or lack of it*, from receiving the benefits of public welfare legislation. While we do not mean to intimate that a state could not provide transportation only to children attending public schools, we must be careful, in protecting the citizens of New Jersey against state-established churches, to be sure that we do not inadvertently prohibit New Jersey from extending its general State law benefits to all its citizens without regard to their religious belief.

Measured by these standards, we cannot say that the First Amendment prohibits New Jersey from spending tax-raised funds to pay the bus fares of parochial school pupils as a part of a general program under which it pays the fares of pupils attending public and other schools. It is undoubtedly true that children are helped to get to church schools. There is even a possibility that some of the children might not be sent to the church schools if the parents were compelled to pay their children's bus fares out of their own pockets when transportation to a public school would have been paid for by the State. The same possibility exists where the state requires a local transit company to provide reduced fares to school children including those attending parochial schools, or where a municipally owned transportation system undertakes to carry all school children free of charge. Moreover, state-paid policemen, detailed to protect children going to and from church schools from the very real hazards of traffic, would serve much the same purpose and accomplish much the same result as state provisions intended to guarantee free transportation of a kind which the state deems to be best for the school children's welfare. And parents might refuse to risk their children to the serious danger of traffic accidents going to and from parochial schools, the approaches to which were not protected by policemen. Similarly, parents might be reluctant to permit their children to attend schools which the state had cut off from such general government services as ordinary police and fire protection, connections for sewage disposal, public highways and sidewalks. Of course, cutting off church schools from these services, so separate and so indisputably marked off from the religious function, would make it far more difficult for the schools to operate. But such is obviously not the purpose of the First Amendment. That Amendment requires the state to be a neutral in its relations with groups of religious believers and non-believers; it does not require the state to be their adversary. State power is no more to be used so as to handicap religions, than it is to favor them.

This Court has said that parents may, in the discharge of their duty under state compulsory education laws, send their children to a religious rather than a public school if the school meets the secular educational requirements which the state has power to impose. See Pierce v. Society of the Sisters of the Holy Names of Jesus and Mary, 268 U.S. 510, 45 S.Ct. 571, 69 L.Ed. 1070, 39 A.L.R. 468. It appears that these parochial schools meet New Jersey's requirements. The State contributes no money to the schools. It does not support them. Its legislation, as applied, does no more than provide a general program to help parents get their children, regardless of their religion, safely and expeditiously to and from accredited schools.

The First Amendment has erected a wall between church and state. That wall must be kept high and impregnable. We could not approve the slightest breach. New Jersey has not breached it here.

Affirmed.

■ MR. JUSTICE JACKSON, dissenting.

II.

Whether the taxpayer constitutionally can be made to contribute aid to parents of students because of their attendance at parochial schools depends upon the nature of those schools and their relation to the Church.

The function of the Church school is a subject on which this record is meager. It shows only that the schools are under superintendence of a priest and that "religion is taught as part of the curriculum." But we know that such schools are parochial only in name—they, in fact, represent a world-wide and age-old policy of the Roman Catholic Church.

It is no exaggeration to say that the whole historic conflict in temporal policy between the Catholic Church and non-Catholics comes to a focus in their respective school policies. The Roman Catholic Church, counseled by experience in many ages and many lands and with all sorts and conditions of men, takes what, from the viewpoint of its own progress and the success of its mission, is a wise estimate of the importance of education to religion. It does not leave the individual to pick up religion by chance. It relies on early and indelible indoctrination in the faith and order of the Church by the word and example of persons consecrated to the task.

Our public school, if not a product of Protestantism, at least is more consistent with it than with the Catholic culture and scheme of values. It is a relatively recent development dating from about 1840. It is organized on the premise that secular education can be isolated from all religious teaching so that the school can inculcate all needed temporal knowledge and also maintain a strict and lofty neutrality as to religion. The assumption is that after the individual has been instructed in worldly wisdom he will be better fitted to choose his religion. Whether such a disjunction is possible, and if possible whether it is wise, are questions I need not try to answer.

I should be surprised if any Catholic would deny that the parochial school is a vital, if not the most vital, part of the Roman Catholic Church. If put to the choice, that venerable institution, I should expect, would forego its whole service for mature persons before it would give up education of the young, and it would be a wise choice. Its growth and cohesion, discipline and loyalty, spring from its schools. Catholic education is the rock on which the whole structure rests, and to render tax aid to its Church school is indistinguishable to me from rendering the same aid to the Church itself.

III.

It is of no importance in this situation whether the beneficiary of this expenditure of tax-raised funds is primarily the parochial school and incidentally the pupil, or whether the aid is directly bestowed on the pupil with indirect benefits to the school. The state cannot maintain a Church and it can no more tax its citizens to furnish free carriage to those who attend a Church. The prohibition against establishment of religion cannot be circumvented by a subsidy, bonus or reimbursement of expense to individuals for receiving religious instruction and indoctrination. . . .

■ MR. JUSTICE RUTLEDGE, with whom MR. JUSTICE FRANKFURTER, MR. JUSTICE JACKSON and MR. JUSTICE BURTON agree, dissenting.

II.

As the Remonstrance discloses throughout, Madison opposed every form and degree of official relation between religion and civil authority. For him religion was a wholly private matter beyond the scope of civil power either to restrain or to support.

In no phase was he more unrelentingly absolute than in opposing state support or aid by taxation. Not even "three pence" contribution was thus to be exacted from any citizen for such a purpose. Tithes had been the lifeblood of establishment before and after other compulsions disappeared. Madison and his coworkers made no exceptions or abridgments to the complete separation they created. Their objection was not to small tithes. It was to any tithes whatsoever. "If it were lawful to impose a small tax for religion, the admission would pave the way for oppressive levies." Not the amount but "the principle of assessment was wrong." And the principle was as much to prevent "the interference of law in religion" as to restrain religious intervention in political matters. In this field the authors of our freedom would not tolerate "the first experiment on our liberties" or "wait till usurped power had strengthened itself by exercise, and entangled the question in precedents." Nor should we.

III.

Does New Jersey's action furnish support for religion by use of the taxing power? Certainly it does, if the test remains undiluted as Jefferson and Madison made it, that money taken by taxation from one is not to be used or given to support another's religious training or belief, or indeed one's own. Today as then the furnishing of "contributions of money for the propagation of opinions which he disbelieves" is the forbidden exaction; and the prohibition is absolute for whatever measure brings that consequence and whatever amount may be sought or given to that end.

The funds used here were raised by taxation. The Court does not dispute, nor could it, that their use does in fact give aid and encouragement to religious instruction. Here parents pay money to send their children to parochial schools and funds raised by taxation are used to reimburse them. This not only helps the children to get to school and the parents to send them. It aids them in a substantial way to get the very thing which they are sent to the particular school to secure, namely, religious training and teaching. New Jersey's action therefore exactly fits the type of exaction and the kind of evil at which Madison and Jefferson struck.

This is not therefore just a little case over bus fares. In paraphrase of Madison, distant as it may be in its present form from a complete establishment of religion, it differs from it only in degree; and is the first step in that direction. Today as in his time "the same authority which can force a citizen to contribute three pence only . . . for the support of any one [religious] establishment, may force him" to pay more; or "to conform to any other establishment in all cases whatsoever."

The judgment should be reversed.

NOTES AND QUESTIONS

1.   In Cochran v. Louisiana State Board of Education, 281 U.S. 370 (1930), Louisiana taxpayers sued the State Board of Education for purchasing textbooks for both public and private school children. The taxpayers argued that the taxation was a taking of property for a private purpose. The Supreme Court upheld the legislation, without mentioning the Establishment Clause, on the grounds that the act had a public purpose.

When the challengers to the New Jersey bill brought their case, they focused on *state* constitutional issues. "Everson's attorney added a Fourteenth Amendment claim as an afterthought," and did not expect it to be important to the case. Daryl F. Fair, The *Everson* Case in the Context of New Jersey Politics, in Jo Renee Formicola & Hubert Morken, eds., *Everson* Revisited: Religion, Education and Law at the Crossroads 1 (1997). The New Jersey Supreme Court (the trial court) invalidated the transportation funding on state constitutional grounds, concluding 2–1 that the state constitution did not allow such funding to nonpublic schools. The dissenting justice argued that the benefit was provided to children and not to non-public schools. The Court of Errors and Appeals reversed and upheld the funding. Cochran's lawyer, Challen B. Ellis, joined Everson's challenge when it went to the United States Supreme Court, and the parties then turned to the religion issues.

What did *Everson* hold? See William Bentley Ball, Litigating *Everson* after *Everson*, in Formicola and Morken, supra, at 219–29: "[T]here are several purported *Everson* cases. One is the *Everson* that upholds the absolute separation of church and state. Another is the *Everson* that justifies unlimited governmental aid to churches. A third *Everson*, in conflict with the first two *Everson's* [sic], is the *Everson* that holds that states may provide free busing, but no greater benefits, for children attending religious schools. A fourth *Everson* holds that government may fully subsidize religious schools; a fifth, that it may reimburse parents for the cost of sending their children to such schools."

2.   Ewing Township, lacking its own public high schools, sent its students to schools in neighboring districts. Because Ewing's buses did not run into those areas, it reimbursed parents for their children's bus fare to those schools. Fair, supra, at 7. Is the fact that the money was paid to the parents and not to the religious schools significant to the *Everson* holding? Should it be? Keep this distinction in mind when considering subsequent readings.

3.   Is there a tension between *Everson's* outcome and its reasoning? Can you reconcile the case's emphasis on separation of church and state with its upholding of the busing program? Who won the case? John Courtney Murray, a Jesuit, Roman Catholic priest and theologian who was involved with writing the church's amicus brief in the case, responded, "We have won on busing but lost on the First Amendment." Was he correct? See Jo Renee Formicola, *Everson* Revisited: "This Is Not . . . Just a Little Case Over Bus Fares," 28 Polity 49, 56 n.32 (Autumn 1995). For Murray's more positive comments on *Everson*, see John Courtney Murray, The Court Upholds Religious Freedom, 76 America 628 (Mar. 8, 1947). Joseph Martin Dawson, who founded Protestants and Other Americans United for Separation of Church and State in response to *Everson*, and out of disappointment with the ruling, claimed to have "lost a battle, but won the war." See Philip Hamburger, Separation of Church and State 462 (2002), but see Joseph Martin Dawson, Separate Church and State Now 53 (1948) (*Everson* "justifies the fear that the breach is likely to be widened"). Justice Black viewed it as a "Pyrrhic victory" for Catholics. See Hamburger, supra. Is it surprising that Catholics criticized the appointment of Hugo Black, a former member of the Ku Klux Klan? Black's son once remarked "The Ku Klux Klan and Daddy, so far as I could tell, only had one thing in common. He suspected the Catholic Church." Id. at 463.

4.   *Establishment or Free Exercise? Everson* is frequently cited as an establishment case and is presented here as the first modern establishment case. Is that a mistake, because the case really involves free exercise? Father Murray, the theologian who was involved in *Everson's* briefing on the Catholic side, argued "there is a hierarchy of purpose and statement" in the religion clauses: "The dominant one is the 'free exercise' clause. It is principally and precisely in order that there may be no restriction on the free exercise of religion that the Amendment forbids the establishment of a religion." See supra, note 4 at 629. William Bentley Ball, who argued numerous First Amendment cases in the state courts and in the United States Supreme Court, observed that, even though the free exercise issue was not raised by the parties, *Everson* was based on free exercise because it held that government cannot exclude people from benefits based on religion. See William Bentley Ball, Litigating *Everson* After *Everson*, in Formicola & Morken, supra. Ball concludes that *Everson's* *holding* is that aid to parents does not violate the Establishment Clause because it promotes the Free Exercise Clause, and its *dictum* is that Establishment requires separation of church and state.

Do you agree with Ball that *Everson* was a free exercise decision? Or with Murray's assertion that the purpose of the Establishment Clause was to promote free exercise? Professor Philip Kurland provided a different interpretation of the clauses, distinguishing toleration, which free exercise promotes, from separation. Separation does more than protect religious liberty, however. According to Kurland,

> Religious toleration, summed up in the second of the two clauses, was, therefore, necessary to preserve the peace. Separation, represented by the first of the two clauses, was necessary to make such religious freedom a reality. But the separation clause had a greater function than the assurance of toleration of dissenting religious beliefs and practices. To suggest but two lessons of the evils resulting from the alliance of church and state, there was abundant evidence of the contributions of the churches to the warfare among nations as well as the conflict within them and equally obvious was the inhibition on scientific endeavor that followed from the acceptance by the state of church dogma. It is not necessary to suggest that the Francophiles in the American community were dedicated to the anti-clericalism that contributed to the French Revolution, but they certainly were not ignorant of the evils that aroused such violent reactions. For them toleration could hardly satisfy the felt needs; separation was a necessary concomitant. But admittedly separation was a new concept in practice. Toleration had a long English history; separation—conceived in the English writings of Roger Williams—had its beginnings as an historical fact only on the shores of this continent. It is justified in Williams' terms by the necessity for keeping the state out of the affairs of the church, lest the church be subordinated to the state; in Jeffersonian terms its function is to keep the church out of the business of government, lest the government be subordinated to the church. Limited powers of government were not instituted to expand the realm of power of religious organizations, but rather in favor of freedom of action and thought by the people.

Philip B. Kurland, Of Church and State in the Supreme Court, 29 U. Chi. L. Rev. 1, 4 (1961). Does any of the justices in the *Everson* case subscribe to Kurland's interpretation of the Establishment Clause?

5. *Garden and Wilderness?* According to Mark DeWolfe Howe, The Garden and the Wilderness: Religion and Government in American Constitutional History 6–7 (1965), there are two different accounts of the wall between church and state, one associated with Thomas Jefferson and the other with Roger Williams. Jefferson's wall protected the state from the influence of the church, while Williams' wall preserved the garden of the church from corruption by the wilderness of the world. Contemporary scholars now doubt that either Jefferson's or Williams' position was so simple or univocal as Howe's characterization; nonetheless the political and theological categories are useful for understanding different concepts of church and state. See Timothy L. Hall, Separating Church and State: Roger Williams and Religious Liberty 2–3 (1998) (approving some aspects of Howe's thesis but noting that Howe and others have "muffled Roger Williams's distinctive voice"); id. at 82–83 ("Williams's writings, however, do not lend themselves to Howe's portrayal of an aggressive partisan of the church's liberty who is otherwise uninterested in the fate of the state. Williams defined for the state a sphere of existence untroubled by religious disputes. He envisioned a notion of the secular as not antagonistic to religion but occupied with fundamentally different concerns from religion."); Philip B. Kurland, The Origins of the Religion Clauses of the Constitution, 27 Wm. & Mary L. Rev. 839, 859–60 (1985–1986) (identifying problems with Howe's thesis); David Little, Roger Williams and the Separation of Church and State, in James E. Wood, Jr., ed., Religion and the State: Essays in Honor of Leo Pfeffer 16 (1985) (arguing that the real Williams recognized that civil society must be governed by common moral standards).

Do the debates about Williams and Jefferson, or the historical materials about Jefferson and Madison, provide any guidance to resolving First Amendment questions, or should the Court "reject history as the foundation for its Religion Clause jurisprudence" because "the historical record does not speak in a unified voice?" See David Reiss, Jefferson and Madison as Icons in Judicial History: A Study of Religion Clause Jurisprudence, 61 U. Md. L. Rev. 94 (2002).

6.   *The No-Aid Principle: State Blaine Amendments.* Representative, Speaker of the House, Senator, and presidential candidate James Blaine of Maine lent his name to a proposed constitutional amendment (1875) that would have banned state funding of religious schools: "no money raised by taxation in any State for the support of public schools, or derived from any public fund therefor, nor any public lands devoted thereto, shall ever be under the control of any religious sect."

Although the federal Blaine amendment failed in the Senate, state Blaine amendments passed in the majority of states. Eventually 36 states had some version of a no-aid-to-religion statute on the books. See Mark Edward DeForrest, An Overview and Evaluation of State Blaine Amendments: Origins, Scope, and First Amendment Concerns, 26 Harv. J.L. & Pub. Pol'y 551, 573 (2003). "Under Blaine Amendments, state courts have struck down busing for religious private school students, college tuition grants, textbook loans, course credit for extracurricular Bible study, released-time programs, and vocational assistance for the blind, but have upheld building grants, funding of charter schools, textbook loans, busing for religious private school students, and public university Bible-related courses." 3 Religious Organizations and the Law § 12:83. We examine the significance of and current constitutional debates about Blaine amendments in Section B3.

7. *The No-Aid Principle: Courts.* Professor Angela Carmella argues that because of the outcome and language of *Everson*, it is not clear if *Everson* stands for strict separation or the accommodation of religion. She identifies two trajectories of Everson: first, *Lemon*, with its strict separation, and second, the equal access line of cases, beginning with Widmar v. Vincent, 454 U.S. 263 (1981). The latter involved access to school facilities and the use of those facilities for worship and religious discussion groups. In *Widmar*, for example, the Court ruled that the University of Missouri may not bar evangelical Christian student groups from using university buildings for extracurricular religious worship and religious teaching. We study *Widmar* and the equal access trajectory in Section C.

On the separationist trajectory, in a line of post-*Everson* cases, the Court rejected numerous state efforts to fund religion, especially religious schools, as violating the Establishment Clause. The most famous of those cases was Lemon v. Kurtzman, 403 U.S. 602 (1971), which we studied in Chapter 2. *Lemon* involved a Pennsylvania effort to provide textbooks and other instructional materials for secular subjects and to supplement teacher salaries at non-public schools. Relying on the third prong of its three-part test, the Court ruled that even though the law had a secular purpose and did not have a primary purpose to advance religion, the aid programs involved too much entanglement between church and state.

During the post-*Lemon* years, the Court inconsistently permitted "government funding of bus rides to private schools but not field trips from private schools; of books but not maps, globes and projectors; of standardized testing in private schools but not tests written by private school officials; of religious universities but not religious elementary and secondary schools. The case law allowed released-time religious instruction on private school but not public school grounds and accepted the presumption that public school teachers do not retain their secular perspective once they enter religious schools. The Court prohibited the funding of secular subjects in religious schools while upholding the constitutionality of religious worship on public school grounds." See Leslie C. Griffin, "Their Own Prepossessions": the Establishment Clause, 1999–2000, 33 Loy. U. Chi. L.J. 237, 239–40 (2001). Some of those cases relied on the reasoning that government aid should not be provided to "pervasively sectarian" schools because the government's money might be used for religious indoctrination. See, e.g., Wolman v. Waters, 433 U.S. 229, 247 (1977).

Some of the anti-aid cases were gradually overruled. In Mitchell v. Helms, 530 U.S. 793 (2000), the Court upheld federal funding for library materials and computer software and hardware to public and private elementary and secondary schools. The plurality favored a "neutrality" Establishment Clause analysis, concluding because "the religious, irreligious, and areligious are all alike eligible for government aid," the program was constitutional. Justice Clarence Thomas, the author of the plurality opinion, took particular aim at the "pervasively sectarian" reasoning of earlier cases: "This doctrine, born of bigotry, should be buried now," he argued. Id. at 829.

Justice O'Connor's controlling concurrence in *Mitchell* warned that neutrality was not the only Establishment Clause value implicated in the case. She criticized the plurality's "approval of actual diversion of government aid to religious indoctrination," id. at 837, and warned the plurality "foreshadows the approval of direct monetary subsidies to religious organizations, even when they use the money to advance their religious objectives." Id. at 844. Justice O'Connor believed the Establishment Clause had never permitted direct funding of religion.

Having opened the door to aid to religious schools in *Mitchell*, the Court then struggled to develop a principle that would protect neutrality. Many commentators saw a crack in the wall and a rejection of *Everson* in the following case, which allowed state vouchers to parents of religious-school children.

2. THE WALL CRUMBLES: SOME AID TO RELIGION

Zelman v. Simmons-Harris

Supreme Court of the United States, 2002.
536 U.S. 639, 122 S.Ct. 2460, 153 L.Ed.2d 604.

■ REHNQUIST, C.J., delivered the opinion of the court, in which O'CONNOR, SCALIA, KENNEDY, and THOMAS, JJ., joined. O'CONNOR, J. and THOMAS, J., filed concurring opinions. STEVENS, J., filed a dissenting opinion. SOUTER, J., filed a dissenting opinion, in which STEVENS, GINSBURG, and BREYER, JJ., joined. BREYER, J., filed a dissenting opinion, in which STEVENS and SOUTER, JJ., joined.

■ CHIEF JUSTICE REHNQUIST delivered the opinion of the Court.

The State of Ohio has established a pilot program designed to provide educational choices to families with children who reside in the Cleveland City School District. The question presented is whether this program offends the Establishment Clause of the United States Constitution. We hold that it does not.

There are more than 75,000 children enrolled in the Cleveland City School District. The majority of these children are from low-income and minority families. Few of these families enjoy the means to send their children to any school other than an inner-city public school. For more than a generation, however, Cleveland's public schools have been among the worst performing public schools in the Nation.

It is against this backdrop that Ohio enacted, among other initiatives, its Pilot Project Scholarship Program (program). The program provides financial assistance to families in any Ohio school district that is or has been "under federal court order requiring supervision and operational management of the district by the state superintendent." Cleveland is the only Ohio school district to fall within that category.

The program provides two basic kinds of assistance to parents of children in a covered district. First, the program provides tuition aid for students in kindergarten through third grade, expanding each year through eighth grade, to attend a participating public or private school of their parent's choosing. Second, the program provides tutorial aid for students who choose to remain enrolled in public school.

The tuition aid portion of the program is designed to provide educational choices to parents who reside in a covered district. Any private school, whether religious or nonreligious, may participate in the program and accept program students so long as the school is located within the boundaries of a covered district and meets statewide educational standards. Participating private schools must agree not to discriminate on the basis of race, religion, or ethnic background, or to "advocate or foster unlawful behavior or teach hatred of any person or group on the basis of race, ethnicity, national origin, or religion." Any public school located in a school district adjacent to the covered district may also participate in the program. Adjacent public schools are eligible to receive a $2,250 tuition grant for each program student accepted in addition to the full amount of per-pupil state funding attributable to each additional student. All participating schools, whether public or private, are required to accept students in accordance with rules and procedures established by the state superintendent.

Tuition aid is distributed to parents according to financial need. Families with incomes below 200% of the poverty line are given priority and are eligible to receive 90% of private school tuition up to $2,250. For these lowest income families, participating private schools may not charge a parental copayment greater than $250. For all other families, the program pays 75% of tuition costs, up to $1,875, with no copayment cap. These families receive tuition aid only if the number of available scholarships exceeds the number of low-income children who choose to participate. Where tuition aid is spent depends solely upon where parents who receive tuition aid choose to enroll their child. If parents choose a private school, checks are made payable to the parents who then endorse the checks over to the chosen school.

The program has been in operation within the Cleveland City School District since the 1996–1997 school year. In the 1999–2000 school year, 56 private schools participated in the program, 46 (or 82%) of which had a religious affiliation. None of the public schools in districts adjacent to Cleveland have elected to participate. More than 3,700 students participated in the scholarship program, most of whom (96%) enrolled in religiously affiliated schools. Sixty percent of these students were from families at or below the poverty line. In the 1998–1999 school year, approximately 1,400 Cleveland public school students received tutorial aid. This number was expected to double during the 1999–2000 school year.

[W]here a government aid program is neutral with respect to religion, and provides assistance directly to a broad class of citizens who, in turn, direct government aid to religious schools wholly as a result of their own genuine and independent private choice, the program is not readily subject to challenge under the Establishment Clause. A program that shares these features permits government aid to reach religious institutions only by way of the deliberate choices of numerous individual recipients.

We believe that the program challenged here is a program of true private choice. There are no "financial incentive[s]" that "ske[w]" the program toward religious schools. . . . no reasonable observer would think a neutral program of private choice, where state aid reaches religious schools solely as a result of the numerous independent decisions of private individuals, carries with it the *imprimatur* of government endorsement.

In sum, the Ohio program is entirely neutral with respect to religion. It provides benefits directly to a wide spectrum of individuals, defined only by financial need and residence in a particular school district. It permits such individuals to exercise genuine choice among options public and private, secular and religious. The program is therefore a program of true private choice. In keeping with an unbroken line of decisions rejecting challenges to similar programs, we hold that the program does not offend the Establishment Clause.

The judgment of the Court of Appeals is reversed.

It is so ordered.

■ JUSTICE O'CONNOR, concurring.

I

These cases are different from prior indirect aid cases in part because a significant portion of the funds appropriated for the voucher program reach religious schools without restrictions on the use of these funds. The share of public resources that reach religious schools is not, however, as significant as respondents suggest. Data from the 1999–2000 school year indicate that 82 percent of schools participating in the voucher program were religious and that 96 percent of participating students enrolled in religious schools, but these data are incomplete. These statistics do not take into account all of the reasonable educational choices that may be available to students in Cleveland public schools. When one considers the option to attend community schools, the percentage of students enrolled in religious schools falls to

62.1 percent. If magnet schools are included in the mix, this percentage falls to 16.5 percent.

Even these numbers do not paint a complete picture. The Cleveland program provides voucher applicants from low-income families with up to $2,250 in tuition assistance and provides the remaining applicants with up to $1,875 in tuition assistance. In contrast, the State provides community schools $4,518 per pupil and magnet schools, on average, $7,097 per pupil. Even if one assumes that all voucher students came from low-income families and that each voucher student used up the entire $2,250 voucher, at most $8.2 million of public funds flowed to religious schools under the voucher program in 1999–2000. Although just over one-half as many students attended community schools as religious private schools on the state fisc, the State spent over $1 million more—$9.4 million—on students in community schools than on students in religious private schools because per-pupil aid to community schools is more than double the per-pupil aid to private schools under the voucher program. Moreover, the amount spent on religious private schools is minor compared to the $114.8 million the State spent on students in the Cleveland magnet schools.

■ JUSTICE THOMAS, concurring.

Frederick Douglass once said that "[e]ducation ... means emancipation. It means light and liberty. It means the uplifting of the soul of man into the glorious light of truth, the light by which men can only be made free." Today many of our inner-city public schools deny emancipation to urban minority students. Despite this Court's observation nearly 50 years ago in *Brown v. Board of Education*, 347 U.S. 483, 493, 74 S.Ct. 686, 98 L.Ed.873 (1954), that "it is doubtful that any child may reasonably be expected to succeed in life if he is denied the opportunity of an education," urban children have been forced into a system that continually fails them. These cases present an example of such failures. Besieged by escalating financial problems and declining academic achievement, the Cleveland City School District was in the midst of an academic emergency when Ohio enacted its scholarship program.

II

While the romanticized ideal of universal public education resonates with the cognoscenti who oppose vouchers, poor urban families just want the best education for their children, who will certainly need it to function in our high-tech and advanced society. As Thomas Sowell noted 30 years ago: "Most black people have faced too many grim, concrete problems to be romantics. They want and need certain tangible results, which can be achieved only by developing certain specific abilities." The same is true today. An individual's life prospects increase dramatically with each successfully completed phase of education. For instance, a black high school dropout earns just over

$13,500, but with a high school degree the average income is almost $21,000. Blacks with a bachelor's degree have an average annual income of about $37,500, and $75,500 with a professional degree. Staying in school and earning a degree generates real and tangible financial benefits, whereas failure to obtain even a high school degree essentially relegates students to a life of poverty and, all too often, of crime. The failure to provide education to poor urban children perpetuates a vicious cycle of poverty, dependence, criminality, and alienation that continues for the remainder of their lives. If society cannot end racial discrimination, at least it can arm minorities with the education to defend themselves from some of discrimination's effects.

* * *

As Frederick Douglass poignantly noted, "no greater benefit can be bestowed upon a long benighted people, than giving to them, as we are here earnestly this day endeavoring to do, the means of an education."

[A dissent by JUSTICE STEVENS is omitted.]

■ JUSTICE SOUTER, with whom JUSTICE STEVENS, JUSTICE GINSBURG, and JUSTICE BREYER join, dissenting.

How can a Court consistently leave *Everson* on the books and approve the Ohio vouchers? The answer is that it cannot. It is only by ignoring *Everson* that the majority can claim to rest on traditional law in its invocation of neutral aid provisions and private choice to sanction the Ohio law. It is, moreover, only by ignoring the meaning of neutrality and private choice themselves that the majority can even pretend to rest today's decision on those criteria.

II

A

In order to apply the neutrality test, then, it makes sense to focus on a category of aid that may be directed to religious as well as secular schools, and ask whether the scheme favors a religious direction. Here, one would ask whether the voucher provisions, allowing for as much as $2,250 toward private school tuition (or a grant to a public school in an adjacent district), were written in a way that skewed the scheme toward benefiting religious schools.

This, however, is not what the majority asks. The majority looks not to the provisions for tuition vouchers, but to every provision for educational opportunity.

The illogic is patent. If regular, public schools (which can get no voucher payments) "participate" in a voucher scheme with schools that can, and public expenditure is still predominantly on public schools, then the majority's reasoning would find neutrality in a scheme of vouchers available for private tuition in districts with no secular private schools at all. "Neutrality" as the majority employs the term is, literally, verbal and nothing more. This, indeed, is the only way the majority can gloss over the very nonneutral feature of the total scheme covering "*all* schools": public tutors may receive from the State no more than $324 per child to support extra tutoring (that is, the State's 90% of a total amount of $360), whereas the tuition voucher schools (which turn out to be mostly religious) can receive up to $2,250.

B

The majority addresses the issue of choice the same way it addresses neutrality, by asking whether recipients or potential recipients of voucher aid have a choice of public schools among secular alternatives to religious schools. Again, however, the majority asks the wrong question and misapplies the criterion. If, contrary to the majority, we ask the right question about genuine choice to use the vouchers, the answer shows that something is influencing choices in a way that aims the money in a religious direction: of 56 private schools in the district participating in the voucher program (only 53 of which accepted voucher students in 1999–2000), 46 of them are religious; 96.6% of all voucher recipients go to religious schools, only 3.4% to nonreligious ones. [T]he $2,500 cap that the program places on tuition for participating low-income pupils has the effect of curtailing the participation of nonreligious schools: "nonreligious schools with higher tuition (about $4,000) stated that they could afford to accommodate just a few voucher students." By comparison, the average tuition at participating Catholic schools in Cleveland in 1999–2000 was $1,592, almost $1,000 below the cap.

There is, in any case, no way to interpret the 96.6% of current voucher money going to religious schools as reflecting a free and genuine choice by the families that apply for vouchers. The 96.6% reflects, instead, the fact that too few nonreligious school desks are available and few but religious schools can afford to accept more than a handful of voucher students.

■ JUSTICE BREYER, with whom JUSTICE STEVENS and JUSTICE SOUTER join, dissenting.

I write separately, however, to emphasize the risk that publicly financed voucher programs pose in terms of religiously based social conflict.

II

The principle underlying these cases—avoiding religiously based social conflict—remains of great concern. As religiously diverse as America had become when the Court decided its major 20th-century Establishment Clause cases, we are exponentially more diverse today. America boasts more than 55 different religious groups and subgroups with a significant number of members. Major religions include, among others, Protestants, Catholics, Jews, Muslims, Buddhists, Hindus, and

Sikhs. And several of these major religions contain different subsidiary sects with different religious beliefs. Newer Christian immigrant groups are "expressing their Christianity in languages, customs, and independent churches that are barely recognizable, and often controversial, for European-ancestry Catholics and Protestants."

Under these modern-day circumstances, how is the "equal opportunity" principle to work—without risking the "struggle of sect against sect" against which Justice Rutledge warned?

Consider the voucher program here at issue. That program insists that the religious school accept students of all religions. Does that criterion treat fairly groups whose religion forbids them to do so? The program also insists that no participating school "advocate or foster unlawful behavior or teach hatred of any person or group on the basis of race, ethnicity, national origin, or religion." And it requires the State to "revoke the registration of any school if, after a hearing, the superintendent determines that the school is in violation" of the program's rules. As one *amicus* argues, "it is difficult to imagine a more divisive activity" than the appointment of state officials as referees to determine whether a particular religious doctrine "teaches hatred or advocates lawlessness."

How are state officials to adjudicate claims that one religion or another is advocating, for example, civil disobedience in response to unjust laws, the use of illegal drugs in a religious ceremony, or resort to force to call attention to what it views as an immoral social practice? What kind of public hearing will there be in response to claims that one religion or another is continuing to teach a view of history that casts members of other religions in the worst possible light? How will the public react to government funding for schools that take controversial religious positions on topics that are of current popular interest—say, the conflict in the Middle East or the war on terrorism? . . .

III

Vouchers also differ in *degree*. The aid programs recently upheld by the Court involved limited amounts of aid to religion. But the majority's analysis here appears to permit a considerable shift of taxpayer dollars from public secular schools to private religious schools. That fact, combined with the use to which these dollars will be put, exacerbates the conflict problem. State aid that takes the form of peripheral secular items, with prohibitions against diversion of funds to religious teaching, holds significantly less potential for social division. In this respect as well, the secular aid upheld in *Mitchell* differs dramatically from the present case. Although it was conceivable that minor amounts of money could have, contrary to the statute, found their way to the religious activities of the recipients, that case is at worst the camel's nose, while the litigation before us is the camel itself. . . .

V

The Court, in effect, turns the clock back. It adopts, under the name of "neutrality," an interpretation of the Establishment Clause that this Court rejected more than half a century ago. In its view, the parental choice that offers each religious group a kind of equal opportunity to secure government funding overcomes the Establishment Clause concern for social concord. An earlier Court found that "equal opportunity" principle insufficient; it read the Clause as insisting upon greater separation of church and state, at least in respect to primary education. In a society composed of many different religious creeds, I fear that this present departure from the Court's earlier understanding risks creating a form of religiously based conflict potentially harmful to the Nation's social fabric. Because I believe the Establishment Clause was written in part to avoid this kind of conflict, and for reasons set forth by Justice SOUTER and Justice STEVENS, I respectfully dissent.

NOTES AND QUESTIONS

1. *No Law Respecting Direct Establishment?* Can you define direct and indirect aid to religion? Should the distinction be of constitutional significance? In *Committee for Public Education and Religious Liberty v. Nyquist*, 413 U.S. 756 (1973), the Court ruled that a New York program providing tuition reimbursement grants or tax deductions to parents of religious school children violated the Establishment Clause. Was that aid direct or indirect? Is giving grants or tax deductions to parents different from allocating money in the state budget for religious schools? Does the parents' choice in *Zelman* sufficiently insulate the church or the state? The Court concluded that the New York program advanced religion in violation of *Lemon*. What is the difference between *Nyquist* and *Zelman*? Has *Nyquist* been overruled? See Ira C. Lupu & Robert W. Tuttle, The Faith-Based Initiative and the Constitution, 55 DePaul L. Rev. 1, 27 (2005) ("To the extent that *Nyquist* or other prior cases had suggested that the quantity of government assistance that made its way to religious providers had any bearing on the scheme's constitutionality, *Zelman* pushes such a notion completely aside. It is the program's qualitative arrangement, not quantitative consequences, that determine its legality.").

2. *The Opinions.*

a.   According to Professors Lupu and Tuttle, Supreme Court opinions should do two things: "provide guidance that is sufficiently clear to enable lawyers and lower court judges to make decisions in future, relevantly similar cases . . . [and] make a reasonable attempt to justify the Court's decision as something more principled than judicial fiat." Ira C. Lupu & Robert W. Tuttle, Zelman's Future: Vouchers, Sectarian Providers, and the Next Round of Constitutional Battles, 78 Notre Dame L. Rev. 917, 927 (2003). The professors concluded that Rehnquist's opinion in Zelman accomplished the first but not the second goal. Do you agree?

b.   Why did Chief Justice Rehnquist's opinion include the argument that there was no endorsement of religion in the voucher program? Was endorsement necessary to his argument, or was it sufficient for him to rely on the argument that the Establishment Clause requires neutrality? See id. at 936–37 ("The Court's focus on endorsement—a concept far better suited to analysis of cases involving religious expression by the government—can be attributed at least in part to the attention the parties in Zelman gave to the concept. Both sides perceived that Justice O'Connor represented the swing vote, and she has long been associated with the endorsement test. Chief Justice Rehnquist, however, reframed the endorsement analysis, and thus the significance of private choice, to match the plurality's reasoning in *Mitchell v. Helms*.").

c.   What is the difference between Justice O'Connor's concurrence and Chief Justice Rehnquist's opinion for the Court? Does she rely upon the endorsement test? Do you agree that "Justice O'Connor is the only member of the Court who thinks that 'genuine and independent choice' has determinative constitutional significance"? See id. at 943–44.

   Did parents really have a choice to send their children to different schools, or was it evident that the adjacent school districts and the magnet schools were not going to admit students? See Steven K. Green, The Illusionary Aspect of "Private Choice" for Constitutional Analysis, 38 Willamette L. Rev. 549 (2002).

d.   Which argument is more persuasive: the majority's claim that, when measuring the effect of the vouchers on religion, it is appropriate to include all of Cleveland's educational funding, or the dissent's argument that only the voucher system itself should be counted? See Mark Tushnet, Vouchers After *Zelman*, 2002 Supreme Court Review 1. According to Chief Justice Rehnquist, the important question was "whether Ohio is coercing parents into sending their children to religious schools, and that question must be answered by evaluating all options Ohio provides Cleveland schoolchildren." Is the Chief Justice persuasive in his claim that the Ohio Program creates a disincentive for religious schools when up to 96 percent of students within the program went to religious schools? See id. at 13.

e.   Is Justice Souter correct that *Zelman* overrules *Everson*? How do you think Justices Black, Jackson and Rutledge, whose opinions you read in *Everson*, would have ruled in the

Zelman case? Does the Memorial and Remonstrance provide any guidance about how Zelman should be decided?

Should Justice Souter and the other dissenters have been more flexible about the content of their argument instead of promoting a strict, *Everson*-like version of separation of church and state? Would it have been more persuasive for the dissenters to argue that Cleveland should have done more to keep parents from being directed to religious schools, perhaps by making the suburban schools and magnet schools more willing to admit students? See Lupu & Tuttle, supra, at 952. Professors Lupu and Tuttle argue that "[h]ad the dissenters been willing to take the Court's own premises at face value—in particular, the argument that the public schooling options had to count in any appraisal of whether the state was responsible for religious indoctrination of voucher students—they might have had a chance of persuading Justice O'Connor, the crucial fifth vote" that "Ohio had not done enough to avoid steering Cleveland schoolchildren into religious experience as the price of escape from the inadequacies of the public system." Id.; see also Thomas C. Berg, Vouchers and Religious Schools: The New Constitutional Questions, 72 U. Cin. L. Rev. 151 (2003). Was Justice Souter's unwillingness to compromise caused by hostility to religion or prejudice against pervasively sectarian or Catholic institutions?

f.   How do you assess Justice Breyer's argument that the provision of vouchers to religious schools fosters political divisiveness? If every religious group received neutral funding, would political division disappear?

g.   Why do both Justices Souter and Breyer quote Justice Rutledge's dissent in *Everson* about the "struggle of sect against sect"? Does government aid to religion really promote wars among religions?

3.   *True Private Choice.* In *Zelman,* Justice Souter criticized the "true private choice" principle as "rhetorical." 536 U.S. at 692–700. He wrote, "If 'choice' is present whenever there is any educational alternative to the religious school to which vouchers can be endorsed, then there will always be a choice and the voucher can always be constitutional, even in a system in which there is not a single private secular school as an alternative to the religious school." Considering that 82 percent of the eligible private schools participating in the voucher program were religious schools, did the parents in Cleveland have "true private choice," or did the lack of educational options mean that they were influenced to choose religious schools? When is true private choice present? Have the lower courts applied *Zelman*'s interpretation of true private choice correctly in the following scenarios?

"InnerChange, a Christian program, describes itself as 'an intensive, voluntary, faith-based program of work and study within a loving community that promotes transformation from the inside out through the miraculous power of God's love. [InnerChange] is committed to Christ and the Bible. We try to base everything we do on biblical truth.' Further, 'Biblical principles are integrated into the entire course curriculum of [InnerChange], rather than compartmentalized in specific classes. In other words, the application of Biblical principles is not an agenda item—it is the agenda.'" After considering other alternatives, the Iowa Department of Corrections signed a contract with InnerChange to provide values-based programs in the Iowa prisons. Inmates were not required to participate in InnerChange, received no reduced sentences or other benefits for participation, and confirmed in writing that their participation was voluntary. InnerChange was the only program available as the state was unable to find other satisfactory programs. Did the prisoners enjoy true private choice? See Americans United for Separation of Church and State v. Prison Fellowship Ministries, 509 F.3d 406, 413–414 (8th Cir. 2007) (no; the money could go only to InnerChange and not to any secular or general programs). For a detailed study of the implications of the InnerChange case for First Amendment jurisprudence, see Winnifred Fallers Sullivan, Prison Religion: Faith-Based Reform and the Constitution (2009).

Wisconsin criminals who violate the terms of their probation may be offered the alternative of living in a halfway house instead of returning to prison. Among the halfway house options offered by the State is Faith Works, which incorporates Christianity into its program by encouraging offenders to develop a relationship with Jesus Christ. Parole officers may recommend Faith Works to parolees but must always explain its Christian character and describe the secular alternatives to the program. Does it violate the Establishment Clause for the parole officers to recommend Faith Works? In Freedom from Religion Foundation v. McCallum, 324 F.3d 880 (7th Cir. 2003), the Seventh Circuit held that parole officers may recommend Faith Works, just as a public high school counselor may recommend Catholic schools or an addiction counselor may recommend Alcoholics Anonymous. Has the state violated the Establishment Clause by coercing parolees if Faith Works is the best program, or the most effective or even most popular program? See id. at 884 ("[i]t is a misunderstanding of freedom . . . to suppose that choice is not free when the objects between which the chooser must choose are not equally attractive to him. It would mean that a person was not exercising his free will when in response to the question whether he preferred vanilla or chocolate ice cream he said vanilla, because it was the only honest answer that he could have given and therefore 'he had no choice.'"). Do you agree or is such an argument "rhetorical" in Justice Souter's meaning? Can the Faith Works decision be reconciled with the InnerChange case?

The AmeriCorps Education Awards Program makes federal grants available to volunteers who participate in national service by teaching. Some volunteers met the program's requirements by working in religious schools, where they taught religious as well as secular subjects. Of the

1,608 pre-approved schools, 328 were religious. Does giving federal grants to these teachers violate the Establishment Clause by funding religious schools? Are the volunteers coerced to work in religious settings? See American Jewish Congress v. Corporation for National and Community Service, 399 F.3d 351 (D.C. Cir. 2005) (volunteers exercised true private choice in their selection of religious schools as their workplace). Would it matter if 1000 or 1500 of the schools were religious? See id. at 358 ("A program may be one of 'true private choice' even when more religious than non-religious choices are available.").

The Michigan Family Independence Agency places children in residential care units; a state employee decides which placement is in the best interests of the child. Should Teen Ranch, a Christian organization, receive state funding to participate in the program? See Teen Ranch v. Udow, 479 F.3d 403 (6th Cir. 2007), cert. denied, 552 U.S. 1039 (2007) (true private choice was not present for vulnerable teens when the decision was made for them by a state employee).

4.   May the government regulate religious schools that participate in the vouchers program? Could it, for example, require the schools to hire members of other faiths as teachers or to admit students of all faiths? Could it require that the schools not discriminate on the basis of race or sex? See Mark Tushnet, Vouchers After Zelman, 2002 Supreme Court Review 1; Thomas C. Berg, Vouchers and Religious Schools: The New Constitutional Questions, 72 U. Cin. L. Rev. 151 (2003).

Once the Court decided states could provide vouchers, litigants soon asked whether states must provide vouchers in order to comply with the First Amendment. The no-aid Blaine amendments discussed in Section B1 were central to the discussion because many of them prohibited voucher programs, as we learn in the next section.

3.   MUST THE WALL BE TORN DOWN?: NEUTRAL AID TO ALL

According to Mark Edward DeForrest,

The importance of state law in evaluating the overall legality of vouchers or other forms of aid for private religious schools should not be underestimated. States provide most of the funding for education in our society, and according to general estimates, eighty-five percent of all private schools are affiliated with religious groups or denominations. If such schools are excluded as options for parents under enacted state voucher programs, the school voucher movement will be effectively dead as a serious option in reforming education. And the strongest legal argument at the state level against providing vouchers to parents to send their children to private religiously-based schools is a collection of state constitutional provisions known collectively and generically as "Blaine Amendments."

Mark Edward DeForrest, An Overview and Evaluation of State Blaine Amendments: Origins, Scope, and First Amendment Concerns, 26 Harv. J.L. & Pub. Pol'y 551, 554 (2003). As we learned in Section B1, state Blaine amendments first passed immediately after the failure of the federal Blaine constitutional amendment in 1875. As DeForrest explains, some 36 states eventually passed Blaine amendments of various rigor, including "less restrictive," "moderate," and "most restrictive" standards. Less restrictive states, like New Jersey, allowed limited governmental assistance, such as busing, to religious schools; this explains why New Jersey was the home of the *Everson* dispute. Moderate states, like Utah and Alabama, allowed indirect but not direct aid to religious schools. And the most restrictive states, like Missouri, banned even indirect aid to religious schools. Id. at 577–88. Thus *Zelman* might have no effect in states whose constitutions banned vouchers.

Washington State agreed to a Blaine amendment as a condition for admission to the Union in 1889. More recently, Washington established a voucher-like, Promise Scholarship program that excluded funding for students pursuing degrees in devotional theology. Joshua Davey, a Northwest College student of pastoral ministries who was denied a scholarship, lost his First Amendment challenge to Washington's refusal of the scholarship. At the time, many critics of the Court's no-aid jurisprudence thought that, given the holding in *Zelman*, the Court might be ready to rule that First Amendment neutrality required that Davey receive his scholarship. However, because of the long American history of opposition to taxes that support churches, wrote Chief Justice Rehnquist, "we can think of few areas in which a State's antiestablishment interests come more into play. Since the founding of our country, there have been popular uprisings against procuring taxpayer funds to support church leaders, which was one of the hallmarks of an 'established' religion." 540 U.S. 712 (2004). Thus although funding was permitted by the Establishment Clause, it was not required by Free Exercise. We read *Davey* in Chapter 10, when we consider the constitutional distinction between devotional theology and religious studies.

Davey's supporters were confident that Washington's ban violated the leading free exercise case, *Lukumi,* which we read in Chapter 1. See Douglas Laycock, The Supreme Court, 2003 Term; Theology Scholarships, The Pledge of Allegiance, and Religious Liberty: Avoiding the Extremes But Missing the Liberty, 118 Harv. L. Rev. 155, 173 (2004) (*Davey* "appeared to be a slam dunk under *Lukumi.* And yet it lost, 7–2."). Do you agree? How can you explain Davey's loss in the Supreme Court? See id. (*Davey* is "not surprising" as a funding case, but "remarkable" as a religious discrimination case.).

In an earlier case from Washington, Larry Witters' application to the Washington Commission for the Blind for state rehabilitation funding was denied because he was studying at a private Christian college to become a pastor, missionary, or youth director. After the Washington Supreme Court ruled that funding Witters would violate the Establishment Clause by advancing religion, the United States Supreme Court held that the First Amendment was not violated because the money was not paid directly to the religious institution, but instead went to an individual who could exercise independent private choice. See Witters v. Washington Dept. of Services for the Blind, 474 U.S. 481 (1986). Soon after, the Washington Court ruled that funding Witters violated the *state constitution*'s ban on aid to religion. See Witters v. State Comm'n for the Blind, 112 Wash.2d 363, 771 P.2d 1119, 1123–24 (1989). Is there any argument that denying aid to Witters post-*Davey* violates the U.S. Constitution? Professor Laycock argues that *Davey* involved the specific question of training for the ministry, and can be distinguished from other forms of aid to religious schools. See Laycock, supra, at 173. Do you agree?

Post-*Davey*, states have continued to follow their own constitutions in determining what support goes to religious organizations. Maine enacted legislation providing state funding to students in public school districts that did not have a public high school, but permitting the money to be used only at non-sectarian schools. In Anderson v. Town of Durham, 895 A.2d 944 (Me. 2006), cert. denied, 549 U.S. 1051 (2006), parents of private religious school children challenged the law, but the Maine Supreme Court upheld the program. The Florida legislature, despite a no-aid provision in its state constitution, passed a voucher program that included religious schools, which the Florida Supreme Court invalidated. See Bush v. Holmes, 919 So.2d 392 (Fla. 2006).

A Colorado scholarship program excluded "pervasively sectarian" schools from funding but allowed scholarships for students of other religious schools. Colorado Christian University challenged its exclusion from the program. Does *Davey* "definitely resolve" the issue in favor of the state? See Colorado Christian University v. Weaver, 534 F.3d 1245, 1250 (10th Cir. 2008) (no, for two reasons: "the program expressly discriminates among religions without constitutional justification, and its criteria for doing so involve unconstitutionally intrusive scrutiny of religious belief and practice [to determine which schools are pervasively sectarian]."). Did the Tenth Circuit misinterpret *Davey*? Do you agree with Justice Thomas, who believes that the "pervasively sectarian" category is a sign of bigotry? Or with Professor Justice, who argues that the

> largest mistake, repeated by Justice Thomas but made by others as well, is that judicial doctrine of preventing sectarian participation in state-funded education was "born of bigotry."

This claim is astonishing, given the clear record the founding generation left of their attempts to *prevent* bigotry by keeping religious sects out of the business of educating citizens. Indeed the primary authors of the Declaration of Independence and the Constitution of the United States, who were also the foremost champions of religious liberty in the founding period, were explicitly critical of a role for religious bodies in public education within a republic, with bigotry being among their top concerns.

Benjamin Justice, The Originalist Case Against Vouchers: The First Amendment, Religion, and American Public Education, 26 Stan. L. & Pol'y Rev. 437, 480–81 (2015); see also Steven K. Green, The Bible, the School, and the Constitution: The Clash That Shaped Modern Church-State Doctrine 13–16 (2012) (Education advocates wanted nonsectarian schools to attract the greatest number of students and avoid religious divisiveness); but see Steven G. Calabresi & Abe Salander, Religion and the Equal Protection Clause: Why the Constitution Requires School Vouchers, 65 Fla. L. Rev. 909, 1033 (2013) (the "fact that Congress and the States felt the need to pass the Blaine Amendment in 1875 to stop government money from going to religious schools and institutions itself shows that members of Congress in 1875 did not think that the Establishment Clause alone barred government funding of religious schools and institutions.").

States continue to disagree about the constitutionality of voucher programs. In 2013, the Supreme Court of Indiana ruled that the Choice Scholarship Program, which gave scholarships for students "to attend private schools instead of the public schools they otherwise would attend," did not violate the Indiana Constitution because the families of eligible students, not religious or theological institutions, *directly* benefitted from the scholarships. See Meredith v. Pence, 984 N.E.2d 1213, 1227 (Ind. 2013) ("We hold today that the proper test for examining whether a government expenditure violates Article 1, Section 6, is not whether a religious or theological institution *substantially* benefits from the expenditure, but whether the expenditure *directly* benefits such an institution."). In contrast, in 2015 the Colorado Supreme Court ruled that a Choice Scholarship Pilot program (CSP), which gave taxpayer-funded scholarships to elementary, middle, and high school students to pay tuition at Private School Partners, including religious schools, violated the Colorado constitution. Unlike Indiana's, the Colorado constitution's

prohibitions are not limited to direct funding. Rather, section 7 bars school districts from "pay[ing] from any public fund or moneys *whatever, anything* in aid of any" religious institution, and from "help[ing] *support or sustain* any school . . . controlled by any church or sectarian denomination *whatsoever*"

> (emphasis added). Given that private religious schools rely on students' attendance (and their corresponding tuition payments) for their ongoing survival, the CSP's facilitation of such attendance necessarily constitutes aid to "support or sustain" those schools.

Taxpayers for Pub. Educ. v. Douglas Cty. Sch. Dist., 2015 CO 50, ¶ 28, 351 P.3d 461, 470. The Colorado court was particularly upset by the idea that religious schools would raise tuition or reduce financial aid after students received a scholarship. Why is this so troubling? Did that turn the program into a direct benefit to religious institutions? The Colorado Supreme Court also rejected the argument that *striking down* the CSP violated the First Amendment.

On January 15, 2016, the Supreme Court stepped back into the funding and Blaine amendment dispute when it granted cert. on a case from Missouri, which is one of the "most restrictive" Blaine states. See Trinity Lutheran Church of Columbia, Inc. v. Pauley, 788 F.3d 779, 787 (8th Cir. 2015), cert. granted, 136 S. Ct. 891 (2016). The Eighth Circuit described the facts of the case as follows:

> Trinity Church operates on its church premises a licensed preschool and daycare called the Learning Center. Initially established as a non-profit corporation, the Learning Center merged into Trinity Church in 1985. The Learning Center has an open admissions policy. It is a ministry of Trinity Church that teaches a Christian world view and incorporates daily religious instruction in its programs.

> The Missouri Department of Natural Resources (DNR) offers Playground Scrap Tire Surface Material Grants, a solid waste management program. The grants provide DNR funds to qualifying organizations for the purchase of recycled tires to resurface playgrounds, a beneficial reuse of this solid waste. In 2012, Trinity Church applied for a grant to replace the Learning Center's playground surface, disclosing that the Learning Center was part of Trinity Church. On May 21, 2012, the Solid Waste Management Program Director wrote the Learning Center's Director, advising:

> [A]fter further review of applicable constitutional limitations, the department is unable to provide this financial assistance directly to the church as contemplated by the grant application. Please note that Article I, Section 7 of the Missouri Constitution specifically provides that "no money shall ever be taken from the public treasury, directly or indirectly, in aid of any church, section or denomination of religion."

Id. The Eighth Circuit rejected Trinity's free exercise, establishment, and equal protection claims, observing that "Trinity Church seeks an unprecedented ruling—that a state constitution violates the First Amendment and the Equal Protection Clause if it bars the grant of public funds to a church." Id. at 783. The Supreme Court granted cert. on the question: "Whether the exclusion of churches from an otherwise neutral and secular aid program violates the Free Exercise and Equal Protection Clauses when the state has no valid Establishment Clause concern."

What do you expect the Court to rule about state funding to religion? Do you think the Court will rule that Missouri must fund Trinity? That it can't fund Trinity? That it can fund or not fund Trinity, as it chooses? Do you expect *Everson*'s wall of separation between church and state to be abolished? See Steven G. Calabresi & Abe Salander, Religion and the Equal Protection Clause: Why the Constitution Requires School Vouchers, 65 Fla. L. Rev. 909, 1034 (2013) ("under a Fourteenth Amendment anti-discrimination analysis, Blaine Amendments should surely be struck down.").

Recall from the discussion of *Everson* that Professor Carmella identified two trajectories from *Everson*, namely, the *Lemon*, no-aid cases that we read in this section, and the "equal access" cases. The latter trajectory began with *Widmar v. Vincent*, 454 U.S. 263 (1981), which follows. Notice two important aspects of this line of cases. First, the plaintiffs argued their *free speech* rights were violated. Second, the Establishment Clause appears in this case as a state *defense* to allowing religious groups to use public facilities. Missouri's refusal to allow religious groups to use public facilities was based on similar no-funding principles that we still see in *Trinity Lutheran*, above, based on the state's Blaine amendment.

C. THE ESTABLISHMENT CLAUSE AS A DEFENSE: EQUAL ACCESS

Widmar v. Vincent

Supreme Court of the United States, 1981.
454 U.S. 263, 102 S.Ct. 269, 70 L.Ed.2d. 440.

■ JUSTICE POWELL delivered the opinion of the Court.

This case presents the question whether a state university, which makes its facilities generally available for the activities of registered student groups, may close its facilities to a registered student group desiring to use the facilities for religious worship and religious discussion.

I

It is the stated policy of the University of Missouri at Kansas City to encourage the activities of student organizations. The University officially recognizes over 100 student groups. It routinely provides

University facilities for the meetings of registered organizations. Students pay an activity fee of $41 per semester (1978–1979) to help defray the costs to the University.

From 1973 until 1977 a registered religious group named Cornerstone regularly sought and received permission to conduct its meetings in University facilities. In 1977, however, the University informed the group that it could no longer meet in University buildings. The exclusion was based on a regulation, adopted by the Board of Curators in 1972, that prohibits the use of University buildings or grounds "for purposes of religious worship or religious teaching."

Eleven University students, all members of Cornerstone, brought suit to challenge the regulation in the Federal District Court for the Western District of Missouri. They alleged that the University's discrimination against religious activity and discussion violated their rights to free exercise of religion, equal protection, and freedom of speech under the First and Fourteenth Amendments to the Constitution of the United States.

Upon cross-motions for summary judgment, the District Court upheld the challenged regulation. It found the regulation not only justified, but required, by the Establishment Clause of the Federal Constitution.

The Court of Appeals for the Eighth Circuit reversed. Rejecting the analysis of the District Court, it viewed the University regulation as a content-based discrimination against religious speech, for which it could find no compelling justification. The court held that the Establishment Clause does not bar a policy of equal access, in which facilities are open to groups and speakers of all kinds. According to the Court of Appeals, the "primary effect" of such a policy would not be to advance religion, but rather to further the neutral purpose of developing students' "'social and cultural awareness as well as [their] intellectual curiosity.'" We now affirm.

II

Through its policy of accommodating their meetings, the University has created a forum generally open for use by student groups. Having done so, the University has assumed an obligation to justify its discriminations and exclusions under applicable constitutional norms. The Constitution forbids a State to enforce certain exclusions from a forum generally open to the public, even if it was not required to create the forum in the first place ... our cases leave no doubt that the First Amendment rights of speech and association extend to the campuses of state universities.

Here the UMKC has discriminated against student groups and speakers based on their desire to use a generally open forum to engage in religious worship and discussion. These are forms of speech and association protected by the First Amendment. In order to justify discriminatory exclusion from a public forum based on the religious content of a group's intended speech, the University must therefore satisfy the standard of review appropriate to content-based exclusions. It must show that its regulation is necessary to serve a compelling state interest and that it is narrowly drawn to achieve that end.

III

In this case the University claims a compelling interest in maintaining strict separation of church and State. It derives this interest from the "Establishment Clauses" of both the Federal and Missouri Constitutions.

A

We agree that the interest of the University in complying with its constitutional obligations may be characterized as compelling. It does not follow, however, that an "equal access" policy would be incompatible with this Court's Establishment Clause cases. Those cases hold that a policy will not offend the Establishment Clause if it can pass a three-pronged test: "First, the [governmental policy] must have a secular legislative purpose; second, its principal or primary effect must be one that neither advances nor inhibits religion . . . ; finally, the [policy] must not foster 'an excessive government entanglement with religion.' "

In this case two prongs of the test are clearly met. Both the District Court and the Court of Appeals held that an open-forum policy, including nondiscrimination against religious speech, would have a secular purpose and would avoid entanglement with religion. But the District Court concluded, and the University argues here, that allowing religious groups to share the limited public forum would have the "primary effect" of advancing religion.

The University's argument misconceives the nature of this case. The question is not whether the creation of a religious forum would violate the Establishment Clause. The University has opened its facilities for use by student groups, and the question is whether it can now exclude groups because of the content of their speech. In this context we are unpersuaded that the primary effect of the public forum, open to all forms of discourse, would be to advance religion.

We are not oblivious to the range of an open forum's likely effects. It is possible—perhaps even foreseeable—that religious groups will benefit from access to University facilities. But this Court has explained that a religious organization's enjoyment of merely "incidental" benefits does not violate the prohibition against the "primary advancement" of religion.

We are satisfied that any religious benefits of an open forum at UMKC would be "incidental" within the meaning of our cases. Two factors are especially relevant.

First, an open forum in a public university does not confer any imprimatur of state approval on religious sects or practices.

Second, the forum is available to a broad class of nonreligious as well as religious speakers; there are over 100 recognized student groups at UMKC. The provision of benefits to so broad a spectrum of groups is an important index of secular effect. If the Establishment Clause barred the extension of general benefits to religious groups, "a church could not be protected by the police and fire departments, or have its public sidewalk kept in repair." At least in the absence of empirical evidence that religious groups will dominate UMKC's open forum, we agree with the Court of Appeals that the advancement of religion would not be the forum's "primary effect."

B

Arguing that the State of Missouri has gone further than the Federal Constitution in proscribing indirect state support for religion, the University claims a compelling interest in complying with the applicable provisions of the Missouri Constitution. [T]he state interest asserted here—in achieving greater separation of church and State than is already ensured under the Establishment Clause of the Federal Constitution—is limited by the Free Exercise Clause and in this case by the Free Speech Clause as well. In this constitutional context, we are unable to recognize the State's interest as sufficiently "compelling" to justify content-based discrimination against respondents' religious speech.

For this reason, the decision of the Court of Appeals is

Affirmed.

■ JUSTICE WHITE, dissenting.

A state university may permit its property to be used for purely religious services without violating the First and Fourteenth Amendments. With this I agree. The Establishment Clause, however, sets limits only on what the State may do with respect to religious organizations; it does not establish what the State is *required* to do.

A large part of respondents' argument, accepted by the court below and accepted by the majority, is founded on the proposition that because religious worship uses speech, it is protected by the Free Speech Clause of the First Amendment. Not only is it protected, they argue, but religious worship *qua* speech is not different from any other variety of protected speech as a matter of constitutional principle. I believe that this proposition is plainly wrong. Were it right, the Religion Clauses would be emptied of any independent meaning in circumstances in which religious practice took the form of speech.

Although I agree that the line [between verbal acts of worship and other verbal acts] may be difficult to draw in many cases, surely the majority cannot seriously suggest that no line may ever be drawn. If that were the case, the majority would have to uphold the University's right to offer a class entitled "Sunday Mass." Under the majority's view, such a class would be—as a matter of constitutional principle—indistinguishable from a class entitled "The History of the Catholic Church."

This case involves religious worship only; the fact that that worship is accomplished through speech does not add anything to respondents' argument. That argument must rely upon the claim that the State's action impermissibly interferes with the free exercise of respondents' religious practices. Although this is a close question, I conclude that it does not.

Respondents complain that compliance with the regulation would require them to meet "about a block and a half" from campus under conditions less comfortable than those previously available on campus. I view this burden on free exercise as minimal. Because the burden is minimal, the State need do no more than demonstrate that the regulation furthers some permissible state end. The State's interest in avoiding claims that it is financing or otherwise supporting religious worship—in maintaining a definitive separation between church and State—is such an end. That the State truly does mean to act toward this end is amply supported by the treatment of religion in the State Constitution. Thus, I believe the interest of the state is sufficiently strong to justify the imposition of the minimal burden on respondents' ability freely to exercise their religious beliefs.

On these facts, therefore, I cannot find that the application of the regulation to prevent Cornerstone from holding religious worship services in University facilities violates the First and Fourteenth Amendments. I would not hold as the majority does that if a university permits students and others to use its property for secular purposes, it must also furnish facilities to religious groups for the purposes of worship and the practice of their religion. Accordingly, I would reverse the judgment of the Court of Appeals.

NOTES AND QUESTIONS

1.   *The Opinion.* Do you agree Cornerstone should have been allowed to use the university's facilities? Why or why not? How do you react to Justice White's dissenting argument that students would have to meet only a block and a half from campus if state aid were denied to them?

What did the Court mean when it characterized the regulation as a "content-based" distinction? Why does the First Amendment prohibit content-based restrictions on speech?

What would happen if the university prevented all student groups from meeting on campus post-*Widmar*?

Why did the Court reject the argument that Missouri had a compelling interest not to fund religion under the establishment tenets of both the federal and state constitutions? How are *Lemon* and its three-part test relevant to the Court's decision?

What do you think of Justice White's argument that the case confuses religious worship and religious speech in a manner that erodes the Religion Clauses? How would this case turn out if it were a free exercise case instead of a free speech case? If the students would lose under free-exercise precedents like *Smith*, why should they win under a different clause of the First Amendment?

2. *The Equal Access Trajectory.* In Board of Education v. Mergens, 496 U.S. 226 (1990), and Lamb's Chapel v. Center Moriches Union Free School District, 508 U.S. 384 (1993), religious groups won their claims that their groups should be allowed to use school facilities during after-school hours as other community groups did. Moreover, in Zobrest v. Catalina Foothills School District, 509 U.S. 1 (1993) the Court upheld funding of an interpreter for a hearing-impaired child at a Catholic school. Then, in Good News Club v. Milford Central School, 533 U.S. 98 (2001), a Christian club for elementary school children, whose activities were primarily prayer and Bible study, challenged its exclusion from the school building after hours, while other clubs were meeting. The school had denied the club access because of the Establishment Clause. The Court again sided with the challengers, holding their free speech rights were violated by the exclusion.

In Rosenberger v. Rector and Visitors of the University of Virginia, 515 U.S. 819 (1995), the Court held that the University of Virginia could not deny funding to *Wide Awake*, a student Christian newspaper. The university had a Student Activities Fund that barred funding to any activity that "primarily promotes or manifests a particular belie[f] in or about a deity or an ultimate reality." *Wide Awake* offered Christian perspectives on a range of topics of importance to the local community. The debate among the justices was reminiscent of Justice White's concern that the *Widmar* majority's rule could not distinguish between a Catholic mass and a class about the history of the Catholic church. Although the majority thought *Rosenberger* fell easily into the equal access line of cases, dissenting Justice David Souter argued that the majority had required the state to fund, "not the discourse of the scholar's study or the seminar room, but [ ] the evangelist's mission station and the pulpit." Id. at 868. We examine *Rosenberger* and its relationship to *Locke v. Davey* in Chapter 10.

3. *Equal Access and Nondiscrimination.* Some universities have policies not to fund religious groups that discriminate in membership on the grounds of religion or sexual orientation. One regulation at the University of California, Hastings College of Law required student organizations to comply with its nondiscrimination policy, which forbids discrimination on the basis of race, color, religion, national origin, ancestry, disability, age, sex or sexual orientation. In applying that policy, Hastings pursued an "all-comers" policy, which required student groups to admit any student who wanted to participate. The Christian Legal Society, in contrast, bars individuals who engage in "unrepentant homosexual conduct" and practices religious discrimination in its membership.

In Christian Legal Society v. Martinez, 130 S.Ct. 2971 (2010), the Court rejected a constitutional challenge to Hastings Law School's all-comers policy for student organizations. Under that policy, "registered student organizations" had to admit all students if they wanted the law school's recognition. Christian Legal Society argued that it should not be forced to admit students who engaged in "unrepentant homosexual conduct" or who refused to sign a Statement of Faith. According to Justice Ginsburg's majority opinion,

> Compliance with Hastings' all-comers policy, we conclude, is a reasonable, viewpoint-neutral condition on access to the student-organization forum. In requiring CLS—in common with all other student organizations—to choose between welcoming all students and forgoing the benefits of official recognition, we hold, Hastings did not transgress constitutional limitations. CLS, it bears emphasis, seeks not parity with other organizations, but a preferential exemption from Hastings' policy. The First Amendment shields CLS against state prohibition of the organization's expressive activity, however exclusionary that activity may be. But CLS enjoys no constitutional right to state subvention of its selectivity.

Should the holding of this case be impacted by what the Court decides in *Trinity Lutheran*, at the end of Section B?

The Court quickly dismissed the argument that Hastings violated CLS's Free Exercise rights because the policy was a neutral law of general applicability according to *Smith*. Do you agree? Is there any problem with allowing religious groups to win on free speech when they lose on free exercise?

4. *Equal Access, Ten Commandments, and Seven Aphorisms.* The Summum religion, which was founded in Utah in 1975, describes itself as a form of Gnostic Christianity, and teaches that God originally gave Moses the Seven Aphorisms. After the Israelites were unprepared to receive the aphorisms, however, Moses destroyed those first tablets and later replaced them with a second set of tablets containing the simpler Ten Commandments. See About Summum, http://www.summum.org/about.shtml. Summum's requests to display its Seven Aphorisms monument in public parks across Utah that contained Ten Commandments displays were denied. Despite its religious facts and the case's implications for establishment and free exercise, *Summum* was not litigated under the Religion Clauses but as a speech case.

The Supreme Court's and Tenth Circuit's case law made it nearly impossible to litigate Summum's challenges on religious grounds. In 1973, the Tenth Circuit ruled in *Anderson v. Salt Lake City* that a Ten Commandments monument at a county courthouse was secular, not religious. See Anderson v. Salt Lake City, 475 F.2d 29 (10th Cir. 1973). That precedent kept Summum's potential claim of religious discrimination from being litigated; if the commandments were secular, the Utah cities could not violate the Establishment Clause by allowing the Ten

Commandments but not the Seven Aphorisms. In subsequent litigation against the City of Ogden, Utah, Summum conceded in 2002 that it could not win an Establishment Clause challenge to another Ten Commandments display without an en banc reconsideration of *Anderson*, and it placed its hopes on free speech. See Summum v. Callaghan, 130 F.3d 906 (10th Cir. 1997); Summum v. City of Ogden, 297 F.3d 995 (10th Cir. 2002).

Summum made another attempt to add its monument to the city park in Pleasant Grove City, Utah, and filed a lawsuit after city officials refused the request. Following the terminology of free speech jurisprudence, the district court originally ruled for the city because the park was a nonpublic forum in which the government could control the content of its own message. The Tenth Circuit, however, ruled for Summum on the grounds that the park was a traditional public forum that the government had opened to private speakers, where the government may not discriminate on the basis of the speaker's (here, the monument's) content. See Summum v. Pleasant Grove City, 483 F.3d 1044, 1050–52 (10th Cir. 2007). Thus *Summum* seemed to fit into the equal access line of cases that prohibit the government from discriminating against religious viewpoints. The question then became whether the Supreme Court would see the issue as the Tenth Circuit had and add *Summum* to the equal access line of cases. It did not.

At the oral argument, even the Supreme Court justices appeared confused that the case was about free speech, not religion; Justice Anthony Kennedy derided the "tyranny of labels" that left the Court speaking about nonpublic and public fora, government and private speech, and the Chief Justice warned the city that "the more you say that the monument is Government speech to get out of the first, free speech—the Free Speech Clause, the more it seems to me you're walking into a trap under the Establishment Clause." Transcript of Oral Argument, Summum, 129 S.Ct. 1125 (No. 07–665). When the Court issued its unanimous ruling for the city, however, the labeling was straightforward; Justice Samuel Alito concluded "although a park is a traditional public forum for speeches and other transitory expressive acts, the display of a permanent monument in a public park is not a form of expression to which forum analysis applies." The monument was government speech. In other words, the government cannot ban Summum's members from reading the Seven Aphorisms aloud in the park while allowing other private speakers to read the Ten Commandments, but the government may choose one monument over another because the government speaks through the monument. See Pleasant Grove City, Utah v. Summum, 129 S.Ct. 1125, 1129 (2009).

As you read the following opinion, consider its implications for Establishment Clause jurisprudence. Is it an Establishment Clause violation for the government to sponsor the Ten Commandments and refuse the Seven Aphorisms? Does the case leave you confused about the interrelationship of free speech, free exercise, and establishment?

The Ten Commandments and the Seven Aphorisms.

Pleasant Grove City, Utah v. Summum

United States Supreme Court, 2009.
555 U.S. 460, 129 S.Ct. 1125, 172 L.Ed.2d 853.

■ JUSTICE ALITO delivered the opinion of the Court.

This case presents the question whether the Free Speech Clause of the First Amendment entitles a private group to insist that a municipality permit it to place a permanent monument in a city park in which other donated monuments were previously erected. The Court of Appeals held that the municipality was required to accept the monument because a public park is a traditional public forum. We conclude, however, that although a park is a traditional public forum for speeches and other transitory expressive acts, the display of a permanent monument in a public park is not a form of expression to which forum analysis applies. Instead, the placement of a permanent monument in a public park is best viewed as a form of government speech and is therefore not subject to scrutiny under the Free Speech Clause.

I

A

Pioneer Park (or Park) is a 2.5 acre public park located in the Historic District of Pleasant Grove City (or City) in Utah. The Park currently contains 15 permanent displays, at least 11 of which were donated by private groups or individuals. These include an historic granary, a wishing well, the City's first fire station, a September 11 monument, and a Ten Commandments monument donated by the Fraternal Order of Eagles in 1971.

Respondent Summum is a religious organization founded in 1975 and headquartered in Salt Lake City, Utah. On two separate occasions in 2003, Summum's president wrote a letter to the City's mayor requesting permission to erect a "stone monument," which would contain "the Seven Aphorisms of SUMMUM" and be similar in size and nature to the Ten Commandments monument. The City denied the requests and explained that its practice was to limit monuments in the Park to those that "either (1) directly relate to the history of Pleasant Grove, or (2) were donated by groups with longstanding ties to the Pleasant Grove community." The following year, the City passed a resolution putting this policy into writing. The resolution also mentioned other criteria, such as safety and esthetics.

In May 2005, respondent's president again wrote to the mayor asking to erect a monument, but the letter did not describe the monument, its historical significance, or Summum's connection to the community. The city council rejected this request.

II

No prior decision of this Court has addressed the application of the Free Speech Clause to a government entity's acceptance of privately donated, permanent monuments for installation in a public park, and the parties disagree sharply about the line of precedents that governs this situation. Petitioners contend that the pertinent cases are those concerning government speech. Respondent, on the other hand, agrees with the Court of Appeals panel that the applicable cases are those that analyze private speech in a public forum. The parties' fundamental disagreement thus centers on the nature of petitioners' conduct when they permitted privately donated monuments to be erected in Pioneer Park. Were petitioners engaging in their own expressive conduct? Or were they providing a forum for private speech?

A

If petitioners were engaging in their own expressive conduct, then the Free Speech Clause has no application. The Free Speech Clause restricts government regulation of private speech; it does not regulate government speech.

B

While government speech is not restricted by the Free Speech Clause, the government does not have a free hand to regulate private speech on government property. This Court long ago recognized that members of the public retain strong free speech rights when they venture into public streets and parks, "which 'have immemorially been held in trust for the use of the public and, time out of mind, have been used for purposes of assembly, communicating thoughts between citizens, and discussing public questions.' "

With the concept of the traditional public forum as a starting point, this Court has recognized that members of the public have free speech rights on other types of government property and in certain other government programs that share essential attributes of a traditional public forum. We have held that a government entity may create "a designated public forum" if government property that has not traditionally been regarded as a public forum is intentionally opened up for that purpose. Government restrictions on speech in a designated public forum are subject to the same strict scrutiny as restrictions in a traditional public forum.

The Court has also held that a government entity may create a forum that is limited to use by certain groups or dedicated solely to the discussion of certain subjects. In such a forum, a government entity may impose restrictions on speech that are reasonable and viewpoint-neutral.

IV

A

In this case, it is clear that the monuments in Pleasant Grove's Pioneer Park represent government speech. Although many of the monuments were not designed or built by the City and were donated in completed form by private entities, the City decided to accept those donations and to display them in the Park. Respondent does not claim that the City ever opened up the Park for the placement of whatever permanent monuments might be offered by private donors. Rather, the City has "effectively controlled" the messages sent by the monuments in the Park by exercising "final approval authority" over their selection. The City has selected those monuments that it wants to display for the purpose of presenting the image of the City that it wishes to project to all who frequent the Park; it has taken ownership of most of the monuments in the Park, including the Ten Commandments monument that is the focus of respondent's concern; and the City has now expressly set forth the criteria it will use in making future selections.

B

Respondent voices the legitimate concern that the government speech doctrine not be used as a subterfuge for favoring certain private speakers over others based on viewpoint. Respondent's suggested solution is to require a government entity accepting a privately donated monument to go through a formal process of adopting a resolution publicly embracing "the message" that the monument conveys.

We see no reason for imposing a requirement of this sort. The parks of this country contain thousands of donated monuments that government entities have used for their own expressive purposes, usually without producing the sort of formal documentation that respondent now says is required to escape Free Speech Clause restrictions. Requiring all of these jurisdictions to go back and proclaim formally that they adopt all of these monuments as their own expressive vehicles would be a pointless exercise that the Constitution does not mandate. . . .

This argument fundamentally misunderstands the way monuments convey meaning. The meaning conveyed by a monument is generally not a simple one like " 'Beef. It's What's for Dinner.' "

What, for example, is "the message" of the Greco-Roman mosaic of the word "Imagine" that was donated to New York City's Central Park in memory of John Lennon? Some observers may "imagine" the musical contributions that John Lennon would have made if he had not been killed. Others may think of the lyrics of the Lennon song that obviously inspired the mosaic and may "imagine" a world without religion, countries, possessions, greed, or hunger.

A striking example of how the interpretation of a monument can evolve is provided by one of the most famous and beloved public monuments in the United States, the Statue of Liberty. The statue was given to this country by the Third French Republic to express republican solidarity and friendship between the two countries. At the inaugural ceremony, President Cleveland saw the statue as an emblem of international friendship and the widespread influence of American ideals. Only later did the statue come to be viewed as a beacon welcoming immigrants to a land of freedom.

C

Respondent and the Court of Appeals analogize the installation of permanent monuments in a public park to the delivery of speeches and the holding of marches and demonstrations, and they thus invoke the rule that a public park is a traditional public forum for these activities. But "public forum principles . . . are out of place in the context of this case." The forum doctrine has been applied in situations in which government-owned property or a government program was capable of accommodating a large number of public speakers without defeating the essential function of the land or the program. For example, a park can accommodate many speakers and, over time, many parades and demonstrations. The Combined Federal Campaign permits hundreds of groups to solicit donations from federal employees. A public university's student activity fund can provide money for many campus activities. See *Rosenberger*, 515 U.S., at 825, 115 S.Ct. 2510. A public university's buildings may offer meeting space for hundreds of student groups. See *Widmar v. Vincent*, 454 U.S. 263, 274–75, 102 S.Ct. 269, 70 L.Ed.2d 440

(1981). A school system's internal mail facilities can support the transmission of many messages to and from teachers and school administrators.

By contrast, public parks can accommodate only a limited number of permanent monuments. Public parks have been used, " 'time out of mind, . . . for purposes of assembly, communicating thoughts between citizens, and discussing public questions,' " but "one would be hard pressed to find a 'long tradition' of allowing people to permanently occupy public space with any manner of monuments." While respondent and some of its *amici* deride the fears expressed about the consequences of the Court of Appeals holding in this case, those concerns are well founded. If government entities must maintain viewpoint neutrality in their selection of donated monuments, they must either "brace themselves for an influx of clutter" or face the pressure to remove longstanding and cherished monuments. Every jurisdiction that has accepted a donated war memorial may be asked to provide equal treatment for a donated monument questioning the cause for which the veterans fought. New York City, having accepted a donated statue of one heroic dog (Balto, the sled dog who brought medicine to Nome, Alaska, during a diphtheria epidemic) may be pressed to accept monuments for other dogs who are claimed to be equally worthy of commemoration. The obvious truth of the matter is that if public parks were considered to be traditional public forums for the purpose of erecting privately donated monuments, most parks would have little choice but to refuse all such donations. And where the application of forum analysis would lead almost inexorably to closing of the forum, it is obvious that forum analysis is out of place.

V

In sum, we hold that the City's decision to accept certain privately donated monuments while rejecting respondent's is best viewed as a form of government speech. As a result, the City's decision is not subject to the Free Speech Clause, and the Court of Appeals erred in holding otherwise. We therefore reverse.

It is so ordered.

■ JUSTICE STEVENS, with whom JUSTICE GINSBURG joins, concurring.

This case involves a property owner's rejection of an offer to place a permanent display on its land. While I join the Court's persuasive opinion, I think the reasons justifying the city's refusal would have been equally valid if its acceptance of the monument, instead of being characterized as "government speech," had merely been deemed an implicit endorsement of the donor's message.

To date, our decisions relying on the recently minted government speech doctrine to uphold government action have been few and, in my view, of doubtful merit. The Court's opinion in this case signals no expansion of that doctrine. And by joining the Court's opinion, I do not mean to indicate agreement with our earlier decisions. Unlike other decisions relying on the government speech doctrine, our decision in this case excuses no retaliation for, or coercion of, private speech. Nor is it likely, given the near certainty that observers will associate permanent displays with the governmental property owner, that the government will be able to avoid political accountability for the views that it endorses or expresses through this means. Finally, recognizing permanent displays on public property as government speech will not give the government free license to communicate offensive or partisan messages. For even if the Free Speech Clause neither restricts nor protects government speech, government speakers are bound by the Constitution's other proscriptions, including those supplied by the Establishment and Equal Protection Clauses. Together with the checks imposed by our democratic processes, these constitutional safeguards ensure that the effect of today's decision will be limited.

■ JUSTICE SCALIA, with whom JUSTICE THOMAS joins, concurring.

As framed and argued by the parties, this case presents a question under the Free Speech Clause of the First Amendment. I agree with the Court's analysis of that question and join its opinion in full. But it is also obvious that from the start, the case has been litigated in the shadow of the First Amendment's *Establishment* Clause.

The city ought not fear that today's victory has propelled it from the Free Speech Clause frying pan into the Establishment Clause fire. Contrary to respondent's intimations, there are very good reasons to be confident that the park displays do not violate *any* part of the First Amendment.

In *Van Orden v. Perry*, 545 U.S. 677 (2005), this Court upheld against Establishment Clause challenge a virtually identical Ten Commandments monument, donated by the very same organization (the Fraternal Order of Eagles), which was displayed on the grounds surrounding the Texas State Capitol. Nothing in that decision suggested that the outcome turned on a finding that the monument was only "private" speech. To the contrary, all the Justices agreed that government speech was at issue, but the Establishment Clause argument was nonetheless rejected. For the plurality, that was because the Ten Commandments "have an undeniable historical meaning" in addition to their "religious significance," Justice BREYER, concurring in the judgment, agreed that the monument conveyed a permissible secular message, as evidenced by its location in a park that contained multiple monuments and historical markers; by the fact that it had been donated by the Eagles "as part of that organization's efforts to combat juvenile delinquency"; and by the length of time (40 years) for which the monument had gone unchallenged.

Even accepting the narrowest reading of the narrowest opinion necessary to the judgment in *Van Orden*, there is little basis to distinguish the monument in this case: Pioneer Park includes "15 permanent displays,"; it was donated by the Eagles as part of its national effort to combat juvenile delinquency, Brief for Respondent 3; and it was erected in 1971, which means it is approaching its (momentous!) 40th anniversary.

The city can safely exhale. Its residents and visitors can now return to enjoying Pioneer Park's wishing well, its historic granary—and, yes, even its Ten Commandments monument—without fear that they are complicit in an establishment of religion.

■ JUSTICE BREYER, concurring.

I agree with the Court and join its opinion. I do so, however, on the understanding that the "government speech" doctrine is a rule of thumb, not a rigid category. Were the City to discriminate in the selection of permanent monuments on grounds unrelated to the display's theme, say solely on political grounds, its action might well violate the First Amendment.

In my view, courts must apply categories such as "government speech," "public forums," "limited public forums," and "nonpublic forums" with an eye towards their purposes—lest we turn "free speech" doctrine into a jurisprudence of labels. Consequently, we must sometimes look beyond an initial categorization. And, in doing so, it helps to ask whether a government action burdens speech disproportionately in light of the action's tendency to further a legitimate government objective.

Were we to do so here, we would find—for reasons that the Court sets forth—that the City's action, while preventing Summum from erecting its monument, does not disproportionately restrict Summum's freedom of expression. The City has not closed off its parks to speech; no one claims that the City prevents Summum's members from engaging in speech in a form more transient than a permanent monument. Rather, the City has simply reserved some space in the park for projects designed to further other than free-speech goals. And that is perfectly proper. After all, parks do not serve speech-related interests alone. To the contrary, cities use park space to further a variety of recreational, historical, educational, aesthetic, and other civic interests. To reserve to the City the power to pick and choose among proposed monuments according to criteria reasonably related to one or more of these legitimate ends restricts Summum's expression, but, given the impracticality of alternatives and viewed in light of the City's legitimate needs, the restriction is not disproportionate. Analyzed either way, as "government speech" or as a proportionate restriction on Summum's expression, the City's action here is lawful.

■ JUSTICE SOUTER, concurring in the judgment.

I have qualms, however, about accepting the position that public monuments are government speech categorically.

Because the government speech doctrine, as Justice STEVENS notes, is "recently minted," it would do well for us to go slow in setting its bounds, which will affect existing doctrine in ways not yet explored. Even though, for example, Establishment Clause issues have been neither raised nor briefed before us, there is no doubt that this case and its government speech claim has been litigated by the parties with one eye on the Establishment Clause. The interaction between the "government speech doctrine" and Establishment Clause principles has not, however, begun to be worked out.

The case shows that it may not be easy to work out. After today's decision, whenever a government maintains a monument it will presumably be understood to be engaging in government speech. If the monument has some religious character, the specter of violating the Establishment Clause will behoove it to take care to avoid the appearance of a flat-out establishment of religion, in the sense of the government's adoption of the tenets expressed or symbolized. In such an instance, there will be safety in numbers, and it will be in the interest of a careful government to accept other monuments to stand nearby, to dilute the appearance of adopting whatever particular religious position the single example alone might stand for. As mementoes and testimonials pile up, however, the chatter may well make it less intuitively obvious that the government is speaking in its own right simply by maintaining the monuments.

If a case like that occurred, as suspicion grew that some of the permanent displays were not government speech at all (or at least had an equally private character associated with private donors), a further Establishment Clause prohibition would surface, the bar against preferring some religious speakers over others. But the government could well argue, as a development of government speech doctrine, that when it expresses its own views, it is free of the Establishment Clause's stricture against discriminating among religious sects or groups. Under this view of the relationship between the two doctrines, it would be easy for a government to favor some private religious speakers over others by its choice of monuments to accept.

To avoid relying on a *per se* rule to say when speech is governmental, the best approach that occurs to me is to ask whether a reasonable and fully informed observer would understand the expression to be government speech, as distinct from private speech the government chooses to oblige by allowing the monument to be placed on public land. Application of this observer test provides the reason I find the monument here to be government expression.

NOTES AND QUESTIONS

1.   What is the difference between a traditional public forum and a limited public forum? What is the difference between public forums and government speech? Arlington Cemetery in Washington D.C. is a government cemetery where veterans are buried. If the graves at Arlington are covered with a wide variety of religious symbols, are the graves government speech? See Summum, 129 S.Ct. at 1192 (Souter, J.) ("there are circumstances in which government maintenance of monuments does not look like government speech at all. Sectarian identifications on markers in Arlington Cemetery come to mind.").

2.   If Summum now files an Establishment Clause lawsuit, should the Court rule that the exclusion of the Seven Aphorisms from the park violates the Establishment Clause?

3.   Do you expect *Summum*'s reasoning to permit discrimination against small, unpopular religions? Or will the Court find a way to protect them under the Establishment Clause? Should the Red River Freethinkers be allowed to post a sign saying "The United States is not in any way founded on the Christian religion" in a park with Ten Commandments? See Judy Keen, Fight Over Thou Shalts Won't Wilt, USA Today, July 8, 2007.

4.   Should it matter to the legal analysis what the Seven Principles of Summum are? The Seven Principles are the principle of psychokinesis, the principle of correspondence, the principle of vibration, the principle of opposition, the principle of rhythm, the principle of cause and effect, and the principle of gender. See Summum: Sealed Except to the Open Mind, at http://www.summum.us/philosophy/principles.shtml. Do these principles persuade you that Summum is a religion, or do you need more data?

5.   Summum lost its Establishment Clause challenge when the case returned to the district court. The court accepted the City's testimony that it did not know Summum was a religion when Summum applied to have the aphorisms installed in the park and had refused the monument only because it lacked a relationship to Pleasant Grove's history. Thus the Ten Commandments and the Fraternal Order of Eagles enjoyed *historical* ties to the City that Summum lacked. The district court then adopted Justice Scalia's conclusion in *Summum* that because the facts of *Summum* matched those of *Van Orden*, the Texas Ten Commandments case, the city's action was constitutional. As the district court explained, "The undisputed facts of record in this case show that—whatever the Eagles' intended message—Pleasant Grove has, since the beginning, displayed the monument for reasons of history, not religion. Moreover, there is no evidence that anyone in Pleasant Grove government had any idea what Summum's religious beliefs were, and thus it cannot be said that the Pleasant Grove government demonstrated a preference for one religion over another." Summum v. Pleasant Grove City, No. 2:05CV638 DAK, 2010 WL 2330336 (D. Utah 2010). Do you agree with the analysis of the district court? What implications does such a ruling have for the Establishment Clause?

6. *State Constitutions.* After the Supreme Court litigation, Summum filed a state court lawsuit arguing that, *by not installing the Summum monument*, the city violated the religious liberty clause of the Utah Constitution, which holds "[n]o public money or property shall be appropriated for or applied to any religious worship, exercise or instruction, or for the support of any ecclesiastical establishment." Utah Const. art. I, § 4. Was Summum asking the state to violate the constitution by providing public money for Summum's monument?

The Utah Supreme Court rejected Summum's claim. The court concluded that adding the Summum monument to the Ten Commandments monument would not serve neutrality because many other religions would be unrepresented. See Summum v. Pleasant Grove City, 345 P.3d 1188, 1191 (Utah 2015) ("Because the allocation of public money or property to a permanent religious monument is per se not neutral, the appropriate remedy for a monument constituting 'religious worship, exercise or instruction' would not be the forced installation of a second monument.").

The Court noted it "was not asked to reach the question whether public use of money for the Ten Commandments monument violated another constitutional provision." Id. at 1193. Is this another situation where Utah's no-funding provision should be invalidated?

————————

In Chapter 4, we return to the Free Exercise clause. After the Court decided the *Smith* case (Chapter 1), Congress determined that the opinion did not adequately protect the free exercise of religion. In response, it passed the Religious Freedom Restoration Act (RFRA). Chapter 4 studies the differences between constitutional and statutory protection of religious freedom.

CHAPTER 4

CONSTITUTIONAL AND STATUTORY PROTECTION OF FREE EXERCISE

No citizen shall "become a law unto himself," wrote Justice Antonin Scalia in *Employment Division v. Smith*, a case from Chapter 1, when the Court denied Native Americans an exemption from the criminal and unemployment compensation statutes for their peyote use; the law applies to all. See Employment Div., Department of Human Resources of Oregon v. Smith, 494 U.S. 872, 885 (1990). *Smith* held that "the right of free exercise does not relieve an individual of the obligation to comply with a 'valid and neutral law of general applicability' on the ground that the law proscribes (or prescribes) conduct that his religion prescribes (or proscribes)." Id. at 880. According to *Smith*'s author, that standard was consistent with the Court's earlier Free Exercise decisions, including *Reynolds*, the 1879 Mormon polygamy case, which we read at the beginning of Chapter 1. *Smith* did not signal the end of exemptions, but rather indicated that Congress, not the Court, may exempt citizens from the law. Thus, exemptions may be statutorily required but not compelled by the Free Exercise Clause of the Constitution.

Other members of the Court disagreed with Justice Scalia about the free exercise standard. They argued *Smith* overturned First Amendment jurisprudence by substituting the neutral law of general applicability standard for the compelling state interest test that the Court had employed in Sherbert v. Verner, 374 U.S. 398 (1963), and other cases. Under the *Sherbert* test, if a general law burdens free exercise, the state may justify it only "by showing that it is the least restrictive means of achieving some compelling state interest." Thus, the Constitution mandates exemptions when the State fails the compelling state interest test. Under this standard, the Court plays an important role in determining when the Constitution requires an exemption for religious believers.

These two tests—the neutral law of general applicability standard of *Smith* and the compelling state interest/least restrictive means test of *Sherbert*—address the question of how much liberty is protected by the Free Exercise Clause. In order to answer that question, the materials in this chapter consider three recurring and interrelated questions. First, what difference does the compelling state interest test make from the *Smith* standard? Second, what is the difference between constitutionally required and statutory exemptions from general laws? Third, what role should courts and legislatures play in protecting religious freedom? Throughout this chapter, you should consider what legal standard best protects the religious liberty of the individual.

These questions are recurring because the legal standards governing free exercise have fluctuated. After *Smith* called into question the *Sherbert* compelling interest test, the United States Congress passed the Religious Freedom Restoration Act of 1993 (RFRA), 42 U.S.C. § 2000bb et seq., directed at both state and federal governments. The Act's stated purposes were:

(1) to restore the compelling interest test as set forth in *Sherbert v. Verner*, 374 U.S. 398 (1963) and *Wisconsin v. Yoder*, 406 U.S. 205 and to guarantee its application in all cases where free exercise of religion is substantially burdened; and

(2) to provide a claim or defense to persons whose religious exercise is substantially burdened by government. Id. § 2000bb(b).

In City of Boerne v. Flores, 521 U.S. 507 (1997), however, the Court ruled that RFRA cannot be applied to the states because Congress lacks the power to pass the Act under Section 5 of the Fourteenth Amendment. Thus, state governments are held to the *Smith* standard in Free Exercise cases, while RFRA still applies to the federal government.

In response to *Boerne*'s ruling that RFRA cannot be applied to the states, many state legislatures passed state RFRAs to hold state governments to the compelling state interest test. In addition, after *Boerne*, Congress used its spending and commerce powers to enact the Religious Land Use and Institutionalized Persons Act of 2000 (RLUIPA), 42 U.S.C. § 2000cc et seq., which applies the compelling state interest test to the state and federal governments in more limited circumstances than RFRA, namely, as the Act's name suggests, to protect religious land use (e.g., zoning) and institutionalized persons (e.g., prisoners). In summary, across the United States, current protection of religion wavers between strict scrutiny and deferential review by the courts. Amid the amalgam of standards, we can continue to question which regime best serves religious liberty.

Once the standards for free exercise are resolved, however, other constitutional questions remain. In *Boerne*, Justice John Paul Stevens argued that RFRA was unconstitutional because it violated the Establishment Clause by giving an advantage to religious citizens that nonreligious citizens lacked. Boerne v. Flores, 521 U.S. 507, 536–537 (1997) (Stevens, J., concurring). Hence every exemption raises a potential establishment violation that must be kept in mind. Moreover, whenever some categories of citizens receive benefits that are denied to others, Equal Protection values are implicated. Does the Free Exercise Clause provide a rational basis for or a compelling state interest in giving benefits to religion? Or, as Professor Gedicks has suggested, does "the commitment of contemporary legal culture (and, indeed, of American society) to equality . . . likely prevent the success" of any effort to justify religious exemptions? See Frederick Mark Gedicks, An Unfirm Foundation: The Regrettable Indefensibility of Religious Exemptions, 20 U. Ark. Little Rock L.J. 555, 557 (1998) ("I emphasize that I am not urging the abandonment of exemptions on the basis of a normative argument, but rather for the pragmatic reason that they can no longer be justified with the theoretical resources available in late 20th century legal culture."). Are there now so many world religions and philosophies that it makes no sense to give exemptions from the law to religious believers? The Supreme Court says no.

Most recently, the Court interpreted RFRA broadly to protect the rights of religious entities who object to neutral statutes. See Burwell v. Hobby Lobby Stores, Inc., 134 S.Ct. 2751 (2014). Analyzing religious objections to the Patient Protection and Affordable Care Act, the majority in *Hobby Lobby* interpreted RFRA to afford greater protection to religious exercise than was previously recognized under the Free Exercise Clause prior to *Smith*.

This chapter is divided into two parts to address the two types of exemption from the law identified above. Section A examines constitutional exemptions from *Sherbert* to *Smith*. Section B identifies the statutory exemptions authorized by RFRA.

A. CONSTITUTIONAL EXEMPTIONS: FROM *SHERBERT* TO *SMITH*

Sherbert v. Verner

Supreme Court of the United States, 1963.
374 U.S. 398, 83 S.Ct. 1790, 10 L.Ed.2d 965.

■ MR. JUSTICE BRENNAN delivered the opinion of the Court.

Appellant, a member of the Seventh-Day Adventist Church, was discharged by her South Carolina employer because she would not work on Saturday, the Sabbath Day of her faith. When she was unable to obtain other employment because from conscientious scruples she would not take Saturday work, she filed a claim for unemployment compensation benefits under the South Carolina Unemployment Compensation Act. That law provides that, to be eligible for benefits, a claimant must be "able to work and * * * is available for work"; and, further, that a claimant is ineligible for benefits "if * * * he has failed, without good cause * * * to accept available suitable work when offered him by the employment office or the employer * * * ." The appellee Employment Security Commission, in administrative proceedings under the statute, found that appellant's restriction upon her availability for

Saturday work brought her within the provision disqualifying for benefits insured workers who fail, without good cause, to accept "suitable work when offered * * * by the employment office or the employer * * *." ... [T]he South Carolina Supreme Court rejected appellant's contention that, as applied to her, the disqualifying provisions of the South Carolina statute abridged her right to the free exercise of her religion secured under the Free Exercise Clause of the First Amendment through the Fourteenth Amendment. The State Supreme Court held specifically that appellant's ineligibility infringed no constitutional liberties because such a construction of the statute "places no restriction upon the appellant's freedom of religion nor does it in any way prevent her in the exercise of her right and freedom to observe her religious beliefs in accordance with the dictates of her conscience." We reverse the judgment of the South Carolina Supreme Court and remand for further proceedings not inconsistent with this opinion.

II.

We turn first to the question whether the disqualification for benefits imposes any burden on the free exercise of appellant's religion. We think it is clear that it does. In a sense the consequences of such a disqualification to religious principles and practices may be only an indirect result of welfare legislation within the State's general competence to enact; it is true that no criminal sanctions directly compel appellant to work a six-day week. But this is only the beginning, not the end, of our inquiry. For "if the purpose or effect of a law is to impede the observance of one or all religions or is to discriminate invidiously between religions, that law is constitutionally invalid even though the burden may be characterized as being only indirect." Here not only is it apparent that appellant's declared ineligibility for benefits derives solely from the practice of her religion, but the pressure upon her to forego that practice is unmistakable. The ruling forces her to choose between following the precepts of her religion and forfeiting benefits, on the one hand, and abandoning one of the precepts of her religion in order to accept work, on the other hand. Governmental imposition of such a choice puts the same kind of burden upon the free exercise of religion as would a fine imposed against appellant for her Saturday worship.

Nor may the South Carolina court's construction of the statute be saved from constitutional infirmity on the ground that unemployment compensation benefits are not appellant's "right" but merely a "privilege." It is too late in the day to doubt that the liberties of religion and expression may be infringed by the denial of or placing of conditions upon a benefit or privilege. Likewise, to condition the availability of benefits upon this appellant's willingness to violate a cardinal principle of her religious faith effectively penalizes the free exercise of her constitutional liberties.

Significantly South Carolina expressly saves the Sunday worshipper from having to make the kind of choice which we here hold infringes the Sabbatarian's religious liberty. When in times of "national emergency" the textile plants are authorized by the State Commissioner of Labor to operate on Sunday, "no employee shall be required to work on Sunday * * * who is conscientiously opposed to Sunday work; and if any employee should refuse to work on Sunday on account of conscientious * * * objections he or she shall not jeopardize his or her seniority by such refusal or be discriminated against in any other manner." S.C. Code, § 64–4. No question of the disqualification of a Sunday worshipper for benefits is likely to arise, since we cannot suppose that an employer will discharge him in violation of this statute. The unconstitutionality of the disqualification of the Sabbatarian is thus compounded by the religious discrimination which South Carolina's general statutory scheme necessarily effects.

III.

We must next consider whether some compelling state interest enforced in the eligibility provisions of the South Carolina statute justifies the substantial infringement of appellant's First Amendment right. It is basic that no showing merely of a rational relationship to some colorable state interest would suffice; in this highly sensitive constitutional area, "only the gravest abuses, endangering paramount interests, give occasion for permissible limitation." No such abuse or danger has been advanced in the present case. The appellees suggest no more than a possibility that the filing of fraudulent claims by unscrupulous claimants feigning religious objections to Saturday work might not only dilute the unemployment compensation fund but also hinder the scheduling by employers of necessary Saturday work. But that possibility is not apposite here because no such objection appears to have been made before the South Carolina Supreme Court, and we are unwilling to assess the importance of an asserted state interest without the views of the state court. Nor, if the contention had been made below, would the record appear to sustain it; there is no proof whatever to warrant such fears of malingering or deceit as those which the respondents now advance. Even if consideration of such evidence is not foreclosed by the prohibition against judicial inquiry into the truth or falsity of religious beliefs, United States v. Ballard, 322 U.S. 78, 64 S.Ct. 882, 88 L.Ed. 1148—a question as to which we intimate no view since it is not before us—it is highly doubtful whether such evidence would be sufficient to warrant a substantial infringement of religious liberties. For even if the possibility of spurious claims did threaten to dilute the fund and disrupt the scheduling of work, it would plainly be incumbent upon the appellees to demonstrate that no alternative forms of regulation would combat such abuses without infringing First Amendment rights.

IV.

Our holding today is only that South Carolina may not constitutionally apply the eligibility provisions so as to constrain a worker to abandon his religious convictions respecting the day of rest. This holding but reaffirms a principle that we announced a decade and a half ago, namely that no State may "exclude individual Catholics, Lutherans, Mohammedans, Baptists, Jews, Methodists, Non-believers, Presbyterians, or the members of any other faith, *because of their faith, or lack of it,* from receiving the benefits of public welfare legislation."

Reversed and remanded.

■ MR. JUSTICE HARLAN, whom MR. JUSTICE WHITE joins, dissenting.

[T]he implications of the present decision are far more troublesome than its apparently narrow dimensions would indicate at first glance. The meaning of today's holding is that the State must furnish unemployment benefits to one who is unavailable for work if the unavailability stems from the exercise of religious convictions. The State, in other words, must *single out* for financial assistance those whose behavior is religiously motivated, even though it denies such assistance to others whose identical behavior (in this case, inability to work on Saturdays) is not religiously motivated.

It has been suggested that such singling out of religious conduct for special treatment may violate the constitutional limitations on state action. My own view, however, is that at least under the circumstances of this case it would be a permissible accommodation of religion for the State, if it *chose* to do so, to create an exception to its eligibility requirements for persons like the appellant. The constitutional obligation of "neutrality" is not so narrow a channel that the slightest deviation from an absolutely straight course leads to condemnation. There are too many instances in which no such course can be charted, too many areas in which the pervasive activities of the State justify some special provision for religion to prevent it from being submerged by an all-embracing secularism. The State violates its obligation of neutrality when, for example, it mandates a daily religious exercise in its public schools, with all the attendant pressures on the school children that such an exercise entails. But there is, I believe, enough flexibility in the Constitution to permit a legislative judgment accommodating an unemployment compensation law to the exercise of religious beliefs such as appellant's.

For very much the same reasons, however, I cannot subscribe to the conclusion that the State is constitutionally *compelled* to carve out an exception to its general rule of eligibility in the present case. Those situations in which the Constitution may require special treatment on account of religion are, in my view, few and far between, and this view is amply supported by the course of constitutional litigation in this area. Such compulsion in the present case is particularly inappropriate in light of the indirect, remote, and insubstantial effect of the decision below on the exercise of appellant's religion and in light of the direct financial assistance to religion that today's decision requires.

For these reasons I respectfully dissent from the opinion and judgment of the Court.

NOTES AND QUESTIONS

1. Justice Brennan observes that South Carolina law exempted Sunday worshippers from working on Sundays during national emergencies. How important is that law to the Court's holding? Would Sherbert's claim for exemption be as strong if the South Carolina law did not have this exemption for Sunday worshippers? Is an act that gives Sunday worshippers, but not Sabbatarians, the day off in national emergencies constitutional? Does a law that exempts both Sunday worshippers and Sabbatarians from working during national emergencies solve the problem? See Estate of Thornton v. Caldor, 472 U.S. 703, 710–11 (1985) (Connecticut law giving employees an absolute and unqualified right not to work on their Sabbath violates the Establishment Clause).

Professors Eisgruber's and Sager's interpretation of the Religion Clauses is based on the principle of Equal Liberty: "First, no members of our political community ought to be devalued on account of the spiritual foundations of their important commitment and projects. And second, all members of our political community ought to enjoy rights of free speech, personal autonomy, associative freedom, and private property that, while neither uniquely relevant to religion nor defined in terms of religion, will allow a broad range of religious beliefs and practices to flourish." Christopher L. Eisgruber & Lawrence G. Sager, Religious Freedom and the Constitution 4 (2007). They argue that the Sunday worshippers' exemption is crucial to interpreting *Sherbert* because a ruling for Sherbert protected her equality with citizens who were allowed to follow their Sunday Sabbath. The compelling state interest test is appropriate in her circumstances (but not for all religious exemption claims) because Sherbert was *discriminated against* under state law. Id. at 41. Do you agree with that analysis?

According to the Collective Bargaining Agreement (CBA) of the Lynn, Massachusetts, school district, Jewish administrators are excused from three days of work without loss of pay on Rosh Hashanah and Yom Kippur. Greek and Russian administrators are excused on Orthodox Good Friday with pay. All administrators have Christmas and regular Good Friday as a holiday. Can you identify potential administrators who would be able successfully to challenge the agreement? A Catholic administrator filed suit after he was denied days off with pay for Holy Thursday and Ascension Thursday. Should he succeed? Why or why not? See Troy v. City of Lynn

Sch. Dept., 2007 WL 1289409 (MCAD) (finding direct evidence of discrimination and awarding $4,857.07).

2. *Burden and Interest.* The State of South Carolina was not compelling Sherbert to worship. Was there really a burden on her free exercise?

Why is the possibility of filing fraudulent claims by unscrupulous claimants feigning religious objection to Saturday work not a sufficiently compelling state interest to defeat Sherbert's claim? How would the state determine if an individual was "feigning religious objection," i.e., that her beliefs were not sincere? Does it violate free exercise for a court to examine how sincere an individual's religious beliefs are? See United States v. Ballard, 322 U.S. 78 (1944) (in mail fraud conviction, jury could consider whether defendants had a good faith belief in their religion but not whether the religion was true); Thomas v. Review Bd. of Indiana Employment Sec. Division, 450 U.S. 707, 719 (1981) (no); Hansard v. Johns-Manville Prods. Corp., No. 1902, 1973 WL 129, *2 (E.D.Tex. 1973) (court dismissed plaintiff's claim not to work Sundays on sincerity grounds because he had previously worked regularly on Sunday).

3. The dissent suggests the State of South Carolina may reasonably accommodate the Sabbatarians' needs but that the Court should not require the exemption under the Free Exercise Clause. Does it matter if the exemption comes from the State or the Court? What are the advantages and disadvantages of having the State identify exemptions instead of the Court? Are different religious groups likely to be protected? Why does an exemption by either the Court or the State not violate the Establishment Clause?

4. Justice Harlan observes that the majority requires the state to "single out" religious groups for benefits while denying similar benefits to non-religious workers. Is it unfair that religious believers receive unemployment benefits under the majority's standard but other people who do not want to work on Saturday do not? Compare the strength of Sherbert's claim for compensation with other hypothetical plaintiffs who:

a)   cannot work on Saturday because they need to be home with their

    i)   newborn baby,

    ii)   teenage children, or

    iii)   noncustodial children whom they can see on Saturday only;

b)   compete in athletic competitions that are held on Saturday only;

c)   like to sleep in late on Saturday;

d)   have a great passion for art and want to devote Saturday mornings to it; or

e)   like to go sailing on Saturday.

Is the burden that the state law places on them different from the burden carried by Sherbert? See Christopher L. Eisgruber & Lawrence G. Sager, The Vulnerability of Conscience: The Constitutional Basis for Protecting Religious Conduct, 61 U. Chi. L. Rev. 1245, 1255, 1264 (1994) ("Of course, burdens upon religious practice differ from burdens upon tastes in fashion and recreation. Do they also differ from the considerably more weighty burdens imposed by secular commitments to one's family, or by secular moral obligations, or by physical disabilities?"); Douglas Laycock, The Remnants of Free Exercise, 1990 S. Ct. Rev. 1, 11 (it would be an error to maintain that "(a) soldier who believes he must cover his head before an omnipresent God is constitutionally indistinguishable from a soldier who wants to wear a Budweiser gimme cap."); Michael W. McConnell, Religious Freedom at a Crossroads, 59 U. Chi. L. Rev. 115 (1992) (a Saturday work schedule places lesser burdens on those who like to go sailing on Saturdays than on those who observe the Sabbath on that day).

    5.   *Cases Following Sherbert: Thomas and Secular Thomas.* Thomas was a Jehovah's Witness who worked at the Blaw-Knox Foundry & Machinery Company. He first worked in the roll foundry, which made sheet steel. After the roll foundry closed, Thomas was transferred to another section of the company that made turrets for military tanks. Thomas objected to weapons-related work on the basis of his religion, and could not find any non-weapons-related work at Blaw-Knox. The roll foundry work did not violate his conscience because it was only indirectly involved with weapons.

    After Thomas's request to be laid off was denied, he quit and applied for unemployment compensation. The Review Board of the Indiana Employment Security Division and the Supreme Court of Indiana denied Thomas's request for benefits because he had "quit voluntarily for personal reasons, and therefore did not qualify for benefits." "The Indiana court concluded that denying Thomas benefits would create only an indirect burden on his free exercise right and that the burden was justified by the legitimate state interest in preserving the integrity of the insurance fund and maintaining a stable work force by encouraging workers not to leave their jobs for personal reasons." See Thomas v. Review Bd. of Ind. Employment Sec. Div., 450 U.S. 707, 713 (1981).

    The U.S. Supreme Court reversed, following *Sherbert.* The Court concluded that the State's interests in avoiding widespread unemployment and the probing of religious beliefs were not strong enough to meet the compelling state interest test.

    One of Thomas's friends, a Jehovah's Witness who also worked at the factory, told Thomas that working on weapons was "not unscriptural." Thomas disagreed, however, because "his friend's view was based upon a less strict reading of Witnesses' principles than his own." Id. at 711. Does that disagreement between the two men suggest that Thomas's views were just "personal" and thus not entitled to First Amendment protection? Should the First Amendment protect Thomas even if most Jehovah's Witnesses would agree with his friend?

Compare the real Thomas with Secular Thomas, whose support for pacifism is nonreligious. Is he entitled to the exemption? See Christopher L. Eisgruber & Lawrence G. Sager, The Vulnerability of Conscience: The Constitutional Basis for Protecting Religious Conduct, 61 U. Chi. L. Rev. 1245, 1292 (1994) (Yes, because a "constitutional jurisprudence that permitted intervention on behalf of one Thomas but not the other would be unacceptable.") Now compare Thomas and Secular Thomas with Labor Thomas. After a strike at the factory, Thomas and Secular Thomas will not work because of their opposition to arms, but Labor Thomas will not work because he thinks it is immoral to cross picket lines. Is Labor Thomas entitled to an exemption? See id. at 1293 (No, because "[l]abor law issues have, by contrast, a more economic focus and a less immediate connection to matters of life and death. The stakes are lower and the imponderables less profound. It is possible, but not likely, that we would deem union sympathy to be reasonably constitutive of moral identity in the same way that pacifism is."). Would Roman Catholic Thomas who opposed crossing picket lines be entitled to an exemption? See Michael McConnell, The Problem of Singling Out Religion, 50 DePaul L. Rev. 1, 33–34 (2000) (Yes, pointing out inconsistencies of Eisgruber & Sager and arguing against coverage for Secular Thomas); but see Steven G. Gey, Symposium Panel, in Law, Religion, and the "Secular" State, at 113 (Proceedings of the Second Annual Symposium of the Constitutional Law Resource Center, Drake University Law School, Apr. 13, 1991) (noting the problem of disallowing benefits to Thomas' "secular-evil twin").

6.   Justice Rehnquist's dissent in *Thomas* cited the Harlan dissent in *Sherbert*, arguing "the statute did not make unlawful any religious practices of appellants; it simply made the practice of their religious beliefs more expensive." Is Justice Rehnquist correct? Should religious believers have to pay a price for their beliefs?

7.   *Additional Unemployment Cases.* What should happen to an employee who converts to a religion after two and a half years on the job? Should her conversion be viewed as the cause of her unemployment, thus disqualifying her from benefits? Or should the conversion be reason for granting her an exemption? See Hobbie v. Unemployment Appeals Comm'n of Florida, 480 U.S. 136 (1987) (following *Sherbert* and *Thomas* in awarding benefits to Seventh-Day Adventist convert).

William Frazee turned down a job that required him to work on Sunday, describing himself as a Christian who could not work on the Lord's Day. Illinois rejected his claim for unemployment benefits because he was "not a member of an established religious sect or church, nor did he claim that his refusal to work resulted from a 'tenet, belief or teaching of an established religious body.' " See Frazee v. Illinois Dep't of Employment Sec., 489 U.S. 829, 831 (1989) (reversing Illinois courts because Frazee's religious belief was sincere). Should the First Amendment protect Frazee? How do courts know when a religious belief is sincere? Do the courts have a right to analyze whether the individual's beliefs are sincere, or would this constitute a free exercise violation? Is Frazee "the boldest leap of all" in terms of extending First Amendment protection because Frazee was only nominally Christian? See Robert M. O'Neil, Religious Freedom and Nondiscrimination: State RFRA Laws Versus Civil Rights, 32 U.C. Davis L. Rev. 785, 790 (1999).

A Chinese citizen's application for refugee protection in Canada was rejected after the administrator concluded "it is implausible that the Applicant is a Christian." Haixhin Zhang was unable to identify all four Gospels, could name only two of Jesus' apostles, and left out two complete sentences of the Lord's Prayer. Nonetheless, he had a baptismal certificate as well as affidavits from a pastor stating that he had attended church services regularly for six years. Do you agree with the administrator that the claimant was not a genuine practicing Christian and probably joined his church "only for the purpose of supporting a fraudulent refugee claim"? See Zhang v. Canada (Minister of Citizenship & Immigration), [2012] F.C. 503, paras. 11–12 (Can. Ont. Fed. Ct.) (reversing ruling because Canadian law holds that "regardless of idiosyncrasy, if a certain view is conscientiously held, it is religious" and that "assessing a genuine Christian by way of 'trivia' is contrary to law"). The appeals court also wrote "a process of questioning religious *knowledge* is a fundamentally flawed fact finding venture to learn about a person's religious *faith*. Learning about the person is the only path to the truth." See id. (emphasis added). Do you agree? What is the difference between religious knowledge and religious faith? Is the Canadian court's approach consistent with *Thomas*?

8. *The Amish Exemption.* Unlike the unemployment compensation cases, *Wisconsin v. Yoder* involved a state compulsory school attendance law that required children to attend school until age 16. Members of the Old Order Amish Religion and the Conservative Amish Mennonite Church, who believed that school attendance after the eighth grade was contrary to their religion and endangered their and their children's salvation, were convicted of violating the school attendance law. Justice Burger concluded that "only those interests of the highest order" could overcome the right of free exercise of religion, and that the State's asserted interest in education (which prepares children to be active and self-sufficient citizens) could not overcome the Amish claim. The convictions were reversed. See Wisconsin v. Yoder, 406 U.S. 205 (1972). The Court's opinion noted that the Amish children received extensive vocational education in their community. Should a religion that did not provide such vocational training receive an exemption?

Is *Yoder* a limited holding with narrow application? If Henry David Thoreau wanted to keep his children from school so that they could learn in the environment of Walden Pond, would he receive the same exemption as the Amish? See id. at 216 (No, because "Thoreau's choice was philosophical and personal rather than religious, and such belief does not rise to the demands of the Religion Clauses"). How does a court determine what is philosophical and personal rather than religious? Was the Court wrong about Thoreau? *Yoder* is reprinted in Chapter 11.

9. *Strict Scrutiny?* Many commentators have asked if the *"Sherbert* Quartet" and *Yoder* really provided extensive protection to religious freedom, noting that in most other cases religious claimants lost because the courts found that the government had demonstrated a compelling state interest. Professor Lupu has argued, for example, that fifty years of Supreme Court cases demonstrate that the "Supreme Court made it a steady practice to honor in the breach the free exercise principles nominally stated in *Sherbert-Yoder.* . . . For fifty years, judges at all levels have avoided privileging religiously motivated behavior over its secular counterparts." Ira C. Lupu, *Hobby Lobby* and the Dubious Enterprise of Religious Exemptions, 38 Harv. J. L. & Gender 35, 71–72 (2015). Can you think of any reasons why strict scrutiny was unsuccessful in the religious freedom area despite its successes in the free speech and racial discrimination contexts? See William P. Marshall, Bad Statutes Make Bad Law: *Burwell v. Hobby Lobby*, 2014 Sup. Ct. Rev. 71, 74 (2014) ("the pre-*Smith* decisions demonstrated that the application of a compelling interest test to religious exercise challenge raises serious problems of coherency and consistency."). Did these arguments provide a justification for the Court to abandon *Sherbert?*

10. Did Justice Scalia adopt the Harlan/Rehnquist standard in the following case, thus reversing *Sherbert?* Or is his opinion consistent with *Sherbert,* as he contends, as well as with the other body of free exercise cases represented by *Reynolds?* Contrast the *Sherbert* compelling state interest test with the test enunciated below by Justice Scalia. Does *Smith* mean that the Court will no longer use the compelling state interest test? Can you identify three circumstances in which *Smith* still allows the Court to use strict scrutiny?

Employment Div., Dept. of Human Resources of Oregon v. Smith

Supreme Court of the United States, 1990.
494 U.S. 872, 110 S.Ct. 1595, 108 L.Ed.2d 876.

■ JUSTICE SCALIA delivered the opinion of the Court, in which REHNQUIST, C.J., and WHITE, STEVENS and KENNEDY, joined.

Respondents Alfred Smith and Galen Black (hereinafter respondents) were fired from their jobs with a private drug rehabilitation organization because they ingested peyote for sacramental purposes at a ceremony of the Native American Church, of which both are members. When respondents applied to petitioner Employment Division (hereinafter petitioner) for unemployment compensation, they were determined to be ineligible for benefits because they had been discharged for work-related "misconduct." [The Oregon Supreme Court declared them eligible for benefits under *Sherbert.*]

II

Respondents' claim for relief rests on our decisions in *Sherbert v. Verner, supra, Thomas v. Review Bd. Of Indiana Employment Sec. Division, supra,* and *Hobbie v. Unemployment Appeals Comm'n of Florida,* in which we held that a State could not condition the availability of unemployment insurance on an individual's willingness to forgo conduct required by his religion. As we observed in *Smith I,* however, the conduct at issue in those cases was not prohibited by law. We held that distinction to be critical, for "if Oregon does prohibit the religious use of peyote, and if that prohibition is consistent with the Federal Constitution, there is no federal right to engage in that conduct in Oregon," and "the State is free to withhold unemployment compensation from respondents for engaging in work-related misconduct, despite its religious motivation." Now that the Oregon Supreme Court has confirmed that Oregon does prohibit the religious use of peyote, we proceed to consider whether that prohibition is permissible under the Free Exercise Clause.

A

We have never held that an individual's religious beliefs excuse him from compliance with an otherwise valid law prohibiting conduct that the State is free to regulate. On the contrary, the record of more than a century of our free exercise jurisprudence contradicts that proposition. As described succinctly by Justice Frankfurter in *Minersville School Dist. v. Gobitis,* 310 U.S. 586, 594–595, 60 S.Ct. 1010, 1012–1013, 84 L.Ed. 1375 (1940): "Conscientious scruples have not, in the course of the long struggle for religious toleration, relieved the individual from obedience to a general law not aimed at the promotion or restriction of religious beliefs. The mere possession of religious convictions which contradict the relevant concerns of a political society does not relieve the citizen from the discharge of political responsibilities (footnote omitted)." We first had occasion to assert that principle in *Reynolds v. United States,* 98 U.S. 145 (1879), where we rejected the claim that criminal laws against polygamy could not be constitutionally applied to those whose religion commanded the practice. "Laws," we said, "are made for the government of actions, and while they cannot interfere with mere religious belief and opinions, they may with practices. . . . Can a man excuse his practices to the contrary because of his religious belief? To permit this would be to make the professed doctrines of religious belief superior to the law of the land, and in effect to permit every citizen to become a law unto himself." *Id.* at 166–167.

Subsequent decisions have consistently held that the right of free exercise does not relieve an individual of the obligation to comply with a "valid and neutral law of general applicability on the ground that the law proscribes (or prescribes) conduct that his religion prescribes (or proscribes)." In *Prince v. Massachusetts*, 321 U.S. 158, 64 S.Ct. 438, 88 L.Ed. 645 (1944), we held that a mother could be prosecuted under the child labor laws for using her children to dispense literature in the streets, her religious motivation notwithstanding. We found no constitutional infirmity in "excluding [these children] from doing there what no other children may do." In *Braunfeld v. Brown*, 366 U.S. 599, 81 S.Ct. 1144, 6 L.Ed.2d 563 (1961) (plurality opinion), we upheld Sunday-closing laws against the claim that they burdened the religious practices of persons whose religions compelled them to refrain from work on other days. In *Gillette v. United States*, 401 U.S. 437, 461, 91 S.Ct. 828, 842, 28 L.Ed.2d 168 (1971), we sustained the military Selective Service System against the claim that it violated free exercise by conscripting persons who opposed a particular war on religious grounds.

Our most recent decision involving a neutral, generally applicable regulatory law that compelled activity forbidden by an individual's religion was *United States v. Lee*, 455 U.S., at 258–261, 102 S.Ct., at 1055–1057. There, an Amish employer, on behalf of himself and his employees, sought exemption from collection and payment of Social Security taxes on the ground that the Amish faith prohibited participation in governmental support programs. We rejected the claim that an exemption was constitutionally required. There would be no way, we observed, to distinguish the Amish believer's objection to Social Security taxes from the religious objections that others might have to the collection or use of other taxes. "If, for example, a religious adherent believes war is a sin, and if a certain percentage of the federal budget can be identified as devoted to war-related activities, such individuals would have a similarly valid claim to be exempt from paying that percentage of the income tax. The tax system could not function if denominations were allowed to challenge the tax system because tax payments were spent in a manner that violates their religious belief."

The only decisions in which we have held that the First Amendment bars application of a neutral, generally applicable law to religiously motivated action have involved not the Free Exercise Clause alone, but the Free Exercise Clause in conjunction with other constitutional protections, such as freedom of speech and of the press, see *Cantwell v. Connecticut*, 310 U.S., at 304–307, 60 S.Ct., at 903–905 (invalidating a licensing system for religious and charitable solicitations under which the administrator had discretion to deny a license to any cause he deemed nonreligious); *Murdock v. Commonwealth of Pennsylvania*, 319 U.S. 105, 63 S.Ct. 870, 87 L.Ed. 1292 (1943) (invalidating a flat tax on solicitation as applied to the dissemination of religious ideas); *Follett v. McCormick*, 321 U.S. 573, 64 S.Ct. 717, 88 L.Ed. 938 (1944) (same), or the right of parents, acknowledged in *Pierce v. Society of the Sisters of the Holy Names of Jesus and Mary*, 268 U.S. 510, 45 S.Ct. 571, 69 L.Ed. 1070 (1925), to direct the education of their children, see *Wisconsin v. Yoder*, 406 U.S. 205, 92 S.Ct. 1526, 32 L.Ed.2d 15 (1972) (invalidating compulsory school-attendance laws as applied to Amish parents who refused on religious grounds to send their children to school). Some of our cases prohibiting compelled expression, decided exclusively upon free speech grounds, have also involved freedom of religion, cf. *Wooley v. Maynard*, 430 U.S. 705, 97 S.Ct. 1428, 51 L.Ed.2d 752 (1977) (invalidating compelled display of a license plate slogan that offended individual religious beliefs); *West Virginia Bd. Of Education v. Barnette*, 319 U.S. 624, 63 S.Ct. 1178, 87 L.Ed. 1628 (1943) (invalidating compulsory flag salute statute challenged by religious objectors). And it is easy to envision a case in which a challenge on freedom of association grounds would likewise be reinforced by Free Exercise Clause concerns. *Cf. Roberts v. United States Jaycees*, 468 U.S. 609, 622, 104 S.Ct. 3244, 3251–52, 82 L.Ed.2d 462 (1984) ("An individual's freedom to speak, to worship, and to petition the government for the redress of grievances could not be vigorously protected from interference by the State [if] a correlative freedom to engage in group effort toward those ends were not also guaranteed").

The present case does not present such a hybrid situation, but a free exercise claim unconnected with any communicative activity or parental right.

B

Respondents argue that even though exemption from generally applicable criminal laws need not automatically be extended to religiously motivated actors, at least the claim for a religious exemption must be evaluated under the balancing test set forth in *Sherbert v. Verner*. Under the *Sherbert* test, governmental actions that substantially burden a religious practice must be justified by a compelling governmental interest. Applying that test we have, on three occasions, invalidated state unemployment compensation rules that conditioned the availability of benefits upon an applicant's willingness to work under conditions forbidden by his religion. See *Sherbert v. Verner*, supra; *Thomas v. Review Bd. Of Indiana Employment Sec. Division*, 450 U.S. 707, 101 S.Ct. 1425, 67 L.Ed.2d 624 (1981); *Hobbie v. Unemployment Appeals Comm'n of Florida*, 480 U.S. 136, 107 S.Ct. 1046, 94 L.Ed.2d 190 (1987). We have never invalidated any governmental action on the basis of the *Sherbert* test except the denial of unemployment compensation. Although we have sometimes purported to apply the *Sherbert* test in contexts other than that, we have always found the test satisfied, [see *United States v. Lee*; *Gillette v. United States*]. In recent years we have abstained from applying the *Sherbert* test (outside the unemployment compensation field) at all. In *Bowen v. Roy*, 476 U.S. 693 (1986), we declined to apply *Sherbert* analysis to a federal statutory scheme that required benefit applicants and recipients to provide their Social Security numbers. The plaintiffs in that case asserted that it would violate their religious beliefs to obtain and provide a Social Security number for their daughter. We held the statute's application to the plaintiffs valid regardless of whether it was necessary to effectuate a compelling interest. See 476 U.S., at 699–701, 106 S.Ct., at 2151–53. In *Lyng v. Northwest Indian Cemetery Protective Assn.*, 485 U.S. 439, 108 S.Ct. 1319, 99 L.Ed.2d 534 (1988), we declined to apply *Sherbert* analysis to the Government's logging and road construction activities on lands used for religious purposes by several Native American Tribes, even though it was undisputed that the activities "could have devastating effects on traditional Indian religious practices," 485 U.S., at 451, 108 S.Ct., at 1326. In *Goldman v. Weinberger*, 475 U.S. 503, 106 S.Ct. 1310, 89 L.Ed.2d 478 (1986), we rejected application of the *Sherbert* test to military dress regulations that forbade the wearing of yarmulkes. In *O'Lone v. Estate of Shabazz*, 482 U.S. 342, 107 S.Ct. 2400, 96 L.Ed.2d 282 (1987), we sustained, without mentioning the *Sherbert* test, a prison's refusal to excuse inmates from work requirements to attend worship services.

Even if we were inclined to breathe into *Sherbert* some life beyond the unemployment compensation field, we would not apply it to require exemptions from a generally applicable criminal law. The *Sherbert* test, it must be recalled, was developed in a context that lent itself to individualized governmental assessment of the reasons for the relevant conduct. As a plurality of the Court noted in *Roy*, a distinctive feature of unemployment compensation programs is that their eligibility criteria invite consideration of the particular circumstances behind an applicant's unemployment: "The statutory conditions [in *Sherbert* and *Thomas*] provided that a person was not eligible for unemployment compensation benefits if, 'without good cause,' he had quit work or refused available work. The 'good cause' standard created a mechanism for individualized exemptions." As the plurality pointed out in *Roy*, our decisions in the unemployment cases stand for the proposition that where the State has in place a system of individual exemptions, it may not refuse to extend that system to cases of "religious hardship" without compelling reason.

Whether or not the decisions are that limited, they at least have nothing to do with an across-the-board criminal prohibition on a particular form of conduct. Although, as noted earlier, we have sometimes used the *Sherbert* test to analyze free exercise challenges to such laws, see *United States v. Lee, supra*, 455 U.S., at 257–260, 102 S.Ct., at 1055–1057; *Gillette v. United States, supra*, 401 U.S., at 462, 91 S.Ct., at 842–43, we have never applied the test to invalidate one. We conclude today that the sounder approach, and the approach in accord with the vast majority of our precedents, is to hold the test inapplicable to such challenges. The government's ability to enforce generally applicable prohibitions of socially harmful conduct, like its ability to carry out other aspects of public policy, "cannot depend on measuring the effects of a governmental action on a religious objector's spiritual development." To make an individual's obligation to obey such a law contingent upon the law's coincidence with his religious beliefs, except where the State's interest is "compelling"—permitting him, by virtue of his beliefs, "to become a law unto himself," *Reynolds v. United States*, 98 U.S., at 167—contradicts both constitutional tradition and common sense.

The "compelling government interest" requirement seems benign, because it is familiar from other fields. But using it as the standard that must be met before the government may accord different treatment on the basis of race, or before the government may regulate the content of speech is not remotely comparable to using it for the purpose asserted here. What it produces in those other fields—equality of treatment and an unrestricted flow of contending speech—are constitutional norms; what it would produce here—a private right to ignore generally applicable laws—is a constitutional anomaly.[3]

Nor is it possible to limit the impact of respondents' proposal by requiring a "compelling state interest" only when the conduct prohibited is "central" to the individual's religion. It is no more appropriate for judges to determine the "centrality" of religious beliefs before applying a "compelling interest" test in the free exercise field, than it would be for them to determine the "importance" of ideas before applying the "compelling interest" test in the free speech field. What principle of law or logic can be brought to bear to contradict a believer's assertion that a particular act is "central" to his personal faith? Judging the centrality of different religious practices is akin to the unacceptable "business of evaluating the relative merits of differing religious claims." Repeatedly and in many different contexts, we have warned that courts must not presume to determine the place of a particular belief in a religion or the plausibility of a religious claim.

If the "compelling interest" test is to be applied at all, then, it must be applied across the board, to all actions thought to be religiously commanded. Moreover, if "compelling interest" really means what it says (and watering it down here would subvert its rigor in the other fields where it is applied), many laws will not meet the test. Any society

---

[3] Justice O'CONNOR suggests that "[t]here is nothing talismanic about neutral laws of general applicability," and that all laws burdening religious practices should be subject to compelling-interest scrutiny because "the First Amendment unequivocally makes freedom of religion, like freedom from race discrimination and freedom of speech, a 'constitutional nor[m],' not an 'anomaly.'" But we have held that race-neutral laws that have the *effect* of disproportionately disadvantaging a particular racial group do not thereby become subject to compelling-interest analysis under the Equal Protection Clause, and we have held that generally applicable laws unconcerned with regulating speech that have the *effect* of interfering with speech do not thereby become subject to compelling-interest analysis under the First Amendment. Our conclusion that generally applicable, religion-neutral laws that have the effect of burdening a particular religious practice need not be justified by a compelling governmental interest is the only approach compatible with these precedents.

adopting such a system would be courting anarchy, but that danger increases in direct proportion to the society's diversity of religious beliefs, and its determination to coerce or suppress none of them. Precisely because "we are a cosmopolitan nation made up of people of almost every conceivable religious preference," and precisely because we value and protect that religious divergence, we cannot afford the luxury of deeming *presumptively invalid*, as applied to the religious objector, every regulation of conduct that does not protect an interest of the highest order. The rule respondents favor would open the prospect of constitutionally required religious exemptions from civic obligations of almost every conceivable kind—ranging from compulsory military service, see, *e.g., Gillette v. United States*, 401 U.S. 437, 91 S.Ct. 828, 28 L.Ed.2d 168 (1971), to the payment of taxes, see, *e.g., United States v. Lee, supra*; to health and safety regulation such as manslaughter and child neglect laws, see, *e.g., Funkhouser v. State*, 763 P.2d 695 (Okla.Crim.App.1988), compulsory vaccination laws, see, *e.g., Cude v. State*, 237 Ark. 927, 377 S.W.2d 816 (1964), drug laws, see, *e.g., Olsen v. Drug Enforcement Administration*, 279 U.S.App.D.C. 1, 878 F.2d 1458 (1989), and traffic laws, see *Cox v. New Hampshire*, 312 U.S. 569, 61 S.Ct. 762, 85 L.Ed. 1049 (1941); to social welfare legislation such as minimum wage laws, see *Tony and Susan Alamo Foundation v. Secretary of Labor*, 471 U.S. 290, 105 S.Ct. 1953, 85 L.Ed.2d 278 (1985), child labor laws, see *Prince v. Massachusetts*, 321 U.S. 158, 64 S.Ct. 438, 88 L.Ed. 645 (1944), animal cruelty laws, see, *e.g., Church of the Lukumi Babalu Aye, Inc. v. City of Hialeah*, 723 F.Supp. 1467 (SD Fla.1989), cf. *State v. Massey*, 229 N.C. 734, 51 S.E.2d 179, appeal dism'd, 336 U.S. 942, 69 S.Ct. 813, 93 L.Ed. 1099 (1949), environmental protection laws, see *United States v. Little*, 638 F.Supp. 337 (Mont.1986), and laws providing for equality of opportunity for the races, see, *e.g., Bob Jones University v. United States*, 461 U.S. 574, 603–604, 103 S.Ct. 2017, 2034–2035, 76 L.Ed.2d 157 (1983). The First Amendment's protection of religious liberty does not require this.[5]

Values that are protected against government interference through enshrinement in the Bill of Rights are not thereby banished from the political process. Just as a society that believes in the negative protection accorded to the press by the First Amendment is likely to

---

[5]   Justice O'CONNOR contends that the "parade of horribles" in the text only "demonstrates . . . that courts have been quite capable of . . . strik[ing] sensible balances between religious liberty and competing state interests." But the cases we cite have struck "sensible balances" only because they have all applied the general laws, despite the claims for religious exemption. In any event, Justice O'CONNOR mistakes the purpose of our parade: it is not to suggest that courts would necessarily permit harmful exemptions from these laws (though they might), but to suggest that courts would constantly be in the business of determining whether the "severe impact" of various laws on religious practice (to use Justice Blackmun's terminology) or the "constitutiona[l] significan[ce]" of the "burden on the specific plaintiffs" (to use Justice O'Connor's terminology) suffices to permit us to confer an exemption. It is a parade of horribles because it is horrible to contemplate that federal judges will regularly balance against the importance of general laws the significance of religious practice.

enact laws that affirmatively foster the dissemination of the printed word, so also a society that believes in the negative protection accorded to religious belief can be expected to be solicitous of that value in its legislation as well. It is therefore not surprising that a number of States have made an exception to their drug laws for sacramental peyote use. But to say that a nondiscriminatory religious-practice exemption is permitted, or even that it is desirable, is not to say that it is constitutionally required, and that the appropriate occasions for its creation can be discerned by the courts. It may fairly be said that leaving accommodation to the political process will place at a relative disadvantage those religious practices that are not widely engaged in; but that unavoidable consequence of democratic government must be preferred to a system in which each conscience is a law unto itself or in which judges weigh the social importance of all laws against the centrality of all religious beliefs.

The decision of the Oregon Supreme Court is accordingly reversed.

It is so ordered.

■ JUSTICE O'CONNOR, concurring in the judgment.

Although I agree with the result the Court reaches in this case, I cannot join its opinion. In my view, today's holding dramatically departs from well-settled First Amendment jurisprudence, appears unnecessary to resolve the question presented, and is incompatible with our Nation's fundamental commitment to individual religious liberty

II

B

Respondents, of course, do not contend that their conduct is automatically immune from all governmental regulation simply because it is motivated by their sincere religious beliefs. . . . Rather, respondents invoke our traditional compelling interest test to argue that the Free Exercise Clause requires the State to grant them a limited exemption from its general criminal prohibition against the possession of peyote. The Court today, however, denies them even the opportunity to make that argument, concluding that "the sounder approach, and the approach in accord with the vast majority of our precedents, is to hold the [compelling interest] test inapplicable to" challenges to general criminal prohibitions.

In my view, however, the essence of a free exercise claim is relief from a burden imposed by government on religious practices or beliefs, whether the burden is imposed directly through laws that prohibit or compel specific religious practices, or indirectly through laws that, in effect, make abandonment of one's own religion or conformity to the religious beliefs of others the price of an equal place in the civil community.

A State that makes criminal an individual's religiously motivated conduct burdens that individual's free exercise of religion in the severest manner possible, for it "results in the choice to the individual of either abandoning his religious principle or facing criminal prosecution." I would have thought it beyond argument that such laws implicate free exercise concerns.

Indeed, we have never distinguished between cases in which a State conditions receipt of a benefit on conduct prohibited by religious beliefs and cases in which a State affirmatively prohibits such conduct. The *Sherbert* compelling interest test applies in both kinds of cases. See, *e.g.*, *Lee*, 455 U.S., at 257–260, 102 S.Ct., at 1055–1057 (applying *Sherbert* to uphold Social Security tax liability); *Gillette*, 401 U.S., at 462, 91 S.Ct., at 842–43 (applying *Sherbert* to uphold military conscription requirement); *Yoder*, 406 U.S., at 215–234, 92 S.Ct., at 1533–1538 (applying *Sherbert* to strike down criminal convictions for violation of compulsory school attendance law). A neutral criminal law prohibiting conduct that a State may legitimately regulate is, if anything, *more* burdensome than a neutral civil statute placing legitimate conditions on the award of a state benefit.

Once it has been shown that a government regulation or criminal prohibition burdens the free exercise of religion, we have consistently asked the government to demonstrate that unbending application of its regulation to the religious objector "is essential to accomplish an overriding governmental interest," or represents "the least restrictive means of achieving some compelling state interest." To me, the sounder approach—the approach more consistent with our role as judges to decide each case on its individual merits—is to apply this test in each case to determine whether the burden on the specific plaintiffs before us is constitutionally significant and whether the particular criminal interest asserted by the State before us is compelling. Even if, as an empirical matter, a government's criminal laws might usually serve a compelling interest in health, safety, or public order, the First Amendment at least requires a case-by-case determination of the question, sensitive to the facts of each particular claim. Given the range of conduct that a State might legitimately make criminal, we cannot assume, merely because a law carries criminal sanctions and is generally applicable, that the First Amendment *never* requires the State to grant a limited exemption for religiously motivated conduct.

There is nothing talismanic about neutral laws of general applicability or general criminal prohibitions, for laws neutral toward religion can coerce a person to violate his religious conscience or intrude upon his religious duties just as effectively as laws aimed at religion. Although the Court suggests that the compelling interest test, as applied to generally applicable laws, would result in a "constitutional anomaly," the First Amendment unequivocally makes freedom of religion, like freedom from race discrimination and freedom of speech, a "constitutional nor[m]," not an "anomaly." The Court's parade of horribles not only fails as a reason for discarding the compelling interest test, it instead demonstrates just the opposite: that courts have been quite capable of applying our free exercise jurisprudence to strike sensible balances between religious liberty and competing state interests.

Finally, the Court today suggests that the disfavoring of minority religions is an "unavoidable consequence" under our system of government and that accommodation of such religions must be left to the political process. In my view, however, the First Amendment was enacted precisely to protect the rights of those whose religious practices are not shared by the majority and may be viewed with hostility. The history of our free exercise doctrine amply demonstrates the harsh impact majoritarian rule has had on unpopular or emerging religious groups such as the Jehovah's Witnesses and the Amish. The compelling interest test reflects the First Amendment's mandate of preserving religious liberty to the fullest extent possible in a pluralistic society. For the Court to deem this command a "luxury" is to denigrate "[t]he very purpose of a Bill of Rights."

[JUSTICE O'CONNOR then upheld the denial of an exemption because Oregon had met the compelling state interest test with its overriding interest in preventing the physical harm caused by controlled substances. JUSTICES BLACKMUN, BRENNAN and MARSHALL concurred with O'CONNOR's identification of the compelling state interest test; they, however, believed the state had not met its burden because there was no evidence that religious peyote use harmed people.]

NOTES AND QUESTIONS

1.   Is Justice Scalia's opinion consistent with *Sherbert* and *Yoder*, or is Justice O'Connor correct that he misinterpreted years of settled Free Exercise jurisprudence? Does Justice O'Connor ignore the line of cases cited by Justice Scalia, ranging from *Reynolds* to *Prince, Braunfeld, Gillette, Lee, Roy,* and *Lyng*?

Based on his research in the justices' personal files, Professor Paul McGreal argues that a *Smith*-like test was percolating among the Justices long before *Smith* was decided. In reviewing a case about a woman who argued for an exemption from a picture on her driver's license because her religion forbade any graven images, for example, Chief Justice Burger expressed concern about the costs of allowing too many exemptions to government licensing laws. See Paul F. McGreal, The Unpublished Free Exercise Opinion in *Jensen v. Quaring*, 33 S. Ill. U. L.J. 1 (2008). McGreal describes the tension concerning *Sherbert* in the following manner:

Given the diversity of religions in the United States and the pervasiveness of the modern regulatory state, a wide array of state and federal laws arguably burden the free exercise of someone's religion. Consequently, several justices worried that the strict scrutiny approach applied in *Sherbert* licensed lower courts to run roughshod over state and federal laws in the name of free exercise. Because the government could be put to strict scrutiny for any law that substantially burdened free exercise, the *Sherbert* approach effectively made each believer a law unto herself. The question was whether the Court would put the brakes on this constitutional runaway train.

Paul McGreal, The Making of the Supreme Court's Free Exercise Clause Jurisprudence: Lessons from the Blackmun and Powell Papers in *Bowen v. Roy*, 34 S. Ill. U. L.J. 469, 471 (2010). Do you agree that *Sherbert* was a "constitutional runaway train"? Did *Smith* effectively put the brakes on *Sherbert*?

2. *Compelling State Interest.* What difference do the *Smith* and *Sherbert* standards make in specific cases? In Rhode Island, the Yangs belonged to the Hmong community, which prohibits any mutilation of the body, including autopsies. After their son, Neng Yang, died from an inexplicable seizure, a hospital resident requested the autopsy required by state law to "ensure that the cause of death was not attributable to some act or agent that posed a threat to the health, safety and welfare of the citizens of . . . Rhode Island." The medical examiner performed an autopsy, but could not determine the cause of death. The Yangs filed suit alleging that their free exercise rights were violated. Medical Examiner William Sturner replied that the health, safety, and welfare of Rhode Island residents were important state interests served by autopsies, which can prevent diseases from spreading across the state.

What should be the result be under *Sherbert* and *Smith*? Compare You Vang Yang v. Sturner, 728 F.Supp. 845 (D.R.I. 1990), where the district court ruled for the Yangs, concluding that the state had not met the compelling state interest test and that the statute was not the least restrictive alternative to meet the state's needs, with You Vang Yang v. Sturner, 750 F.Supp. 558 (D.R.I. 1990) (siding with the government). *Smith* was decided before the court's order issued; accordingly Judge Pettine "with deep regret" recalled the earlier opinion because the autopsy law was a neutral law of general applicability, and dismissed the case.

3. *Exemptions.* Are religious exemptions from general laws defensible? If so, who should award them, the Court or Congress? Is Justice Scalia correct that it is "inappropriate for judges to determine the centrality of religious beliefs"?

What arguments can you give for and against exemptions for religious believers? Professor Gedicks identifies five traditional justifications for exemptions: the text of the First Amendment, its history, transcendent consequences, preventing violence and persecution, and the "God is good" argument. See Frederick Mark Gedicks, An Unfirm Foundation: The

Regrettable Indefensibility of Religious Exemptions, 20 U. Ark. Little Rock L.J. 555, 560–66 (1998).

Professor McConnell's work is frequently cited for the textual and historical arguments; Justice Scalia cited it to support his conclusion that the Free Exercise Clause permits but does not compel exemptions. See *Smith*, 494 U.S. at 902; Michael McConnell, Accommodation of Religion, 1985 S. Ct. Rev. 1, 9; Michael McConnell, The Origins and Historical Understanding of Free Exercise of Religion, 103 Harv. L. Rev. 1409, 1415 (1990). Gedicks concludes that the First Amendment text is inconclusive, because it is as likely to prohibit discrimination against religions as to compel exemptions. Meanwhile, about the historical argument he concludes that the early cases, including *Reynolds*, did not grant exemptions. See also Philip Hamburger, A Constitutional Right of Religious Exemption: An Historical Perspective, 60 Geo. Wash. L. Rev. 915 (1992) (arguing that historical evidence supports *Smith*'s interpretation of free exercise); Ellis West, The Case Against a Right to Religion-Based Exemptions, 4 Notre Dame J. L. Ethics & Pub. Pol'y 591, 624 (1990); William P. Marshall, The Case Against the Constitutionally Compelled Free Exercise Exemption, 40 Case W. Res. L. Rev. 357 (1990); Marci A. Hamilton, God vs. the Gavel: Religion and the Rule of Law 219 (2005) (disagreeing with McConnell).

Under the transcendent consequences argument, religious people are entitled to exemptions because they face worse consequences (like hell, or the loss of salvation) than secular people. (This explains the difference between Thomas and Secular Thomas, supra.) Gedicks concludes that this argument is both over- and under-inclusive, because some religious people will fear the consequences of their actions less than other intense secular people. Finally, the "God is good" argument states that religion is a "uniquely valuable human activity" and so entitled to special exemption. Gedicks at 566 (citing John H. Garvey, All Things Being Equal, 1996 BYU L. Rev. 588). See also John Garvey, What Are Freedoms For? (1997). Gedicks rejects this last argument because of the many moral nonreligious people he has met.

Gedicks concludes that these five traditional grounds cannot justify exemptions, and that as a pragmatic matter they should not be allowed because they are inconsistent with our legal culture of equality. See Frederick Mark Gedicks, An Unfirm Foundation: The Regrettable Indefensibility of Religious Exemptions, 20 U. Ark. Little Rock L. J. 555 (1998); see also William P. Marshall, The Case Against the Constitutionally Compelled Free Exercise Exemption, 40 Case W. Res. 357 (1990). Does giving exemptions to religious believers violate the rule of law? Do you agree "as a society Americans have ignored the likely harms that can result from religious accommodation" and that courts have given exemptions without attention to their negative consequences? See Marci A. Hamilton, A Response to Professor Greenawalt, 30 Cardozo L. Rev. 1535, 1535 (2009). Can a business or a corporation have religious beliefs under the First Amendment? If so, are they entitled to exemptions?

4. *Oregon Post*-Smith. Oregon eventually recognized religious belief as a defense against prosecution for use of peyote, see Or. Rev. Stat. § 475.992. Should all religious use of drugs be exempt from prosecution or penalty? Congress may be more protective of religious freedom than the states or the Court. In the past, congressional legislation has provided exemptions that permit soldiers to wear religious headgear, 10 U.S.C. § 774; allow Native Americans to hunt bald and golden eagles for religious rituals, 16 U.S.C. § 668a; allowed churches to use sacramental wine during Prohibition, National Prohibition Act (Volstead Act) ch. 85, 41 Stat. 305 (1919) (repealed 1933); free churches from paying social security taxes, U.S.C. § 3121(w)(1); allow religious organizations to discriminate among employees on religious grounds, 42 U.S.C.A. § 2000e–1; allow ritual use of peyote, 42 U.S.C. § 1996; and allow conscientious objection to military service, 50 U.S.C. App. § 456(j) (1994). See also Christopher L. Eisgruber & Lawrence G. Sager, Why the Religious Freedom Restoration Act is Unconstitutional, 69 N.Y.U. L. Rev. 437, 459 (1994); Eugene Volokh, A Common-Law Model for Religious Exemptions, 46 UCLA L. Rev. 1465, 1472 (1999); Louis Fisher, Religious Liberty in America: Political Safeguards (2002). Moreover, in a little-known exemption to federal pension law, religious organizations may either follow the law or opt out. This means that religious employers, for example, do not have to pay pension insurance premiums. Moreover, although regular companies may not back out on benefit plans, churches may. Some pension money has gone to pay off church sexual abuse claims, which would be prohibited to employers governed by the regular pension law. See Mary Williams Walsh, Pensions in Peril Over Exemptions Tied to Churches, N.Y. Times, May 2, 2006, at A1. Is this fair? What are the competing policy reasons for this practice?

5. *Strict Scrutiny.* Both Justices Scalia and O'Connor refer to race and speech and compare free exercise protection to equal protection and free speech. How should religion be protected in comparison with those two constitutional rights? Should race, religion, and speech get heightened scrutiny by the courts? What should the nature of that scrutiny be? In equal protection cases, for example, the discriminatory impact of laws does not prove a constitutional violation; instead, a plaintiff must prove discriminatory intent. See Village of Arlington Heights v. Metropolitan Housing Dev. Corp., 429 U.S. 252 (1977). As Justice Scalia explains in *Smith*:

> But we have held that race-neutral laws that have the *effect* of disproportionately disadvantaging a particular racial group do not thereby become subject to compelling-interest analysis under the Equal Protection Clause, and we have held that generally applicable laws unconcerned with regulating speech that have the *effect* of interfering with speech do not thereby become subject to compelling-interest analysis under the First Amendment. Our conclusion that generally applicable, religion-neutral laws that have the effect of burdening a particular religious practice need

not be justified by a compelling governmental interest is the only approach compatible with these precedents.

494 U.S. at 886 n.3. Without the same standard, protection of religious freedom would become a "constitutional anomaly." Justice O'Connor disagreed with an intentional discrimination standard for religion because "laws neutral toward religion can coerce a person to violate his religious conscience or intrude upon his religious duties just as effectively as laws aimed at religion." Which argument is more persuasive?

Should race and religion have the same standards, while speech is treated differently? See Christopher L. Eisgruber & Lawrence G. Sager, The Vulnerability of Conscience: The Constitutional Basis for Protecting Religious Conduct, 61 U. Chi. L. Rev. 1245, 1251–52 (1997) (Under the Constitution, free speech is privileged, while race and religion are protected against discrimination. "A claim for constitutional privilege requires a showing of virtue or precedence, while a claim for constitutional protection requires a showing of vulnerability or victimization." Therefore free exercise should not be privileged but should, like race, be protected when it is vulnerable.).

Recall that Professor Gedicks mentioned "preventing violence and persecution" as one reason to award exemptions under the Free Exercise Clause. Should members of racial minorities receive exemptions from neutral and general laws because they have confronted violence and persecution? See Frederick Mark Gedicks, An Unfirm Foundation: The Regrettable Indefensibility of Religious Exemptions, 20 U. Ark. Little Rock L.J. 555 (1998) (comparison with race cases is an additional reason not to grant exemptions).

Although *Smith* set a standard upholding neutral laws of general applicability, it also suggested that the application of strict scrutiny remains appropriate in three circumstances: first, if the law is not neutral and of general applicability; second, if the challenged law contains some exemptions, but exemptions are denied to cases of religious hardship; and third, in so-called "hybrid" situations, when First Amendment claims are joined with another constitutional right. In all three circumstances, the courts hold the government to the compelling state interest test. These three exceptions have contributed extensive controversy about *Smith's* application in the lower courts and are examined in detail in the following three notes.

6.   *Neutral Laws of General Applicability.* Although critics of *Smith* worried that its test could not protect free exercise, *Lukumi* demonstrated that some laws (namely, Florida's ban on animal sacrifice) are neither neutral nor general and so violate the Free Exercise Clause. Recall that in *Lukumi*, in Chapter 1, the Court concluded that because "suppression of the central element of the Santeria worship service was the object of the ordinances," the Hialeah ordinances violated the Free Exercise Clause. See Church of the Lukumi Babalu Aye, Inc. v. City of Hialeah, 508 U.S. 520, 534 (1993).

In his majority opinion in *Lukumi*, Justice Kennedy wrote that laws that are not neutral or general "must be justified by a compelling governmental interest and must be narrowly tailored to advance that interest." Id. at 531. Strict scrutiny survives *Smith*.

The difficult question becomes, what do *neutral* and *general* mean? According to Justice Kennedy, "If the object of a law is to infringe upon or restrict practices because of their religious motivation, the law is not neutral." Id. at 533. Because Santeria animal sacrifice was targeted by the Hialeah ordinances (while other killing of animals, including hunting, fishing, slaughter of animals for food and euthanasia, was permitted), the law was not neutral. In defining neutrality, Justice Kennedy looked for guidance to the Equal Protection standards, noting that hostility toward Santeria characterized the local hearings and that such animus indicates lack of neutrality.

Although failing to provide an explicit definition of general applicability, Justice Kennedy observed that the animal sacrifice ordinances were under-inclusive toward their goals of protecting public health and preventing cruelty to animals. The acts failed to protect most other animals from killing and did not regulate other killing of animals to make sure that the public's health interest was protected. Such under-inclusiveness indicated that the laws were not of general applicability.

In his concurrence in *Lukumi*, Justice Scalia wrote that, in contrast to Kennedy, he did not distinguish between "neutral" and "general" because the terms "substantially overlap." Scalia then added:

> In my view, the defect of lack of neutrality applies primarily to those laws that *by their terms* impose disabilities on the basis of religion (e.g., a law excluding members of a certain sect from public benefits, cf. *McDaniel v. Paty*, 435 U.S. 618 (1978)), see *Bowen v. Roy*, 476 U.S. 693 (1986) (opinion of Burger, C.J.); whereas the defect of lack of general applicability applies primarily to those laws which, though neutral in their terms, through their design, construction, or enforcement target the practices of a particular religion for discriminatory treatment, see *Fowler v. Rhode Island*, 345 U.S. 67 (1953). But certainly a law that is not of general applicability (in the sense I have described) can be considered "nonneutral"; and certainly no law that is nonneutral (in the relevant sense) can be thought to be of general applicability.

Id. at 557–58. For that reason, he joined Justice Kennedy's analysis of neutral and general applicability except for the portion that analyzed the intent of the state actors. "The First Amendment does not refer to the purposes for which legislators enact laws, but to the effects of the laws enacted." Id. at 558.

What is the difference between Justice Kennedy's and Justice Scalia's definitions of neutral laws of general applicability? Use their tests to determine if the following laws are neutral and general—or not. What standard of scrutiny should the Court employ in each case?

a. *Social Security Numbers and Drivers' Licenses.* Recall that in a pre-*Smith* case, Bowen v. Roy, 476 U.S. 693 (1986), the Court ruled that a statutory requirement that the government use a Social Security number in administering a food stamp program did not violate the free exercise rights of the parents of a Native American child who believed the numbers would rob their daughter's spirit. Some states require a Social Security number in order to qualify for a driver's license. Should these laws be upheld against free exercise challenges? Members of the March of Ides' Foundation, for example, object to providing Social Security numbers because the acquisition of such numbers probably condemns the member to death. They also fear that an omnipotent state will usurp God and destroy those who do not obey the state. They base this belief upon the New Testament's Book of Revelations. See Brunson v. Department of Motor Vehicles, 72 Cal.App.4th 1251, 85 Cal.Rptr.2d 710 (1999). Scott McDonald believes that a Social Security number is a precursor to, or is itself, the "Mark of the Beast" referred to in the Book of Revelation, and that he is not to accept such a mark. He taught his sons to believe this, and they have never been issued Social Security numbers. See McDonald v. Alabama Dep't of Public Safety, 756 So.2d 880 (Ala. Civ. App. 1999). Should Brunson and the McDonalds receive drivers' licenses without having Social Security numbers?

b. *Autopsies.* Kickapoo Tribe member Norma Rodriguez died suddenly of unexplained causes. After the decedent's mother told Justice of the Peace Martha Chacon "somebody killed her, I know somebody killed her," Chacon ordered an autopsy. The body had been removed from the state office and buried; Chacon ordered disinterment and autopsy. Raul Garza, the Tribe's chief, insisted that no autopsy be done because the Tribe believes autopsy and disruption of a grave damage the spirit of the deceased and negatively affect the family. Which side should prevail? See Kickapoo Traditional Tribe of Texas v. Chacon, 46 F.Supp.2d 644 (W.D. Tex. 1999).

c. *Public Accommodations.* An engaged same-sex couple visited Masterpiece Cakeshop to order a cake for their upcoming wedding reception. The owner of the store informed the couple that because of his religious beliefs, it was against the shop's policy to provide baked goods to customers who wished to use them to celebrate same-sex marriages. The couple sued the shop under Colorado's Anti-Discrimination Act, which prohibits public accommodations (such as bakeries) from denying services on the basis of factors such as race, sex, marital status, or sexual orientation. The Colorado Court of Appeals held in favor of the couple, declining to find that Masterpiece Cakeshop's religious position excused its violation of the Anti-Discrimination Act. See Craig v. Masterpiece Cakeshop, 370 P.3d 272 (Colo. App. 2015). Is Colorado's Anti-Discrimination Act a neutral law of general applicability?

d.   *Ritual Circumcision.* As part of ritual circumcision, some Orthodox Jews perform Metzitzah B'peh (MBP), which places direct oral suction on the circumcision wound. New York City health officials determined that MBP spreads the herpes virus; some New York infants died from the infection. After attempting an educational program about MBP's risks, city officials passed a regulation prohibiting MBP without obtaining informed consent from one of the infant's parents. Is the circumcision law a neutral law of general applicability? See Central Rabbinical Congress of U.S. & Canada v. New York City Dep't of Health & Mental Hygiene, 763 F.3d 183 (2d Cir. 2014) (regulation is neither neutral nor generally applicable and strict scrutiny applies). Do you agree with the Second Circuit that the MBP regulation is not neutral because it "purposefully and exclusively targets a religious practice for special burdens"? Id. at 186. That the regulation is not generally applicable because "it is underinclusive in relation to its asserted secular goals: the Regulation pertains to religious conduct associated with a small percentage of HSV infection cases among infants, while leaving secular conduct associated with a larger percentage of such infection unaddressed"? Id.

7.   *Individualized Exemptions. Smith* said that the *Sherbert* test "was developed in a context that lent itself to individualized governmental assessment of the reasons for the relevant conduct. . . . [O]ur decisions in the unemployment cases stand for the proposition that where the State has in place a system of individual exemptions, it may not refuse to extend that system to cases of 'religious hardship' without compelling reason." *Smith,* 494 U.S. at 884. Do the following cases invite strict scrutiny because they exempt non-religious persons but not religious?

a.   *Beards.* The Newark Police Department forbids police officers to wear beards, but exempts officers with medical conditions from the regulation. Two Sunni Muslims who believe the Qur'an requires them to wear beards were disciplined and told they might be required to leave the department. The Department argued that the Americans with Disabilities Act was the reason for the medical exemption. Who should win? Why? See Fraternal Order of Police v. City of Newark, 170

F.3d 359 (3d Cir. 1999) (Alito, J.) (finding free exercise violation in allowing medical but not religious exemption).

b. *Zoning.* Grace United Methodist Church sought to operate a daycare center on its land in the City of Cheyenne, which is zoned for residential use with limited exceptions for churches, schools, and other similar uses. The zoning ordinance prohibits an entity from operating a day care with twelve children or more. The City of Cheyenne denied Grace United a license to operate the day care. Grace United argued it was entitled to an exception because secular exceptions to the zoning ordinance were already granted on a "case-by-case" basis. The City contended that while exceptions to the zoning ordinance generally were sometimes granted, no exceptions to the specific day care prohibition in question were granted to anyone—secular or religious. See Grace United Methodist Church v. City of Cheyenne, 451 F.3d 643 (10th Cir. 2006) (finding in favor of the City of Cheyenne; " . . . we have already refused to interpret *Smith* as standing for the proposition that a secular exemption automatically creates a claim for a religious exemption.").

c. *Black Bears.* Dennis Black Hawk is a Native American who conducts ceremonies with black bears, who are believed to be sacred and to give spiritual strength. Hair shed by the bears is used in Native American medicine bags. The Pennsylvania Game Code requires ownership permits for owners of black bears. Under the statute, the Game Commission may waive the annual permit fee of $200 for hardship or extraordinary circumstances that are consistent with sound game or wildlife management. Excluded from the permit fee by statute are public zoological gardens that receive government grants or appropriations, private zoological parks or gardens that are open to the public and that are accredited by the American Association of Zoological Parks, and nationally recognized circuses. The Commission also does not charge a fee for educational exhibits of wildlife. Black Hawk had trouble raising the money for the fee, and asked for an exemption because he owned the bears for religious reasons. His request was denied. Without a permit, he could be prosecuted and the bears confiscated. Should the prosecution be upheld? See Black Hawk v. Commonwealth, 225 F.Supp.2d 465 (M.D. Pa. 2002), aff'd by Blackhawk v. Pennsylvania, 381 F.3d 202 (3d Cir. 2004) (Alito, J.) (law not neutral and generally applicable). See also Horen v. Commonwealth, 23 Va.App. 735, 479 S.E.2d 553 (1997) (regulation about wild bird parts was not religiously neutral toward Native American possession of owl parts).

8. *Hybrids.* Justice Scalia's opinion in *Smith* noted strict scrutiny is appropriate in so-called "hybrid" situations, when the free exercise right is combined with another constitutional right. In *Lukumi*, Justice Souter argued that the hybrid was "ultimately untenable":

> Though *Smith* sought to distinguish the free-exercise cases in which the Court mandated exemptions from secular laws of general application, I am not persuaded. *Wisconsin v. Yoder*, and *Cantwell v. Connecticut*, according to *Smith*, were not true free-exercise cases but "hybrid[s]" involving "the Free Exercise Clause in conjunction with other constitutional protections, such as freedom of speech and of the press, or the right of parents . . . to direct the education of their children." Neither opinion, however, leaves any doubt that "fundamental claims of religious freedom [were] at stake." And the distinction *Smith* draws strikes me as ultimately untenable. If a hybrid claim is simply one in which another constitutional right is implicated, then the hybrid exception would probably be so vast as to swallow the *Smith* rule, and, indeed, the hybrid exception would cover the situation exemplified by *Smith*, since free speech and associational rights are certainly implicated in the peyote ritual. But if a hybrid claim is one in which a litigant would actually obtain an exemption from a formally neutral, generally applicable law under another constitutional provision, then there would have been no reason for the Court in what *Smith* calls the hybrid cases to have mentioned the Free Exercise Clause at all.

508 U.S. at 566–67. Is the hybrid untenable? Does it really mean that "two loser constitutional claims = one winner constitutional claim"? See William L. Esser IV, Note, Religious Hybrids in the Lower Courts: Free Exercise Plus or Constitutional Smoke Screen?, 74 Notre Dame L. Rev. 211, 242 (1998).

Since *Smith* was decided, the circuit courts have taken three approaches to the hybrid theory of religious freedom: the dicta, independent claim, and colorable claim approaches. The Second, Third, and Sixth Circuits have refused to adopt the hybrid theory, treating it as dicta, as Justice Souter suggested. The First and D.C. Circuits have adopted the independent claim approach, which holds that a hybrid can succeed only if an independently viable constitutional claim is part of the hybrid. The Ninth and Tenth Circuits require that the related constitutional claim have a colorable or probable chance of success. Ryan S. Rummage, In Combination: Using Hybrid Rights to Expand Religious Liberty, 64 Emory L.J. 1175, 1189–97 (2015). The Supreme Court has never clarified the hybrid theory.

Identify the hybrid presented in the following sets of facts. Should these cases qualify for strict scrutiny? If there were no hybrid, would there be a free exercise violation in these cases?

   a. A veterinary student requested an alternative to the Operative Practice class because it required healthy animals to be anesthetized, operated on and killed. The Veterinary College developed an alternative curriculum, to which the student objected as well. She withdrew from the class, forcing her withdrawal from school. See Kissinger v. Ohio State Univ., 5 F.3d 177 (6th Cir. 1993).

b. A nurse consultant in the State Department of Public Health interviewed patients in their homes in order to collect the data needed for her job. She was suspended after visiting the home of a gay couple, whom she told "although God created us and loves us, He doesn't like the homosexual lifestyle." See Knight v. Connecticut Dep't of Pub. Health, 275 F.3d 156 (2d Cir. 2001).

c. High school students attended a mandatory assembly about AIDS. The speaker gave sexually explicit monologues and performed sexually suggestive skits. She

   1) told the students that they were going to have a "group sexual experience, with audience participation";

   2) used profane, lewd and lascivious language to describe body parts and excretory functions;

   3) advocated and approved oral sex, masturbation, homosexual sexual activity and condom use during promiscuous premarital sex;

   4) simulated masturbation;

   5) characterized the loose pants worn by one minor as "erection wear";

   6) referred to being in "deep sh—" after anal sex;

   7) had a male minor lick an oversized condom with her, after which she had a female minor pull it over the male minor's entire head and blow it up;

   8) encouraged a male minor to display his "orgasm face" with her for the camera;

   9) informed a male minor that he was not having enough orgasms;

   10) closely inspected a minor and told him he had a "nice butt"; and

   11) made eighteen references to orgasms, six references to male genitals, and eight references to female genitals.

The parents filed suit, complaining that the show violated their constitutional rights. See Brown v. Hot, Sexy and Safer Productions, 68 F.3d 525, 529 (1st Cir. 1995).

Massachusetts parents sued because they did not receive advance notice and exemption from their children's elementary school's use of books presenting gay families in a favorable light. See Parker v. Hurley, 514 F.3d 87 (1st Cir.

2008), cert. denied, 129 S.Ct. 56 (2008). Where is the hybrid? Is it relevant that the state had a statute giving parents notice and exemption from classes involving human sexuality, but did not give notice to the parents because the gay family materials involved diversity and not sexuality?

d.   Annie was homeschooled by her parents for religious reasons. When she reached seventh grade, her parents asked that she be enrolled as a part-time student in several public school classes (music, science and foreign language) that they could not duplicate. The school refused. The school district policy permitted full-time enrollment only because part-time students could not be counted for state financial aid purposes. See Swanson v. Guthrie Ind. Sch. Dist. No. I–L, 135 F.3d 694 (10th Cir. 1998). Where is the hybrid in religious parents' argument that compliance with a state home schooling law requiring them to submit their children's educational schedule and samples of their work violated their constitutional rights? See Combs v. Homer-Center School Dist., 540 F.3d 231 (3d Cir. 2008).

e.   Christina Axson-Flynn, a Mormon, enrolled in the University of Utah's Actor Training Program. She told the directors that she would not take off her clothes, use the word "fuck" or take the Lord's name in vain. As part of a class exercise performing the play "The Quadrangle," Axson-Flynn refused to use the words "goddam" and "fucking." Although the professors scolded Axson-Flynn, on several occasions they allowed her to use substitute words without penalty. At her end-of-semester review, however, the directors told her that if she wanted to continue in the program she would have to modify her values. See Axson-Flynn v. Johnson, 356 F.3d 1277 (10th Cir. 2004).

f.   Donald Miller refused to divulge his Social Security number on his application to renew his driver's license because he believes that revealing the number is "tantamount to a sin." The Department of Motor Vehicles denied his application, and now he cannot drive legally anywhere in the United States. See Miller v. Reed, 176 F.3d 1202, 1204 (9th Cir. 1999).

g.   Gregory Green belongs to The Church of the Living God The Pillar and Ground of the Truth, which prohibits photographs as a form of idolatry. The City of Philadelphia requires pictures for gun permits. Although originally there were some exceptions to the statutory requirement, after 2001 the Gun Permit unit did not grant any exemptions. See Green v. Philadelphia, No. Civ.A. 03–1476, 2004 WL 1170531 (E.D. Pa. 2004). Should Green get his exemption?

h.   Evangelical Christian Plaintiffs Henderson and Phillips wanted to sell t-shirts on the National Mall in Washington, D.C., an activity that was prohibited by a National Park Service regulation forbidding commercial transactions from the Mall. Henderson v. Kennedy, 253 F.3d 12, 13 (D.C. Cir. 2001).

9.   Sherbert *or* Smith? Nurse worked alternating Saturdays and Sundays at Hospital. Then she was rebaptized as a Seventh Day Adventist and requested Saturdays off. Hospital said she could keep working if she found other nurses to take her Saturday shifts. Hospital has a policy that dismisses employees after ten instances of absenteeism. Absenteeism is defined as either one missed day or five instances of tardiness. In 2010, Nurse was absent 5 times (2 for religious reasons) and tardy 23 times. The next year, she was tardy 50 times. The tardiness was usually due to trouble with child care. Hospital issued warnings to Nurse on these occasions. Finally, in 2012, Nurse had 58 tardies and one absence when her supervisor informed her that she would be fired after either one more absence or two tardies. Nurse missed the next Saturday and was fired. Hospital argued that Nurse was not entitled to unemployment compensation because she was fired for misconduct. A state unemployment law judge agreed. Were Nurse's free exercise rights violated? Which precedent applies, *Sherbert* or *Smith*? See Nyaboga v. Evangelical Lutheran Good Samaritan Soc., 2012 WL 3641017, *2 (Minn.App. Aug. 27, 2012) (under *Sherbert*, the state cannot force an applicant to choose between religious beliefs and employment; despite tardiness, "the conduct that triggered her discharge was an absence for religious reasons" and free exercise was violated.).

10.   *Joint Resolution on American Indian Religious Freedom.* Congress passed the 1978 Joint Resolution on American Indian Religious Freedom (AIRFA) based on its findings that many federal policies, especially environmental ones, abridged the free exercise of religion of Native Americans. Worship and access to sacred sites and objects, for example, were often limited by government construction projects that did not consider the impact on religion. Federal agencies were deemed too ignorant of American Indian religious practices and were ordered to attend to them in enacting their policies. Henceforth, Congress declared:

> it shall be the policy of the United States to protect and preserve for American Indians their inherent right of freedom to believe, express, and exercise the traditional religions of the American Indian, Eskimo, Aleut, and Native Hawaiians, including but not limited to access to sites, use and possession of sacred objects, and the freedom to worship through ceremonials and traditional rites.

42 U.S.C. § 1996 (2003).

Does the language of AIRFA suggest that Smith should have won the peyote case? Does AIRFA mandate a compelling state interest test as RFRA did? If so, why was AIRFA not applied in *Smith*? See Sharon O'Brien, A Legal Analysis of the American Indian Religious Freedom Act, in Christopher Vecsey, ed., Handbook of American Indian Religious Freedom 29 (1991) (Congress did not want to exempt American Indians from existing law but only wanted to provide them the same First Amendment protections as other citizens); 124 Cong. Rec. 21444 (July 18, 1978) (expressing fears that special benefits for Native American religions violate the Establishment Clause). The bill's sponsor, Representative Morris Udall, acknowledged on the floor of the House that "it is not the intent of my bill to wipe out laws passed for the benefit of the general public or to confer special religious rights on Indians." 124 Cong. Rec. 21444 (July 18, 1978). What else could AIRFA do?

After AIRFA's passage, a Jimmy Carter Administration task force of nine federal agencies sent a thirty-seven page report to Congress that identified 522 agency actions that burdened Native American religious freedom. See Rita Sabina Mandosa, Another Promise Broken, Fed. Bar News & J. (February 1993); Barbara Falcone, Legal Protections (or the Lack of Thereof) of American Indian Sacred Religious Sites, Fed. Bar News & J. (September 1994); Ann E. Beeson, Dances With Justice: Peyotism in the Courts, 41 Emory L.J. 1121, 1162–63 (1992). There was little follow-up on those recommendations, however. In litigation after the Act's passage, the federal courts interpreted it narrowly, often concluding that the government's interest overrode religious freedom. In *Bowen v. Roy*, the Social Security case, supra, the government's interests were upheld over the Native Americans' spiritual opposition to Social Security numbers, despite the existence of the Act. Then in Lyng v. Northwest Indian Cemetery Protective Ass'n, 485 U.S. 439 (1988), the United States Forest Service planned to build roads and allow timber harvesting in sections of land that were important sacred sites for three tribes of Native Americans. Following *Bowen*, Justice O'Connor upheld the government's interest against a free exercise claim, stating:

> Even if we assume that we should accept the Ninth Circuit's prediction, according to which the G–O road [a road linking two California towns, Gasquet and Orleans] will "virtually destroy the . . . Indians' ability to practice their religion," the Constitution simply does not provide a principle that could justify upholding respondents' legal claims. However much we might wish that it were otherwise, government simply could not operate if it were required to satisfy every citizen's religious needs and desires. . . . The First Amendment must apply to all citizens alike, and it can give to none of them a veto over public programs that do not prohibit the free exercise of religion. . . . Whatever rights the Indians may have to the use of the area, however, those rights do not divest the Government of its right to use what is, after all, *its* land.

Id. at 451–53.

Justice O'Connor noted in *Lyng* that AIRFA did not create any enforceable rights. Although AIRFA was not mentioned in the *Smith* majority opinions and concurrence, Justice Blackmun's dissent observed that even though the Act did not create enforceable rights: "this Court must scrupulously apply its free exercise analysis to the religious claims of Native Americans, however unorthodox they may be. Otherwise, both the First Amendment and the stated policy of Congress will offer to Native Americans merely an unfulfilled and hollow promise." *Smith*, 494 U.S. at 921.

Congressman Morris Udall, the sponsor of AIRFA, observed that the bill had "no teeth." See Sequoyah v. T.V.A., 620 F.2d 1159 (6th Cir. 1980) (Cherokee Indians failed to show the centrality and indispensability of the Little Tennessee River to Cherokee religious ceremonies and practices); Badoni v. Higginson, 638 F.2d 172 (10th Cir. 1980) (impounding water to form Lake Powell did not deny Navajo Indians access to a sacred prayer spot and allowing tourists to visit Rainbow Bridge did not desecrate the sacred nature of the prayer spot or prevent Native Americans from conducting religious ceremonies at the prayer spot); and Wilson v. Block, 708 F.2d 735 (D.C. Cir. 1983) (decision to develop and expand a government-owned ski area did not deny Navajo and Hopi Indian tribes access to the San Francisco Peaks or hinder their ability to gather sacred objects or perform ceremonies). Why did Congress not do more to protect Native American religious freedom? Is prior discrimination against Native American religion a good reason to apply strict scrutiny to every governmental action that affects their religious practices?

B. STATUTORY EXEMPTIONS: RFRA

Smith was a controversial case that raised significant questions about the interpretation of the Free Exercise Clause. The opinion immediately attracted extensive critical commentary from academic commentators who preferred the *Sherbert* exemption model. See Michael W. McConnell, Free Exercise Revisionism and the Smith Decision, 57 U. Chi. L. Rev. 1109 (1990); Douglas Laycock, The Remnants of Free Exercise, 1990 Sup. Ct. Rev. 1; but see William P. Marshall, In Defense of Smith and Free Exercise Revisionism, 58 U. Chi. L. Rev. 308 (1991). Critics of *Smith* argued that *Sherbert* was the sole correct interpretation of free exercise and was wrongly demolished by Justice Scalia. Defenders of *Smith* identified "two competing strands of thought in religious free exercise cases." The "predominant" approach was the line of cases upholding neutral laws including *Reynolds* (polygamy), *Lee* (Social Security), *Gillette* (military conscription laws), *Braunfeld* (Sunday closing laws), *Roy* (Social Security identification requirements), *Lyng* (federal oversight of federal land), *Shabazz* (prison regulations), and *Swaggart* (state taxation of sales by religious organizations). The second line included *Sherbert*, the other unemployment compensation cases, and *Yoder*. See Marci A. Hamilton, *Employment Division v. Smith* at the Supreme Court: The Justices, the Litigants and the Doctrinal Discourse, 32 Cardozo L. Rev. 1671, 1694

(2011). If there were two lines of free exercise cases, why did so many academics complain that *Smith* was wrongly decided?

The debate was much more than academic. Congress, with the support of a broad array of religious groups, in 1993 passed the Religious Freedom Restoration Act (RFRA), in an attempt to reinstate the compelling state interest test whenever religion was substantially burdened by a state or federal government. As Professors Sager and Eisgruber explain:

> Self-congratulatory hoopla is the norm in Washington, but the trumpets heralding RFRA's enactment were unusual. The Act sailed through both houses of Congress, passing unanimously in the House of Representatives and drawing only three votes in opposition in the Senate. President Clinton declared that the signing ceremony had a "majestic quality" because the new law affirmed "the historic role that people of faith have played in the history of this country and the constitutional protections those who profess and express their faith have always demanded and cherished." Vice President Al Gore avowed that "the Religious Freedom Restoration Act is something that all Americans can support" and pronounced it "one of the most important steps to reaffirm religious freedom in my lifetime." The *New York Times* gushed that "[t]he Religious Freedom Restoration Act reasserts a broadly accepted American concept of giving wide latitude to religious practices that many might regard as odd or unconventional."

Christopher L. Eisgruber & Lawrence G. Sager, Why the Religious Freedom Restoration Act Is Unconstitutional, 69 N.Y.U. L. Rev. 437, 438 (1994).

The text of RFRA specifically addressed *Smith, Sherbert,* and *Yoder:*

(1) The framers of the Constitution, recognizing free exercise of religion as an unalienable right, secured its protection in the First Amendment to the Constitution;

(2) laws "neutral" toward religion may burden religious exercise as surely as laws intended to interfere with religious exercise;

(3) governments should not substantially burden religious exercise without compelling justification;

(4) in Employment Division v. Smith, 494 U.S. 872 (1990), the Supreme Court virtually eliminated the requirement that the government justify burdens on religious exercise imposed by laws neutral toward religion; and

(5) the compelling interest test as set forth in prior Federal court rulings is a workable test for striking sensible

balances between religious liberty and competing prior governmental interests.

42 U.S.C. § 2000bb(a). The Act's stated purposes were:

(1) to restore the compelling interest test as set forth in Sherbert v. Verner, 374 U.S. 398 (1963) and Wisconsin v. Yoder, 406 U.S. 205 (1972) and to guarantee its application in all cases where free exercise of religion is substantially burdened; and

(2) to provide a claim or defense to persons whose religious exercise is substantially burdened by government.

Id. § 2000bb(b). RFRA prohibited both state and federal governments from substantially burdening a person's exercise of religion, even if the burden resulted from a rule of general applicability, unless the government could demonstrate that the burden "(1) is in furtherance of a compelling governmental interest; and (2) is the least restrictive means of furthering that compelling governmental interest." Id. § 2000bb–1(a)(b).

RFRA applied to all federal and state law. Id. § 2000bb–3(a). In City of Boerne v. Flores, 521 U.S. 507 (1997), however, the Court ruled that RFRA could not be applied to the states because Congress lacked the power to pass the Act under Section 5 of the Fourteenth Amendment. The Act was not congruent or proportional with the problem of religious discrimination and so was beyond Congress' Fourteenth Amendment powers. "In contrast to the record which confronted Congress and the Judiciary in the voting rights cases," the Court observed, "RFRA's legislative record lacks examples of modern instances of generally applicable laws passed because of religious bigotry." *Boerne*, 521 U.S. at 530. The Court explained why applying strict scrutiny to state governments intruded on the states' sovereignty:

Claims that a law substantially burdens someone's exercise of religion will often be difficult to contest. Requiring a State to demonstrate a compelling interest and show that it has adopted the least restrictive means of achieving that interest is the most demanding test known to constitutional law. If "'compelling interest' really means what it says, ... many laws will not meet the test. [The test] would open the prospect of constitutionally required religious exemptions from civic obligations of almost every conceivable kind." Laws valid under *Smith* would fall under RFRA without regard to whether they had the object of stifling or punishing free exercise. We make these observations not to reargue the position of the majority in *Smith* but to illustrate the substantive alteration of its holding attempted by RFRA. Even assuming RFRA would be interpreted in effect to mandate some lesser test, say one equivalent to intermediate scrutiny,

> the statute nevertheless would require searching judicial
> scrutiny of state law with the attendant likelihood of
> invalidation. This is a considerable congressional intrusion
> into the States' traditional prerogatives and general authority
> to regulate for the health and welfare of their citizens.

Boerne, 521 U.S. at 534. Hence, post-*Boerne*, state governments are
held to the *Smith* standard in Free Exercise cases.

Many states, however, enacted state RFRAs to hold state
governments to the compelling state interest test. Therefore, the federal
and state governments may be held to the *Smith* standard in Free
Exercise cases and to the compelling state interest/least restrictive
means test for statutory claims. Because plaintiffs frequently raise both
types of challenges to a law, a court in one case may apply *Smith*, the
exceptions to *Smith* that invoke strict scrutiny, and the statutory
compelling state interest test to the same set of facts.

RFRA still applies to the federal government. See Gonzales v. O
Centro Espirita Beneficente Uniao do Vegetal, 546 U.S. 418 (2006). In
O Centro, a Brazilian religion, O Centro Espirita Beneficente Uniao do
Vegetal, sued the federal government under RFRA to challenge its
interference with the church's use of the drug *hoasca* as a sacrament.
Usage of *hoasca* is prohibited by the Controlled Substances Act, having
been found by Congress to be unsafe and in violation of an international
treaty when imported or distributed. If O Centro had sued under the
First Amendment as interpreted by *Smith*, what result would you
predict?

Analyzing O Centro's claim under RFRA, the Court unanimously
held that O Centro was entitled to an exemption from the Controlled
Substances Act's prohibition on *hoasca*. Specifically, the Court found
that the government had not met its burden of demonstrating that the
prohibition on *hoasca* use for religious purposes served a compelling
government interest, having failed to submit sufficient evidence of
health and safety risks associated with *hoasca* or the need for
compliance with an international treaty.

Does RFRA unfairly privilege religion over non-religion by giving
religion a "trump card"? Why does O Centro receive an exemption for
hoasca while cancer patients do not have a legal right to use marijuana
to relieve the discomfort of chemotherapy? See Richard Dawkins, The
God Delusion 22 (2006) ("Imagine members of an art appreciation
society pleading in court that they 'believe' they need a hallucinogenic
drug in order to enhance their understanding of Impressionist or
Surrealist paintings. Yet, when a church claims an equivalent need, it
is backed by the highest court in the land. Such is the power of religion
as a talisman.").

At the oral argument in *O Centro*, after the Deputy Solicitor
General argued that "making an exception (beyond peyote) under the

Controlled Substances Act, would 'turn over to 700 District judges' the judgment about enforcing federal drug law, Justice David H. Souter retorted: 'That's exactly what the Act does.' Justice O'Connor chimed in that Congress, in enacting RFRA, 'did seem to indicate that the courts are supposed to examine each instance.'" After the government's lawyer warned that administrative procedures, not judges, were best suited to remove drugs from Schedule I, Justice Scalia "immediately shot back: 'RFRA overrides all of that. It says there can be an exception to all federal statutes where there is a religious objection and a court makes a finding there can be an exception.'" See Lyle Denniston, Herbal Tea Case: A Government Loss?, Nov. 1, 2005, http://www.scotus blog.com/2005/11/herbal-tea-case-a-government-loss/.

Is it unwise to leave so many decisions about federal drug laws in the hands of the courts? Should the courts be allowed to make decisions granting citizens exemptions from laws regulating dangerous drugs when they have no idea how dangerous the drugs are? Is the difference between peyote and *hoasca* that much more is known about peyote because of its long history of use in the United States? Did the Supreme Court really understand the health dangers of *hoasca* when it ruled in favor of O Centro? See Marci A. Hamilton, A Response to Professor Greenawalt, 30 Cardozo L. Rev. 1535, 1537–39 (2009) ("Because Congress had never considered whether to make use of DMT an exception to the Controlled Substances Act for religious purposes, the federal government had no studies or other sources of information regarding this particular drug.").

Who would be likely to file a lawsuit arguing that RFRA is unconstitutional as applied to the federal government? Who would have standing to do so? Are you persuaded that RFRA is necessary to protect religious freedom? Or does it give religious believers unfair advantages over non-religious citizens and the opportunity to become a law unto themselves?

Should RFRA protections extend from individuals and churches to businesses and other entities? In the following case, for-profit corporations challenged the contraceptive mandate of the Affordable Care Act under RFRA.

Burwell v. Hobby Lobby Stores, Inc.

Supreme Court of the United States, 2014.
134 S.Ct. 2751, 189 L.Ed.2d 675.

■ ALITO, J., delivered the opinion of the Court, in which ROBERTS C.J., and SCALIA, KENNEDY, and THOMAS, JJ., joined. KENNEDY, J., filed a concurring opinion. GINSBURG, J., filed a dissenting opinion, in which SOTOMAYOR, J., joined, and in which BREYER and KAGAN, JJ., joined as to all but Part III-C-1. BREYER and KAGAN, JJ., filed a dissenting opinion.

■ JUSTICE ALITO delivered the opinion of the Court.

We must decide in these cases whether the Religious Freedom Restoration Act of 1993 (RFRA) permits the United States Department of Health and Human Services (HHS) to demand that three closely held corporations provide health-insurance coverage for methods of contraception that violate the sincerely held religious beliefs of the companies' owners. We hold that the regulations that impose this obligation violate RFRA, which prohibits the Federal Government from taking any action that substantially burdens the exercise of religion unless that action constitutes the least restrictive means of serving a compelling government interest.

In holding that the HHS mandate is unlawful, we reject HHS's argument that the owners of the companies forfeited all RFRA protection when they decided to organize their businesses as corporations rather than sole proprietorships or general partnerships. The plain terms of RFRA make it perfectly clear that Congress did not discriminate in this way against men and women who wish to run their businesses as for-profit corporations in the manner required by their religious beliefs.

Since RFRA applies in these cases, we must decide whether the challenged HHS regulations substantially burden the exercise of religion, and we hold that they do. The owners of the businesses have religious objections to abortion, and according to their religious beliefs the four contraceptive methods at issue are abortifacients. If the owners comply with the HHS mandate, they believe they will be facilitating abortions, and if they do not comply, they will pay a very heavy price—as much as $1.3 million per day, or about $475 million per year, in the case of one of the companies. If these consequences do not amount to a substantial burden, it is hard to see what would.

Under RFRA, a Government action that imposes a substantial burden on religious exercise must serve a compelling government interest, and we assume that the HHS regulations satisfy this requirement. But in order for the HHS mandate to be sustained, it must also constitute the least restrictive means of serving that interest, and the mandate plainly fails that test. There are other ways in which Congress or HHS could equally ensure that every woman has cost-free access to the particular contraceptives at issue here and, indeed, to all FDA-approved contraceptives.

In fact, HHS has already devised and implemented a system that seeks to respect the religious liberty of religious nonprofit corporations while ensuring that the employees of these entities have precisely the same access to all FDA-approved contraceptives as employees of companies whose owners have no religious objections to providing such coverage. The employees of these religious nonprofit corporations still have access to insurance coverage without cost sharing for all FDA-approved contraceptives; and according to HHS, this system imposes no net economic burden on the insurance companies that are required to provide or secure the coverage.

Although HHS has made this system available to religious nonprofits that have religious objections to the contraceptive mandate, HHS has provided no reason why the same system cannot be made available when the owners of for-profit corporations have similar religious objections. We therefore conclude that this system constitutes an alternative that achieves all of the Government's aims while providing greater respect for religious liberty. And under RFRA, that conclusion means that enforcement of the HHS contraceptive mandate against the objecting parties in these cases is unlawful.

As this description of our reasoning shows, our holding is very specific. We do not hold, as the principal dissent alleges, that for-profit corporations and other commercial enterprises can "opt out of any law (saving only tax laws) they judge incompatible with their sincerely held religious beliefs." Nor do we hold, as the dissent implies, that such corporations have free rein to take steps that impose "disadvantages . . . on others" or that require "the general public [to] pick up the tab." And we certainly do not hold or suggest that "RFRA demands accommodation of a for-profit corporation's religious beliefs no matter the impact that accommodation may have on . . . thousands of women employed by Hobby Lobby." The effect of the HHS-created accommodation on the women employed by Hobby Lobby and the other companies involved in these cases would be precisely zero. Under that accommodation, these women would still be entitled to all FDA-approved contraceptives without cost sharing.

I

B

At issue in these cases are HHS regulations promulgated under the Patient Protection and Affordable Care Act of 2010 (ACA). ACA generally requires employers with 50 or more full-time employees to offer "a group health plan or group health insurance coverage" that provides "minimum essential coverage." Any covered employer that does not provide such coverage must pay a substantial price. Specifically, if a covered employer provides group health insurance but its plan fails to comply with ACA's group-health-plan requirements, the employer may be required to pay $100 per day for each affected "individual." And if the employer decides to stop providing health insurance altogether and at least one full-time employee enrolls in a health plan and qualifies for a subsidy on one of the government-run ACA exchanges, the employer must pay $2,000 per year for each of its full-time employees.

Unless an exception applies, ACA requires an employer's group health plan or group-health-insurance coverage to furnish "preventive care and screenings" for women without "any cost sharing requirements." Congress itself, however, did not specify what types of preventive care must be covered. Instead, Congress authorized the Health Resources and Services Administration (HRSA), a component of HHS, to make that important and sensitive decision. The HRSA in turn consulted the Institute of Medicine, a nonprofit group of volunteer advisers, in determining which preventive services to require.

In August 2011, based on the Institute's recommendations, the HRSA promulgated the Women's Preventive Services Guidelines. The Guidelines provide that nonexempt employers are generally required to provide "coverage, without cost sharing" for "[a]ll Food and Drug Administration [(FDA)] approved contraceptive methods, sterilization procedures, and patient education and counseling." Although many of the required, FDA-approved methods of contraception work by preventing the fertilization of an egg, four of those methods (those specifically at issue in these cases) may have the effect of preventing an already fertilized egg from developing any further by inhibiting its attachment to the uterus.

HHS also authorized the HRSA to establish exemptions from the contraceptive mandate for "religious employers." That category encompasses "churches, their integrated auxiliaries, and conventions or associations of churches," as well as "the exclusively religious activities of any religious order."

In addition, HHS has effectively exempted certain religious nonprofit organizations, described under HHS regulations as "eligible organizations," from the contraceptive mandate. An "eligible organization" means a nonprofit organization that "holds itself out as a religious organization" and "opposes providing coverage for some or all of any contraceptive services required to be covered ... on account of religious objections." To qualify for this accommodation, an employer must certify that it is such an organization. When a group-health-insurance issuer receives notice that one of its clients has invoked this provision, the issuer must then exclude contraceptive coverage from the employer's plan and provide separate payments for contraceptive services for plan participants without imposing any cost-sharing requirements on the eligible organization, its insurance plan, or its employee beneficiaries. Although this procedure requires the issuer to bear the cost of these services, HHS has determined that this obligation will not impose any net expense on issuers because its cost will be less than or equal to the cost savings resulting from the services.

II

A

Norman and Elizabeth Hahn and their three sons are devout members of the Mennonite Church, a Christian denomination. The Mennonite Church opposes abortion and believes that "[t]he fetus in its earliest stages . . . shares humanity with those who conceived it."

Fifty years ago, Norman Hahn started a wood-working business in his garage, and since then, this company, Conestoga Wood Specialties, has grown and now has 950 employees. Conestoga is organized under Pennsylvania law as a for-profit corporation. The Hahns exercise sole ownership of the closely held business; they control its board of directors and hold all of its voting shares. One of the Hahn sons serves as the president and CEO.

The Hahns believe that they are required to run their business "in accordance with their religious beliefs and moral principles." To that end, the company's mission, as they see it, is to "operate in a professional environment founded upon the highest ethical, moral, and Christian principles." The company's "Vision and Values Statements" affirms that Conestoga endeavors to "ensur[e] a reasonable profit in [a] manner that reflects [the Hahns'] Christian heritage."

As explained in Conestoga's board-adopted "Statement on the Sanctity of Human Life," the Hahns believe that "human life begins at conception." It is therefore "against [their] moral conviction to be involved in the termination of human life" after conception, which they believe is a "sin against God to which they are held accountable." The Hahns have accordingly excluded from the group-health-insurance plan they offer to their employees certain contraceptive methods that they consider to be abortifacients.

The Hahns and Conestoga sued HHS and other federal officials and agencies under RFRA and the Free Exercise Clause of the First Amendment, seeking to enjoin application of ACA's contraceptive mandate insofar as it requires them to provide health-insurance coverage for four FDA-approved contraceptives that may operate after the fertilization of an egg. These include two forms of emergency contraception commonly called "morning after" pills and two types of intrauterine devices.

In opposing the requirement to provide coverage for the contraceptives to which they object, the Hahns argued that "it is immoral and sinful for [them] to intentionally participate in, pay for, facilitate, or otherwise support these drugs." The District Court denied a preliminary injunction, and the Third Circuit affirmed in a divided opinion, holding that "for-profit, secular corporations cannot engage in religious exercise" within the meaning of RFRA or the First Amendment.

B

David and Barbara Green and their three children are Christians who own and operate two family businesses. Forty-five years ago, David Green started an arts-and-crafts store that has grown into a nationwide chain called Hobby Lobby. There are now 500 Hobby Lobby stores, and the company has more than 13,000 employees. Hobby Lobby is organized as a for-profit corporation under Oklahoma law.

One of David's sons started an affiliated business, Mardel, which operates 35 Christian bookstores and employs close to 400 people. Mardel is also organized as a for-profit corporation under Oklahoma law.

Though these two businesses have expanded over the years, they remain closely held, and David, Barbara, and their children retain exclusive control of both companies. David serves as the CEO of Hobby Lobby, and his three children serve as the president, vice president, and vice CEO.

Hobby Lobby's statement of purpose commits the Greens to "[h]onoring the Lord in all [they] do by operating the company in a manner consistent with Biblical principles." Each family member has signed a pledge to run the businesses in accordance with the family's religious beliefs and to use the family assets to support Christian ministries. In accordance with those commitments, Hobby Lobby and Mardel stores close on Sundays, even though the Greens calculate that they lose millions in sales annually by doing so. The businesses refuse to engage in profitable transactions that facilitate or promote alcohol use; they contribute profits to Christian missionaries and ministries; and they buy hundreds of full-page newspaper ads inviting people to "know Jesus as Lord and Savior."

Like the Hahns, the Greens believe that life begins at conception and that it would violate their religion to facilitate access to contraceptive drugs or devices that operate after that point. They specifically object to the same four contraceptive methods as the Hahns and, like the Hahns, they have no objection to the other 16 FDA-approved methods of birth control. Although their group-health-insurance plan predates the enactment of ACA, it is not a grandfathered plan because Hobby Lobby elected not to retain grandfathered status before the contraceptive mandate was proposed.

Contrary to the conclusion of the Third Circuit, the Tenth Circuit held that the Greens' two for-profit businesses are "persons" within the meaning of RFRA and therefore may bring suit under that law. . ..[and] that the corporations had established a likelihood of success on their RFRA claim.

III

A

RFRA prohibits the "Government [from] substantially burden[ing] a person's exercise of religion even if the burden results from a rule of general applicability" unless the Government "demonstrates that application of the burden to the person—(1) is in furtherance of a compelling governmental interest; and (2) is the least restrictive means of furthering that compelling governmental interest." The first question that we must address is whether this provision applies to regulations that govern the activities of for-profit corporations like Hobby Lobby, Conestoga, and Mardel.

B

1

Under the Dictionary Act, "the wor[d] 'person' ... include[s] corporations, companies, associations, firms, partnerships, societies, and joint stock companies, as well as individuals." We have entertained RFRA and free-exercise claims brought by nonprofit corporations. No known understanding of the term "person" includes some but not all corporations. The term "person" sometimes encompasses artificial persons (as the Dictionary Act instructs), and it sometimes is limited to natural persons. But no conceivable definition of the term includes natural persons and nonprofit corporations, but not for-profit corporations.

2

According to HHS and the dissent, these corporations are not protected by RFRA because they cannot exercise religion. Neither HHS nor the dissent, however, provides any persuasive explanation for this conclusion.

Is it because of the corporate form? The corporate form alone cannot provide the explanation because, as we have pointed out, HHS concedes that nonprofit corporations can be protected by RFRA. If the corporate form is not enough, what about the profit-making objective? In Braunfeld, 366 U.S. 599, 81 S.Ct. 1144, 6 L.Ed.2d 563, [a Sunday closing case] we entertained the free-exercise claims of individuals who were attempting to make a profit as retail merchants, and the Court never even hinted that this objective precluded their claims. If, as Braunfeld recognized, a sole proprietorship that seeks to make a profit may assert a free-exercise claim, why can't Hobby Lobby, Conestoga, and Mardel do the same?

Some lower court judges have suggested that RFRA does not protect for-profit corporations because the purpose of such corporations is simply to make money. This argument flies in the face of modern corporate law. While it is certainly true that a central objective of for-profit corporations is to make money, modern corporate law does not require for-profit corporations to pursue profit at the expense of everything else, and many do not do so. For-profit corporations, with ownership approval, support a wide variety of charitable causes, and it is not at all uncommon for such corporations to further humanitarian and other altruistic objectives. Many examples come readily to mind. So long as its owners agree, a for-profit corporation may take costly pollution-control and energy-conservation measures that go beyond what the law requires. A for-profit corporation that operates facilities in other countries may exceed the requirements of local law regarding working conditions and benefits. If for-profit corporations may pursue such worthy objectives, there is no apparent reason why they may not further religious objectives as well.

4

Finally, HHS contends that Congress could not have wanted RFRA to apply to for-profit corporations because it is difficult as a practical matter to ascertain the sincere "beliefs" of a corporation. HHS goes so far as to raise the specter of "divisive, polarizing proxy battles over the religious identity of large, publicly traded corporations such as IBM or General Electric."

These cases, however, do not involve publicly traded corporations, and it seems unlikely that the sort of corporate giants to which HHS refers will often assert RFRA claims. And if, as HHS seems to concede, Congress wanted RFRA to apply to nonprofit corporations, what reason is there to think that Congress believed that spotting insincere claims would be tougher in cases involving for-profits?

IV

Because RFRA applies in these cases, we must next ask whether the HHS contraceptive mandate "substantially burden[s]" the exercise of religion. We have little trouble concluding that it does.

A

If the Hahns and Greens and their companies do not yield to this demand, the economic consequences will be severe. If the companies continue to offer group health plans that do not cover the contraceptives at issue, they will be taxed $100 per day for each affected individual. For Hobby Lobby, the bill could amount to $1.3 million per day or about $475 million per year; for Conestoga, the assessment could be $90,000 per day or $33 million per year; and for Mardel, it could be $40,000 per day or about $15 million per year. These sums are surely substantial.

It is true that the plaintiffs could avoid these assessments by dropping insurance coverage altogether and thus forcing their employees to obtain health insurance on one of the exchanges established under ACA. But if at least one of their full-time employees were to qualify for a subsidy on one of the government-run exchanges, this course would also entail substantial economic consequences. The companies could face penalties of $2,000 per employee each year. These penalties would amount to roughly $26 million for Hobby Lobby, $1.8 million for Conestoga, and $800,000 for Mardel.

B

Although these totals are high, amici supporting HHS have suggested that the $2,000 per-employee penalty is actually less than the average cost of providing health insurance, and therefore, they claim, the companies could readily eliminate any substantial burden by forcing their employees to obtain insurance in the government exchanges. We do not generally entertain arguments that were not raised below and are not advanced in this Court by any party, ... In sum, we refuse to sustain the challenged regulations on the ground— never maintained by the Government—that dropping insurance coverage eliminates the substantial burden that the HHS mandate imposes. We doubt that the Congress that enacted RFRA—or, for that matter, ACA—would have believed it a tolerable result to put family-run businesses to the choice of violating their sincerely held religious beliefs or making all of their employees lose their existing healthcare plans.

C

In taking the position that the HHS mandate does not impose a substantial burden on the exercise of religion, HHS's main argument (echoed by the principal dissent) is basically that the connection between what the objecting parties must do (provide health-insurance coverage for four methods of contraception that may operate after the fertilization of an egg) and the end that they find to be morally wrong (destruction of an embryo) is simply too attenuated. HHS and the dissent note that providing the coverage would not itself result in the destruction of an embryo; that would occur only if an employee chose to take advantage of the coverage and to use one of the four methods at issue.

This argument dodges the question that RFRA presents (whether the HHS mandate imposes a substantial burden on the ability of the objecting parties to conduct business in accordance with their religious beliefs) and instead addresses a very different question that the federal courts have no business addressing (whether the religious belief asserted in a RFRA case is reasonable). The Hahns and Greens believe that providing the coverage demanded by the HHS regulations is connected to the destruction of an embryo in a way that is sufficient to make it immoral for them to provide the coverage. This belief implicates a difficult and important question of religion and moral philosophy, namely, the circumstances under which it is wrong for a person to perform an act that is innocent in itself but that has the effect of enabling or facilitating the commission of an immoral act by another. Arrogating the authority to provide a binding national answer to this religious and philosophical question, HHS and the principal dissent in effect tell the plaintiffs that their beliefs are flawed. For good reason, we have repeatedly refused to take such a step.

Moreover, in Thomas v. Review Bd. of Indiana Employment Security Div., 450 U.S. 707, 101 S.Ct. 1425, 67 L.Ed.2d 624 (1981), we considered and rejected an argument that is nearly identical to the one now urged by HHS and the dissent.

Similarly, in these cases, the Hahns and Greens and their companies sincerely believe that providing the insurance coverage demanded by the HHS regulations lies on the forbidden side of the line, and it is not for us to say that their religious beliefs are mistaken or insubstantial. Instead, our "narrow function . . . in this context is to determine" whether the line drawn reflects "an honest conviction," and there is no dispute that it does. . . .

V

Since the HHS contraceptive mandate imposes a substantial burden on the exercise of religion, we must move on and decide whether HHS has shown that the mandate both "(1) is in furtherance of a compelling governmental interest; and (2) is the least restrictive means of furthering that compelling governmental interest."

A

We will assume that the interest in guaranteeing cost-free access to the four challenged contraceptive methods is compelling within the meaning of RFRA, and we will proceed to consider the final prong of the RFRA test, i.e., whether HHS has shown that the contraceptive mandate is "the least restrictive means of furthering that compelling governmental interest."

B

The least-restrictive-means standard is exceptionally demanding, and it is not satisfied here.

The most straightforward way of [providing contraceptive insurance] would be for the Government to assume the cost of providing the four contraceptives at issue to any women who are unable to obtain them under their health-insurance policies due to their employers' religious objections. This would certainly be less restrictive of the plaintiffs' religious liberty, and HHS has not shown that this is not a viable alternative. If, as HHS tells us, providing all women with cost-free access to all FDA-approved methods of contraception is a Government interest of the highest order, it is hard to understand HHS's argument that it cannot be required under RFRA to pay anything in order to achieve this important goal.

HHS contends that RFRA does not permit us to take this option into account because "RFRA cannot be used to require creation of entirely new programs." But we see nothing in RFRA that supports this argument, and drawing the line between the "creation of an entirely new program" and the modification of an existing program (which RFRA surely allows) would be fraught with problems.

In the end, however, we need not rely on the option of a new, government-funded program in order to conclude that the HHS regulations fail the least-restrictive-means test. HHS itself has demonstrated that it has at its disposal an approach that is less restrictive than requiring employers to fund contraceptive methods that violate their religious beliefs. As we explained above, HHS has already established an accommodation for nonprofit organizations with religious objections. Under that accommodation, the organization can self-certify that it opposes providing coverage for particular contraceptive services. If the organization makes such a certification, the organization's insurance issuer or third-party administrator must "[e]xpressly exclude contraceptive coverage from the group health insurance coverage provided in connection with the group health plan" and "[p]rovide separate payments for any contraceptive services required to be covered" without imposing "any cost-sharing requirements . . . on the eligible organization, the group health plan, or plan participants or beneficiaries."

We do not decide today whether an approach of this type complies with RFRA for purposes of all religious claims. . . .

C

HHS and the principal dissent argue that a ruling in favor of the objecting parties in these cases will lead to a flood of religious objections regarding a wide variety of medical procedures and drugs, such as vaccinations and blood transfusions, but HHS has made no effort to substantiate this prediction. HHS points to no evidence that insurance plans in existence prior to the enactment of ACA excluded coverage for such items. Nor has HHS provided evidence that any significant number of employers sought exemption, on religious grounds, from any of ACA's coverage requirements other than the contraceptive mandate.

In any event, our decision in these cases is concerned solely with the contraceptive mandate. Our decision should not be understood to hold that an insurance-coverage mandate must necessarily fall if it conflicts with an employer's religious beliefs. Other coverage requirements, such as immunizations, may be supported by different interests (for example, the need to combat the spread of infectious diseases) and may involve different arguments about the least restrictive means of providing them.

The principal dissent raises the possibility that discrimination in hiring, for example on the basis of race, might be cloaked as religious practice to escape legal sanction. Our decision today provides no such shield. The Government has a compelling interest in providing an equal opportunity to participate in the workforce without regard to race, and prohibitions on racial discrimination are precisely tailored to achieve that critical goal.

* * *

The contraceptive mandate, as applied to closely held corporations, violates RFRA. Our decision on that statutory question makes it unnecessary to reach the First Amendment claim raised by Conestoga and the Hahns.

The judgment of the Tenth Circuit in No. 13–354 is affirmed; the judgment of the Third Circuit in No. 13–356 is reversed, and that case is remanded for further proceedings consistent with this opinion.

It is so ordered.

■ JUSTICE KENNEDY concurring.

It is important to confirm that a premise of the Court's opinion is its assumption that the HHS regulation here at issue furthers a legitimate and compelling interest in the health of female employees.

But the Government has not made the second showing required by RFRA, that the means it uses to regulate is the least restrictive way to further its interest. As the Court's opinion explains, the record in these cases shows that there is an existing, recognized, workable, and already-implemented framework to provide coverage.

Among the reasons the United States is so open, so tolerant, and so free is that no person may be restricted or demeaned by government in exercising his or her religion. Yet neither may that same exercise unduly restrict other persons, such as employees, in protecting their own interests, interests the law deems compelling. In these cases the means to reconcile those two priorities are at hand in the existing accommodation the Government has designed, identified, and used for circumstances closely parallel to those presented here. . . . For these reasons and others put forth by the Court, I join its opinion.

■ JUSTICE GINSBURG with whom JUSTICE SOTOMAYOR joins, and with whom JUSTICE BREYER and JUSTICE KAGAN join as to all but Part III-C-1, dissenting.

In a decision of startling breadth, the Court holds that commercial enterprises, including corporations, along with partnerships and sole proprietorships, can opt out of any law (saving only tax laws) they judge incompatible with their sincerely held religious beliefs. Compelling governmental interests in uniform compliance with the law, and disadvantages that religion-based opt-outs impose on others, hold no sway, the Court decides, at least when there is a "less restrictive alternative." And such an alternative, the Court suggests, there always will be whenever, in lieu of tolling an enterprise claiming a religion-based exemption, the government, i.e., the general public, can pick up the tab.

In the Court's view, RFRA demands accommodation of a for-profit corporation's religious beliefs no matter the impact that accommodation may have on third parties who do not share the corporation owners' religious faith—in these cases, thousands of women employed by Hobby Lobby and Conestoga or dependents of persons those corporations employ. Persuaded that Congress enacted RFRA to serve a far less radical purpose, and mindful of the havoc the Court's judgment can introduce, I dissent.

I

"The ability of women to participate equally in the economic and social life of the Nation has been facilitated by their ability to control their reproductive lives." Congress acted on that understanding when, as part of a nationwide insurance program intended to be comprehensive, it called for coverage of preventive care responsive to women's needs. Carrying out Congress' direction, the Department of Health and Human Services (HHS), in consultation with public health experts, promulgated regulations requiring group health plans to cover all forms of contraception approved by the Food and Drug Administration (FDA). The genesis of this coverage should enlighten the Court's resolution of these cases.

A

As altered by the Women's Health Amendment's passage, the ACA requires new insurance plans to include coverage without cost sharing of "such additional preventive care and screenings . . . as provided for in comprehensive guidelines supported by the Health Resources and Services Administration [(HRSA)]," a unit of HHS. . . . Consistent with the findings of "[n]umerous health professional associations" and other organizations, the IOM [Institute of Medicine] experts determined that preventive coverage should include the "full range" of FDA-approved contraceptive methods.

In making that recommendation, the IOM's report expressed concerns similar to those voiced by congressional proponents of the Women's Health Amendment. The report noted the disproportionate burden women carried for comprehensive health services and the adverse health consequences of excluding contraception from preventive care available to employees without cost sharing.

III

C

With RFRA's restorative purpose in mind, I turn to the Act's application to the instant lawsuits. That task, in view of the positions taken by the Court, requires consideration of several questions, each potentially dispositive of Hobby Lobby's and Conestoga's claims: Do for-profit corporations rank among "person[s]" who "exercise . . . religion"? Assuming that they do, does the contraceptive coverage requirement "substantially burden" their religious exercise? If so, is the requirement "in furtherance of a compelling government interest"? And last, does the requirement represent the least restrictive means for furthering that interest?

Misguided by its errant premise that RFRA moved beyond the pre-*Smith* case law, the Court falters at each step of its analysis.

1

Until this litigation, no decision of this Court recognized a for-profit corporation's qualification for a religious exemption from a generally applicable law, whether under the Free Exercise Clause or RFRA. The absence of such precedent is just what one would expect, for the exercise of religion is characteristic of natural persons, not artificial legal entities. As Chief Justice Marshall observed nearly two centuries ago, a corporation is "an artificial being, invisible, intangible, and existing only in contemplation of law." Corporations, Justice Stevens more recently reminded, "have no consciences, no beliefs, no feelings, no thoughts, no desires." [U]ntil today, religious exemptions had never been extended to any entity operating in "the commercial, profit-making world." Amos, 483 U.S., at 337.

The reason why is hardly obscure. Religious organizations exist to foster the interests of persons subscribing to the same religious faith. Not so of for-profit corporations. Workers who sustain the operations of those corporations commonly are not drawn from one religious community. Indeed, by law, no religion-based criterion can restrict the work force of for-profit corporations.

Reading RFRA, as the Court does, to require extension of religion-based exemptions to for-profit corporations surely is not grounded in the pre-Smith precedent Congress sought to preserve. Had Congress intended RFRA to initiate a change so huge, a clarion statement to that effect likely would have been made in the legislation. To reiterate, "for-profit corporations are different from religious non-profits in that they use labor to make a profit, rather than to perpetuate [the] religious value[s] [shared by a community of believers.

The Court's determination that RFRA extends to for-profit corporations is bound to have untoward effects. Although the Court attempts to cabin its language to closely held corporations, its logic extends to corporations of any size, public or private. Little doubt that RFRA claims will proliferate, for the Court's expansive notion of corporate personhood—combined with its other errors in construing RFRA—invites for-profit entities to seek religion-based exemptions from regulations they deem offensive to their faith.

2

The Court barely pauses to inquire whether any burden imposed by the contraceptive coverage requirement is substantial. Undertaking the inquiry that the Court forgoes, I would conclude that the connection between the families' religious objections and the contraceptive coverage requirement is too attenuated to rank as substantial. The requirement carries no command that Hobby Lobby or Conestoga purchase or provide the contraceptives they find objectionable. Instead, it calls on the companies covered by the requirement to direct money into undifferentiated funds that finance a wide variety of benefits under comprehensive health plans. Those plans, in order to comply with the ACA, must offer contraceptive coverage without cost sharing, just as they must cover an array of other preventive services.

Importantly, the decisions whether to claim benefits under the plans are made not by Hobby Lobby or Conestoga, but by the covered employees and dependents, in consultation with their health care providers. Should an employee of Hobby Lobby or Conestoga share the religious beliefs of the Greens and Hahns, she is of course under no compulsion to use the contraceptives in question. But "[n]o individual decision by an employee and her physician—be it to use contraception, treat an infection, or have a hip replaced—is in any meaningful sense [her employer's] decision or action." It is doubtful that Congress, when it specified that burdens must be "substantia[l]," had in mind a linkage thus interrupted by independent decisionmakers (the woman and her health counselor) standing between the challenged government action and the religious exercise claimed to be infringed. Any decision to use contraceptives made by a woman covered under Hobby Lobby's or Conestoga's plan will not be propelled by the Government, it will be the woman's autonomous choice, informed by the physician she consults.

3

. . . To recapitulate, the mandated contraception coverage enables women to avoid the health problems unintended pregnancies may visit on them and their children. The coverage helps safeguard the health of women for whom pregnancy may be hazardous, even life threatening. And the mandate secures benefits wholly unrelated to pregnancy, preventing certain cancers, menstrual disorders, and pelvic pain. . . .the cost of an IUD is nearly equivalent to a month's full-time pay for workers earning the minimum wage, that almost one-third of women would change their contraceptive method if costs were not a factor, and that only one-fourth of women who request an IUD actually have one inserted after finding out how expensive it would be.

The Court ultimately acknowledges a critical point: RFRA's application "must take adequate account of the burdens a requested accommodation may impose on nonbeneficiaries." No tradition, and no prior decision under RFRA, allows a religion-based exemption when the accommodation would be harmful to others—here, the very persons the contraceptive coverage requirement was designed to protect.

4

After assuming the existence of compelling government interests, the Court holds that the contraceptive coverage requirement fails to satisfy RFRA's least restrictive means test. But the Government has shown that there is no less restrictive, equally effective means that would both (1) satisfy the challengers' religious objections to providing insurance coverage for certain contraceptives (which they believe cause abortions); and (2) carry out the objective of the ACA's contraceptive coverage requirement, to ensure that women employees receive, at no cost to them, the preventive care needed to safeguard their health and well being. A "least restrictive means" cannot require employees to relinquish benefits accorded them by federal law in order to ensure that their commercial employers can adhere unreservedly to their religious tenets.

Then let the government pay (rather than the employees who do not share their employer's faith), the Court suggests. "The most straightforward [alternative]," the Court asserts, "would be for the Government to assume the cost of providing . . . contraceptives . . . to any women who are unable to obtain them under their health-insurance policies due to their employers' religious objections." The ACA, however, requires coverage of preventive services through the existing employer-based system of health insurance "so that [employees] face minimal logistical and administrative obstacles." Impeding women's receipt of benefits "by requiring them to take steps to learn about, and to sign up for, a new [government funded and administered] health benefit" was scarcely what Congress contemplated. Moreover, Title X of the Public Health Service Act, "is the nation's only dedicated source of federal funding for safety net family planning services." "Safety net programs like Title X are not designed to absorb the unmet needs of . . . insured individuals." Note, too, that Congress declined to write into law the preferential treatment Hobby Lobby and Conestoga describe as a less restrictive alternative.

And where is the stopping point to the "let the government pay" alternative? Suppose an employer's sincerely held religious belief is offended by health coverage of vaccines, or paying the minimum wage, see Tony and Susan Alamo Foundation v. Secretary of Labor, 471 U.S. 290, 303, 105 S.Ct. 1953, 85 L.Ed.2d 278 (1985), or according women equal pay for substantially similar work, see Dole v. Shenandoah Baptist Church, 899 F.2d 1389, 1392 (C.A.4 1990)? Does it rank as a less restrictive alternative to require the government to provide the money or benefit to which the employer has a religion-based objection? Because the Court cannot easily answer that question, it proposes something else: Extension to commercial enterprises of the accommodation already afforded to nonprofit religion-based organizations.

Ultimately, the Court hedges on its proposal to align for-profit enterprises with nonprofit religion-based organizations. "We do not decide today whether [the] approach [the opinion advances] complies with RFRA for purposes of all religious claims." Counsel for Hobby Lobby was similarly noncommittal. Asked at oral argument whether the Court-proposed alternative was acceptable, counsel responded: "We haven't been offered that accommodation, so we haven't had to decide what kind of objection, if any, we would make to that."

IV

Hobby Lobby and Conestoga surely do not stand alone as commercial enterprises seeking exemptions from generally applicable laws on the basis of their religious beliefs. See, e.g., Newman v. Piggie Park Enterprises, Inc., 256 F.Supp. 941, 945 (SC 1966) (owner of restaurant chain refused to serve black patrons based on his religious beliefs opposing racial integration), aff'd in relevant part and rev'd in part on other grounds, 377 F.2d 433 (C.A.4 1967), aff'd and modified on other grounds, 390 U.S. 400, 88 S.Ct. 964, 19 L.Ed.2d 1263 (1968); In re Minnesota ex rel. McClure, 370 N.W.2d 844, 847 (Minn.1985) (born-again Christians who owned closely held, for-profit health clubs believed that the Bible proscribed hiring or retaining an "individua[l] living with but not married to a person of the opposite sex," "a young, single woman working without her father's consent or a married woman working without her husband's consent," and any person "antagonistic to the Bible," including "fornicators and homosexuals" (internal quotation marks omitted)), appeal dismissed, 478 U.S. 1015, 106 S.Ct. 3315, 92 L.Ed.2d 730 (1986); Elane Photography, LLC v. Willock, 2013–NMSC–040, ___ N.M. ___, 309 P.3d 53 (for-profit photography business owned by a husband and wife refused to photograph a lesbian couple's commitment ceremony based on the religious beliefs of the company's owners), cert. denied, 572 U.S. ___ (2014). Would RFRA require exemptions in cases of this ilk? And if not, how does the Court divine which religious beliefs are worthy of accommodation, and which are not? Isn't the Court disarmed from making such a judgment given its recognition that "courts must not presume to determine . . . the plausibility of a religious claim"?

Would the exemption the Court holds RFRA demands for employers with religiously grounded objections to the use of certain contraceptives extend to employers with religiously grounded objections to blood transfusions (Jehovah's Witnesses); antidepressants (Scientologists); medications derived from pigs, including anesthesia, intravenous fluids, and pills coated with gelatin (certain Muslims, Jews, and Hindus); and vaccinations (Christian Scientists, among others)? According to counsel for Hobby Lobby, "each one of these cases . . .

would have to be evaluated on its own . . . apply [ing] the compelling interest-least restrictive alternative test." Not much help there for the lower courts bound by today's decision.

The Court, I fear, has ventured into a minefield, by its immoderate reading of RFRA. I would confine religious exemptions under that Act to organizations formed "for a religious purpose," "engage[d] primarily in carrying out that religious purpose," and not "engaged . . . substantially in the exchange of goods or services for money beyond nominal amounts."

■ JUSTICE BREYER and JUSTICE KAGAN, dissenting.

We agree with JUSTICE GINSBURG that the plaintiffs' challenge to the contraceptive coverage requirement fails on the merits. We need not and do not decide whether either for-profit corporations or their owners may bring claims under the Religious Freedom Restoration Act of 1993. Accordingly, we join all but Part III-C-1 of JUSTICE GINSBURG's dissenting opinion.

NOTES AND QUESTIONS

1. *Person.* How many justices concluded corporations are persons under RFRA? How many justices concluded that corporations are not persons under RFRA? How many justices did not decide that question?

Which argument about corporations do you find more compelling, the majority's or the dissent's? Justice Alito views corporations as organizations that protect the rights of people because "corporations, 'separate and apart from' the human beings who own, run, and are employed by them, cannot do anything at all." He also relies on the Dictionary Act, and then concludes "no conceivable definition of the term includes natural persons and nonprofit corporations, but not for-profit corporations."

In contrast, Justice Ginsburg argues that no past decision of the Court recognized for-profit corporations as RFRA or First Amendment persons because "the exercise of religion is characteristic of natural persons, not artificial legal entities." Justice Ginsburg then argues that the distinction between nonprofit and for-profit corporations makes sense, because "[r]eligious organizations exist to foster the interests of persons subscribing to the same religious faith. Not so of for-profit corporations."

What did Justices Breyer and Kagan conclude about this question? Do you agree with Professor Goforth's argument:

> The majority opinion in *Hobby Lobby* fails to acknowledge the nature of the business corporation. The doctrine of piercing [the veil] holds that when individuals in control of a corporation use that corporation to express their views and to advance their interests, rather than those of the corporation, those actions are improper because they fail to respect the separate existence and legal personality of the corporation . . . the essential notion that

corporations have personhood and legal status distinct from that of their shareholders and directors has long been a bulwark of business organizations laws in this country. It is regrettable that the majority opinion in *Hobby Lobby* overlooked or ignored this particular aspect of corporate existence, as exemplified in piercing jurisprudence in every state.

Carol Goforth, A Corporation Has No Soul, and Doesn't Go to Church: Relating the Doctrine of Piercing the Veil to *Burwell v. Hobby Lobby*, 67 S.C. L. Rev. 73, 97 (2015).

Or does Professor Goforth overstate her case because "[f]or-profit organizations are quite unlikely to raise a large number of religious liberty claims post-*Hobby Lobby*."? Eric Rassbach, Is *Hobby Lobby* Really A Brave New World? Litigation Truths About Religious Exercise by for-Profit Organizations, 42 Hastings Const. L.Q. 625, 636 (2015); but see William P. Marshall, Bad Statutes Make Bad Law: *Burwell v. Hobby Lobby*, 2014 Sup. Ct. Rev. 71, 118–19 (2014) ("For-profit corporations and other commercial entities will also have incentives to file RFRA challenges for another reason—*Hobby Lobby* substantially increases the likelihood that they will prevail. *Hobby Lobby*'s holding that courts must defer to the claimant's characterization of the burden, combined with its rejection of the categorical exclusions from RFRA of for-profit corporations and commercial activities, means that the government will no longer be able to defeat RFRA claims at their threshold.").

Post-*Hobby Lobby*, several states, including Indiana and Arkansas, discussed amending their state RFRAs to define all corporations as persons. These amendments were perceived to offer corporations a right to refuse customers, especially same-sex couples looking for wedding services. What should a state RFRA cover?

2. *Exercise of Religion.* According to Justice Alito, RLUIPA amended RFRA's definition of the exercise of religion to be broader than the First Amendment, and to include "any exercise of religion, whether or not compelled by, or central to, a system of religious belief." § 2000cc–5(7)(A). And Congress mandated that this concept 'be construed in favor of a broad protection of religious exercise, to the maximum extent permitted by the terms of this chapter and the Constitution.' " § 2000cc–3(g). In contrast, Justice Ginsburg argues that RFRA incorporates the definition of exercise of religion included in pre-RFRA First Amendment cases. Who has the better argument? Is Justice Alito correct that RFRA can be interpreted more expansively than the First Amendment case law that existed when RFRA was passed? See Micah Schwartzman, Richard Schragger and Nelson Tebbe, The New Law of Religion: *Hobby Lobby* Rewrites Religious-Freedom Law in Ways that Ignore Everything that Came Before, Slate, Jul. 2014, http://www.slate.com/articles/news_and_politics/jurisprudence/2014/07/after_hobby_lobby_there_is_only_rfra_and_that_s_all_you_need.html (Justice Alito wrote a "radical" new interpretation of RFRA, a "revolution," not a "restoration," a "total break" from First Amendment jurisprudence).

Justice Alito dismisses the argument that for-profit corporations cannot exercise religion because they make money. Was his argument persuasive? How do you assess his descriptions of how corporations exercise religion? See Carol Goforth, A Corporation Has No Soul, and Doesn't Go to Church: Relating the Doctrine of Piercing the Veil to *Burwell v. Hobby Lobby*, 67 S.C. L. Rev. 73, 97 (2015) ("A corporation has no religious views of its own. It has no soul; it does not go to church. The legal personality that it possesses does not and cannot extend so far. Only individuals have religious views and rights. While corporations act through individuals, when a religious viewpoint is expressed, it is necessarily that of those individuals and not that of the corporation itself.").

3. *Substantial Burden.* Why did Justice Alito think the plaintiffs' religion was substantially burdened? Was it because of the economic consequences of not complying with the mandate? Was it because they said their religion was substantially burdened? Under Justice Alito's analysis, can a court ever question a plaintiff's assertion that her religion was substantially burdened, or must courts always defer to that belief? Is anything left of the substantial burden prong of RFRA? See Erwin Chemerinsky, On *Hobby Lobby*, L.A. Times, Jul. 1, 2014, at A15 ("Never before has the Supreme Court found a substantial burden on a person's religious exercise where the individual is not himself required to take or forgo action that violates his or her religious beliefs but is merely required to take action that might enable other people to do things that are at odds with the person's religious beliefs.").

Why did Justice Ginsburg think the link between the employers' beliefs and the employees' decisions to use contraception was too "attenuated" to constitute a substantial burden? The Greens and Hahns sincerely believed that four of the contraceptives covered by the mandate were abortifacients. Government studies and science suggest otherwise. Should the plaintiffs have had to prove that the contraceptives caused abortions in order to show their religion was substantially burdened? How would Justice Alito respond to that question?

Why didn't the Court accept the amici's argument that the penalty was less than the cost of providing insurance and therefore there was no substantial burden? Do you agree with Professor Greenawalt that Justice Alito's substantial burden analysis "both fails to consider how its approach will work for a range of RFRA claims and effectively eliminates the burden requirement as a genuine limit on claims that can be made"? Kent Greenawalt, *Hobby Lobby*: Its Flawed Interpretive Techniques and Standards of Application, 115 Colum. L. Rev. Sidebar 153, 171 (2015).

4. *Compelling Governmental Interest.* Why did Justice Kennedy write a separate concurrence? Was the most important accomplishment of the concurrence "to confirm that a premise of the Court's opinion is its assumption that the HHS regulation here at issue furthers a legitimate and compelling interest in the health of female employees"? What did the majority conclude about the compelling governmental interest in this case?

Do you agree that by not addressing the compelling interest, the majority did not "address[ ] the importance of birth control for women's health and the course of their life" and that the opinion "was stunningly bad for women's health and starkly dismissive of women's own religious beliefs." See Marcia Greenberger, *Hobby Lobby* symposium: A decision based on conclusory assertions and results-oriented reasoning, SCOTUSblog (Jul. 2, 2014, 12:30 PM), http://www.scotusblog.com/2014/07/hobby-lobby-symposium-a-decision-based-on-conclusory-assertions-and-results-oriented-reasoning/. Or was it a big day for religious liberty, with the proper balance struck between women's rights and religious rights? See Jonathan Keim, A Big day for Religious Liberty in *Hobby Lobby* & *Conestoga Wood*, National Review Online, Jun. 30, 2014, at http://www.nationalreview.com/bench-memos/381576/big-day-religious-liberty-hobby-lobby-and-conestoga-wood-jonathan-keim.

Did the majority's analysis forget that some women use contraceptive prescriptions for non-contraceptive health care? See Zoe Fenson, For Me, Birth Control is Medicine First, Contraceptive Second, The New Republic, Jun. 30, 2014 (describing experience of young woman who suffers from Polycystic Ovary Syndrome (PCOS); "I've known women who take birth control to limit pain from endometriosis, to stave off migraines, to address skin-scarring cases of acne.").

5. *Least Restrictive Means.* During the oral argument in this case, Justice Scalia observed that the pre-*Smith* case law had never included the least restrictive means test, and the Court agreed in this opinion. Does that insight affect your assessment of RFRA's constitutionality? See Marci A. Hamilton, The Case for Evidence-Based Free Exercise Accommodation: Why the Religious Freedom Restoration Act Is Bad Public Policy, 9 Harv. L. & Pol'y Rev. 129, 138 (2015) ("In 2014, the Court yet again stated that the least restrictive means requirement 'was not used in the pre-*Smith* jurisprudence RFRA purported to codify' and that RFRA 'does not accurately convey the Court's pre-*Smith* First Amendment doctrine.' ")

The least restrictive means test is a very hard test to pass. Why did the Court say the government failed to meet it here? What are the two alternatives that are less restrictive than the contraceptive mandate? Which one would you prefer?

What do you think of the dissent's argument that "there is no less restrictive, equally effective means that would both (1) satisfy the challengers' religious objections to providing insurance coverage for certain contraceptives (which they believe cause abortions); and (2) carry out the objective of the ACA's contraceptive coverage requirement, to ensure that women employees receive, at no cost to them, the preventive care needed to safeguard their health and well being. A 'least restrictive means' cannot require employees to relinquish benefits accorded them by federal law in order to ensure that their commercial employers can adhere unreservedly to their religious tenets."? Do you agree with Professor Hamilton's criticism of the least-restrictive-means test, noting in this case:

the government had not provided in the law that it would pay for contraceptive coverage for millions of American women who work for closely held corporations that could raise a challenge under RFRA to covering some or all contraception, as such coverage is not politically feasible in an era of budget shortfalls and the movement among some to turn back not only abortion laws but also the availability of contraception. Therefore, the Court concluded that there is a pie-in-the-sky least restrictive means for the government's compelling interest to be served, where least restrictive means apparently do not need to take into account economic or political feasibility of the lesser restrictive means. If the supposed lesser restrictive means is impossible to achieve, it should not be considered an alternative.

Marci A. Hamilton, The Case for Evidence-Based Free Exercise Accommodation: Why the Religious Freedom Restoration Act Is Bad Public Policy, 9 Harv. L. & Pol'y Rev. 129, 140 (2015).

6. *Establishment Clause.* Should the Court have considered the argument that an accommodation for Hobby Lobby would violate the Establishment Clause? "In a line of cases going back decades, the Supreme Court has held that the government may not grant religious exemptions when doing so would impose significant burdens on third parties who are not beneficiaries of the religious accommodation." Micah Schwartzman, Richard Schragger & Nelson Tebbe, The Establishment Clause and the Contraceptive Mandate, Balkinization (Nov. 27, 2013, 2:05PM), http:// balkin.blogspot.com/2013/11/the-establishment-clause-and.html, archived at http://perma.cc/A9YN-XZRW; see also Frederick Mark Gedicks & Rebecca G. Van Tassell, RFRA Exemptions from the Contraception Mandate: An Unconstitutional Accommodation of Religion, 49 Harv. C.R.-C.L. L. Rev. 343, 363 (2014) ("broad consensus that the Establishment Clause prohibits permissive accommodations that shift the costs of the accommodated religious practices onto third parties"). Did the Court's accommodation of Hobby Lobby impose significant burdens on women employees in violation of the Establishment Clause? See Ira C. Lupu, *Hobby Lobby* and the Dubious Enterprise of Religious Exemptions, 38 Harv. J. L. & Gender 35, 77 (2015) ("the Establishment Clause requires a construction of RFRA that does not permit the imposition of significant harms on third parties—in this case, female employees and female dependents of all employees. Loss of no-cost coverage of pregnancy prevention services, even for an interim period, is precisely one such harm."). Why do you think the Establishment Clause issue wasn't litigated in the Supreme Court?

7. *Other For-Profits Opposed to Contraception.* In circuit court decisions issued before *Hobby Lobby*, the courts had split on whether Catholic business owners who oppose all contraceptives required by the mandate should win their RFRA cases. The Court remanded the cases where owners had lost and denied review on cases where the owners had won. What does this mean about *Hobby Lobby*'s reach? See Lyle Denniston,

Wider impact of Hobby Lobby ruling?, SCOTUSblog (Jul. 1, 2014, 12:05 PM), at http://www.scotusblog.com/2014/07/wider-impact-of-hobby-lobby-ruling/; see, e.g., Gilardi v. U.S. Dep't of Health & Human Servs., 575 F. App'x 1 (D.C. Cir. 2014) ("ORDERED and ADJUDGED that the case be remanded to the district court with instructions to enter a preliminary injunction for the Freshway companies and to reconsider the denial of the preliminary injunction as to the individual owners in light of *Burwell v. Hobby Lobby Stores, Inc.*, ___ U.S. ___, 134 S.Ct. 2751, 189 L.Ed.2d 675 (2014)."). What should the court have done in *Gilardi* post-*Hobby Lobby*?

8. *Broad or Narrow?* The justices and commentators disagree whether this opinion is very narrow or a "a decision of startling breadth." What do you think? What kind of RFRA cases would you expect corporations to file now? Do you think Justice Ginsburg is exaggerating the types of lawsuits that will be filed, or is Justice Alito underestimating them? Do you agree with Professor Greenawalt "Justice Alito's opinion in *Hobby Lobby* adopts an approach that is excessively formalistic, that it treats as separate certain elements of the statute that should be seen as interrelated, and that it takes inadequate account of concerns about administrability."? Kent Greenawalt, *Hobby Lobby*: Its Flawed Interpretive Techniques and Standards of Application, 115 Colum. L. Rev. Sidebar 153, 155 (2015).

What should happen to lawsuits by employers refusing to provide health insurance coverage for same-sex partners and spouses? See Ira Lupu and Robert Tuttle, Hobby Lobby in the Long Run, Cornerstone, Jul. 1, 2014, at http://www.religiousfreedominstitute.org/cornerstone/2016/6/30/hobby-lobby-in-the-long-run.

Robert Soto is a Native American who is not a member of a federally recognized Indian tribe. He was prosecuted for possession of eagle feathers and denied a permit for possessing feathers. Only members of the recognized tribes gain access to the feathers. Should his RFRA claim succeed post-Hobby Lobby? See McAllen Grace Brethren Church v. Salazar, 764 F.3d 465 (5th Cir. 2014). Think through the steps the statute requires: Was a sincere religious belief substantially burdened? See id. at 472 (government did not contest burden on a man whose ministry uses eagle feathers in worship). Did the government have a compelling interest? See id. at 472–75 (court assumed government had two compelling interests in protecting eagles and fulfilling its responsibilities to federally recognized tribes). Did the government use the least restrictive means? See id. at 475 (the government had not provided sufficient evidence of least restrictive means).

Why do you think the government failed the least restrictive means test? See id. at 476–78 (the government had not presented evidence that expanding the permitting process would increase poaching and black market in feathers).

During an investigation into child labor violations in the Fundamentalist Church of Jesus Christ of Latter-day Saints (FLDS), Vernon Steed objected to the government's questioning him about the church's organization and internal affairs. Sneed asserted that his religious views about church secrecy did not allow him to discuss the church's internal affairs and organization. The district court ruled that requiring Steed to testify would violate RFRA. Perez v. Paragon Contractors, Corp., No. 2:13CV00281-DS, 2014 WL 4628572 (D. Utah Sept. 11, 2014). Is that ruling consistent with *Hobby Lobby*?

9. *To Accommodate or Not?* According to Professor Horwitz, the "*Hobby Lobby* moment" has witnessed a shift in attitudes toward religious accommodations. Until very recently, he argues, there was "widespread approval for religious accommodation," but the "past few years have witnessed a significant weakening of this consensus":

> Contestation over religious accommodations has moved rapidly from the background to the foreground. Accommodations by *anyone*—courts *or* legislatures—have been called into question, including by those who acknowledge that until recently those accommodations would have been uncontroversial. Whether religion is "a good thing"—whether it ought to enjoy any kind of unique status, and whether that status should find meaningful constitutional protection—has itself come up for grabs.

Paul Horwitz, The *Hobby Lobby* Moment, 128 Harv. L. Rev. 154, 159–60 (2014). Should that question be up for grabs or are religious accommodations definitely a good thing? What do you think of Professor Hamilton's proposal that RFRA be repealed and that, in its place, legislatures should adopt "evidence-based" accommodations with the following characteristics:

> Legislative and executive accommodation of religious practices (or any other) should not proceed unless legislators have a minimum quantum of information:
>
> *First*, which law or laws in particular would be affected by this accommodation?
>
> *Second*, who seeks to overcome these laws and for what practices?
>
> *Third*, who will be harmed if the accommodation is permitted?
>
> *Fourth*, what do experts in the field and the public think about the proposal?

Marci A. Hamilton, The Case for Evidence-Based Free Exercise Accommodation: Why the Religious Freedom Restoration Act Is Bad Public Policy, 9 Harv. L. & Pol'y Rev. 129, 153–54 (2015).

After reading this entire chapter on free exercise and statutory exemptions and accommodations for religion, do you agree with Professor Lupu's comment that "a generalized exemption regime will be rhetorically strong, experientially weak, and relentlessly ad hoc in its results."? Ira C. Lupu, *Hobby Lobby* and the Dubious Enterprise of Religious Exemptions, 38 Harv. J. L. & Gender 35, 39 (2015). Does this history suggest that post-*Hobby Lobby*, "at best, the Court's interpretation of RFRA will lead to a jumbled jurisprudence beset by the same problems that plagued the Court's pre-*Smith* free exercise decisions. At worst it may lead to results that are normatively problematic and constitutionally unsound."? William P. Marshall, Bad Statutes Make Bad Law: *Burwell v. Hobby Lobby*, 2014 Sup. Ct. Rev. 71, 75 (2014).

10. *Religious Nonprofits.* As the decision explains, the original contraceptive mandate exempted churches, mosques, and other purely religious organizations from its coverage. After numerous lawsuits were filed by religious nonprofits arguing that the mandate violated RFRA, the Obama administration offered the accommodation described in Hobby Lobby, whereby the employers notify third party administrators of their refusal to provide contraceptive coverage, which is then provided by the insurer.

Pre-*Hobby Lobby*, the religious nonprofits continued to litigate the new accommodation. Many of them argued that even signing the form notifying the third party insurer of their decision not to cover contraception violated their conscience because it "triggered" contraception, of which they disapproved. The Sixth and Seventh Circuits ruled that the nonprofits' religions were not substantially burdened by the signature because the law, not the signature, triggered the coverage. See Michigan Catholic Conference and Catholic Family Services v. Burwell, 755 F.3d 372 (6th. Cir. 2014); University of Notre Dame v. Sebelius, 743 F.3d 547 (7th Cir. 2014). Should religious nonprofits lose those cases now? Or does the decision, by recognizing the accommodation as a less restrictive means, mean that the accommodation does not violate RFRA?

Right after the Court issued *Hobby Lobby*, one of those non-profits, Wheaton College, a Christian school in Illinois, applied for an injunction against the mandate. The Court issued an injunction that the mandate could not be applied to Wheaton if it told the Secretary of Health and Human Services that it objected to contraception; Wheaton College need not use the government form or send copies to health insurers and third-party administrators. Wheaton College v. Burwell, 134 S.Ct. 2806 (2014).

Three dissenting Justices (Sotomayor, joined by Ginsburg and Kagan) wrote that Wheaton had no viable claim because the law, not the signature, triggered the coverage, and because, as the Court had just ruled in *Hobby Lobby*, the accommodation is the least restrictive means. Justice Sotomayor wrote the following: "Those who are bound by our decisions usually believe they can take us at our word. Not so today. After expressly relying on the availability of the religious-nonprofit accommodation to hold that the contraceptive coverage requirement violates RFRA as applied to closely held for-profit corporations, the Court now, as the dissent in *Hobby Lobby* feared it might, . . . retreats from that position." The dissent emphasized the extraordinary nature of injunctive relief in these circumstances, given the lack of a record in the lower courts. Do you agree *Wheaton College* is inconsistent with *Hobby Lobby*? Why do you think Justice Breyer didn't join the dissent? Does this mean six justices believe that the substantial burden standard was met in *Notre Dame*, *Michigan Catholic,* and *Wheaton College*?

The dissenters argued that the majority "craft[ed] a new administrative regime" by telling the government that it could contact the insurance companies without receiving a form from Wheaton. Do you agree? How will HHS identify who the third-party administrators are for all the religious nonprofits across the country?

———————————

We examine the religious nonprofits' claims of conscience in Chapter 5, which considers conscience, complicity, and conscientious objection in medicine, the military, and the law and government.

CHAPTER 5

CONSCIENCE, COMPLICITY, AND CONSCIENTIOUS OBJECTION

The tension between religion and government is most evident when individuals assert their religion obligates them to disagree with or disobey the law. Both parties are then faced with choices: on the individual's side, whether to comply with the government's demands or to object to them; on the state's side, whether to accommodate dissenters or to punish them. This chapter focuses on the individual's conscientious objection to actions of the state.

Different religions may disagree about many matters of doctrine while agreeing that the state does not have the last word on matters of justice and morality. The readings in this chapter examine conflicts between loyalty to God and obedience to the law in three areas: in Section A, medicine and reproductive health; in Section B, the military; and in Section C, law and government. From the experience of these areas we can examine how religion should and does influence the choices individuals make about obedience to the law, and whether the law should accommodate those choices. In each area you should consider how to balance the claims of individual conscience against the demands of the state. Recall that we read in Chapters 1 and 4, in the *Smith* decision, that the Free Exercise Clause does not allow the citizen to become a law unto himself. Are conscientious objectors citizens who try to set the law for themselves? Are they ever justified in doing so? How does RFRA, the statute discussed in Chapter 4, impact the viability of conscientious objection claims?

The conscientious objection cases are about citizens who request an exemption from law due to the demands of conscience. What should conscientious objectors do when the government fails to exempt them? Should they disobey the law? And, if so, how should they do so? Conscientious objection can be distinguished from civil disobedience, which is "[t]he political tactic of disobeying a law deliberately, in order to bring about some change. The disobedience should ideally be public, non-violent, and committed by activists willing to face the penalties of the law." Simon Blackburn, ed., The Oxford Dictionary of Philosophy 62 (2005). Religious believers may engage in both conscientious objection and civil disobedience because of their belief that the claims of conscience are more important than the requirements of the state. Many religious traditions believe that unjust laws do not bind the conscience. We examine the idea of civil disobedience at the end of the chapter.

Recently *conscience* and *complicity* have received significant attention in debates about believers' obligations to follow neutral laws of general applicability. Conscience clauses have long relieved objectors of their obligation to obey laws they find objectionable. Moreover, federal and state RFRAs, which we explored in Chapter 4, have encouraged numerous individuals and institutions to argue that a government law or regulation substantially burdens their conscience. An increasing number of those conscience claims also involve the argument that conscience is violated through complicity with the government's or third parties' wrongdoing. See generally Douglas NeJaime, Reva B. Siegel, Conscience Wars: Complicity-Based Conscience Claims in Religion and Politics, 124 Yale L.J. 2516 (2015).

A. MEDICINE AND REPRODUCTIVE HEALTH

As we learned in Chapter 4, since the passage of the Affordable Care Act, an employer's statutory duty to provide health insurance benefits that conflicts with his religious beliefs has become a source of significant controversy. *Hobby Lobby* dealt with for-profit corporations seeking the accommodation received by religious nonprofit organizations. In this section, we examine cases in which these very religious nonprofit institutions sought full exemption from the ACA's contraception mandate.

The primary discussions about conscientious objection and *medical personnel* have also involved reproductive health, especially sterilization, contraception, abortion, and assisted reproductive technologies. Medical participation in the death and dying process, including euthanasia, assisted suicide, and withdrawal of feeding, has also become a subject of moral concern. Do you think there should be a constitutional right to obey conscience for medical personnel? In all these areas, the usual legal solution has been for state and federal governments to draft legislation containing conscience clauses, which protect employees who refuse to perform abortion, euthanasia, and other contested procedures from firing or demotion. Many conscience clauses shield individuals from sanction for adhering to their religious beliefs; others protect religious hospitals and health care institutions from any obligation to perform the contested services.

Such conscience clauses are controversial. They may protect the conscience of the medical provider but not the needs of the patient who conscientiously desires a certain form or level of treatment. Furthermore, religious institutions that enjoy the protections of conscience may receive government funding for some of their programs, raising difficult questions of Establishment and Free Exercise. On one side are religious health care providers who have moral reasons not to perform a medical service; on the other are citizens who desire that medical treatment.

As you read the following materials, consider how the courts and the legislatures should strike the proper balance between those two groups. Keep in mind four recurring themes. First, is the protection of conscience a constitutional right or a statutory privilege that can be given or taken away by the state? Second, should both individuals and institutions enjoy rights of conscience? Third, what jobs warrant conscience protection—doctors, nurses, pharmacists, administrators, janitors? Fourth, what procedures warrant conscience protection—abortion, sterilization, provision of contraceptive insurance, sale of pharmaceuticals, euthanasia? We start with the same issue we studied in Chapter 4: contraception.

1. CLAIMS OF CONSCIENCE AND COMPLICITY

Are religious nonprofit employers entitled to institutional conscience protection? As explained in *Hobby Lobby*, the original Affordable Care Act contraceptive mandate exempted churches, mosques, and other purely religious organizations from its coverage. After numerous lawsuits were filed by religious nonprofits arguing the mandate violated RFRA, the Obama administration offered the accommodation described in *Hobby Lobby*, whereby the employers notify third party administrators of their refusal to provide contraceptive coverage, which is then provided by the insurer.

Pre-*Hobby Lobby*, religious nonprofits objected to this very accommodation. Many of them argued that even signing the form notifying the third party insurer of their decision not to cover contraception violated their conscience because it "triggered" contraception, of which they disapproved. The Seventh Circuit ruled against religious nonprofit Notre Dame in the case below. Then the case was remanded to the Seventh Circuit to review the case in light of the Court's opinion in *Hobby Lobby*. Who did a better job of interpreting *Hobby Lobby* in the following case, the majority or the dissent?

University of Notre Dame v. Burwell

United States Court of Appeals for the Seventh Circuit, 2015.
786 F.3d 606.

■ Before POSNER, FLAUM and HAMILTON CIRCUIT JUDGES.

■ POSNER, CIRCUIT JUDGE.

The Affordable Care Act requires providers of health insurance (including both health insurance companies and companies that administer self-insured employer health plans on behalf of the employer—such companies are called "third party administrators") to cover certain preventive services without cost to the insured, including, "with respect to women, such additional preventive care . . . as provided for in comprehensive guidelines supported by the Health Resources and Services Administration" of the Department of Health and Human Services. Guidelines specifying such care have been promulgated by the Department and include, so far as bears on this case, "all Food and Drug Administration approved contraceptive methods."

About half of all pregnancies in the United States are unintended, and 40 percent of them end in abortion and many others in premature births or other birth problems. Many of the unintended pregnancies are teen pregnancies, and contraceptive use has been found to be positively correlated with decreased teen pregnancy. Because out-of-pocket expenditures on female contraceptives can be substantial for many women, the provision of such contraceptives without cost to the user can be expected to increase contraceptive use and so reduce the number both of unintended pregnancies and of abortions. Furthermore, "women who can successfully delay a first birth and plan the subsequent timing and spacing of their children are more likely than others to enter or stay in school and to have more opportunities for employment and for full social or political participation in their community."

The University of Notre Dame provides health benefits to both its employees and its students. It self-insures its employees' medical expenses, but has hired Meritain Health, Inc. to administer the employee health plan without providing any insurance coverage; Meritain is therefore the third-party administrator of the university's employee health plan. To take care of its students' medical needs, Notre Dame has a contract with Aetna, Inc., the well-known health care and health insurance company (and Meritain's parent); the contract gives the students the option of obtaining health insurance from Aetna at rates negotiated by Notre Dame. Meritain administers coverage for some 4600 employees of Notre Dame (out of a total of 5200) and 6400 dependents of employees. Aetna insures 2600 students and 100 dependents; Notre Dame has about 11,000 students, most of whom have coverage under either their parents' health insurance policies or under their own policies rather than under the Aetna Notre Dame Health Plan.

Because Catholic doctrine forbids the use of contraceptives to prevent pregnancy (the "rhythm" method of avoiding pregnancy, which is permitted, is a form of abstention, not of contraception), Notre Dame has never paid for contraceptives for its employees or permitted Aetna to insure students under the Aetna Notre Dame Health Plan (or any other Aetna plan) for the expense of contraceptives. Cognizant of the religious objections of Catholic and a number of other religious institutions to contraception, and mindful of the dictate of the Religious Freedom Restoration Act, 42 U.S.C. §§ 2000bb–1(a), (b), that "Government shall not substantially burden a person's exercise of religion even if the burden results from a rule of general applicability," unless "it demonstrates that application of the burden to the person— (1) is in furtherance of a compelling governmental interest; and (2) is the least restrictive means of furthering that compelling governmental interest," some months after the enactment of the Affordable Care Act the government offered a religious exemption from the contraception guidelines.

At first the exemption was limited to churches and so excluded religious institutions that are incorporated as nonprofit (rather than as religious) institutions, such as Notre Dame. The exclusion precipitated the filing in 2012 of a federal suit by the university against the government, claiming that the contraceptive regulations infringed rights conferred on the university by both the First Amendment and the Religious Freedom Restoration Act. That suit was dismissed on standing and ripeness grounds, the government having promised that Notre Dame wouldn't have to comply with the regulations for one year, during which new regulations would be issued. The new regulations were issued as promised—and as expected they enlarged the exemption. As a result, Notre Dame now came within its scope.

But to exercise its right conferred by the new regulations to opt out of having to pay for contraceptive coverage either directly (with or without the administrative assistance of a third-party administrator, such as Meritain) or through a health insurer, such as Aetna, the university had to fill out "EBSA Form 700—Certification." The form (http://www.dol.gov/ebsa/pdf/preventiveserviceseligibleorganizationcerti ficationform.pdf) is short, its meat the following sentence: "I certify that, on account of religious objections, the organization opposes providing coverage for some or all of any contraceptive services that would otherwise be required to be covered; the organization is organized and operates as a nonprofit entity; and the organization holds itself out as a religious organization." The form states that "the organization or its plan must provide a copy of this certification to the plan's health insurance issuer (for insured health plans) or a third party administrator (for self-insured health plans) in order for the plan to be accommodated with respect to the contraceptive coverage requirement." So Notre Dame, if it decided to sign the exemption form, would have to give copies to both Aetna and Meritain.

As noted at the outset of this opinion, the Affordable Care Act requires providers of health insurance (including third-party administrators of self-insured health plans, even though they are conduits rather than ultimate payors of plan benefits) to provide contraceptive coverage for women. The exemption form if signed by Notre Dame and sent to Aetna and Meritain would therefore inform them that since Notre Dame was not going to pay for contraceptive coverage of its students and staff, Aetna and Meritain would have to pay. Aetna (including its Meritain subsidiary) has neither religious nor financial objections to paying for contraception. Regarding the cost to these companies, the government will reimburse at least 110 percent of the third-party administrator's (Meritain's) costs, while Aetna can expect to recoup its costs of contraceptive coverage from savings on pregnancy medical care (since there will be fewer pregnancies if contraception is more broadly available, at no cost, to Notre Dame's female employees and students) as well as from other regulatory offsets.

The regulations required Aetna and Meritain, if Notre Dame signed and sent the exemption form—but not Notre Dame—to inform the university's female employees and students that those companies would be covering their contraceptive costs. The companies could either "provide payments for contraceptive services" themselves or, alternatively, "arrange for an insurer or other entity to provide payments for" those services, but they could not "impos[e] any cost-sharing requirements (such as a copayment, coinsurance, or a deductible), or impos[e] a premium, fee, or other charge, or any portion thereof, directly or indirectly, on the eligible organization, the group health plan, or plan participants or beneficiaries."

The regulations thus sought an accommodation between the secular interests that had motivated the requirement to provide contraceptive services to women free of charge and the interests of religious objectors. Accommodation is consistent with the balancing act required by the Religious Freedom Restoration Act, which as we noted requires consideration of "substantial burden" (on the institution unwilling to provide contraceptive services), a "compelling governmental interest" in that provision, and the "least restrictive means" that is feasible for realizing the government's interest. . . .

Our previous opinion had expressed puzzlement about what exactly the university wanted us to enjoin. It had by that time signed EBSA Form 700 and sent copies to Aetna and Meritain, thus obtaining the statutory accommodation, and the companies had notified Notre Dame's employees and students that they (the companies, not the university) would be providing contraceptive coverage. We now have (we think) a clearer idea of what the university wants. It wants us to enjoin the government from forbidding Notre Dame to bar Aetna and Meritain from providing contraceptive coverage to any of the university's students or employees. Because of its contractual relations with the two companies, which continue to provide health insurance coverage and administration for medical services apart from contraception as a method of preventing pregnancy, Notre Dame claims to be complicit in the sin of contraception. It wants to dissolve that complicity by forbidding Aetna and Meritain—with both of which, to repeat, it continues to have contractual relations—to provide any contraceptive coverage to Notre Dame students or staff. The result would be that the students and staff currently lacking coverage other than from Aetna or Meritain would have to fend for themselves, seeking contraceptive coverage elsewhere in the health insurance market.

Notre Dame does not forbid its students or staff to use contraception or to obtain reimbursement from health insurance companies for their purchase of contraceptives. Its objection that it asks us to ratify by issuing a preliminary injunction is to Aetna's and Meritain's being legally obligated to make contraceptive coverage available to Notre Dame students and staff. It regards its contractual relationship with those companies as making the university a conduit between the suppliers of the coverage and the university's students and employees. In the university's words, the contraception regulation imposes a substantial burden on it by forcing the university to "identify[ ] and contract[ ] with a third party willing to provide the very services Notre Dame deems objectionable."

But the scanty record contains no evidence to support the conduit theory. Although Notre Dame is the final arbiter of its religious beliefs, it is for the courts to determine whether the law actually forces Notre Dame to act in a way that would violate those beliefs. As far as we can determine from the very limited record, the only "conduit" is between the companies and Notre Dame students and staff; the university has stepped aside. Thus it tells its students (and we assume its staff as well) that "the University of Notre Dame honors the moral teachings of the Catholic Church. Therefore, for example, University Health Services may prescribe contraceptive medications to treat approved medical conditions, but not to prevent pregnancy. To comply with federal law, Aetna Student Health provides coverage for additional women's health products or procedures that the University objects to based on its religious beliefs. *This coverage is separate from Notre Dame.* Students enrolled in Aetna Student Health may call Aetna customer service at 877-378-9492 for more information. Students not covered by Aetna Student Health should check with their own insurance plans regarding federally-mandated women's health coverage." University of Notre Dame Health Services, "FAQ–Aetna Student Health," http://uhs.nd.edu/insurance-billing/faq-aetna-student-health-ans/ (emphasis added). There thus is no suggestion that Notre Dame is involved at all in Aetna's and Meritain's contraception coverage.

When the case was last before us, in 2014, the university's lawyer had similarly argued that Notre Dame's health plans were the "conduit" through which the employees and students obtained contraceptive coverage, making Notre Dame complicit in sin. But the lawyer also had said that his client would have no problem if each of its female employees signed and mailed to Meritain (and its students mailed to Aetna) a form saying "I have insurance through Notre Dame, but the university won't cover contraceptive services, so now you must cover them." It's difficult to see how that would make the health plan any less of a "conduit" between Notre Dame and Aetna/Meritain.

It's not even clear that by forcing Aetna/Meritain to provide Notre Dame's students and staff with contraception coverage the government is forcing Notre Dame to do business with an entity that is providing an objectionable service to the Notre Dame community. For the government authorizes a third-party administrator to "arrange for an issuer or other entity" to pay for contraception coverage and bill the expense to the government. Notre Dame thus could ask Meritain to outsource contraception coverage for both students and staff to an entity that does no business with Notre Dame. The university would have no contractual relationship with that entity and so would not be involved even indirectly in the provision of contraceptive coverage to its students and employees.

A further problem with Notre Dame's quest for a preliminary injunction is the absence from the record of its contracts with Aetna and Meritain. We are not told what the duration of the contracts is, whether or in what circumstances they are terminable by Notre Dame before their expiration date, or what the financial consequences to the companies might be given that the federal government reimburses health insurers' contraception payouts generously. So far as contraception is concerned, health insurers are merely intermediaries between the federal government and the consumers. We are led in turn to wonder whether the government—which rarely provides health services directly to patients but rather uses health care companies to provide those services as the government's agents—might without offending Notre Dame's religious scruples hire Aetna and Meritain to provide that coverage. That would be simpler and more direct than the government's shopping for other health insurance companies to be its agents in dealing with Notre Dame's students and staff.

It is irregular, moreover, for a court to be asked to enjoin nonparties. For all we know, Aetna and its subsidiary value the opportunity to provide contraception coverage with generous reimbursement by the federal government. (The record, consistent with its sparseness, contains almost nothing about Aetna or Meritain.) Their business is providing health care, health care administration, and health insurance, and Notre Dame wants unilaterally to exclude them from a possibly lucrative chunk of that business. When the university, albeit under protest, signed and mailed the exemption form, Aetna and Meritain reasonably believed that they had an economic opportunity—that for the first time they would be providing contraceptive coverage to the Notre Dame community. (Remember that before the Affordable Care Act was passed they provided no such coverage to the community.) They have had no opportunity to intervene in the district court, where proceedings have been suspended pending Notre Dame's appellate submissions culminating in this case.

Notre Dame takes particular umbrage at the regulation under the Affordable Care Act which states that "if the eligible organization provides a copy of the self-certification [EBSA Form 700] of its objection to administering or funding any contraceptive benefits ... to a third party administrator [Meritain], the self-certification shall be an instrument under which the plan is operated, [and] shall be treated as a designation of the third party administrator as the plan administrator under section 3(16) of ERISA for any contraceptive services required to be covered under § 2590.715–2713(a)(1)(iv) of this chapter to which the eligible organization objects on religious grounds." (What a mouthful!) Notre Dame treats this regulation as having made its mailing of the certification form to its third-party administrator (Meritain) the *cause* of the provision of contraceptive services to its employees in violation of its religious beliefs. That's not correct. Since there is now a federal right, unquestioned by Notre Dame, to contraceptive services, the effect of the university's exercise of its religious exemption is to throw the entire burden of administration on the entities (Aetna and Meritain) that now provide contraceptive coverage to Notre Dame's students and staff. The university is permitted to opt out of providing federally mandated contraceptive services, and the federal government determines (enlists, drafts, conscripts) substitute providers, and it is not surprising that they are the providers who already are providing health services to university students and staff.

The university argues that by conditioning its right not to provide contraceptive coverage for its students and staff on its signing EBSA Form 700 and giving copies to Aetna and Meritain, the government has, in violation of RFRA, "substantially burden[ed] a person's exercise of religion" (the university is a nonprofit corporate "person"), and that no "compelling governmental interest" justifies that burdening. It notes that the Catholic concept of "scandal" forbids the encouragement (equivalent to aiding and abetting) of sinful acts; a 2013 affidavit by Notre Dame's executive vice-president defines " 'scandal' ... in the theological context ... as encouraging by words or example other persons to engage in wrongdoing." Of course in invoking the exemption the university also throws the entire administrative and financial burden of providing contraception on the health insurer and third-party administrator, which are secular organizations that unlike the university have no aversion to providing contraceptive coverage. The result is to lift a burden from the university's shoulders.

Alternatively Notre Dame charges that the government has "coerce[d] [it] into serving as the crucial link between contraceptive providers and recipients." That's a recursion to the "conduit" theory, and ignores that as a result of the university's signing the exemption form, students and staff now deal directly with Aetna and Meritain, bypassing Notre Dame. It is federal law, rather than the religious organization's signing and mailing the form, that requires health-care insurers, along with third-party administrators of self-insured health plans, to cover contraceptive services. By refusing to fill out the form Notre Dame would subject itself to penalties, but Aetna and Meritain would still be required to provide the services to the university's students and employees.

Notre Dame says no—that had it not filled out the form, Meritain wouldn't have been *authorized* to provide contraceptive services because it would have been a "plan administrator" under section 3(16) of ERISA, and thus not a plan fiduciary entitled to make expenditures (as for contraception coverage) on behalf of the plan. The university argues that it alone is authorized to designate a plan fiduciary, and that it made that designation in the form that it mailed to the company and thus is complicit in the provision of contraceptives to the university's staff. This version of Notre Dame's "triggering" argument does not apply to Aetna, which is the students' health insurer and so already a plan fiduciary, required therefore by the Affordable Care Act to provide contraceptive coverage to plan members whether or not Notre Dame signs the form. Even as to Meritain, although "many agreements between third party administrators and plan sponsors prohibit third party administrators from serving as fiduciaries," "many" is not "all" or even "most." Notre Dame has presented no evidence that its contract with Meritain forbids the latter to be a plan fiduciary (remember that the contract is not in the record).

Nor has the university been ordered to name Meritain as a plan fiduciary. Rather, the signed form "*shall be treated as* a designation of the third party administrator as the plan administrator under section 3(16) of ERISA for any contraceptive services required to be covered." Treated and designated by whom? By the government. The delivery of a copy of the form to Meritain reminds it of an obligation that the *law*, not the university, imposes on it—the obligation to pick up the ball if Notre Dame decides, as is its right, to drop it. Notre Dame's signing the form no more "triggers" Meritain's obligation to provide contraceptive services than a tortfeasor's declaring bankruptcy "triggers" his co-tortfeasors' joint and several liability for damages. Meritain must provide the services no matter what; signing the form simply shifts the financial burden from the university to the government, as desired by the university.

Suppose the United States, like the United Kingdom, Canada, and many other foreign nations, had a "single payer" health care system. In such a system, the government pays the cost of specified medical services (if the United States had such a system, it would be the equivalent of Medicare for everyone), rather than employers, health insurers, and patients, though patients may be charged directly for some of the expense of the medical care provided by the system, as distinct from indirectly through taxes. If our hypothetical single-payer system paid the full expense of female contraceptives, Notre Dame couldn't argue that the system placed a "substantial burden" on the university's compliance with Catholic doctrine, for Notre Dame does not deny the existence of the legitimate secular interests noted at the outset of this opinion that justify a federal program of paying for contraceptive expenses. It even advised the district court that to "achieve its asserted interests without forcing Notre Dame to violate its religious beliefs" the government could "directly provide contraceptive[s]" to the university's staff and students or, alternatively, "directly offer insurance coverage for contraceptive services." The consequence in either case would be a single-payer system for contraceptives. The main difference between such a system and the Affordable Care Act is that under the Act the government, instead of providing medical services directly, uses private insurance providers and health plan administrators as its agents to provide medical services subsidized by the government.

If the government is entitled to require that female contraceptives be provided to women free of charge, it is unclear how signing the form that declares Notre Dame's authorized refusal to pay for contraceptives for its students or staff, and its mailing the authorization document to those companies, which under federal law are obligated to pick up the tab, could be thought to "trigger" the provision of contraceptive coverage.

But we must—we have been ordered by the Supreme Court to—consider the bearing on our analysis of *Hobby Lobby*. The Supreme Court did leave open in *Hobby Lobby* the possibility that the accommodation sought and obtained there would not prevent religious beliefs or practices from being substantially burdened in some cases. But it gave no examples; perhaps it remanded our case for further consideration of that possibility. We've suggested in this opinion that Notre Dame could as an alternative to the official accommodation direct Meritain to delegate to companies that have no contractual relationship with Notre Dame (as Aetna and Meritain do) the provision of contraception coverage to the university's students and staff. Then Notre Dame would be outside the loop.

Notre Dame does note possible alternatives, such as a single-payer system in which Notre Dame women would apply directly to the government for reimbursement of their costs of buying contraceptives. But at this stage in the litigation, with no trial having been conducted, we have no basis for concluding that any of the university's proposed alternatives would avoid imposing an unreasonable cost either on the government or on Notre Dame's students and employees. The government, as we said, typically provides medical services, including reimbursement of costs incurred by medical providers, indirectly, through health insurance companies such as Aetna. Does Notre Dame expect the government to establish a federal contraception agency to which Notre Dame women should send the bills for the contraceptives they buy? Alternatively, must every woman who wants reimbursement of contraceptive costs pick a health insurance company, maybe on the basis of a Google search, to contract with? This seem to be what the university has in mind when it says in its position statement that it has no "objection to a system in which its employees or students coordinated with an *independent* insurer to provide coverage that 'would not involve Notre Dame'" (emphasis in original). But because it's a bother for a person to shop for the "best" contraceptive coverage, the proposed solution would reduce the number of women with such coverage, compared to their being entitled to such coverage automatically by virtue of being Notre Dame students or employees.

The Supreme Court pertinently observed in its *Hobby Lobby* opinion that the official accommodation (the accommodation that Notre Dame wants to escape from) would not impede "women's receipt of benefits by requiring them to take steps to learn about, and to sign up for, a new government funded and administered health benefit." So far as we can tell from an undeveloped record, the alternatives suggested by Notre Dame would impede the receipt of such benefits.

Notre Dame says in its position statement that the government has "*many* alternative ways of providing free contraceptive coverage without using the health plans of objecting religious non-profits as the conduit" (emphasis added). Put to one side the question in what sense students and staff dealing directly as they now do with Aetna and Meritain are "using" Notre Dame's health plans—plans that exclude contraception coverage. Our present concern is that Notre Dame has thus far failed to explain the "many alternative ways" (elsewhere it refers to "the myriad ways" or "any number of ways" in which the government can provide free contraceptive coverage to Notre Dame's students and staff)—and it admits that it (that is, Notre Dame) "opposes many of these alternatives on policy grounds."

It lists the following "myriad ways": The government could

> (i) directly provide contraceptive services to the few individuals who do not receive it under their health plans;

> (ii) offer grants to entities that already provide contraceptive services at free or subsidized rates and/or work with these entities to expand delivery of the services;

> (iii) directly offer insurance coverage for contraceptive services;

> (iv) grant tax credits or deductions to women who purchase contraceptive services; or

(v) allow Notre Dame and other Catholic non-profit organizations to comply with the Mandate [what we are calling the accommodation or official accommodation] by providing coverage for methods of family planning consistent with Catholic beliefs (i.e., Natural Family Planning training and materials).

Number v is not contraception at all; iv elides all consideration of the costs and complications of the administrative machinery for providing tax incentives to consumers; options i through iii similarly would involve cumbersome administrative machinery and at the same time impose a burden on Notre Dame's female students and employees who want to obtain contraceptives.

Nor does Notre Dame explain how a government program that directly or indirectly provided contraception coverage to Notre Dame employees—as Notre Dame suggests—would avoid complicity in sin. Were Notre Dame to hire an unemployed person who, by virtue of becoming employed by Notre Dame, obtained contraception coverage for the first time, would not the university be "triggering" the new employee's access to contraception?

We point out, finally, that a religious institution does not have to sign ESBA 700 in order to exempt itself from the requirement of providing contraceptive coverage to employees and (if the institution is a college or university) students. It can in the alternative notify the Department of Health and Human Services. That was the alternative chosen by another institution of higher learning that was unwilling to provide contraceptive coverage or even sign the ESBA 700. In *Wheaton College v. Burwell*, ___ U.S. ___, 134 S.Ct. 2806, 189 L.Ed.2d 856 (2014) (per curiam), the Supreme Court said that "if the applicant informs the Secretary of Health and Human Services in writing that it is a nonprofit organization that holds itself out as religious and has religious objections to providing coverage for contraceptive services, the respondents are enjoined from enforcing against the applicant the challenged provisions of the Patient Protection and Affordable Care Act and related regulations pending final disposition of appellate review. To meet the condition for injunction pending appeal, the applicant need not use the form prescribed by the Government, EBSA Form 700, and need not send copies to health insurance issuers or third-party administrators." We assume that Notre Dame could ask Aetna and Meritain to ignore its submission to them of the signed ESBA 700, and instead could itself inform the Secretary of Health and Human Services of its desire to be exempt on religious grounds from providing contraceptive coverage; undoubtedly the Secretary would agree.

Notre Dame tells us that it likewise objects to that alternative. But based on the sparse record before us, there is a strong argument that given the government's legitimate interest in the provision of contraceptive coverage to women without cost to them, notice to the government would strike the proper balance between legitimate governmental and sincere religious interests. That was the accommodation sought and received by Wheaton College.

We are put in mind of *Bowen v. Roy,* 476 U.S. 693, 106 S.Ct. 2147, 90 L.Ed.2d 735 (1986). Roy objected that any use of his daughter's Social Security number would substantially burden his religious beliefs because he believed that use of that unique identifier would harm her spirit. He wanted an accommodation that would relieve him of the burden of providing the number in his applications for welfare and food stamps and prevent the government from using the number in its internal administration. The Supreme Court refused. It said that "Roy may no more prevail on his religious objection to the Government's use of a Social Security number for his daughter than he could on a sincere religious objection to the size or color of the Government's filing cabinets." The very word "accommodation" implies a balance of competing interests; and when we compare the burden on the government or third parties of having to establish some entirely new method of providing contraceptive coverage with the burden on Notre Dame of simply notifying the government that the ball is now in the government's court, we cannot conclude that Notre Dame has yet established its right to the injunctive relief that it is seeking before trial. The mandate to cover contraceptive care as part of any broad health insurance package provided by employers (or in the case of educational institutions, students as well) was intended to minimize financial, administrative, and logistical obstacles to such coverage. All of Notre Dame's suggested alternatives would impose significant financial, administrative, and logistical obstacles by requiring women to sign up for separate coverage either with a government agency or with another private insurer. Such obstacles were considered by the Supreme Court in *Hobby Lobby* in support of the same accommodation that Notre Dame refuses to accept.

We emphasize in closing the tentative character of the analysis in this opinion. The record is insufficiently developed to enable us to rule definitively on Notre Dame's claims. The burden of establishing an entitlement to a preliminary injunction was of course on the university, not on the government. The burden has not been carried. Chief Judge Simon's denial of preliminary relief is therefore once again

AFFIRMED.

■ FLAUM, CIRCUIT JUDGE, dissenting.

By requiring health insurers to provide contraceptive coverage, the Patient Protection and Affordable Care Act ("ACA") forces Notre Dame to act in ways it says violate its religious beliefs. The resultant burden on Notre Dame's rights is substantial: because Notre Dame offers health insurance to its students, and especially because it acts as a self-insurer for its employees, the law turns Notre Dame into a conduit for the provision of cost-free contraception. It also compels Notre Dame to contract with parties—Meritain and Aetna—in a manner in which Notre Dame believes makes it complicit in moral wrong. Notre Dame's only alternative is to endure crippling fines.

In light of the Supreme Court's ruling in *Hobby Lobby*—the decision the Court cited in asking us to reconsider this case—Notre Dame has articulated a substantial burden for purposes of the Religious Freedom Restoration Act ("RFRA"). As a result, strict scrutiny governs our consideration of Notre Dame's challenge here, and the government has the burden of demonstrating that the challenged accommodation is the least restrictive means of serving a compelling interest. In my view, the government has not satisfied that charge. Accordingly, I respectfully dissent, concluding that Notre Dame is entitled to a preliminary injunction pending the district court's decision of this case on the merits.

In Notre Dame's view, the ACA alters its relationships with both Meritain and Aetna in a way that renders Notre Dame morally complicit in the provision of contraception. Put simply, Notre Dame is too engaged in a process—the very premise of which offends its religion—that the church itself is exempted from entirely.

The majority appears to minimize the significance of Notre Dame's position by focusing on its continued objection to the mandate in the face of a proffered accommodation. I believe that any inquiry into the rationality of that position is precluded by the Supreme Court's decision in *Hobby Lobby*, which in my view underscores the legitimacy of Notre Dame's religious objection. There, as here, HHS's main argument was "basically that the connection between what the objecting parties must do . . . and the end that they find to be morally wrong . . . [was] simply too attenuated." However, the Supreme Court made clear that this position, at least in this narrow context, is untenable. That's because it "dodges the question that RFRA presents (whether the HHS mandate imposes a substantial burden on the ability of the objecting parties to conduct business in accordance with *their religious beliefs*) and instead addresses a very different question that the federal courts have no business addressing (whether the religious belief asserted in a RFRA case is reasonable)."

Like the plaintiffs' challenge in *Hobby Lobby*, Notre Dame's deeply held religious beliefs about contraception and the formation and prevention of human life "implicate[ ] a difficult and important question of religion and moral philosophy, namely, the circumstances under which it is wrong for a person to perform an act that is innocent in itself but that has the effect of enabling or facilitating the commission of an immoral act by another." Notre Dame is no doubt differently situated than the *Hobby Lobby* plaintiffs, who had to directly provide contraceptive insurance. Nevertheless, the ACA also places Notre Dame in a position that contravenes its belief system. Yet the majority here sides with HHS, and "in effect tell[s] the plaintiff[ ] that [its] beliefs are flawed." The *Hobby Lobby* Court, however, rejected that position. And so do I.

As the Court noted, "[t]he least-restrictive-means standard is exceptionally demanding," and it is the government's burden to demonstrate that "it lacks other means of achieving its desired goal without imposing a substantial burden on the exercise of religion by the objecting part[y]." Here again, the majority in our case sets aside *Hobby Lobby*, instead assigning Notre Dame this burden because it seeks a preliminary injunction.

The majority observes that Notre Dame has presented "possible alternatives" to the accommodation that would not infringe its religious exercise. Yet it concludes that Notre Dame has failed to present an adequate proposal for how the government can efficiently (and conveniently) implement and administer an alternative program. But to reiterate, *Hobby Lobby* expressly informs that it is the government's, not Notre Dame's, burden to establish that the accommodation is the least restrictive means of advancing a compelling government interest. Moreover, the suggestion by the majority that any alternative method of advancing the government's interests would likely be too costly or cumbersome to the government turns a blind eye to the Supreme Court's latest teachings. What matters under RFRA is whether the means by which the government is attempting to advance its compelling interest is the least burdensome on Notre Dame's religious beliefs. Accordingly, RFRA may require the government to start over and "creat[e] ... entirely new programs," and it "may in some circumstances require the Government to expend additional funds to accommodate citizens' religious beliefs." For those reasons, the Supreme Court made clear that, in this sphere, "[t]he most straightforward way" of serving the Government's interests would be for it to assume the cost of providing contraception "to any women who are unable to obtain them under their health-insurance policies due to their employers' religious objections." Here, as in *Hobby Lobby*, "HHS has not shown ... that this is not a viable alternative." For that reason, I would reverse the decision of the district court denying Notre Dame a preliminary injunction.

NOTES AND QUESTIONS

1.   *Conscience and Complicity.* What was the objection of conscience that Notre Dame had to the ACA? Do you understand the complicity argument? With what evil did Notre Dame say it was complicit? What did the concept of scandal have to do with Notre Dame's argument? The opinion "notes that the Catholic concept of 'scandal' forbids the encouragement of sinful acts; a 2013 affidavit by Notre Dame's executive

vice-president defines ' "scandal" ... in the theological context ... as encouraging by words or example other persons to engage in wrongdoing.' "

Does RFRA place any limits on claims of complicity and scandal? Should the courts accept only "reasonable" claims of complicity and scandal? Or must courts accept these claims at face value? See generally Amy J. Sepinwall, Conscience and Complicity: Assessing Pleas for Religious Exemptions in *Hobby Lobby*'s Wake, 82 U. Chic. L. Rev. 1897 (2015).

2. *RFRA Analysis: Substantial Burden.* You read *Hobby Lobby* in Chapter 4. Who did a better job of following the Court's guidance on what constitutes a substantial burden, Judge Posner or Judge Flaum? How do you assess what Judge Posner wrote about Notre Dame in the following paragraphs? Is he too dismissive of the school's complicity argument?

> Notre Dame treats this regulation as having made its mailing of the certification form to its third-party administrator (Meritain) the *cause* of the provision of contraceptive services to its employees in violation of its religious beliefs. That's not correct.

> Notre Dame's signing the form no more "triggers" Meritain's obligation to provide contraceptive services than a tortfeasor's declaring bankruptcy "triggers" his co-tortfeasors' joint and several liability for damages.

> Alternatively Notre Dame charges that the government has "coerce[d] [it] into serving as the crucial link between contraceptive providers and recipients." That's a recursion to the "conduit" theory, and ignores that as a result of the university's signing the exemption form, students and staff now deal directly with Aetna and Meritain, bypassing Notre Dame. It is federal law, rather than the religious organization's signing and mailing the form, that requires health-care insurers, along with third-party administrators of self-insured health plans, to cover contraceptive services.

What do you think of Judge Flaum's argument that Posner did exactly what the Court rejected in *Hobby Lobby*, namely address whether Notre Dame's religious belief was reasonable rather than whether it was substantially burdened?

3. *RFRA Analysis: Least Restrictive Means.* How many least restrictive means of providing contraceptive coverage are identified in the opinion? The court listed the following five options that were acceptable to Notre Dame; the government could:

> (i) directly provide contraceptive services to the few individuals who do not receive it under their health plans;

> (ii) offer grants to entities that already provide contraceptive services at free or subsidized rates and/or work with these entities to expand delivery of the services;

(iii) directly offer insurance coverage for contraceptive services;

(iv) grant tax credits or deductions to women who purchase contraceptive services; or

(v) allow Notre Dame and other Catholic non-profit organizations to comply with the Mandate [what we are calling the accommodation or official accommodation] by providing coverage for methods of family planning consistent with Catholic beliefs (i.e., Natural Family Planning training and materials).

In the opinion, Posner also suggested that "Notre Dame thus could ask Meritain to outsource contraception coverage for both students and staff to an entity that does no business with Notre Dame." Or, perhaps, Judge Posner wondered "whether the government—which rarely provides health services directly to patients but rather uses health care companies to provide those services as the government's agents—might without offending Notre Dame's religious scruples hire Aetna and Meritain to provide that coverage." Moreover, he wrote:

Notre Dame does note possible alternatives, such as a single-payer system in which Notre Dame women would apply directly to the government for reimbursement of their costs of buying contraceptives. Does Notre Dame expect the government to establish a federal contraception agency to which Notre Dame women should send the bills for the contraceptives they buy? Alternatively, must every woman who wants reimbursement of contraceptive costs pick a health insurance company, maybe on the basis of a Google search, to contract with? This seem to be what the university has in mind when it says in its position statement that it has no "objection to a system in which its employees or students coordinated with an *independent* insurer to provide coverage that 'would not involve Notre Dame' " (emphasis in original)

How do you assess these possibilities? Should Notre Dame win the case if any one of them is a possibility?

4. *Bowen v. Roy.* Do you agree that the Social Security number case is comparable to this one?

5. *Circuit Split.* Eight of nine appeals courts ruled for the government in the religious nonprofit cases. After the Eighth Circuit ruled for the nonprofits, see Sharpe Holdings, Inc. v. Department of Health and Human Servs., 801 F.3d 927 (8th Cir. 2015), the Court granted certiorari and consolidated appeal in seven cases from the Third, Fifth, Tenth, and D.C. Circuits in Zubik v. Burwell, 136 S.Ct. 444 (2015). The court granted cert. on the issue "whether the contraception coverage mandate and its accommodation violate the Religious Freedom Restoration Act by forcing religious nonprofits to act in violation of their sincerely held religious beliefs, when the government has not proven that this compulsion is the least restrictive means of advancing any compelling interest."

6. *Oral Argument.* Early in the oral argument in *Zubik*, Paul Clement for the nonprofit petitioners argued the government is going to "hijack our health plans and provide the coverage against our will." Zubik v. Burwell, 2016 WL 1134578 (U.S.), 14 (U.S.Oral.Arg., 2016). What do you think of the hijacking metaphor? Do you agree the ACA hijacked the nonprofits' plans? Is there any metaphor that the government should have used to counter the concept of hijacking?

The hijacking language seemed to take hold among the Justices.

CHIEF JUSTICE ROBERTS: Petitioner has used the phrase 'hijacking,' and it seems to me that that's an accurate description of what the government wants to do. They want to use the mechanism that the Little Sisters and the other Petitioners have set up to provide services because they want the coverage to be seamless.

JUSTICE KENNEDY, to the Solicitor General: "That's why it's necessary to hijack the plans."

JUSTICE BREYER: "Do I have the other part right, which is this is not hijacking because there is a Federal regulation that says the infrastructure of the insurers' contraceptive-related plan belongs to the insurer, not to the person who buys the insurance? Am I correct about that?"

GENERAL VERRILLI: And that's all—that's all correct, Your Honor. And that's why when I say when we make an arrangement with Aetna or Blue Cross, we are not making an arrangement with Petitioners or anything that Petitioners own.

JUSTICE SOTOMAYOR: General, the—we've used—the hijack analogy has been mentioned. Can you explain why you don't see this as a hijacking?

GENERAL VERRILLI: All right. I think what we've tried to—the—the way I've tried to explain that, Your Honor, is that we have tried—and I think the Court recognized this in *Hobby Lobby*, that the goal of this is to exempt the employer from providing the contraceptive coverage, to exempt them and to provide it as separate means through separate funds without their involvement, and therefore, it's not hijacking.

Is there a better answer to Justice Sotomayor's question? Justice Sotomayor also wondered if the logic of the nonprofits' argument meant that conscientious objectors to war should have a right not to notify the government of their objection because someone else would be sent to war in their place.

How should Mr. Clement have answered the following question from Justice Kagan:

> But what happens if somebody did just object to objecting? It seems all your arguments would apply the same way. In other words, somebody comes in and says, I do object to objecting because objecting will make it easier for the government to fill my slot. That's a perfectly understandable thing to say. And that's

part of my sincere religious belief. And you say the sincere religious belief is what controls. And there too it would seem under your very theory you would have to say that that's a substantial burden, even if it's objecting to objecting.

7. *Supplemental Briefing.* After oral arguments, in an unusual action, the Court requested supplemental briefing to address how the female employees of the religious nonprofits might obtain contraceptive coverage in a way that requires no involvement—not even notice—on the part of their employers. The Court's order read:

> The parties are directed to file supplemental briefs that address whether and how contraceptive coverage may be obtained by petitioners' employees through petitioners' insurance companies, but in a way that does not require any involvement of petitioners beyond their own decision to provide health insurance without contraceptive coverage to their employees.

> Petitioners with insured plans are currently required to submit a form either to their insurer or to the Federal Government (naming petitioners' insurance company), stating that petitioners object on religious grounds to providing contraceptive coverage. The parties are directed to address whether contraceptive coverage could be provided to petitioners' employees, through petitioners' insurance companies, without any such notice from petitioners.

> For example, the parties should consider a situation in which petitioners would contract to provide health insurance for their employees, and in the course of obtaining such insurance, inform their insurance company that they do not want their health plan to include contraceptive coverage of the type to which they object on religious grounds. Petitioners would have no legal obligation to provide such contraceptive coverage, would not pay for such coverage, and would not be required to submit any separate notice to their insurer, to the Federal Government, or to their employees. At the same time, petitioners' insurance company—aware that petitioners are not providing certain contraceptive coverage on religious grounds—would separately notify petitioners' employees that the insurance company will provide cost-free contraceptive coverage, and that such coverage is not paid for by petitioners and is not provided through petitioners' health plan. . . .

Order, Zubik v. Burwell, 194 L. Ed. 2d 599 (March 29, 2016). If you were a religious nonprofit like Notre Dame, what would you have written in your brief? What would you have written if you were defending the government?

After assessing the parties' supplemental briefs, the Court unexpectedly declined to reach the merits of the case. Instead, finding that the parties had some common ground, the Court issued the following per curiam opinion remanding the cases to the circuit courts to determine an appropriate resolution. Was conscience protected in the Court's decision? Was the Petitioners' complicity argument accepted?

Zubik v. Burwell

Supreme Court of the United States, 2016.
578 U.S. ___, 136 S.Ct. 1557, 194 L.Ed.2d 696.

■ PER CURIAM.

Petitioners are primarily nonprofit organizations that provide health insurance to their employees. Federal regulations require petitioners to cover certain contraceptives as part of their health plans, unless petitioners submit a form either to their insurer or to the Federal Government, stating that they object on religious grounds to providing contraceptive coverage. Petitioners allege that submitting this notice substantially burdens the exercise of their religion, in violation of the Religious Freedom Restoration Act of 1993.

Following oral argument, the Court requested supplemental briefing from the parties addressing "whether contraceptive coverage could be provided to petitioners' employees, through petitioners' insurance companies, without any such notice from petitioners." Both petitioners and the Government now confirm that such an option is feasible. Petitioners have clarified that their religious exercise is not infringed where they "need to do nothing more than contract for a plan that does not include coverage for some or all forms of contraception," even if their employees receive cost-free contraceptive coverage from the same insurance company. The Government has confirmed that the challenged procedures "for employers with insured plans could be modified to operate in the manner posited in the Court's order while still ensuring that the affected women receive contraceptive coverage seamlessly, together with the rest of their health coverage."

In light of the positions asserted by the parties in their supplemental briefs, the Court vacates the judgments below and remands to the respective United States Courts of Appeals for the Third, Fifth, Tenth, and D. C. Circuits. Given the gravity of the dispute and the substantial clarification and refinement in the positions of the parties, the parties on remand should be afforded an opportunity to arrive at an approach going forward that accommodates petitioners' religious exercise while at the same time ensuring that women covered by petitioners' health plans "receive full and equal health coverage, including contraceptive coverage." We anticipate that the Courts of Appeals will allow the parties sufficient time to resolve any outstanding issues between them.

The Court finds the foregoing approach more suitable than addressing the significantly clarified views of the parties in the first instance. Although there may still be areas of disagreement between the parties on issues of implementation, the importance of those areas of potential concern is uncertain, as is the necessity of this Court's involvement at this point to resolve them.

The Court expresses no view on the merits of the cases. In particular, the Court does not decide whether petitioners' religious exercise has been substantially burdened, whether the Government has a compelling interest, or whether the current regulations are the least restrictive means of serving that interest.

Nothing in this opinion, or in the opinions or orders of the courts below, is to affect the ability of the Government to ensure that women covered by petitioners' health plans "obtain, without cost, the full range of FDA approved contraceptives." *Wheaton College v. Burwell,* 573 U.S. ___, ___, 134 S.Ct. 2806, 2807, 189 L.Ed.2d 856 (2014). Through this litigation, petitioners have made the Government aware of their view that they meet "the requirements for exemption from the contraceptive coverage requirement on religious grounds." *Id.,* at ___, 134 S.Ct., at 2807. Nothing in this opinion, or in the opinions or orders of the courts below, "precludes the Government from relying on this notice, to the extent it considers it necessary, to facilitate the provision of full contraceptive coverage" going forward. *Ibid.* Because the Government may rely on this notice, the Government may not impose taxes or penalties on petitioners for failure to provide the relevant notice.

The judgments of the Courts of Appeals are vacated, and the cases are remanded for further proceedings consistent with this opinion.

It is so ordered.

■ JUSTICE SOTOMAYOR, with whom JUSTICE GINSBURG joins, concurring.

I join the Court's *per curiam* opinion because it expresses no view on "the merits of the cases," "whether petitioners' religious exercise has been substantially burdened," or "whether the current regulations are the least restrictive means of serving" a compelling governmental interest. *Ante,* at 1560–1561. Lower courts, therefore, should not construe either today's *per curiam* or our order of March 29, 2016, as signals of where this Court stands. We have included similarly explicit disclaimers in previous orders. See, *e.g., Wheaton College v. Burwell,* 573 U.S. ___, 134 S.Ct. 2806, 189 L.Ed.2d 856 (2014) ("[T]his order should not be construed as an expression of the Court's views on the merits"). Yet some lower courts have ignored those instructions. See, *e.g., Sharpe Holdings, Inc. v. Department of Health and Human Servs.,* 801 F.3d 927, 944 (C.A.8 2015) ("[I]n *Wheaton College, Little Sisters of the Poor,* and *Zubik,* the Supreme Court approved a method of notice to HHS that is arguably less onerous than [existing regulations] yet permits the government to further its interests. Although the Court's orders were not final rulings on the merits, they at the very least collectively constitute a signal that less restrictive means exist by which the government may further its interests"). On remand in these cases, the Courts of Appeals should not make the same mistake.

I also join the Court's opinion because it allows the lower courts to consider only whether existing or modified regulations could provide seamless contraceptive coverage " 'to petitioners' employees, through petitioners' insurance companies, without any . . . notice from petitioners.' " The opinion does not, by contrast, endorse the petitioners' position that the existing regulations substantially burden their religious exercise or that contraceptive coverage must be provided through a "separate policy, with a separate enrollment process." Such separate contraceptive-only policies do not currently exist, and the Government has laid out a number of legal and practical obstacles to their creation. Requiring standalone contraceptive-only coverage would leave in limbo all of the women now guaranteed seamless preventive-care coverage under the Affordable Care Act. And requiring that women affirmatively opt into such coverage would "impose precisely the kind of barrier to the delivery of preventive services that Congress sought to eliminate."

Today's opinion does only what it says it does: "afford[s] an opportunity" for the parties and Courts of Appeals to reconsider the parties' arguments in light of petitioners' new articulation of their religious objection and the Government's clarification about what the existing regulations accomplish, how they might be amended, and what such an amendment would sacrifice. As enlightened by the parties' new submissions, the Courts of Appeals remain free to reach the same conclusion or a different one on each of the questions presented by these cases.

Recall that the Supreme Court originally remanded the *Notre Dame* case to the Seventh Circuit to be reconsidered in light of *Hobby Lobby*. On May 16, 2016, the Court again granted cert. in *Notre Dame v. Burwell*. This time the case was remanded for reconsideration in light of *Zubik*. See Univ. of Notre Dame v. Burwell, 136 S. Ct. 2007 (2016). How should the Seventh Circuit rule now?

Next we consider statutes passed specifically to protect medical conscience.

2.   CONSCIENCE CLAUSES

Elizabeth B. Deutsch, Expanding Conscience, Shrinking Care
124 Yale L.J. 2470, 2477–83 (2015).

A.   Origins of the Conscience Clause

Immediately after *Roe v. Wade* announced a right to abortion, Congress responded to concerns that medical staff would have to perform abortions despite religious objections by passing the Church Amendment. Under this Amendment, individual healthcare providers cannot be required to perform abortion or sterilization procedures. Further, the federal government cannot, as a condition of receipt of federal funds, require providers to make their facilities available for such procedures if they contravene the provider's "religious beliefs or moral convictions." The Amendment actually protects healthcare providers on both sides of the abortion issue: it prevents entities that receive certain federal funding from discriminating against medical personnel who either perform or refuse to perform abortion or sterilization procedures. The Amendment's legacy, however, has not been so even-handed.

Following the passage of the Church Amendment, more than half of the states enacted laws mirroring the federal protections by the end of 1974. Within four years, nearly all states had enacted such laws. With these protections in place, the issue was dormant until the mid-1990s, when changes to the structure of the healthcare industry catalyzed new exemptions.

B.   The Expansion of Federal Laws and the Ethical and Religious Directives

The Balanced Budget Act of 1997 protected two new forms of conscientious objection: (1) insurance companies administering Medicare and Medicaid benefits (payors) could now object in addition to practitioners; and (2) payors could now object to the provision of information, not just services. The Act provided that Medicaid managed-care plans and Medicare Choice plans may object to providing counseling or referral services on moral or religious grounds. In all other contexts, Medicaid managed-care organizations are explicitly prohibited from imposing "gag rules" on doctors.

The Coats Amendment in 1996 and the Weldon Amendment in 2005 further extended federal religious accommodation. The Coats Amendment prohibited the federal government and recipients of government funding from discriminating against providers that refuse to offer training in abortion services due to religious objections. The Weldon Amendment prohibited Department of Health and Human Services (HHS) appropriations from being made available to any state or local government discriminating against any healthcare entity that "does not provide, pay for, provide coverage of, or refer for abortions." This Amendment defined "health care entity" to include HMOs and insurance plans. These expansions further entrenched payors into the conscientious objection system.

The expanding exemptions reached their peak in 2008, in the waning hours of the Bush Administration. Secretary of Health and Human Services Mike Leavitt adopted the so-called "Midnight Regulations" that specifically aimed to expand (or "clarify") the definitions of "assistance" and "health care entity" in the Church Amendment. The regulation expanded "assistance" to include referrals and "health care entity" to include "an individual physician, a postgraduate physician training program, and a participant in a program of training in the health professions," as well as "hospitals and other entities" such as HMOs and health insurers. A leaked earlier draft would have expanded the definition of "abortion" to include so-called "abortifacient" forms of contraception, though the final text did not do so. The Midnight Regulations attempted to broaden federal accommodations to match expansive state laws until the Obama Administration reversed them in 2011. Because these regulations were reversed, federal law does not currently extend these provisions to information given to patients by their healthcare providers.

C. The Reach of State Conscience Clauses

Recent years have seen a wave of conscience-clause expansions at the state level, matching and sometimes outpacing the activity at the federal level. These state laws tend to allow more objections without ensuring meaningful protections for patients. Today, according to a Guttmacher Institute report, forty-six states allow individual objections to abortion; forty-four allow institutional objections; ten allow individual provider refusals of contraception; six allow pharmacist refusals of contraception; nine allow institutional refusals of contraception; seventeen allow individual refusals of sterilization services; and sixteen allow institutional refusals of sterilization services. Almost all state conscience clauses allow nurses or doctors to refuse to treat a patient even in an emergency or other time-sensitive situation.

The aggressive expansion of these state refusal laws began in the mid-1990s. The laws broadened exemptions in two respects. First, they expanded beyond abortion and sterilization to apply to contraception, then to end-of-life care, stem-cell research, and even, in some cases, to any unspecified health service to which a religious or moral objection may be raised, including counseling or the provision of information to patients about their health status. Second, they granted religious accommodation to more kinds of entities.

The most sweeping new state laws extend protection to any individual involved in healthcare regarding any part of any service to which he or she objects. For example, in 2004, Mississippi enacted the Health Care Rights of Conscience Act, which extends the protection afforded to doctors and nurses to all providers, institutions, and payors. This Act typifies the latest trend by establishing "the right not to participate . . . in a health care service that violates [one's] conscience." It defines health care service as "any phase of patient medical care, treatment or procedure, including, but not limited to . . . patient referral, counseling, therapy, testing, diagnosis or prognosis, research, instruction, prescribing, dispensing or administering any device, drug, or medication, surgery, or any other care or treatment rendered by health care providers or health care institutions." The Mississippi act further defines to "participate" as actions including "to counsel, advise, provide, perform, assist in, refer for, admit for purposes of providing, or participate in providing, any healthcare service or any form of such service." Moreover, it provides complete immunity from liability to healthcare providers who refuse to provide services or information.

What do you think about the interpretation of the Church Amendment in the following case? How much legal protection should Cenzon-DeCarlo enjoy? Which of the types of conscience clauses identified in the Deutsch reading should protect her?

Cenzon-DeCarlo v. Mount Sinai Hospital

United States District Court for the Eastern District of New York, 2010.
No. 09 CV 3120 (RJD), 2010 WL 169485 (Jan. 15, 2010).

■ DEARIE, J.

Plaintiff has worked as an operating room nurse at Mount Sinai since August of 2004. In addition to her full-time work week, she typically has been assigned an extra eight or nine "on-call" work shifts per month on weekends and holidays.[1] When hired, plaintiff made her objection to participating in abortion procedures known and filled out a form given to her by the hospital to register her religious objection. According to plaintiff, abortion procedures at Mount Sinai are generally scheduled for Saturday mornings.

Plaintiff alleges that on Sunday, May 24, 2009, while working an on-call shift, she was forced to assist in an abortion procedure against her known religious objection. She complained to her supervisors and filed a grievance under her union's collective bargaining agreement. She alleges that as a consequence of and in retaliation for her complaints and grievance, she was assigned only one on-call shift for the month of August.

Plaintiff further alleges that on July 16, 2009, her attorney accompanied her to a scheduled meeting to discuss her grievance, but the union refused to conduct the meeting with her attorney present. Shortly after the cancelled meeting, her manager told her that she would not be assigned to work on-call shifts in September unless she signed a statement that she would assist in abortions designated emergencies by the hospital. Plaintiff refused to sign.

---

[1]   Qualified nurses volunteer for these additional shifts, for additional pay, as a benefit of their employment, but in the absence of a sufficient number of volunteers, the hospital assigns the shifts.

Plaintiff commenced this action on July 21, 2009, claiming that Mount Sinai's actions constitute prohibited discrimination under the Church Amendment, 42 U.S.C. § 300a–7(c). She seeks a declaratory judgment that Mount Sinai has violated and continues to violate the Church Amendment and her rights thereunder. In addition, she seeks an injunction (1) prohibiting Mount Sinai from receiving any further qualifying federal funds under 42 U.S.C. § 300a–7(c) until it demonstrates compliance with the Church Amendment's non-discrimination provisions; (2) requiring Mount Sinai to disgorge qualifying federal funds it received under 42 U.S.C. § 300a–7(c); and (3) ordering Mount Sinai to restore plaintiff's access to on-call surgical team assignments and to refrain from forcing plaintiff and other health care personnel to participate in abortion procedures against their objections. Finally, plaintiff asks for damages from Mount Sinai for violating her rights under the Church Amendment.

The Church Amendment provides:

(c) Discrimination prohibition

(1) No entity which receives a grant, contract, loan, or loan guarantee under the Public Health Service Act [42 U.S.C.A. § 201 et seq.], the Community Mental Health Centers Act [42 U.S.C.A. § 2689 et seq.], or the Developmental Disabilities Services and Facilities Construction Act [42 U.S.C.A. § 6000 et seq.] after June 18, 1973, may—

(A) discriminate in the employment, promotion, or termination of employment of any physician or other health care personnel, or

(B) discriminate in the extension of staff or other privileges to any physician or other health care personnel,

because he performed or assisted in the performance of a lawful sterilization procedure or abortion, because he refused to perform or assist in the performance of such a procedure or abortion on the grounds that his performance or assistance in the performance of the procedure or abortion would be contrary to his religious beliefs or moral convictions, or because of his religious beliefs or moral convictions respecting sterilization procedures or abortions.

(2) No entity which receives after July 12, 1974, a grant or contract for biomedical or behavioral research under any program administered by the Secretary of Health and Human Services may—

> (A) discriminate in the employment, promotion, or termination of employment of any physician or other health care personnel, or
>
> (B) discriminate in the extension of staff or other privileges to any physician or other health care personnel,

because he performed or assisted in the performance of any lawful health service or research activity, because he refused to perform or assist in the performance of any such service or activity on the grounds that his performance or assistance in the performance of such service or activity would be contrary to his religious beliefs or moral convictions, or because of his religious beliefs or moral convictions respecting any such service or activity.

42 U.S.CA. § 300a–7(c). The parties agree that the Church Amendment contains no express private right of action to seek relief for alleged violations of the statute. Defendant moves to dismiss on the ground that no implied private right of action exists. . . .

Conclusion

The Court finds no basis for implying a private right of action under the Church Amendment. Accordingly, defendant's motion to dismiss pursuant to Rule 12(b)(6) of the Federal Rules of Civil Procedure is granted. The Court declines to exercise supplemental jurisdiction over the remaining state-law claims plaintiff added by amendment on November 30, 2009, and they are dismissed. In addition, plaintiff's application for a stay pending her addition of a Title VII claim, recently filed with the EEOC and with respect to which she has not yet received a right-to-sue letter, is denied.

NOTES AND QUESTIONS

1.   The Second Circuit upheld the district court's ruling that the Church Amendment does not provide a private right of action. See Cenzon-DeCarlo v. Mount Sinai Hosp., 626 F.3d 695 (2d Cir. 2010). Does Cenzon-DeCarlo have any other legal recourse? In the last paragraph of the opinion, the district court referred to possible state law and Title VII lawsuits. See also id. at 699 ("appellant has preserved state discrimination claims"). What type of lawsuit, if any, should Cenzon-DeCarlo be allowed to bring? Do you think she is entitled to damages from Mount Sinai?

Is it relevant to your analysis of this case whether the abortion was an emergency procedure? Whether other employees were available to take Cenzon-DeCarlo's place? Whether there was a six-hour window before the medical procedure was medically necessary? See James Nathaniel, Note, The Church Amendment: In Search of Enforcement, 68 Wash. & Lee L. Rev. 717, 718–23 (2011).

2. Is it appropriate for health care providers who have voluntarily entered the medical profession to refuse treatment to patients? For a review of the ethics of conscientious objection in medicine, see Julian Savulescu, Conscientious Objection in Medicine, 332 Brit. Med. J. 294 (Feb. 4, 2006).

3. *The Church Amendment.* In October 1972, James and Gloria Taylor went to St. Vincent's Hospital in Billings, Montana, to deliver their second child. Earlier that year, St. Vincent's, a Roman Catholic hospital run by the Sisters of Charity, had combined its maternity department with that of the only other hospital in town, the Billings Deaconess Hospital. During the merger negotiations, St. Vincent's had told Deaconess that it would not provide surgical sterilizations, which violate the "Ethical and Religious Directives for Catholic Hospitals." Instead, the two hospitals had an agreement that St. Vincent's would send patients desiring sterilization to Deaconess. The Taylors wanted to have a sterilization operation during Mrs. Taylor's cesarean section, but St. Vincent's refused their request.

The Taylors sued St. Vincent's for violation of their constitutional rights under 42 U.S.C. § 1983, arguing that St. Vincent's was a state actor because it received tax benefits from the State of Montana and federal funding under the Hill-Burton Act, 42 U.S.C. § 291, which had paid for some of the hospital's construction. The district court of Montana took jurisdiction of the case.

In response, Congress passed the Church Amendment to the Health Programs Extension Act of 1973 (see current version at 42 U.S.C. § 300a–7). The Church Amendment provided that a hospital that receives federal funding is not a state actor. Specifically, under that amendment courts could not order an entity that received federal funding to "make its facilities available for the performance of any sterilization procedure or abortion if the performance of such procedure or abortion in such facilities is prohibited by the entity on the basis of religious beliefs or moral convictions." Accordingly, the district court then refused jurisdiction over the Taylors' case because St. Vincent's was not a state actor. See Taylor v. St. Vincent's Hospital, 369 F.Supp. 948, 951 (D. Mont. 1973), aff'd by 523 F.2d 75 (9th Cir. 1975), cert. denied, 424 U.S. 948 (1976). The courts did not reach the Taylors' argument that the Church Amendments violated the Establishment Clause. St. Vincent's was not forced to perform a sterilization that contradicted Catholic principles and modern conscience clauses were born.

The Church Amendment was also prompted by the Supreme Court's January 1973 decision, Roe v. Wade, 410 U.S. 113 (1973), which held that the decision whether to abort or bear a pregnancy is protected by the constitutional right to privacy. Several religious groups, including Catholics, Mormons, Seventh-Day Adventists, Baptists and Muslims, have moral objections to abortion and have insisted on the necessity of conscience clauses as a matter of free exercise. See Lloyd Steffen, ed., Abortion: A Reader (1996) for denominational statements and attitudes toward abortions. See also Ronald M. Green, Religions' "Bioethical

Sensibility:" A Research Agenda, in Dena S. Davis & Laurie Zoloth, eds., Notes from a Narrow Ridge: Religion and Bioethics 165–81 (1999).

Now that you know the purpose of the Church Amendment, do you think Cenzon-DeCarlo should have been allowed a private right of action under the statute?

4. *The Ethical and Religious Directives.* Note that in the *Taylor* case, supra note 3, St. Vincent's subscribed to the Ethical and Religious Directives for Catholic hospitals. In a part of the article you didn't read, Deutsch explains that, at the same time conscience clauses were increasing in scope, most Catholic hospitals adopted the directives, which ban birth control, emergency contraception, tubal ligation, artificial insemination, in vitro fertilization, and abortion. The directives also require Catholic hospitals to impose those norms any time they merge with another hospital or health care service.

One in six hospital beds in the United States is in a Catholic hospital. Is it good that Catholic conscience is protected by a wide range of conscience clauses? Does your answer depend on how much money Catholic hospitals receive from government sources? Or do you agree with Deutsch that the "expansion of the Directives in lockstep with the expansion of conscience protections has produced a new crisis in reproductive care?" How would you decide the following cases?

Women commonly undergo sterilization by tubal ligation following a C-section. About 600,000 women in the United States have this procedure every year. The American College of Obstetricians and Gynecologists says "tubal ligation immediately after a woman's last intended childbirth is such a safe and effective procedure that it should be considered 'urgent' medical care." Having the procedure separately from the C-section is not recommended because the woman would have to undergo another round of anesthesia and surgery.

California law allows hospitals to refuse to perform abortions, but not sterilizations. The Catholic Church's Ethical and Religious Directives prohibit sterilization. The ACLU sued Mercy Medical Center in Redding, California, for sex discrimination after it refused tubal ligation to Rachel Miller. Although the hospital settled Miller's case and performed the surgery, it later denied tubal ligations to two other women. See Bob Egelko, Two More Women Denied Tubal Ligation, S.F. Chron., Dec. 7, 2015, at C1. Should those women be able to bring successful lawsuits against Mercy? The hospital says it will perform sterilizations "when necessary for 'the cure or alleviation of a present and serious pathology.'" What does that mean?

In Muskegon, Michigan, Tamara Means went to Mercy Health Partners at the eighteen-week mark of her pregnancy. Although doctors knew her fetus would not survive and that continuing her pregnancy posed serious risks to her health, they did not tell her that abortion was her safest medical choice. Instead, they told her to go home and return for follow-up care in a week. The next day, Means reappeared at the hospital with signs of a possibly-lethal bacterial infection, but was sent home again. On her third trip to the hospital she was about to be sent home when she went into delivery; her baby died immediately.

> The Directives instructed Mercy Health Partners not to facilitate miscarriage for Tamesha Means, even if there was no chance that the pregnancy would result in a viable live birth. The Directives also prevented the hospital's physicians from informing Means about treatment options that were inconsistent with the Directives but might be available elsewhere. Compounding the problem, Means was given no indication that Mercy Health Partners, as a religiously affiliated hospital, might withhold information, so she continued to seek treatment from the same doctors as she grew sicker.

Deutsch, supra, at 2473–74. Should Means have a successful lawsuit against Mercy Health or should the hospital be protected by conscience clauses?

Michigan Catholic Genesys Hospital also refused Jessica Mann a post-C-section tubal ligation. Mann and her doctor requested the sterilization after she was diagnosed with a brain tumor and advised not to have any more children. Mann's doctor has admitting privileges at only that Catholic hospital. The ACLU filed a complaint with the Michigan Department of Licensing and Public Affairs, which oversees hospitals. What should the state do with the complaint? Was it a good outcome that Mann, at the last moment, found a new doctor and a new hospital and had the procedure? See ACLU Files Complaint after Catholic Hospital Refuses Care to Pregnant Woman with Brain Tumor, Chattanooga Courier (Tennessee), Oct. 20, 2015, at 2.

Another ACLU lawsuit against Trinity Health Corporation alleged the corporation's hospitals deny appropriate emergency care to women who suffer miscarriages and other pregnancy complications. The complaint alleged specifically that women suffering from pregnancy complications did not receive the emergency care required by EMTALA, the Emergency Medical Treatment and Active Labor Act, 42 U.S.C. § 1395dd. Can EMTALA require hospitals to perform abortion in medical circumstances even if that violates their conscience? See Howard Friedman, ACLU Sues Catholic Hospitals Over Denial of Abortions to Treat Serious Medical Complications, ReligionClause, Oct. 6, 2015, available at http://religion clause.blogspot.com/2015/10/aclu-sues-catholic-hospitals-over.html.

What do these cases teach you about the balance between conscience clauses and patient health?

5. *Uneven Refusal Clauses?* The cases in the last note involved doctors who wanted to perform sterilizations for their patients at Catholic hospitals. What should happen to their claims of conscience to ignore the hospitals' prohibitions on sterilization? Professor Sepper has demonstrated that refusal clauses tend to privilege the consciences of medical professionals who refuse health care over those who seek to provide it.

Sepper describes the differences between a hypothetical Dr. Abbott, who wants to refuse services, and Dr. Baker, who is eager to provide them:

> The first, Dr. Abbott, refuses to administer contraception, but works at a hospital committed to delivering all necessary care to patients. By contrast, the second, Dr. Baker, feels a moral imperative to ensure his patients have autonomy over their reproductive lives, but his employer has moral policies against contraceptives. Under the approach taken by most legislation, Dr. Abbott can refuse to prescribe emergency contraception to a rape victim in violation of her institution's policy -without consequence. Dr. Baker, however, can be fired for prescribing emergency contraception to a rape victim—even if he acts in good conscience—because he has violated the institutional policy of refusal.

Elizabeth Sepper, Taking Conscience Seriously, 98 Va. L. Rev. 1501, 1525–26 (2012). How could conscience clause legislation address this problem?

6. *Penalties.* In addition to protection of her own job status, Cenzon-DeCarlo sought an injunction prohibiting Mount Sinai from receiving any further qualifying federal funds until it demonstrated compliance with the Church Amendment's non-discrimination provisions and requiring Mount Sinai to disgorge qualifying federal funds it received. Would that have been an appropriate remedy for the kind of violation Cenzon-DeCarlo was alleging?

Sara Hellwege, a nurse who applied for a job as a nurse-midwife at the Tampa Family Health Centers ("TFHC"), does not believe in prescribing some "hormonal" birth control drugs, which she would have to do as part of her job at the health center. Hellwege "believes that 'birth control can cause the death of a human embryo.'" Katie McDonough, Nurse Won't Prescribe Birth Control, Sues Because She Didn't Get a Job that Requires Prescribing Birth Control, Salon, Jul. 21, 2014, at http://www.salon.com/2014/07/21/nurse_wont_prescribe_birth_control_sues_because_she_didnt_get_a_job_that_requires_prescribing_birth_control/. Hellwege wrote in her application to TFHC that she had no religious objections to counseling women about contraception. After Hellwege did not get an interview for the job, she filed a lawsuit alleging religious discrimination against TFHC, in particular discrimination because she is pro-life. The lawsuit lists violations of a federal public health law and two Florida statutes. Id.

Title X of the Public Health Service Act, 42 U.S.C. § 300, provides federal funding for family planning services. TFHC is a Title X organization, which receives federal funding to provide family planning services to clients. Hellwege's lawsuit relies on one Title X provision, stating that an individual cannot be required to "perform or assist in the performance of any sterilization procedure or abortion if his performance or assistance in the performance of such part of such program or activity would be contrary to his religious beliefs or moral convictions." 42 U.S.C. § 300a–7(a)(1). Florida has similar laws preventing retaliation against employees for refusal to participate in family planning or abortion services.

See Complaint, Hellwege v. Tampa Family Health Ctrs., Case No. 8:14-cv-01576-VMC-AEP (M.D. Fla. Jun. 27, 2014), available at http://www.adfmedia.org/files/HellwegeComplaint.pdf. The complaint asks for $400,000 and attorneys' fees in damages and asks the court to divest Tampa Family Health Centers of its federal funding, which could possibly involve millions of dollars. Id. What do you think the result of the lawsuit should be? See Hellwege v. Tampa Family Health Centers, 103 F. Supp. 3d 1303 (M.D. Fla. 2015) (Hellwege has no private right of action under the Church Amendment (citing *Cenzon-DeCarlo*) but can sue for Title VII religious discrimination). We learn the elements of a religious discrimination claim in Chapter 6.

7.   *The Affordable Care Act.* The Affordable Care Act prohibits qualified health plans from discriminating against health care providers due to their "unwillingness to provide, pay for, provide coverage of, or refer for abortions." Does that give too much protection to providers who refuse abortion care? Why should referral be included on the list?

8.   In Mrs. Spellacy v. Tri-County Hospital, Equity Number 77–1788, 1978 WL 3437 (Pa. Com. Pl. 1978), Cecelia Spellacy was hired as a part-time cashier at Tri-County Hospital in Pennsylvania; she worked weekends from 8 A.M. to 4 P.M. She then requested and received a transfer to become a part-time admissions clerk. As a part-time admissions clerk, she had the following responsibilities: "(a) Handled reservations for admissions; (b) Contacted patients prior to admission to secure patient information; (c) Contacted patients by telephone to inform them as to specific time they were to be admitted; (d) Secured patients' signatures on all hospital admission documents at the time of patients' admissions; (e) Explained the hospital procedures to patients with respect to its billing and insurance; (f) Directed admission patients to X-ray or laboratory facilities and when necessary, to hospital EKG facilities; (g) Notified the hospital departments when to expect an admitting patient; (h) Occasionally escorted the patients to his or her room." Four months later she told her supervisor that her religious beliefs did not allow her to admit patients for abortions. In response, the hospital agreed that she would not be required to have personal contact with abortion patients or to accompany them to their rooms.

Spellacy continued voluntarily typing up abortion patients' admissions forms until a year later, when she told her employer that even this clerical work violated her conscience. Then she asked to work evening hours to avoid contact with these patients and waited for a different job at the hospital to open up. There were no other jobs, however, and she was given a three-month leave of absence and placed on call until a job consistent with her beliefs would open.

After Spellacy refused four jobs (as a full-time PBX telephone operator, a part-time pharmacy technician, a part-time position as an outpatient clerk in the hospital's business office and a part-time dietary aide), she filed a Charge of Discrimination with the Pennsylvania Human Relations Commission alleging a violation of a Pennsylvania statute that provided:

> No hospital or other health care facility shall be required to, or held liable for refusal to, perform or permit the performance of abortion or sterilization contrary to its state ethical policy. *No physician, nurse, staff member or employee of a hospital* or other health care facility, *who shall state in writing to such hospital* or health care facility *his objection to performing, participating in, or cooperating in abortion or sterilization on moral, religious—or professional grounds, shall be required to, or held liable for refusal to, perform, participate in, or cooperate in such abortion or sterilization.*

Id. at *3. According to the Regulations interpreting the statute, only employees who were *"directly involved and in attendance"* at the abortion procedure or those *"without whose services the procedure itself could not be performed"* were protected by the statute. The Court ruled that Mrs. Spellacy was not protected by the act because her duties were "ancillary" and "clerical." Do you agree or disagree with the Court's ruling? Should the law be amended to protect employees like Mrs. Spellacy? If so, how far would you expand the radius of protection? Should the law protect an employee who refuses to translate abortion information into Spanish? See Moncivaiz v. DeKalb Cnty, No. 03–CV 50226, 2004 WL 539994 (N.D. Ill. 2003). What about an ambulance driver who refuses to transport a woman who had abdominal pain to an elective abortion? See Tresa Baldas, Fighting Refusal to Treat, Nat'l L. J., Feb. 7, 2005.

In *Spellacy*, the court noted that even if Spellacy had been covered by the act, the hospital had made a reasonable accommodation of Spellacy's religious objections by offering her alternative employment. Do you agree? We examine the accommodation of religious employees in more detail in Chapter 6.

9.   Jehovah's Witnesses refuse blood transfusions because they believe they are forbidden by scriptural passages, including Genesis 9:4, Leviticus 17:12, Deuteronomy 12:23–25 and Acts 15:28–29. Receiving a transfusion jeopardizes their everlasting life with God. Should Jehovah's Witnesses be allowed to refuse medical treatment that will save their lives? See generally Heather Payne & Norman Doe, Public Health and the Limits of Religious Freedom, 19 Emory Int'l L. Rev. 539 (2005) (explaining that adult refusal is usually accepted because of the informed consent requirements). What should happen if medical personnel wish to give transfusions to a Jehovah's Witness because they want to save their patient's life? Should the conscience of the provider overcome the conscience of the adult in some circumstances? See Application of President and Directors of Georgetown College, Inc., 331 F.2d 1000 (D.C. Cir. 1964), reh'g denied by Application of President and Dirs. of Georgetown Coll., Inc., 331 F.2d 1010 (D.C.Cir. 1964), cert. denied, Jones v. President and Dirs. of Georgetown Coll., Inc., 377 U.S. 978 (1964) (allowing transfusion over the objection of the patient and her husband because she was the mother of a seven-month-old child).

Should doctors try to persuade their Jehovah's Witnesses patients that their religion may allow some transfusions? See Raanan Gillon, Refusal of Potentially Life-Saving Blood Transfusions by Jehovah's Witnesses: Should Doctors Explain That Not All JWs Think It's Religiously Required?, 26 J. Med. Ethics 299, 299–301 (2000). What should happen if parents refuse transfusions for their ill children? See, e.g., In the Matter of Elisha McCauley, 409 Mass. 134, 565 N.E.2d 411 (1991) (ordering transfusions for an eight-year-old girl with leukemia over her parents' objections).

10. Should a rape survivor be allowed to sue a religious hospital for failing to advise her about emergency contraception? See Brownfield v. Daniel Freeman Marina Hosp., 208 Cal.App.3d 405, 256 Cal.Rptr. 240 (1989) (a rape survivor could state a cause of action by showing that: (1) a skilled practitioner of good standing would have provided her with information about emergency contraception under similar circumstances; (2) she would have utilized such treatment if it had been available; and (3) she suffered damages as a result of the hospital's failure to provide her with information about this treatment option.). What about suing a pharmacist for failure to provide post-rape contraception?

11. Zubik *and the Military.* One of several amicus briefs submitted on behalf of the Department of Health and Human Services in *Zubik* came from military historians especially familiar with conscientious objector law. The military historians asserted that, contrary to the religious nonprofits' claims, "religious accommodations have often required religious objectors to play a far more active role in shifting that responsibility than does the accommodation here, for example requiring religious objectors opposed to war to pay for a substitute to serve or take some other action to satisfy the important interests of the government." For example, conscientious objectors to the American Revolution were exempted from fighting, but not from furnishing the equivalent in funds to assist the government. The historians noted how this balance shaped the Bill of Rights. The historians therefore argued that the religious nonprofits' position was "profoundly inconsistent with how religious accommodation has long been understood in this country, as evidenced by the history of conscientious objector laws enacted over the entire sweep of our nation's history." Brief for Military Historians as Amici Curiae Supporting Respondents, Zubik v. Burwell, Inc., 194 L. Ed. 2d 696 (2016), 2016 U.S. S. Ct. Briefs LEXIS 751. Conscientious objection in the context of military service is discussed in the next section.

B. THE MILITARY

The main source of law about conscientious objection is a line of United States Supreme Court cases construing the Selective Service Act, which exempts conscientious objectors from military service because of their religious opposition to war. That statutory exemption, passed by Congress, allowed the objectors to fulfill their military service in an alternative, non-violent manner. Such legislation is a good reminder that the claims of conscience and religion are traditionally significant enough that states may try to accommodate them in some manner. Recognition of conscientious objection to war by pacifists has a long history in the United States. The right to conscientious objection has also been recognized in the United Nations Universal Declaration of Human Rights and the European Convention on Human Rights, which we study in Chapter 8.

It was in cases deciding who qualified to be a conscientious objector to the Vietnam War that the Supreme Court provided its clearest definition of religion. As we saw in the *Seeger* opinion in Chapter 1, courts have not always been explicit about what "religion" is protected by the Free Exercise Clause. The Supreme Court's fullest effort to define religion can be found in the cases that interpreted the Selective Service Act, which protected anyone "who, by reason of religious training and belief, is conscientiously opposed to participation in war in any form" from military service." The Selective Service cases that arose during the Vietnam War—United States v. Seeger, 380 U.S. 163 (1965) (studied in Chapter 1), Welsh v. United States, 398 U.S. 333 (1970), and Gillette v. United States, 401 U.S. 437 (1971)—set the stage for modern conscientious objection law.

What do you think of the Army's process of identifying conscientious objectors as explained in the following opinion?

Hanna v. Secretary of the Army

United States Court of Appeals for the First Circuit, 2008.
513 F.3d 4.

■ Before BOUDIN and TORRUELLA CIRCUIT JUDGES, and SCHWARZER, DISTRICT JUDGE.

■ SCHWARZER, DISTRICT JUDGE.

Schwarzer, District Judge. Captain Mary Hanna sought discharge from the Army as a conscientious objector. The Department of the Army Conscientious Objector Review Board ("DACORB") denied Hanna's application. Hanna then petitioned the district court for a writ of habeas corpus which the court granted, holding that there was no basis in fact for the DACORB's decision. The Army appealed. We hold that the DACORB's decision was without a basis in fact, and we therefore affirm.

FACTUAL AND PROCEDURAL HISTORY

Mary Hanna joined the Army in 1997 as a member of the Army Health Professions Scholarship Program ("HPSP") and thereafter attended medical school. In exchange for financial assistance with medical school, Hanna promised to serve on active duty in the Army for four years and to remain in the Army Reserve for an additional four years. After Hanna finished medical school, the Army deferred her active duty obligation for four years while she completed a residency in anesthesiology. On October 20, 2005, the Army sent Hanna a letter directing her to report for active duty in August 2006. Hanna was later scheduled to report to William Beaumont Army Medical Center in El Paso, Texas.

On December 23, 2005, Hanna filed an application for discharge as a conscientious objector ("CO"). In her application, Hanna declared that she sought discharge because, as a Christian, she believed in the inherent sanctity of human life and that it "would be committing a crime against God" to take another human's life. She further explained:

> I ... believe that violence and killing are in direct contradiction to all of Jesus' teachings. I am unable to put Christ's words into practice while simultaneously participating, whether directly or indirectly, in war, violence, and killing. All of Jesus' preaching reiterates love, peace, forgiveness and cautions against anger, hatred, and their end product, murder. Based on Christ's example, I believe that I must take things one step further and constantly strive to eliminate conflict with others by seeking prompt reconciliation with adversaries. Love of God and love of fellow humans drives Christian life, and I have incorporated this principle into my own life.

Hanna declared that she would be "incapable of attaining these qualities" by participating in "war and killing" and would "betray these moral and religious principles by participating in war in any way." She explained that her parents were "deeply involved" in the Coptic Orthodox Church ("COC") and that her father had planned to become a monk and her mother a nun until they met each other and chose to marry. As a child, Hanna attended church weekly in Los Angeles, where she grew up. Her parents taught her to believe in "love for God first, love for all other humans as a direct reflection of our love for God, respect for elders, respect for the traditions of our Church, honesty, sincerity of heart, and constant striving for goodness." Hanna became a Coptic hymn teacher in high school and later served as a Sunday school teacher while she attended UCLA. She also participated in the Coptic Club at UCLA.

In 1997, in her senior year of college, Hanna applied and was accepted for medical school at Tufts University. In her CO application, Hanna described her last year of college as a time that "greatly tested" her faith and her "proximity to the Church." At the time she applied for the HPSP, Hanna was experiencing a period of "change and uncertainty" during which she "questioned everything." She "turned to atheism for several months, followed by agnosticism for several more months." During this time, she had "no particular convictions one way or the other regarding war."

Hanna's father died in 2003, and during the mourning period that followed his death, Hanna's faith was "rekindled" and she found herself "again drawn to God." She explained that "I had lived both without God and with him, and I liked myself immensely more when striving to emulate his nature, his mercy, his love, his generosity, his forgiveness." Hanna further explained that it "took some time" for her to "make the connection between this newly rekindled faith and its incompatibility with certain aspects" of her life. For example, she became increasingly concerned about her participation in elective abortions as an anesthesiology resident because she felt she was "participating in an act in direct contradiction to the Bible's teachings." She asked her floor manager if she could abstain from abortion procedures and her request was granted.

During the summer of 2005, Hanna watched several war documentaries and "growingly began to view all war from a Christian perspective: complete separation from God." She explained that she "started to gradually understand the spectrum Christ described which connects anger to hatred to violence to murder (war on a larger scale)." After watching the documentaries, she "finally understood how Christ equated them all as the same sin, with anger being the stem." Her new understanding motivated her to participate in a war protest in September 2005, where she realized that she "was no longer able to play a role in propagating violence." In early October 2005, Hanna watched a television program during which a man discussed the "destructive role" of war and violence, citing the Beatitudes. She then realized that "to live the rest of my life with integrity, in harmony with God's nature of love and compassion, I could not participate in military service." Reflecting on her choice to join the Army, Hanna commented, "I realized then the full implications of the path I had chosen years earlier and the incompatibility of war and violence with Christ's teachings."

Hanna submitted six letters in support of her CO application, four from Coptic Orthodox priests who knew her personally, and two from supervisors in her residency program. One of the priests, who had known Hanna since infancy, stated that he had spoken with Hanna recently about her belief that war is "the direct opposite of Christ's call to peace and love." The priest wrote:

> I have read her application for conscientious objector status, and it is consistent with her character, ethics, and approach to Christianity. I know Mary well, and she is both honest and sincere in her application. I strongly urge you to approve her application in order to allow her to live a life that does not contradict her beliefs.

A second priest, who had known Hanna for more than 15 years, wrote that Hanna was "both honest and sincere in her application," that he knew Hanna well, and that she was "trying to live a life consistent with her beliefs." He urged the Army to approve her application. A third priest, who had known Hanna for 12 years, described her as "one of the most dedicated conscientious and compassionate young ladies in our church." He described her as "trustworthy, honest and sincere." A fourth priest wrote that Hanna had been a member of St. Mark Coptic Orthodox Church in Natick, Massachusetts since 1997. Hanna attended church there regularly during medical school and as often as her call schedule allowed during her residency. Hanna's supervisors wrote that her CO application was "a sincere representation of who she is, and what she believes," described Hanna as "a gentle soul" and " 'the mother to all our sickest patients' " and urged the Army to approve her application.

After Hanna submitted her application for discharge, Colonel John Powers in the Office of the Surgeon General issued a memorandum regarding her application. Powers commented that "[t]he Army is under-strength in anesthesiologists." Turning to Hanna's application, he noted that he "did not question [Hanna's] religious belief" but that he found "some aspects" of her application "troubling." Powers stated that although Hanna stated in her CO application that she was experiencing doubts about her religious faith at the time she applied to the Army, her 1997 HPSP application indicated that she had been teaching Sunday school during the same time period. Powers also noted the late timing of Hanna's CO application, commenting that she never raised concerns about conscientious objection during medical school or her residency. Powers observed that Hanna's application was received around the same time as a CO application submitted by another anesthesiologist and shortly after the Army approved the CO application of a third anesthesiologist. He pointed out that all three applicants were represented by the same attorney. Powers also commented that the Army had paid more than $ 180,000 for Hanna's medical school expenses. He recommended that the Army either deny Hanna's application and order her to active duty, or grant the application with recoupment of her medical school costs plus interest.

Pursuant to Army regulations, Hanna was interviewed by a military chaplain and a psychiatrist. The chaplain's report stated that the Coptic Orthodox Church does not teach pacifism. He reported that, based on his research, he believed the COC "endorses military service through the example of [its] Saints and religious leaders." The chaplain also questioned Hanna's sincerity because she worked in a hospital that provided abortions. He added that Hanna had not made significant lifestyle changes since becoming a conscientious objector.

The psychiatrist found that Hanna did not suffer from any psychiatric disorders. He also found that Hanna's application was "a convenient, if not opportunistic choice in refuting her basic military contract based on her newly found faith." During her interview with the psychiatrist, Hanna related that her father had served in the Egyptian military for six years and was very proud of her decision to join the Army. She told him that her father would have been "devastated" to know of her decision to file for discharge as a conscientious objector. Hanna also told him that she was prepared to repay the Army for her medical school costs plus interest.

Hanna's application was assigned to an Investigating Officer ("IO"). The IO conducted a hearing lasting more than six hours at which he heard testimony from Hanna, two Coptic Orthodox priests who knew Hanna personally, and the Army psychiatrist who had interviewed Hanna. One of the priests, who had known Hanna for six years, testified that she was "an honest and sincere person" and that her application accurately described the source of her beliefs. The priest also testified that there is no uniform position on military service in the Coptic Orthodox Church. Rather, the Church supports both conscientious objectors and those who choose military service. The priest disagreed with the chaplain's conclusion that the COC endorses military service and also with the chaplain's statement that some COC saints were "warriors." He testified that military service by these saints occurred before their religious phase. The second priest, who had known Hanna since she was seven or eight years old, testified that she is a "truthful person" and that he supported her CO application. He also testified that the COC supports both conscientious objectors and those who serve in the military. The IO credited the testimony of both priests.

In his summary of Hanna's testimony, the IO stated that when Hanna applied to the HPSP in 1997, "she was naive and her personal belief system was not fully developed. She did not give much thought to the morality of war." During college, "her religious faith waxed and waned" and she "began to question her religious beliefs" and this "caused discord with her father." When she watched the war documentaries in 2005, she was " 'shocked' " by the civilian deaths. After watching the movies, she "adopted a pacifist approach. She began praying more. She read scripture and the writings of religious philosophers. She noted that Jesus Christ was a pacifist." Hanna testified that by treating soldiers, "she would be repleting the force and assisting it [in] waging war." She stated that her objection to war was based on her "religious upbringing, her personal belief system and Christian theology."

Hanna further testified that there was a distinction between serving in the Army and working at a civilian hospital that provides abortions. Hanna reasoned that a civilian hospital is "not an organization that is dedicated to war." By treating soldiers, she would be assisting the Army to wage war, whereas at a civilian hospital, she had the option to refrain from participating in abortions. She stated that she had "no offer or prospects for private practice" if her CO application was granted.

In addition to hearing the testimony of witnesses, the IO reviewed Hanna's CO application, her 1997 HPSP application, the reports of the chaplain and psychiatrist, the Powers memorandum and attached documents, the letters of support from Coptic clergy members and Hanna's professional supervisors, and various research materials related to Eastern Orthodox churches.

The IO concluded that Hanna sincerely opposed participation in war in any form because of her religious, moral and ethical beliefs. In his report, the IO observed that Hanna was "open, cooperative, courteous and sincere during the hearing." He concluded that she was "sincere and very credible . . . I was impressed by CPT Hanna's sincere expressions of her beliefs and her interaction with Father Bishara (in person) and Father Henein (by telephone) at the hearing. I was left with the impression that she was a devout member of the COC and sincerely held the beliefs she professed in her CO application."

The IO found that Hanna's objection to war became fixed in 2005. He credited Hanna's testimony that "when she applied to join the military in 1997 her belief system was still developing and, in fact, she was experiencing doubts as to the existence of God." He also credited her explanation of how her beliefs developed from the death of her father in 2003 through the summer and fall of 2005, when she began to view war from "a Christian perspective." The IO concluded his report by stating:

> I assessed [Hanna's] credibility at the hearing and considered the opinions as to her sincerity and/or honesty proffered by Fathers Bishara and Henein, Philip Hess, M.D., Father Megally, and Stephanie Jones, M.D. I concluded that CPT Hanna is an honest and truthful person and credited her statements that her beliefs became incompatible with military service in October 2005.

The IO also discussed the reports of the chaplain and the psychiatrist, as well as the Powers memorandum. The IO concluded that the chaplain was incorrect in his opinion that the COC is not supportive of conscientious objectors. He noted that two Coptic priests had testified that the COC supports conscientious objectors, and that this testimony was consistent with materials he reviewed regarding the treatment of war by Eastern Orthodox religions. The IO also noted that, under Army regulations, an applicant's personal convictions dominate over the teachings of her church, "so long as they derive from the person's moral, ethical, or religious beliefs." The IO found that "[i]n addition to her involvement with the COC, CPT Hanna made reference to her personal research into Christian philosophy and the development of her own, individual beliefs as to God and morality and her personal moral belief system. I find that in the case of CPT Hanna, her opposition to war in all forms is derived from moral, ethical and religious beliefs and that her beliefs are sincerely held."

Regarding the chaplain's views on Hanna's work at a hospital that provides abortions, the IO credited Hanna's explanation that serving in the military is not analogous to working in a civilian hospital. The IO concluded that Hanna's work at a hospital that provides abortions and her willingness to treat police officers and gang members had no bearing on the sincerity of her objection to war.

Turning to the Powers memorandum, the IO credited Hanna's testimony that she did not know the other anesthesiologists who had submitted CO applications. The IO also commented that no adverse inference could be drawn from the fact that Hanna had hired an attorney experienced in CO applications because a prudent person would not pay attorney's fees to someone who did not have the requisite experience to provide effective representation. The IO further noted that Hanna's attorney was a West Point graduate, that he had served on active duty, and that he had previously represented numerous soldiers who were seeking to be retained by the Army.

Regarding the psychiatrist's report, the IO stated that the psychiatrist admitted during testimony that his report contained several errors, including an incorrect characterization of Hanna's beliefs as "not based on any religious conviction." In his testimony, the psychiatrist clarified his opinion that "while CPT Hanna's beliefs were not anchored in the tenets of a particular religion they were a product of her personal faith system." The IO commented that he interpreted the psychiatrist's testimony to mean that Hanna's beliefs were a product of "her personal relationship with God." The IO also noted that the Powers memorandum, which the psychiatrist reviewed before Hanna's interview, may have prompted the psychiatrist to "engage in an unnecessarily involved discussion" of the issues in the memo, particularly her choice of attorney, putting Hanna "on the defensive" and possibly influencing Hanna's demeanor during the interview, which the psychiatrist reported as tense and guarded. The IO found that, in contrast, Hanna's demeanor during the hearing was "open, cooperative, courteous and sincere."

The IO's report was forwarded to officers up the chain of command, each of whom recommended approval of Hanna's application based on their findings that Hanna sincerely opposed participation in war because of her religious beliefs. Colonel Robert Marsh found that Hanna's "life-long church involvement does not appear to be a recent effort to avoid military service." Colonel Marsh further stated that "[t]he strength and intensity of her evolving convictions against war and violence, beginning with the death of her father in May 2003 and becoming firm by October 2005, are reflective of sincere belief and are supported by clear and convincing evidence." A Staff Judge Advocate ("SJA") recommended approval after concluding that "[t]he investigating officer conducted a thorough inquiry into [Hanna's] convictions. Numerous witnesses were called on her behalf." The SJA noted that after the death of her father, Hanna "felt free to consider the contradiction in her religious beliefs and the Army mission." The SJA further commented that Hanna's application "is not a means to avoid her military commitment." Brigadier General Todd Semonite found, after "thoroughly" reviewing the file, that Hanna's objection was "sincerely held" and that "[t]he solemnity of her convictions is clear throughout the investigation and they do not appear to have been born of a desire to avoid service." General Semonite emphasized that his conclusion was based on "the investigating officer's credibility determination, CPT Hanna's testimony, and the opinions of the leaders of her church."

Hanna's application was ultimately reviewed by the DACORB, which voted 2–1 to reject it. The President of the Board voted to disapprove the application, stating:

> Applicant has shown that she is a devout Coptic Christian but has failed to show that she sincerely meets the CO criteria. Her statements are logical but lack passion and sincerity; they appear as repetition rather than personally held beliefs.

The Chaplain voted to disapprove the application, stating:

> The statement by the priest that the COC does not teach pacifism leads one to believe that there is more to Cpt. Hanna's position then merely religious conviction. Also, her timing is too convenient w/the completion of her schooling and her entry on [active duty].

The Staff Judge Advocate voted to approve the application, finding that the applicant "has a firm, fixed and sincere objection to participation in war in any form."

Hanna petitioned for a writ of habeas corpus. The district court, after a lengthy and detailed review of the record, held that there was no "basis in fact" for the DACORB's decision and granted Hanna's petition permanently enjoining the Army from ordering Hanna to active duty.

The Army timely appealed.

DISCUSSION

II. WHETHER THERE WAS A BASIS IN FACT FOR THE DACORB'S DECISION

The Army's attack on the district court's decision is narrowly focused. It argues first that the timing of her application casts doubt on her sincerity and that her explanations for the change in her beliefs were inconsistent. Second, it argues that her beliefs were not gained through rigorous training, study or contemplation. We address each of those contentions in turn.

A. The Army's first argument is that the late crystallization of Hanna's opposition to war coupled with inconsistencies in her explanations for the change in her beliefs provide a "basis in fact" for the decision.

The Army concedes, as it must, that "[t]he timing of [an] application alone . . . is never enough to furnish a basis in fact to support a disapproval." A sincere conscientious objector is entitled to release from his service obligations whether his view crystallizes late or early.

In an effort to fortify its timing argument, the Army points to what it regards as inconsistencies in Hanna's explanation as evidence of insincerity. In her CO application, Hanna stated that in 1997, when she applied for the HPSP scholarship, she was experiencing a period of "change and uncertainty" that "greatly tested [her] faith and [her] proximity to the Church." She further stated that during this time, she "questioned everything," turning to atheism for several months, followed by agnosticism. The Army contrasts this description with her 1997 application, in which Hanna described her activities and achievements as an undergraduate and expressed a desire to "take on the myriad challenges" of serving in the Army and practicing medicine. The Army argues that Hanna's 1997 motivation statement, which reflects Hanna's high-achieving, driven nature and her ability to "overcome obstacles in her life" based on her "strength and determination" is inconsistent with the statement in her CO application that she applied for the HPSP scholarship during a time of "change and uncertainty." The Army argues that the DACORB could have found Hanna's explanations to be inconsistent and hence evidence of insincerity.

The first response to this argument is that it rests on pure speculation. Nothing in the DACORB decision suggests that any DACORB member had found Hanna's explanations to be inconsistent. The statements of the President and the Chaplain are sufficiently specific that had they found Hanna to be insincere on the basis of inconsistencies in her explanations, one would have expected one or the other to have said so. Moreover, the Army's after-the-fact interpretive gloss on Hanna's statements cannot pass muster as "hard, reliable provable facts which would provide a basis for disbelieving the applicant's sincerity . . . something concrete in the record."

In any event, we do not find Hanna's explanations to be inconsistent. That Hanna might have questioned her religious beliefs at the time when she applied for the HPSP is not inconsistent with her being highly motivated to attend medical school and join the military during that same period. The IO credited Hanna's testimony that her "personal belief system was not fully developed" and that she had "not give[n] much thought to the morality of war" at the time she applied to the HPSP. As the IO noted, eight years had passed between Hanna's application to join the Army and her application for discharge. We think that was more than sufficient time for crystallization.

Here, "the [Army] has blotted out entirely the finding of sincerity made by its own Investigating Officer." After conducting a hearing at which he heard testimony from Hanna and other witnesses and examined documentary evidence, the IO "concluded that CPT. Hanna is an honest and truthful person and credited her statements that her beliefs became incompatible with military service in October 2005." He found Hanna "to be sincere and her beliefs to be sincerely held." When the IO's recommendation was forwarded to the officers in the chain of command, it was endorsed at each level. At the first level, the commanding officer of the human resources command found that Hanna "has provided clear and convincing evidence supporting her request for conscientious objector (CO) status and discharge." The staff judge advocate found that "the evidence supports the findings of the investigating officer." Finally, the commanding general, in his recommendation to the DACORB, stated that Hanna "has put forth clear and convincing evidence that she is opposed to participation in war in any form based on her religious, moral and ethical beliefs." Where, as here, the applicant has established her sincerity to the satisfaction of the officer charged with investigating her application and has provided a plausible explanation for the late crystallization of her beliefs, "inferences of insincerity drawn from the timing of the application are insufficient 'objective facts' to provide a basis-in-fact for rejecting the claim."

B. The Army's second argument in support of the DACORB's decision is that Hanna's application does not comply with Army regulations. Citing the regulations, it argues that Hanna's beliefs were not gained through rigorous training, study or contemplation. Instead, it points out, according to her application, her beliefs crystallized in October 2005 when she watched war documentaries and a television program discussing war and violence and their destructive roles. Thus, she has failed to show that her beliefs were developed through "activity comparable in rigor and dedication to the processes by which traditional religious convictions are formulated."

This argument too is an after-the-fact rationalization which finds no support in the DACORB decision or in the record. In any event, it lacks merit.

The regulation on which the Army relies states:

(ii) Relevant factors to be considered in determining an applicant's claim of conscientious objection include: Training in the home and church; general demeanor and pattern of conduct; participation in religious activities; whether ethical or moral convictions were gained through training, study, contemplation, or other activity comparable in rigor and dedication to the processes by which traditional religious convictions are formulated; credibility of the applicant; and credibility of persons supporting the claim. 32 C.F.R. § 75.5(c)(2)(ii)(emphasis added).

The Army's argument misreads its regulation. The reference to "rigor and dedication" appears in the context of comparing "traditional religious convictions" with "ethical or moral convictions." The "rigor and dedication" consideration applies only to applicants whose objections stem purely from secular beliefs, i.e. ethical and moral convictions, as opposed to those whose objections are based on "traditional religious conviction." See Welsh v. United States, 398 U.S. 333, 340, 90 S. Ct. 1792, 26 L. Ed. 2d 308 (1970) (holding that an applicant whose beliefs "are purely ethical or moral in source and content" is "as much entitled to a 'religious' conscientious objector exemption . . . as is someone who derives his conscientious opposition to war from traditional religious convictions"). The Army's reading would obliterate the distinction between objectors asserting purely moral or ethical grounds and those whose objection is based on traditional religious convictions and would render the regulation nonsensical.

The dissent acknowledges Hanna's religious convictions but argues that her objection to war cannot be religious because "pacifist views are not part of her church's doctrine." It is well settled that membership in a church that does not teach conscientious objection does not render an applicant's beliefs non-religious. United States v. Seeger, 380 U.S. 163, 171–72, 85 S. Ct. 850, 13 L. Ed. 2d 733 (1965). An applicant's objection may be religious though she belongs to no church at all, or an applicant may "through religious reading reach a conviction against participation in war" though she belongs to a church that is not opposed to war. Id. See also Clay v. United States, 403 U.S. 698, 702–03, 91 S. Ct. 2068, 29 L. Ed. 2d 810 (1971) (holding applicant's objection sincere where based on "tenets of the Muslim religion as he understands them") (emphasis added). The Army must evaluate "whether the beliefs professed by a registrant are sincerely held and whether they are, in his own scheme of things, religious." Seeger, 380 U.S. at 185. Indeed, the Army's own regulations recognize that an applicant's opposition to war may be religious in nature even though her church does not teach conscientious objection. See AR 600-43 1–5.b.;32 C.F.R. § 75.5 (c)(2)(iii)(d) (disagreement with tenets of church does not necessarily discredit claim, so long as objection derives "from the person's moral, ethical, or religious beliefs").

In her CO application, Hanna identified herself as Christian and Christianity as the source of her objection to war. She explained in detail her belief that Christianity required her to refrain from participation in war. The IO found, based on Hanna's testimony and the testimony and letters of several Coptic priests that knew her personally, that Hanna was a "devout member" of the Coptic Orthodox Church. He found her to be sincerely opposed to war in any form because of religious as well as moral and ethical beliefs. The fact that non-religious documentaries contributed to Hanna's view that there is a conflict between her religious faith and her military service does not mean that her beliefs are purely ethical or moral or that they lack religious grounding. As Hanna explained in her CO application, the documentaries caused her to "view all war from a Christian perspective: complete separation from God." Indeed, the DACORB did not question Hanna's religious belief. The President acknowledged that Hanna is a "devout Coptic Christian," and the Chaplain thought that "there is more to Cpt. Hanna's position than merely religious conviction."

Thus the Army's citation of Aguayo v. Harvey, 375 U.S. App. D.C. 38, 476 F.3d 971, 980–81 (D.C. Cir. 2007), is inapposite. There the court upheld a denial of CO status where the applicant's beliefs did not have a religious foundation and the applicant had failed to identify the source of his non-religious objection to war. The court reasoned that the applicant had failed to show that his ethical objection to war had developed through activity comparable in rigor to the processes by which religious convictions are formed. Id. Here, because Hanna's objection to war stems from religious convictions, the regulation provides no basis in fact for the Army's decision to deny Hanna's application.

Affirmed.

NOTES AND QUESTIONS

1.   Recall *Seeger* from Chapter 1. How is *Hanna* similar to *Seeger*? How is it different? Does it correctly apply the Court's definition of "religion"?

2.   *The Process.* Summarize the process that Hanna had to follow in order to achieve C.O. status. What did the regulations require? What was the role of DACORB in the process? What is the importance of the "basis in fact" standard? Do you think the Army has a good process for identifying COs, or was the process too burdensome on Hanna? Too lenient on Hanna? How does the process compare with the burden on the *Zubik* petitioners to prove their claims of conscience and complicity? Do you think it would be hard or easy for other C.O.s to achieve C.O. status following *Hanna's* standard?

Do you agree with DACORB there was no basis in fact for Hanna to receive C.O. status? Or with the district and appellate courts? What is the basis for your conclusion? Did you believe Hanna's decision to seek C.O.

status was sincere? What is the "late crystallization" argument? Did it influence your reaction to the case?

3. As you learned in the opinion, C.O. applicants must fill out detailed applications that are sent to the Department of the Army Conscientious Objector Review Board (DACORB) for review. They must establish that their beliefs are "sincere" and "deeply held." The applications include interviews with chaplains, psychiatrists, fellow soldiers, and officers. Applicants may submit a personal statement and letters of recommendations from family, friends, professors, and clergy. DACORB then provides a decision explaining the reasons for granting or denying C.O. status. Although unsuccessful applicants may file a writ of habeas corpus, the courts defer to DACORB if there is some "basis in fact" for its decision. See Alexander Drylewski, Note, When Fighting Is Impossible: A Contractual Approach to the Military's Conscientious Objection Rules, 74 Brooklyn L. Rev. 1445, 1449–52 (2009); Dep't of the Army, Army Regulation 600–43, Conscientious Objection (Sept. 21, 2006), at http://www. apd.army.mil/pdffiles/r600_43.pdf.

The court identified the applicant's sincerity in her belief as the threshold question in every C.O. case. What advice would you give to a client who is seeking military exemption as a C.O.? What could your client say to the military that would demonstrate his or her sincerity? What type of demeanor would be most favorable to your client? Do you think it is fair that an applicant's ability to demonstrate sincerity is a threshold question in these cases? How sincere do you believe the applicants in the following cases were?

Rasheed Alhassan joined the Marine Corps in July 2002, when he submitted a form stating he was not a C.O. He attended boot camp in October 2002, and in January 2003 found out that he would be sent to Iraq. When he learned about the deployment, he told an officer that he was worried about his mother's divorce and whether he would be able to attend college. He did not mention his religion. Six days later, in February 2003, he sought discharge as a C.O. In interviews with a Navy psychiatrist that are required by the C.O. application, Alhassan said that he had " 'found Jesus' and accepted Him. Alhassan also stated that he had attended a few Sunday services but had not chosen a particular religion to follow and had not been baptized in any church. Alhassan also mentioned that he had not discussed this recent religious 'conversion' with his girlfriend." The Navy chaplain decided Alhassan's "faith . . . [was] very immature at this point and not well developed," and his application for C.O. status was denied. Alhassan v. Hagee, 424 F.3d 518, 520–521 (7th Cir. 2005). Does this inquiry into Alhassan's faith violate *Seeger*? The Free Exercise Clause? See id. (upholding the denial of C.O. status). Is it significant that Alhassan did not make his C.O. claim until he was deployed to Iraq?

In February 2004, fifteen months after he joined the military, Agustin Aguayo applied for C.O. status, stating his moral views did not allow him to take life and that military training caused him "great anguish and guilt." Aguayo said that his family upbringing and time in the military influenced his desire to become a C.O., and that he was an agnostic who admired Jesus Christ, Gandhi, and Martin Luther King, Jr. Although an army investigator and Aguayo's Company Commander recommended that his request be approved, other commanders disagreed and rejected his application. Aguayo's writ for habeas corpus was denied by the district court, a decision upheld in Aguayo v. Harvey, 476 F.3d 971 (D.C. Cir. 2007). The appeals court, following *Seeger*, stated it would not disturb the Army's decision unless "there is no factual basis for the decision." Because some of the Army's reviewers expressed doubt about the "depth and source" of Aguayo's opposition to war, there was enough evidence in the record to uphold the denial of Aguayo's application. Should the appeals court have been so deferential to the army on a matter of such constitutional significance? Why did the First Circuit distinguish *Aguayo* from Hanna's case?

Watson v. Geren involved a medical student, Timothy Watson, who joined the Army during his first year of medical school. The Army subsequently paid for Watson's remaining 3 years of medical school and a one-year internship. Afterwards, the Army also paid for Watson to enroll in a four-year residency program; however, during his final year of residency, Watson petitioned for release from the Army as a C.O. In his application, Watson described his reaction to the September 11 attacks and his evolving opposition to violence and warfare, preemptive warfare in particular. He quoted inspiration from sources such as Dr. Martin Luther King, the Dalai Lama, the Christian Bible, and the Qur'an. He submitted letters from family and colleagues to document his "feelings about war," his "unwillingness to participate with activities he deems improper, inaccurate or immoral" and his "ethically and politically unwavering" personality. Finally, Watson proclaimed as a matter of conviction that he would not treat wounded soldiers.

After DACORB denied Watson's application, the district court granted Watson's writ of habeas corpus challenging the Army's denial of his application. On appeal to the Second Circuit, the Army argued that there were four bases in fact to support the denial of Watson's application:

1.   "[T]he timing of Watson's application, as his residency was ending and active duty was approaching, indicates that his professed belief was merely expedient, rather than sincerely held";

2.   "[T]he application and supporting materials make clear that Watson does not truly oppose war in all forms, but is specifically opposed to the wars in Iraq and Afghanistan";

3.   "Watson's application explains the development of his conscientious objection by what can reasonably be characterized as a grab-bag of references to various political and religious figures";

4.   "Watson purportedly delayed between the time his conscientious objector views crystallized in the early summer 2005

and the time his application for discharge as a conscientious objector was initially filed, in January 2006."

Watson v. Geren, 569 F.3d 115, 131–132 (2d Cir. 2009). The Second Circuit rejected those arguments and affirmed the district court because there was no basis in fact for denial of the application on any valid ground. Watson was required to remit all costs incurred by the Army to pay for his medical training. Was this ruling consistent with *Hanna*?

Do you agree that there was no basis in fact to support denial of Watson's application? Which proffered bases do you find most persuasive for grounds to deny C.O. status? Which do you find least persuasive? Is reaction to the September 11 attacks good reason to grant C.O. status? Are you sympathetic toward Watson or do you think the timing of his request suggests opportunism? Do you think Watson's claim that he could not morally treat a wounded soldier contradicts his belief in the sanctity of human life or the Hippocratic Oath? Should all in-service C.O.s be required to repay the government for their training and education?

4.   *Sincerely Held Religion.* Why did the Army argue Hanna "failed to show that her beliefs were developed through 'activity comparable in rigor and dedication to the processes by which traditional religious convictions are formulated.' "? Why did the dissent argue Hanna's "objection to war cannot be religious because 'pacifist views are not part of her church's doctrine.' "? Why did the court think both these approaches to Hanna's religious belief violated *Seeger* and other Court precedents?

In *Seeger*, the Court concluded "the test of belief 'in a relation to a Supreme Being' is whether a given belief that is sincere and meaningful occupies a place in the life of its possessor parallel to that filled by the orthodox belief in God of one who clearly qualifies for the exemption. Where such beliefs have parallel positions in the lives of their respective holders we cannot say that one is "in a relation to a Supreme Being" and the other is not." What should Congress have done after the Court decided *Seeger*: (1) abolished the exemption altogether; (2) limited the exemption to those who oppose military service on the basis of their belief in a traditional concept of God; or (3) simply let it stand? See Robert L. Rabin, When is a Religious Belief Religious: *United States v. Seeger* and the Scope of Free Exercise, 51 Cornell L.Q. 231, 241–42 (1966). What are the arguments for and against following each of these options? Do the arguments in *Hanna* affect your answer to that question?

The Military Selective Service Act of 1967 deleted the reference to a Supreme Being, so that the statute read: "Nothing contained in this title shall be construed to require any person to be subject to combatant training and service in the armed forces of the United States who, by reason of religious training and belief, is conscientiously opposed to participation in war in any form. As used in this subsection, the term 'religious training and belief' does not include essentially political, sociological, or philosophical views, or a merely personal moral code." Military Selective Service Act of 1967, Pub. L. No. 90–40, § 7, 81 Stat. 100, 104 (1967). How does this text compare with the 1948 statute? Is it constitutional?

A few years after *Seeger*, the Court revisited the issue of conscientious objection to military service in Welsh v. United States, 398 U.S. 333 (1970). On his exemption application, Welsh wrote:

"I believe that human life is valuable in and of itself; in its living; therefore I will not injure or kill another human being. This belief (and the corresponding 'duty' to abstain from violence toward another person) is not 'superior to those arising from any human relation.' On the contrary: *it is essential to every human relation.* I cannot, therefore, conscientiously comply with the Government's insistence that I assume duties which I feel are immoral and totally repugnant."

Welsh, however, indicated on his Selective Service System form that his beliefs were not religious in nature, and even crossed out the words "religious training" on the form. Nonetheless, as in *Seeger*, the Court found that deep, conscientious opposition to taking part in war on moral and ethical grounds was sufficient to constitute a religious objection to participation in the draft. Conscientious objector status applies to "all those whose consciences, spurred by deeply held moral, ethical, or religious beliefs, would give them no rest or peace if they allowed themselves to become a part of an instrument of war." In other words, to determine whether to grant an exemption on religious grounds, courts must inquire into whether "beliefs play the role of a religion and function as a religion" in the life of the applicant seeking an exemption.

In a dissent to *Welsh*, Justice Byron White wrote that, if Congress exempted religious conscientious objectors from military service because of its "purely practical judgment that religious objectors, however admirable, would be of no more use in combat than many others unqualified for military service," there would be no constitutional violation because Congress had acted from a secular purpose. Do you agree?

Was the First Circuit consistent with these cases when it wrote in *Hanna* that the " 'rigor and dedication' consideration applies only to applicants whose objections stem purely from secular beliefs, i.e. ethical and moral convictions, as opposed to those whose objections are based on 'traditional religious conviction' "? Does that mean it is easier for members of traditional religions to achieve C.O. status?

5. *Selective Conscientious Objection.* In the third of the three major Vietnam-era cases that shaped conscientious objector law, *Gillette v. United States*, the Court examined the question "whether conscientious objection to a particular war, rather than objection to war as such, relieves the objector from responsibilities of military training and service." The Court held that allowing exemptions on the basis of an objector's view that some wars are "just" and others "unjust" went a step too far. Rather, "conscientious scruples relating to war and military service must amount to conscientious opposition to participating personally in any war and all war."

The Court concluded that valid neutral reasons justified this limitation. The government must not only be able to obtain the manpower, but also to maintain a fair system for determining "who serves when not all serve." The Court explained:

> When the Government exacts so much, the importance of fair, evenhanded, and uniform decisionmaking is obviously intensified. The Government argues that the interest in fairness would be jeopardized by expansion of [an exemption] to include conscientious objection to a particular war. The contention is that the claim to relief on account of such objection is intrinsically a claim of uncertain dimensions, and that granting the claim in theory would involve a real danger of erratic or even discriminatory decisionmaking in administrative practice.
>
> A virtually limitless variety of beliefs are subsumable under the rubric, "objection to a particular war."

Justice Douglas' dissent noted that, unlike a pacifist, a "Catholic has a moral duty not to participate in unjust wars." Did *Gillette* therefore discriminate between religions by requiring C.O.s to object to war in any form? Would *Gillette* have been decided differently under RFRA? Do you think that free exercise and/or establishment are violated by allowing some religious C.O.s but not others?

6. *War in Any Form.* Boxing champion Muhammad Ali made headlines for a different reason when in 1966 he declared his objection to the Vietnam War. Just two years prior, Ali had joined Elijah Muhammad's Nation of Islam and changed his name from Cassius Clay to Muhammad Ali. He was imprisoned in 1967 when he refused to be inducted into the Army. The Selective Service System denied his conscientious objector application but gave no reason other than reliance on a letter from the Department of Justice. The DOJ letter contended Clay did not object to military service in any form, but only "to military service in the Armed Forces of the United States." It also stated his opposition to induction was "because of political and racial objections to policies of the United States as interpreted by Elijah Muhammad."

Was the DOJ correct that Ali was disqualified from C.O. status under *Gillette?* Should Ali lose under *Gillette* if he said that he would fight theocratic wars or wars in which he was commanded to fight by his God? Apparently Justice Harlan's clerk, Thomas Krattenmaker, researched Islam's teachings on war and discovered that the prospect of a holy or theocratic war was "entirely abstract and hypothetical." Thus, "Ali was, as a *practical* matter, religiously opposed to fighting in any wars that might actually occur." After Krattenmaker persuaded Harlan to side with Ali, Justice Douglas told the justices that Muslims were willing to fight *jihad* and therefore were selective C.O.s. Douglas, however, had rejected the Court's holding in *Gillette* and so sided with Ali on other grounds. Other justices thought Douglas was unfair in attributing the *jihad* theory to Ali's branch of Islam. Meanwhile Chief Justice Burger complained that Harlan had "become an apologist for the Black Muslims." Marty Lederman, Muhammad

Ali, conscientious objection, and the Supreme Court's struggle to understand "jihad" and "holy war": The story of Cassius Clay v. United States, SCOTUSBLOG (Jun. 8, 2016, 9:15 AM), http://www.scotusblog.com/ 2016/06/muhammad-ali-conscientious-objection-and-the-supreme-courts-struggle-to-understand-jihad-and-holy-war-the-story-of-cassius-clay-v-united-states/.

After Justice Stewart worked out a minimalist compromise, see id., the Supreme Court unanimously overturned Ali's conviction in a per curiam decision based on the government's failure to specify a reason for the denial of his application. Clay v. United States, 403 U.S. 698 (1971). Thus the "Court thereby avoided the need to ever decide whether the theoretical prospect of participating in a 'holy war' against Islam meant that members of the Nation of Islam were, or were not, 'conscientiously opposed to participation in war in any form.'" Lederman, infra. Do you think this issue would arise today?

7.   *An All-Volunteer Military.* Congress abolished the draft and established an all-volunteer military force in 1973. Federal law still requires men to register for the draft within thirty days of their eighteenth birthday. If the draft were reinstated, would the Court have to overrule *Seeger*, *Welsh*, and *Gillette*? Can the Selective Service Act survive constitutional scrutiny under *Lemon*, the endorsement test, the coercion test, and the neutrality test? Why or why not? See Matthew G. Lindenbaum, Religious Conscientious Objection and the Establishment Clause in the Rehnquist Court: Seeger, Welsh, Gillette and § 6(j) Revisited, 36 Colum. J.L. & Soc. Probs. 237 (2003) (concluding that the statute has no secular purpose, entangles church and state, and endorses religion).

Should C.O. status be available only when individuals are *drafted* by the government into military service, or should it be allowed as well for *voluntary, in-service* C.O.s who were not C.O.s at the time they joined the military? Do you agree that "to dismiss the need for an in-service program for volunteers would be to under-appreciate the strong belief in individual freedom of thought and capacity for individuals to change their views over time," and that "a person who volunteered for military service and affirmatively denied being a conscientious objector can subsequently have a fundamental change in core values and beliefs that are radically inconsistent with military service"? Or should in-service C.O. status be completely eliminated? See Major Joseph B. Mackey, Reclaiming the In-Service Conscientious Objection Program: Proposals for Creating a Meaningful Limitation to the Claim of Conscientious Objection, 2008–Aug Armlaw 31, 34–35 (2008); see also Alhassan v. Hagee, 424 F.3d 518, 524 (7th Cir. 2005), supra ("Alhassan argues that there is no difference between cases in which a soldier volunteers in the military versus cases in which a soldier is drafted. We disagree.").

8.   What impact does RFRA have on conscientious objector claims? A Sikh soldier sought a religious accommodation allowing him to wear a religious head covering with his army combat helmet and protective mask. The Army required that, to receive this accommodation, the soldier submit

to specialized testing at a cost of $32,000 to ensure "that his Sikh articles of faith, namely a cloth head covering and unshorn hair and beard, will not interfere with the helmet's ability 'to withstand ballistic and blunt forces' and the mask's ability 'to provide protection from toxic chemical and biological agents.' " The soldier sued under RFRA. Does this specialized testing requirement constitute a substantial burden? If so, is it the least restrictive means for the Army to achieve a compelling purpose? See Singh v. Carter, No. 16-399. 2016 WL 837924, *1 (D. D.C., Mar. 3, 2016) (holding that the soldier demonstrated a prima facie case under RFRA sufficient for the court to grant his TRO).

In the next section, we ask if RFRA has authorized a new system of conscientious objector status for government officials.

C. LAW AND GOVERNMENT

In the military section, Section B, we asked if voluntary (as opposed to drafted) members of the armed services can legitimately claim C.O. status. If they volunteer to join the military, does it follow that they cannot conscientiously object to all wars? Now we examine individuals who voluntarily join the profession of law or assume positions of government power. Lawyers take oaths to uphold the law; their professional rules require them not to break the law. Can a lawyer legitimately object to the law? Does it make sense to give lawyers and public officials exemptions from some laws? Which ones?

Should public employees who certify marriages be allowed to register their disapproval of homosexuality by refusing to participate in same-sex marriages? How would you handle the case of an employee who refuses to grant a marriage license to a same-sex couple? See generally Douglas Laycock, Anthony R. Picarello, Jr. & Robin Fretwell Wilson, eds., Same-Sex Marriage and Religious Liberty: Emerging Conflicts (2008). What do you think of the argument that religious exemptions from marriage laws will eventually undermine antidiscrimination laws that protect gay rights? See Douglas NeJaime, Marriage Inequality: Same-Sex Relationships, Religious Exemptions and the Production of Sexual Orientation Discrimination, 100 Cal. L. Rev. 1169 (2012).

After the Supreme Court recognized a constitutional right to same-sex marriage in *Obergefell v. Hodges,* Kentucky clerk Kim Davis refused to issue same-sex marriage licenses as a matter of personal conscience and religious liberty. Are you surprised by the result of her case?

Miller v. Davis

U.S. District Court for the Eastern District of Kentucky, Northern Division.
August 12, 2015.
123 F.Supp.3d 924.

■ DAVID L. BUNNING, DISTRICT JUDGE.

I. Introduction

This matter is before the Court on Plaintiffs' Motion for Preliminary Injunction. Plaintiffs are two same-sex and two opposite-sex couples seeking to enjoin Rowan County Clerk Kim Davis from enforcing her own marriage licensing policy. On June 26, 2015, just hours after the U.S. Supreme Court held that states are constitutionally required to recognize same-sex marriage, Davis announced that the Rowan County Clerk's Office would no longer issue marriage licenses to any couples. Davis, an Apostolic Christian with a sincere religious objection to same-sex marriage, specifically sought to avoid issuing licenses to same-sex couples without discriminating against them. Plaintiffs now allege that this "no marriage licenses" policy substantially interferes with their right to marry because it effectively forecloses them from obtaining a license in their home county. Davis insists that her policy poses only an incidental burden on Plaintiffs' right to marry, which is justified by the need to protect her own free exercise rights.

At its core, this civil action presents a conflict between two individual liberties held sacrosanct in American jurisprudence. One is the fundamental right to marry implicitly recognized in the Due Process Clause of the Fourteenth Amendment. The other is the right to free exercise of religion explicitly guaranteed by the First Amendment. Each party seeks to exercise one of these rights, but in doing so, they threaten to infringe upon the opposing party's rights. The tension between these constitutional concerns can be resolved by answering one simple question: Does the Free Exercise Clause likely excuse Kim Davis from issuing marriage licenses because she has a religious objection to same-sex marriage? For reasons stated herein, the Court answers this question in the negative.

IV. Analysis

B. Plaintiffs' Motion for Preliminary Injunction

1. Plaintiffs' likelihood of success on the merits

a. The fundamental right to marry

The state action at issue in this case is Defendant Davis' refusal to issue any marriage licenses. Plaintiffs contend that Davis' "no marriage licenses" policy significantly interferes with their right to marry because they are unable to obtain a license in their home county. Davis insists that her policy does not significantly discourage Plaintiffs from marrying because they have several other options for obtaining licenses:

(1) they may go to one of the seven neighboring counties that are issuing marriage licenses; (2) they may obtain licenses from Rowan County Judge Executive Walter Blevins; or (3) they may avail themselves of other alternatives being considered post-*Obergefell*.

Davis is correct in stating that Plaintiffs can obtain marriage licenses from one of the surrounding counties; thus, they are not totally precluded from marrying in Kentucky. However, this argument ignores the fact that Plaintiffs have strong ties to Rowan County. They are long-time residents who live, work, pay taxes, vote and conduct other business in Morehead. Under these circumstances, it is understandable that Plaintiffs would prefer to obtain their marriage licenses in their home county. And for other Rowan County residents, it may be more than a preference. The surrounding counties are only thirty minutes to an hour away, but there are individuals in this rural region of the state who simply do not have the physical, financial or practical means to travel.

This argument also presupposes that Rowan County will be the only Kentucky county not issuing marriage licenses. While Davis may be the only clerk currently turning away eligible couples, 57 of the state's 120 elected county clerks have asked Governor Beshear to call a special session of the state legislature to address religious concerns related to same-sex marriage licenses. If this Court were to hold that Davis' policy did not significantly interfere with the right to marry, what would stop the other 56 clerks from following Davis' approach? What might be viewed as an inconvenience for residents of one or two counties quickly becomes a substantial interference when applicable to approximately half of the state.

As for her assertion that Judge Blevins may issue marriage licenses, Davis is only partially correct. KRS § 402.240 provides that, "[i]n the absence of the county clerk, or during a vacancy in the office, the county judge/executive may issue the license and, in so doing, he shall perform the duties and incur all the responsibilities of the clerk." The statute does not explicitly define "absence," suggesting that a traditional interpretation of the term is appropriate. However, Davis asks the Court to deem her "absent," for purposes of this statute, because she has a religious objection to issuing the licenses. While this is certainly a creative interpretation, Davis offers no legal precedent to support it.

This proposal also has adverse consequences for Judge Blevins. If he began issuing marriage licenses while Davis continued to perform her other duties as Rowan County Clerk, he would likely be exceeding the scope of his office. After all, KRS § 402.240 only authorizes him to issue marriage licenses when Davis is unable to do so; it does not permit him to assume responsibility for duties that Davis does not wish to perform. Such an arrangement not only has the potential to create tension between the next judge executive and county clerk, it sets the stage for further manipulation of statutorily defined duties. Under these circumstances, the Court simply cannot count this as a viable option for Plaintiffs to obtain their marriage licenses.

Davis finally suggests that Plaintiffs will have other avenues for obtaining marriage licenses in the future. For example, county clerks have urged Governor Beshear to create an online marriage licensing system, which would be managed by the State of Kentucky. While these options may be available someday, they are not feasible alternatives at present. Thus, they have no impact on the Court's "substantial interference" analysis.

Having considered Davis' arguments in depth, the Court finds that Plaintiffs have one feasible avenue for obtaining their marriage licenses—they must go to another county. Davis makes much of the fact that Plaintiffs are able to travel, but she fails to address the one question that lingers in the Court's mind. Even if Plaintiffs are able to obtain licenses elsewhere, why should they be required to? The state has long entrusted county clerks with the task of issuing marriage licenses. It does not seem unreasonable for Plaintiffs, as Rowan County voters, to expect their elected official to perform her statutorily assigned duties. And yet, that is precisely what Davis is refusing to do. Much like the statutes at issue in *Loving* and *Zablocki*, Davis' "no marriage licenses" policy significantly discourages many Rowan County residents from exercising their right to marry and effectively disqualifies others from doing so. The Court must subject this policy apply heightened scrutiny.

b.   The absence of a compelling state interest

When pressed to articulate a compelling state interest served by her "no marriage licenses" policy, Davis responded that it serves the State's interest in protecting her religious freedom. The State certainly has an obligation to "observe the basic free exercise rights of its employees," but this is not the extent of its concerns. In fact, the State has some priorities that run contrary to Davis' proffered state interest. Chief among these is its interest in preventing Establishment Clause violations. Davis has arguably committed such a violation by openly adopting a policy that promotes her own religious convictions at the expenses of others. In such situations, "the scope of the employees' rights must [ ] yield to the legitimate interest of governmental employer in avoiding litigation."

The State also has a countervailing interest in upholding the rule of law. Our form of government will not survive unless we, as a society, agree to respect the U.S. Supreme Court's decisions, regardless of our personal opinions. Davis is certainly free to disagree with the Court's opinion, as many Americans likely do, but that does not excuse her from complying with it. To hold otherwise would set a dangerous precedent.

For these reasons, the Court concludes that Davis' "no marriage licenses" policy likely infringes upon Plaintiffs' rights without serving a compelling state interest. Because Plaintiffs have demonstrated a strong likelihood of success on the merits of their claim, this first factor weighs in favor of granting their request for relief.

3.   Potential for substantial harm to Kim Davis

a.   The right to free exercise of religion

For purposes of this inquiry, the state action at issue is Governor Beshear's post-*Obergefell* directive, which explicitly instructs county clerks to issue marriage licenses to same-sex couples. Davis argues that the Beshear directive not only substantially burdens her free exercise rights by requiring her to disregard sincerely-held religious beliefs, it does not serve a compelling state interest. She further insists that Governor Beshear could easily grant her a religious exemption without adversely affecting Kentucky's marriage licensing scheme, as there are readily available alternatives for obtaining licenses in and around Rowan County.

This argument proceeds on the assumption that Governor Beshear's policy is not neutral or generally applicable, and is therefore subject to strict scrutiny. However, the text itself supports a contrary inference. Governor Beshear first describes the legal impact of the Court's decision in *Obergefell*, then provides guidance for all county clerks in implementing this new law. His goal is simply to ensure that the activities of the Commonwealth are consistent with U.S. Supreme Court jurisprudence.

While facial neutrality is not dispositive, Davis has done little to convince the Court that Governor Beshear's directive aims to suppress religious practice. She has only one piece of anecdotal evidence to demonstrate that Governor Beshear "is picking and choosing the conscience-based exemptions to marriage that he deems acceptable." In 2014, Attorney General Jack Conway declined to appeal a federal district court decision striking down Kentucky's constitutional and statutory prohibitions on same-sex marriage. He openly stated that he could not, in good conscience, defend discrimination and waste public resources on a weak case. Instead of directing Attorney General Conway to pursue the appeal, regardless of his religious beliefs, Governor Beshear hired private attorneys for that purpose. He has so far refused to extend such an "exemption" to county clerks with religious objections to same-sex marriage.

However, Davis fails to establish that her current situation is comparable to Attorney General Conway's position in 2014. Both are elected officials who have voiced strong opinions about same-sex marriage, but the comparison ends there. Governor Beshear did not actually "exempt" Attorney General Conway from pursuing the same-sex marriage appeal. Attorney General Conway's decision stands as an exercise of prosecutorial discretion on an unsettled legal question. By contrast, Davis is refusing to recognize the legal force of U.S. Supreme Court jurisprudence in performing her duties as Rowan County Clerk. Because the two are not similarly situated, the Court simply cannot conclude that Governor Beshear treated them differently based upon their religious convictions. There being no other evidence in the record to suggest that the Beshear directive is anything but neutral and generally applicable, it will likely be upheld if it is rationally related to a legitimate government purpose.

The Beshear directive certainly serves the State's interest in upholding the rule of law. However, it also rationally relates to several narrower interests identified in Obergefell. By issuing licenses to same-sex couples, the State allows them to enjoy "the right to personal choice regarding marriage [that] is inherent in the concept of individual autonomy" and enter into "a two-person union unlike any other in its importance to the committed individuals." It also allows same-sex couples to take advantage of the many societal benefits and fosters stability for their children. Therefore, the Court concludes that it likely does not infringe upon Davis' free exercise rights. .

d.   The Kentucky Religious Freedom Act

Kentucky courts have held that Kentucky Constitution § 5 does not grant more protection to religious practice than the First Amendment. Such a finding would normally permit the Court to collapse its analysis of state and federal constitutional provisions. However, the Kentucky Religious Freedom Act, patterned after the federal RFRA, subjects state free exercise challenges to heightened scrutiny.

Davis again argues that the Beshear directive substantially burdens her religious freedom without serving a compelling state interest. The record in this case suggests that the burden is more slight. As the Court has already pointed out, Davis is simply being asked to signify that couples meet the legal requirements to marry. The State is not asking her to condone same-sex unions on moral or religious grounds, nor is it restricting her from engaging in a variety of religious activities. Davis remains free to practice her Apostolic Christian beliefs. She may continue to attend church twice a week, participate in Bible Study and minister to female inmates at the Rowan County Jail. She is even free to believe that marriage is a union between one man and one woman, as many Americans do. However, her religious convictions cannot excuse her from performing the duties that she took an oath to perform as Rowan County Clerk. The Court therefore concludes that Davis is unlikely to suffer a violation of her free exercise rights.

4.   Public interest

"[I]t is always in the public interest to prevent the violation of a party's constitutional rights." Because Davis' "no marriage licenses" policy likely infringes upon Plaintiffs' fundamental right to marry, and because Davis herself is unlikely to suffer a violation of her free speech or free exercise rights if an injunction is issued, this fourth and final factor weighs in favor of granting Plaintiffs' Motion.

NOTES AND QUESTIONS

1. *The Opinion.* How do you assess the district court's reasoning? Do you think it struck the proper balance between the right to marry and free exercise? Why did the court say the right to marry is "implicitly recognized" in the Constitution but free exercise is "explicitly guaranteed" by the First Amendment? Why didn't an explicit guarantee trump an implicitly recognized right in this case?

Do you agree there was no substantial burden on Davis' religion in this case? Is that conclusion consistent with *Hobby Lobby*'s and *Zubik*'s reasoning about substantial burden? Should Kentucky courts adopt the same or different reasoning as the federal RFRA cases about their state RFRAs?

2. *The Appeal.* Davis refused to issue licenses even after she lost in the district court. She appealed to the U.S. Court of Appeals for the Sixth Circuit, which declined to grant a stay of removal. The Sixth Circuit stated:

> In light of the binding holding of *Obergefell*, it cannot be defensibly argued that the holder of the Rowan County Clerk's office, apart from who personally occupies that office, may decline to act in conformity with the United States Constitution as interpreted by a dispositive holding of the United States Supreme Court.

Miller v. Davis, 2015 WL 10692640, at *1 (6th Cir. Aug. 26, 2015).

Do you agree with the Sixth Circuit's reasoning about *Obergefell*? How do you think the dissenting justices in *Obergefell* would assess the Sixth Circuit's and the district court's reasoning?

After Davis refused to issue licenses, Judge Bunning sentenced her to jail for contempt of court. She stayed in jail until the judge determined her office was issuing marriage licenses. Do you agree Davis should have spent time in jail? What do you think of the argument "she needs to either resign or come to grips with the fact that her official duties in government must not carry any hint of personal religious favoritism or bias"? Tod Robberson, Kim Davis' Jail Release Still Doesn't Clarify the Line Between Religion and Official Duties, Dallas Morning News Blogs, Sept. 8, 2015.

Governor Beshear's successor, Matt Bevins, ordered county clerks' names removed from state marriage licenses "to ensure that the sincerely held religious beliefs of all Kentuckians are honored." Steve Bittenbender, New Kentucky Governor Orders Clerks' Names Off Marriage Licenses, Las Vegas Rev.-J., Dec. 22, 2015. Is this a good outcome for everyone? Should Kentucky legislators pass a conscience clause that would protect government workers who oppose same-sex marriage?

3. In Walker v. City of Birmingham, 388 U.S. 307 (1967), the Reverend Martin Luther King, Jr. and other African-American ministers led protest demonstrations in Birmingham, Alabama, on Good Friday and Easter Sunday 1963. Before the marches began, the ministers had applied for the parade permit required by a city ordinance, but their requests were refused by Commissioner Bull Connor, who said "No you will not get a permit in Birmingham, Alabama to picket. I will picket you over to the City Jail," and he repeated that twice. Id. at 318 n. 9. The city immediately sought an injunction to stop the protests, which the state court granted. Nonetheless, the protesters proceeded with their demonstrations, announcing their "intention to disobey the injunction because it was 'raw tyranny under the guise of maintaining law and order.' " Id. at 310. When the city asked the state court to hold the ministers in contempt for violating the injunction, the protest leaders replied that the city ordinance was unconstitutionally vague as well as applied in a discriminatory manner, and that they should not be convicted for violating an unconstitutional law. Upholding the state courts' conviction of the ministers, the U.S. Supreme Court ruled that the ministers could be held in contempt and could not raise their constitutional challenges to the law because they had not appealed the injunction. The majority asserted "no man can be judge in his own case":

> The rule of law that Alabama followed in this case reflects a belief that in the fair administration of justice no man can be judge in his own case, however exalted his station, however righteous his motives, and irrespective of his race, color, politics, or religion. This Court cannot hold that the petitioners were constitutionally free to ignore all the procedures of the law and carry their battle to the streets. One may sympathize with the petitioners' impatient commitment to their cause. But respect for judicial process is a small price to pay for the civilizing hand of law, which alone can give abiding meaning to constitutional freedom.

Id. at 321–22.

Chief Justice Warren dissented that " 'the civilizing hand of law' would [not] be hampered in the slightest by enforcing the First Amendment in this case."

> These facts lend no support to the court's charges that petitioners were presuming to act as judges in their own case, or that they had a disregard for the judicial process. They did not flee the jurisdiction or refuse to appear in the Alabama courts. Having violated the injunction, they promptly submitted themselves to the courts to test the constitutionality of the injunction and the ordinance it parroted. . . . Indeed, it shows no disrespect for law to violate a statute on the ground that it is unconstitutional and then to submit one's case to the courts with the willingness to accept the penalty if the statute is held to be valid.

Id. at 327.

After this conviction, King wrote his famous *Letter from Birmingham Jail*, which includes the following passages about unjust laws:

> You express a great deal of anxiety over our willingness to break laws. This is certainly a legitimate concern. Since we so diligently urge people to obey the Supreme Court's decision of 1954 outlawing segregation in the public schools, at first glance it may seem rather paradoxical for us consciously to break laws. One may ask: "How can you advocate breaking some laws and obeying others?" The answer lies in the fact that there are two types of laws: just and unjust. I would be the first to advocate obeying just laws. One has not only a legal but a moral responsibility to obey just laws. Conversely, one has a moral responsibility to disobey unjust laws. I would agree with St. Augustine that "an unjust law is no law at all."
>
> Now, what is the difference between the two? How does one determine whether a law is just or unjust? A just law is a man-made code that squares with the moral law or the law of God. An unjust law is a code that is out of Harmony with the moral law. To put it in the terms of St. Thomas Aquinas: An unjust law is a human law that is not rooted in eternal law and natural law. Any law that uplifts human personality is just. Any law that degrades human personality is unjust. All segregation statutes are unjust because segregation distorts the soul and damages the personality. It gives the segregator a false sense of superiority and the segregated a false sense of inferiority. Segregation, to use the terminology of the Jewish philosopher Martin Buber, substitutes an "I-it" relationship for an "I-thou" relationship and ends up relegating persons to the status of things. Hence segregation is not only politically, economically and sociologically unsound, it is morally wrong and sinful. Paul Tillich has said that sin is separation. Is not segregation an existential expression of man's tragic separation, his awful estrangement, his terrible sinfulness? Thus is it that I can urge men to obey the 1954 decision of the Supreme Court, for it is morally right; and I can urge them to disobey segregation ordinances, for they are morally wrong.

Martin Luther King, Jr., Letter from a Birmingham Jail (Apr. 16, 1963) (on file with the King Center, Atlanta, Georgia). Whose interpretation of the law do you prefer, Dr. King's or the Supreme Court's *Walker* decision? See David Luban, Legal Storytelling: Difference Made Legal: The Court and Dr. King, 87 Mich. L. Rev. 2152 (1989).

Are Kim Davis' actions similar to Martin Luther King's?

4.   Gandhi, who influenced Dr. King and the Civil Rights Movement, made similar remarks about obedience to unjust laws:

READER: You would then disregard laws—this is rank disloyalty. We have always been considered a law-abiding nation. You seem to be going even beyond the extremists. They say that we must obey the laws that have been passed, but that if the laws be bad, we must drive out the law-givers even by force.

[GANDHI]: Whether I go beyond them or whether I do not is a matter of no consequence to either of us. We simply want to find out what is right and to act accordingly. The real meaning of the statement that we are a law-abiding nation is that we are passive resisters. When we do not like certain laws, we do not break the heads of law-givers but we suffer and do not submit to the laws. That we should obey laws whether good or bad is a new-fangled notion. There was no such thing in former days. The people disregarded those laws they did not like and suffered the penalties for their breach. It is contrary to our manhood if we obey laws repugnant to our conscience. Such teaching is opposed to religion and means slavery. If the Government were to ask us to go about without any clothing, should we do so? If I were a passive resister, I would say to them that I would have nothing to do with their law. But we have so forgotten ourselves and become so compliant that we do not mind any degrading law.

A man who has realized his manhood, who fears only God, will fear no one else. Man-made laws are not necessarily binding on him. Even the Government does not expect any such thing from us. They do not say: "You must do such and such a thing," but they say: "If you do not do it, we will punish you." We are sunk so low that we fancy that it is our duty and our religion to do what the law lays down. If man will only realize that it is unmanly to obey laws that are unjust, no man's tyranny will enslave him. This is the key to self-rule or home-rule.

M.K. Gandhi, Indian Home Rule (1909) in Homer A. Jack, ed., The Gandhi Reader: A Source Book of His Life and Writings 112–13 (1956). See also Rabbi Abraham Joshua Heschel, The Reasons for My Involvement in the Peace Movement, in Abraham Joshua Heschel, Moral Grandeur and Spiritual Audacity 224–26 (1997) ("Although Jewish tradition enjoins our people to obey scrupulously the decrees issued by the government of the land, whenever a decree is unambiguously immoral, one nevertheless has a duty to disobey it."). What does it mean to be a passive resister? Do you agree that it is wrong to obey an unjust law? If it is wrong to obey an unjust law, why should there be a penalty for disobeying?

5. How can an individual tell if a law is unjust? When do you think civil disobedience was most justified: in the Civil Rights Movement, in protests against the Vietnam War, in opposition to new immigration laws, or to protest *Obergefell*? What criteria can you suggest for deciding when a law is just or unjust?

6. Dr. King and Gandhi led non-violent movements. Should all conscientious objection and civil disobedience be non-violent? Does religion require non-violence? Consider the following reflections from Gandhi:

> Passive resistance is a method of securing rights by personal suffering; it is the reverse of resistance by arms. When I refuse to do a thing that is repugnant to my conscience, I use soul-force. For instance, the Government of the day has passed a law which is applicable to me. I do not like it. If by using violence I force the Government to repeal the law, I am employing what may be termed body-force. If I do not obey the law and accept the penalty for its breach, I use soul-force. It involves sacrifice of self. . . .

M.K. Gandhi, supra, at 112. See also Judith M. Brown, Gandhi and Civil Disobedience: The Mahatma in Indian Politics 1928–34 (1977) and Mohammed Abu-Nimer, A Framework for Nonviolence and Peacebuilding in Islam, 15 J. L. & Rel. 217 (2000–2001) (discussing Islamic resources for non-violent civil disobedience).

While leading India in its quest for independence from the British Empire, Gandhi outlined the following rules for civil disobedience:

1) A civil resister will express no anger.

2) He will sometimes suffer the anger of the opponent.

3) In so doing, he will put up with assaults from the opponent, never retaliate; but he will not submit, out of fear of punishment or the like, to any order given in anger.

4) When any person in authority seeks to arrest a civil resister, he will voluntarily submit to the arrest, and he will not resist the attachment or removal of his own property, if any, when confiscated by authorities.

5) If a civil resister has any property in his possession as a trustee, he will refuse to surrender it, even though in defending it he might lose his life. He will, however, never retaliate.

6) Retaliation includes swearing and cursing.

7) Therefore a civil resister will never insult his opponent, and therefore also not take part in many of the newly coined cries, which are contrary to the spirit of ahimsa. (Ahimsa is a rule of conduct that bars the killing or injuring of human beings).

8) A civil resister may not salute the flag of Britain, but he will not insult it or officials, English or Indian.

9) In the course of the struggle if anyone insults an official or commits an assault upon him, a civil resister will protect such official or officials from the insult or attack even at the risk of his life.

Mohandas Karamchand Gandhi, Non-Violent Resistance (Satyagraha) 79 (1961). Would anyone in the contemporary American professions of the military, medicine and the law be capable of following these rules?

7. *Constitutional Resistance to Obergefell?* A group of prominent legal academics and attorneys issued a statement calling for "constitutional resistance" to *Obergefell*. According to their statement:

> We stand with James Madison and Abraham Lincoln in recognizing that the Constitution is not whatever a majority of Supreme Court justices say it is.
>
> We remind all officeholders in the United States that they are pledged to uphold the Constitution of the United States, not the will of five members of the Supreme Court.
>
> We call on all federal and state officeholders:
>
> > To refuse to accept *Obergefell* as binding precedent for all but the specific plaintiffs in that case.
> >
> > To recognize the authority of states to define marriage, and the right of federal and state officeholders to act in accordance with those definitions.
> >
> > To pledge full and mutual legal and political assistance to anyone who refuses to follow *Obergefell* for constitutionally protected reasons.
> >
> > To open forthwith a broad and honest conversation on the means by which Americans may constitutionally resist and overturn the judicial usurpations evident in *Obergefell*.
>
> We emphasize that the course of action we are here advocating is neither extreme nor disrespectful of the rule of law. Lincoln regarded the claim of supremacy for the Supreme Court in matters of constitutional interpretation as incompatible with the republican principles of the Constitution.

American Principles Project, Statement Calling for Constitutional Resistance to *Obergefell v. Hodges*, Oct. 8, 2015, at https://american principlesproject.org/founding-principles/statement-calling-for-constitutional-resistance-to-obergefell-v-hodges.

How do you assess their argument? Are they recommending conscientious objection? Civil disobedience? Do you agree that the statement may be dangerous because the "ethical restraint that is supposed to keep a lawyer in check as an adversary of the courts may be sorely tested if, acting as legal professionals, they join in or originate a campaign to treat a Supreme Court ruling as non-binding across the country in all similar cases, and thus advocate explicitly that it be defied."? Lyle Denniston, May Lawyers Lead a Campaign to Defy the Supreme Court?, Constitution Daily, Oct. 13, 2015, at http://blog.constitutioncenter.org/2015/10/constitution-check-may-lawyers-lead-a-campaign-to-defy-the-supreme-court/. Are lawyers different from other C.O.s? Do you think the same guidelines should apply to military and medical C.O.s? Why or why not? How would you explain to your clients that you are a C.O.?

8. *More than Military, Medicine, and Law?* Professor Sawicki argues that a "more comprehensive" account of conscientious objection is needed than the traditional one that emphasizes the military, medicine and law. Conscientious objectors include parents who opt out of medical or educational norms for their children, individuals who discriminate on the basis of sexual orientation, tax evaders, and terrorists who turn to violence to make their messages heard. Do you think the United States has too much conscience protection, or too little? See Nadia N. Sawicki, The Hollow Promise of Freedom of Conscience, 33 Cardozo L. Rev. 1389, 1410–29 (2012).

———————

In Chapter 6, we examine whether the Court's Religion Clause jurisprudence has been equally protective of individual and institutional religious freedom.

CHAPTER 6

CONFLICTS BETWEEN INDIVIDUAL AND INSTITUTIONAL RELIGIOUS FREEDOM

In this chapter, we study the relationship between the freedom of religious individuals and the organizations to which they belong. How much freedom should religious institutions enjoy? Should they, for example, enjoy immunity from lawsuits by their members? This chapter examines property, employment, and tort law to determine the range of institutional religious freedom against individual members.

The Supreme Court's cases about church property involve disputes between warring factions of churches who ask the civil courts to determine which group holds title to the property. Should the courts tell these groups they must decide such controversies on their own? Do courts have legal authority to back one religious group's claims to property over another's? The Supreme Court has both observed the importance of court abstention from ecclesiastical disputes and stated courts may decide such property disputes according to "neutral principles of law." Can such neutral principles really protect churches from government interference? We explore church property disputes in Section A.

Title VII of the Civil Rights Act protects individuals from employment discrimination on the basis of race, color, religion, sex, and national origin. Does the application of Title VII to religious organizations constitute unconstitutional government interference in religious practice? Congress anticipated that question; the Act, for example, includes the following exemption from religious discrimination lawsuits for religious organizations that hire on the basis of religion:

> This subchapter shall not apply . . . to a religious corporation, association, educational institution, or society with respect to the employment of individuals of a particular religion to perform work connected with the carrying on by such corporation, association, educational institution, or society of its activities.

42 U.S.C. § 2000e–1(a). That exemption, however, raises as many questions as it answers. Should churches be liable for racial or sexual discrimination if it accords with their beliefs? Should a church be liable for sex discrimination if it refuses to ordain women, or racial

discrimination if it refuses to hire African Americans? Does the exemption extend to all employment at church-run institutions, from janitors to clergy? Are all religious organizations, from the local mosque to the YMCA, protected from discrimination suits on the basis of religion?

We explore such questions of employment law in Section B. Section B1 explains Title VII religious discrimination law. Section B2 focuses on the ministerial exception, which is a constitutionally-required exemption that bans some lawsuits by ministers against their church employers.

What should happen when church members desire to sue their churches for tortious conduct, ranging from negligence to defamation to intentional infliction of emotional distress or assault? Does the First Amendment prohibit all tort lawsuits against the churches, or only some of them? In recent years, sexual misconduct and abuse by clergy have focused attention on a no-harm principle as ecclesiastical tort liability has expanded. We examine the scope of churches' civil liability for such harms in Section C.

As you read this chapter, keep in mind the questions raised in Chapter 4 about the implications of *Employment Div. v. Smith*. Does *Smith* apply to religious institutions or should they be exempt from neutral laws of general applicability? If religious institutions are exempt from neutral laws, is there a violation of the Establishment Clause? Also consider how the rights of individuals should be balanced with the rights of religious organizations. Is it correct to assume that the protection of church institutions promotes religious freedom, even when individual rights are restricted? Consider the following reflection by Professor Laura Underkuffler:

> I have never been a fan of the *Smith* opinion. It is my view that freedom of religion—or freedom of conscience, as I have defined it—has very distinct value, which is recognized in our constitutional scheme. By affording individual religious exercise no special protection, *Smith* denies this principle. However, frustration with *Smith* should not blind us to the deep problems that an aggressive vision of religious-group autonomy presents. The prospect of religious groups with broad, autonomous power poses special dangers, both to dissenting individuals and to the goals of government, which should impel us to view it cautiously. Indeed, our reservations about the supremacy of religious claims should, if anything, be stronger when we consider the claims of religious groups.

Laura S. Underkuffler, Thoughts on Smith and Religious-Group Autonomy, 2004 BYU L. Rev. 1773, 1776. Professor Michael McConnell argues that in recent years the Court has moved to a much more vigorous defense of institutional over individual religious freedom. The

Court's decision in *Hosanna-Tabor*, which we study in Section B2, particularly reflects this shift, according to McConnell:

> Taken together, the establishment and free exercise holdings of *Hosanna-Tabor* suggest a shift in Religion Clauses jurisprudence from a focus on individual believers to a focus on the autonomy of organized religious institutions. Although the Court never confined the protections of the Religion Clauses to natural persons, opinions gave the impression that, to the Court, religion is essentially a matter between individuals and their God (however conceived). Free exercise cases emphasized individual sincerity and rejected the idea that religious exercise must be rooted in the teachings of a faith community. In some of the parochial school cases, members of the Court gave the impression they regarded the "inculcat[ion]" of church "dogma" as a threat to the freedom of individuals to form their own beliefs. Now, however, as interpreted in *Smith* and *Hosanna-Tabor*, the Free Exercise Clause provides far greater protection to the "faith and mission" of religious institutions than to individual acts of religious exercise, and the Establishment Clause bars the government from interfering in "ecclesiastical" decisionmaking. Perhaps it is a coincidence, but this shift in emphasis corresponds very roughly to the old divide between individualistic Protestantism and institutional Catholicism and might be the first evident fruit of the new Catholic majority on the Court. The "freedom of the church" was the first kind of religious freedom to appear in the western world, but got short shrift from the Court for decades. Thanks to *Hosanna-Tabor*, it has again taken center stage.

Michael W. McConnell, Reflections on *Hosanna-Tabor*, 35 Harv. J.L. & Pub. Pol'y 821, 835–36 (2012). Does this suggest a bigger influence by the Catholic justices on the Supreme Court?

As you read the following opinion, ask yourself which legal test best protects litigants against government entanglement with churches.

A. DISPUTES OVER CHURCH PROPERTY

Episcopal Church Cases
Supreme Court of California, 2009.
45 Cal.4th 467, 198 P.3d 66, 87 Cal.Rptr.3d 275.

■ CHIN, J.

In this case, a local church has disaffiliated itself from a larger, general church with which it had been affiliated. Both the local church and the general church claim ownership of the local church building and the property on which the building stands. The parties have asked the courts of this state to resolve this dispute. When secular courts are asked to resolve an internal church dispute over property ownership, obvious dangers exist that the courts will become impermissibly entangled with religion. Nevertheless, when called on to do so, secular courts must resolve such disputes. We granted review primarily to decide how the secular courts of this state should resolve disputes over church property.

State courts must not decide questions of religious doctrine; those are for the church to resolve. Accordingly, if resolution of the property dispute involves a doctrinal dispute, the court must defer to the position of the highest ecclesiastical authority that has decided the doctrinal point. But to the extent the court can resolve the property dispute without reference to church doctrine, it should use what the United States Supreme Court has called the "neutral principles of law" approach. (*Jones v. Wolf* (1979) 443 U.S. 595, 597, 99 S.Ct. 3020, 61 L.Ed.2d 775.) The court should consider sources such as the deeds to the property in dispute, the local church's articles of incorporation, the general church's constitution, canons, and rules, and relevant statutes, including statutes specifically concerning religious property, such as Corporations Code section 9142.

Applying the neutral principles of law approach, we conclude, on this record, that the general church, not the local church, owns the property in question. Although the deeds to the property have long been in the name of the local church, that church agreed from the beginning of its existence to be part of the greater church and to be bound by its governing documents. These governing documents make clear that church property is held in trust for the general church and may be controlled by the local church only so long as that local church remains a part of the general church. When it disaffiliated from the general church, the local church did not have the right to take the church property with it.

I.   FACTS AND PROCEDURAL HISTORY

"The Protestant Episcopal Church in the United States of America . . . , organized in 1789, was the product of secession of the Anglican church in the colonies from the Church of England, the latter church itself being the product of secession from the Church of Rome in 1534." The church (hereafter the Episcopal Church) is governed by a general convention and a presiding bishop. In the United States, the Episcopal Church is divided geographically into dioceses, including the Episcopal Diocese of Los Angeles (Los Angeles Diocese). Each diocese is governed by a diocesan convention and a bishop. A diocese is itself divided into missions and parishes, which are individual churches where members meet to worship. A parish is governed by a rector and a board of elected lay persons called the vestry. One such parish within the Los Angeles Diocese was St. James Parish in Newport Beach (St. James Parish).

St. James Parish began as a mission of the Episcopal Church in 1946. In 1947, members of the mission sought permission from the Los Angeles Diocese to organize as a parish. The members' handwritten application "promise[d] and declare[d] that the said Parish shall be forever held under, and conform to and be bound by, the Ecclesiastical authority of the Bishop of Los Angeles, and of his successor in office, the Constitution and Canons of the [Episcopal Church], and the Constitution and Canons of the Diocese of Los Angeles." Articles of Incorporation of St. James Parish, filed with the California Secretary of State on March 1, 1949, stated that the corporation was formed "[t]o establish and maintain a Parish which shall form a constituent part of the Diocese of Los Angeles in [the Episcopal Church]; and so that the Constitution and Canons, Rules, Regulations and Discipline of said Church ... and the Constitution and Canons in the Diocese of Los Angeles, for the time being shall, unless they be contrary to the laws of this State, always form a part of the By-Laws and Articles of Incorporation of the corporation hereby formed and shall prevail against and govern anything herein contained that may appear repugnant to such Constitutions, Canons, Rules, Regulations and Discipline. . . . " In 1991, St. James Parish amended its articles of incorporation, but it did not modify these provisions.

In 1950, the "Bishop of the Protestant Episcopal Church in Los Angeles" deeded the property on which the church building stands to St. James Parish for consideration of "less than $100.00." The deeds to the property have been in the name of the local church ever since.

Canon II.6 of the canons of the general convention of the Episcopal Church provides: "Sec. 1. No Church or Chapel shall be consecrated until the Bishop shall have been sufficiently satisfied that the building and the ground on which it is erected are secured for ownership and use by a Parish, Mission, Congregation, or Institution affiliated with this Church and subject to its Constitution and Canons.

"Sec. 2. It shall not be lawful for any Vestry, Trustees, or other body authorized by laws of any State or Territory to hold property for any Diocese, Parish or Congregation, to encumber or alienate any dedicated and consecrated Church or Chapel, or any Church or Chapel which has been used solely for Divine Service, belonging to the Parish or Congregation which they represent, without the previous consent of the Bishop, acting with the advice and consent of the Standing Committee of the Diocese.

"Sec. 3. No dedicated and consecrated Church or Chapel shall be removed, taken down, or otherwise disposed of for any worldly or common use, without the previous consent of the Standing Committee of the Diocese.

"Sec. 4. Any dedicated and consecrated Church or Chapel shall be subject to the trust declared with respect to real and personal property held by any Parish, Mission, or Congregation as set forth in Canon I.7.4."

The record shows, and no one disputes, that the Episcopal Church first adopted the original versions of sections 2 and 3 of Canon II.6 in 1868. It added section 1 of that Canon in 1871 and section 4 in 1979 when it amended Canon I.7.

In 1979, in apparent response to that year's United States Supreme Court opinion in *Jones v. Wolf, supra,* 443 U.S. 595, 99 S.Ct. 3020, the Episcopal Church added section 4 to Canon I.7 (Canon I.7.4), which provides: "All real and personal property held by or for the benefit of any Parish, Mission or Congregation is held in trust for this Church and the Diocese thereof in which such Parish, Mission or Congregation is located. The existence of this trust, however, shall in no way limit the power and authority of the Parish, Mission or Congregation otherwise existing over such property so long as the particular Parish, Mission or Congregation remains a part of, and subject to, this Church and its Constitution and Canons."

Recently, as a result of a doctrinal dispute, St. James Parish disaffiliated itself from the Episcopal Church. It appears that the dispute leading to the decision to disaffiliate arose after the national church ordained an openly gay man as a bishop in New Hampshire in 2003. Some members of the Episcopal Church, including members of St. James Parish, disagreed with this ordination. In July 2004, the board of St. James Parish voted to end its affiliation with the Episcopal Church and to affiliate with the Anglican Church of Uganda. A majority of the congregation voted to support the decision. After the disaffiliation, a further dispute arose as to who owned the church building that St. James Parish used for worship and the property on which the building stands—the local church that left the Episcopal Church or the higher church authorities.

II. DISCUSSION

B. Resolving the Dispute Over the Church Property

We will first consider what method the secular courts of this state should use to resolve disputes over church property. We will then apply that method to analyze the dispute of this case.

1. How California Courts Should Resolve Disputes Over Church Property

Decisions from both this court and the United States Supreme Court have made clear that, when asked to do so, secular courts may, indeed must, resolve internal church disputes over ownership of church property. As the high court put it in the seminal 19th-century case involving a church property dispute, "an appeal is made to the secular authority; the courts when so called on must perform their functions as in other cases. Religious organizations come before us in the same attitude as other voluntary associations for benevolent or charitable purposes, and their rights of property, or of contract, are equally under the protection of the law, and the actions of their members subject to its restraints." (*Watson v. Jones* (1871) 80 U.S. (13 Wall.) 679, 714, 20 L.Ed. 666.) Similarly, in its most recent decision involving a church property dispute, the court stated, "There can be little doubt about the general authority of civil courts to resolve this question. The State has an obvious and legitimate interest in the peaceful resolution of property disputes, and in providing a civil forum where the ownership of church property can be determined conclusively." (*Jones v. Wolf, supra,* 443 U.S. at p. 602, 99 S.Ct. 3020.)

But when called on to resolve church property disputes, secular courts must not entangle themselves in disputes over church doctrine or infringe on the right to free exercise of religion. In this regard, the United States Supreme Court has made two points clear: (1) how state courts resolve church property disputes is a matter of state law; but (2) the method a state chooses must not violate the First Amendment to the United States Constitution. "[T]he First Amendment prohibits civil courts from resolving church property disputes on the basis of religious doctrine and practice. As a corollary to this commandment, the Amendment requires that civil courts defer to the resolution of issues of religious doctrine or polity by the highest court of a hierarchical church organization. Subject to these limitations, however, the First Amendment does not dictate that a State must follow a particular method of resolving church property disputes. Indeed, 'a State may adopt *any* one of various approaches for settling church property disputes so long as it involves no consideration of doctrinal matters, whether the ritual and liturgy of worship or the tenets of faith.'" (*Jones v. Wolf, supra,* 443 U.S. at p. 602.)

The high court found invalid, for example, a method used in Georgia whereby "the right to the property previously used by the local churches was made to turn on a civil court jury decision as to whether the general church abandoned or departed from the tenets of faith and practice it held at the time the local churches affiliated with it." (*Presbyterian Church v. Hull Church, supra,* 393 U.S. at p. 441, 89 S.Ct. 601.) The court held that "the civil courts [have] *no* role in determining ecclesiastical questions in the process of resolving property disputes." It explained that the First Amendment "commands civil courts to decide church property disputes without resolving underlying controversies over religious doctrine. Hence, States, religious organizations, and individuals must structure relationships involving church property so as not to require the civil courts to resolve ecclesiastical questions." The court concluded that the "departure-from-doctrine" approach "requires the civil court to determine matters at the very core of a religion—the interpretation of particular church doctrines and the importance of those doctrines to the religion. Plainly, the First Amendment forbids civil courts from playing such a role." (*Id.* at p. 450, 89 S.Ct. 601; see also *Serbian Eastern Orthodox Diocese v. Milivojevich* (1976) 426 U.S. 696, 698, 96 S.Ct. 2372, 49 L.Ed.2d 151 ["inquiries made by the Illinois Supreme Court into matters of ecclesiastical cognizance and polity and the court's actions pursuant thereto contravened the First and Fourteenth Amendments"].) The court remanded the matter to the Georgia Supreme Court to develop a new method for resolving church property disputes.

The high court has approved two methods for adjudicating church property disputes. The first approach is one the court itself adopted in the 19th century. (*Watson v. Jones, supra*, 80 U.S. 679.) This approach is often called the "principle of government" approach. The *Watson v. Jones* court distinguished between two types of church disputes. One "has reference to the case of a church of a strictly congregational or independent organization, governed solely within itself . . . ; and to property held by such a church, either by way of purchase or donation, with no other specific trust attached to it in the hands of the church than that it is for the use of that congregation as a religious society." "In such cases," the court explained, "where there is a schism which leads to a separation into distinct and conflicting bodies, the rights of such bodies to the use of the property must be determined by the ordinary principles which govern voluntary associations." Another type, which the court said "is the one which is oftenest found in the courts," involves a hierarchical structure, i.e., a "religious congregation which is itself part of a large and general organization of some religious denomination, with which it is more or less intimately connected by religious views and ecclesiastical government." In the latter case, the court said, "we are bound to look at the fact that the local congregation is itself but a member of a much larger and more important religious organization, and is under its government and control, and is bound by its orders and judgments."

The court adopted this test for a hierarchical church: "[W]henever the questions of discipline, or of faith, or ecclesiastical rule, custom, or law have been decided by the highest of these church judicatories to which the matter has been carried, the legal tribunals must accept such decisions as final, and as binding on them, in their application to the case before them."

The second approach the high court has approved is what it called the "neutral principles of law" approach. (*Jones v. Wolf, supra*, 443 U.S. at p. 597, 99 S.Ct. 3020.) . . . The high court definitively approved the neutral principles approach in *Jones v. Wolf*, a 1979 decision that is the high court's most recent on this subject and, hence, is of critical importance to the instant dispute. . . "The primary advantages of the neutral-principles approach are that it is completely secular in operation, and yet flexible enough to accommodate all forms of religious organization and polity. The method relies exclusively on objective, well-established concepts of trust and property law familiar to lawyers and judges. It thereby promises to free civil courts completely from entanglement in questions of religious doctrine, polity, and practice. Furthermore, the neutral-principles analysis shares the peculiar genius of private-law systems in general-flexibility in ordering private rights and obligations to reflect the intentions of the parties. Through appropriate reversionary clauses and trust provisions, religious societies can specify what is to happen to church property in the event of a particular contingency, or what religious body will determine the ownership in the event of a schism or doctrinal controversy. In this manner, a religious organization can ensure that a dispute over the ownership of church property will be resolved in accord with the desires of the members." (*Jones v. Wolf, supra*, 443 U.S. at pp. 603–604, 99 S.Ct. 3020.)

The court also recognized potential difficulties inherent in the neutral principles approach. "The neutral-principles method, at least as it has evolved in Georgia, requires a civil court to examine certain religious documents, such as a church constitution, for language of trust in favor of the general church. In undertaking such an examination, a civil court must take special care to scrutinize the document in purely secular terms, and not to rely on religious precepts in determining whether the document indicates that the parties have intended to create a trust. In addition, there may be cases where the deed, the corporate charter, or the constitution of the general church incorporates religious concepts in the provisions relating to the ownership of property. If in such a case the interpretation of the instruments of ownership would require the civil court to resolve a religious controversy, then the court must defer to the resolution of the doctrinal issue by the authoritative ecclesiastical body." (*Jones v. Wolf, supra*, 443 U.S. at p. 604, 99 S.Ct. 3020.)

Despite these potential difficulties, the high court concluded that "the promise of nonentanglement and neutrality inherent in the neutral-principles approach more than compensates for what will be occasional problems in application. These problems, in addition, should be gradually eliminated as recognition is given to the obligation of 'States, religious organizations, and individuals [to] structure relationships involving church property so as not to require the civil courts to resolve ecclesiastical questions.' [Citation.] We therefore hold that a State is constitutionally entitled to adopt neutral principles of law as a means of adjudicating a church property dispute." (*Jones v. Wolf, supra*, 443 U.S. at p. 604, 99 S.Ct. 3020, quoting *Presbyterian Church v. Hull Church, supra*, 393 U.S. at p. 449, 89 S.Ct. 601.) . . .

Subject to the proviso that secular courts may not decide questions of church doctrine, we believe that California courts should use neutral principles of law to decide church property disputes.

Accordingly, we conclude that secular courts called on to resolve church property disputes should proceed as follows: State courts must not decide questions of religious doctrine; those are for the church to resolve. Accordingly, if resolution of a property dispute involves a point of doctrine, the court must defer to the position of the highest ecclesiastical authority that has decided the point. But to the extent the court can resolve a property dispute without reference to church doctrine, it should apply neutral principles of law. The court should consider sources such as the deeds to the property in dispute, the local church's articles of incorporation, the general church's constitution, canons, and rules, and relevant statutes, including statutes specifically concerning religious property, such as Corporations Code section 9142.

2. Resolving the Dispute of This Case

St. James Parish holds record title to the property in question. That is the fact that defendants rely on most heavily in claiming ownership. On the other hand, from the beginning of its existence, St. James Parish promised to be bound by the constitution and canons of the Episcopal Church. Such commitment is found in the original application to the higher church authorities to organize as a parish and in the articles of incorporation. Canon I.7.4, adopted in 1979, provides that property held by a local parish "is held in trust" for the general church and the diocese in which the local church is located. The same canon states that the trust does not limit the authority of the parish over the property "so long as the particular Parish . . . remains a part of, and subject to, this Church and its Constitution and Canons." Other canons adopted long before St. James Parish existed also contained substantial restrictions on the local use of church property.

The question before us is, which prevails—the fact that St. James Parish holds record title to the property, or the facts that it is bound by the constitution and canons of the Episcopal Church and the canons impress a trust in favor of the general church? . . .

[According to *Jones v. Wolf*,], [u]nder the neutral-principles approach, the outcome of a church property dispute is not foreordained. *At any time before the dispute erupts*, the parties can ensure, if they so desire, that the faction loyal to the hierarchical church will retain the church property. They can modify the deeds or the corporate charter to include a right of reversion or trust in favor of the general church. *Alternatively, the constitution of the general church can be made to recite an express trust in favor of the denominational church.* The burden involved in taking such steps will be minimal. *And the civil courts will be bound to give effect to the result indicated by the parties*, provided it is embodied in some legally cognizable form."

Shortly after this decision, and in apparent reaction to it, the Episcopal Church added Canon I.7.4, which recites an express trust in favor of the denominational church. This occurred some 25 years before the instant dispute erupted. Defendants focus on the high court's reference to what the "parties" can do, and argue that Canon I.7.4, to be effective, had to have been enacted by the parties—in other words, that some kind of agreement must have been reached between the general church and St. James Parish (and presumably every other parish in the country) ratifying Canon I.7.4. We do not so read the high court's words. Use of the passive voice in describing the possible "alternative[ ]" of making the general church's constitution recite the trust suggests the high court intended that this could be done by whatever method the church structure contemplated. Requiring a particular method to change a church's constitution—such as requiring every parish in the country to ratify the change—*would* infringe on the free exercise rights of religious associations to govern themselves as they see fit. It would impose a major, not a "minimal," burden on the church governance.

Thus, the high court's discussion in *Jones v. Wolf, supra*, together with the Episcopal Church's adoption of Canon I.7.4 in response, strongly supports the conclusion that, once defendants left the general church, the property reverted to the general church.

This conclusion is bolstered by a review of out-of-state cases that involved similar church property disputes within the Episcopal Church and that, with near unanimity, awarded the disputed property to the general church when a local church disaffiliated itself from that general church. These out-of-state decisions are not binding on this court, but we find them persuasive, especially in the aggregate.

■ Concurring and Dissenting Opinion by KENNARD, J.

I agree with the majority that the Protestant Episcopal Church in the United States of America (Episcopal Church) owns the property to which St. James Parish in Newport Beach (St. James Parish) has held title since 1950. This conclusion is compelled by Corporations Code section 9142, subdivision (c)(2). But I disagree with the majority that this provision, which applies only to religious corporations, reflects a "neutral principles of law" approach. . . .

II

In 1982, the California Legislature amended Corporations Code section 9142 by adding, as relevant here, subdivision (c)(2). That provision permits the assets of a religious corporation to be made subject to a trust when "the articles or bylaws of the corporation, or the governing instruments of a superior religious body or general church of which the corporation is a member, so expressly provide." Thus, as the majority notes, through legislative fiat a "superior religious body or general church" may *unilaterally* create trusts in its favor over property held by the smaller church that was a member of the general church when the trust was created. That occurred here when in 1979 the Episcopal Church added section 4 to its Canon I.7 to unilaterally provide that all property held by any parish is held in trust for the Episcopal Church.

Applying California's statute in resolving church property disputes, the majority concludes that the Episcopal Church now is the owner of the St. James Parish property in question. I agree.

But that conclusion is not based on neutral principles of law. No principle of trust law exists that would allow the unilateral creation of a trust by the declaration of a nonowner of property that the owner of the property is holding it in trust for the nonowner. If a neutral principle of law approach were applied here, the Episcopal Church might well lose because the 1950 deed to the disputed property is in the name of St. James Parish, and the Episcopal Church's 1979 declaration that the parish was holding the property in trust for the Episcopal Church is of no legal consequence.

But under the principle of government approach, the Episcopal Church wins because that method makes the decision of the highest authority of a hierarchical church, here the Episcopal Church, binding on a civil court. This result is constitutional, but only because the dispute involves religious bodies and then only because the principle of government approach, permissible under the First Amendment, allows a state to give unbridled deference to the superior religious body or general church.

In my view, Corporations Code section 9142 reflects the principle of government approach. That statute allows a hierarchical church, such as the Episcopal Church here, through its bylaws to unilaterally impose a trust on the property of a local member parish. The statute does not state a neutral principle of law; rather, it creates a special principle applicable solely to religious corporations.

NOTES AND QUESTIONS

1.   *Hands Off.* The basic constitutional idea in the church property cases "is that secular courts must not determine questions of religious doctrine and practice. Not only must they refrain from deciding which doctrines and practices are correct or wise, they must also avoid deciding which are faithful to a group's traditions." See Kent Greenawalt, Hands Off! Civil Court Involvement in Conflicts Over Religious Property, 98 Colum. L. Rev. 1843, 1846 (1998). Why does the First Amendment require this "hands off" approach to doctrinal questions? What would you say to someone who made the following argument: The Christian tradition has clearly opposed homosexuality for 2000 years, so it should be no problem for a court to determine that the local church is more Christian than the national church and to award property to the local church. Does the First Amendment allow that line of reasoning? Or would such reasoning reflect

the "departure from doctrine" approach to property disputes rejected by the Supreme Court in *Hull*?

2. *Two Standards.* What is the difference between the two approaches to resolving church property disputes recognized by the U.S Supreme Court, namely the neutral principles of law test and the principle of government standard? Do you agree with Justice Chin that neutral principles of law favor the national church? Do you agree with Justice Kennard that the court applied the principle of government approach while pretending to apply neutral principles? In a follow-up to this case, the California Supreme Court refined its holding to allow St. James Parish to continue its lawsuit in the trial court. Although the first opinion seemed to hold that the national church owned the disputed property, the court clarified that St. James could proceed with its factual claim that a 1991 letter gave the local church ownership of the property. Rasmussen v. Super. Ct., 51 Cal.4th 804, 808–09 (2011). In dissent, Justice Kennard reaffirmed her concurring and dissenting opinion in the original case that the property belonged to the national church under the "principles of government" approach. Id. at 809–10. Does this second ruling suggest that the court didn't understand its first ruling under neutral principles of law?

The breakaway local Episcopal groups also lost in New York, which applied neutral principles of law in favor of the national church. The Court of Appeals explained that in 1979—in response to *Jones v. Wolf*—the national church had adopted the Dennis Canons, which state that the real and personal property of the parishes is held in trust for the national church. The Court explained that because the legal deeds did not clearly establish a trust, it was appropriate for the court to consider church constitutions. Episcopal Diocese of Rochester v. Harnish, 11 N.Y.3d 340, 870 N.Y.S.2d 814, 899 N.E.2d 920 (2008). Did the California and New York courts accurately apply the neutral principles of law approach? Or is Justice Kennard correct that the church governance rule applied?

In contrast, the South Carolina Supreme Court applied neutral principles in favor of the local church. The court explained that in 1903 the South Carolina Diocese had executed a quit-claim deed transferring its interests in the property to the local congregation, All Saints Parish. In 1987, the diocese amended its constitution to include the same Dennis Canons involved in the California and New York cases, which stated that the local property was held in trust for the diocese and the national church. Worried about its ownership status, the local congregation investigated the title records in 2000 and found that the 1903 deed was the latest document filed. In response, the diocese then—in 2000—filed a legal notice that the parish held its property in trust for the diocese and the national church. The court rejected the diocese's claim of ownership with the following argument: "It is an axiomatic principle of law that a person or entity must hold title to property in order to declare that it is held in trust for the benefit of another or transfer legal title to one person for the benefit of another. The Diocese did not, at the time it recorded the 2000 Notice, have any interest in the congregation's property. Therefore, the recordation of the 2000 Notice could not have created a trust over the property." All Saints Parish Waccamaw v. Protestant Episcopal Church in Diocese of South Carolina, 385 S.C. 428, 685 S.E.2d 163 (2009). Does South Carolina have a better understanding of neutral principles than New York and California? Is the South Carolina opinion consistent with Justice Kennard's reasoning?

In 2005 a majority of the local Waccamaw congregation voted to leave the national church. The South Carolina trial court applied the principle of government standard and ruled for the minority that had remained faithful to the national church. In contrast, the Supreme Court followed the South Carolina Non-Profit Act and the church's bylaws, concluding that a majority of the church had legitimately voted to sever ties with the national church. The court believed that its decision was made independently of doctrinal issues because it was based on the number of votes cast and the church's rules about voting. Do you agree? See id.

Should a state court enforce the Dennis Canons in favor of the national Episcopal church even if state law outlines more specific ways to create a trust and makes those means available to religious organizations? See Rector, Wardens, Vestrymen of Christ Church in Savannah v. Bishop of Episcopal Diocese of Georgia, 290 Ga. 95, 102, 718 S.E.2d 237, 244–45 (2011) (church groups' free exercise of religion would be burdened by a requirement that they amend all their documents in accordance with state law instead of allowing them to amend their own constitutions to create a trust).

In another Episcopal Church case, the Texas Supreme Court ruled that Texas would apply *only* the neutral principles approach to church property disputes, rejecting the hierarchical deference approach. The Court stated that using only one test would lead to "greater predictability" in the law and was consistent with the state's constitutional duty to hear cases within its jurisdiction. The case was remanded because the Episcopal Diocese had relied primarily on its hierarchical status in its motion for summary judgment. Masterson v. Diocese of Northwest Texas, 422 S.W.3d 594 (Tex. 2013).

The Montana Supreme Court also relied upon the neutral principles of law approach in an intra-Lutheran dispute. The local congregation, Faith Lutheran Church, was affiliated with the Evangelical Lutheran Church of America (ELCA), but wanted to disaffiliate after ELCA backed gay ordination. Church documents stated:

> If a 90% majority of the voting members of this congregation present at a regularly called and conducted special meeting of this congregation vote to transfer to another Lutheran Church body, title to property shall continue to reside in this congregation. Before this congregation takes action to transfer to another Lutheran Church body, it shall consult the representatives of the Montana Synod.

71% of the Faith Lutheran voters voted to disaffiliate. The minority, New Hope, said it was entitled to the property because the motion had failed to reach 90%.

Faith Lutheran argued the court could not review its claims that the constitution establishing the 90% rule was invalid or the vote itself. The Supreme Court, however, reviewed the events surrounding the constitution's adoption, noted that Faith Lutheran had not challenged the adoption until after New Hope questioned the vote, and ruled that the 90% language was secular language that a court could apply without any interference with religion. Thus New Hope was entitled to the church property. New Hope Lutheran Ministry v. Faith Lutheran Church of Great Falls, 328 P.3d 586 (Mont. 2014). Does the Montana court's detailed review of the record convince you that courts are able to apply neutral principles of law?

3. *Neutral Principles of Law.* Professors McConnell and Goodrich argue that in practice courts apply two different types of neutral principles analysis in property disputes, the "strict approach" and the "hybrid approach." The authors note that in "any given church property dispute, there will typically be at least three types of ownership evidence: (1) legal documents, such as the deed, corporate charter, state laws governing trusts, and any formal contracts or trusts; (2) church governance documents, such as the church constitution and canons; and (3) evidence of church practice, such as who typically controls local property and how the church constitution and canons are applied in practice." The strict approach allows only consideration of the first category of evidence, while the hybrid approach allows a combination of all three. Michael W. McConnell & Luke W. Goodrich, On Resolving Church Property Disputes, 58 Ariz. L. Rev. 307, 309 (2016).

McConnell and Goodrich argue church property disputes should be resolved under the strict approach by property, trust, or contract law. Depending on the nature of the dispute and the claims of the parties, different principles of civil law may apply. For example, "[I]f there is a dispute over the language of a deed or the validity of a conveyance, courts will apply state property law. If there is a dispute over an express or implied trust, courts will apply state trust law. And if there is a dispute over the validity of a contract or the locus of corporate control, courts will apply state contract or corporations law." Id.

The authors prefer the strict approach. Which approach do you prefer? Go back to the cases included in Note 2 and decide which approach the state courts used in each case.

4. *Hierarchical or Congregational Churches.* Is it acceptable for courts to distinguish between hierarchical and congregational churches in property disputes? Do you agree that this principle of government test (also called the polity test) has "grave defects"? "Most important among the defects are (1) the extreme deference to higher church authorities, even when they have violated their own rules, and (2) the indefensible differentiation between congregational and hierarchical churches in respect

to requirements of fair process." Kent Greenawalt, Religion and the
Constitution: Free Exercise and Fairness 277 (2006). Is it unconstitutional
for a court to decide if a church is hierarchical or congregational because it
then becomes involved in studying church doctrine? Should the principle of
government rule be declared unconstitutional?

5. *Express Trusts.* Trust law has become increasingly important to
church property disputes because three of the largest American Christian
denominations—Episcopalians, Presbyterians, and Methodists—have not
only amended their church constitutions to include an express trust in
favor of the national church but also been hit by controversies over LGBT
rights. "Under black letter trust law, those internal church rules, standing
alone, could not create a valid trust, because a trust can only be created by
the legal titleholder," which is frequently the local congregation. Michael
W. McConnell & Luke W. Goodrich, On Resolving Church Property
Disputes, 58 Ariz. L. Rev. 307, 319–22 (2016). Should the courts rely on
black letter trust law or the intent of the churches as expressed in the
church constitutions? Should the courts set a rule that a trust is present
only if the local congregations declare that they are forming a trust?

Should churches be encouraged to establish express trusts? If property
were given to a church for "exclusive use of those who believe in the
doctrine of the Holy Trinity," could the courts prevent the property from
being used to disseminate Unitarian doctrine? If property were given on the
condition that women not be ordained, would that provision be enforceable?
Are there any limits on express trusts? Would it be permissible for
churches to write express trusts barring gays or African-Americans from
ministry? See Kent Greenawalt, Hands Off! Civil Court Involvement in
Conflicts Over Religious Property, 98 Colum. L. Rev. 1843, 1846–48 (1998).

In 1959, a majority of the Congregation Beth Tefilas Moses, a Jewish
Synagogue located in the city of Mt. Clemens, Michigan, voted to allow
mixed seating of men and women. A minority filed suit, arguing that mixed
seating violated Orthodox Judaism. The defendant majority did not
challenge the plaintiffs' evidence that Orthodox Judaism prohibits mixed
seating, and so the court read that conclusion as undisputed. The court
ruled for the minority, even though there was no express trust. See Davis v.
Scher, 356 Mich. 291, 97 N.W.2d 137, 141 (1959) ("The weight of authority
in Michigan is to the effect that the majority faction of a local congregation
or society, being one part of a large church unit, however regular its action
or procedure in other respects, may not, as against a faithful minority,
divert the property of the society to another denomination or to the support
of doctrines fundamentally opposed to the characteristic doctrines of the
society, although the property is subject to no expressed trust."). Is that
ruling accurate today? See Berkaw v. Mayflower Congregational Church,
18 Mich.App. 245, 170 N.W.2d 905 (1969) (refusing jurisdiction in a case
where there was a dispute about which party was faithful to original
church doctrine).

6. Kathleen E. Reeder argues that the two tests, polity deference
and neutral principles, are inadequate to deal with the facts of the

Episcopal Church disputes. Instead of focusing on a "few basic documents," as courts traditionally do, "a court must look beyond official church canons and consider questions such as: Who paid for the property? What were the true expectations of parishioners, who, after all, are the body of the church? What was the balance of bargaining power when coercive church laws were passed?" Kathleen E. Reeder, Whose Church Is It Anyway? Property Disputes and Episcopal Church Splits, 40 Colum. J.L. & Soc. Probs. 125, 170 (2006). Do you think the California Supreme Court was attentive enough to these questions?

7. Do the property cases in this section have any relevance for employment disputes in which a member of a religious organization sues her religious employer?

B. DISPUTES ABOUT RELIGIOUS EMPLOYMENT

In 1964, Congress passed the Civil Rights Act, which prohibits discrimination by public and private employers on the basis of religion. According to Title VII,

> It shall be an unlawful employment practice for an employer—
>
> (1) to fail or refuse to hire or to discharge any individual, or otherwise to discriminate against any individual with respect to his compensation, terms, conditions, or privileges of employment, because of such individual's race, color, religion, sex, or national origin; or
>
> (2) to limit, segregate, or classify his employees or applicants for employment in any way which would deprive or tend to deprive any individual of employment opportunities or otherwise adversely affect his status as an employee, because of such individual's race, color, religion, sex, or national origin.

42 U.S.C.A. § 2000e–2.

The Act defines "religion" to include "all aspects of religious observance and practice, as well as belief, unless an employer demonstrates that he is unable to reasonably accommodate to an employee's or prospective employee's religious observance or practice without undue hardship on the conduct of the employer's business." 42 U.S.C. § 2000e(j). A high percentage of Title VII cases involve workers who demand changes in their work schedule to accommodate their religious worship. See Vikram David Amar, State RFRAs and the Workplace, 32 U.C. Davis L. Rev. 513 (1999).

As you read the following case, ask what it says about how an employee can prove the presence of religious discrimination in the workplace. How can employers win such lawsuits? What is undue hardship for employers?

1. RELIGIOUS DISCRIMINATION

Reed v. The Great Lakes Companies, Inc.

United States Court of Appeals for the Seventh Circuit, 2003.
330 F.3d 931.

■ POSNER, CIRCUIT JUDGE.

Melvin Reed, the plaintiff in this Title VII religious-discrimination suit, appeals from the grant of summary judgment to his former employer, Great Lakes. Construed as favorably to Reed as the record permits, the facts of the case are as follows. He was hired to be the executive housekeeper of a newly opened Holiday Inn that Great Lakes operates in Milwaukee. One of his duties was to see to it that a copy of the Bible, supplied free of charge to the hotel by the Gideons, was placed in every room. It is customary for representatives of management to meet with the Gideons when they deliver Bibles to a newly opened hotel. Reed had been working for Great Lakes for less than a month when the Gideons showed up to deliver the Bibles. A few days before their scheduled arrival, the manager of the Holiday Inn had told Reed in a joking manner that they were going to "pray with the Gideons," which Reed understood to mean that, given his responsibility for the distribution of the Bibles to the rooms, he was to accompany the manager to the meeting at which they would receive the Bibles from the Gideons. Reed did not object to attending the meeting. But, to the manager's surprise, at the meeting the Gideons, besides delivering Bibles, did some Bible reading and some praying. Reed was offended by the religious character of the meeting and left in the middle, to the manager's chagrin. Later in the day, the manager ran into Reed and told him: "Don't do that again, you embarrassed me." Reed riposted: "You can't compel me to a religious event," to which the manager replied that Reed would do what he was told to do. Reed responded, "Oh, hell no, you won't, not when it comes to my spirituality," whereupon the manager fired him for insubordination.

Oddly, Reed at his deposition refused to indicate what if any religious affiliation or beliefs (or nonbeliefs) he has; refused even to deny that he might be a Gideon! His position was that Title VII forbids an employer to require an employee to attend a religious meeting, period.

Title VII does forbid an employer, unless it is a religious organization, which Great Lakes is not, to discriminate against an employee on the basis of the employee's religion. And for these purposes, as assumed by the parties, as strongly intimated in [many cases], and as supported by analogy to cases under the free-exercise clause of the First Amendment,—cases which hold that religious freedom includes the freedom to reject religion—"religion" includes antipathy to religion. And so an atheist (which Reed may or may not be) cannot be fired because his employer dislikes atheists. If we think of religion as taking a position on divinity, then atheism is indeed a form of religion.

But there is no indication that Reed was fired because of his religious beliefs, identity, or observances or because of his aversion to religion, to Christianity, or to the Gideons, whatever the case may be (remember that we don't know anything about his religion or lack of religion). Great Lakes accepts Bibles from the Gideons because the Bibles are free, not because any of Great Lakes' owners or managers, including the manager of the Holiday Inn who fired Reed, is a Gideon. So far as appears, none is. The manager's joking reference to "pray[ing] with the Gideons" makes it pretty clear that he is not one of them; anyway there is no contention that he is. For that matter, there is no evidence that he expected to encounter prayers and Bible reading at the meeting with them. At previous such meetings the Gideons had handed over the Bibles and the manager had thanked them, and that was that. The religious service was a surprise. It is apparent that the manager fired Reed because Reed's sudden departure from the meeting was embarrassing to the manager, who would be in trouble with his superiors if the Gideons became huffy and cut off the supply of free Bibles to Great Lakes hotels, and also because Reed's refusal to see the manager's point of view indicated that he was unlikely to be a cooperative employee.

The manager *must* have been indifferent to Reed's religious views, because Reed never expressed them to the manager; to this day we do not know what his religion is, as he refused to say at his deposition. It is difficult to see how an employer can be charged with discrimination on the basis of an employee's religion when he doesn't know the employee's religion (or lack thereof, which, as we have noted, is in the eyes of the law a form of religion), though the employee can survive summary judgment if, while declining to specify his religious beliefs, he attests that they differ from his employer's and that that is why he was fired.

Reed has utterly failed to make a prima facie case of intentional religious discrimination. But he has another string to his bow. Besides forbidding intentional discrimination, Title VII requires an employer to try to accommodate the religious needs of its employees, that is, to try to adjust the requirements of the job so that the employee can remain employed without giving up the practice of his religion, provided the adjustment would not work an undue hardship on the employer. 42 U.S.C. § 2000e(j); *Ansonia Board of Education v. Philbrook*, 479 U.S. 60, 70, 107 S.Ct. 367, 93 L.Ed.2d 305 (1986). And again for these purposes hostility to religion counts as a form of religion. So if attending a meeting at which Gideons might pray or read from the Bible would offend Reed's religious or antireligious sensibilities, he might be entitled to an accommodation.

We say "might be" rather than "would be" for two reasons. First, the duty to accommodate is not absolute; the cost to the employer must be considered. *Ansonia Board of Education v. Philbrook, supra,* 479 U.S. at 70, 107 S.Ct. 367; Second, an employee is not permitted to redefine a purely personal preference or aversion as a religious belief. Otherwise he could announce without warning that white walls or venetian blinds offended his "spirituality," and the employer would have to scramble to see whether it was feasible to accommodate him by repainting the walls or substituting curtains for venetian blinds. This case is not so extreme, because compelled attendance at sectarian religious services is the sort of thing that is likely to offend someone who does not belong to the sect in question, though we repeat that for all we know Reed is a Gideon and his claim for accommodation therefore completely spurious.

But putting that possibility to one side and assuming that it would have been no sort of hardship for Great Lakes to have excused Reed from attendance at meetings with the Gideons, who are hardly likely to ask, "Why isn't the executive housekeeper here?" we think the district court was right to grant summary judgment for Great Lakes with respect to this claim as well as the disparate-treatment claim. There is a line, indistinct but important, between an employee who seeks an accommodation to his religious faith and an employee who asserts as Reed did an unqualified right to disobey orders that he deems inconsistent with his faith though he refuses to indicate at what points that faith intersects the requirements of his job. Today he storms out of a meeting with the Gideons; tomorrow he may refuse to place their Bibles in the rooms; the day after that he may announce that he will not come to work on the day when the Gideons visit. Reed failed to give any indication of what future occurrences at the Holiday Inn would impel him to make a scene embarrassing to the manager and potentially injurious to the employer.

Title VII imposes a duty on the employer but also a reciprocal duty on the employee to give fair warning of the employment practices that will interfere with his religion and that he therefore wants waived or adjusted. A person's religion is not like his sex or race—something obvious at a glance. Even if he wears a religious symbol, such as a cross or a yarmulka, this may not pinpoint his particular beliefs and observances; and anyway employers are not charged with detailed knowledge of the beliefs and observances associated with particular sects. Suppose the employee is an Orthodox Jew and believes that it is deeply sinful to work past sundown on Friday. He does not tell his employer, the owner of a hardware store that is open from 9 a.m. to 6 p.m. on Fridays, who leaves the employee in sole charge of the store one

Friday afternoon in mid-winter, and at 4 p.m. the employee leaves the store. The employer could fire him without being thought guilty of failing to accommodate his religious needs. This case is similar.

The grant of summary judgment to Great Lakes is affirmed.

NOTES AND QUESTIONS

1. *Reed's Religion.* What is the relevance of the fact that the court had no idea what Reed's religion was? Why did the court reject Reed's argument that "Title VII forbids an employer to require an employee to attend a religious meeting, period."? Why did the court conclude Reed had failed to make a prima facie case of intentional discrimination? What do you think Reed would have had to prove in order to make a successful intentional discrimination case?

2. *Accommodation.* Why did the court have to reach the question of accommodation if there was no intentional discrimination by Great Lakes? Wouldn't it have been easy for the employer to accommodate Reed in these circumstances?

Donald Thornton told his employer (Caldor) that he could not work on Sunday because of his religious beliefs. Caldor offered Thornton several options, including a transfer to a management job in a Massachusetts store that closed on Sundays or to a nonsupervisory job in Connecticut at a lower salary. When he refused, he was then transferred to a clerical position. Thornton resigned and sued under a Connecticut law that stated "No person who states that a particular day of the week is observed as his Sabbath may be required by his employer to work on such day. An employee's refusal to work on his Sabbath shall not constitute grounds for his dismissal." Should Thornton win or lose his case? See Estate of Thornton v. Caldor, 472 U.S. 703, 706 (1985) (Connecticut law giving employees an absolute and unqualified right not to work on their Sabbath violates the Establishment Clause). What should happen to a Muslim school teacher who wants an accommodation for his Friday prayer schedule? See T. Jeremy Gunn, Adjudicating Rights of Conscience Under the European Convention on Human Rights, in Johan D. van der Vyver and John Witte, Jr., eds., Religious Human Rights in Global Perspective: Legal Perspectives 314 (1996) (discussing Ahmad v. United Kingdom, App. No. 8160/78, 4 Eur. H.R. Rep. 126 (1981) (Eur. Comm'n)). The European Commission ruled against the Muslim teacher's request on the grounds that he had accepted his position voluntarily and was free to resign. Would he also lose his case in the United States? Should he?

Is Title VII unconstitutional following *Caldor*? See Estate of Thornton v. Caldor, 472 U.S. 703, 711–12 (1985) (O'Connor, J., concurring) ("In my view, a statute outlawing employment discrimination based on race, color, religion, sex, or national origin has the valid secular purpose of assuring employment opportunity to all groups in our pluralistic society. Since Title VII calls for reasonable rather than absolute accommodation and extends that requirement to all religious beliefs and practices rather than protecting only the Sabbath observance, I believe an objective observer would perceive it as an anti-discrimination law rather than an endorsement of religion or a particular religious practice.").

3. *Supreme Court Cases.* The Supreme Court has decided three cases about Title VII religious discrimination. In the first two cases, the Court sided with the employer. In Trans World Airlines, Inc. v. Hardison, 432 U.S. 63, 80–82 (1977), a Sabbatarian pilot who did not want to fly on Saturdays was fired after requesting a four-day work week. The Court upheld the employer's use of a seniority system for allocation of employee schedules even though the system had some discriminatory effects. In Ansonia Bd. of Educ. v. Philbrook, 479 U.S. 60 (1986), a high school teacher requested six days off for religious observance. The collective bargaining agreement allowed three paid days off for religious observance and three personal days, but did not allow the use of personal days for religious observance. The court ruled that unpaid leave was a reasonable accommodation instead of the requested six days of paid religious leave.

According to Professor Kaminer, in those cases the Court relied on the "concept of formal equality, ignoring the fact that [Title VII] was enacted to mandate accommodation or differential treatment of religious employees. The Court was concerned that requiring TWA to violate a valid seniority agreement would amount to discrimination in favor of religious employees. . . . The Court held that Philbrook was not entitled to any special treatment based on his specific religious convictions; he was entitled to the three paid religious days that all employees were entitled to, plus three unpaid days off. However, the Court also emphasized that Philbrook could not be treated worse than nonreligious employees requesting time off." Debbie N. Kaminer, Religious Accommodation in the Workplace: Why Federal Courts Fail to Provide Meaningful Protection of Religious Employees, 20 Tex. Rev. L. & Pol. 107, 122–25 (2015). Are you sympathetic to the argument that religious employees are entitled to special protection, or do you think formal equality is a good idea in the workplace?

A driver for the United Parcel Service (UPS) is a member of the Seventh-Day Adventist Church, which forbids work between sundown Friday and sundown Saturday. "He suggested as possible accommodations starting early on Fridays, working Sundays through Thursdays, working longer shifts on Mondays through Thursdays and shorter shifts on Fridays, using vacation time to cover a shorter Friday workday, relief from making next-day air deliveries on Fridays, or no lunch breaks on Fridays." Should UPS be expected to accommodate his schedule? Should his schedule be accommodated even during UPS's peak delivery season between Thanksgiving and Christmas? See Sturgill v. United Parcel Service, Inc., 512 F.3d 1024 (8th Cir. 2008) (upholding jury's verdict for employee).

4. *Employers' and Employees' Duties.* In *Reed*, Judge Posner wrote that employers and employees have reciprocal duties in the workplace. In particular, the employee must "give fair warning of the employment practices that will interfere with his religion and that he therefore wants waived or adjusted." Posner thought fair warning was necessary because a person's religion is not "obvious at a glance." Re-read the last full paragraph of the opinion. Did the Supreme Court adopt a different perspective on employers' and employees' duties in the following case?

EEOC v. Abercrombie & Fitch Stores, Inc.

Supreme Court of the United States, 2015.
135 S.Ct. 2028, 192 L.Ed.2d 35.

■ SCALIA, J., delivered the opinion of the Court, in which ROBERTS C.J., and KENNEDY, GINSBURG, BREYER, SOTOMAYOR and KAGAN, JJ., joined. ALITO J., filed an opinion concurring in the judgment. THOMAS J., filed an opinion concurring in part and dissenting in part.

■ JUSTICE SCALIA delivered the opinion of the Court.

Title VII of the Civil Rights Act of 1964 prohibits a prospective employer from refusing to hire an applicant in order to avoid accommodating a religious practice that it could accommodate without undue hardship. The question presented is whether this prohibition applies only where an applicant has informed the employer of his need for an accommodation.

I

We summarize the facts in the light most favorable to the Equal Employment Opportunity Commission (EEOC), against whom the Tenth Circuit granted summary judgment. Respondent Abercrombie & Fitch Stores, Inc., operates several lines of clothing stores, each with its own "style." Consistent with the image Abercrombie seeks to project for each store, the company imposes a Look Policy that governs its employees' dress. The Look Policy prohibits "caps"—a term the Policy does not define—as too informal for Abercrombie's desired image.

Samantha Elauf is a practicing Muslim who, consistent with her understanding of her religion's requirements, wears a headscarf. She applied for a position in an Abercrombie store, and was interviewed by Heather Cooke, the store's assistant manager. Using Abercrombie's ordinary system for evaluating applicants, Cooke gave Elauf a rating that qualified her to be hired; Cooke was concerned, however, that Elauf's headscarf would conflict with the store's Look Policy.

Cooke sought the store manager's guidance to clarify whether the headscarf was a forbidden "cap." When this yielded no answer, Cooke turned to Randall Johnson, the district manager. Cooke informed Johnson that she believed Elauf wore her headscarf because of her faith. Johnson told Cooke that Elauf's headscarf would violate the Look Policy, as would all other headwear, religious or otherwise, and directed Cooke not to hire Elauf.

The EEOC sued Abercrombie on Elauf's behalf, claiming that its refusal to hire Elauf violated Title VII. The District Court granted the

EEOC summary judgment on the issue of liability, held a trial on damages, and awarded $20,000. The Tenth Circuit reversed and awarded Abercrombie summary judgment. It concluded that ordinarily an employer cannot be liable under Title VII for failing to accommodate a religious practice until the applicant (or employee) provides the employer with actual knowledge of his need for an accommodation.

II

Title VII of the Civil Rights Act of 1964 78 Stat. 253, as amended, prohibits two categories of employment practices. It is unlawful for an employer:

"(1) to fail or refuse to hire or to discharge any individual, or otherwise to discriminate against any individual with respect to his compensation, terms, conditions, or privileges of employment, because of such individual's race, color, religion, sex, or national origin; or

(2) to limit, segregate, or classify his employees or applicants for employment in any way which would deprive or tend to deprive any individual of employment opportunities or otherwise adversely affect his status as an employee, because of such individual's race, color, religion, sex, or national origin." 42 U.S.C. § 2000e–2(a).

These two proscriptions, often referred to as the "disparate treatment" (or "intentional discrimination") provision and the "disparate impact" provision, are the only causes of action under Title VII. The word "religion" is defined to "includ[e] all aspects of religious observance and practice, as well as belief, unless an employer demonstrates that he is unable to reasonably accommodate to" a "religious observance or practice without undue hardship on the conduct of the employer's business."

Abercrombie's primary argument is that an applicant cannot show disparate treatment without first showing that an employer has "actual knowledge" of the applicant's need for an accommodation. We disagree. Instead, an applicant need only show that his need for an accommodation was a motivating factor in the employer's decision.

The disparate-treatment provision forbids employers to: (1) "fail . . . to hire" an applicant (2) "because of" (3) "such individual's . . . religion" (which includes his religious practice). Here, of course, Abercrombie (1) failed to hire Elauf. The parties concede that (if Elauf sincerely believes that her religion so requires) Elauf's wearing of a headscarf is (3) a "religious practice." All that remains is whether she was not hired (2) "because of" her religious practice.

The term "because of" appears frequently in antidiscrimination laws. It typically imports, at a minimum, the traditional standard of but-for causation. Title VII relaxes this standard, however, to prohibit even making a protected characteristic a "motivating factor" in an employment decision. . . .

Thus, the rule for disparate-treatment claims based on a failure to accommodate a religious practice is straightforward: An employer may not make an applicant's religious practice, confirmed or otherwise, a factor in employment decisions. For example, suppose that an employer thinks (though he does not know for certain) that a job applicant may be an orthodox Jew who will observe the Sabbath, and thus be unable to work on Saturdays. If the applicant actually requires an accommodation of that religious practice, and the employer's desire to avoid the prospective accommodation is a motivating factor in his decision, the employer violates Title VII.

Abercrombie urges this Court to adopt the Tenth Circuit's rule "allocat[ing] the burden of raising a religious conflict." This would require the employer to have actual knowledge of a conflict between an applicant's religious practice and a work rule. The problem with this approach is the one that inheres in most incorrect interpretations of statutes: It asks us to add words to the law to produce what is thought to be a desirable result. That is Congress's province. We construe Title VII's silence as exactly that: silence. Its disparate-treatment provision prohibits actions taken with the *motive* of avoiding the need for accommodating a religious practice. A request for accommodation, or the employer's certainty that the practice exists, may make it easier to infer motive, but is not a necessary condition of liability.

Nor does the statute limit disparate-treatment claims to only those employer policies that treat religious practices less favorably than similar secular practices. Abercrombie's argument that a neutral policy cannot constitute "intentional discrimination" may make sense in other contexts. But Title VII does not demand mere neutrality with regard to religious practices—that they be treated no worse than other practices. Rather, it gives them favored treatment, affirmatively obligating employers not "to fail or refuse to hire or discharge any individual . . . because of such individual's" "religious observance and practice." An employer is surely entitled to have, for example, a no-headwear policy as an ordinary matter. But when an applicant requires an accommodation as an "aspec[t] of religious . . . practice," it is no response that the subsequent "fail[ure] . . . to hire" was due to an otherwise-neutral policy. Title VII requires otherwise-neutral policies to give way to the need for an accommodation.

* * *

The Tenth Circuit misinterpreted Title VII's requirements in granting summary judgment. We reverse its judgment and remand the case for further consideration consistent with this opinion.

It is so ordered.

■ JUSTICE ALITO concurring in the judgment.

The opinion of the Court states that "§ 2000e–2(a)(1) does not impose a knowledge requirement," but then reserves decision on the question whether it is a condition of liability that the employer know or suspect that the practice he refuses to accommodate is a religious practice, but in my view, the answer to this question, which may arise on remand, is obvious. I would hold that an employer cannot be held liable for taking an adverse action because of an employee's religious practice unless the employer knows that the employee engages in the practice for a religious reason. If § 2000e–2(a)(1) really "does not impose a knowledge requirement," it would be irrelevant in this case whether Abercrombie had any inkling that Elauf is a Muslim or that she wore the headscarf for a religious reason. That would be very strange.

The scarves that Elauf wore were not articles of clothing that were designed or marketed specifically for Muslim women. Instead, she generally purchased her scarves at ordinary clothing stores. In this case, the Abercrombie employee who interviewed Elauf had seen her wearing scarves on other occasions, and for reasons that the record does not make clear, came to the (correct) conclusion that she is a Muslim. But suppose that the interviewer in this case had never seen Elauf before. Suppose that the interviewer thought Elauf was wearing the scarf for a secular reason. Suppose that nothing else about Elauf made the interviewer even suspect that she was a Muslim or that she was wearing the scarf for a religious reason. If "§ 2000e–2(a)(1) does not impose a knowledge requirement," Abercrombie would still be liable. The EEOC, which sued on Elauf's behalf, does not adopt that interpretation, and it is surely wrong.

The statutory text does not compel such a strange result. It is entirely reasonable to understand the prohibition against an employer's taking an adverse action because of a religious practice to mean that an employer may not take an adverse action because of a practice that the employer knows to be religious. . . . This interpretation makes sense of the statutory provisions. Those provisions prohibit intentional discrimination, which is blameworthy conduct, but if there is no knowledge requirement, an employer could be held liable without fault. The prohibition of discrimination because of religious practices is meant to force employers to consider whether those practices can be accommodated without undue hardship. See § 2000e(j). But the "no-knowledge" interpretation would deprive employers of that opportunity. For these reasons, an employer cannot be liable for taking adverse action because of a religious practice if the employer does not know that the practice is religious.

A plaintiff need not show, however, that the employer took the adverse action because of the religious nature of the practice. Suppose, for example, that an employer rejected all applicants who refuse to work on Saturday, whether for religious or nonreligious reasons. Applicants whose refusal to work on Saturday was known by the employer to be based on religion will have been rejected because of a religious practice.

This conclusion follows from the reasonable accommodation requirement imposed by § 2000e(j). If neutral work rules (*e.g.*, every employee must work on Saturday, no employee may wear any head covering) precluded liability, there would be no need to provide that defense, which allows an employer to escape liability for refusing to make an exception to a neutral work rule if doing so would impose an undue hardship. . . .

In sum, the EEOC was required in this case to prove that Abercrombie rejected Elauf because of a practice that Abercrombie knew was religious. It is undisputed that Abercrombie rejected Elauf because she wore a headscarf, and there is ample evidence in the summary judgment record to prove that Abercrombie knew that Elauf is a Muslim and that she wore the scarf for a religious reason. The Tenth Circuit therefore erred in ordering the entry of summary judgment for Abercrombie. On remand, the Tenth Circuit can consider whether there is sufficient evidence to support summary judgment in favor of the EEOC on the question of Abercrombie's knowledge. The Tenth Circuit will also be required to address Abercrombie's claim that it could not have accommodated Elauf's wearing the headscarf on the job without undue hardship.

■ JUSTICE THOMAS, concurring in part and dissenting in part.

Unlike the majority, I adhere to what I had thought before today was an undisputed proposition: Mere application of a neutral policy cannot constitute "intentional discrimination." Because the Equal Employment Opportunity Commission (EEOC) can prevail here only if Abercrombie engaged in intentional discrimination, and because Abercrombie's application of its neutral Look Policy does not meet that description, I would affirm the judgment of the Tenth Circuit.

I

I would hold that Abercrombie's conduct did not constitute "intentional discrimination." Abercrombie refused to create an exception to its neutral Look Policy for Samantha Elauf's religious practice of wearing a headscarf. In doing so, it did not treat religious practices less favorably than similar secular practices, but instead remained neutral with regard to religious practices. To be sure, the *effects* of Abercrombie's neutral Look Policy, absent an accommodation, fall more harshly on those who wear headscarves as an aspect of their faith. But that is a classic case of an alleged disparate impact. It is not what we have previously understood to be a case of disparate treatment because Elauf received the *same* treatment from Abercrombie as any other applicant who appeared unable to comply with the company's

Because I cannot classify Abercrombie's conduct as "intentional discrimination," I would affirm.

II

A

But inserting the statutory definition of religion into § 2000e–2(a) does not answer the question whether Abercrombie's refusal to hire Elauf was "because of her religious practice." At first glance, the phrase "because of such individual's religious practice" could mean one of two things. Under one reading, it could prohibit taking an action because of the religious nature of an employee's particular practice. Under the alternative reading, it could prohibit taking an action because of an employee's practice that *happens* to be religious.

The distinction is perhaps best understood by example. Suppose an employer with a neutral grooming policy forbidding facial hair refuses to hire a Muslim who wears a beard for religious reasons. Assuming the employer applied the neutral grooming policy to all applicants, the motivation behind the refusal to hire the Muslim applicant would not be the religious nature of his beard, but its existence. Under the first reading, then, the Muslim applicant would lack an intentional-discrimination claim, as he was not refused employment "because of" the religious nature of his practice. But under the second reading, he would have such a claim, as he was refused employment "because of" a practice that happens to be religious in nature.

One problem with the second, more expansive reading is that it would punish employers who have no discriminatory motive. If the phrase "because of such individual's religious practice" sweeps in any case in which an employer takes an adverse action because of a practice that happens to be religious in nature, an employer who had no idea that a particular practice was religious would be penalized. That strict-liability view is plainly at odds with the concept of intentional discrimination. Surprisingly, the majority leaves the door open to this strict-liability theory, reserving the question whether an employer who does not even "suspec[t] that the practice in question is a religious practice" can nonetheless be punished for *intentional* discrimination.

For purposes of today's decision, however, the majority opts for a compromise, albeit one that lacks a foothold in the text and fares no better under our precedents. The majority construes § 2000e–2(a)(1) to punish employers who refuse to accommodate applicants under neutral policies when they act "with the motive of avoiding accommodation." But an employer who is aware that strictly applying a neutral policy will have an adverse effect on a religious group, and applies the policy anyway, is not engaged in intentional discrimination, at least as that term has traditionally been understood. As the Court explained many decades ago, " 'Discriminatory purpose' "—*i.e.,* the purpose necessary for a claim of intentional discrimination—demands "more than . . .

awareness of consequences. It implies that the decisionmaker ... selected or reaffirmed a particular course of action at least in part 'because of,' not merely 'in spite of,' its adverse effects upon an identifiable group."

I do not dispute that a refusal to accommodate can, in some circumstances, constitute intentional discrimination. If an employer declines to accommodate a particular religious practice, yet accommodates a similar secular (or other denominational) practice, then that may be proof that he has "treated a particular person less favorably than others because of [a religious practice]." But merely refusing to create an exception to a neutral policy for a religious practice cannot be described as treating a particular applicant "less favorably than others." The majority itself appears to recognize that its construction requires something more than equal treatment. But equal treatment is not disparate treatment, and that basic principle should have disposed of this case.

B

The majority's novel theory of intentional discrimination is also inconsistent with the history of this area of employment discrimination law. As that history shows, cases arising out of the application of a neutral policy absent religious accommodations have traditionally been understood to involve only disparate-impact liability.

When Title VII was enacted in 1964, it prohibited discrimination "because of ... religion" and did not include the current definition of "religion" encompassing "religious observance and practice" that was added to the statute in 1972. Shortly thereafter, the EEOC issued guidelines purporting to create "an obligation on the part of the employer to accommodate to the religious needs of employees." From an early date, the EEOC defended this obligation under a disparate-impact theory.

This Court's first decision to discuss a refusal to accommodate a religious practice, *Trans World Airlines, Inc. v. Hardison*, 432 U.S. 63, 97 S.Ct. 2264, 53 L.Ed.2d 113 (1977), similarly did not treat such conduct as intentional discrimination. *Hardison* involved a conflict between an employer's neutral seniority system for assigning shifts and an employee's observance of a Saturday Sabbath. The employer denied the employee an accommodation, so he refused to show up for work on Saturdays and was fired. This Court held that the employer was not liable under Title VII because the proposed accommodations would have imposed an undue hardship on the employer. To bolster its conclusion that there was no statutory violation, the Court relied on a provision of Title VII shielding the application of a " 'bona fide seniority or merit system' " from challenge unless that application is " 'the result of an intention to discriminate because of ... religion.' In applying that provision, the Court observed that "[t]here ha[d] been no suggestion of discriminatory intent in th[e] case." But if the majority's view were correct—if a mere refusal to accommodate a religious practice under a neutral policy could constitute intentional discrimination—then the Court in *Hardison* should never have engaged in such reasoning. After all, the employer in *Hardison* knew of the employee's religious practice and refused to make an exception to its neutral seniority system, just as Abercrombie arguably knew of Elauf's religious practice and refused to make an exception to its neutral Look Policy.

Lower courts following *Hardison* likewise did not equate a failure to accommodate with intentional discrimination. . . .. At least before we granted a writ of certiorari in this case, the EEOC too understood that merely applying a neutral policy did not automatically constitute intentional discrimination giving rise to a disparate-treatment claim. For example, the Commission explained in a recent compliance manual, "A religious accommodation claim is distinct from a disparate treatment claim, in which the question is whether employees are treated equally." Indeed, in asking us to take this case, the EEOC dismissed one of Abercrombie's supporting authorities as "a case addressing intentional discrimination, not religious accommodation." Once we granted certiorari in this case, however, the EEOC altered course and advanced the intentional-discrimination theory now adopted by the majority. The Court should have rejected this eleventh-hour request to expand our understanding of "intentional discrimination" to include merely applying a religion-neutral policy.

* * *

The Court today rightly puts to rest the notion that Title VII creates a freestanding religious-accommodation claim, but creates in its stead an entirely new form of liability: the disparate-treatment-based-on-equal-treatment claim. Because I do not think that Congress' 1972 redefinition of "religion" also redefined "intentional discrimination," I would affirm the judgment of the Tenth Circuit. I respectfully dissent from the portions of the majority's decision that take the contrary view.

NOTES AND QUESTIONS

1. *Disparate Treatment or Disparate Impact.* What is the difference between a disparate treatment and a disparate impact case of religious discrimination? Why did the majority consider *Abercrombie* to be a disparate treatment case while only Justice Thomas argued it was a disparate impact case? According to Professor Harper,

> Disparate treatment analysis asks whether an agent of an employer, with or without animus, has considered one of the five protected statuses specified in Title VII [race, color, religion, sex, and national origin] in taking some employment action. Disparate impact analysis asks whether an employer has taken some action under a policy or practice that has disproportionately adverse

effects on members of a group defined by a protected status. The former is illegal regardless of any business justification, except in rare cases where a protected status (other than race or color) is considered a bona fide occupational qualification ("BFOQ"). The latter is illegal only where an employer cannot demonstrate that the policy or practice serves a necessary business goal or where the plaintiff can demonstrate an alternate means to achieve such a demonstrated goal without the adverse effects.

Michael C. Harper, Confusion on the Court: Distinguishing Disparate Treatment from Disparate Impact in *Young v. UPS* and *EEOC v. Abercrombie & Fitch*, Inc., 96 B.U. L. Rev. 543, 543–44 (2016). How do the facts of *Abercrombie* fit into each category?

    2.   *The Conceptual Question in* Abercrombie. Professor Harper also identified a key conceptual question in the opinion about the differences between disparate treatment and disparate impact analysis. "Does disparate treatment include assigning members of a protected group, based on their protected status, to a larger disfavored group that is defined by neutral principles and that includes others who are not members of the protected group? Or, in the alternative, does such an assignment have only a disparate impact on the protected group?" Id. at 545. How did the Court answer this question? Who is the "larger disfavored group" in this case? Who is the "protected group"? See id. at 545–46 ("eight members of the Court held that consideration of a protected religious practice under a general policy that defined a larger disfavored group was illegal disparate treatment, absent the availability of a statutory defense. These eight Justices concluded that disparate treatment analysis was appropriate for Abercrombie's application of its neutral "Look Policy," which prohibited the wearing of caps, to deny employment to Samantha Elauf, a young Muslim woman who wore a hijab scarf to her job interview. This was despite the fact that the neutral policy defined a larger disfavored group that included non-religious cap-wearers.").

    3.   *Actual Knowledge or Motivating Factor.* According to the opinion, must the employer have actual knowledge of a potential employee's need for an accommodation? Or is it sufficient for a Title VII case that religion was a motivating factor in the employer's decision? What arguments can you give on behalf of each standard?

    What evidence would be necessary to prove religion was a motivating factor in an employer's decision? According to Justice Alito's concurrence, "[t]here is sufficient evidence in the summary judgment record to support a finding that Abercrombie's decisionmakers knew that Elauf was a Muslim and that she wore the headscarf for a religious reason." E.E.O.C. v. Abercrombie & Fitch Stores, Inc., 135 S. Ct. 2028, 2034 (2015). In a footnote to the majority opinion, Justice Scalia wrote "[w]hile a knowledge requirement cannot be added to the motive requirement, it is arguable that the motive requirement itself is not met unless the employer at least suspects that the practice in question is a religious practice—*i.e.*, that he cannot discriminate 'because of' a 'religious practice' unless he knows or suspects it to be a religious practice." Justice Scalia then added that the Court should not decide that issue (as Alito's concurrence did) because neither side in the litigation had addressed it. Id. at 2033, n. 3. How would you apply this rule in future cases?

4. *Application of* Abercrombie. Should the employer or the employee win the following religious discrimination lawsuit? Kelsey Nobach was a nursing home activities aide at Woodland Village Nursing Center. Over her time there, Nobach had accumulated four negative employment write-ups: two for tardiness, one for stealing a resident's nail polish, and one for false accusations against a fellow worker. One night, Nobach refused a coworker's request to read the rosary to a patient. Nobach told her coworker that reading the rosary was against her religion.

After the patient complained to management, supervisory staff told Nobach she was fired for failing to assist a resident with the rosary. The supervisor told Nobach: "I don't care if it's your fifth write-up or not. I would have fired you for this instance alone." After the firing, Nobach informed the supervisor that performing the rosary was against her religion; she was a former Jehovah's Witness. The jury awarded damages to Nobach in her Title VII religious discrimination lawsuit. Pre-*Abercrombie*, the Fifth Circuit reversed the jury's verdict because there was insufficient evidence of religious discrimination. The Supreme Court then granted certiorari and remanded the case so the appeals court would apply *Abercrombie*. How should the case turn out post-*Abercrombie*? Do you think Nobach's firing was motivated by religion even though the employer did not have actual knowledge that Nobach had been a Jehovah's Witness who did not want to engage in a Catholic form of prayer? See Nobach v. Woodland Vill. Nursing Ctr., Inc., 799 F.3d 374, 376–79 (5th Cir. 2015), cert. denied sub nom. Nobach v. Woodland Vill. Nursing Ctr., LLC, 136 S. Ct. 1166 (2016) (Woodland Village wins on summary judgment because "Nobach has offered no evidence that Woodland came to know of or suspect her bona-fide religious belief until after she was actually discharged.")

Are there any circumstances under which Nobach could win her lawsuit? See id. ("If Nobach had presented any evidence that Woodland knew, suspected, or reasonably should have known the cause for her refusing this task was her conflicting religious belief—and that Woodland was motivated by this knowledge or suspicion—the jury would certainly have been entitled to reject Woodland's explanation for Nobach's termination. But, no such evidence was ever provided to the jury.").

Was the Fifth Circuit's reasoning similar to that employed by Judge Posner in the *Reed v. Great Lakes* case? Would *Reed* come out differently post-*Abercrombie*?

5. *Neutrality or Favoritism.* The majority opinion also asserts "Title VII does not demand mere neutrality with regard to religious practices— that they be treated no worse than other practices. Rather, it gives them favored treatment, affirmatively obligating employers not 'to fail or refuse to hire or discharge any individual . . . because of such individual's "religious observance and practice." ' " See also Jeffrey M. Hirsch, EEOC v.

Abercrombie & Fitch Stores, Inc.: Mistakes, Same-Sex Marriage, and Unintended Consequences, 94 Tex. L. Rev. See Also 95, 95–96 (2016) ("[R]eligious employees enjoy a protection under Title VII that no other protected class under that statute enjoys: a right to reasonable accommodation of religious beliefs and practices. As the Supreme Court emphasized in *Abercrombie*, this accommodation duty means that employers cannot hide behind facially neutral job rules, like the clothing policy at issue in the case. Rather, the accommodation requirement requires employers at times to favor religious beliefs and practices."). How is this interpretation of Title VII consistent with the requirements of the First Amendment? Why isn't religious favoritism always prohibited by the Establishment Clause?

6. *Unintended Consequences.* Do you agree with Professor Hirsch's criticism of *Abercrombie* that "the decision might decrease the employment opportunities of all applicants who display subtle signs of religion, even if they have no intention of ever seeking accommodations."? Consider Professor Hirsch's possible hypothetical involving Kim Davis, the Kentucky marriage clerk whose religious opposition to same-sex marriage was presented in Chapter 5.

> Consider then, a hypothetical situation in which Davis applies to a bakery and is rejected, allegedly because of the bakery's belief that she will seek a religious accommodation allowing her to refuse to work on orders for same-sex weddings.

> Unless the bakery admitted the allegation, the most obvious challenge for Davis in this hypothetical would be proving that the bakery was motivated by a desire to avoid a religious accommodation. Unlike Elauf's headscarf in *Abercrombie*, an applicant's religious belief about same-sex marriage will often not be discernable. But there may be some signs. Davis, for example, is an Apostolic Christian—a faith in which female followers typically wear long, modest dresses; do not cut their hair; and do not wear makeup. Much like an applicant wearing a headscarf, if Davis appeared for a job interview, an employer that was aware of the religious motivations for these garb and grooming choices would suspect that she is a member of a conservative Christian faith that typically opposes same-sex marriage But what if instead of Davis, the applicant was a conservative Christian who also has religious objections to same-sex marriage, but displays fewer signs of her faith? For instance, the applicant may wear only a cross on a necklace or note church service on her resume. From the employer's point of view, the cross and church reference could indicate a religious objection to same-sex marriage, but they could also simply be an indication that the individual is a Christian, many of whom support same-sex marriage. In short, applicants with subtle signs of religious belief send a signal to employers that there is a chance that accommodation will be requested; however, without further information, it is very

difficult for employers to accurately distinguish applicants with accommodation needs from those without.

Do you agree that "employers are better able to engage in this behavior when faced with applicants with only subtle religious symbols, such as a cross, rather than those with more conspicuous signs. The garb and grooming of certain Muslim, Christian, and other faiths with clear displays of religiosity make it more difficult for employers to deny knowledge of applicants' religious beliefs and thereby improve the chances of any subsequent refusal-to-hire claims. This reality means that accommodation-avoiding employers may be more willing to hire applicants with obvious signs of religion than applicants with more subtle displays. The irony is that the Supreme Court's decision in *Abercrombie* may enhance this tendency."? Jeffrey M. Hirsch, EEOC v. Abercrombie & Fitch Stores, Inc.: Mistakes, Same-Sex Marriage, and Unintended Consequences, 94 Tex. L. Rev. See Also 95, 101–03 (2016).

Although Title VII exempted religious institutions from the religious discrimination lawsuits described in this section, on its face Title VII's prohibition of race, color, sex, and national origin discrimination applies to churches. We address the constitutionality of suing religious institutions for discrimination in the next section.

2.   THE MINISTERIAL EXCEPTION

Hosanna-Tabor Evangelical Lutheran Church and School v. EEOC

Supreme Court of the United States, 2012.
132 S.Ct. 694, 181 L.Ed.2d 650, 80 USLW 4056.

■ CHIEF JUSTICE ROBERTS delivered the opinion of the Court.

Certain employment discrimination laws authorize employees who have been wrongfully terminated to sue their employers for reinstatement and damages. The question presented is whether the Establishment and Free Exercise Clauses of the First Amendment bar such an action when the employer is a religious group and the employee is one of the group's ministers.

I

A

Petitioner Hosanna-Tabor Evangelical Lutheran Church and School is a member congregation of the Lutheran Church-Missouri Synod, the second largest Lutheran denomination in America. Hosanna-Tabor operated a small school in Redford, Michigan, offering a "Christ-centered education" to students in kindergarten through eighth grade.

The Synod classifies teachers into two categories: "called" and "lay." "Called" teachers are regarded as having been called to their vocation by God through a congregation. To be eligible to receive a call from a congregation, a teacher must satisfy certain academic requirements. One way of doing so is by completing a "colloquy" program at a Lutheran college or university. The program requires candidates to take eight courses of theological study, obtain the endorsement of their local Synod district, and pass an oral examination by a faculty committee. A teacher who meets these requirements may be called by a congregation. Once called, a teacher receives the formal title "Minister of Religion, Commissioned." A commissioned minister serves for an open-ended term; at Hosanna-Tabor, a call could be rescinded only for cause and by a supermajority vote of the congregation.

"Lay" or "contract" teachers, by contrast, are not required to be trained by the Synod or even to be Lutheran. At Hosanna-Tabor, they were appointed by the school board, without a vote of the congregation, to one-year renewable terms. Although teachers at the school generally performed the same duties regardless of whether they were lay or called, lay teachers were hired only when called teachers were unavailable.

Respondent Cheryl Perich was first employed by Hosanna-Tabor as a lay teacher in 1999. After Perich completed her colloquy later that school year, Hosanna-Tabor asked her to become a called teacher. Perich accepted the call and received a "diploma of vocation" designating her a commissioned minister.

Perich taught kindergarten during her first four years at Hosanna-Tabor and fourth grade during the 2003–2004 school year. She taught math, language arts, social studies, science, gym, art, and music. She also taught a religion class four days a week, led the students in prayer and devotional exercises each day, and attended a weekly school-wide chapel service. Perich led the chapel service herself about twice a year.

Perich became ill in June 2004 with what was eventually diagnosed as narcolepsy. Symptoms included sudden and deep sleeps from which she could not be roused. Because of her illness, Perich began the 2004–2005 school year on disability leave. On January 27, 2005, however, Perich notified the school principal, Stacey Hoeft, that she would be able to report to work the following month. Hoeft responded that the school had already contracted with a lay teacher to fill Perich's position for the remainder of the school year. Hoeft also expressed concern that Perich was not yet ready to return to the classroom.

On January 30, Hosanna-Tabor held a meeting of its congregation at which school administrators stated that Perich was unlikely to be physically capable of returning to work that school year or the next. The congregation voted to offer Perich a "peaceful release" from her call, whereby the congregation would pay a portion of her health insurance premiums in exchange for her resignation as a called teacher. Perich refused to resign and produced a note from her doctor stating that she would be able to return to work on February 22. The school board urged Perich to reconsider, informing her that the school no longer had a position for her, but Perich stood by her decision not to resign.

On the morning of February 22—the first day she was medically cleared to return to work—Perich presented herself at the school. Hoeft asked her to leave but she would not do so until she obtained written documentation that she had reported to work. Later that afternoon, Hoeft called Perich at home and told her that she would likely be fired. Perich responded that she had spoken with an attorney and intended to assert her legal rights.

Following a school board meeting that evening, board chairman Scott Salo sent Perich a letter stating that Hosanna-Tabor was reviewing the process for rescinding her call in light of her "regrettable" actions. Salo subsequently followed up with a letter advising Perich that the congregation would consider whether to rescind her call at its next meeting. As grounds for termination, the letter cited Perich's "insubordination and disruptive behavior" on February 22, as well as the damage she had done to her "working relationship" with the school by "threatening to take legal action." The congregation voted to rescind Perich's call on April 10, and Hosanna-Tabor sent her a letter of termination the next day.

B

Perich filed a charge with the Equal Employment Opportunity Commission, alleging that her employment had been terminated in violation of the Americans with Disabilities Act. The ADA prohibits an employer from discriminating against a qualified individual on the basis of disability. It also prohibits an employer from retaliating "against any individual because such individual has opposed any act or practice made unlawful by [the ADA] or because such individual made a charge, testified, assisted, or participated in any manner in an investigation, proceeding, or hearing under [the ADA]."

The EEOC brought suit against Hosanna-Tabor, alleging that Perich had been fired in retaliation for threatening to file an ADA lawsuit. Perich intervened in the litigation, claiming unlawful retaliation under both the ADA and the Michigan Persons with Disabilities Civil Rights Act. The EEOC and Perich sought Perich's reinstatement to her former position (or frontpay in lieu thereof), along with backpay, compensatory and punitive damages, attorney's fees, and other injunctive relief.

Hosanna-Tabor moved for summary judgment. Invoking what is known as the "ministerial exception," the Church argued that the suit was barred by the First Amendment because the claims at issue concerned the employment relationship between a religious institution and one of its ministers. According to the Church, Perich was a minister, and she had been fired for a religious reason—namely, that her threat to sue the Church violated the Synod's belief that Christians should resolve their disputes internally.

The District Court agreed that the suit was barred by the ministerial exception and granted summary judgment in Hosanna-Tabor's favor. The court explained that "Hosanna-Tabor treated Perich like a minister and held her out to the world as such long before this litigation began," and that the "facts surrounding Perich's employment in a religious school with a sectarian mission" supported the Church's characterization. In light of that determination, the court concluded that it could "inquire no further into her claims of retaliation."

The Court of Appeals for the Sixth Circuit vacated and remanded, directing the District Court to proceed to the merits of Perich's retaliation claims. The Court of Appeals recognized the existence of a ministerial exception barring certain employment discrimination claims against religious institutions—an exception "rooted in the First Amendment's guarantees of religious freedom." The court concluded, however, that Perich did not qualify as a "minister" under the exception, noting in particular that her duties as a called teacher were identical to her duties as a lay teacher. Judge White concurred. She viewed the question whether Perich qualified as a minister to be closer than did the majority, but agreed that the "fact that the duties of the contract teachers are the same as the duties of the called teachers is telling."

II

Both Religion Clauses bar the government from interfering with the decision of a religious group to fire one of its ministers.

A

Familiar with life under the established Church of England, the founding generation sought to foreclose the possibility of a national church. See 1 Annals of Cong. 730–731 (1789) (noting that the Establishment Clause addressed the fear that "one sect might obtain a pre-eminence, or two combine together, and establish a religion to which they would compel others to conform" (remarks of J. Madison)). By forbidding the "establishment of religion" and guaranteeing the "free exercise thereof," the Religion Clauses ensured that the new Federal Government—unlike the English Crown—would have no role in filling ecclesiastical offices. The Establishment Clause prevents the Government from appointing ministers, and the Free Exercise Clause prevents it from interfering with the freedom of religious groups to select their own.

This understanding of the Religion Clauses was reflected in two events involving James Madison, " 'the leading architect of the religion clauses of the First Amendment.' " The first occurred in 1806, when John Carroll, the first Catholic bishop in the United States, solicited the

Executive's opinion on who should be appointed to direct the affairs of the Catholic Church in the territory newly acquired by the Louisiana Purchase. After consulting with President Jefferson, then-Secretary of State Madison responded that the selection of church "functionaries" was an "entirely ecclesiastical" matter left to the Church's own judgment. Letter from James Madison to Bishop Carroll (Nov. 20, 1806), reprinted in 20 Records of the American Catholic Historical Society 63 (1909). The "scrupulous policy of the Constitution in guarding against a political interference with religious affairs," Madison explained, prevented the Government from rendering an opinion on the "selection of ecclesiastical individuals." *Id.*, at 63–64.

The second episode occurred in 1811, when Madison was President. Congress had passed a bill incorporating the Protestant Episcopal Church in the town of Alexandria in what was then the District of Columbia. Madison vetoed the bill, on the ground that it "exceeds the rightful authority to which Governments are limited, by the essential distinction between civil and religious functions, and violates, in particular, the article of the Constitution of the United States, which declares, that 'Congress shall make no law respecting a religious establishment.'" 22 Annals of Cong. 982–983 (1811).

B

[The Court concluded that the old church property cases [Section A] "confirm that it is impermissible for the government to contradict a church's determination of who can act as its ministers."]

C

Until today, we have not had occasion to consider whether this freedom of a religious organization to select its ministers is implicated by a suit alleging discrimination in employment . . . We agree that there is such a ministerial exception. The members of a religious group put their faith in the hands of their ministers. Requiring a church to accept or retain an unwanted minister, or punishing a church for failing to do so, intrudes upon more than a mere employment decision. Such action interferes with the internal governance of the church, depriving the church of control over the selection of those who will personify its beliefs. By imposing an unwanted minister, the state infringes the Free Exercise Clause, which protects a religious group's right to shape its own faith and mission through its appointments. According the state the power to determine which individuals will minister to the faithful also violates the Establishment Clause, which prohibits government involvement in such ecclesiastical decisions.

The EEOC and Perich acknowledge that employment discrimination laws would be unconstitutional as applied to religious groups in certain circumstances. They grant, for example, that it would violate the First Amendment for courts to apply such laws to compel the ordination of women by the Catholic Church or by an Orthodox Jewish seminary. According to the EEOC and Perich, religious organizations could successfully defend against employment discrimination claims in those circumstances by invoking the constitutional right to freedom of association—a right "implicit" in the First Amendment. The EEOC and Perich thus see no need—and no basis—for a special rule for ministers grounded in the Religion Clauses themselves.

We find this position untenable. The right to freedom of association is a right enjoyed by religious and secular groups alike. It follows under the EEOC's and Perich's view that the First Amendment analysis should be the same, whether the association in question is the Lutheran Church, a labor union, or a social club. That result is hard to square with the text of the First Amendment itself, which gives special solicitude to the rights of religious organizations. We cannot accept the remarkable view that the Religion Clauses have nothing to say about a religious organization's freedom to select its own ministers.

The EEOC and Perich also contend that our decision in *Employment Div., Dept. of Human Resources of Ore. v. Smith,* 494 U.S. 872, 110 S.Ct. 1595, 108 L.Ed.2d 876 (1990), precludes recognition of a ministerial exception. In *Smith,* two members of the Native American Church were denied state unemployment benefits after it was determined that they had been fired from their jobs for ingesting peyote, a crime under Oregon law. We held that this did not violate the Free Exercise Clause, even though the peyote had been ingested for sacramental purposes, because the "right of free exercise does not relieve an individual of the obligation to comply with a valid and neutral law of general applicability on the ground that the law proscribes (or prescribes) conduct that his religion prescribes (or proscribes)."

It is true that the ADA's prohibition on retaliation, like Oregon's prohibition on peyote use, is a valid and neutral law of general applicability. But a church's selection of its ministers is unlike an individual's ingestion of peyote. *Smith* involved government regulation of only outward physical acts. The present case, in contrast, concerns government interference with an internal church decision that affects the faith and mission of the church itself. See *id.,* at 877 (distinguishing the government's regulation of "physical acts" from its "lend[ing] its power to one or the other side in controversies over religious authority or dogma"). The contention that *Smith* forecloses recognition of a ministerial exception rooted in the Religion Clauses has no merit.

III

Having concluded that there is a ministerial exception grounded in the Religion Clauses of the First Amendment, we consider whether the exception applies in this case. We hold that it does.

Every Court of Appeals to have considered the question has concluded that the ministerial exception is not limited to the head of a religious congregation, and we agree. We are reluctant, however, to adopt a rigid formula for deciding when an employee qualifies as a minister. It is enough for us to conclude, in this our first case involving the ministerial exception, that the exception covers Perich, given all the circumstances of her employment.

To begin with, Hosanna-Tabor held Perich out as a minister, with a role distinct from that of most of its members. When Hosanna-Tabor extended her a call, it issued her a "diploma of vocation" according her the title "Minister of Religion, Commissioned." She was tasked with performing that office "according to the Word of God and the confessional standards of the Evangelical Lutheran Church as drawn from the Sacred Scriptures." The congregation prayed that God "bless [her] ministrations to the glory of His holy name, [and] the building of His church." In a supplement to the diploma, the congregation undertook to periodically review Perich's "skills of ministry" and "ministerial responsibilities," and to provide for her "continuing education as a professional person in the ministry of the Gospel."

Perich's title as a minister reflected a significant degree of religious training followed by a formal process of commissioning. To be eligible to become a commissioned minister, Perich had to complete eight college-level courses in subjects including biblical interpretation, church doctrine, and the ministry of the Lutheran teacher. She also had to obtain the endorsement of her local Synod district by submitting a petition that contained her academic transcripts, letters of recommendation, personal statement, and written answers to various ministry-related questions. Finally, she had to pass an oral examination by a faculty committee at a Lutheran college. It took Perich six years to fulfill these requirements. And when she eventually did, she was commissioned as a minister only upon election by the congregation, which recognized God's call to her to teach. At that point, her call could be rescinded only upon a supermajority vote of the congregation—a protection designed to allow her to "preach the Word of God boldly."

Perich held herself out as a minister of the Church by accepting the formal call to religious service, according to its terms. She did so in other ways as well. For example, she claimed a special housing allowance on her taxes that was available only to employees earning their compensation " 'in the exercise of the ministry.' " App. 220 ("If you are not conducting activities 'in the exercise of the ministry,' you cannot take advantage of the parsonage or housing allowance exclusion" (quoting Lutheran Church-Missouri Synod Brochure on Whether the IRS Considers Employees as a Minister (2007)). In a form she submitted to the Synod following her termination, Perich again indicated that she regarded herself as a minister at Hosanna-Tabor, stating: "I feel that God is leading me to serve in the teaching ministry . . . I am anxious to be in the teaching ministry again soon."

Perich's job duties reflected a role in conveying the Church's message and carrying out its mission. Hosanna-Tabor expressly charged her with "lead[ing] others toward Christian maturity" and "teach[ing] faithfully the Word of God, the Sacred Scriptures, in its truth and purity and as set forth in all the symbolical books of the Evangelical Lutheran Church." In fulfilling these responsibilities, Perich taught her students religion four days a week, and led them in prayer three times a day. Once a week, she took her students to a school-wide chapel service, and—about twice a year—she took her turn leading it, choosing the liturgy, selecting the hymns, and delivering a short message based on verses from the Bible. During her last year of teaching, Perich also led her fourth graders in a brief devotional exercise each morning. As a source of religious instruction, Perich performed an important role in transmitting the Lutheran faith to the next generation.

In light of these considerations—the formal title given Perich by the Church, the substance reflected in that title, her own use of that title, and the important religious functions she performed for the Church—we conclude that Perich was a minister covered by the ministerial exception.

In reaching a contrary conclusion, the Court of Appeals committed three errors. First, the Sixth Circuit failed to see any relevance in the fact that Perich was a commissioned minister. Although such a title, by itself, does not automatically ensure coverage, the fact that an employee has been ordained or commissioned as a minister is surely relevant, as is the fact that significant religious training and a recognized religious mission underlie the description of the employee's position. It was wrong for the Court of Appeals—and Perich, who has adopted the court's view—to say that an employee's title does not matter.

Second, the Sixth Circuit gave too much weight to the fact that lay teachers at the school performed the same religious duties as Perich. We express no view on whether someone with Perich's duties would be covered by the ministerial exception in the absence of the other considerations we have discussed. But though relevant, it cannot be dispositive that others not formally recognized as ministers by the church perform the same functions—particularly when, as here, they did so only because commissioned ministers were unavailable.

Third, the Sixth Circuit placed too much emphasis on Perich's performance of secular duties. It is true that her religious duties consumed only 45 minutes of each workday, and that the rest of her day was devoted to teaching secular subjects. The EEOC regards that as conclusive, contending that any ministerial exception "should be limited to those employees who perform exclusively religious functions." We cannot accept that view. Indeed, we are unsure whether any such employees exist. The heads of congregations themselves often have a mix of duties, including secular ones such as helping to manage the congregation's finances, supervising purely secular personnel, and overseeing the upkeep of facilities.

Although the Sixth Circuit did not adopt the extreme position pressed here by the EEOC, it did regard the relative amount of time Perich spent performing religious functions as largely determinative. The issue before us, however, is not one that can be resolved by a stopwatch. The amount of time an employee spends on particular activities is relevant in assessing that employee's status, but that factor cannot be considered in isolation, without regard to the nature of the religious functions performed and the other considerations discussed above.

Because Perich was a minister within the meaning of the exception, the First Amendment requires dismissal of this employment discrimination suit against her religious employer. The EEOC and Perich originally sought an order reinstating Perich to her former position as a called teacher. By requiring the Church to accept a minister it did not want, such an order would have plainly violated the Church's freedom under the Religion Clauses to select its own ministers.

Perich no longer seeks reinstatement, having abandoned that relief before this Court. But that is immaterial. Perich continues to seek frontpay in lieu of reinstatement, backpay, compensatory and punitive damages, and attorney's fees. An award of such relief would operate as a penalty on the Church for terminating an unwanted minister, and would be no less prohibited by the First Amendment than an order overturning the termination. Such relief would depend on a determination that Hosanna-Tabor was wrong to have relieved Perich of her position, and it is precisely such a ruling that is barred by the ministerial exception.

The EEOC and Perich suggest that Hosanna-Tabor's asserted religious reason for firing Perich—that she violated the Synod's commitment to internal dispute resolution—was pretextual. That suggestion misses the point of the ministerial exception. The purpose of the exception is not to safeguard a church's decision to fire a minister only when it is made for a religious reason. The exception instead ensures that the authority to select and control who will minister to the faithful—a matter "strictly ecclesiastical," *Kedroff*, 344 U.S., at 119—is the church's alone.[4]

IV

The EEOC and Perich foresee a parade of horribles that will follow our recognition of a ministerial exception to employment discrimination

---

[4] We conclude that the exception operates as an affirmative defense to an otherwise cognizable claim, not a jurisdictional bar. . . .

suits. According to the EEOC and Perich, such an exception could protect religious organizations from liability for retaliating against employees for reporting criminal misconduct or for testifying before a grand jury or in a criminal trial. What is more, the EEOC contends, the logic of the exception would confer on religious employers "unfettered discretion" to violate employment laws by, for example, hiring children or aliens not authorized to work in the United States.

Hosanna-Tabor responds that the ministerial exception would not in any way bar criminal prosecutions for interfering with law enforcement investigations or other proceedings. Nor, according to the Church, would the exception bar government enforcement of general laws restricting eligibility for employment, because the exception applies only to suits by or on behalf of ministers themselves. Hosanna-Tabor also notes that the ministerial exception has been around in the lower courts for 40 years, see *McClure v. Salvation Army,* 460 F.2d 553, 558 (C.A.5 1972), and has not given rise to the dire consequences predicted by the EEOC and Perich.

The case before us is an employment discrimination suit brought on behalf of a minister, challenging her church's decision to fire her. Today we hold only that the ministerial exception bars such a suit. We express no view on whether the exception bars other types of suits, including actions by employees alleging breach of contract or tortious conduct by their religious employers. There will be time enough to address the applicability of the exception to other circumstances if and when they arise.

The interest of society in the enforcement of employment discrimination statutes is undoubtedly important. But so too is the interest of religious groups in choosing who will preach their beliefs, teach their faith, and carry out their mission. When a minister who has been fired sues her church alleging that her termination was discriminatory, the First Amendment has struck the balance for us. The church must be free to choose those who will guide it on its way.

The judgment of the Court of Appeals for the Sixth Circuit is reversed.

It is so ordered.

■ JUSTICE THOMAS, concurring.

I join the Court's opinion. I write separately to note that, in my view, the Religion Clauses require civil courts to apply the ministerial exception and to defer to a religious organization's good-faith understanding of who qualifies as its minister ... the evidence demonstrates that Hosanna-Tabor sincerely considered Perich a minister. That would be sufficient for me to conclude that Perich's suit is properly barred by the ministerial exception.

■ JUSTICE ALITO, with whom JUSTICE KAGAN joins, concurring.

I join the Court's opinion, but I write separately to clarify my understanding of the significance of formal ordination and designation as a "minister" in determining whether an "employee" of a religious group falls within the so-called "ministerial" exception. . . . Because virtually every religion in the world is represented in the population of the United States, it would be a mistake if the term "minister" or the concept of ordination were viewed as central to the important issue of religious autonomy that is presented in cases like this one. Instead, courts should focus on the function performed by persons who work for religious bodies.

The First Amendment protects the freedom of religious groups to engage in certain key religious activities, including the conducting of worship services and other religious ceremonies and rituals, as well as the critical process of communicating the faith. Accordingly, religious groups must be free to choose the personnel who are essential to the performance of these functions.

The "ministerial" exception should be tailored to this purpose. It should apply to any "employee" who leads a religious organization, conducts worship services or important religious ceremonies or rituals, or serves as a messenger or teacher of its faith. If a religious group believes that the ability of such an employee to perform these key functions has been compromised, then the constitutional guarantee of religious freedom protects the group's right to remove the employee from his or her position.

II

A

The Court's opinion today holds that the "ministerial" exception applies to Cheryl Perich (hereinafter respondent), who is regarded by the Lutheran Church—Missouri Synod as a commissioned minister. But while a ministerial title is undoubtedly relevant in applying the First Amendment rule at issue, such a title is neither necessary nor sufficient. As previously noted, most faiths do not employ the term "minister," and some eschew the concept of formal ordination. And at the opposite end of the spectrum, some faiths consider the ministry to consist of all or a very large percentage of their members. Perhaps this explains why, although every circuit to consider the issue has recognized the "ministerial" exception, no circuit has made ordination status or formal title determinative of the exception's applicability.

B

The ministerial exception applies to respondent because, as the Court notes, she played a substantial role in "conveying the Church's message and carrying out its mission." She taught religion to her students four days a week and took them to chapel on the fifth day. She led them in daily devotional exercises, and led them in prayer three times a day. She also alternated with the other teachers in planning and leading worship services at the school chapel, choosing liturgies, hymns, and readings, and composing and delivering a message based on Scripture.

It makes no difference that respondent also taught secular subjects. While a purely secular teacher would not qualify for the "ministerial" exception, the constitutional protection of religious teachers is not somehow diminished when they take on secular functions in addition to their religious ones. What matters is that respondent played an important role as an instrument of her church's religious message and as a leader of its worship activities. Because of these important religious functions, Hosanna-Tabor had the right to decide for itself whether respondent was religiously qualified to remain in her office.

Hosanna-Tabor discharged respondent because she threatened to file suit against the church in a civil court. This threat contravened the Lutheran doctrine that disputes among Christians should be resolved internally without resort to the civil court system and all the legal wrangling it entails. In Hosanna-Tabor's view, respondent's disregard for this doctrine compromised her religious function, disqualifying her from serving effectively as a voice for the church's faith. Respondent does not dispute that the Lutheran Church subscribes to a doctrine of internal dispute resolution, but she argues that this was a mere pretext for her firing, which was really done for nonreligious reasons.

For civil courts to engage in the pretext inquiry that respondent and the Solicitor General urge us to sanction would dangerously undermine the religious autonomy that lower court case law has now protected for nearly four decades. In order to probe the *real reason* for respondent's firing, a civil court—and perhaps a jury—would be required to make a judgment about church doctrine. The credibility of Hosanna-Tabor's asserted reason for terminating respondent's employment could not be assessed without taking into account both the importance that the Lutheran Church attaches to the doctrine of internal dispute resolution and the degree to which that tenet compromised respondent's religious function. If it could be shown that this belief is an obscure and minor part of Lutheran doctrine, it would be much more plausible for respondent to argue that this doctrine was not the real reason for her firing. If, on the other hand, the doctrine is a central and universally known tenet of Lutheranism, then the church's asserted reason for her discharge would seem much more likely to be nonpretextual. But whatever the truth of the matter might be, the mere adjudication of such questions would pose grave problems for religious autonomy: It would require calling witnesses to testify about the importance and priority of the religious doctrine in question, with a civil factfinder sitting in ultimate judgment of what the accused church really believes, and how important that belief is to the church's overall mission.

At oral argument, both respondent and the United States acknowledged that a pretext inquiry would sometimes be prohibited by principles of religious autonomy, and both conceded that a Roman Catholic priest who is dismissed for getting married could not sue the church and claim that his dismissal was actually based on a ground forbidden by the federal antidiscrimination laws. But there is no principled basis for proscribing a pretext inquiry in such a case while permitting it in a case like the one now before us. The Roman Catholic Church's insistence on clerical celibacy may be much better known than the Lutheran Church's doctrine of internal dispute resolution, but popular familiarity with a religious doctrine cannot be the determinative factor.

What matters in the present case is that Hosanna-Tabor believes that the religious function that respondent performed made it essential that she abide by the doctrine of internal dispute resolution; and the civil courts are in no position to second-guess that assessment. This conclusion rests not on respondent's ordination status or her formal title, but rather on her functional status as the type of employee that a church must be free to appoint or dismiss in order to exercise the religious liberty that the First Amendment guarantees.

NOTES AND QUESTIONS

1. Before the Supreme Court issued this opinion on the ministerial exception, the Sixth Circuit had employed the "primary duties" test. If Perich's primary duties were religious, she was a minister. If her primary duties were secular, she was not. Why would the Sixth Circuit conclude that Perich's primary duties were secular? What does the Supreme Court say about the primary duties test? What test for a minister does the Court provide in its place?

2. *Reaction.* Are you surprised the opinion was unanimous? Do you agree the decision was " 'a major win for religious freedom' and 'a resounding defeat for those who seek to deny [it].'. . . 'an occasion for celebration, for dancing in the streets,' . . . 'truly a shout of praise to first principles of the First Amendment.' "? Richard W. Garnett & John M. Robinson, *Hosanna-Tabor*, Religious Freedom, and the Constitutional Structure, Cato Sup. Ct. Rev., 2011–2012, at 307, 323. Or, in contrast, do you think it "subverts individual autonomy to protect church autonomy. It affords greater free exercise protection to churches than is enjoyed by their members. It is so broad and absolute that its doctrinal limitation seems inevitable, yet its compound jurisprudential architecture is impervious to limitation. In the crowning irony, the exception does all of this to safeguard an experience of religious practice and belief that is rapidly passing away. It is fair to wonder whether the ministerial exception will outlast the churches it shields."? Frederick Mark Gedicks, Narrative Pluralism and

Doctrinal Incoherence in *Hosanna-Tabor*, 64 Mercer L. Rev. 405, 435 (2013).

Post-*Hosanna-Tabor*, do you agree with Professor Horwitz that churches have a moral obligation to treat their ministerial employees with love and compassion? Professor Horwitz also argues that everyone should ask "what sorts of nonlegal levers—from internal debate within the church to external public criticism—might encourage churches to exercise their authority sensitively and appropriately." Paul Horwitz, Act III of the Ministerial Exception, 106 Nw. U. L. Rev. 973, 976 (2012). Do you agree? What non-legal mechanisms would you recommend when churches and ministers get into disputes about employment?

3.   What purposes do the concurrences serve? Are their tests of a minister different from that provided by the opinion of the Court?

4.   *Smith*. Do you agree with the Court that Perich's case is different from *Employment Division v. Smith*? How does the Court distinguish *Smith*? Is the distinction persuasive? Do you agree with Professor McConnell that the decision "create[d] uncertainty" because

> Future litigants will want to know: What are "outward physical acts"? Are some acts "inward"? Are some acts not "physical"? How broad is the term "acts"? Are there any religiously motivated acts by individuals, as opposed to religious organizations, that qualify for protection because they are not outward or physical? Future litigants also will want to know: What is "an internal church decision that affects the faith and mission of the church itself"? "Internal" presumably means that the action affects only the church, its members, its employees, and others who voluntarily associate with it. That distinction makes sense, though there may be cases on the boundary. But what is meant by the qualifier, "affects the faith and mission of the church itself"? Are there internal church decisions that do not affect "the faith and mission of the church itself"?

Michael W. McConnell, Reflections on *Hosanna-Tabor*, 35 Harv. J.L. & Pub. Pol'y 821, 834–35 (2012). Do you agree with Professor Griffin that the decisions are backwards in protecting the church's freedom to discriminate for a non-religious reason but not protecting the religious ritual of peyote?. See Leslie C. Griffin, The Sins of *Hosanna-Tabor*, 88 Ind. L.J. 981, 993–94 (2013) ("In terms of religious freedom, the ingestion of peyote is a profound religious ritual with a long American history predating the Constitution. In sharp contrast, the ministerial exception involves cases where employees allege disabilities discrimination, retaliation, pregnancy discrimination, sexual harassment, hostile work environment, unequal pay, race discrimination, gender discrimination, and other civil rights violations.")

5.   Is the result of *Hosanna-Tabor* that courts must now become *more* entangled in religious questions than if the ministerial exception were not involved? See Caroline Mala Corbin, The Irony of *Hosanna-Tabor Evangelical Lutheran Church & School v. EEOC*, 106 Nw. U. L. Rev. 951,

965–69 (2012) ("The very nature of the question—is this person a 'minister'?—invites courts to become entangled with theological and doctrinal issues beyond their institutional competence."). If schools required all their employees, from janitors to bookkeepers to P.E. teachers, to lead prayer once or twice during the school year, would the courts have to rule that all these employees were ministers? Id.

6. Can you identify church employees who *clearly* would not be ministers under the Supreme Court's ruling? Does it matter if you rely on the Chief Justice's test, Justice Thomas's test, or Justice Alito's test for a minister? Do you agree that "[e]ven if, for example, Perich had taught only math, the context in which she taught it, and the pervasive, animating religious mission of the school, would still suggest that she expressed, carried, and 'personified' the faith commitments and aspirations of Hosanna-Tabor—commitments and aspirations she could no longer personify effectively given her public departure from Lutheran doctrine," and would therefore be a math-teacher-minister? Richard W. Garnett & John M. Robinson, *Hosanna-Tabor*, Religious Freedom, and the Constitutional Structure, Cato Sup. Ct. Rev., 2011–2012, at 307, 326.

7. One of the reasons Perich was declared a minister is because she claimed ministerial status on her tax return. According to the Internal Revenue Code:

> In the case of a minister of the gospel, gross income does not include—
>
> (1) the rental value of a home furnished to him as part of his compensation; or
>
> (2) the rental allowance paid to him as part of his compensation, to the extent used by him to rent or provide a home and to the extent such allowance does not exceed the fair rental value of the home, including furnishing and appurtenances such as a garage, plus the cost of utilities. 26 U.S.C. § 107.

Does this provision violate the Establishment Clause by favoring ministers over regular taxpayers? See Freedom from Religion Foundation v. Geithner, 715 F.Supp.2d 1051 (E.D. Cal. 2010) (ruling that tax provisions violate prong two of the *Lemon* test by advancing religion). The court observed that religious employers receive a benefit from the tax by being able to pay their employees lower wages: "While §107 is a tax exemption to be claimed by ministers, churches as employers clearly benefit by being able to pay their ministers more, for less. The financial effect of the exemption is the same as if the government were giving direct subsidies to ministers or churches to hire ministers." Id. at 1064–65; see also Freedom From Religion Foundation v. Lew, 773 F.3d 815 (7th Cir. 2014) (atheists lacked standing to bring Establishment Clause challenge to the parsonage exemption "because they never asked for it.").

Do you think the Establishment Clause is violated by the exemption? Or do you agree with Professor Zelinsky that the allowance is "a permitted, though not compelled, choice to accept one form of church-state entanglement over others and to accommodate the autonomy of churches and religious personnel by excluding their housing and housing allowances from clergy members' gross incomes"? See Edward A. Zelinsky, The First Amendment and the Parsonage Allowance, 142 Tax Notes 413 (Jan. 27, 2014)

8. What should happen to the following lawsuits under the reasoning of *Hosanna-Tabor*? Consider what additional facts you might need to make your decision.

  a.   In two separate cases, a pastor with the Presbyterian Church and a pastor with the African Methodist Episcopal Church were fired by their employers. The pastors filed breach of contract lawsuits arguing that their employers had not paid their wages for work completed before the firing and requesting the courts to order payment of the wages. Can the two cases survive the ministerial exception? See Crymes v. Grace Hope Presbyterian Church, Inc., 2012 WL 3236290 (Ky.App.); Second Episcopal District African Methodist Episcopal Church v. Prioleau, 49 A.3d 812 (D.C. 2012).

  b.   Lexington Theological Seminary is a Disciples of Christ school that trains students for Christian ministry. Laurence Kant is a tenured Jewish professor of Jewish Studies who taught academic courses about the history of religion. Jimmy Kirby is a Methodist Episcopal Church pastor and teacher who taught religious courses at the Seminary and occasionally preached there. Both men were fired after a financial restructuring at the Seminary. Can a Jewish man be a Christian minister? See Kant v. Lexington Theological Seminary 426 S.W.3d 587 (Ky. 2014); Kirby v. Lexington Theological Seminary 426 S.W.3d 597 (Ky. 2014). We examine the constitutionality of academic teaching about religion in Chapter 10.

  c.   Christa Dias, a non-Catholic Technology Coordinator at a Catholic school, oversaw computers at the school and instructed students on computer usage. Non-Catholics were not allowed to teach religion at the school. Dias was fired after becoming pregnant by means of artificial insemination, which is prohibited by Catholic teaching. Can Dias' pregnancy discrimination lawsuit proceed without running afoul of the ministerial exception? See Dias v. Archdiocese of Cincinnati, No. 1:11–CV–00251, 2012 WL 1068165 (S.D.Ohio Mar. 29, 2012).

      What do you think of the argument that the "seemingly broad scope of Hosanna-Tabor's ministerial exception is likely to have a disproportionate effect on female employees of religiously-affiliated employers. The majority of Catholic schoolteachers are female, and, of course, only women can get pregnant."? Jessica L. Waters, Testing Hosanna-Tabor: The

Implications for Pregnancy Discrimination Claims and Employees' Reproductive Rights, 9 Stan. J. Civ. Rts. & Civ. Liberties 47, 71–72 (2013).

d.   Two cases involving Catholic seminarians were decided before *Hosanna-Tabor*. Would they come out differently today? John Bollard was studying to become a Roman Catholic priest as a novice with the Jesuit order. He alleged that his superiors made unwanted sexual advances and sent him pornographic materials; he sued for sexual harassment under Title VII. See Bollard v. California Province of the Soc'y of Jesus, 196 F.3d 940 (9th Cir. 1999) (harassment was not part of church doctrine so lawsuit could proceed). The New Jersey Supreme Court followed *Bollard* in a case involving another Catholic seminarian, Christopher McKelvey, who was subjected to unwanted homosexual advances and repeatedly asked to discuss masturbation and other sexual acts. After McKelvey left the seminary, the diocese presented him with a $69,000 bill for his education, and he sued in contract and tort alleging breach of an implied contract by the creation of a hostile education and work environment, breach of the covenant of good faith and fair dealing, breach of fiduciary duty, intentional infliction of emotional distress and fraud and deceit. McKelvey sought damages in the form of reimbursement for his tuition costs and student loans and for his emotional suffering, loss of employment and loss of employability as a Roman Catholic priest. See McKelvey v. Pierce, 173 N.J. 26, 800 A.2d 840, 844 (2002) (lawsuit is permitted as long as religious decisions about ministry were not reached).

e.   Another *cert.* petition before the Court while *Hosanna-Tabor* was argued involved Michigan elementary school teacher Madeline Weishuhn, who was fired by a Catholic school principal for reporting possible sexual abuse of a student's friend to state authorities. Even though Weishuhn was a required reporter of abuse under state law, Michigan state courts dismissed her whistleblowers lawsuit under the ministerial exception. Weishuhn v. Catholic Diocese of Lansing, 756 N.W.2d 483 (Mich. Ct. App. 2008). Why do you think the Court agreed to hear *Hosanna-Tabor* instead of *Weishuhn*? Should Weishuhn's case fall within the tort exception to *Hosanna-Tabor*?

f.   Emily Herx (who taught junior high school level literature and language arts at St. Vincent de Paul School in Fort Wayne, Indiana) was fired after she and her husband used in vitro fertilization to start their family. She alleged Title VII sex discrimination and Americans With Disabilities Act disability discrimination. Does it matter that Herx was a lay teacher? Herx v. Diocese of Ft. Wayne-S. Bend Inc., 48 F. Supp. 3d 1168, 1177 (N.D. Ind.) appeal dismissed sub nom. Herx v. Diocese of Fort Wayne-S. Bend, Inc., 772 F.3d 1085 (7th Cir. 2014).

g. Kimberly Bohnert was a biology teacher in the science department at Junipero Serra High School, who alleged that her employer did nothing to protect her from sexual harassment by male students. Bohnert had participated in the school's Campus Ministry and Kairos Retreat programs by "assist[ing] with the logistics of student trips and help[ing] facilitate the programs." Bohnert v. Roman Catholic Archbishop of San Francisco, 136 F. Supp. 3d 1094 (N.D. Cal. 2015).

h. Matthew Barrett's job offer as Food Service Director at Fontbonne Academy (a private Catholic school for girls) was rescinded after Barrett listed his husband as emergency contact, and filed a sexual orientation discrimination lawsuit. Barrett v. Fontbonne Acad., No. NOCV2014-751, 2015 WL 9682042 (Mass. Super. Dec. 16, 2015).

i. Can Catholic schools turn all their teachers into ministers by asking them to sign a contract renewal stating they are ministers? The Archbishop of San Francisco proposed such a contract for the San Francisco Catholic schools. Lee Romney, Cleric Goes Old School; Morality Clauses Outrage Many in Bay Area, L.A. Times, Feb. 12, 2015, at A1 ("The teachers union is 'very, very, concerned' about the proposed change to the collective bargaining agreement that would deem them 'ministers.' "). Are there any limits as to who can be defined as a minister?

9. *Contract and Tort*. What did the Court say about whether the ministerial exception bars actions by employees alleging tortious conduct by their religious employers? What do you think of Professor Lund's argument that churches should be subject to assumed but not imposed (or involuntary) legal obligations? Assumed legal obligations include contract, property, and corporate law, while imposed legal obligations include tort and criminal law. Christopher C. Lund, Free Exercise Reconceived: The Logic and Limits of *Hosanna-Tabor*, 108 Nw. U. L. Rev. 1183, 1233 (2014). Would that mean that the ministerial exception would allow churches to be sued for breach of contract but not for tort? Do you agree with Professor Laycock's description of how contract and tort lawsuits should be resolved post-*Hosanna Tabor*:

A minister's contract claim for unpaid salary or retirement benefits surely can proceed to the merits. A minister discharged for cause, suing in contract on the theory that the church lacked adequate cause to discharge him, should be squarely within the rationale of *Hosanna-Tabor*. He would be directly challenging the church's right to evaluate and select its own ministers, and he would be asking the court to substitute its evaluation of his job performance for the church's evaluation.

Similarly, in tort, a minister's workers' compensation claim for physical injury surely can proceed to the merits. A defamation claim alleging that church officials made false statements in the proceedings leading to his discharge, or when they explained the discharge to the congregation, should be barred. A church cannot evaluate its ministers without making statements about their performance, and it is in no one's interest—not the church's and certainly not the minister's—to encourage them to make such decisions without discussion and deliberation. Statements evaluating a minister's performance should be within the ministerial exception.

Douglas Laycock, *Hosanna-Tabor* and the Ministerial Exception, 35 Harv. J.L. & Pub. Pol'y 839, 861–62 (2012).

C. TORT SUITS AGAINST RELIGIOUS ORGANIZATIONS

We read in Section B that courts and legislatures are reluctant to intervene in employment disputes among church members. In this section we examine a related but different question: what should happen to individuals who desire to sue their pastors and other church personnel for tortious conduct? Are such lawsuits barred by the same principles that keep employment cases out of court, or should a different legal standard apply? Should tort suits for malpractice, breach of fiduciary duty, negligent hiring and supervision, or defamation, for example, be allowed against ministers, bishops and other church administrators?

As you read the following materials, consider what standard the Religion Clauses set for lawsuits against church employees and administrators. Should the courts decide cases according to a principle of no-harm, of neutrality or equality, or by a structural-separation model? See Marci A. Hamilton, Religious Institutions, the No-Harm Doctrine, and the Public Good, 2004 BYU L. Rev. 1099, 1115 ("The Supreme Court's religious institution cases operate from the principle of no-harm, which is part and parcel of the core principle of ordered liberty embedded in republicanism—the maximal amount of liberty is calibrated to achieve the minimal amount of harm. They reflect the Constitution's larger orientation towards republican democracy, which rests on the no-harm rule, not a principle of autonomy."); William P. Marshall, Separation, Neutrality, and Clergy Liability for Sexual Misconduct, 2004 BYU L. Rev. 1921, 1923–24 ("Generally, as Lupu and Tuttle note, First Amendment law posits that religion and nonreligion are indistinct for constitutional purposes (the 'neutrality' or 'equality' model). Accordingly, the central constitutional inquiry is whether religion and nonreligion are being treated equally with respect to the matter at hand. Thus, in the case of the clergy-congregant sexual misconduct issue, the neutrality model would simply inquire whether leaders of nonreligious organizations would be subject to liability for similar conduct with their members. Professors Lupu and Tuttle's structural-separation model, however, is premised on the notion that religion should be considered constitutionally distinct with respect to clergy-congregant sexual misconduct cases. How a neutrality analysis would resolve such cases is therefore irrelevant to their analysis. Rather, it is a competing way to understand the question."); Ira C. Lupu & Robert W. Tuttle, Sexual Misconduct and Ecclesiastical Immunity, 2004 BYU L. Rev. 1789, 1896 ("Religious institutions should have no sweeping immunities from any body of law, civil or criminal, dealing with any kind of misconduct. In most circumstances, courts should treat such institutions and their agents in the same manner as their secular counterparts. In some highly particularized legal contexts, however, the First Amendment may indeed limit the state's decision-making bodies. The state may not impose unique legal responsibilities on religious bodies, expose such entities to an unreasonable risk of jury discrimination against them, or adjudicate the answers to questions that are internal to a religious community, including the crucial question of who may serve as a spokesperson for the faith.").

Should the First Amendment protect religious organizations from being sued in tort, as in the following case?

Pleasant Glade Assembly of God v. Schubert

Supreme Court of Texas, 2008.
264 S.W.3d 1, 51 Tex. Sup. Ct. J. 1086.

■ JUSTICE MEDINA delivered the opinion of the Court, in which JUSTICE HECHT, JUSTICE O'NEILL, JUSTICE WAINWRIGHT, JUSTICE BRISTER, and JUSTICE WILLETT joined.

This appeal concerns the tension between a church's right to protection under the Free Exercise Clause of the First Amendment and a church member's right to judicial redress under a claim for intentional tort. We further conclude the case, as tried, presents an ecclesiastical dispute over religious conduct that would unconstitutionally entangle the court in matters of church doctrine and, accordingly, reverse the court of appeals' judgment and dismiss the case.

I

On Saturday June 8, 1996, Tom and Judy Schubert left town, leaving their three teenage children at home. While the Schuberts were away, their seventeen-year-old daughter, Laura, spent much of her time at the family's church, Pleasant Glade Assembly of God, participating in church-related activities.

On Friday evening, before her parents left town, Laura attended a youth group activity at Pleasant Glade in preparation for a garage sale the next day. The atmosphere during this event became spiritually charged after one of the youth announced he had seen a demon near the sanctuary. The youth minister, Rod Linzay, thereupon called the group together to hear the story, and after hearing it, agreed that demons were indeed present. Linzay instructed the youth to anoint everything in the church with holy oil and led a spirited effort throughout the night to cast out the demons. Finally, on Saturday morning at about 4:30 a.m., Linzay gathered the exhausted youth together to announce that he had seen a cloud of the presence of God fill the church and that God had revealed a vision to him. Although exhausted, the young people assisted with the garage sale later that morning.

At the Sunday morning worship service the next day, several young people gave testimonials about the spiritual events of the preceding day. At the conclusion of the service, the youth, including Laura and her brother, prayed at the altar. During these prayers, Laura's brother became "slain in the spirit,"[2] collapsing to the floor where church members continued to pray into the early afternoon.

Later that afternoon, Laura returned to church for another youth activity and the Sunday evening worship service. During the evening service, Laura collapsed. After her collapse, several church members took Laura to a classroom where they "laid hands" on her and prayed. According to Laura, church members forcibly held her arms crossed over her chest, despite her demands to be freed. According to those present, Laura clenched her fists, gritted her teeth, foamed at the mouth, made guttural noises, cried, yelled, kicked, sweated, and hallucinated. The parties sharply dispute whether these actions were the cause or the result of her physical restraint.

Church members, moreover, disagreed about whether Laura's actions were a ploy for attention or the result of spiritual activity. Laura stated during the episode that Satan or demons were trying to get her. After the episode, Laura also allegedly began telling other church members about a "vision." Yet, her collapse and subsequent reaction to being restrained may also have been the result of fatigue and hypoglycemia. Laura had not eaten anything substantive that day and had missed sleep because of the spiritual activities that weekend. Whatever the cause, Laura was eventually released after she calmed down and complied with requests to say the name "Jesus."

---

[2] Lloyd McCutchen, Pleasant Glade's senior pastor, explained "slain in the spirit" as:

[A] biblical experience related in several accounts of the Bible. When this happens, a person often faints into semi-consciousness, and sometimes lies down on the floor of our church. It is our belief that this is a positive experience in which the holy spirit comes over a person and influences them. It is our belief that the holy spirit is not the only spirit that can influence a person. Evil spirits can move and can torment persons.

On Monday and Tuesday, Laura continued to participate in church-related activities without any problems, raising money for Vacation Bible School and preparing for youth drama productions. Her parents returned from their trip on Tuesday afternoon.

On Wednesday evening, Laura attended the weekly youth service presided by Rod Linzay. According to Linzay, Laura began to act in a manner similar to the Sunday evening episode. Laura testified that she curled up into a fetal position because she wanted to be left alone. Church members, however, took her unusual posture as a sign of distress. At some point, Laura collapsed and writhed on the floor. Again, there is conflicting evidence about whether Laura's actions were the cause or result of being physically restrained by church members and about the duration and force of the restraint. According to Laura, the youth, under the direction of Linzay and his wife, Holly, held her down. Laura testified, moreover, that she was held in a "spread eagle" position with several youth members holding down her arms and legs. The church's senior pastor, Lloyd McCutchen, was summoned to the youth hall where he played a tape of pacifying music, placed his hand on Laura's forehead, and prayed. During the incident, Laura suffered carpet burns, a scrape on her back, and bruises on her wrists and shoulders. Laura's parents were subsequently called to the church. After collecting their daughter, the Schuberts took her out for a meal and then home. Laura did not mention her scrapes and bruises to her parents that night.

In July, Laura's father, himself an Assembly of God pastor and missionary, met twice with Senior Pastor McCutchen to discuss the June incidents and the youth ministry. Following those conversations, Senior Pastor McCutchen took the matter to the board of deacons and met with Linzay to discuss theology. Linzay assured McCutchen "that neither he nor Holly believe that Christians can be demon possessed." After meeting with Linzay, McCutchen spent an hour with the youth group to clarify the biblical doctrine of angels, fallen angels, and demonic possession. McCutchen reported his actions to Laura's father in a letter on July 22.

A few days later, Laura's father responded to McCutchen's letter, discussing at length Laura's version of the spiritually charged atmosphere surrounding the weekend of June 7–9 and the following Wednesday evening youth service on June 12. In addition, he stated that Laura "ha[d] started having terrible nightmares" and had felt "that a demon [was] in her room at night." Because missionaries "can not get into local church affairs," Laura's father concluded by asking the senior pastor to investigate the matter further, adding "I am placing this situation in your hands and hope God gives you wisdom." The Schuberts subsequently left Pleasant Glade to attend another church.

Over the next months, several psychologists and psychiatrists examined Laura, documenting her multiple symptoms, such as angry outbursts, weight loss, sleeplessness, nightmares, hallucinations, self-mutilation, fear of abandonment, and agoraphobia. Despite the psychiatric counseling, Laura became increasingly depressed and suicidal, eventually dropping out of her senior year of high school and abandoning her former plan to attend Bible College and pursue missionary work. Finally, in November 1996, Laura was diagnosed as suffering from traumatic stress disorder, which the doctors associated with her physical restraint at the church in June 1996. One of the expert witnesses at trial testified that Laura would "require extensive time to recover trust in authorities, spiritual leaders, and her life-long religious faith." Ultimately, Laura was classified as disabled by the Social Security Administration and began drawing a monthly disability check.

Thereafter, Laura and her parents sued Pleasant Glade, the senior pastor, the youth minister, and other members of the church, alleging negligence, gross negligence, professional negligence, intentional infliction of emotional distress, false imprisonment, assault, battery, loss of consortium, and child abuse. The Schuberts further claimed that the defendants' conduct had caused Laura "mental, emotional and psychological injuries including physical pain, mental anguish, fear, humiliation, embarrassment, physical and emotional distress, post-traumatic stress disorder[,] and loss of employment." The Schuberts' petition detailed the June spiritual events at the church leading to Laura's breakdown.

In response, Pleasant Glade and the other defendants sought a protective order and moved to dismiss the Schuberts' lawsuit as an unconstitutional burden on their religious practices, describing the litigation as "a dispute regarding how services should be conducted within a church, including the practice of 'laying on of hands.'" The trial court denied both motions.

In the mandamus proceeding that followed, the court of appeals granted the church's request for relief, agreeing that the Schuberts' "religious" claims were barred by the First Amendment because they "involve[d] a searching inquiry into Assembly of God beliefs and the validity of such beliefs." The court defined "religious" claims to include the Schuberts' claims of negligence, gross negligence, professional negligence, intentional infliction of emotional distress, child abuse, and loss of Laura's consortium. The church did not ask for mandamus protection from Laura's claims of false imprisonment and assault, and those claims were not included in the court's definition of religious claims.

Following the mandamus proceeding, the trial court signed a protective order, prohibiting the Schuberts from inquiring into or debating the religious teachings, practices, or beliefs of the Pentecostal or Assembly of God churches. Laura's remaining claims proceeded to trial, where a jury found that Laura had been assaulted and falsely imprisoned by the senior pastor, the youth minister, and several church members. The jury apportioned liability among these defendants, attributing fifty percent to the senior pastor, twenty-five percent to the youth minister, and the remainder to the other defendants. Finally, the jury awarded Laura damages of $300,000 for her pain and suffering, loss of earning capacity, and medical expenses. Following the verdict, Laura moved for judgment, and Pleasant Glade moved for judgment notwithstanding the verdict, asserting once again its free exercise rights under the state and federal constitutions. The trial court rendered judgment on the jury's verdict of false imprisonment, awarding Laura the damages found by the jury and adding Pleasant Glade as a judgment debtor with joint and several liability for the amounts apportioned to its senior pastor and youth minister. Pleasant Glade and the other defendants appealed.

The court of appeals eliminated the damages awarded for lost earning capacity, concluding that these damages were too remote and speculative, but otherwise affirmed the trial court's judgment in Laura's favor.

III

[W]e next consider whether the church's religious practice of "laying hands" is entitled to First Amendment protection. Pleasant Glade contends the First Amendment protects it against claims of intangible harm derived from its religious practice of "laying hands." The church relies on *Paul v. Watchtower Bible & Tract Society of New York, Inc.*, 819 F.2d 875 (9th Cir. 1987), for this proposition.

In *Paul*, the Ninth Circuit was asked to determine whether the Jehovah's Witness' practice of shunning was protected by the Free Exercise Clause. After being excommunicated from the church, the plaintiff brought suit against the congregation, alleging common law torts of defamation, invasion of privacy, fraud, and outrageous conduct. Because the church's practice of shunning was exclusively based on their interpretation of canonical text, the court found "[t]he harms suffered by Paul as a result of her shunning by the Jehovah's Witnesses are clearly not of the type that would justify the imposition of tort liability for religious conduct." In particular, the Ninth Circuit held that "[i]ntangible or emotional harms cannot ordinarily serve as a basis for maintaining a tort cause of action against a church for its practice—or against its members." Therefore, "[a] religious organization has a defense of constitutional privilege to claims that it has caused intangible harms—in most, if not all, circumstances."

Laura asserted, however, that the events at the church caused her both physical and emotional injury, and the church concedes that the

First Amendment does not protect it from Laura's claim of physical injury. But Laura's case was not about her physical injuries. Although she suffered scrapes and bruises during these events, her proof at trial related solely to her subsequent emotional or psychological injuries. Laura testified about her fear and anxiety during these events, recalling that she had hallucinated, had trouble breathing, feared that her leg might be broken, and feared that she might die. Her memory of the experience also included many details. She could name the people who held her, where they had placed their hands, and even in whose lap her head rested during part of her ordeal. She also remembered being given water to drink, being walked with, and having a cold compress held to her forehead. Her final memory of the Wednesday evening episode was of her parents coming to take her home and walking with her father in the sanctuary. She could not recall events after that, including her family's stop at a restaurant for dinner on the way home. Laura did not assert that the church-related events had caused her any physical impairment or disfigurement. She did not complain of physical injury that night, and her scrapes and bruises went unnoticed until the next morning when she showed them to her parents. Her medical proof at trial was also not about physical injury but about her psychological evaluations and treatment. Under this record, any claim of physical pain appears inseparable from that of her emotional injuries.

Indeed, her case at trial was not significantly different from what she would have presented under her claim of intentional infliction of emotional distress, a claim the court of appeals agreed should be dismissed. We have previously said that adjudication of this type of claim "would necessarily require an inquiry into the truth or falsity of religious beliefs that is forbidden by the Constitution." This type of intangible, psychological injury, without more, cannot ordinarily serve as a basis for a tort claim against a church or its members for its religious practices.

[E]ven Laura's psychological expert, Dr. Arthur Swen Helge, admitted that he could not separate the damages resulting from Laura's physical restraint and the psychological trauma resulting from the discussion of demons at the church. . . . In this case, although Laura's secular injury claims might theoretically be tried without mentioning religion, the imposition of tort liability for engaging in religious activity to which the church members adhere would have an unconstitutional "chilling effect" by compelling the church to abandon core principles of its religious beliefs.

According to Pentecostal religious doctrine, whenever a person is believed to be under "spiritual influence," the church "lays hands" on the person and anoints oil to combat "evil forces." Senior Pastor McCutchen, in an affidavit supporting the church's motion for summary judgment, explained the practice:

. . . Many people did "lay hands" on Laura Schubert and pray [sic] for her, according to the custom of our church. This type of activity happens on a very regular basis in our church, since we believe in the physical conduct of laying hands on persons in order to pray for them.

Within our church, it is not unusual for a person to be "slain in the spirit." This is a biblical experience, related in several accounts of the Bible. When this happens, a person often faints into semi-consciousness, and sometimes lies down on the floor of our church. It is our belief that this is a positive experience in which the holy spirit comes over a person and influences them. It is our belief that the holy spirit is not the only spirit that can influence a person. Evil spirits can move and can torment persons. Also, it is possible that a person (particularly a young dramatic person such as Laura Schubert) can take advantage of the attention that this activity brings. They can fake the entire experience in order to draw attention to themselves.

When a person comes forward in the service and begins having one of these experiences, it is sometimes difficult to discern whether: (1) the person is having a positive experience with the holy spirit, (2) whether there might be evil spirits engaged in warfare against the holy spirit, (3) whether there are emotional issues are [sic] involved, or (4) whether the person is faking the entire process in order to gain attention. Discerning between these various influences and factors is a matter on which even pastors within the church might disagree. . . .

Clearly, the act of "laying hands" is infused in Pleasant Glade's religious belief system.

Before the mandamus proceeding, the Schuberts sought discovery about the defendants' beliefs and practices, and, even before the litigation, Tom Schubert and Senior Pastor McCutchen discussed demonic possession and the appropriateness of exorcism in the church. This discussion caused McCutchen to meet with Rod Linzay to confirm the youth minister's theological understanding of church tenets, including the "laying of hands." In their original petition, the Schuberts alleged that Laura was in serious emotional and physical distress during the Wednesday night youth service and did not want anyone touching her or praying for her. They further alleged she was restrained and held to the floor against her will and that an exorcism was performed in which the youth minister led the youth group in prayer, demanding that the Devil leave Laura's body. The Schuberts alleged that this restraint caused Laura's emotional injuries. However, because the religious practice of "laying hands" and church beliefs about demons are so closely intertwined with Laura's tort claim, assessing emotional damages against Pleasant Glade for engaging in these religious practices would unconstitutionally burden the church's right to free exercise and embroil this Court in an assessment of the propriety of those religious beliefs.

The Free Exercise Clause prohibits courts from deciding issues of religious doctrine. Here, the psychological effect of church belief in demons and the appropriateness of its belief in "laying hands" are at issue. Because providing a remedy for the very real, but religiously motivated emotional distress in this case would require us to take sides in what is essentially a religious controversy, we cannot resolve that dispute. Accordingly, we reverse the court of appeals' judgment and dismiss the case.

■ CHIEF JUSTICE JEFFERSON filed a dissenting opinion, in which JUSTICE GREEN joined, and in Parts II-A, III, and IV of which JUSTICE JOHNSON joined.

After today, a tortfeasor need merely allege a religious motive to deprive a Texas court of jurisdiction to compensate his fellow congregant for emotional damages. This sweeping immunity is inconsistent with United States Supreme Court precedent and extends far beyond the protections our Constitution affords religious conduct. The First Amendment guards religious liberty; it does not sanction intentional abuse in religion's name. Because the Court's holding precludes recovery of emotional damages—even for assault and other serious torts—where the defendant alleges that the underlying assault was religious in nature, I respectfully dissent.

II

A

The rights contained in the Free Exercise and Establishment Clauses are among our most cherished constitutional freedoms. As broad as these protections are, I agree with the Court that " 'under the cloak of religion, persons may [not], with impunity,' commit intentional torts upon their religious adherents." Unfortunately, this is precisely what the Court's holding allows. Here, assuming all facts favorable to the verdict, members of Pleasant Glade restrained Schubert on two separate occasions against her will. During the first encounter, seven members pinned her to the floor for *two hours* while she cried, screamed, kicked, flailed, and demanded to be released. This violent act caused Schubert multiple bruises, carpet burns, scrapes, and injuries to her wrists, shoulders, and back. As she testified, "I was being grabbed by my wrists, on my ankles, on my shoulders, everywhere. I was fighting with everything I had to get up, I was telling them, no. I was telling them, let go, leave me alone. They did not respond at all." After Schubert "complied with what they wanted [her] to do," she was temporarily released. Fifteen minutes later, at the direction of Pleasant

Glade's youth pastor, a different group of seven church members physically restrained her for an hour longer. After this experience, Schubert was "weak from exhaustion" and could hardly stand.

Three days later, a male church member approached Schubert after a service and put his arm around her shoulders. At this point, Schubert was still trying to figure out "what had happened" at the previous incident, "wasn't interested in being touched," and resisted him. As Schubert testified, "I tried to scoot away from him. He scooted closer. He was more persistent. Finally, his grasp on me just got hard . . . before I knew it, I was being grabbed again." Eight members of Pleasant Glade then proceeded to hold the crying, screaming, seventeen-year-old Schubert spread-eagle on the floor as she thrashed, attempting to break free. After this attack, Schubert was unable to stand without assistance and has no recollection of events immediately afterward. On both occasions, Schubert was scared and in pain, feeling that she could not breathe and that "somebody was going to break [her] leg," not knowing "what was going to happen next."

The jury found that petitioners assaulted and falsely imprisoned Schubert, and the trial court rendered judgment for her on the false imprisonment claim. Although this case presents an unusual set of facts, involving physical restraint not proven to be part of any established church practice, at its core the case is about secular, intentional tort claims squarely within our jurisdiction, and I believe the Court errs in dismissing for want thereof. I will address each of the Court's arguments in turn. First, the Court states that because Schubert's "proof at trial related solely to her subsequent emotional or psychological injuries," her "case at trial then was not significantly different from what she would have presented under her claim of intentional infliction of emotional distress . . . [a] type of claim [that] would necessarily require an inquiry into the truth or falsity of religious beliefs that is forbidden by the Constitution." As an initial matter, this is factually inaccurate. Schubert testified that she suffered *physical* as well as emotional injuries from the assaults. Furthermore, the jury awarded damages for unsegregated past "physical pain and mental anguish." Pleasant Glade did not request that the damages be segregated, and so waived any complaint that her physical injuries were not compensable.

More importantly, the Court's allusion to intentional infliction of emotional distress fails to explain how submitting Schubert's emotional damages claim would "require an inquiry into the truth or falsity of religious beliefs," "embroil this Court in an assessment of the propriety of . . . religious beliefs," or "decid[e] issues of religious doctrine." In *Tilton v. Marshall*, 925 S.W.2d 672, 682 (Tex. 1996), we held that intentional infliction of emotional distress claims based on insincere religious representations and breached promises to read, touch, and pray over tithes and prayer requests were barred by the First Amendment. We explained:

> One of the elements that a plaintiff must prove to establish intentional infliction of emotional distress is that the conduct was "so outrageous in character, and so extreme in degree, as to go beyond all possible bounds of decency, and to be regarded as atrocious, and utterly intolerable in a civilized community." With regard to religious representations, we conclude that no conscientious fact finder would make such a determination without at least considering the objective truth or falsity of the defendants' beliefs, regardless of what evidentiary exclusions or limiting instructions were attempted. After all, the outrageousness and extremity of a representation is, under almost any circumstance, aggravated by being false or mitigated by being true.

This case is not like *Tilton*. False imprisonment does not require a showing of outrageous conduct.[3] Evaluating whether Pleasant Glade falsely imprisoned Schubert does not require the factfinder to determine "the objective truth or falsity of the defendants' belief," and neither does awarding her emotional damages. It is a basic tenet of tort law that emotional damages may be recovered for intentional torts involving physical invasions, such as assault, battery, and false imprisonment. This is common sense: many experiences—including some sexual assaults and certain forms of torture—are extremely traumatic yet result in no serious physical injury.

Given this, it is not surprising that the Court cites no case holding that the First Amendment bars claims for emotional damages arising from assault, battery, false imprisonment, or similar torts.

I agree with the Court that certain claims for emotional damages are barred by the First Amendment—if Schubert were merely complaining of being expelled from the church, she would have no claim in the civil courts. But again, this case, as it was tried, is not about beliefs or "intangible harms"—it is about violent action—specifically, twice pinning a screaming, crying teenage girl to the floor for extended periods of time. That was how it was presented to the jury, which *heard almost nothing about religion during the trial* due to the trial court's diligent attempt to circumvent First Amendment problems and to honor the court of appeals' mandamus ruling that neither side introduce religion as a reason for Laura's restraint. . . . Thus, the Court's assertion that assessing emotional damages against Pleasant Glade for engaging in these religious practices "would . . . embroil this Court in

---

[3] The elements of intentional infliction of emotional distress are: "(1) the defendant acted intentionally or recklessly; (2) the conduct was extreme and outrageous; (3) the defendant's actions caused the plaintiff emotional distress; and (4) the emotional distress that the plaintiff suffered was severe." The elements of false imprisonment, on the other hand, are "(1) willful detention; (2) without consent; and (3) without authority of law."

an assessment of the propriety of those religious beliefs" is belied by the conduct of this very case: Schubert testified that she was "grabbed" after collapsing due to illness; Pleasant Glade contested that version of events without reference to demons, "laying of hands," or other religious subjects, and the jury was able to award damages without considering—or even being informed of—Pleasant Glade's beliefs.

Further, although the Court chooses to conduct its own inquiry into the role of "laying hands" in Pleasant Glade's religion, and attempts to limit its holding by stating that "religious practices that threaten the public's health, safety, or general welfare cannot be tolerated," and thus that there may be some cases in which emotional damages are available as a consequence of religiously motivated conduct, any religious motivation Pleasant Glade may have had is irrelevant to our consideration. The tort of false imprisonment is a religiously neutral law of general applicability, and the First Amendment provides no protection against it. *Employment Div. v. Smith*, 494 U.S. 872, 879, 110 S.Ct. 1595, 108 L.Ed.2d 876 (1990) ("[T]he right of free exercise does not relieve an individual of the obligation to comply with a valid and neutral law of general applicability on the ground that the law proscribes (or prescribes) conduct that his religion prescribes (or proscribes).") . . . The *Smith* Court emphatically rejected the proposition that the First Amendment alone—without being coupled to another constitutional protection, such as the freedom of speech, the press, or to direct the education of one's children, "could excuse [an individual] from compliance" with a general applicable law.

To be clear, even if it had been proven at trial that Pleasant Glade's religion demanded that Schubert be restrained, the First Amendment would provide no defense—we simply need not evaluate the validity of Pleasant Glade's religious beliefs, or even inquire into the assailants' motives, to hold Pleasant Glade liable for its intentionally tortious conduct. And while the Court suggests that imposing this liability would have a "chilling effect" on the church's beliefs, constitutional protection for illegal or tortious conduct cannot be bootstrapped from the protection of beliefs where it does not otherwise exist. Further, the Court's threat to "health, safety, or general welfare" test for liability for religiously motivated acts is almost identical to the "substantial threat to public safety, peace or order" language from *Sherbert v. Verner*, 374 U.S. 398, 403, 83 S.Ct. 1790, 10 L.Ed.2d 965 (1963). In *Smith*, however, the Court expressly rejected the application of *Sherbert*, which developed out of an unemployment compensation case, to "generally applicable prohibitions of socially harmful conduct."

And even under the Court's erroneous standard, it is hard to see why this case would not qualify. The torts of false imprisonment and assault both have substantially similar criminal analogs, and it cannot be seriously argued from this record that Pleasant Glade's conduct did not threaten Schubert's welfare. It is difficult to determine what *would* meet the Court's standard, not least because the Court offers no analysis beyond its declaration that "this is not such a case."

[T]he Court treats church membership as an across the board buffer to tort liability. The problems with this approach are obvious. It is impossible to apply the Court's standard in the absence of factual development or determination in the trial court. We are in no position to decide that the ordeal to which Schubert was subjected was so "expected" and "accepted by those in the church" as to overcome Schubert's vehement denial of consent at the time of the incidents. Further, the scant evidence does not support the Court's conclusion. Senior Pastor McCutchen, in his affidavit quoted by the Court, speaks of "lay[ing] hands" and of church members "faint [ing] into semi-consciousness, and sometimes l[ying] down on the floor of our church." This is far removed from the incident described by Schubert, which we must take as true even if Pleasant Glade had properly raised this issue, and lends no credence to the Court's consent theory.

B

To the extent that this case presents any First Amendment problems, I believe they lie in the fact that Schubert was traumatized not only by the false imprisonment viewed in isolation, but also by the religious content of that experience.

A jury could then be instructed to award damages only for the mental anguish the plaintiff would have suffered had the tort been committed by a secular actor in a secular setting. Juries are frequently asked to exclude certain sources of injury—in this case religious sources—when calculating damages, and this procedure would allow plaintiffs' secular claims to go forward while protecting defendants' First Amendment rights.

V

The Court today essentially bars all recovery for mental anguish damages stemming from allegedly religiously motivated, intentional invasions of bodily integrity committed against members of a religious group. This overly broad holding not only conflicts with well-settled legal and constitutional principles, it will also prove to be dangerous in practice. Texas courts have been and will continue to be confronted with cases in which a congregant suffers physical or psychological injury as a result of violent or unlawful, but religiously sanctioned, acts. In these cases, the Court's holding today will force the lower courts to deny the plaintiff recovery of emotional damages if the defendant alleges that some portion thereof stemmed from the religious content of the experience—unless the trial court is able to anticipate that the case will fall under the Court's rather vague exception.

I would affirm the court of appeals' judgment. Because the Court instead dismisses the case for lack of jurisdiction, I respectfully dissent.

■ JUSTICE GREEN filed a dissenting opinion.

Because the fundamental principles of Texas common law do not conflict with the Free Exercise Clause, courts can and should decide cases like this according to neutral principles of tort law. If a plaintiff's case can be made without relying on religious doctrine, the defendant must be required to respond in kind.[1] Though not always a simple task for courts, "the promise of nonentanglement and neutrality inherent in the neutral-principles approach more than compensates for what will be occasional problems in application." In contrast, today's decision ignores the rule that "courts must not presume to determine the place of a particular belief in a religion or the plausibility of a religious claim," *Smith*, replacing it with a far more dangerous practice: a judicial attempt to "balance against the importance of general laws the significance of religious practice," "The First Amendment's protection of religious liberty does not require this." The trial court heeded these admonishments, but the Court today does not. For these reasons, and for those expressed by the Chief Justice, I respectfully dissent.

■ JUSTICE JOHNSON, dissenting.

. . . The Court says that intangible, psychological injury, without more, "cannot ordinarily serve as a basis for a tort claim against a church or its members for its religious practices." I agree. But rather than preclude recovery for physical injuries and pain such as are involved in this case in which there are also claims for subsequently-occurring emotional injuries that relate to both the physical restraint and religious practices, I would preclude damages for those emotional injuries for which there is any evidence of causation by religious beliefs or teachings. This would prevent the "entanglement" with First Amendment issues with which the Court is properly concerned. I would not make that preclusion an affirmative defense as Chief Justice Jefferson advocates because it is hard to see how such an affirmative defense would work in a practical sense. It would require presenting evidence of and, at least to some degree, evaluating the religious beliefs involved. And religious beliefs in many, if not most, instances are not just beliefs—they are among individuals' most deeply-held convictions. Asking jurors to separate themselves from convictions as to their own or another's religious beliefs and to dispassionately evaluate damages related to those beliefs, in my view, asks too much of them.

---

[1] This case is not about sanctioning voluntary religious practices. If Schubert had consented to the church's actions, the consent—under our familiar, neutral principles of tort law—would have completely defeated her claims. The jury, however, found that Schubert had not consented, and Pleasant Glade does not challenge that conclusion. When faced with an otherwise valid tort claim, Pleasant Glade's religious motivation is not a defense.

I would hold that whether alleged mental and emotional damages resulted to any degree from religious beliefs and teachings should be determined by the trial court as a matter of law. Evidence of religious practices and beliefs should be precluded by means of pretrial hearings or motions in limine, as was done for the most part in this case. If the question could not be decided until after all the evidence was presented, the trial court could either direct a verdict as to damages other than those from physical injury and pain or submit separate questions as to each element of damages so the First Amendment issue as to emotional or psychological damages could be properly isolated. The trial court could then consider granting judgment notwithstanding the verdict as to emotional damages. Limiting evidence and submitting a separate damage question for physical injuries and pain protects all interests involved: the individual claiming damages, the church, and members of the church.

NOTES AND QUESTIONS

1.   What is the holding of *Schubert*? Does *Schubert* hold that the First Amendment protects assault and battery? If a church believed that its practice of "laying on hands" justified lightly choking people during religious rituals, would the church be immune from liability?

2.   Who offers the more accurate interpretation of *Smith* and the requirements of free exercise, the majority or the dissents? According to Chief Justice Jefferson, "[t]his sweeping immunity is inconsistent with United States Supreme Court precedent and extends far beyond the protections our Constitution affords religious conduct." Is that argument correct?

3.   Does consideration of a consent defense in a tort case against a religious organization always involve entanglement with religious doctrine? Do you agree with Professor Lund that if "Schubert consented to the exorcism, then her intentional tort claims should fail for reasons unrelated to the religious context of her injuries. If Schubert did not consent, then her claims should succeed because the elements of the tort are satisfied and because that same lack of consent simultaneously vitiates any claim of church autonomy."? Christopher C. Lund, Free Exercise Reconceived: The Logic and Limits of *Hosanna-Tabor*, 108 Nw. U. L. Rev. 1183, 1219 (2014).

4.   Justice Medina's opinion relied on the reasoning of a Ninth Circuit case, Paul v. Watchtower Bible & Tract Soc'y, 819 F.2d 875 (9th Cir. 1987), cert. denied, 484 U.S. 926 (1987). Janice Paul sued the Jehovah's Witnesses for the common-law torts of defamation, invasion of privacy, fraud, and outrageous conduct when church members shunned her after she withdrew from church membership. Under Jehovah's Witnesses doctrine, members who voluntarily disassociate themselves from the church are shunned by other church members who are not allowed to associate with them or even to say hello. The Ninth Circuit ruled that the Jehovah's Witnesses enjoyed a First Amendment privilege to engage in the

religious practice of shunning and dismissed the lawsuit. Does *Paul* govern *Schubert*?

According to the Ninth Circuit opinion, "The harms suffered by Paul as a result of her shunning by the Jehovah's Witnesses are clearly not of the type that would justify the imposition of tort liability for religious conduct. No physical assault or battery occurred. Intangible or emotional harms cannot ordinarily serve as a basis for maintaining a tort cause of action against a church for its practices—or against its members." Id. at 883. Did assault and battery occur in *Schubert*? Was the *Schubert* majority confused about the connection between the physical injury and the intangible harm of the exorcism when it stated Laura's case was "not about her physical injuries"? See Thomas Clark, Exorcising Our Free Exercise Jurisprudence: A New Interpretation of Free Exercise in *Pleasant Glade Assembly of God v. Schubert*, 7 First Amend. L. Rev. 350 (2009) (explaining the confusion in the majority's treatment of the relationship between the physical and intangible injuries in *Schubert*).

Marian Guinn joined the Church of Christ when she moved to Collinsville, Oklahoma. Several years later the Elders confronted her with a rumor that she was having sexual relations with a man who was not a member of the church, and Guinn admitted fornication. Under church rules, she was then subject to discipline consistent with the New Testament's Gospel of St. Matthew, 18:13–17. The Elders confronted Guinn several times outside the church, and then warned her that they would "withdraw fellowship" unless she stopped sinning, meaning that they would read to the congregation the scriptures Guinn had violated and then refuse to acknowledge her presence. Guinn and her lawyer wrote to the church abandoning her membership, but the disciplinary process continued because Church Elders believe that one can never withdraw from membership. The Elders told the congregation about Guinn's sin. The jury awarded $205,000 in actual and $185,000 in punitive damages for the torts of outrage and invasion of privacy. Is the verdict consistent with the First Amendment? See Guinn v. Church of Christ, 775 P.2d 766 (Okla. 1989) (upholding verdict for post-membership claims). Should Guinn be allowed to recover damages for the Elders' pre-withdrawal meetings when they explained what withdrawal of fellowship entails? According to the dissenting judge in *Guinn*:

> upon joining the Church of Christ, Parishioner expressly and impliedly consented to the Church's doctrine and was subject to its disciplinary procedures. The actions of the Elders taken against her were consistent with Church rules and laws both prior to and after her attempted unilateral withdrawal of membership. In my view, her withdrawal has no effect on the Elders' actions. . . . I therefore would hold the Elders of the Church of Christ are free to discipline Parishioner as a Church member (and former member) under the protection of the First Amendment without State interference and Parishioner may not escape such discipline by unilaterally withdrawing her membership.

Guinn, 775 P.2d at 797. Do you agree with the majority or the dissent in *Guinn*? Can *Guinn* be reconciled with *Paul* and *Schubert*? Did Laura Schubert "impliedly consent" to the assault and battery connected with the exorcism?

Did Guinn possess a First Amendment right to change her religion? Should this right be protected in international law, even if some religions, such as Islam, recognize that "Muslims have full religious freedom to practice Islam, but there is no right to leave Islam"? See Abdullahi A. An-Na'im, Religious Minorities under Islamic Law and the Limits of Cultural Relativism, 9 Hum. Rts. Q. 1, 11–12 (1987).

5. A jury awarded Judith Dadd $317,255.68 for claims against Mount Hope Church and David Williams (Mount Hope's pastor) for negligence, false light, libel, and slander. Dadd was injured after responding to Pastor Williams' altar call, when Williams and other ministers pray over parishioners who approach the altar. "Sometimes, congregants who answer the altar call fall to the ground, a phenomenon referred to as 'slain in the spirit.'" While being slain in the spirit, Dadd fell over and injured her head. Dadd and others testified that Williams had assured congregants that ushers were trained to catch people as they fell and that ushers had caught other congregants on the day Dadd was injured. The appeals court held that the defendants owed Dadd a duty under state tort law and upheld the damages for negligence. See Dadd v. Mount Hope Church & International Outreach Ministries, Not Reported in N.W.2d, 2009 WL 961516 (Mich.App. 2009). The decision never mentioned the First Amendment. Was that a mistake in analysis? Would the damages be overturned under *Schubert*? Should the negligence lawsuit have been dismissed?

Dorothy Kubala sued the Hartford, Connecticut Diocese after she attended a Catholic Charismatic healing service at St. Augustine's Church. After she approached the altar and was prayed over, she fell backwards and injured her head. A Connecticut court dismissed the lawsuit, concluding Kubala cannot rely on neutral principles of secular law to resolve the dispute because her claims cannot be taken out of the religious context in which the incident occurred. Kubala v. Hartford Roman Catholic Diocesan, 41 A.3d 351 (Conn. Super. 2011). Is an altar call like an exorcism?

In another Connecticut case, Kathleen Brady sought to light a votive candle at Saint Mary's Star of the Sea Church. As she climbed up a set of stairs with loose pads to reach the candles, a pad slipped and Brady fell, setting her blouse on fire. Should her lawsuit be dismissed as *Kubala* was? Church officials argued that lighting candles is a religious exercise "in remembrance that our prayers are rising to God." See Brady v. Star of the Sea Church Corp. of Unionville, No. HHDCV085022030S, 2012 WL 6846403, at *4 (Conn. Super. Ct. Dec. 14, 2012) (distinguishing *Kubala* because "[a]ccording to the undisputed facts supported by the submitted affidavits and as presented by counsel for both parties at oral argument, the church was open for the lighting of votive candles, prior to Mass; the lighting of the candles was invited, but not required, and was outside the context of an organized religious service as there was no religious ceremony taking place at the time."). What do you think of Professor Lund's argument:

> *Kubala* illustrates all the dangers that can arise from thoughtlessly applying regular tort rules to constitutionally protected behavior. The plaintiff probably sees this case as easy. She was injured, the church caused her injuries, and so the church should pay. But her suit really claims that the healing service here was illegal. That is strong language, but it is the right language. Torts are illegal acts. Tort liability is government regulation, legally indistinguishable from a civil fine. If Dorothy Kubala wins this case, it is a judicial declaration that the way the church conducted this healing service was illegal. And it will threaten charismatic healing services everywhere.
>
> My problem is with courts that fail to appreciate what is at stake. There is a case [*Dadd*] whose facts are almost identical to *Kubala*, where liability was upheld on appeal without the appellate court detecting even the slightest constitutional problem.

Christopher C. Lund, Free Exercise Reconceived: The Logic and Limits of *Hosanna-Tabor*, 108 Nw. U. L. Rev. 1183, 1212–13 (2014). How would Professor Lund analyze the result in *Brady*?

6. *Faith Healing.* The Christian Science Church was founded in Boston in 1879 by Mary Baker Eddy, after Eddy recovered from an injury while reading about Jesus. Her book, *Science and Health with Key to the Scriptures*, describes the philosophy of Christian Science. See David Levinson, Religion: A Cross-Cultural Dictionary 42 (1996). "Christian Scientists hold that behind all diseases are mental factors rooted in the human mind's blindness to God's presence and our authentic relation to God, revealed in the life of Christ. They hold that treatment is a form of prayer or communion with God in which God's reality and power, admitted and witnessed to, become so real as to eclipse the temporal 'reality' of disease and pain." Stephen Gottschalk, Spiritual Healing on Trial: A Christian Scientist Reports, Christian Century, June 22–29, 1988, at 602.

Twelve-year-old Andrew Wantland, the son of Gayle Quigley, suffered from juvenile diabetes. He became sick while living with his father and grandmother, who put him under the care of Christian Science practitioners. Prayer treatment can be done from a distance, over the telephone, as it was in Andrew's case for several days until an on-call Christian Scientist nurse visited him. After feeling sick for three days, Andrew was emaciated, vomiting and unable to eat or drink when his father and grandmother called 911. Andrew was pronounced dead at the hospital after the ambulance picked him up in response to the 911 call. No one called Quigley. Quigley sued the grandmother and the Christian Scientists arguing that the church members owed her a duty. Do you agree? Should Quigley be able to succeed in a lawsuit against the church?

See Quigley v. First Church of Christ, Scientist, 65 Cal.App.4th 1027, 76 Cal.Rptr.2d 792 (1998) (dismissing lawsuit).

Some states exempt Christian Scientist parents from liability for the death of their children from prayer treatment. Mass. Gen. Law ch. 273, § 1 (1986). Do such statutes violate the First Amendment? See Walker v. Superior Court, 47 Cal.3d 112, 253 Cal.Rptr. 1, 763 P.2d 852 (1988). What balance should the courts and legislatures strike between their concern to promote children's health and the religious freedom of Christian Scientist parents? According to Christian Scientists, "healing in Christian Science has been regular and tangible—not the exception—and it cannot be dismissed as merely 'doing nothing' or waiting on natural processes." Christian Science: A Sourcebook of Contemporary Materials 183 (1990). See also Gottschalk, supra (arguing that parents, like the state, want to protect their children and have good reason to believe that Christian Science healing is as or more effective than other medicine).

Medical treatment does not always work. Are courts competent to determine if Christian Science prayer is effective? Or must every lawsuit about Christian Science healing be dismissed because the courts lack the competence to review prayer?

7.   *Clergy Malpractice.* In his book about a "landmark" tort case, *Nally v. Grace Community Church of the Valley*, Mark Weitz explained that before the case was filed in 1980, "the notion of suing a priest, clergyman, or a church would have been almost sacrilegious for the vast majority of Americans throughout our 200-year history. If such a thing were even suggested to most Americans in prior generations they would have replied that 'No one sues God, or any of God's servants, for goodness' sake.'" See Mark A. Weitz, Clergy Malpractice in America: Nally v. Grace Community Church of the Valley 1 (2001). After considering the following history of the case, do you think that clergy malpractice should be recognized as a tort today?

The parents of Kenneth Nally filed a wrongful death and intentional infliction of emotional distress lawsuit against Grace Community Church alleging that their son committed suicide due to the negligent failure of church counselors to refer Kenneth for psychiatric counseling after he demonstrated suicidal tendencies. Among the contested items in the case was a biblical counseling tape that included one of the church's pastors preaching "suicide is one of the ways that the Lord takes home a disobedient believer." The case went through several appeals as the California courts struggled to identify the relationship between tort law and religious freedom.

As the Weitz book explains in detail, *Nally* had many stages between its initial filing on March 31, 1980, and the California Supreme Court's final decision dismissing the lawsuit on November 23, 1988. See id. After the first trial judge, Thomas C. Murphy, dismissed the Nallys' lawsuit, the Court of Appeal reinstated it in a 1984 decision holding that the First Amendment "does not license intentional infliction of emotional distress in the name of religion and cannot shield defendants from liability for wrongful death for a suicide caused by such conduct." See Nally v. Grace Community Church of the Valley, 157 Cal.App.3d 912, 204 Cal.Rptr. 303 (1984) (depublished), hearing denied. Although the California Supreme Court did not grant review of that decision, it ordered the decision depublished, for reasons that are unclear. See Weitz, supra at 97 (perhaps they did not want a case recognizing the tort of clergy malpractice on the books). Why would it be a problem for a court to recognize a tort of clergy malpractice?

The second time around, the California Supreme Court granted review and decided the case for Grace on tort law grounds without reaching the First Amendment issues, holding that nontherapist counselors do not have a duty to refer persons to licensed mental health professionals once suicide becomes a foreseeable risk. See Nally v. Grace Cmty. Church of the Valley, 47 Cal.3d 278, 763 P.2d 948 (1988). Concurring Justice Kaufman believed that although there was a duty, Grace's ministers had not breached it.

Although Kenneth Nally's case against Grace Community Church was eventually dismissed, since then, according to Professor Idleman, cultural, institutional and doctrinal developments have increased plaintiffs' chances of success in lawsuits against religious organizations and the "general rule of not adjudicating tort claims against religious defendants" has eroded. See Scott C. Idleman, Tort Liability, Religious Entities, and the Decline of Constitutional Protection, 75 Ind. L.J. 219, 271 (2000). Those developments include increases in tort litigation, extensive publicity about sexual abuse by members of the clergy, and a change in the Supreme Court's First Amendment jurisprudence, which now emphasizes equal treatment of religious and non-religious organizations instead of distinctive legal treatment for churches. See id.

After *Nally*, however, courts consistently refused to recognize a tort of clergy malpractice in "pure" counseling cases. New questions about tort liability arose, however, after repeated lawsuits were filed about clergy sexual misconduct with their parishioners. The courts have split over the extent of civil liability by clergy and their employers for reasons spelled out in *Nally*. What kinds of lawsuit, if any, should be available to adult church members who have sexual relations with clergy? Should any charges of sexual misconduct by clergy against adult church members be justiciable, or does church autonomy require that complaints be resolved by internal church disciplinary rules only? What about individuals who do not belong to the church, but who speak to clergy in order to receive counseling? Should they be allowed to sue? If lawsuits are acceptable, who are the appropriate defendants: the minister alone, or the minister's employers as well? See Ira C. Lupu & Robert W. Tuttle, Sexual Misconduct and Ecclesiastical Immunity, 2004 BYU L. Rev. 1789, 1820–21 (2004) ("Where courts can identify and apply criteria that encompass secular as well as religious roles, the liability of clergy for noncriminal sexual relationships may appropriately follow. By contrast, clergy-specific triggers of liability offend constitutional norms against disfavoring religion.").

How do you think the courts should handle tort liability in cases like the following lawsuit for negligent hiring, supervision and retention, and breach of fiduciary duty, in the sexual abuse context?

Redwing v. Catholic Bishop for the Diocese of Memphis

Supreme Court of Tennessee, 2012.
363 S.W.3d 436.

■ WILLIAM C. KOCH, JR., J., delivered the opinion of the Court, in which CORNELIA A. CLARK, C.J., JANICE M. HOLDER, GARY R. WADE, and SHARON G. LEE, J.J., joined.

This appeal involves a dispute regarding the civil liability of the Catholic Diocese of Memphis for acts of child sexual abuse allegedly perpetrated by one of its priests in the 1970s. A victim of this alleged abuse filed suit against the Bishop of the Catholic Diocese of Memphis in the Circuit Court for Shelby County seeking monetary damages. The Diocese moved to dismiss the complaint, arguing that the ecclesiastical abstention doctrine deprived state courts of subject matter jurisdiction and that the victim's claims were barred by the statute of limitations. We have concluded that the Court of Appeals erred by concluding that the state courts lack subject matter jurisdiction over the victim's claims and that the victim's claims are barred by the statute of limitations.

I

The facts in this opinion are drawn from the allegations in the complaint. Norman Redwing was born in August 1960 and was raised in a Roman Catholic home. His childhood was turbulent. He was raped by an adult male when he was seven years old. The trauma remained long after the event, and by the time he was twelve, Mr. Redwing began to run away from home on a regular basis.

Between 1972 and 1974, Mr. Redwing attended mass regularly at Holy Names Catholic Church in Memphis. There he came to know Father Milton Guthrie. On the occasions when Mr. Redwing ran away from home, Fr. Guthrie allowed him to stay at the church. These acts of kindness caused Mr. Redwing to admire and respect priests in general and Fr. Guthrie in particular. Mr. Redwing respected Fr. Guthrie not only for his acts of kindness but also for his involvement in the civil rights movement.

Eventually, Mr. Redwing confided to Fr. Guthrie that he had been raped when he was seven years old. At first, Fr. Guthrie responded with kindness and understanding. He made breakfast for Mr. Redwing when he spent the night at the church and gave him pocket money from time to time. However, after a time, Mr. Redwing alleges that Fr. Guthrie began to take advantage of him. He states that Fr. Guthrie began to touch him in inappropriate ways and eventually inveigled him into a physical relationship that included oral sex.

In August 2008, over thirty years after the alleged acts of sexual abuse occurred, Mr. Redwing filed suit in the Circuit Court for Shelby County against the "Catholic Bishop for the Diocese of Memphis." He did not name Fr. Guthrie as a defendant based on his understanding that Fr. Guthrie had died. The Diocese denied the allegations in Mr. Redwing's complaint.

This case squarely presents two issues. The first issue is whether, pursuant to the ecclesiastical abstention doctrine, Tennessee's courts should decline to adjudicate Mr. Redwing's claims for breach of fiduciary duty and for negligent hiring, supervision, and retention against the Diocese. If Tennessee's courts possess subject matter jurisdiction to adjudicate all or any of these claims, the second issue is whether Mr. Redwing's claims are barred by the statute of limitations.

II

[The court reviewed the church property cases covered in Section A and described the ecclesiastical abstention policy of *Watson v. Jones* and the neutral principles of law approach of *Jones v. Wolf.*] Over the course of more than a century, Tennessee's courts have continued to recognize ecclesiastically required jurisdictional limitations on civil courts. Thus, the ecclesiastical abstention doctrine has been applied to preclude judicial review of matters involving religious institutions that are ecclesiastical and internal in nature. However, the application of the ecclesiastical abstention doctrine has not been extended to "questions of property or personal rights."

There can be little question that the state and federal courts are currently sharply divided regarding the courts' subject matter jurisdiction over suits involving claims similar to those asserted by Mr. Redwing in this case. Our analysis begins with the recognition that religious institutions exist and function in the context of the broader secular community. The courts do not inhibit the free exercise of religion simply by opening their doors to a suit involving a religious organization. Thus, the weight of authority recognizes that religious institutions are not above the law, and that, like other societal institutions, they may be amenable to suits involving property rights, torts, and criminal conduct.

In civil cases, the ecclesiastical abstention doctrine is implicated only when the alleged improper conduct that gave rise to the lawsuit is "rooted in religious belief." . . . Adopting a more expansive application of the ecclesiastical abstention doctrine runs the risk of placing religious institutions in a preferred position, . . . and favoring religious institutions over secular institutions could give rise to Establishment Clause concerns. . . . [T]he justifications for the ecclesiastical abstention doctrine are "at their lowest ebb" in circumstances where religious institutions or their employees "harm innocent and unconsenting third parties."

In this case, the Diocese has not asserted any religious foundation for the alleged conduct upon which Mr. Redwing's claims are based. In fact, the Diocese strongly insists that any such actions would be directly contrary to the beliefs, teachings, and principles of the Roman Catholic Church. The Diocese does contend, however, that any adjudication of Mr. Redwing's negligent hiring, supervision, and retention claims will necessarily require addressing church doctrine and practices.

Mr. Redwing is not free to convert his tort claims into an assault on the religious doctrines, practices, and customs of the Roman Catholic Church. Several of the allegations in Mr. Redwing's amended complaint stray into the protected domain of religious liberty. However, determining whether the ecclesiastical abstention doctrine requires the dismissal of a complaint does not depend on whether the complaint contains some allegations that would be improper for adjudication. Rather, it depends on whether the complaint contains claims that Tennessee's courts may properly adjudicate. If the complaint contains one or more of these claims, then Tennessee's civil courts are not entirely without subject matter jurisdiction over this case.

We find that Mr. Redwing's amended complaint contains claims over which Tennessee's civil courts plainly have subject matter jurisdiction. Mr. Redwing asserts that the Diocese was aware or should have been aware that Fr. Guthrie presented a danger to children and, nevertheless, placed him in a position where it was foreseeable that he would sexually abuse a child, as he allegedly did Mr. Redwing, on church property. The Diocese denies the existence of any religious basis for enabling sexual predators. Accordingly, based on the record before us, it appears that Mr. Redwing will be able to pursue his negligent hiring, supervision, and retention claims without asking the trial court to resolve any religious disputes or to rely on religious doctrine. In other words, Mr. Redwing's claims can be pursued based upon breach of a secular duty by the Diocese without requiring the court to resolve disputes over religious questions.

We have [also] concluded that the ecclesiastical abstention doctrine does not impose an absolute bar on claims for breach of fiduciary duty against religious institutions ... A religious institution's fiduciary obligations cannot be predicated on a religious duty and cannot arise solely from the relationship between the institution and its members. Thus, breach of fiduciary obligation claims against religious institutions remain quite rare. However, the status of a defendant as a religious institution does not, by itself, preclude the existence of a fiduciary relationship and the possibility of a breach of fiduciary duty claim. Accordingly, we find that Tennessee's civil courts may exercise jurisdiction over a breach of fiduciary duty claim against a religious institution, as long as the fiduciary relationship is not based on a religious duty or is not inextricably tied to a religious duty.

IV

Turning to the three elements to be considered in the context of a statute of limitations defense, there is no question in this case regarding the applicable statute of limitations or the length of the limitations period. Even though Mr. Redwing's complaint is less than specific about when the alleged sexual abuse occurred, there is no dispute that Mr. Redwing was a minor at the time. It is also undisputed that Mr. Redwing's eighteenth birthday occurred on August 18, 1978 and that, in accordance with Tenn. Code Ann. § 28–1–106, he had one year from that date to file suit against Fr. Guthrie and any other person or entity that caused the alleged abuse. There is likewise no dispute that Mr. Redwing did not file suit against the Diocese until August 15, 2008—almost twenty-nine years after the statute of limitations would have expired. [Redwing then argued that equitable estoppel and fraudulent concealment should prevent the diocese from using the statute of limitations defense.]

[T]he essence of an equitable estoppel claim when it is used to defeat a statute of limitations defense is that the defendant intentionally induced the plaintiff to delay filing suit within the time required by the statute of limitations . . . The factual allegations in Mr. Redwing's amended complaint are inconsistent with an equitable estoppel claim.

Mr. Redwing's complaint contains allegations that both the Roman Catholic Church and the Diocese knew, but covered up, the clergy's sexual abuse of minors and that the Diocese was aware that Fr. Guthrie sexually abused minors *and* misled Mr. Redwing and his family about its knowledge and involvement. Considered in the light most favorable to Mr. Redwing, the allegation that the Diocese misled Mr. Redwing and his family could be construed to mean that at some point, Mr. Redwing or his family asked the Diocese about its knowledge of Fr. Guthrie's conduct and that the Diocese's response misled them. The Court of Appeals has correctly recognized that this circumstance could amount to fraudulent concealment.

For the purposes of both the discovery rule and the doctrine of fraudulent concealment, the pivotal issue is whether Mr. Redwing would have discovered the Diocese's allegedly wrongful acts had he exercised reasonable care and diligence . . . We must, at least at this juncture, take the allegations in Mr. Redwing's complaint as true and draw all reasonable inferences in Mr. Redwing's favor.

V

For the reasons discussed above, we conclude that the Court of Appeals correctly determined that the trial court has subject matter jurisdiction over Mr. Redwing's negligent supervision claims against the Diocese but that the Court of Appeals erred by holding that the trial court lacked subject matter jurisdiction over Mr. Redwing's negligent hiring and retention claims. Additionally, we find that the trial court has subject matter jurisdiction over Mr. Redwing's breach of fiduciary duty claim but caution that Mr. Redwing may not proceed with this claim if it is based solely on duties that are either religious or inextricably intertwined with religious duties. We also conclude that the Court of Appeals erred by finding that the statute of limitations barred Mr. Redwing's negligent hiring, retention, and supervision claims against the Diocese. We remand this case to the trial court for further proceedings consistent with this opinion.

NOTES AND QUESTIONS

1. *Respondeat Superior, Negligent Hiring, Retention, and Supervision.* Why would the Court of Appeals have distinguished between negligent supervision and negligent hiring and retention claims? Should one tort be more protected by the First Amendment than the others? Why did the Diocese argue that these claims would inevitably implicate court review of religious doctrine? Is a religious issue at stake any time a church gives its reasons for hiring or retaining a priest? Or is the court correct that these claims can be adjudicated without encroaching upon religious freedom?

Are negligent selection and training lawsuits equivalent to negligent ordination and so always barred by the First Amendment? See Swanson v. Roman Catholic Bishop, 692 A.2d 441 (Me. 1997) ("'it would . . . be inappropriate and unconstitutional for this Court to determine after the fact that the ecclesiastical authorities negligently supervised or retained the defendant . . . *Any award of damages would have a chilling effect leading indirectly to state control over the future conduct of affairs of a religious denomination.*'") but see Malicki v. Doe, 814 So.2d 347, 361 (Fla. 2002) (In case where priest engaged in sexual assault and battery of a minor and an adult, court allowed negligent hiring and supervision lawsuit to proceed; "we thus give no greater or lesser deference to tortious conduct committed on third parties by religious organizations than we do to tortious conduct committed on third parties by non-religious entities."). Should they be barred by the holding of *Hosanna-Tabor*, p. 344, infra?

Respondeat superior is the tort theory that holds an employer "liable for the employee's or agent's wrongful acts committed within the scope of the employment." Black's Law Dictionary (8th ed. 2004). Religious organizations employ some clergy who engage in the types of sexual misconduct described in *Redwing*. Should the organizations be subject to lawsuits based on *respondeat superior*?

Edna and Robert Destefano went to Roman Catholic Father Dennis Grabrian for marital counseling, during which Grabrian began an affair with Edna. Edna sued Father Grabrian's employer, the Roman Catholic

Diocese of Colorado Springs, for negligence. On what theory of liability, if any, should that lawsuit proceed? See Destefano v. Grabrian, 763 P.2d 275 (Colo. 1988) (*respondeat superior* not allowed because Grabrian's conduct was not within the scope of his employment, but the diocese could be sued for negligent supervision). Should *respondeat superior* be allowed if the priest used sex in order to teach the sacraments ("at least one sexual encounter was presented . . . as similar to Holy Communion")? See Martinelli v. Bridgeport, 989 F.Supp. 110, 118 (D. Conn. 1997) (yes, because there was a genuine dispute as to whether the priest's activities represented a "total departure from the diocese's business").

Grandmaster Lu founded the True Buddha School and is recognized by his followers as a living Buddha. S.H.C., a follower of Lu's, became sick with headaches and went to the temple for blessings. Lu told her that he could cure the headaches and save her life through the "Twin Body Blessing," which was sexual intercourse. S.H.C. later sued the Buddhist temple for negligent supervision. The Buddhists believed that they had an "obligation of obedience" to the grandmaster. Moreover, Buddhist precepts stated that, if one believes the guru is phony, he should leave the guru but never criticize or slander him. May the court hear the negligent supervision case? See S.H.C. v. Sheng-Yen Lu, 113 Wash.App. 511, 54 P.3d 174 (2002) (case dismissed because there was no way to resolve the case without reviewing religious doctrine: "Thus, although the alleged activities of Grandmaster Lu may be secular in this case, that does not address whether a civil court may avoid interpreting doctrine of the True Buddha religion to address whether the Temple is liable for negligent supervision.").

Mary Moses Tenantry had a long history of mental illness. She was sexually abused as a child and had multiple personality disorder, but her disease appeared to be in remission when she became a parishioner at St. Philip and St. James Episcopal Church in Denver. Father Paul Robinson became her counselor there and engaged in oral sex with her during their counseling sessions. Her mental illness was reaggravated after her affair with Father Robinson ended, and she and her husband divorced. Is the diocese liable under respondeat superior? See Moses v. Diocese of Colo., 863 P.2d 310 (Colo. 1993) (en banc) (no *respondeat superior* because sex was not within the scope of Father Robinson's employment). In the Episcopal Church, it is the local vestry and not the diocese that hires Episcopal priests. Father Myers, the priest who hired Robinson at St. Philip and St. James, believed that Bishop Frey considered Robinson to be "bishop material"; neither Bishop Frey nor the Diocese told Myers that Robinson's personnel file "indicated Father Robinson had problems with depression, low self-esteem, and possessed a 'sexual identification ambiguity.' " Id. at 315. When Moses' relatives told Father Myers about the sexual relationship between Moses and Robinson, he urged them to keep it quiet because "there were worse things a priest could do." After Myers eventually informed the bishop of the relationship, the bishop urged Moses to keep her relationship with Robinson secret and told her he would take care of things. Moses felt guilty about the relationship and believed the bishop could influence her salvation. The bishop ordered counseling for Robinson, but did nothing for Moses, who later broke down when she encountered Father Robinson and learned he had received another promotion in the church.

Robinson was bankrupt; should Moses' lawsuit against Bishop Frey and the Diocese succeed? See id. at 318 (upholding jury verdict of $728,100 for breach of fiduciary duty and negligent hiring and supervision). Are there good reasons to hold the bishop and the diocese liable for a priest's misconduct with a mentally disturbed woman? See id. at 321 (the facts of *Moses* "indicate that an organization, confronted with the misdeeds of one of its agents, assumed control of the matter and in the process of protecting itself injured a vulnerable individual"); see also Martinelli, infra, (basing liability of diocese on numerous connections between the diocese and the abused youth. "For example, the diocese ran the high school that Martinelli attended, knew that Martinelli participated with a group of boys in sessions with Father Brett who acted as a mentor and spiritual advisor, encouraged Brett to work with the youth of the church, and received reports from other victims whom Brett had abused.").

Do you agree with the following commentary on the *Moses* case?

The *Moses* opinion is full of danger signs for religious organizations. It is not hard to see the ways in which [Moses's] troubled past would lead the courts, and jurors, to be sympathetic to her plight. But it is equally easy to see, if one is willing to look, that the bishop did not hold himself out as her counselor, nor did he represent that he was acting in her interest rather than the institutional interests of the church in clergy management and crisis control. The expert's testimony that the bishop did not listen to [Moses's] side of the story or help her explore her feelings or her planned course of action, is quite inconsistent with a claim that he was acting as her spiritual counselor rather than the caretaker of the church's interests. When courts allow juries, under vague and general instructions, to permit the institutional position of bishop or pastoral leader to become dispositive factors in the imposition of fiduciary duties, courts are effectively imposing upon religious organizations a state-backed vision of how religious organizations should conduct pastoral relations. As understandable as those normative expectations may be, their application to religious organizations in cases like Moses is in serious tension with the First Amendment considerations associated with the doctrines of ecclesiastical immunity.

Lupu & Tuttle, supra, p. 251, at 1838. Do you agree with Lupu and Tuttle that *Moses* goes too far, and that the following standard offers a better way to balance the important interests at stake?

We believe this balancing is best accomplished by limiting liability for supervisory wrongs to situations in which supervisors, with requisite authority to act, have actual knowledge of clergy propensity for wrongdoing, or in which such supervisors act in reckless disregard of the risks of such wrongdoing. A similar standard already reconciles tort considerations and First

Amendment concerns in the law of libel, and we argue that a similar structure of reconciliation can operate successfully here.

Id. at 1795. How could that standard be applied in *Redwing*?

2.   *Suits Against the Clergy Member: Clergy Malpractice and Breach of Fiduciary Duty.* In Colorado, Edna and Robert Destefano went to Roman Catholic Father Dennis Grabrian for marital counseling, during which Grabrian began an affair with Edna. Both Edna and Robert later sued Grabrian for negligence and breach of fiduciary duty. The court dismissed Edna's negligence claim against Grabrian because it did not recognize the tort of clergy malpractice, and Robert's negligence claim against Grabrian, because it was a heart balm lawsuit prohibited by Colorado law. (A heart balm statute is a "state law that abolishes the rights of action for monetary damages as solace for the emotional trauma occasioned by a loss of love and relationship. The abolished rights of action include alienation of affections, breach of promise to marry, criminal conversation, and seduction of a person over the legal age of consent." Black's Law Dictionary 740 (8th ed. 2004)). Both parties' breach of fiduciary lawsuits against Grabrian were allowed to proceed, however, because examining a fiduciary relationship does not involve review of church doctrine. See Destefano v. Grabrian, 763 P.2d 275 (Colo. 1988). In New Jersey, F.G. alleged inappropriate physical contact with the minister but no sexual intercourse; should the lawsuit proceed? See F.G. v. MacDonell, 150 N.J. 550, 696 A.2d 697 (1997) (allowing lawsuit for breach of fiduciary duty).

Should courts bar lawsuits for clergy malpractice but allow them for breach of fiduciary duty, as Colorado and New Jersey did? Is there a real difference between the two types of lawsuit? See Moses v. Diocese of Colo., 863 P.2d 310, 321 n.13 (Colo. 1993) ("The fundamental difference between the two causes of action is the former is a breach of trust and does not require a professional relationship or a professional standard of care, while the latter is an action for negligence based on a professional relationship and a professional standard of care."); Janna Satz Nugent, Note and Comment: A Higher Authority: The Viability of Third Party Tort Actions Against a Religious Institution Grounded on Sexual Misconduct by a Member of the Clergy, 30 Fla. St. U. L. Rev. 957, 963 (2003) ("Beyond the bond shared between a parent and child, it is difficult to imagine a more sacred relationship than the one shared by a faithful parishioner and his or her church. Even the term 'Father,' as used by members of the clergy, invites trust and lulls loyal followers into feeling safe. This relationship must be guarded at all costs, and the Church hierarchy should be liable for failing to protect it."); but see Lupu & Tuttle, supra (arguing that courts treat religion unfairly when they find a fiduciary duty for ministers when they would not do so for other professionals in similar situations).

In Michigan, Linda Teadt sued Lutheran minister Robert Garbisch about their five-year affair. The two met when Garbisch visited Teadt's home before she underwent back surgery. She stated that he made sexual advances to her during counseling, while he argued that the affair was consensual and that he was her friend, not her counselor. Michigan does not recognize a tort of clergy malpractice. Should Teadt be allowed to sue for breach of fiduciary duty? See Teadt v. Lutheran Church Missouri Synod, 237 Mich.App. 567, 603 N.W.2d 816 (1999) (no, because the breach of fiduciary duty claim "sounded in clergy malpractice" and thus was prohibited).

In New York, Adina Marmelstein went to Orthodox Rabbi Mordecai Tendler for personal and spiritual counseling, including advice about how to find a husband. Tendler told Marmelstein that engaging in a sexual relationship with him would open her up to the world and make her more attractive to men. The two engaged in a sexual affair for three and a half years. Can Marmelstein bring a successful tort claim? Why or why not? See Marmelstein v. Kehillat New Hempstead, 11 N.Y.3d 15, 862 N.Y.S.2d 311, 892 N.E.2d 375 (2008) (case dismissed; New York does not allow heart balm torts and Marmelstein did not prove she was "uniquely vulnerable and incapable of self-protection" as a breach of fiduciary duty lawsuit requires). Were these facts outrageous enough to sustain a lawsuit for intentional infliction of emotional distress? See id. (no). Another New Yorker, Susan Langford, was diagnosed with multiple sclerosis and sought spiritual assistance. Monsignor Sivillo visited her home, where he held her hand while telling her "how he spoke to God and how as God's emissary he would see to it that the disease would go into remission." Langford said that "she lacked the power to resist the defendant's physical advances because she 'was addicted to him and the [religious] power he possessed to halt the spread of the multiple sclerosis . . . [she believed that if she angered him, she] would lose her lifeline to God and continued health.'" Presumably, unlike Marmelstein, Langford was "uniquely vulnerable and incapable of self-protection." Why would New York disallow the breach of fiduciary duty suit in these sad circumstances? See Langford v. Roman Catholic Diocese of Brooklyn, 177 Misc.2d 897, 677 N.Y.S.2d 436 (1998) ("In order to consider the validity of plaintiff's claims of dependency and vulnerability, the jury would have to weigh and evaluate, *inter alia*, the legitimacy of plaintiff's beliefs, the tenets of the faith insofar as they reflect upon a priest's ability to act as God's emissary and the nature of the healing powers of the church. . . . On the other hand, if we try to salvage plaintiff's claim by stripping her narrative of all religious nuance, what is left makes out a cause of action in seduction—a tort no longer recognized in New York—but not in breach of a fiduciary duty.").

Shelby Baucum worked for the Casa View Baptist Church in Texas as the Minister of Education and Administration (MEA). Baucum was not part of the church's spiritual counseling staff and knew that the church referred non-pastoral counseling to professionals. Church receptionist Lisa Mullinix and secretary Robyn Sanders both went to Baucum for marital counseling. They believed he was authorized by the church to provide counseling and that he had the requisite experience and training to provide marital counseling. Both women engaged in sexual relations with him; Baucum also disclosed their sexual histories to others. Baucum testified that he referred to scripture during the counseling sessions. Can the women sue him for the marital counseling, even though it was not "purely secular" because of the scriptural references? See Sanders v. Casa View Baptist Church, 134 F.3d 331, 335 (5th Cir. 1998), reh'g denied (Mar. 26, 1998), cert. denied sub nom. Baucum v. Sanders, 525 U.S. 868 (1998) (yes, the First Amendment does not require a purely secular standard; Baucum could be held to the standard of a prudent marriage counselor); see also Odenthal v. Minnesota Conf. of Seventh-Day Adventists, 649 N.W.2d 426, 434 (Minn. 2002) (minister who became sexually involved with parishioner could be held liable as "an unlicensed mental health practitioner").

Given the outcome of these breach of fiduciary duty cases against clergy, how would you describe the fiduciary duty owed to Redwing by the Diocese? According to the Tennessee Supreme Court, the court "may exercise jurisdiction over a breach of fiduciary duty claim against a religious institution, as long as the fiduciary relationship is not based on a religious duty or is not inextricably tied to a religious duty." What would be the non-religious duty owed to Redwing by the Diocese?

3. *Statute of Limitations.* Statute of limitations [SOL] laws have been changed around the country in response to the sexual abuse crisis. One major reason for the change is that victims take many years to recognize that they were abused. Courts and legislatures have recognized the need to distinguish between "the acts of abuse themselves and the injuries that result years later for many victims of childhood sexual abuse, . . . in recognition of the unique nature of childhood sexual assaults." Earle v. State, 743 A.2d 1101, 1106 (Vt. 1999).

What should happen to someone like Redwing, who suffered abuse at an early age but may not have remembered or recognized the effects of the abuse until thirty years later? Should the SOL be two years from the date of abuse, so that a 7-year-old must sue by age 9? Should it be two years from the age of majority, 18? Should it be suspended completely? California passed "window legislation," which opened the civil courts for a one year window during which all victims could file their lawsuits. Should all states pass window legislation? Or should all states abolish child abuse SOL entirely? See Marci Hamilton, Justice Denied: What American Must Do to Protect Its Children (2008). A list of state SOL legislation is available at Reform the Statute of Limitations on Child Sexual Abuse, http://www.sol-reform.com.

Catholic Church officials argue that it is unfair to church defendants to extend SOL far beyond the time of alleged abuse and that churches risk bankruptcy by being sued by multiple victims. Do you agree that expanding SOL is unfair to defendants? See, e.g., Colomb v. Roman Catholic Diocese of Burlington, Vermont, No. 2:10–cv–254, 2012 WL 4479758, *3 (D.Vt. 2012) (church argued that tort liability could interfere with the church's mission or put it out of business; court rejected church's argument that "[i]f the protections of the First Amendment are to mean anything, the government should not be allowed to shut the doors of a church and put it up for sale."). Do you think religious institutions should enjoy special protections that make it harder to sue them for sex abuse?

4. *Suing the Vatican.* Should the Vatican be subject to suit in American courts for tort suits involving Catholic priests and dioceses? In a tort lawsuit by victims of sexual abuse against the Holy See—which is both a foreign state and the central government of the Roman Catholic Church—the Sixth Circuit considered the Holy See's immunity from lawsuit under the Foreign Sovereign Immunities Act [FSIA], 28 U.S.C. § 1602 et seq. Although the Act provides foreign sovereigns with immunity from lawsuits, it contains an exception for tortious acts (1) "occurring in the United States"; (2) "caused by [a] tortious act or omission"; (3) where the alleged acts or omissions were those of a "foreign state or of any official or employee of that foreign state"; and (4) those acts or omissions were done within the scope of tortfeasor's employment. See 28 U.S.C. § 1605(a)(5); O'Bryan v. Holy See, 556 F.3d 361, 381 (6th Cir. 2009), cert. denied, 130 S.Ct. 361 (2009). The victims alleged that the Holy See's policy of complete secrecy, which required American church officials not to report the abusers' identities to criminal authorities even when the law required reporting, had contributed to their injuries. The court concluded that any actions that took place outside the United States (in particular, the decisions made by the Holy See itself including any negligent supervision based on Holy See policies) enjoyed immunity from suit. Moreover, any claims directly involving sexual abuse were outside the scope of employment. This ended the jurisdiction of the court over the Holy See and the priest abusers. The court allowed lawsuits against bishops and archbishops to proceed for their supervision of abusive clergy. Id. at 386. Why would those lawsuits be permitted? The plaintiffs in *O'Bryan* asked the court to dismiss their lawsuit. The plaintiffs' attorney explained that prior rulings about the Vatican's sovereign immunity would make a victory difficult. See Dylan T. Lovan, Plaintiffs Give Up Sexual Abuse Case Against Vatican, Associated Press, Aug. 10, 2010.

In another sexual abuse case against the Holy See, the Ninth Circuit ruled that John Doe could pursue a respondeat superior case against the Holy See based on the sexual abuse conducted by Father Ronan, an employee of the Holy See, but that Doe's claims against the Holy See for negligent retention and supervision and failure to warn were barred by the discretionary function exclusion of the FSIA. See Doe v. Holy See, 557 F.3d 1066 (9th Cir. 2009), cert. denied, 130 S.Ct. 3497 (2010). How could the Holy See be liable under respondeat superior when other cases against church officials have been dismissed on that theory because the priest was not acting within the scope of employment? See id. at 1082 (the court relied on Oregon case law, which allowed respondeat superior if conduct within the scope of employment, namely a priest's pastoral duties toward abuse victims, was "a necessary precursor to the sexual abuse and that the assaults thus were a direct outgrowth of and were engendered by conduct that was within the scope of . . . employment."). The district court eventually dismissed the lawsuit on the grounds that Ronan was not an employee of the Holy See. Do you agree? See John Breslin & Breda Heffernan, U.S. Ruling Means Vatican Not Liable Over Paedophile Priest, Belfast Telegraph, Aug. 22, 2012. John Doe withdrew his appeal of the district court's ruling that Ronan was not employed by the Vatican after Doe grew "weary of the long legal odyssey." Steven Dubois, Plaintiff Drops Abuse Case Against Vatican, (Albany) Times Union, Aug. 6, 2013.

————————

Now that you have learned about constitutional and statutory protection of religious freedom, the religious freedom of institutions and individuals, and the scope of the Establishment Clause, Chapter 7 examines the Religious Land Use and Institutionalized Persons Act (RLUIPA), which Congress passed after the Court invalidated RFRA in *Boerne v. Flores*.

CHAPTER 7

RLUIPA:
THE RELIGIOUS LAND USE AND INSTITUTIONALIZED PERSONS ACT

In Chapter 4, we studied RFRA (the Religious Freedom Restoration Act), which Congress passed in response to the Court's free exercise decision in *Smith*. This chapter focuses on congressional action to support religious freedom in the states after the Supreme Court ruled in *Boerne* that RFRA could not be applied to the states. According to RFRA's text:

(1) The framers of the Constitution, recognizing free exercise of religion as an unalienable right, secured its protection in the First Amendment to the Constitution;

(2) laws "neutral" toward religion may burden religious exercise as surely as laws intended to interfere with religious exercise;

(3) governments should not substantially burden religious exercise without compelling justification;

(4) in Employment Division v. Smith, 494 U.S. 872 (1990), the Supreme Court virtually eliminated the requirement that the government justify burdens on religious exercise imposed by laws neutral toward religion; and

(5) the compelling interest test as set forth in prior Federal court rulings is a workable test for striking sensible balances between religious liberty and competing prior governmental interests.

42 U.S.C. § 2000bb(a). The Act's stated purposes were:

(1) to restore the compelling interest test as set forth in Sherbert v. Verner, 374 U.S. 398 (1963) and Wisconsin v. Yoder, 406 U.S. 205 (1972) and to guarantee its application in all cases where free exercise of religion is substantially burdened; and

(2) to provide a claim or defense to persons whose religious exercise is substantially burdened by government.

Id. § 2000bb(b). RFRA prohibited both state and federal governments from substantially burdening a person's exercise of religion, even if the burden resulted from a rule of general applicability, unless the government could demonstrate that the burden "(1) is in furtherance of a compelling governmental interest; and (2) is the least restrictive means of furthering that compelling governmental interest." Id. § 2000bb–1(a)(b).

RFRA applied to all federal and state law. Id. § 2000bb–3(a). In City of Boerne v. Flores, 521 U.S. 507 (1997), however, the Court ruled RFRA could not be applied to the states because Congress lacked the power to pass the Act under Section 5 of the Fourteenth Amendment. The Act was not congruent or proportional with the problem of religious discrimination and so was beyond Congress' Fourteenth Amendment powers. "In contrast to the record which confronted Congress and the Judiciary in the voting rights cases," the Court observed, "RFRA's legislative record lacks examples of modern instances of generally applicable laws passed because of religious bigotry." Boerne, 521 U.S. at 530. The Court explained why applying strict scrutiny to state governments intruded on the states' sovereignty:

> Claims that a law substantially burdens someone's exercise of religion will often be difficult to contest. Requiring a State to demonstrate a compelling interest and show that it has adopted the least restrictive means of achieving that interest is the most demanding test known to constitutional law. If " 'compelling interest' really means what it says . . . many laws will not meet the test. . . . [The test] would open the prospect of constitutionally required religious exemptions from civic obligations of almost every conceivable kind." Laws valid under Smith would fall under RFRA without regard to whether they had the object of stifling or punishing free exercise. We make these observations not to reargue the position of the majority in Smith but to illustrate the substantive alteration of its holding attempted by RFRA. Even assuming RFRA would be interpreted in effect to mandate some lesser test, say one equivalent to intermediate scrutiny, the statute nevertheless would require searching judicial scrutiny of state law with the attendant likelihood of invalidation. This is a considerable congressional intrusion into the States' traditional prerogatives and general authority to regulate for the health and welfare of their citizens.

Boerne, 521 U.S. at 534. Hence, post-Boerne, state governments are held to the Smith standard in Free Exercise cases.

As we learned in Chapter 4, RFRA still applies to the federal government. See Gonzales v. O Centro Espirita Beneficente Uniao do Vegetal, 546 U.S. 418 (2006). Why? Who would be likely to file a lawsuit arguing that RFRA is unconstitutional as applied to the federal government? Who would have standing to do so?

In response to *Boerne*, Congress passed another bill protecting religious freedom, the Religious Land Use and Institutionalized Persons Act (RLUIPA), 42 U.S.C. § 2000cc et seq., which holds that the government shall not implement land use regulations that impose a substantial burden on the religious exercise of a person, or impose a substantial burden on the religious exercise of a person confined to an institution, unless the government's action "is in furtherance of a compelling governmental interest; and is the least restrictive means of furthering that compelling governmental interest." Section A focuses on the Court's RLUIPA cases about prisoners. Section B examines RLUIPA's treatment of land use.

Aware of the unconstitutionality of RFRA, Congress relied on its commerce and spending powers to enact RLUIPA; every state receives federal money for its prisons. See Marci A. Hamilton, Federalism and the Public Good: The True Story Behind the Religious Land Use and Institutionalized Persons Act, 78 Ind. L.J. 311 (2003). The narrow focus on land use and institutionalized persons was meant to respond to *Boerne*'s criticism that RFRA was a disproportionate response to the states' history of discrimination against women. Yet, as the last reading in this chapter explains, RLUIPA's effects have been anything but narrow.

We start with institutionalized persons—usually prisoners.

A. INSTITUTIONALIZED PERSONS

One criticism of RFRA was that it increased unnecessary prisoner litigation with frivolous claims about religious rights. Indeed, California Governor Pete Wilson vetoed his state's RFRA because it allowed prisoner lawsuits, which he believed would undermine the deferential standard of Turner v. Safley, 482 U.S. 78 (1987), and O'Lone v. Estate of Shabazz, 482 U.S. 342 (1987). In *Turner*, the Supreme Court clarified the standard of review for the violation of prisoners' constitutional rights, namely "when a prison regulation impinges on inmates' constitutional rights, the regulation is valid if it is reasonably related to legitimate penological interests." 482 U.S. at 89. *Shabazz* applied that deferential standard to a Free Exercise claim. See *Shabazz*, 482 U.S. at 349.

Commentators disagreed about how much extra prisoner litigation RFRA triggered before it was ruled unconstitutional. Compare Lee Boothby and Nicholas P. Miller, Prisoner Claims for Religious Freedom and State RFRAs, 32 U.C. Davis L. Rev. 573, 595–602 (1999) ("The numbers from all sources show that the impact of prisoner claims generated by the Federal RFRA was de minimis, given the overall backdrop of prisoner claims generally.") with Marci A. Hamilton, God vs. the Gavel: Religion and the Rule of Law 156–159 (2005) (listing extensive accommodations requested by prisoners, including types of diet, grooming and dress restrictions (facial hair, medals, crosses, and head coverings), religious literature and religious items (tarot cards, feathers, trees, saunas, prayer rugs, and wine) and observing that religious accommodation in prisons can be "enormously problematic."). The enactment of RLUIPA suggests that Congress did not view extra prisoner litigation as Governor Wilson did; indeed, several Senators expressed strong support for statutory protection of prisoners' religious freedom. See 139 Cong. Rec. S14,465 (daily ed. Oct. 27, 1993) (statement of Sen. Hatch) ("[E]xposure to religion is the best hope we have for rehabilitation of a prisoner. Most prisoners, like it or not, will eventually be returning to our communities. I want to see a prisoner exposed to religion while in prison. We should accommodate efforts to bring religion to prisoners."); id. at S14,466 (statement of Sen. Dole) ("[I]f religion can help just a handful of prison inmates get back on track, then the inconvenience of accommodating their religious beliefs is a very small price to pay.").

In *Boerne*, Justice John Paul Stevens argued that RFRA was unconstitutional because it violated the Establishment Clause by giving an advantage to religious citizens that nonreligious citizens lacked. Boerne v. Flores, 521 U.S. 507, 536–537 (1997) (Stevens, J., concurring). Why do you think no justice, even Justice Stevens, found an Establishment Clause violation in the interpretation of RLUIPA in the following prisoners' case?

Cutter v. Wilkinson

Supreme Court of the United States, 2005.
544 U.S. 709, 125 S.Ct. 2113, 161 L.Ed.2d 1020.

■ GINSBURG, J. delivered the opinion for a unanimous Court. THOMAS, J. filed a concurring opinion.

Section 3 of the Religious Land Use and Institutionalized Persons Act of 2000 (RLUIPA or Act), 114 Stat. 804, 42 U.S.C. § 2000cc–1(a)(1)–(2), provides in part: "No government shall impose a substantial burden on the religious exercise of a person residing in or confined to an institution," unless the burden furthers "a compelling governmental interest," and does so by "the least restrictive means." Plaintiffs below, petitioners here, are current and former inmates of institutions operated by the Ohio Department of Rehabilitation and Correction and assert that they are adherents of "nonmainstream" religions: the Satanist, Wicca, and Asatru religions, and the Church of Jesus Christ Christian. They complain that Ohio prison officials (respondents here), in violation of RLUIPA, have failed to accommodate their religious exercise "in a variety of different ways, including retaliating and discriminating against them for exercising their nontraditional faiths, denying them access to religious literature, denying them the same opportunities for group worship that are granted to adherents of mainstream religions, forbidding them to adhere to the dress and appearance mandates of their religions, withholding religious ceremonial items that are substantially identical to those that the adherents of mainstream religions are permitted, and failing to provide a chaplain trained in their faith." For purposes of this litigation at its current stage, respondents have stipulated that petitioners are members of bona fide religions and that they are sincere in their beliefs.

The appeals court held, as the prison officials urged, that the portion of RLUIPA applicable to institutionalized persons, 42 U.S.C. § 2000cc–1, violates the Establishment Clause. We reverse the Court of Appeals' judgment.

"This Court has long recognized that the government may . . . accommodate religious practices . . . without violating the Establishment Clause." Just last Term, in *Locke v. Davey*, the Court reaffirmed that "there is room for play in the joints between" the Free Exercise and Establishment Clauses, allowing the government to accommodate religion beyond free exercise requirements, without offense to the Establishment Clause. "At some point, accommodation may devolve into 'an unlawful fostering of religion.'" But § 3 of RLUIPA, we hold, does not, on its face, exceed the limits of permissible government accommodation of religious practices.

I

A

Less sweeping than RFRA, and invoking federal authority under the Spending and Commerce Clauses, RLUIPA targets two areas: Section 2 of the Act concerns land-use regulation, 42 U.S.C. § 2000cc;[3] § 3 relates to religious exercise by institutionalized persons, § 2000cc–1. Section 3, at issue here, provides that "[n]o [state or local] government shall impose a substantial burden on the religious exercise of a person residing in or confined to an institution," unless the government shows that the burden furthers "a compelling governmental interest" and does so by "the least restrictive means." § 2000cc–1(a)(1)–(2). The Act defines "religious exercise" to include "any exercise of religion, whether or not compelled by, or central to, a system of religious belief." § 2000cc–5(7)(A). Section 3 applies when "the substantial burden [on religious exercise] is imposed in a program or activity that receives Federal financial assistance," or "the substantial burden affects or removal of that substantial burden would affect, commerce with foreign nations, among the several States, or with Indian tribes." § 2000cc–1(b)(1)–(2). "A person may assert a violation of [RLUIPA] as a claim or defense in a judicial proceeding and obtain appropriate relief against a government." § 2000cc–2(a).

---

[3]   Section 2 of RLUIPA is not at issue here. We therefore express no view on the validity of that part of the Act.

Before enacting § 3, Congress documented, in hearings spanning three years, that "frivolous or arbitrary" barriers impeded institutionalized persons' religious exercise.[5]

B

Petitioners initially filed suit against respondents asserting claims under the First and Fourteenth Amendments. After RLUIPA's enactment, petitioners amended their complaints to include claims under § 3. Respondents moved to dismiss the statutory claims, arguing, *inter alia*, that § 3 violates the Establishment Clause.

Citing *Lemon v. Kurtzman*, the [Sixth Circuit] Court of Appeals held that § 3 of RLUIPA "impermissibly advanc[es] religion by giving greater protection to religious rights than to other constitutionally protected rights." Affording "religious prisoners rights superior to those of nonreligious prisoners," the court suggested, might "encourag[e] prisoners to become religious in order to enjoy greater rights."

II

A

Our decisions recognize that "there is room for play in the joints" between the Clauses, some space for legislative action neither compelled by the Free Exercise Clause nor prohibited by the Establishment Clause. [W]e hold that § 3 of RLUIPA fits within the corridor between the Religion Clauses: On its face, the Act qualifies as a permissible legislative accommodation of religion that is not barred by the Establishment Clause.

Foremost, we find RLUIPA's institutionalized-persons provision compatible with the Establishment Clause because it alleviates exceptional government-created burdens on private religious exercise. Furthermore, the Act on its face does not founder on shoals our prior decisions have identified: Properly applying RLUIPA, courts must take adequate account of the burdens a requested accommodation may impose on nonbeneficiaries, and they must be satisfied that the Act's prescriptions are and will be administered neutrally among different faiths.

---

[5]   The hearings held by Congress revealed, for a typical example, that "[a] state prison in Ohio refused to provide Moslems with Hallal food, even though it provided Kosher food." . . . Across the country, Jewish inmates complained that prison officials refused to provide sack lunches, which would enable inmates to break their fasts after nightfall. . . . The "Michigan Department of Corrections . . . prohibit[ed] the lighting of Chanukah candles at all state prisons" even though "smoking" and "votive candles" were permitted. *Id.*, at 41 (same). A priest responsible for communications between Roman Catholic dioceses and corrections facilities in Oklahoma stated that there "was [a] nearly yearly battle over the Catholic use of Sacramental Wine . . . for the celebration of the Mass," and that prisoners' religious possessions, "such as the Bible, the Koran, the Talmud or items needed by Native Americans[,] . . . were frequently treated with contempt and were confiscated, damaged or discarded" by prison officials.

Section 3 covers state-run institutions—mental hospitals, prisons, and the like—in which the government exerts a degree of control unparalleled in civilian society and severely disabling to private religious exercise. RLUIPA thus protects institutionalized persons who are unable freely to attend to their religious needs and are therefore dependent on the government's permission and accommodation for exercise of their religion.[10]

We note in this regard the Federal Government's accommodation of religious practice by members of the military.

We do not read RLUIPA to elevate accommodation of religious observances over an institution's need to maintain order and safety. Our decisions indicate that an accommodation must be measured so that it does not override other significant interests.

We have no cause to believe that RLUIPA would not be applied in an appropriately balanced way, with particular sensitivity to security concerns.

Finally, RLUIPA does not differentiate among bona fide faiths.

B

Were the Court of Appeals' view the correct reading of our decisions, all manner of religious accommodations would fall. Congressional permission for members of the military to wear religious apparel while in uniform would fail, as would accommodations Ohio itself makes. Ohio could not, as it now does, accommodate "traditionally recognized" religions: The State provides inmates with chaplains "but not with publicists or political consultants," and allows "prisoners to assemble for worship, but not for political rallies."

---

[10] Respondents argue, in line with the Sixth Circuit, that RLUIPA goes beyond permissible reduction of impediments to free exercise. The Act, they project, advances religion by encouraging prisoners to "get religion," and thereby gain accommodations afforded under RLUIPA. Brief for Respondents 15–17; see 349 F.3d, at 266 ("One effect of RLUIPA is to induce prisoners to adopt or feign religious belief in order to receive the statute's benefits."). While some accommodations of religious observance, notably the opportunity to assemble in worship services, might attract joiners seeking a break in their closely guarded day, we doubt that all accommodations would be perceived as "benefits." For example, congressional hearings on RLUIPA revealed that one state corrections system served as its kosher diet "a fruit, a vegetable, a granola bar, and a liquid nutritional supplement—each and every meal." Protecting Religious Freedom, pt. 3, at 38 (statement of Jaroslawicz).

The argument, in any event, founders on the fact that Ohio already facilitates religious services for mainstream faiths. The State provides chaplains, allows inmates to possess religious items, and permits assembly for worship. See App. 199 (affidavit of David Schwarz, Religious Services Administrator for the South Region of the Ohio Dept. of Rehabilitation and Correction (Oct. 19, 2000)) (job duties include "facilitating the delivery of religious services in 14 correctional institutions of various security levels throughout . . . Ohio"); Ohio Dept. of Rehabilitation and Correction, Table of Organization (Apr. 2005), available at http://www.drc. state.oh.us/web/DRCORG1.pdf (as visited May 27, 2005, and available in Clerk of Court's case file) (department includes "Religious Services" division); Brief for United States 20, and n. 8 (citing, inter alia, Gawloski v. Dallman, 803 F.Supp. 103, 113 (S.D.Ohio 1992) (inmate in protective custody allowed to attend a congregational religious service, possess a Bible and other religious materials, and receive chaplain visits); Taylor v. Perini, 413 F.Supp. 189, 238 (N.D.Ohio 1976) (institutional chaplains had free access to correctional area)).

In upholding RLUIPA's institutionalized-persons provision, we emphasize that respondents "have raised a facial challenge to [the Act's] constitutionality, and have not contended that under the facts of any of [petitioners'] specific cases . . . [that] applying RLUIPA would produce unconstitutional results."

Should inmate requests for religious accommodations become excessive, impose unjustified burdens on other institutionalized persons, or jeopardize the effective functioning of an institution, the facility would be free to resist the imposition. In that event, adjudication in as-applied challenges would be in order.

[JUSTICE THOMAS's concurrence offered a different reading of the Establishment Clause, writing that its purpose is to "make clear that Congress could not interfere with state establishments." He also wrote that RLUIPA may exceed Congress's Spending and Commerce Clause authority.]

NOTES AND QUESTIONS

1. In *Boerne*, Justice Stevens argued that RFRA was unconstitutional because it violated the Establishment Clause:

> If the historic landmark on the hill in Boerne happened to be a museum or an art gallery owned by an atheist, it would not be eligible for an exemption from the city ordinances that forbid an enlargement of the structure. Because the landmark is owned by the Catholic Church, it is claimed that RFRA gives its owner a federal statutory entitlement to an exemption from a generally applicable, neutral civil law. Whether the Church would actually prevail under the statute or not, the statute has provided the Church with a legal weapon that no atheist or agnostic can obtain. This governmental preference for religion, as opposed to irreligion, is forbidden by the First Amendment.

521 U.S. at 536–37. Why did Justice Stevens argue that RFRA violated the Establishment Clause in *Boerne* but join the Court's opinion in *Cutter*?

2. "Given the variety of religions practiced by institutionalized persons, no one single fact pattern emerges as the 'typical' RLUIPA case. Sometimes, for example, institutionalized persons seek recognition of their religion by the prison and request group worship accommodation. In other cases, offenders sue under RLUIPA because the prison does not provide them food that accommodates their religious dietary restrictions." See Joseph E. Bredehoft, Religious Expression and the Penal Institution: The Role of Damages in RLUIPA Enforcement, 74 Mo. L. Rev. 153, 153 (2009). Must prisons meet every food request of religious prisoners? May the state set any limits on the religious worship of prisoners? In the prison setting, does RLUIPA undermine the deferential standard of Turner v. Safley, 482 U.S. 78 (1987), which upholds prison regulations as long as they are reasonably related to legitimate penological interests? *Turner* identified four criteria for determining reasonableness: "(1) the connection between the

prison regulation and a legitimate, neutral government interest, (2) the presence or absence of alternatives for the prisoners to exercise their claimed right, (3) the effect of unfettered exercise of the right on other inmates, guards, and the allocation of prison resources, and (4) the presence or absence of ready alternatives." *Turner*, 482 U.S. at 89.

Aaron K. Marsh, a Zen Buddhist and an involuntary civil detainee under Florida's violent sexual predator law, alleged that the Florida Department of Corrections violated his First Amendment rights with its policy prohibiting the practice of martial arts. Marsh practices Nisei GoJu-Ryu Karate, a form of martial arts that is practiced by Zen Buddhists as a form of spiritual enlightenment. As a civil rather than criminal detainee, Marsh argued that the court should apply strict scrutiny to his free exercise claim. What standard should the court use? See Marsh v. Florida Dep't. of Corrections, 330 Fed.Appx. 179 (11th Cir. 2009). The court ruled the martial arts ban was a neutral law of general applicability and there was no free exercise violation. The court did not address the RLUIPA claim because Marsh did not raise it until his appeal. Should Marsh win or lose under RLUIPA?

Should prisoners be allowed to receive monetary damages as well as injunctive relief for successful RLUIPA cases? See Joseph E. Bredehoft, Religious Expression and the Penal Institution: The Role of Damages in RLUIPA Enforcement, 74 Mo. L. Rev. 153, 153 (2009). The Supreme Court ruled that Texas did not have to pay monetary damages to a prisoner in his RLUIPA suit. Sossamon v. Texas, 131 S.Ct. 1651 (2011).

3. Do you agree with the congressional sponsors of RLUIPA that religion is the best thing that can happen to a prisoner, or with the State of Ohio, which argued that RLUIPA advances religion by encouraging prisoners to "get religion"?

4. Prison officials reasonably believe inmates can hide weapons and contraband in long hair. Facial hair is frequently restricted in prison regulations. Do you agree with the Court that such regulations may violate RLUIPA, as the following opinion holds? Are you surprised the decision was unanimous?

Holt v. Hobbs

Supreme Court of the United States, 2015.
135 S.Ct. 853, 190 L.Ed.2d 747, 83 USLW 4065.

■ ALITO, J., delivered the opinion for a unanimous Court. GINSBURG, J., filed a concurring opinion, in which SOTOMAYOR, J., joined. SOTOMAYOR, J., filed a concurring opinion.

■ JUSTICE ALITO delivered the opinion of the Court.

Petitioner Gregory Holt, also known as Abdul Maalik Muhammad, is an Arkansas inmate and a devout Muslim who wishes to grow a ½-inch beard in accordance with his religious beliefs. Petitioner's objection to shaving his beard clashes with the Arkansas Department of

Correction's grooming policy, which prohibits inmates from growing beards unless they have a particular dermatological condition. We hold that the Department's policy, as applied in this case, violates the Religious Land Use and Institutionalized Persons Act of 2000 (RLUIPA), which prohibits a state or local government from taking any action that substantially burdens the religious exercise of an institutionalized person unless the government demonstrates that the action constitutes the least restrictive means of furthering a compelling governmental interest.

We conclude in this case that the Department's policy substantially burdens petitioner's religious exercise. Although we do not question the importance of the Department's interests in stopping the flow of contraband and facilitating prisoner identification, we do doubt whether the prohibition against petitioner's beard furthers its compelling interest about contraband. And we conclude that the Department has failed to show that its policy is the least restrictive means of furthering its compelling interests. We thus reverse the decision of the United States Court of Appeals for the Eighth Circuit.

I

B

Petitioner, as noted, is in the custody of the Arkansas Department of Correction and he objects on religious grounds to the Department's grooming policy, which provides that "[n]o inmates will be permitted to wear facial hair other than a neatly trimmed mustache that does not extend beyond the corner of the mouth or over the lip." The policy makes no exception for inmates who object on religious grounds, but it does contain an exemption for prisoners with medical needs: "Medical staff may prescribe that inmates with a diagnosed dermatological problem may wear facial hair no longer than one quarter of an inch." The policy provides that "[f]ailure to abide by [the Department's] grooming standards is grounds for disciplinary action."

Petitioner sought permission to grow a beard and, although he believes that his faith requires him not to trim his beard at all, he proposed a "compromise" under which he would grow only a ½-inch beard. Prison officials denied his request, and the warden told him: "[Y]ou will abide by [Arkansas Department of Correction] policies and if you choose to disobey, you can suffer the consequences."

Petitioner filed a *pro se* complaint in Federal District Court challenging the grooming policy under RLUIPA. We refer to the respondent prison officials collectively as the Department. In October 2011, the District Court granted petitioner a preliminary injunction and remanded to a Magistrate Judge for an evidentiary hearing. At the hearing, the Department called two witnesses. Both expressed the belief that inmates could hide contraband in even a ½-inch beard, but neither pointed to any instances in which this had been done in

Arkansas or elsewhere. Both witnesses also acknowledged that inmates could hide items in many other places, such as in the hair on their heads or their clothing. In addition, one of the witnesses—Gaylon Lay, the warden of petitioner's prison—testified that a prisoner who escaped could change his appearance by shaving his beard, and that a prisoner could shave his beard to disguise himself and enter a restricted area of the prison. Neither witness, however, was able to explain why these problems could not be addressed by taking a photograph of an inmate without a beard, a practice followed in other prison systems. Lay voiced concern that the Department would be unable to monitor the length of a prisoner's beard to ensure that it did not exceed one-half inch, but he acknowledged that the Department kept track of the length of the beards of those inmates who are allowed to wear a ¼-inch beard for medical reasons.

As a result of the preliminary injunction, petitioner had a short beard at the time of the hearing, and the Magistrate Judge commented: "I look at your particular circumstance and I say, you know, it's almost preposterous to think that you could hide contraband in your beard." Nevertheless, the Magistrate Judge recommended that the preliminary injunction be vacated and that petitioner's complaint be dismissed for failure to state a claim on which relief can be granted. The Magistrate Judge emphasized that "the prison officials are entitled to deference," and that the grooming policy allowed petitioner to exercise his religion in other ways, such as by praying on a prayer rug, maintaining the diet required by his faith, and observing religious holidays.

The District Court adopted the Magistrate Judge's recommendation in full, and the Court of Appeals for the Eighth Circuit affirmed in a brief *per curiam* opinion.

II

The Department's grooming policy requires petitioner to shave his beard and thus to "engage in conduct that seriously violates [his] religious beliefs." If petitioner contravenes that policy and grows his beard, he will face serious disciplinary action. Because the grooming policy puts petitioner to this choice, it substantially burdens his religious exercise. Indeed, the Department does not argue otherwise.

The District Court reached the opposite conclusion, but its reasoning (adopted from the recommendation of the Magistrate Judge) misunderstood the analysis that RLUIPA demands. First, the District Court erred by concluding that the grooming policy did not substantially burden petitioner's religious exercise because "he had been provided a prayer rug and a list of distributors of Islamic material, he was allowed to correspond with a religious advisor, and was allowed to maintain the required diet and observe religious holidays." In taking this approach, the District Court improperly imported a strand of reasoning from cases involving prisoners' First Amendment rights.

Under those cases, the availability of alternative means of practicing religion is a relevant consideration, but RLUIPA provides greater protection. RLUIPA's "substantial burden" inquiry asks whether the government has substantially burdened religious exercise (here, the growing of a ½-inch beard), not whether the RLUIPA claimant is able to engage in other forms of religious exercise.

Second, the District Court committed a similar error in suggesting that the burden on petitioner's religious exercise was slight because, according to petitioner's testimony, his religion would "credit" him for attempting to follow his religious beliefs, even if that attempt proved to be unsuccessful. RLUIPA, however, applies to an exercise of religion regardless of whether it is "compelled."

Finally, the District Court went astray when it relied on petitioner's testimony that not all Muslims believe that men must grow beards. Petitioner's belief is by no means idiosyncratic. But even if it were, the protection of RLUIPA, no less than the guarantee of the Free Exercise Clause, is "not limited to beliefs which are shared by all of the members of a religious sect."

III

The Department argues that its grooming policy represents the least restrictive means of furthering a " 'broadly formulated interes[t],' " see *Hobby Lobby,* namely, the Department's compelling interest in prison safety and security. But RLUIPA, like RFRA, contemplates a " 'more focused' " inquiry and " 'requires the Government to demonstrate that the compelling interest test is satisfied through application of the challenged law "to the person"—the particular claimant whose sincere exercise of religion is being substantially burdened.' " RLUIPA requires us to " 'scrutiniz[e] the asserted harm of granting specific exemptions to particular religious claimants' " and "to look to the marginal interest in enforcing" the challenged government action in that particular context. In this case, that means the enforcement of the Department's policy to prevent petitioner from growing a ½-inch beard.

The Department contends that enforcing this prohibition is the least restrictive means of furthering prison safety and security in two specific ways.

A

The Department first claims that the no-beard policy prevents prisoners from hiding contraband. The Department worries that prisoners may use their beards to conceal all manner of prohibited items, including razors, needles, drugs, and cellular phone subscriber identity module (SIM) cards.

We readily agree that the Department has a compelling interest in staunching the flow of contraband into and within its facilities, but the argument that this interest would be seriously compromised by allowing an inmate to grow a ½-inch beard is hard to take seriously. As noted, the Magistrate Judge observed that it was "almost preposterous to think that [petitioner] could hide contraband" in the short beard he had grown at the time of the evidentiary hearing. An item of contraband would have to be very small indeed to be concealed by a ½-inch beard, and a prisoner seeking to hide an item in such a short beard would have to find a way to prevent the item from falling out. Since the Department does not demand that inmates have shaved heads or short crew cuts, it is hard to see why an inmate would seek to hide contraband in a ½-inch beard rather than in the longer hair on his head.

Although the Magistrate Judge dismissed the possibility that contraband could be hidden in a short beard, the Magistrate Judge, the District Court, and the Court of Appeals all thought that they were bound to defer to the Department's assertion that allowing petitioner to grow such a beard would undermine its interest in suppressing contraband. RLUIPA, however, does not permit such unquestioning deference. RLUIPA, like RFRA, "makes clear that it is the obligation of the courts to consider whether exceptions are required under the test set forth by Congress." That test requires the Department not merely to explain why it denied the exemption but to prove that denying the exemption is the least restrictive means of furthering a compelling governmental interest. Prison officials are experts in running prisons and evaluating the likely effects of altering prison rules, and courts should respect that expertise. But that respect does not justify the abdication of the responsibility, conferred by Congress, to apply RLUIPA's rigorous standard. And without a degree of deference that is tantamount to unquestioning acceptance, it is hard to swallow the argument that denying petitioner a ½-inch beard actually furthers the Department's interest in rooting out contraband.

Even if the Department could make that showing, its contraband argument would still fail because the Department cannot show that forbidding very short beards is the least restrictive means of preventing the concealment of contraband..

The Department failed to establish that it could not satisfy its security concerns by simply searching petitioner's beard. The Department already searches prisoners' hair and clothing, and it presumably examines the ¼-inch beards of inmates with dermatological conditions. It has offered no sound reason why hair, clothing, and ¼-inch beards can be searched but ½-inch beards cannot. The Department suggests that requiring guards to search a prisoner's beard would pose a risk to the physical safety of a guard if a razor or needle was concealed in the beard. But that is no less true for searches of hair, clothing, and ¼-inch beards. And the Department has failed to prove that it could not adopt the less restrictive alternative of having the prisoner run a comb through his beard. For all these reasons, the Department's interest in eliminating contraband cannot sustain its refusal to allow petitioner to grow a ½-inch beard.

B

The Department contends that its grooming policy is necessary to further an additional compelling interest, *i.e.*, preventing prisoners from disguising their identities. The Department tells us that the no-beard policy allows security officers to identify prisoners quickly and accurately. It claims that bearded inmates could shave their beards and change their appearance in order to enter restricted areas within the prison, to escape, and to evade apprehension after escaping.

We agree that prisons have a compelling interest in the quick and reliable identification of prisoners, and we acknowledge that any alteration in a prisoner's appearance, such as by shaving a beard, might, in the absence of effective countermeasures, have at least some effect on the ability of guards or others to make a quick identification. But even if we assume for present purposes that the Department's grooming policy sufficiently furthers its interest in the identification of prisoners, that policy still violates RLUIPA as applied in the circumstances present here. The Department contends that a prisoner who has a beard when he is photographed for identification purposes might confuse guards by shaving his beard. But as petitioner has argued, the Department could largely solve this problem by requiring that all inmates be photographed without beards when first admitted to the facility and, if necessary, periodically thereafter. Once that is done, an inmate like petitioner could be allowed to grow a short beard and could be photographed again when the beard reached the ½-inch limit. Prison guards would then have a bearded and clean-shaven photo to use in making identifications. In fact, the Department (like many other States) already has a policy of photographing a prisoner both when he enters an institution and when his "appearance changes at any time during [his] incarceration."

The Department argues that the dual-photo method is inadequate because, even if it might help authorities apprehend a bearded prisoner who escapes and then shaves his beard once outside the prison, this method is unlikely to assist guards when an inmate quickly shaves his beard in order to alter his appearance within the prison. The Department contends that the identification concern is particularly acute at petitioner's prison, where inmates live in barracks and work in fields. Counsel for the Department suggested at oral argument that a prisoner could gain entry to a restricted area by shaving his beard and swapping identification cards with another inmate while out in the fields.

We are unpersuaded by these arguments for at least two reasons. First, the Department failed to show, in the face of petitioner's evidence, that its prison system is so different from the many institutions that allow facial hair that the dual-photo method cannot be employed at its institutions. Second, the Department failed to establish why the risk that a prisoner will shave a ½-inch beard to disguise himself is so great that ½-inch beards cannot be allowed, even though prisoners are allowed to grow mustaches, head hair, or ¼-inch beards for medical reasons. All of these could also be shaved off at a moment's notice, but the Department apparently does not think that this possibility raises a serious security concern.

C

In addition to its failure to prove that petitioner's proposed alternatives would not sufficiently serve its security interests, the Department has not provided an adequate response to two additional arguments that implicate the RLUIPA analysis.

First, the Department has not adequately demonstrated why its grooming policy is substantially underinclusive in at least two respects. Although the Department denied petitioner's request to grow a ½-inch beard, it permits prisoners with a dermatological condition to grow ¼-inch beards. The Department does this even though both beards pose similar risks. And the Department permits inmates to grow more than a ½-inch of hair on their heads. With respect to hair length, the grooming policy provides only that hair must be worn "above the ear" and "no longer in the back than the middle of the nape of the neck." Hair on the head is a more plausible place to hide contraband than a ½-inch beard—and the same is true of an inmate's clothing and shoes. Nevertheless, the Department does not require inmates to go about bald, barefoot, or naked.

In an attempt to demonstrate why its grooming policy is underinclusive in these respects, the Department emphasizes that petitioner's ½-inch beard is longer than the ¼-inch beard allowed for medical reasons. But the Department has failed to establish (and the District Court did not find) that a ¼-inch difference in beard length poses a meaningful increase in security risk. The Department also asserts that few inmates require beards for medical reasons while many may request beards for religious reasons. But the Department has not argued that denying petitioner an exemption is necessary to further a compelling interest in cost control or program administration. At bottom, this argument is but another formulation of the "classic rejoinder of bureaucrats throughout history: If I make an exception for you, I'll have to make one for everybody, so no exceptions." We have rejected a similar argument in analogous contexts, and we reject it again today.

Second, the Department failed to show, in the face of petitioner's evidence, why the vast majority of States and the Federal Government permit inmates to grow ½-inch beards, either for any reason or for religious reasons, but it cannot. . . . We do not suggest that RLUIPA requires a prison to grant a particular religious exemption as soon as a few other jurisdictions do so. But when so many prisons offer an accommodation, a prison must, at a minimum, offer persuasive reasons why it believes that it must take a different course, and the Department failed to make that showing here.

We emphasize that although RLUIPA provides substantial protection for the religious exercise of institutionalized persons, it also affords prison officials ample ability to maintain security. We highlight three ways in which this is so. First, in applying RLUIPA's statutory standard, courts should not blind themselves to the fact that the analysis is conducted in the prison setting. Second, if an institution suspects that an inmate is using religious activity to cloak illicit conduct, "prison officials may appropriately question whether a prisoner's religiosity, asserted as the basis for a requested accommodation, is authentic." Third, even if a claimant's religious belief is sincere, an institution might be entitled to withdraw an accommodation if the claimant abuses the exemption in a manner that undermines the prison's compelling interests.

IV

In sum, we hold that the Department's grooming policy violates RLUIPA insofar as it prevents petitioner from growing a ½-inch beard in accordance with his religious beliefs. The judgment of the United States Court of Appeals for the Eighth Circuit is reversed, and the case is remanded for further proceedings consistent with this opinion.

It is so ordered.

■ JUSTICE GINSBURG, with whom JUSTICE SOTOMAYOR joins, concurring.

Unlike the exemption this Court approved in *Hobby Lobby*, accommodating petitioner's religious belief in this case would not detrimentally affect others who do not share petitioner's belief. On that understanding, I join the Court's opinion.

■ JUSTICE SOTOMAYOR, concurring.

I do not understand the Court's opinion to preclude deferring to prison officials' reasoning when that deference is due—that is, when prison officials offer a plausible explanation for their chosen policy that is supported by whatever evidence is reasonably available to them. But the deference that must be "extend[ed to] the experience and expertise of prison administrators does not extend so far that prison officials may declare a compelling governmental interest by fiat." Indeed, prison policies "'grounded on mere speculation'" are exactly the ones that motivated Congress to enact RLUIPA.

... nothing in the Court's opinion suggests that prison officials must refute every conceivable option to satisfy RLUIPA's least restrictive means requirement. Nor does it intimate that officials must prove that they considered less restrictive alternatives at a particular point in time. Instead, the Court correctly notes that the Department inadequately responded to the less restrictive policies that petitioner brought to the Department's attention during the course of the litigation, including the more permissive policies used by the prisons in New York and California.

Because I understand the Court's opinion to be consistent with the foregoing, I join it.

NOTES AND QUESTIONS

1. *Unanimous.* Are you surprised the Court's decision was unanimous? Recall that the Court's RFRA case, *Hobby Lobby*, was a 5–4 decision, where Justice Alito wrote the majority opinion and Justice Ginsburg the dissent. Is Justice Alito's reasoning in *Holt* consistent with what he wrote in *Hobby Lobby*? If so, how could Justices Ginsburg, Breyer, Sotomayor, and Kagan, who dissented in *Hobby Lobby*, join the opinion?

2. *Ginsburg Concurrence.* Justice Ginsburg distinguished *Hobby Lobby* by noting "accommodating petitioner's religious belief in [*Holt*] would not detrimentally affect others who do not share petitioner's belief." Could a case arise in the prison setting where someone else's religion would be detrimentally affected by accommodating religious freedom? Were third party harms present in the contraceptive cases that we studied in Chapters 4 and 5, *Hobby Lobby* and *Zubik*?

Do you agree "[n]o one suffers when Mr Holt lets his stubble grow a bit. But when a corporation with 23,000 employees refuses to provide a benefit available under federal law, thousands of women are directly impacted. They have to buy their own birth control pills, for example, or shell out $1,000 for their own IUDs"? Is that the difference that Justice Ginsburg's concurrence targets? Steven Mazie, Religious Liberty: Of Beards and Brevity, The Economist, Jan. 21, 2015, available at http://www.economist.com/blogs/democracyinamerica/2015/01/religious-liberty. Do you agree "Those seeking clarity for future claims of religious free exercise will not find it in Justice Ginsburg's haiku-like concurrence in this case. But for all of its brevity, her opinion today reinforces how radical the court's ruling in *Hobby Lobby* was"? Id.

3. *Prison Security.* According to Justice Alito,

We emphasize that although RLUIPA provides substantial protection for the religious exercise of institutionalized persons, it also affords prison officials ample ability to maintain security. We highlight three ways in which this is so. First, in applying

RLUIPA's statutory standard, courts should not blind themselves to the fact that the analysis is conducted in the prison setting. Second, if an institution suspects that an inmate is using religious activity to cloak illicit conduct, "prison officials may appropriately question whether a prisoner's religiosity, asserted as the basis for a requested accommodation, is authentic." Third, even if a claimant's religious belief is sincere, an institution might be entitled to withdraw an accommodation if the claimant abuses the exemption in a manner that undermines the prison's compelling interests.

Do you agree *Holt* leaves adequate room for prison officials to protect security?

4. *Least Restrictive Means.* Could prison officials ever survive the least restrictive means test as described by Justice Alito? Why do you think Justice Sotomayor wrote her concurrence stating: "nothing in the Court's opinion suggests that prison officials must refute every conceivable option to satisfy RLUIPA's least restrictive means requirement"? Does Justice Alito's opinion suggest otherwise?

5. *Religious Liberty.* Do you agree that this case is an important victory for religious freedom? Do you agree with the following commentary about the decision's importance?

But this case is significant for another reason: It affirms our belief that religious liberty is intricately connected to and flows from our inherent human dignity. It cannot be taken away from us, even if we are imprisoned. While prisons have legitimate interests of their own, incarceration does not eliminate the fundamental human right of freedom of religion.

This case is a win for Mr. Holt. But the next time an inmate (perhaps with different beliefs) is facing some other burdensome regulation, he'll be able to draw support from Mr. Holt's precedent. In this way, a bulwark of religious liberty protections continues to be built, one component at a time. As it is said, a win for religious liberty for one is a win for religious liberty for all.

Travis Weber, The Supreme Court, Prisoner Rights, Religious Liberty, and Human Dignity, Jan. 20, 2015, at http://www.frcblog.com/2015/01/supreme-court-prisoner-rights-religious-liberty-and-human-dignity/.

6. *Overactive Court.* Did the Court step into a realm that it doesn't understand when it took upon itself the decision about what practices best protect prison security? Should the Court have shown more deference to prison authorities? Do you agree the Court is now "dictating public policy from the bench"? Marci A. Hamilton, The Supreme Court Decides *Holt v. Hobbs* the Way It Decided *Burwell v. Hobby Lobby*: With a License to Dictate Public Policy from the Bench, Hamilton and Griffin on Rights, Jan. 21, 2015, at http://hamilton-griffin.com/the-supreme-court-decides-holt-v-hobbs-the-way-it-decided-burwell-v-hobby-lobby-with-a-license-to-dictate-public-policy-from-the-bench-justia-com/.

7. *Beards.* Are prisoners now entitled to grow any length beard? Or does the decision still leave open the possibility that some beards are too long? If the Arkansas prison ended the medical exemption policy, would it still have to grant Muslim prisoners the right to wear beards?

In response to *Holt*, Texas changed its old policy requiring prisoners to shave and now allows ½-inch beards. A Muslim Texas prisoner, David Rasheed Ali, sought permission to grow a "fist-length" (i.e., four-inch) beard and wear a kufi, a knit skullcap, as required by his religious beliefs. See Ali v. Stephens, 822 F.3d 776 (5th Cir. 2016). Should Ali win his RLUIPA challenge post-*Holt v. Hobbs*? Texas argued it had compelling interests in "(1) preventing the transfer of contraband within prison; (2) facilitating identification of inmates within prison and in the event an inmate escapes; and (3) controlling costs and, relatedly, maintaining orderly prison administration." Id. at 786. Is it relevant to your analysis that "when searching male inmates, TDCJ's procedure is to have COs visually inspect short hair and 'require inmates with longer hair to shake out their own hair with their fingers' "? See id. at 787 (ruling for Ali because shaking beard was a less restrictive means). What should happen with Ali's kufi challenge?

Frank Staples is a New Hampshire prisoner who wants to wear a full-length beard for religious reasons. The prison has three security classifications—C-5, C-4, and C-3—which determine where a prisoner is housed. The prisoner's classification can change during his time in prison. From most to least restrictive, the units are: (1) Special Housing Unit (SHU) (for inmates classified as C-5); (2) the "closed custody unit" or "CCU" (for inmates classified as C-4); and (3) the medium-security units, also referred to as the units housing "the general population" (for inmates classified as C-3). Staples is housed in SHU. SHU keeps inmates in single cells (where they eat meals alone), allows them out of their cells for limited reasons only (e.g., attorneys, medical visits), handcuffs them during those times, and does not permit any socializing among inmates. CCU has more socializing, and allows inmates out of their cells in groups of 20, three times a day. CCU prisoners eat together in the dining hall. They also move around with less supervision than in SHU. There is also a higher ratio of security guards to prisoners in SHU.

The prison argued that Staples, who had a history of concealing drugs and razor blades in his beard, needed to be kept in SHU so his beard could be monitored. Prison officials are especially worried about Suboxone, a drug that can be produced in the form of a thin, wafer-like strip and therefore hidden in long beards. The court concluded that prison officials had not met their burden under the least restrictive means test to keep Staples in SHU because "the prison could house Staples in CCU, which, because of its smaller size and closer supervision of inmates, would enable the prison to monitor Staples's conduct and his safety while he maintains his full-length beard." Staples v. N.H. State Prison, Warden, No. 14-CV-473-LM, 2015 WL 4067139, at *4 (D.N.H. July 2, 2015). Did the court show appropriate deference to prison authorities under the *Holt* precedent? Under Justice Sotomayor's concurrence?

8. *Hair.* Native American prisoners who do not cut their hair for religious reasons requested a complete exemption from Alabama's short-hair policy, which requires hair to be "off neck and ears." Knight v. Thompson, 797 F.3d 934, 937 (11th Cir. 2015). Before *Holt* was decided, the Eleventh Circuit upheld the short-hair policy. Should the case come out differently now? Do you agree Alabama has compelling interests in security, discipline, hygiene, and safety? Who should win on the least restrictive means analysis? See id. at 945–46 ("Plaintiffs' proposed alternative—allowing an exemption for Native American inmates, requiring exempted inmates to search their own hair, and using a computer program to manipulate inmate photographs—does not eliminate the ADO's security, discipline, hygiene, and safety concerns. As the District Court found, inmates can manipulate searches of their own hair to conceal weapons and contraband, and using a computer program to alter photographs does nothing to address the impediments that long hair causes for the identification of inmates within the prisons. Alternatively, even assuming that the proposed alternative could eliminate the ADOC's concerns as to concealment of weapons and contraband and inmate identification, Plaintiffs' proposed alternative does nothing to assuage the ADOC's concerns about gang-formation and hair-pulling during fights, or the concealment of infections and infestations.").

Are you surprised the Supreme Court denied cert. after the Eleventh Circuit upheld Alabama's policy? See Knight v. Thompson, 796 F.3d 1289 (11th Cir. 2015), cert. denied, 136 S. Ct. 1824 (2016), reh'g denied, 136 S.Ct. 2534 (2016).

9. *Transgender Prisoners.* Jessika Ellen Stover, a male-to-female transgender Native American prisoner, was denied permission to participate in a sweat lodge ceremony. Stover had female hormone therapy but not sex reassignment surgery, leaving her with breasts as well as male genitals. Stover was assaulted several times by other prisoners. The court acknowledged that prison officials had a compelling government interest in protecting Stover from physical and sexual assault. As a less restrictive means, however, she could go to the sweat lodge alone, with a prison volunteer.

Prison officials countered that they had a compelling government interest not to allow the solitary use of the sweat lodge, because other Native Americans objected to Stover's use of the sweat lodge. They believe a "two-spirited person. . .would desecrate the religious sanctity of the lodge." The court concluded that prison officials "have not establish[ed] that burdening one individual's religious practice in an attempt to avoid burdening another's religious practice is a compelling governmental interest under RLUIPA." Stover v. Corr. Corp. of Am., No. 1:12-CV-00393-EJL, 2015 WL 874288, at *29 (D. Idaho Feb. 27, 2015). Is that ruling consistent with *Hobby Lobby*?

B. Land Use

Supporters of RLUIPA also argued that churches suffer under zoning laws, which are usually viewed by the courts as neutral laws of general applicability, and thus difficult to attack under *Smith*. According to Professor Douglas Laycock, who testified on behalf of RLUIPA, land use regulation is "not benign" toward religion, and small religious groups are "vastly overrepresented" in church zoning cases. Douglas Laycock, State RFRAs and Land Use Regulation, 32 U.C. Davis L. Rev. 755, 770–71 (1999).

> Land use regulation has become the most widespread obstacle to the free exercise of religion. Part of the problem is discrimination against churches and among churches; part of the problem is highly intrusive and burdensome regulation, imposed for modest public purposes and without regard to the effect on constitutional rights. Part of the problem is persistent failure of land use authorities in many jurisdictions to recognize that they are even dealing with a constitutional right.

Id. at 783. Government officials who ignore the importance of zoning regulations for churches, Laycock states, forget how important a place to worship is to the free exercise of religion. See also Von G. Keetch & Matthew K. Richards, The Need for Legislation to Enshrine Free Exercise in the Land Use Context, 32 U.C. Davis L. Rev. 725, 729 (1999) (citing a 1997 study finding that minority religions, who are 9 percent of the population, were involved in more than 49 percent of cases on church location and 33 percent on accessory uses of land, as proof that minority religions have a harder time with zoning laws than majorities do).

In contrast, Professor Marci Hamilton observes that churches are no longer simple neighborhood churches as they were in the past; they may be megachurches or churches with needs that disrupt neighborhoods. They offer soup kitchens, homeless shelters, and day care centers, and frequently need a lot of parking. They are powerful political actors who cast fear into zoning boards. Letting the churches escape from zoning regulations may ruin the one investment that other citizens value the most—their home. Like other citizens, Hamilton argues, churches, mosques, and synagogues should follow the neutral and generally applicable laws of zoning. See Marci A. Hamilton, God vs. the Gavel: Religion and the Rule of Law 78–110 (2005).

As you read the following materials, keep in mind two basic questions. First, how should the important words of the statute (e.g., land use, substantial burden, exercise of religion, and equal terms) be interpreted? Second, is RLUIPA unconstitutional because privileging religion violates the Establishment Clause?

When reading RLUIPA, consider that the statute identifies four possible RLUIPA violations in the land use context: substantial burden, equal terms, nondiscrimination, and exclusion. How should the courts interpret these four provisions? Does substantial burden have the same meaning here that it does in RFRA and the First Amendment cases? Does equal terms have the same meaning as the Equal Protection Clause? Does the nondiscrimination section restate the rule of *Lukumi*? What does the exclusion rule cover? What kind of facts would you need to prove that any of the four standards was violated?

(a) Substantial burdens

(1) General rule

No government shall impose or implement a land use regulation in a manner that imposes a substantial burden on the religious exercise of a person, including a religious assembly or institution, unless the government demonstrates that imposition of the burden on that person, assembly, or institution—

(A) is in furtherance of a compelling governmental interest; and

(B) is the least restrictive means of furthering that compelling governmental interest. . . .

(b) Discrimination and exclusion

(1) Equal terms

No government shall impose or implement a land use regulation in a manner that treats a religious assembly or institution on less than equal terms with a nonreligious assembly or institution.

(2) Nondiscrimination

No government shall impose or implement a land use regulation that discriminates against any assembly or institution on the basis of religion or religious denomination.

(3) Exclusions and limits

No government shall impose or implement a land use regulation that—

(A) totally excludes religious assemblies from a jurisdiction; or

(B) unreasonably limits religious assemblies, institutions, or structures within a jurisdiction.

42 U.S.C.A. § 2000cc. The following case focuses on the meaning of the "equal terms" provision of the statute, (b)(1). Do you agree with the Seventh Circuit's standard or prefer one of the other circuit tests criticized by the opinion?

River of Life Kingdom Ministries v. Village of Hazel Crest, Illinois

United States Court of Appeals, Seventh Circuit, en banc, 2010.
611 F.3d 367.

■ POSNER, CIRCUIT JUDGE.

The court granted rehearing en banc to consider the proper standard for applying the equal-terms provision of the Religious Land Use and Institutionalized Persons Act, 42 U.S.C. § 2000cc. That provision states that "no government shall impose or implement a land use regulation in a manner that treats a religious assembly or institution on less than equal terms with a nonreligious assembly or institution." § 2000cc(b)(1).

The appellant, River of Life, is a small church (it has 67 members, only about half of whom attend services on an average Sunday) that at present operates out of rented space in a cramped, dirty warehouse in Chicago Heights, a town 27 miles south of downtown Chicago. It wanted to relocate to a building in the Village of Hazel Crest, a town of some 15,000 people located two miles north and slightly west of Chicago Heights. The building, however, is in a part of the town designated by the town's zoning ordinance as a commercial district. The district is in the town's oldest part, which is run down; indeed the entire town has been in economic decline for years. The area designated as a commercial district is close to the train station, and the presence of commuters might enable the district to be revitalized as a commercial center. The zoning ordinance has therefore been amended to exclude new noncommercial uses from the district, including not only churches but also community centers, schools, and art galleries.

River of Life sued the Village under the equal-terms provision and moved for a preliminary injunction against the enforcement of the zoning ordinance. The district judge denied the motion and a panel of this court affirmed, mainly on the ground that the church was unlikely to prevail when the case was fully litigated. The existence of an intercircuit conflict with respect to the proper test for applying the equal-terms provision, combined with uncertainty about the consistency of our decisions, persuaded the full court to hear the case in order to decide on a test.

Two of our sister courts of appeals have proposed tests. The Third Circuit in *Lighthouse Institute for Evangelism, Inc. v. City of Long Branch,* 510 F.3d 253, 266 (3d Cir.2007), ruled that "a regulation will violate the Equal Terms provision only if it treats religious assemblies or institutions less well than secular assemblies or institutions that are similarly situated *as to the regulatory purpose* " (emphasis in original). The court must identify first the goals of the challenged zoning ordinance and second the secular assemblies (meeting places) that are comparable to the plaintiff's religious assembly in the sense of having roughly the same relation to those goals. If the reasons for excluding some category of secular assembly—whether traditional reasons such as effect on traffic or novel ones such as creating a "Street of Fun," are applicable to a religious assembly, the ordinance is deemed neutral and therefore not in violation of the equal-terms provision. But if a secular assembly is allowed and the religious assembly banned even though the two assemblies don't differ in any way material to the regulatory purpose behind the ordinance, then neutrality has been violated and equality denied. That was the situation in the *Lighthouse* case. The zoning ordinance permitted meeting halls in the district in which the church wanted to locate and there was no way to distinguish between meeting halls and churches on the basis of the purpose of the ordinance. The Third Circuit therefore ordered summary judgment in favor of the church with respect to its challenge to the ordinance (though not its challenge to a newer redevelopment plan), saying that "Long Branch [the defendant] has failed to create a genuine issue of material fact as to whether the Ordinance treated religious assemblies or institutions on less than equal terms with non-religious assemblies or institutions that caused equivalent harm to its governmental objectives."

An alternative test was adopted by the Eleventh Circuit in *Midrash Sephardi, Inc. v. Town of Surfside,* 366 F.3d 1214, 1230–31 (11th Cir.2004). The Eleventh Circuit reads the language of the equal-terms provision literally: a zoning ordinance that permits *any* "assembly," as defined by dictionaries, to locate in a district must permit a church to locate there as well even if the only secular assemblies permitted are hospital operating theaters, bus terminals, air raid shelters, restaurants that have private dining rooms in which a book club or professional association might meet, and sports stadiums. In *Midrash* the court held that where private clubs are allowed, so must churches be.

Pressed too hard, this approach would give religious land uses favored treatment—imagine a zoning ordinance that permits private clubs but not meeting halls used by political advocacy groups. The court indicated, however, that a seemingly unequal treatment of religious uses that nevertheless is consistent with the "strict scrutiny" standard for determining the propriety of a regulation affecting religion would not violate the equal-terms provision. *Midrash Sephardi, Inc. v. Town of Surfside, supra,* 366 F.3d at 1232.

Neither the Third Circuit's nor the Eleventh Circuit's approach, though in application they might yield similar or even identical results—and results moreover that would strike most judges as proper—is entirely satisfactory. We are troubled by the Eleventh Circuit's rule that mere "differential treatment" between a church and some other "company of persons collected together in one place ...

usually for some common purpose" (the court's preferred dictionary definition of "assembly") violates the equal-terms provision. "Assembly" so understood would include most secular land uses—factories, nightclubs, zoos, parks, malls, soup kitchens, and bowling alleys, to name but a few (visitors to each of these institutions have a "common purpose" in visiting)—even though most of them have different effects on the municipality and its residents from a church; consider just the difference in municipal services required by different land uses, including differences in the amount of police protection. The land use that led the Eleventh Circuit in *Midrash* to find a violation of the equal-terms provision was, however, a private club, and it is not obvious that it has different effects on a municipality or its residents from those of a church. Thus our quarrel is not with the result in *Midrash* but with the Eleventh Circuit's test.

A subtler objection to the test is that it may be *too* friendly to religious land uses, unduly limiting municipal regulation and maybe even violating the First Amendment's prohibition against establishment of religion by discriminating in favor of religious land uses. Suppose a zoning ordinance forbids all assemblies except gymnasiums. Then because a gymnasium is an assembly as defined by the Eleventh Circuit, a church could locate in the district but a secular humanist reading room could not, unless secular humanist organizations (such as American Atheists, the American Humanist Association, the Freedom from Religion Foundation, the Godless Americans Political Action Committee, Internet Infidels, and the Skeptics Society—these are all real organizations) were defined as religions. (Nor could the local chapter of the Cat Fanciers' Association, which might have 67 dues-paying local members, only about half of whom show up on average at the chapter's meetings.) It was to avoid making its test overprotect religious assembles in comparison to their closest secular counterparts that the Eleventh Circuit added its "strict scrutiny" gloss—municipalities can bar religious land uses from particular zones if the regulation satisfies the "strict scrutiny" test for regulations that treat religious and secular activities differently. There is no textual basis for the gloss, and religious discrimination is expressly prohibited elsewhere in the statute. The gloss was needed only to solve a problem of the court's own creation.

A further objection to the Eleventh Circuit's test is that "equality," except when used of mathematical or scientific relations, signifies not equivalence or identity but proper relation to relevant concerns. It would not promote equality to require that all men wear shirts that have 15-inch collars, or that the number of churches in a state equal the number of casinos, or that all workers should have the same wages. But it does promote equality to require equal pay for equal work, even though workers differ in a variety of respects, such as race and sex. If a church and a community center, though different in many respects, do not differ with respect to any accepted zoning criterion, then an ordinance that allows one and forbids the other denies equality and violates the equal-terms provision.

This understanding of the equal-terms provision is imperfectly realized by the Third Circuit's test as well. That test centers on identifying the zoning authorities' "regulatory purpose" in adopting an ordinance that excludes a church. Our concern is not that the equal-terms provision as drafted by Congress omits the term "regulatory purpose" or some cognate term. As we explained, "equality" is a complex concept. The fact that two land uses share a dictionary definition doesn't make them "equal" within the meaning of a statute. But the use of "regulatory purpose" as a guide to interpretation invites speculation concerning the reason behind exclusion of churches; invites self-serving testimony by zoning officials and hired expert witnesses; facilitates zoning classifications thinly disguised as neutral but actually systematically unfavorable to churches (as by favoring public reading rooms over other forms of nonprofit assembly); and makes the meaning of "equal terms" in a federal statute depend on the intentions of local government officials.

The problems that we have identified with the Third Circuit's test can be solved by a shift of focus from regulatory *purpose* to accepted zoning *criteria*. The shift is not merely semantic. "Purpose" is subjective and manipulable, so asking about "regulatory purpose" might result in giving local officials a free hand in answering the question "equal with respect to what?" "Regulatory criteria" are objective—and it is federal judges who will apply the criteria to resolve the issue.

As explained in *Skokie Town House Builders, Inc. v. Village of Morton Grove,* 16 Ill.2d 183, 157 N.E.2d 33, 36 (1959), " . . . In short, whether industry and commerce are excluded from the residential areas, or residences from industrial and commercial areas, it is not unreasonable for a legislative body to assume that separation of the areas would tend in the long run to insure a better and a more economical use of municipal services, such as schools, providing police protection, preventing and fighting fires, and better use of street facilities. The general welfare of the public may be enhanced if industry and commerce are provided with a favorable climate. The sale of a few lots at important points in a district may make industrial or commercial expansion impossible or prohibitively expensive. To protect the residents in the district, traffic may be slowed down unduly and thus detract from the efficiency of production and trade. In final analysis, it seems clear that industry and commerce are also necessary and desirable and that a proper environment for them will promote the general welfare of the public."

Exclusion of churches from a commercial zone (though generally not from every commercial zone in the municipality), along with other noncommercial assemblies, such as exhibition halls, clubs, and homeless shelters, is thus not unique to the Village of Hazel Crest. . . . A reader might worry that "commercial" is a synonym for "secular." It is not. There are many secular noncommercial land uses, and if the Village of Hazel Crest were concerned for example about the sufficiency of parking space in some part of the village, the commercial or noncommercial character of land uses that generated similar vehicular traffic flows would be irrelevant. Suppose maintenance of regular (as opposed to sporadic and concentrated) vehicular traffic were the zoning objective. From that standpoint, a church is more like a movie theater, which also generates groups of people coming and going at the same time, than like a public library, which generates a smoother flow of traffic throughout the day. The equal-terms provision would therefore require the zoning authorities to allow the church in the zone with the movie theater because the church was more like the for-profit use (the movie theater) than the not-for-profit use (the public library).

Parking space and traffic control are not the only concerns of land-use regulation. Another is generating municipal revenue and providing ample and convenient shopping for residents, and can be promoted by setting aside some land for commercial uses only, which generate tax revenues. Hazel Crest has therefore created a commercial district that excludes churches *along with* community centers, meeting halls, and libraries because these secular assemblies, like churches, do not generate significant taxable revenue or offer shopping opportunities. Similar assemblies are being treated the same. The permitted land use that is most like the plaintiff's is a commercial gymnasium, and that's not close enough because a commercial assembly belongs in an all-commercial district and a noncommercial assembly, secular or religious, does not.

Of course we can't be certain, or even confident, that a particular zoning decision was actually motivated by a land-use concern that is neutral from the standpoint of religion. But if religious and secular land uses that are treated the same (such as the noncommercial religious and secular land uses in the zoning district that River of Life wants to have its church in) from the standpoint of an accepted zoning criterion, such as "commercial district," or "residential district," or "industrial district," that is enough to rebut an equal-terms claim and thus, in this case, to show that River of Life is unlikely to prevail in a full litigation.

Indeed, this case is straightforward because, after the amendment to its zoning ordinance, Hazel Crest really was applying conventional criteria for commercial zoning in banning noncommercial land uses from a part of the village suitable for a commercial district because of proximity to the train station. We are likely to have cases in the future challenging zoning ordinances that are harder to classify, as variances and special-use permits and grandfathered nonconforming uses blur the character of particular zoning districts. But should a municipality create what purports to be a pure commercial district and then allow other uses, a church would have an easy victory if the municipality kept it out.

If the test we are adopting seems less than airtight, bear in mind that the equal-terms provision is not the only or even the most important protection against religious discrimination by zoning authorities. (Think of the religious clauses of the First Amendment.) It is not even the only protection in the Religious Land Use and Institutionalized Persons Act. For the Act provides that a land-use regulation "that imposes a substantial burden on the religious exercise of a . . . religious assembly or institution" is unlawful "unless the government demonstrates that imposition of the burden . . . is in furtherance of a compelling governmental interest; and is the least restrictive means of furthering that compelling governmental interest." 42 U.S.C. § 2000cc(a)(1). And it further provides that "no government shall impose or implement a land use regulation in a manner that discriminates against any assembly or institution on the basis of religion or religious denomination," § 2000cc(b)(2); or that "totally excludes religious assemblies from a jurisdiction." § 2000cc(b)(3)(A). But as none of these other provisions is before us on this appeal, the appeal must fail.

AFFIRMED.

NOTES AND QUESTIONS

1. *Equal Terms.* What do you think of Judge Posner's accepted zoning criteria test? Is it preferable to the Third and Eleventh Circuits' standards? Do you agree this case is a "straightforward" loss for River of Life? Does this case persuade you that RLUIPA encourages unnecessary litigation harmful to municipal governments?

Would the outcome be different if Hazel Crest had allowed meeting halls and community centers in the commercial zone? See id. at 375, n.1 (Manion, J., concurring) (equal terms would be violated in those circumstances).

Do you agree with Judge Cudahy's concurrence (omitted here) that "the practical distinction between [the Third Circuit's] 'regulatory purpose' and 'regulatory criteria' may not be as pronounced as the majority opinion suggests"? Id. at 374. Can you identify a circumstance in which the tests would lead to different results? Judge Williams argued in another concurrence that the Third Circuit's test (which was applied by the panel that originally heard the case) was preferable and "simpler." Under that test,

> the village's regulatory purpose in establishing the commercial zone was to create a tax revenue-generating commercial district centered near the mass transit area; because the church was not

similar to the non-religious entities permitted in the zone—all of which were commercial in nature—the panel found that the church had not been treated on less than equal terms with the commercial non-religious entities.

Id. at 376. How is that different from Judge Posner's standard?

Do you agree with Judge Sykes' dissent that the new test "dooms most, if not all, equal-term claims," and that the court should have used the Eleventh Circuit's formulation? See id. at 386. The Hazel Crest zoning laws allowed commercial gymnasiums, health clubs, salons, hotels, motels, restaurant, taverns, and day-care centers (as an allowed "special use") in the commercial zone. Are they comparators that easily proved an equal terms violation? Are cities now free to exclude churches from commercial zones?

Should religious institutions and municipalities enjoy equal power in the zoning process? Which court test equalizes religion and government? Do you agree that, unlike the Third and Eleventh Circuit tests, *River of Life* "shifts control over land-use regulations out of the hands of religious institutions and into those of the courts and municipalities"? See Tokufumi J. Noda, Incommensurable Uses: RLUIPA's Equal Terms Provision and Exclusionary Zoning in *River of Life Kingdom Ministries v. Village of Hazel Crest*, 52 B.C. L. Rev. E-Supp. 71, 80–81 (2011).

2.   *Other Circuits.* Post-*River of Life*, the Ninth Circuit addressed the equal terms provision in an Arizona case. Centro Familiar Cristiano Buenas Nuevas bought an old J.C. Penney store building in the Old Town Main Street area of Yuma. Arizona law prohibits bars, nightclubs, and liquor stores from being located within 300 feet of a church. The city denied the church a conditional use permit because of concerns that the inability to get a liquor license would "blight a whole block for purposes of an entertainment district." Centro Familiar Cristiano Buenas Nuevas v. City of Yuma, 651 F.3d 1163, 1166 (9th Cir. 2011). Accepting the Third Circuit's test as modified by the Seventh Circuit, the Ninth Circuit wrote:

> the city may be able to justify some distinctions drawn with respect to churches, if it can demonstrate that the less-than-equal-terms are on account of a legitimate regulatory purpose, not the fact that the institution is religious in nature. In this respect, our analysis is about the same as the Third Circuit's: we look to see if the church is "similarly situated as to the regulatory purpose." The Seventh Circuit, en banc, has refined this test to avoid inappropriate subjectivity by requiring equality with respect to "accepted zoning criteria," such as parking, vehicular traffic, and generation of tax revenue. That refinement is appropriate where necessary to prevent evasion of the statutory requirement, though it makes no practical difference in this case.

Id. at 1172–73. Why do you think the court ruled for the church instead of the city? See id. at 1174–75 ("many of the uses permitted as of right would have the same practical effect as a church of blighting a potential block of bars and nightclubs. An apartment building taking up the whole block may be developed as of right, and so may a post office or prison. Prisons have bars, but not the kind promoting 'entertainment.' ").

In the Fifth Circuit, Opulent Life Church leased property in Holly Springs, Mississippi's business district, on the courthouse square, to use as a church. Opulent Life challenged city ordinances that required churches to get neighboring property owners' and public officials' approval for the property use. In deciding the case, the court distinguished its test from the Third, Seventh, and Ninth Circuits:

> our precedent calls for a test that differs slightly from the Third Circuit's "regulatory purpose" test and the Seventh and Ninth Circuits' "accepted zoning criteria" test. In this circuit, "[t]he 'less than equal terms' must be measured by the ordinance itself and the criteria by which it treats institutions differently." In accord with this instruction, and building on the similar approaches of our sister circuits, we must determine: (1) the regulatory purpose or zoning criterion behind the regulation at issue, as stated explicitly in the text of the ordinance or regulation; and (2) whether the religious assembly or institution is treated as well as every other nonreligious assembly or institution that is "similarly situated" with respect to the stated purpose or criterion. Where, as here, the religious assembly or institution establishes a prima facie case, the government must affirmatively satisfy this two-part test to bear its burden of persuasion on this element of the plaintiff's Equal Terms Clause claim.

Opulent Life Church v. City of Holly Springs, Miss., 697 F.3d 279, 292–93 (5th Cir. 2012). Would this standard have made a difference in *River of Life*? How might the Supreme Court decide which one of these standards to adopt?

3. Could River of Life have filed a successful lawsuit under the other provisions of RLUIPA mentioned by Judge Posner, namely substantial burden, antidiscrimination, and exclusion?

4. *Substantial Burden.* Should the substantial burden test under RLUIPA be the same as it was for RFRA? Consider the following "sliding scale" of tests that the courts have used to identify substantial burden:

> At one end of the scale, with the highest threshold, rests a case decided by the Seventh Circuit, *City League of Urban Believers v. Chicago* (CLUB) in which the court stated "a land-use regulation that imposes a substantial burden on religious exercise is one that necessarily bears direct, primary, and fundamental responsibility for rendering religious exercise—including the use of real property for the purpose thereof within the regulated jurisdiction generally—effectively impracticable."
>
> Next in line, we have cases that discuss "substantial burden" as pressure that directly "coerces" individuals to modify their religious belief. In *Midrash Sephardi, Inc. v. Surfside*, the

Eleventh Circuit held that "a 'substantial burden' must place more than an inconvenience on religious exercise; a 'substantial burden' is akin to significant pressure which directly coerces the religious adherent to conform his or her behavior accordingly." The Second Circuit has adopted the *Midrash* test as well, and in an unpublished decision, the Sixth Circuit adopted a similar standard.

Several courts rest in the middle of the scale. The Ninth Circuit is the only circuit to adopt a dictionary definition of a "substantial burden." Looking to the plain language of the statute, the court held that a substantial burden must be " 'oppressive' to a 'significantly great' extent . . . and must impose a significantly great restriction or onus." The Third and Fifth Circuits have addressed RLUIPA's substantial burden language in the prison context and share identical standards, speaking of "substantial pressure" that alters religiously motivated behavior.

Finally, at the far end of the scale, lies a second Seventh Circuit opinion. In *Saints Constantine & Helen Greek Orthodox Church, Inc. v. City of New Berlin*, the court stated that "delay, uncertainty, and expense" may impose a substantial burden, and that even if a burden is not "insuperable," it is not necessarily "insubstantial." Although the *Saints Constantine & Helen* and *CLUB* standards appear a world apart, the Seventh Circuit did not directly address the apparent disparity in two subsequent cases.

See Karla L. Chaffee and Dwight H. Merriam, Six Fact Patterns of Substantial Burden in RLUIPA: Lessons for Potential Litigants, 2 Alb. Gov't L. Rev. 437, 449–51 (2009). Which test would you adopt? How much financial hardship to a church would constitute a substantial burden? Should churches always be able to expand so that they can seat all their members at one worship service? If the church could relocate to a new site big enough to meet its expansion needs, has its religious exercise been substantially burdened by the denial of a building permit?

5. *Religious Exercise.* RLUIPA defines "religious exercise" to encompass "any exercise of religion, whether or not compelled by, or central to, a system of religious belief," including "(t)he use, building, or conversion of real property for the purpose of religious exercise." 42 U.S.C. § 2000cc–5(7)(A). Should the following land uses qualify as religious exercises?

a. Building a church? See Cottonwood Christian Ctr. v. Cypress Redev. Agency, 218 F.Supp.2d 1203 (C.D. Cal. 2002) (yes).

b. Adding classrooms to an Orthodox Jewish day school? (yes). A gymnasium? (no). A headmaster's residence? (no). More office space? (no). See Westchester Day School v. Village of Mamaroneck, 504 F.3d 338 (2d Cir. 2007).

c. Operating a homeless shelter or a food bank? See Daytona Rescue Mission v. City of Daytona Beach, 885 F.Supp. 1554 (M.D. Fla. 1995) (yes under RFRA).

d. Building an apartment complex to provide housing to local citizens? See Greater Bible Way Temple v. City of Jackson, 478 Mich. 373, 733 N.W.2d 734 (2007), cert. denied, 128 S.Ct. 1894 (2008) (no; ownership of a commercial building by a religious institution does not transform it into a religious exercise).

e. Leasing a religious property as a venue for commercial events in order to raise money for the religion? See Scottish Rite Cathedral v. Los Angeles, 156 Cal.App.4th 108, 67 Cal.Rptr.3d 207 (2007) (no). Is Freemasonry a religion for purposes of RLUIPA? See id. (yes).

f. Opening a day care center? See Grace United Methodist Church v. City of Cheyenne, 451 F.3d 643 (10th Cir. 2006) (yes, although jury found the exercise was not sincere).

g. Little League baseball? See Cash v. Brookshire United Methodist Church, 61 Ohio App.3d 576, 573 N.E.2d 692, 693 (1988) (yes, pre-RLUIPA case finding "[i]t is the fundamental tenet of the Methodist Church that worship involves not only religious services, but reaching out into the community through sponsorship of activities such as scouting, Little League and Head Start programs.").

h. Social events, including a Saturday night concert series, for college students? See Episcopal Student Foundation v. City of Ann Arbor, 341 F.Supp.2d 691 (E.D. Mich. 2004) (yes).

i. Alcoholics Anonymous meetings? See Glenside Center v. Abington Township Zoning Hearing Bd., 973 A.2d 10 (Pa.Cmwlth. 2009) (no).

j. Use of space in a high school for a commercial fitness center and dance studio? See New Life Worship Center v. Town of Smithfield Zoning Board of Review, C.A. No. 09–0924, 2010 R.I. Super. LEXIS 101 (July 7, 2010) (not a religious exercise).

k. Leasing church space to a private school for disabled children? See Calvary Christian Ctr. v. City of Fredericksburg, 832 F.Supp.2d 635 (E.D. Va. 2011) (No. "Calvary stated that operating Fairwinds on its premises is an exercise of its 'sincere religious belief to minister to emotionally and mentally disabled children.' The Court finds that Calvary has not pled any facts demonstrating that the operation of the day school by a third party is a religious exercise. Talismanic assertions lacking factual support are insufficient to satisfy the pleading standard. . . . ").

The statutory definition is broader than the meaning of free exercise under the First Amendment. "Generally, the Supreme Court has limited free exercise claims to religious beliefs or practices that are central or fundamental to a person's religion." Is RLUIPA's definition of religious exercise so broad that it violates the Establishment Clause or exceeds Congress's powers?

6. *Compelling State Interest.* What should count as a compelling state interest in the land use context? Protecting agricultural space? Avoiding traffic and congestion? Parking? Preserving property values? Regulating aesthetic impacts? Preserving the harmony of the neighborhood? Enacting and enforcing a comprehensive system of zoning and land use? Encouraging economic development and the rehabilitation of deteriorated neighborhoods? Revenue generation? Combating urban blight? Preventing urban sprawl? See Patricia E. Salkin and Amy Lavine, The Genesis of RLUIPA and Federalism: Evaluating the Creation of a Federal Statutory Right and Its Impact on Local Government, 40 Urb. Law. 195, 235–38 (2008).

How compelling is the government interest in protecting the environment? According to Professor Zale, "by allowing religious entities to use their property in ways that no other land users can, [RLUIPA] threatens to undermine local environmental protection efforts nationwide . . . RLUIPA could lead to a 'death by a thousand cuts' for environmental protection efforts across the nation." Kellen Zale, God's Green Earth? The Environmental Impacts of Religious Land Use, 64 Me. L. Rev. 207, 210, 222 (2011).

Churches are tax-exempt. Does the government have a compelling state interest in collecting tax revenue that justifies favoring tax-paying entities over churches? See Douglas Laycock & Luke W. Goodrich, RLUIPA: Necessary, Modest, and Under-Enforced, 39 Fordham Urb. L.J. 1021, 1036 (2012) (tax rationale wrongly gives government reason to exclude every religious group in zoning decisions).

7. *The Establishment Clause.* Does RLUIPA violate the Establishment Clause by privileging religion over non-religion as Professor Hamilton suggests in the following example:

> For example, [churches] can buy property in a residential district at prices below those in the commercial or institutional sections of the city and then force a conversion of the zoning to their advantage. There is not a secular developer who would not covet this extraordinary financial benefit, yet they may not engage in the same economic transaction because they lack the legal weapon of RLUIPA to force the permission that will make their purchase profitable.

See Marci A. Hamilton, The Constitutional Limitations on Congress's Power Over Local Land Use: Why the Religious Land Use and Institutionalized Persons Act is Unconstitutional, 2 Alb. Gov't L. Rev. 366 (2009). In another article, Professor Hamilton argues that whenever courts rule that inconvenience and cost are sufficient to establish a substantial burden violation of RLUIPA, churches receive a "financial privilege that violates the Establishment Clause." Marci A. Hamilton, RLUIPA is a Bridge Too Far: Inconvenience Is Not Discrimination, 39 Fordham Urb. L.J. 959, 983–84 (2012). Do you agree?

There are also unresolved constitutional questions about whether Congress possessed power under the commerce and spending clauses, as well as Section 5 of the Fourteenth Amendment, to pass RLUIPA.

The following essay asks you to consider the impact of the institutional trend in religious freedom cases on land use. Recall that in Chapter 6 we asked if the Court's case law currently favors institutional religious freedom over that of individuals. Is RLUIPA protecting big institutions instead of individuals and smaller churches?

Zachary Bray, RLUIPA and the Limits of Religious Institutionalism

2016 Utah L. Rev. 41.

I.   INTRODUCTION

There are two constants regarding the legal treatment of religious belief and exercise in America, at least in recent years: first, it is almost perpetually unsettled; and second, pretty much everyone claims to hate the current state of the doctrine. The Religious Land Use and Institutionalized Persons Act of 2000 ("RLUIPA") is a particularly loathed target. Many commentators wish it had never been passed, and even those who appreciate the statute's purpose or potential think it is a terrible mess. RLUIPA's many critics are right to point out its flaws: the statute's substantive provisions have created a rash of circuit splits, while exacerbating incentives for conflict in an area that previously saw relatively little federal litigation. Nevertheless, in an odd and stubborn way the statute has not only survived but thrived. Indeed, as this Article will show, new arguments promise (or, perhaps more accurately, threaten) to give RLUIPA additional support, a wider scope, and an even greater impact than it presently enjoys.

By design, RLUIPA covers a wide and diverse range of potential disputes about religious exercise, which range from the religious exercise of individuals "residing in or confined to an institution," to disputes that involve religious land use, the latter of which are the focus of this Article. In the land use context, RLUIPA provides religious landowners with special protections from land use regulations; an array of potential legal claims to make if governments violate these special protections; and a powerful set of tools, in addition to litigation, to employ in negotiations with local governments. RLUIPA's wide range means that the statute has played a role in almost every significant legal controversy and academic debate about religious exercise since its passage in 2000—including the present debate about the importance of and proper roles for religious institutions.

Much recent work addressing law and religious exercise now revolves around this latter debate—the debate over "religious institutionalism," a collection of related theories that have resonated with recent developments in recent high-profile litigation such as *Burwell v. Hobby Lobby Stores, Inc.* The theories grouped together here and elsewhere under the umbrella of religious institutionalism may take many forms. For now, the following may serve as a working definition: theories of religious institutionalism revolve around the central claim that religious institutions, independent from the individual people that make up religious institutions, are actors with key roles to play in determining the nature and limits of protection for religious exercise.

Other versions of religious institutionalism maintain that the problems associated with the legal treatment of religious exercise stem from a fundamental misconception. Under these "stronger" institutional theories, religious institutions should enjoy deference not because they help to safeguard individual religious liberties, but rather because religious institutions, in their own right, ought to be the primary foci for religious protection. Stated simply, what this Article refers to as "strong" religious institutionalism claims that protection for religious exercise ought to be about protection for "churches" first and foremost.

When put into practice, theories of religious institutionalism can pack a powerful punch. Their impact can be seen in recent high-profile litigation, including the Supreme Court's recent decision [*Hosanna-Tabor*] regarding the employment relationship between religious institutions and their ministers, as well as its opinion in *Hobby Lobby*. As a result, arguments drawing on religious institutionalism have begun to seep into numerous new areas—including the current debate about RLUIPA and religious land use. These arguments in favor of an institutional approach to RLUIPA have emerged at roughly the same time that other scholars have begun to recognize the true magnitude of the stakes in this context: courts' increasing willingness to accord special solicitude to religious institutions has, among other problems, threatened to subvert many legitimate aims of local government in the land use context.

This is all troubling. Yet, as this Article will show, it actually understates the problem. When religious institutionalism is combined with an expansive view of RLUIPA, what emerges is far worse than the sum of the already ungainly parts.

III. RLUIPA AND ITS DISCONTENTS

RLUIPA's critics are legion, and even those who defend aspects of the statute and its present or potential future interpretation are usually quick to point out RLUIPA's many flaws. There is relatively more disagreement about *how bad* RLUIPA really is in practice: some commentators have pointed out that the amount of actual litigation under RLUIPA is roughly equivalent to other similar kinds of land use that raise First Amendment issues, and while religious plaintiffs generally do relatively well in RLUIPA suits, they do not win every time or even most of the time. Still, other commentators have suggested that RLUIPA's many critics have overstated the problems with both the statute itself and its practical application, or even that the statute should be reinforced against its many critics.

The long-running debates about RLUIPA can be boiled down to two areas of conflict. The most fundamental criticism of RLUIPA is the claim that it is unconstitutional. While the Supreme Court has ruled that RLUIPA's institutionalized persons provisions are constitutional [see *Cutter v. Wilkinson*, Section A], it has not directly addressed the constitutionality of RLUIPA's land use provisions.

Accordingly, the problems with RLUIPA's practical application will be discussed at much greater length in this Article than the debate about RLUIPA's constitutionality briefly noted immediately above. At the most general level, RLUIPA's exemptions for a wide range of religious land uses make it more difficult to achieve workable and local solutions to land use problems that are, after all, inherently local in nature. More specifically, the most immediate set of problems that RLUIPA creates are related to the sheer impact that certain large-scale religious uses may have on local communities and on systems of local land use regulation, which are effectively exempted under the statute.

A.   The Impact of RLUIPA and Religious Land Use

As one scholar has pointed out, a 200,000-square-foot megachurch is likely to create the same kinds of externalities as a 200,000-square-foot Wal-Mart. Thanks to RLUIPA, however, the religious development may be effectively immune from local land use controls—including, but not necessarily limited to regulations imposed to control externalities arising from large-scale development in environmentally sensitive areas. The comparison of large-scale contemporary religious development to large-scale contemporary commercial development is an apt one because increasingly the two forms of land use mirror one another. In many instances, the increasing similarity between many forms of religious and commercial land use today is no accident. Rather, the convergence of religious and nonreligious land development is often the product of careful design and deliberate imitation, as the leaders of religious organizations and the architects and real estate professionals they employ deliberately seek to replicate the large-scale commercial, educational, and residential institutions that have increasingly shaped American life in recent decades.

Yet even as American religious land use increasingly mirrors other forms of large-scale and intensive land use, RLUIPA's special protections have made American religious land use increasingly exempt from scrutiny and control by local governments. The combination of these trends presents obvious problems. For example, whether the purpose they serve is commercial, residential, or religious in nature, large parking lots lead to increased mobile source air pollution, stormwater runoff, and erosion; large and multiple-use buildings require increased water, sewage, and trash disposal capacity; and large multi-acre complexes sited at or beyond the outskirts of the suburbs may exceed traffic capacity in the short term and exacerbate sprawl and impinge upon planned greenbelts in the medium to long-term. In sum, therefore, the environmental implications for religious land use are often at least as significant as those for structures or developments of equivalent size that are put to nonreligious purposes.

Moreover, the size, scope, and intensity of much religious land use has been steadily increasing in recent decades. But even as the environmental impact of religious land development has steadily grown in recent years, to the point where it now approximates or exceeds the environmental impact of large-scale commercial land development in many instances, RLUIPA has steadily eroded local governments' ability to monitor and regulate religious land use. Whatever RLUIPA's merits may be—and this Article will argue that they are few, far between, and outweighed by RLUIPA's many negative effects—the combination of these background trends is deeply problematic.

Although the problems that RLUIPA creates for local environmental and natural resource regulations are significant, the problems caused by RLUIPA-exempted religious land development are not limited to environmental issues alone. Nor are the problems RLUIPA causes necessarily limited to the impacts that religious land use can have on its immediate neighbors. Rather, the large-scale religious land use that RLUIPA frees from local regulation may have "ripple effects" that can wash over neighboring landowners in unpredictable ways.

For example, the development of land by a religious landowner may dramatically change the character of a residential neighborhood, or dampen foot traffic during business hours in a pedestrian-friendly zone downtown, or preclude certain kinds of commercial development that a community might wish to encourage in certain areas. Moreover, the costs of religious land use are not always limited to a single neighborhood. As with any other kind of significant, intensive, or large-scale land use, in some situations contemporary religious land development may impose particularly wide-ranging externalities or dramatically change the character of a community far beyond the land use's neighbors. The fact that religious land use increasingly causes the same kinds of externalities as other forms of land use is not, in itself, necessarily a problem. But such wide-ranging externalities may be particularly difficult to resolve when they arise from religious land use because RLUIPA frequently inhibits or entirely prevents neighbors and local governments from working toward the types of solutions that might be applied to analogous situations involving nonreligious land use.

In addition to concerns about the size and impact of protected religious land uses, some critics of RLUIPA have raised concerns about the *kinds* of religious land use that may be exempted by the statute. More specifically, some of RLUIPA's many critics are concerned that certain "auxiliary uses" that do not appear to be particularly religious in nature will be exempted by a broad reading of the statute from otherwise controlling land use regulations. Today, common auxiliary uses of land by religious organizations include relatively familiar religious land uses such as schools, but also community centers, health care facilities, homeless shelters and halfway houses, food pantries, food preparation and dining areas, TV and radio broadcasting facilities, credit unions and banks, and various forms of housing. So, for example, courts have considered RLUIPA claims related to proposed or actual land uses that include commercial real estate development, night clubs, GED placement and training centers, day care facilities, fraternal lodges, residential rehabilitation facilities, and commercial wedding businesses. Moreover, courts have applied RLUIPA to protect proposed or actual land uses that include homeless shelters, hospitals, retreat facilities with overnight lodging, crisis centers for addiction or domestic disputes, and, in one recent case, a 5,000-square-foot residence for a religious minister that includes an indoor swimming pool.

None of these land uses may be problematic, at least in certain locations. Indeed, many may be worthy projects, at least in the right spot. But they all impose costs upon their neighbors, and RLUIPA causes many of these costs to be considered and regulated in a less searching way, if at all, when they are arising out of religious land use.

Each of these individual examples of the special treatment religious land use enjoys under RLUIPA may have only local significance. However, in the aggregate these kinds of exceptions have altered the nature of local land use controls, and not for the better—they make it much harder for local governments to manage the externalities that land use inevitably produces. Yet these examples, taken from RLUIPA cases that made it to court, are only the beginning of the practical problem RLUIPA poses for local governments, because the most practically significant aspect of the statute may be the discretion it affords courts to award prevailing religious claimants their attorneys' fees.

Thus, the threat of recovering their attorneys' fees connected with RLUIPA litigation gives religious claimants substantial leverage when disputes arise. This leverage may be disproportionate to the substantive merits of the claim under the statute because both fee awards and the related cost of settlements to resolve RLUIPA cases can be significant, frequently rising into six or seven figures—sums that far outstrip many local governments' ability to pay or even realistically contemplate. Thus, the prospect of having to make such a payment, combined with the murky nature of the statute's substantive provisions, frequently creates substantial pressure on local governments to compromise or settle even relatively weak RLUIPA claims. Indeed, even some attorneys who represent religious organizations in land use disputes note that the combination of RLUIPA's fees provision and the unpredictability attached to the statute's substantive provisions provide strong, often irresistible incentives for local governments to capitulate that bear little relation to the substantive merits of the landowner's claim.

Moreover, the edge that RLUIPA's fee awards provision gives to religious claimants is exacerbated by such claimants' potential access to assistance from expert outside assistance provided by nonprofits that focus on religious legal disputes. As a result, local governments frequently settle RLUIPA disputes on terms favorable to religious plaintiffs, and when they settle, local governments frequently cite RLUIPA's fees provisions as the determinative factor. When local governments are compelled to settle RLUIPA disputes based on the prospect of a fee award, their representatives often acknowledge the fact in stark and honest terms—especially if the local government and the community are relatively small, and facing claimant's counsel from larger legal markets or expert nongovernmental organizations. As the attorney for a local government in one recent settlement put it:

> This settlement was done due to the risk involved with litigation. We were concerned about other cases along the same line that had been litigated in other states. Some had won significant attorney's fees. One was in excess of $1 million . . . . It boiled down to the decision of: 'Is it worth the risk to take it to trial?' Especially in light of the fact attorney's fees could be substantial.

For now, it is enough to note that local government officials and lawyers on both sides of religious land use disputes believe that the prospect of RLUIPA fee awards compels local governments to settle disputes that should not be settled and deters them from regulating religious land use as they otherwise would and should. Again, each individual compromise may have only local significance; however, in the aggregate the compelling threat and deterrent effect of RLUIPA's fees provisions make it much harder for local governments to manage the externalities that religious land use, like every other kind of land use, inevitably produces. . . .

C.   Religious Exercise and Substantial Burdens Under RLUIPA

Two of RLUIPA's specific components are worth particular attention at the outset of this focused review of the statute: first, the statute's use and definition of the term *religious exercise* itself; and second, the provision of the statute that prohibits local governments from imposing a *substantial burden* on religious exercise. Aside from the provisions creating the possibility for attorneys' fee awards for religious claimants, the religious exercise and substantial burden components of RLUIPA are the most important parts of the statute. The breadth of both terms and their relationship to each other makes resolving inquiries into the relevant religious exercise and whether it has been substantially burdened the critical inquiry in many disputes resolved by the statute.

The statute's drafters intended that the term religious exercise should be interpreted as broadly as possible—indeed, the statute expressly does not limit inquiry to practices "compelled by" or "central to" the religious beliefs at issue It is, for example, broader than analogous provisions in the tax code, which extend favorable treatment to religious organizations only if the relevant conduct is "substantially related" to the organization's religious, charitable, or educational purpose. More importantly, RLUIPA's term "religious exercise" is also intended to include and protect more kinds of religious land use than were previously recognized: RLUIPA expressly amended the definition of the "exercise of religion" provided by RFRA "in an obvious effort to effect a complete separation from First Amendment case law" and its predecessor statutes. The intention behind this deliberate rupture with previous First Amendment case law was to make "the exercise of religion" a term that would be as broad as possible, explicitly untethering "the exercise of religion" from any inquiry into that exercise's relative importance to a system of religious belief.

Accordingly, the expansive nature of "religious exercise" under RLUIPA means that defining the outer limits of "a substantial burden on the religious exercise of a person" has proved to be the most important and the most complicated component of the statute. As Judge Posner recently noted, "[i]t's hard to imagine a vaguer criterion for a violation of religious rights." The murky nature of any inquiry into religious exercise and substantial burden under the general and expansive language of the statute has been exacerbated by the mare's nest of opinions that have tried, and spectacularly failed, to sort out consistent interpretations of these terms in RLUIPA cases. Nevertheless, a few general points of consensus have emerged.

In general, courts will not find a substantial burden based on purely procedural requirements that ultimately allow the relevant religious exercise to proceed, or when other sites are available for the religious exercise at issue. On the other hand, local governments are likely to run afoul of the substantial burden prong of RFRA when they entirely reject compromise, or avenues of potential compromise, with religious groups. Similarly, local governments are highly likely to run into RLUIPA-related problems if the record reflects any measure of animus against either the faith in question or the individual believers impacted by the relevant land use controls.

But beyond situations that involve intransigence or outright hostility, what counts as a substantial burden under RLUIPA varies considerably across—and sometimes within—the circuits. So, for example, the Seventh Circuit has recently held that religious exercise must be "effectively impracticable" under a local land use regulation in order to be substantially burdened under RLUIPA; however, the Seventh Circuit has also held that a substantial burden may be found when there is merely "delay, uncertainty, and expense." In contrast, the Eleventh Circuit has deliberately rejected the Seventh Circuit's approach(es), focusing instead on individual believers for whom substantial burdens are "akin to significant pressure which directly coerces the religious adherent to conform his or her behavior accordingly." Meanwhile, courts in the Ninth Circuit have rejected all of the above approaches, holding instead that religious exercise must be burdened to a "significantly great extent"—something less than rendering religious exercise effectively impracticable, but something more than mere delay, uncertainty, and expense. These are only examples: cataloguing the range of recent approaches to substantial burden and religious exercise would take many more pages.

This uncertainty means that courts often reach wildly inconsistent results in RLUIPA cases involving similarly situated religious claimants and local governments. So, for example, some courts have held that land use regulations that effectively restrict the time of religious services and the size of the congregation that can meet may not be a substantial burden, while others have held that a lack of meeting space in auxiliary buildings besides those used for religious services may be a substantial burden. Similarly, although some courts have held that land use controls that entirely prevent construction of a church of any size on rural land impose a substantial burden, other courts require religious organizations in such a situation to also show that they "could not reasonably locate and acquire an alternative site for its proposed combined uses."

As a result, it is hard for local governments and their counsel to predict what might or might not be a substantial burden of religious exercise under RLUIPA. This unpredictability only exacerbates the problematic incentives created by RLUIPA's attorneys' fees provision. Local governments must contend with the procedural risk of RLUIPA's fees provisions and the uncertainty surrounding the substantial terms provision, both of which deter local governments from implementing useful land use regulation in the first place or compel local governments to settle individual disputes where enforcement of existing regulations is badly needed.

D. Equal Terms, Nondiscrimination, Unreasonable Limits, and Total Exclusion Under RLUIPA

In addition to its prohibition on substantially burdening religious exercise, RLUIPA also prohibits local governments from "impos[ing] or implement[ing] a land use regulation in a manner that" treats religious organizations "on less than equal terms" with nonreligious organizations, or discriminates against any religious organization, or totally excludes religious organizations from a jurisdiction, or places unreasonable limits on religious organizations within a jurisdiction. Unlike section 2(a) of the statute, these sections essentially mirror previous constitutional precedent or provisions of other statutes such as the Fair Housing Act, and as a result, they have attracted far less attention from RLUIPA's many critics. For similar reasons, these provisions have also attracted less attention from litigants and from courts than the substantial burden provision discussed above.

Of these remaining substantive provisions of RLUIPA, by far the most significant is the "equal terms" section of the statute, which has begun to be more frequently litigated in recent years. The chief problem with the equal terms provision is that the statutory text contains literally no limiting principle. Accordingly, most courts have read in the limiting term "similarly situated" into the statutory text of 42 U.S.C. § 2000cc(b)(1), because without it, then "if a town allows a local, ten-member book club to meet in the senior center, it must also permit a large church with a thousand members ... to locate in the same neighborhood regardless of the [differential] impact" such a religious land use might have compared with the secular permitted land use. Most, but not all have followed this reasoning: the Eleventh Circuit reads the statutory term literally, effectively giving religious land users a blanket waiver from local land use controls, because under the literal language of the statute a zoning ordinance "that permits *any* 'assembly' ... to locate in a district must permit a church to locate there as well even if the only secular assemblies permitted are hospital operating theaters, bus terminals, air raid shelters," and other assemblies that are dissimilar to religious organizations. Moreover, even among those courts that do effectively read the words "similarly situated" into the statute, there is great variety about how the statutory provision should be interpreted.

Again, the uncertainty and unpredictability that attaches to RLUIPA's equal terms provision only exacerbates the problematic incentives created by RLUIPA's attorneys' fees provision, which may deter local governments from implementing useful land use regulation in the first place or compel local governments to settle individual disputes where enforcement of existing regulations is badly needed. . . .

IV. FROM BAD TO WORSE: THE PROBLEMS WITH AN INSTITUTIONAL APPROACH TO RLUIPA

B. The Practical Problems Caused by RLUIPA's Increasingly Institutional Tendencies

[S]ome scholars have pointed out the ways in which megachurches and other expanding religious institutions have secured or defended novel and expansive forms of land use, despite the presence of environmental land use regulations that otherwise ought to apply, based on little more than the institutions' allegedly distinctive religious nature. In other words, thanks to RLUIPA a religious claimant can push forward plans for development that include over one hundred thousand new square feet of construction, comprising a gymnasium, a gallery, a multipurpose building, and five hundred parking spaces (in addition to a school and facilities for religious worship), on land designated as an agricultural buffer zone where nonreligious claimants would be barred from similarly intensive development. In addition, several critics have identified the "tremendous leverage" that RLUIPA's fee-shifting provisions, combined with the murkiness attached to its substantive components, provide to religious claimants in negotiations with local governments. As attorneys who have been involved *on both sides* of religious land use disputes recognize, RLUIPA allows religious claimants to "bully" or "strong arm" local governments, to a degree "that would be tolerated from no other land user," thanks to the one-sided practical application of the statute's fees provision and the murky nature of the statute's key substantive provisions.

As a result, while bargaining in RLUIPA's shadow, religious claimants can negotiate on such favorable terms with local governments that they become a "law unto themselves," even regarding auxiliary uses like food courts, bookstores, and broadcasting facilities. Furthermore, religious institutions' enhanced bargaining power vis-à-vis local governments under RLUIPA may not be limited to compellent threats in settlement negotiations; rather, as several scholars have pointed out, the specter of RLUIPA's fees provisions may deter local governments from imposing land use regulation in the first place. In other words, the enhanced influence outside of court that RLUIPA gives religious institutions is not just a significant weapon to compel local governments to settle disputes when they arise: the threat of RLUIPA litigation may also chill local governments' willingness to impose desirable land use controls in the first place.

In a similar vein, some scholars have highlighted the costs that expanding religious land use imposes on religious institutions' neighbors, and the reluctance of many institutions to account for concerns related to those costs given RLUIPA's protections. Still, other critics of the statute's land use provisions have described the chasm between the statute's stated purpose—to address and prevent discrimination against particularly vulnerable religious believers—and the special protections that it practically affords to all religious organizations, whether or not they are vulnerable to or have faced discrimination. Regardless of the particular focus of their criticism, a common thread runs through most past critical examinations of RLUIPA: namely, the way in which the statute, as it is often applied, picks out religious institutions that own land for distinctively favorable treatment because of what they are rather than what they are doing or why they are doing it.

Of course, as noted above, some defenders of RLUIPA reject this critical picture of RLUIPA—they argue that religious institutions receive an appropriate amount of deference and protection under the statute, and some even argue that religious institutions receive too little protection under the statute as currently applied.

As a result, the debate about RLUIPA's practical effect has stagnated, leaving both sides to chew over the same evidence while reaching different conclusions. In part this stagnation is a function of the evidence relied upon by both sides. It is true that religious institutions lose RLUIPA suits that are decided on substantive grounds in federal court more often than they win. On the other hand, RLUIPA plaintiffs still win around half the time, and they tend to win more often and with bigger victories than plaintiffs with similar sorts of religious land use claims brought prior to RLUIPA's enactment. Similarly, although the rate of litigation in federal court regarding RLUIPA is not dramatically higher than for other kinds of land use disputes involving rights associated with the First Amendment, such as signs or adult uses, the rate of litigation for religious land use disputes has been higher since RLUIPA than it was before the statute was enacted. In short, data about the outcomes of RLUIPA suits in the courts has failed to resolve the long-standing, though relatively one-sided, debate about the statute's merits. This should not be surprising: due to selection effects and other related variables, litigation success rates often reveal relatively little reliable and interesting information.

In sum, therefore, RLUIPA tilts the balance in negotiation and conflict over land use regulation toward religious institutions. This does not mean that religious institutions win every time in court, nor that local governments are driven to capitulate outside of court in every situation. But RLUIPA's substantive uncertainty, the statute's fee provisions, and the stakes of the conflict for local government defendants do provide religious institutions with distinctive deference and protection from local land use regulation. Moreover, this deference and protection is neither based upon nor entirely reducible to concerns or regard for the institution's individual members, but rather focused on the institutional plaintiffs in their own right.

C. *Hosanna-Tabor and Hobby Lobby Will Exacerbate the Practical Problems RLUIPA Causes*

[J]ust as the ministerial exception, at least for the time being, appears to be growing without readily discernible limits in the wake of the organizational free exercise claims advanced in *Hosanna-Tabor*, it is reasonable to expect that the same principles, incorporated into the land use context, will cause distension of RLUIPA's already expansive definition of "religious exercise" in the land use context. If all teachers in a religious school may be deemed religious ministers, regardless of what they teach or what their own beliefs might be, then similarly every kind of land use activity that school engages in might be deemed religious exercise under RLUIPA, at least according to an institutional theory.

The potential effects of *Hobby Lobby* on religious land use, and the ways in which that decision might lead to an increasingly institutional interpretation of RLUIPA, are a bit harder to explain, although the ultimate impact may be even more significant. *Hobby Lobby* has the potential to influence religious land use disputes in an institutional direction in at least two ways. First, as noted by amici and Justice Ginsburg's dissent, *Hobby Lobby* might lead to a dramatic expansion in the types of organizations that could claim protection under RLUIPA. If closely held commercial corporations count as "persons" under RFRA, then they might equally well count as "persons" under RLUIPA, and lawyers who represent both local governments and religious organizations are already advising their clients of this possibility.

Second, and beyond this potential expansion of potential RLUIPA plaintiffs, *Hobby Lobby* might alter the related inquiries into "religious exercise" and "substantial burden" under the statute, shifting both even closer to an institutional approach. To see how, it is probably easiest to turn first to an extremely recent RLUIPA case that postdates *Hobby Lobby*, albeit one involving a prisoner's religious exercise rather than religious land use. In *Holt v. Hobbs*, the Court drew upon *Hobby Lobby*, and the common history of RFRA and RLUIPA, to underscore the statutes' "expansive protection for religious liberty" and "capacious[ ]" definition of religious exercise. In addition, in *Holt* the Court applied the same analysis for a substantial burden under RLUIPA that it applied to substantial burdens under RFRA in *Hobby Lobby*.

In the land use context, similar trends are likely to further discourage local governments, which in turn will increasingly enable religious organizations to effectively become a "law unto themselves" with respect to local land use controls. Although *Hobby Lobby* is less than a year old, courts already rely on it in RLUIPA cases to justify their decisions to avoid any inquiry into whether the land use activity is religious in nature. In other words, if the claimant is a religious institution, and if its relevant activity involves land, then courts have begun to simply conclude that RLUIPA should apply without any further analysis, relying upon *Hobby Lobby*.

In addition, sophisticated counsel for religious organizations in RLUIPA cases are beginning to invoke *Hobby Lobby* for the same sorts of purposes: to establish the extremely generous limits of religious exercise under the statute; to show how courts must accept, without further inquiry, a religious institution's claim that its activity constitutes religious exercise; and finally, to demonstrate how this nearly unlimited conception of religious exercise should contribute to an equally expansive interpretation of substantial burdens under the statute. In sum, courts and counsel for religious plaintiffs are already using *Hobby Lobby* to advance increasingly institutional interpretations of RLUIPA.

As practically applied, therefore, some recent interpretations of RLUIPA already approximate an institutional approach to religious land use. Even without an institutional gloss on the statute, under RLUIPA, religious institutions already receive substantial deference and protection in the courts, which are not reducible to the beliefs, practice, or the burdens imposed upon their individual members. Outside of court, the practical effects of this institutional turn are even easier to discern: practitioners on both sides of religious land use disputes note the ways that religious organizations are able to obtain the level of deference and protection advocated by institutionalists thanks to the leverage that RLUIPA's substantive ambiguity and attorneys' fees provisions provides. Unfortunately, the many problems associated with this one-sided approach to religious land use are likely to increase as the institutional chords sounded by *Hosanna-Tabor* and *Hobby Lobby* are incorporated into RLUIPA doctrine in the coming years.

NOTES AND QUESTIONS

1.   *RLUIPA's Impact.* Why is Professor Bray so critical of RLUIPA? Summarize his best arguments criticizing the impact of RLUIPA on local land use. Do you believe RLUIPA has as big an impact on local land use as Professor Bray suggests? Or do you think RLUIPA's impact has been overstated by its critics?

Why did the article conclude the attorney's fees portions of RLUIPA favor religious landowners over local governments? If you were a local government official, would you settle RLUIPA cases instead of litigating them? How would you balance your obligations to the community with the demands of RLUIPA?

2.   *Hosanna-Tabor.* You read the ministerial exception case, which rejected Cheryl Perich's disabilities discrimination lawsuit, in Chapter 6.

Why did Bray think *Hosanna-Tabor* was relevant to land use analysis under RLUIPA? Do you agree the ministerial exception cases can be read to implicate broad protection of religious institutions in the land use context?

3. *Holt v. Hobbs.* Professor Bray also argued that the prisoner's beard case, which you read in Section A, might expand RLUIPA's scope. Why? Do you agree? If the *Holt* analysis were applied to every land use case, could the government ever win a RLUIPA challenge?

4. *Hobby Lobby.* Do you recall how the Court analyzed the elements of a RFRA claim in *Hobby Lobby*, in Chapter 4? If the Court was deferential to plaintiffs' substantial burden claims in RFRA cases, does that guarantee RLUIPA review will be equally deferential? How do you think a local government's interests in environmental quality, traffic, and zoning compare to the interest in women's health that was involved in *Hobby Lobby*?

Does RLUIPA affect your assessment of RFRA? Is it a good or bad idea to interpret RFRA and RLUIPA equivalently? Did Justice Alito conclude they must be interpreted equivalently when he wrote "[RLUIPA] enacted under Congress's Commerce and Spending Clause powers, imposes the same general test as RFRA but on a more limited category of governmental actions."? Hobby Lobby, 134 S.Ct. at 2761.

Do you think it is "passing strange" that whenever Justice Alito mentioned RLUIPA in *Hobby Lobby*, he referred to the institutionalized persons section and not to land use? See Hobby Lobby, 134 S.Ct. at 2794, n. 12 (Ginsburg, J., dissenting) ("it is passing strange to attribute to RLUIPA any purpose to cover entities other than 'religious assembl[ies] or institutions[s].' "). Do you think *Hobby Lobby* will become a major precedent for land use cases? Do you think a local Hobby Lobby arts and crafts store should enjoy RLUIPA protection?

How do you react to the following advice about *Hobby Lobby* in the RLUIPA context written by a land use lawyer:

> What should municipalities do if a privately held corporation asserts that it is protected by RLUIPA? Consider, for example, the frozen yogurt establishment sweetFrog.™ According to the company's website, sweetFrog premium frozen yogurt strives to "create the best frozen yogurt experience you've ever had!" It adds that "[t]he F.R.O.G. in sweetFrog stands for Fully Rely on God." What happens if sweetFrog seeks zoning approval to operate at a certain location it asserts is of religious significance? Does RLUIPA apply? Out of an abundance of caution, municipalities may now wish to proceed as though the statute does apply.

Evan J. Seeman, RLUIPA Defense Tactics; How to Avoid & Defend Against RLUIPA Claims, 37:11 Zoning and Planning Law Report 1, 11 (2014). What would you do if sweetFrog filed a zoning request with your government office?

5. *Establishment.* Recall in Section A we learned that RLUIPA was originally challenged in the prison setting as an Establishment Clause violation for preferring religion to non-religion. Do you think the land use provisions of RLUIPA violate the Establishment Clause? Is it clear from Bray's article that RLUIPA favors religious claimants and confers an unfair advantage on them? What argument could you make that RLUIPA extends beyond religious accommodation to religious establishment? In Section A, in *Cutter v. Wilkinson*, the Court ruled RLUIPA did not violate the Establishment Clause because "it alleviates exceptional government-created burdens on private religious exercise." Is that true in the land use setting?

In *Zubik*, the nonprofits' contraceptive mandate case that you read in Chapter 5, many amici argued that the Establishment Clause is violated whenever government accommodations of religion harm third parties. Was there any indication in the RLUIPA cases in this chapter that RLUIPA allows courts to consider the interests of third parties in neighboring landowners, residential neighborhoods, and commercial development? What does Bray say about these issues? What does he argue about the externalities associated with RLUIPA? Are there any other points in the article that suggest an Establishment Clause violation?

Now that you have learned about constitutional and statutory protection of religious freedom, the religious freedom of institutions and individuals, and the scope of the Establishment Clause in the United States, Chapter 8 presents several cases from non-U.S. courts that address issues previously studied in this casebook. As you read Chapter 8, think about how these other courts and nations differ, if at all.

CHAPTER 8

COMPARATIVE RELIGIOUS FREEDOM

You learned throughout the preceding chapters that, within the United States alone, the protection of religious freedom is complex and controversial. In this chapter, we consider religious freedom in the international context. A threshold question regarding international religious freedom relates to the Free Exercise Clause, namely, should all governments recognize a human right to religious freedom, or should the protection of religious freedom be left to the determination of individual nations? Should religious freedom be protected in international law? As a second issue, in the American setting, many constitutional lawyers have argued that the Establishment Clause exists to protect free exercise. Does this mean that every nation should ban establishment? Or are there other relationships between church and state that can protect religious freedom?

In order to encourage you to think comparatively, this chapter presents several cases from non-U.S. courts that address issues previously studied in this casebook. Section A looks at the wearing of religious garb in different national settings. Recall that in Chapter 6, we learned that Abercrombie & Fitch faced a Title VII lawsuit for discriminating against a prospective employee who wore a hijab. This chapter begins with the case of Leyla Şahin v. Turkey, App. No. 44774/98 (GC) 19 Eur. H.R. Rep. 590 (2005). Şahin, a Muslim medical student, argued that the Istanbul University's ban on religious headscarves violated her religious rights under the European Convention on Human Rights. The outcome of the case was affected by the fact that Turkey's government is secular, or *laik*. Thus the case also allows us to explore relationships between church and state that differ from the U.S. Establishment Clause.

In Chapter 3 we learned that the Free Speech Clause of the First Amendment has been used extensively to protect religious freedom. Section B examines the international law of blasphemy and defamation of religion. Although prosecution for blasphemy now seems unimaginable in the United States, at the beginning of Section B you will read excerpts from some nineteenth-century state cases allowing prosecutions for speech offenses against Christianity. The chapter then turns to international debates concerning whether criticism of religion should be illegal.

Section C returns to the statutory and constitutional protection of religious freedom and conscience that we studied in Chapters 4 and 5. Section C is divided into three sections that parallel United States case law that we read in earlier chapters. Section C1 presents *Bayatyan v. Armenia*, in which the European Court of Human Rights recognized a religious freedom right to military conscientious objection for a Jehovah's Witness who objected to military service. Section C2 presents a British case similar in reasoning to the Kentucky clerk's case, *Miller v. Davis*. The European court affirmed a British court holding that an English registrar of marriages had no religious freedom right to refuse to perform same-sex marriages. Finally, Section C3 introduces a case that has been described as "Australia's *Hobby Lobby*." Thus we consider the role of religious exemptions in international law.

Consider throughout the chapter how principles of religious freedom compare and contrast throughout the world. Was freedom of religion and belief protected in the following case?

A. RELIGIOUS GARB

Burqa: A woman wearing a burqa walking with a child by the road in northern Afghanistan.

Photograph by Steve Evans.

Niqab: Muslim woman in Yemen wearing a niqab.

Photograph by Steve Evans.

Leyla Şahin v. Turkey

The European Court of Human Rights, Grand Chamber, 2005.
App. No. 44774/98.

The European Court of Human Rights, sitting as a Grand Chamber composed of:

Mr. L. WILDHABER, *President*,

Mr. C.L. ROZAKIS,

Mr. J.P. COSTA,

Mr. B.M. ZUPANI,

Mr. R. TÜRMEN,

Mrs. F. TULKENS,

Mr. C. BRSAN,

Mr. K. JUNGWIERT,

Mr. V. BUTKEVYCH,

Mrs. N. VAJIĆ,

Mr. M. UGREKHELIDZE,

Mrs. A. MULARONI,

Mr. J. BORREGO,

Mrs. E. FURA-SANDSTRÖM,

Mrs. A. GYULUMYAN,

Mr. E. MYJER,

Mr. S.E. JEBENS, *judges*,

and Mr. T.L. EARLY, *Deputy Grand Chamber Registrar*.

THE FACTS

I.   THE CIRCUMSTANCES OF THE CASE

1.   The applicant was born in 1973 and has lived in Vienna since 1999, when she left Istanbul to pursue her medical studies at the Faculty of Medicine at Vienna University. She comes from a traditional family of practising Muslims and considers it her religious duty to wear the Islamic headscarf.

2.   On 26 August 1997 the applicant, then in her fifth year at the Faculty of Medicine at Bursa University, enrolled at the Cerrahpaşa Faculty of Medicine at Istanbul University. She says that she wore the Islamic headscarf during the four years she spent studying medicine at the University of Bursa and continued to do so until February 1998.

3.   On 23 February 1998 the Vice Chancellor of Istanbul University issued a circular, the relevant part of which provides:

"By virtue of the Constitution, the law and regulations, and in accordance with the case-law of the Supreme

Administrative Court and the European Commission of Human Rights and the resolutions adopted by the university administrative boards, students whose 'heads are covered' (who wear the Islamic headscarf) and students (including overseas students) with beards must not be admitted to lectures, courses or tutorials. Consequently, the name and number of any student with a beard or wearing the Islamic headscarf must not be added to the lists of registered students. However, students who insist on attending tutorials and entering lecture theatres although their names and numbers are not on the lists must be advised of the position and, should they refuse to leave, their names and numbers must be taken and they must be informed that they are not entitled to attend lectures. If they refuse to leave the lecture theatre, the teacher shall record the incident in a report explaining why it was not possible to give the lecture and shall bring the incident to the attention of the university authorities as a matter of urgency so that disciplinary measures can be taken."

4.   On 12 March 1998, in accordance with the aforementioned circular, the applicant was denied access by invigilators to a written examination on oncology because she was wearing the Islamic headscarf. On 20 March 1998 the secretariat of the chair of orthopaedic traumatology refused to allow her to enrol because she was wearing a headscarf. On 16 April 1998 she was refused admission to a neurology lecture and on 10 June 1998 to a written examination on public health, again for the same reason.

5.   On 29 July 1998 the applicant lodged an application for an order setting aside the circular of 23 February 1998. In her written pleadings, she submitted that the circular and its implementation had infringed her rights guaranteed by Articles 8, 9 and 14 of the Convention and Article 2 of Protocol No. 1, in that there was no statutory basis for the circular and the Vice-Chancellor's Office had no regulatory power in that sphere.

6.   In a judgment of 19 March 1999, the Istanbul Administrative Court dismissed the application, holding that by virtue of section 13(b) of the Higher-Education Act (Law no. 2547) a university vice chancellor, as the executive organ of the university, had power to regulate students' dress for the purposes of maintaining order. That regulatory power had to be exercised in accordance with the relevant legislation and the judgments of the Constitutional Court and the Supreme Administrative Court. Referring to the settled case-law of those courts, the Administrative Court held that neither the regulations in issue, nor the measures taken against the applicant, could be considered illegal.

7.   On 19 April 2001 the Supreme Administrative Court dismissed an appeal on points of law by the applicant.

C.   The disciplinary measures taken against the applicant

[Şahin first received a warning, then was suspended for a semester, and lost an appeal of the suspension in the Istanbul Administrative Court. After Law no. 4584 entered into force on 28 June 2000, she was granted an amnesty releasing her from all penalties imposed for the violation. On 16 September 1999 she left Turkey and enrolled at Vienna University.]

II.   RELEVANT LAW AND PRACTICE

A.   The Constitution

8.   The relevant provisions of the Constitution provide:

Article 2

"The Republic of Turkey is a democratic, secular (*laik*) and social State based on the rule of law that is respectful of human rights in a spirit of social peace, national solidarity and justice, adheres to the nationalism of Atatürk and is underpinned by the fundamental principles set out in the Preamble."

Article 10

"All individuals shall be equal before the law without any distinction based on language, race, colour, sex, political opinion, philosophical belief, religion, membership of a religious sect or other similar grounds.

Men and women shall have equal rights. The State shall take action to achieve such equality in practice.

No privileges shall be granted to any individual, family, group or class.

State bodies and administrative authorities shall act in compliance with the principle of equality before the law in all circumstances. . . . "

Article 13

"Fundamental rights and freedoms may be restricted only by law and on the grounds set out in special provisions of the Constitution, provided always that the essence of such rights and freedoms must remain intact. Any such restriction shall not conflict with the letter or spirit of the Constitution or the requirements of a democratic, secular social order and shall comply with the principle of proportionality."

Article 14

"The rights and freedoms set out in the Constitution may be not exercised with a view to undermining the territorial integrity of the State, the unity of the Nation or the democratic and secular Republic founded on human rights.

No provision of this Constitution shall be interpreted in a manner that would grant the State or individuals the right to engage in activities intended to destroy the fundamental rights and freedoms embodied in the Constitution or to restrict them beyond what is permitted by the Constitution.

The penalties to which persons who engage in activities that contravene these provisions are liable shall be determined by law."

Article 24

"Everyone shall have the right to freedom of conscience, belief and religious conviction.

Prayers, worship and religious services shall be conducted freely, provided that they do not violate the provisions of Article 14.

No one shall be compelled to participate in prayers, worship or religious services or to reveal his or her religious beliefs and convictions; no one shall be censured or prosecuted for his religious beliefs or convictions.

Education and instruction in religion and ethics shall be provided under the supervision and control of the State. Instruction in religious culture and in morals shall be a compulsory part of the curricula of primary and secondary schools. Other religious education and instruction shall be a matter for individual choice, with the decision in the case of minors being taken by their legal guardians.

No one shall exploit or abuse religion, religious feelings or things held sacred by religion in any manner whatsoever with a view to causing the social, economic, political or legal order of the State to be based on religious precepts, even if only in part, or for the purpose of securing political or personal interest or influence thereby."

Article 42

"No one may be deprived of the right to instruction and education.

The scope of the right to education shall be defined and regulated by law.

Instruction and teaching shall be provided under the supervision and control of the State in accordance with the principles and reforms of Atatürk and contemporary scientific and educational methods. No educational or teaching institution may be set up that does not follow these rules.

Citizens are not absolved from the duty to remain loyal to the Constitution by freedom of instruction and teaching.

Primary education shall be compulsory for all citizens of both sexes and provided free of charge in State schools.

The rules governing the functioning of private primary and secondary schools shall be regulated by law in keeping with the standards set for State schools.

The State shall provide able pupils of limited financial means with the necessary aid in the form of scholarships or other assistance to enable them to pursue their studies. It shall take suitable measures to rehabilitate those in need of special training so as to render them useful to society.

Education, teaching, research, and study are the only activities that may be pursued in educational and teaching institutions. These activities shall not be impeded in any way. . . . "

B.   History and background

1.   *Religious dress and the principle of secularism*

9.   The Turkish Republic was founded on the principle that the State should be secular (*laik*). Before and after the proclamation of the Republic on 29 October 1923, the public and religious spheres were separated through a series of revolutionary reforms: the abolition of the caliphate on 3 March 1923; the repeal of the constitutional provision declaring Islam the religion of the State on 10 April 1928; and, lastly, on 5 February 1937 a constitutional amendment according constitutional status to the principle of secularism (see Article 2 of the Constitution of 1924 and Article 2 of the Constitutions of 1961 and 1982, as set out above).

10.   The principle of secularism was inspired by developments in Ottoman society in the period between the nineteenth century and the proclamation of the Republic. The idea of creating a modern public society in which equality was guaranteed to all citizens without distinction on grounds of religion, denomination or sex had already been mooted in the Ottoman debates of the nineteenth century. Significant advances in women's rights were made during this period (equality of treatment in education, the introduction of a ban on polygamy in 1914, the transfer of jurisdiction in matrimonial cases to the secular courts that had been established in the nineteenth century).

11.   The defining feature of the Republican ideal was the presence of women in public life and their active participation in society. Consequently, the ideas that women should be freed from religious constraints and that society should be modernised had a common origin. Thus, on 17 February 1926 the Civil Code was adopted, which provided for equality of the sexes in the enjoyment of civic rights, in particular with regard to divorce and succession. Subsequently, through

a constitutional amendment of 5 December 1934 (Article 10 of the 1924 Constitution), women obtained equal political rights with men.

12. The first legislation to regulate dress was the Headgear Act of 28 November 1925 (Law no. 671), which treated dress as a modernity issue. Similarly, a ban was imposed on wearing religious attire other than in places of worship or at religious ceremonies, irrespective of the religion or belief concerned, by the Dress (Regulations) Act of 3 December 1934 (Law no. 2596).

13. Under the Education Services (Merger) Act of 3 March 1924 (Law no. 430), religious schools were closed and all schools came under the control of the Ministry for Education. The Act is one of the laws with constitutional status that are protected by Article 174 of the Turkish Constitution.

14. In Turkey wearing the Islamic headscarf to school and university is a recent phenomenon which only really began to emerge in the 1980s. There has been extensive discussion on the issue and it continues to be the subject of lively debate in Turkish society. Those in favour of the headscarf see wearing it as a duty and/or a form of expression linked to religious identity. However, the supporters of secularism, who draw a distinction between the *basörtüsü* (traditional Anatolian headscarf, worn loosely) and the *türban* (tight, knotted headscarf hiding the hair and the throat), see the Islamic headscarf as a symbol of a political Islam. As a result of the accession to power on 28 June 1996 of a coalition government comprising the Islamist *Refah Partisi*, and the centre-right *Doğru Yol Partisi*, the debate has taken on strong political overtones. The ambivalence displayed by the leaders of the *Refah Partisi*, including the then Prime Minister, over their attachment to democratic values, and their advocacy of a plurality of legal systems functioning according to different religious rules for each religious community was perceived in Turkish society as a genuine threat to republican values and civil peace (see *Refah Partisi (the Welfare Party) and Others v. Turkey* [GC], nos. 41340/98, 41342/98, 41343/98 and 41344/98, ECHR 2003–II). . . .

> 2. *The rules on dress in institutions of higher education and the case-law of the Constitutional Court .*

15. On 25 October 1990 transitional section 17 of Law no. 2547 entered into force. It provides:

> "Choice of dress shall be free in institutions of higher education, provided that it does not contravene the laws in force."

16. In a judgment of 9 April 1991, which was published in the Official Gazette of 31 July 1991, the Constitutional Court noted that, in the light of the principles it had established in its judgment of 7 March 1989, the aforementioned provision did not allow headscarves to be

worn in institutions of higher education on religious grounds and so was consistent with the Constitution. It stated, *inter alia*:

> " ... the expression 'laws in force' refers first and foremost to the Constitution. .... In institutions of higher education, it is contrary to the principles of secularism and equality for the neck and hair to be covered with a veil or headscarf on grounds of religious conviction. In these circumstances, the freedom of dress which the impugned provision permits in institutions of higher education 'does not concern dress of a religious nature or the act of covering one's neck and hair with a veil and headscarf'.... The freedom afforded by this provision [transitional section 17] is conditional on its not being contrary 'to the laws in force'. The judgment [of 7 March 1989] of the Constitutional Court establishes that covering one's neck and hair with the headscarf is first and foremost contrary to the Constitution. Consequently, the condition set out in the aforementioned section requiring [choice of] dress not to contravene the laws in force removes from the scope of freedom of dress the act of 'covering one's neck and hair with the headscarf.... .'"

3.   Application of the regulations at Istanbul University

[The University passed regulations prohibiting religious headgear that it argued were consistent with these laws. The regulations allowed a variety of sanctions, including a warning, a reprimand, temporary suspension of between a week and a month, temporary suspension of one or two semesters and expulsion.]

D.   Comparative law

17.   For more than twenty years the place of the Islamic headscarf in State education has been the subject of debate across Europe. In most European countries, the debate has focused mainly on primary and secondary schools. However, in Turkey, Azerbaijan and Albania it has concerned not just the question of individual liberty, but also the political meaning of the Islamic headscarf. These are the only member States to have introduced regulations on wearing the Islamic headscarf in universities.

18.   In France, where secularism is regarded as one of the cornerstones of republican values, legislation was passed on 15 March 2004 regulating, in accordance with the principle of secularism, the wearing of signs or dress manifesting a religious affiliation in State primary and secondary schools. The legislation inserted a new Article L. 141–5–1 in the Education Code which provides: "In State primary and secondary schools, the wearing of signs or dress by which pupils overtly manifest a religious affiliation is prohibited. The school rules shall state that the institution of disciplinary proceedings shall be preceded by dialogue with the pupil."

The Act applies to all State schools and educational institutions, including post-baccalaureate courses (preparatory classes for entrance to the *grandes écoles* and vocational training courses). It does not apply to State universities. In addition, as the circular of 18 May 2004 makes clear, it only concerns " . . . signs . . . , such as the Islamic headscarf, however named, the kippa or a cross that is manifestly oversized, which make the wearer's religious affiliation immediately identifiable."

19. In Belgium there is no general ban on wearing religious signs at school. In the French Community a decree of 13 March 1994 stipulates that education shall be neutral within the Community. Pupils are in principle allowed to wear religious signs. However, they may do so only if human rights, the reputation of others, national security, public order, and public health and morals are protected and internal rules complied with. Further, teachers must not permit religious or philosophical proselytism under their authority or the organisation of political militancy by or on behalf of pupils. The decree stipulates that restrictions may be imposed by school rules. On 19 May 2004 the French Community issued a decree intended to institute equality of treatment. In the Flemish Community, there is no uniform policy among schools on whether to allow religious or philosophical signs to be worn. Some do, others do not. When pupils are permitted to wear such signs, restrictions may be imposed on grounds of hygiene or safety.

20. In other countries (Austria, Germany, the Netherlands, Spain, Sweden, Switzerland and the United Kingdom), in some cases following a protracted legal debate, the State education authorities permit Muslim pupils and students to wear the Islamic headscarf.

21. In Germany, where the debate focused on whether teachers should be allowed to wear the Islamic headscarf, the Constitutional Court stated on 24 September 2003 in a case between a teacher and the *Land* of Baden-Württemberg that the lack of any express statutory prohibition meant that teachers were entitled to wear the headscarf. Consequently, it imposed a duty on the *Länder* to lay down rules on dress if they wished to prohibit the wearing of the Islamic headscarf in State schools.

22. In Austria there is no special legislation governing the wearing of the headscarf, turban or kippa. In general, it is considered that a ban on wearing the headscarf will only be justified if it poses a health or safety hazard for pupils.

23. In the United Kingdom a tolerant attitude is shown to pupils who wear religious signs. Difficulties with respect to the Islamic headscarf are rare. The issue has also been debated in the context of the elimination of racial discrimination in schools in order to preserve their multicultural character (see, in particular, *Mandla v. Dowell*, "The Law Reports" 1983, 548–570). The Commission for Racial Equality, whose

opinions have recommendation status only, also considered the issue of the Islamic headscarf in 1988 in the *Altrincham Grammar School* case, which ended in a compromise between a private school and members of the family of two sisters who wished to be allowed to wear the Islamic headscarf at the school. The school agreed to allow them to wear the headscarf provided it was navy blue (the colour of the school uniform), kept fastened at the neck and not decorated.

In the case of *R (On the application of Begum) v. Headteacher and Governors of Denbigh High School* [2004], the High Court had to decide a dispute between the school and a Muslim pupil wishing to wear the jilbab (a full-length gown). The school required pupils to wear a uniform, one of the possible options being the headscarf and a shalwar kameeze (long traditional garments from the Indian subcontinent). In June 2004 the High Court dismissed the pupil's application, holding that there had been no violation of her freedom of religion. However, that judgment was reversed in March 2005 by the Court of Appeal, which accepted that there had been interference with the pupil's freedom of religion, as a minority of Muslims in the United Kingdom considered that a religious duty to wear the jilbab from the age of puberty existed and the pupil was genuinely of that opinion. No justification for the interference had been provided by the school authorities, as the decision-making process was not compatible with freedom of religion.

24. In Spain, there is no express statutory prohibition on pupils' wearing religious head coverings in State schools. By virtue of two royal Decrees of 26 January 1996, which are applicable in primary and secondary schools unless the competent authority—the autonomous community—has introduced specific measures, the school governors have power to issue school rules which may include provisions on dress. Generally speaking, State schools allow the headscarf to be worn.

25. In Finland and Sweden the veil can be worn at school. However, a distinction is made between the burka (the term used to describe the full veil covering the whole of the body and the face) and the niqab (a veil covering all the upper body with the exception of the eyes). In Sweden mandatory directives were issued in 2003 by the National Education Agency. These allow schools to prohibit the burka and niqab, provided they do so in a spirit of dialogue on the common values of equality of the sexes and respect for the democratic principle on which the education system is based.

26. In the Netherlands, where the question of the Islamic headscarf is considered from the standpoint of discrimination rather than of freedom of religion, it is generally tolerated. In 2003 a non-binding directive was issued. Schools may require pupils to wear a uniform provided that the rules are not discriminatory and are included in the school prospectus and that the punishment for transgressions is

not disproportionate. A ban on the burka is regarded as justified by the need to be able to identify and communicate with pupils. In addition, the Equal Treatment Commission ruled in 1997 that a ban on wearing the veil during general lessons for safety reasons was not discriminatory.

27. In a number of other countries (the Czech Republic, Greece, Hungary, Poland or Slovakia), the issue of the Islamic headscarf does not yet appear to have given rise to any detailed legal debate.

THE LAW

I. ALLEGED VIOLATION OF ARTICLE 9 OF THE CONVENTION

28. The applicant submitted that the ban on wearing the Islamic headscarf in institutions of higher education constituted an unjustified interference with her right to freedom of religion, in particular, her right to manifest her religion.

She relied on Article 9 of the Convention, which provides:

"1. Everyone has the right to freedom of thought, conscience and religion; this right includes freedom to change his religion or belief and freedom, either alone or in community with others and in public or private, to manifest his religion or belief, in worship, teaching, practice and observance.

2.   Freedom to manifest one's religion or beliefs shall be subject only to such limitations as are prescribed by law and are necessary in a democratic society in the interests of public safety, for the protection of public order, health or morals, or for the protection of the rights and freedoms of others."

C.   The Court's assessment

[The Court assumed there was an interference with Şahin's religious desire to wear a headscarf, and concluded that, under paragraph 2, the ban was prescribed by law which had a number of legitimate aims, namely, the protection of the rights and freedoms of others and of public order. The parties argued whether the ban was "necessary in a democratic society." Şahin argued that her quiet wearing of the scarf did not disrupt social order and the government emphasized the importance of secularism to the state's continuance.]

(i)   General principles

29. The Court reiterates that as enshrined in Article 9, freedom of thought, conscience and religion is one of the foundations of a "democratic society" within the meaning of the Convention. This freedom is, in its religious dimension, one of the most vital elements that go to make up the identity of believers and their conception of life, but it is also a precious asset for atheists, agnostics, sceptics and the unconcerned. The pluralism indissociable from a democratic society, which has been dearly won over the centuries, depends on it. That

freedom entails, *inter alia*, freedom to hold or not to hold religious beliefs and to practise or not to practise a religion.

30. While religious freedom is primarily a matter of individual conscience, it also implies, *inter alia*, freedom to manifest one's religion, alone and in private, or in community with others, in public and within the circle of those whose faith one shares. Article 9 lists the various forms which manifestation of one's religion or belief may take, namely worship, teaching, practice and observance.

Article 9 does not protect every act motivated or inspired by a religion or belief.

31. In democratic societies, in which several religions coexist within one and the same population, it may be necessary to place restrictions on freedom to manifest one's religion or belief in order to reconcile the interests of the various groups and ensure that everyone's beliefs are respected. This follows both from paragraph 2 of Article 9 and the State's positive obligation under Article 1 of the Convention to secure to everyone within its jurisdiction the rights and freedoms defined in the Convention.

32. The Court has frequently emphasised the State's role as the neutral and impartial organiser of the exercise of various religions, faiths and beliefs, and stated that this role is conducive to public order, religious harmony and tolerance in a democratic society. It also considers that the State's duty of neutrality and impartiality is incompatible with any power on the State's part to assess the legitimacy of religious beliefs or the ways in which those beliefs are expressed and that it requires the State to ensure mutual tolerance between opposing groups. Accordingly, the role of the authorities in such circumstances is not to remove the cause of tension by eliminating pluralism, but to ensure that the competing groups tolerate each other.

33. Pluralism, tolerance and broadmindedness are hallmarks of a "democratic society." Although individual interests must on occasion be subordinated to those of a group, democracy does not simply mean that the views of a majority must always prevail: a balance must be achieved which ensures the fair and proper treatment of people from minorities and avoids any abuse of a dominant position. Pluralism and democracy must also be based on dialogue and a spirit of compromise necessarily entailing various concessions on the part of individuals or groups of individuals which are justified in order to maintain and promote the ideals and values of a democratic society. Where these "rights and freedoms" are themselves among those guaranteed by the Convention or its Protocols, it must be accepted that the need to protect them may lead States to restrict other rights or freedoms likewise set forth in the Convention. It is precisely this constant search for a balance between the fundamental rights of each individual which constitutes the foundation of a "democratic society."

34. Where questions concerning the relationship between State and religions are at stake, on which opinion in a democratic society may reasonably differ widely, the role of the national decision-making body must be given special importance. This will notably be the case when it comes to regulating the wearing of religious symbols in educational institutions, especially (as the comparative-law materials illustrate— see paragraphs 17–27 above) in view of the diversity of the approaches taken by national authorities on the issue. It is not possible to discern throughout Europe a uniform conception of the significance of religion in society, and the meaning or impact of the public expression of a religious belief will differ according to time and context. Rules in this sphere will consequently vary from one country to another according to national traditions and the requirements imposed by the need to protect the rights and freedoms of others and to maintain public order. Accordingly, the choice of the extent and form such regulations should take must inevitably be left up to a point to the State concerned, as it will depend on the domestic context concerned.

35. This margin of appreciation goes hand in hand with a European supervision embracing both the law and the decisions applying it. The Court's task is to determine whether the measures taken at national level were justified in principle and proportionate. In delimiting the extent of the margin of appreciation in the present case the Court must have regard to what is at stake, namely the need to protect the rights and freedoms of others, to preserve public order and to secure civil peace and true religious pluralism, which is vital to the survival of a democratic society.

36. The Court also notes that in the decisions of *Karaduman v. Turkey* (no. 16278/90, Commission decision of 3 May 1993, DR 74, p. 93) and *Dahlab v. Switzerland* (no. 42393/98, ECHR 2001–V) the Convention institutions found that in a democratic society the State was entitled to place restrictions on the wearing of the Islamic headscarf if it was incompatible with the pursued aim of protecting the rights and freedoms of others, public order and public safety. In the *Karaduman* case, measures taken in universities to prevent certain fundamentalist religious movements from exerting pressure on students who did not practise their religion or who belonged to another religion were found to be justified under Article 9 § 2 of the Convention. Consequently, it is established that institutions of higher education may regulate the manifestation of the rites and symbols of a religion by imposing restrictions as to the place and manner of such manifestation with the aim of ensuring peaceful co-existence between students of various faiths and thus protecting public order and the beliefs of others (see, among other authorities, *Refah Partisi and Others*, cited above, § 95). In the *Dahlab* case, which concerned the teacher of a class of small children, the Court stressed among other matters the "powerful external symbol" which her wearing a headscarf represented and

questioned whether it might have some kind of proselytising effect, seeing that it appeared to be imposed on women by a religious precept that was hard to reconcile with the principle of gender equality. It also noted that wearing the Islamic headscarf could not easily be reconciled with the message of tolerance, respect for others and, above all, equality and non-discrimination that all teachers in a democratic society should convey to their pupils.

(ii) Application of the foregoing principles to the present case

37. The interference in issue caused by the circular of 23 February 1998 imposing restrictions as to place and manner on the rights of students such as Ms Şahin to wear the Islamic headscarf on university premises was, according to the Turkish courts based in particular on the two principles of secularism and equality.

38. After examining the parties' arguments, the Grand Chamber sees no good reason to depart from the approach taken by the Chamber as follows:

> " ... The Court ... notes the emphasis placed in the Turkish constitutional system on the protection of the rights of women.... Gender equality—recognised by the European Court as one of the key principles underlying the Convention and a goal to be achieved by member States of the Council of Europe—was also found by the Turkish Constitutional Court to be a principle implicit in the values underlying the Constitution....

> ... In addition, like the Constitutional Court ..., the Court considers that, when examining the question of the Islamic headscarf in the Turkish context, there must be borne in mind the impact which wearing such a symbol, which is presented or perceived as a compulsory religious duty, may have on those who choose not to wear it. As has already been noted, the issues at stake include the protection of the "rights and freedoms of others" and the "maintenance of public order" in a country in which the majority of the population, while professing a strong attachment to the rights of women and a secular way of life, adhere to the Islamic faith. Imposing limitations on freedom in this sphere may, therefore, be regarded as meeting a pressing social need by seeking to achieve those two legitimate aims, especially since, as the Turkish courts stated ..., this religious symbol has taken on political significance in Turkey in recent years.

> ... The Court does not lose sight of the fact that there are extremist political movements in Turkey which seek to impose on society as a whole their religious symbols and conception of a society founded on religious precepts.... It has previously said that each Contracting State may, in accordance with the

Convention provisions, take a stance against such political movements, based on its historical experience. The regulations concerned have to be viewed in that context and constitute a measure intended to achieve the legitimate aims referred to above and thereby to preserve pluralism in the university."

39. Having regard to the above background, it is the principle of secularism, as elucidated by the Constitutional Court, which is the paramount consideration underlying the ban on the wearing of religious symbols in universities. In such a context, where the values of pluralism, respect for the rights of others and, in particular, equality before the law of men and women are being taught and applied in practice, it is understandable that the relevant authorities should wish to preserve the secular nature of the institution concerned and so consider it contrary to such values to allow religious attire, including, as in the present case, the Islamic headscarf, to be worn.

[The Court then decided that there was a reasonable relationship of proportionality between the means employed and the legitimate objectives pursued by the interference.]

40. In the light of the foregoing and having regard to the Contracting States' margin of appreciation in this sphere, the Court finds that the interference in issue was justified in principle and proportionate to the aim pursued.

41. Consequently, there has been no breach of Article 9 of the Convention. . . .

FOR THESE REASONS, THE COURT

1.   *Holds*, by sixteen votes to one, that there has been no violation of Article 9 of the Convention; . . .

Done in English and in French, and delivered at a public hearing in the Human Rights Building, Strasbourg, on 10 November 2005.

LUZIUS WILDHABER
PRESIDENT

DISSENTING OPINION OF JUDGE TULKENS

(Translation)

A.   Freedom of religion

4.   On what grounds was the interference with the applicant's right to freedom of religion through the ban on wearing the headscarf based? In the present case, relying exclusively on the reasons cited by the national authorities and courts, the majority put forward, in general and abstract terms, two main arguments: secularism and equality. While I fully and totally subscribe to each of these principles, I disagree with the manner in which they were applied here and to the way they were interpreted in relation to the practice of wearing the headscarf. In

a democratic society, I believe that it is necessary to seek to harmonise the principles of secularism, equality and liberty, not to weigh one against the other.

5.   As regards, firstly, *secularism*, I would reiterate that I consider it an essential principle and one which, as the Constitutional Court stated in its judgment of 7 March 1989, is undoubtedly necessary for the protection of the democratic system in Turkey. Religious freedom is, however, also a founding principle of democratic societies. Accordingly, the fact that the Grand Chamber recognised the force of the principle of secularism did not release it from its obligation to establish that the ban on wearing the Islamic headscarf to which the applicant was subject was necessary to secure compliance with that principle and, therefore, met a "pressing social need." Only indisputable facts and reasons whose legitimacy is beyond doubt—not mere worries or fears— are capable of satisfying that requirement and justifying interference with a right guaranteed by the Convention. Moreover, where there has been interference with a fundamental right, the Court's case-law clearly establishes that mere affirmations do not suffice: they must be supported by concrete examples. Such examples do not appear to have been forthcoming in the present case.

6.   Under Article 9 of the Convention, the freedom with which this case is concerned is not freedom to have a religion (the internal conviction) but to manifest one's religion (the expression of that conviction). If the Court has been very protective (perhaps over- protective) of religious sentiment, it has shown itself less willing to intervene in cases concerning religious practices, which only appear to receive a subsidiary form of protection. This is, in fact, an aspect of freedom of religion with which the Court has rarely been confronted up to now and on which it has not yet had an opportunity to form an opinion with regard to external symbols of religious practice, such as particular items of clothing, whose symbolic importance may vary greatly according to the faith concerned.

7.   Referring to the *Refah Partisi and Others v. Turkey* judgment of 13 February 2003, the judgment states: "An attitude which fails to respect that principle [of secularism] will not necessarily be accepted as being covered by the freedom to manifest one's religion." The majority thus consider that wearing the headscarf contravenes the principle of secularism. In so doing, they take up position on an issue that has been the subject of much debate, namely the signification of wearing the headscarf and its relationship with the principle of secularism.

In the present case, a generalised assessment of that type gives rise to at least three difficulties. Firstly, the judgment does not address the applicant's argument—which the Government did not dispute—that she had no intention of calling the principle of secularism, a principle with which she agreed, into doubt. Secondly, there is no evidence to show that the applicant, through her attitude, conduct or acts, contravened that principle. This is a test the Court has always applied in its case-law. Lastly, the judgment makes no distinction between teachers and students, whereas in the *Dahlab v. Switzerland* decision of 15 February 2001, which concerned a teacher, the Court expressly noted the role-model aspect which the teacher's wearing the headscarf had. While the principle of secularism requires education to be provided without any manifestation of religion and while it has to be compulsory for teachers and all public servants, as they have voluntarily taken up posts in a neutral environment, the position of pupils and students seems to me to be different.

8.   Freedom to manifest a religion entails everyone being allowed to exercise that right, whether individually or collectively, in public or in private, subject to the dual condition that they do not infringe the rights and freedoms of others and do not prejudice public order (Article 9 § 2).

As regards the first condition, this could have been satisfied if the headscarf the applicant wore as a religious symbol had been ostentatious or aggressive or was used to exert pressure, to provoke a reaction, to proselytise or to spread propaganda and undermined—or was liable to undermine—the convictions of others. However, the Government did not argue that this was the case and there was no evidence before the Court to suggest that Ms Şahin had any such intention. As to the second condition, it has been neither suggested nor demonstrated that there was any disruption in teaching or in everyday life at the University, or any disorderly conduct, as a result of the applicant's wearing the headscarf. Indeed, no disciplinary proceedings were taken against her.

9.   The majority maintain, however that "when examining the question of the Islamic headscarf in the Turkish context, there must be borne in mind the impact which wearing such a symbol, which is presented or perceived as a compulsory religious duty, may have on those who choose not to wear it."

Unless the level of protection of the right to freedom of religion is reduced to take account of the context, the possible effect which wearing the headscarf, which is presented as a symbol, may have on those who do not wear it does not appear to me, in the light of the Court's case-law, to satisfy the requirement of a pressing social need. *Mutatis mutandis*, in the sphere of freedom of expression (Article 10), the Court has never accepted that interference with the exercise of the right to freedom of expression can be justified by the fact that the ideas or views concerned are not shared by everyone and may even offend some people. Recently, in the *Gündüz v. Turkey* judgment of 4 December 2003, the Court held that there had been a violation of freedom of expression in a case in which a Muslim religious leader had been convicted for violently criticising the secular regime in Turkey, calling for the introduction of the sharia and referring to children born of marriages celebrated solely before the secular authorities as "bastards." Thus, manifesting one's religion by peacefully wearing a headscarf may be prohibited whereas, in the same context, remarks which could be construed as incitement to religious hatred are covered by freedom of expression.

10. In fact, it is the threat posed by "extremist political movements" seeking to "impose on society as a whole their religious symbols and conception of a society founded on religious precepts" which, in the Court's view, serves to justify the regulations in issue, which constitute "a measure intended to . . . to preserve pluralism in the university." The Court had already made this clear in its *Refah Partisi and Others v. Turkey* judgment of 13 February 2003, when it stated: "In a country like Turkey, where the great majority of the population belong to a particular religion, measures taken in universities to prevent certain fundamentalist religious movements from exerting pressure on students who do not practise that religion or on those who belong to another religion may be justified under Article 9 § 2 of the Convention" (§ 95).

While everyone agrees on the need to prevent radical Islamism, a serious objection may nevertheless be made to such reasoning. Merely wearing the headscarf cannot be associated with fundamentalism and it is vital to distinguish between those who wear the headscarf and "extremists" who seek to impose the headscarf as they do other religious symbols. Not all women who wear the headscarf are fundamentalists and there is nothing to suggest that the applicant held fundamentalist views. She is a young adult woman and a university student and might reasonably be expected to have a heightened capacity to resist pressure, it being noted in this connection that the judgment fails to provide any concrete example of the type of pressure concerned. The applicant's personal interest in exercising the right to freedom of religion and to manifest her religion by an external symbol cannot be wholly absorbed by the public interest in fighting extremism.

11. Turning to *equality*, the majority focus on the protection of women's rights and the principle of sexual equality. By converse implication, wearing the headscarf is considered synonymous with the alienation of women. The ban on wearing the headscarf is therefore seen as promoting equality between men and women. However, what, in fact, is the connection between the ban and sexual equality? The judgment does not say. Indeed, what is the signification of wearing the headscarf? As the German Constitutional Court noted in its judgment of 24 September 2003, wearing the headscarf has no single meaning; it is a practise that is engaged in for a variety of reasons. It does not necessarily symbolise the submission of women to men and there are those who maintain that, in certain cases, it can even be a means of

emancipating women. What is lacking in this debate is the opinion of women, both those who wear the headscarf and those who choose not to.

13. Since, to my mind, the ban on wearing the Islamic headscarf on the university premises was not based on reasons that were relevant and sufficient, it cannot be considered to be interference that was "necessary in a democratic society" within the meaning of Article 9 § 2 of the Convention. In these circumstances, there has been a violation of the applicant's right to freedom of religion, as guaranteed by the Convention.

NOTES AND QUESTIONS

1. *European Convention on Human Rights.* There are three sources of European human rights: the Charter of Fundamental Rights of the European Union ("Charter"), the European Convention on Human Rights ("ECHR"), and the General Principles of European Union's law. "Article 9 of the ECHR, which provides that 'Everyone has the right to freedom of thought, conscience and religion; this right includes freedom to change his religion or belief, and freedom, either alone or in community with others and in public or private, to manifest his religion or belief in teaching, practice, worship, and observance,' is the common ground between the three sources of European human rights protection." Antonios Kouroutakis, Islamic Terrorism: The Legal Impact on the Freedom of Religion in the United States and Europe, 34 B.U. Int'l L.J. 113, 119–20 (2016)

Why did the European Court of Human Rights hear this case if the Court really believes that local governments are best situated to determine the government's interest? How much religious freedom does Article 9 of the Convention protect? Does the European Convention protect more religious liberty than the Turkish Constitution? Or did the Court merely defer to the Turkish Constitution and not enforce Article 9? How does Article 9, and its interpretation by the Court, compare to the First Amendment? For further information about the European Convention, see Paul M. Taylor, Freedom of Religion: UN and European Human Rights Law and Practice (2005).

Professor Bennoune explains that the Court employed the "margin of appreciation" approach in *Şahin*, "according to which a government's claim of necessity for limiting particular rights receives special deference from the European Court, where such a limitation is permitted by the Convention." Was this an appropriate case in which to apply the margin of appreciation, or would it have been more appropriate not to defer to the government because an individual right was at stake? Or is secularism a value that deserves deference? In similar circumstances, would American courts apply strict scrutiny or rational basis review? See Karima Bennoune, Secularism and Human Rights: A Contextual Analysis of Headscarves, Religious Expression, and Women's Equality Under International Law, 45 Colum. J. Transnat'l L. 367, 382 (2007).

2. *Developments in Turkey.* After the Turkish Parliament adopted constitutional amendments permitting headscarves on university campuses, the Constitutional Court invalidated the amendments as inconsistent with the secular principles of the Constitution. As in the *Şahin* case, supporters and critics of the decision disagreed whether the ban on headscarves promotes or violates human rights. See Ali Aslan Kilic & Aysegul Aybar, Top Court Decision Cripples Parliament, Today's Zaman, Oct. 23, 2008. In November 2012, Turkey lifted the ban on religious headscarves in education. Will this development have a positive effect, or "have a negative impact on the psychology of developing children"?

In October 2013, Turkey also lifted the ban on headscarves for state employees. The military, police force, and judiciary will keep the ban. Do you see the lifting of the ban as a "democratic move" or "the government's attempt to push an Islamic agenda"? Should the new rule apply to the military, police force, and judiciary as well as to public employees? See Sebnem Arsu and Dan Bilefsky, Turkey Lifts Longtime Ban on Head Scarves in State Offices, N.Y. Times, Oct. 8, 2013. In June 2014, Turkey's Constitutional Court ruled that a Muslim woman lawyer had the right to wear a headscarf in the courtroom. See Howard Friedman, Turkey's Constitutional Court Says Female Lawyers Can Wear Headscarves in Courtrooms, Religion Clause, Jun. 27, 2014, at http://religionclause.blogspot.com/2014/06/turkeys-constitutional-court-says.html. Are such developments good or bad for religious freedom?

On February 23, 2010, the European Court of Human Rights decided *Ahmet Arslan v. Turkey*, which involved 127 Turkish nationals who met in Ankara for a religious ceremony at a mosque. "They toured the streets of the city while wearing the distinctive dress of their group, which evoked that of the leading prophets and was made up of a turban, 'salvar' (baggy 'harem' trousers), a tunic and a stick." After they were arrested, they wore their group's dress in the State Security Court, where they were convicted "for a breach both of the law on the wearing of headgear and of the rules on the wearing of certain garments, specifically religious garments, in public other than for religious ceremonies." Is this conviction consistent with *Şahin*?

The ECHR ruled that the convictions violated the freedom of conscience and religion. The court distinguished *Arslan* from *Şahin* for several reasons. First, "this case concerned punishment for the wearing of particular dress in public areas that were open to all, and not, as in other cases that it had had to judge, regulation of the wearing of religious symbols in public establishments, where religious neutrality might take precedence over the right to manifest one's religion." Second, there was "no evidence that the applicants represented a threat for public order or that they had been involved in proselytism by exerting inappropriate pressure on passers-by during their gathering." Therefore the court concluded that the Turkish government had not established the necessity of the restriction and ordered it to pay 10 euros to each individual and 2000 euros jointly for their legal fees. Can *Arslan* be reconciled with *Şahin?* See Ahmet Arslan v.

Turkey, No. 41135/98, at http://www.strasbourgconsortium.org/document.php? DocumentID=4732. Does *Arslan* undermine Turkey's secular government? Do you think the cases were affected by the gender of the parties?

3.   *Religious Duty.* Is Islam a religion? Should Şahin's claim qualify as a religious belief protected under the language of the Convention? Some Muslim women wear the *hijab*, a head, face, or body covering that is worn in different styles. A *chador* or *burqa* is a full-length covering from head to foot, usually in black. See John L. Esposito, The Oxford Dictionary of Islam (2003). Some Muslim women wear the coverings, but others do not. Some women wear them for religious reasons, and others as cultural or even fashion statements. See Dina Alsowayel, The Elephant in the Room: A Commentary on Steven Gey's Analysis of the French Headscarf Ban, 42 Hous. L. Rev. 103 (2005); Mary Elaine Hegland, Gender and Religion in the Middle East and South Asia: Women's Voices Rising, in Margaret L. Meriwether & Judith E. Tucker, eds., Social History of Women and Gender in the Modern Middle East 188–95 (1999) (explaining women's different attitudes toward veiling). Should Şahin's belief that she has a religious duty to wear a headscarf suffice to establish a religious freedom claim, or is her claim really cultural in nature?

Scholars disagree whether the Qur'an requires women to wear the headscarf. Can Şahin have a religious duty if Muslims disagree about the obligation? In a Florida case about a Muslim woman and her driver's license, the court relied on expert testimony by the government's witness, Dr. Khaled Abou El Fadl, a UCLA law professor who testified that there are exceptions, based on necessity, to the veiling requirement in Islamic countries, including for identity cards. See Freeman v. Department of Highway Safety and Motor Vehicles, 924 So.2d 48 (Fla. Dist. Ct. App. 2006). If testimony were required about Şahin's beliefs, who should testify? Turkish Muslims? European scholars of religion? Şahin's fellow students at the university?

4.   *Women's Equality.* The European Court identified the importance of women's equality to the laws and Constitution of Turkey. Which system best promotes women's equality—one that requires the headscarf, forbids the headscarf, or makes the headscarf a matter of women's choice? See Dina Alsowayel, The Elephant in the Room: A Commentary on Steven Gey's Analysis of the French Headscarf Ban, 42 Hous. L. Rev. 103 (2005) (asking if women's equality is protected by the creation of a religion-free zone or if women are patronized by the state instead of religion when their choice is taken away); Leila Ahmed, Women and Gender in Islam: Historical Roots of a Modern Debate 150 (1999) ("[I]t gave women a kind of liberty, for it enabled them not to be recognized.").

Does the opinion suggest that women's equality is inconsistent with religious freedom, or with Islam? If a woman, government employee or citizen, desires to wear the *chador*, should the state be able to stop her because of a concern for women's equality? Is religious freedom a more fundamental right than equality? Are gender equality and religious freedom of equal importance? Are they mutually exclusive? Do you agree with Professor Bennoune's assertion that the law "may require some limitation of religious expression in the service of protecting women's rights, in accordance with international human rights norms"? Karima Bennoune, Secularism and Human Rights: A Contextual Analysis of Headscarves, Religious Expression, and Women's Equality Under International Law, 45 Colum. J. Transnat'l L. 367, 374 (2007). Or do you think instead "there are certainly heavy feminist arguments from both those who criticize the wearing of the headscarf as an oppressive practice and therefore encourage restrictions on it, and those who oppose such restrictions. Regrettably, the ECtHR ignored both" in Şahin? Cochav Elkayam-Levy, Women's Rights and Religion—the Missing Element in the Jurisprudence of the European Court of Human Rights, 35 U. Pa. J. Int'l L. 1175, 1215–16 (2014). How could a court "develop a legal methodology to address women rights in the religious context"? Id. Did the U.S. Supreme Court strike a similar balance between women's equality and religious liberty in *Hobby Lobby* in Chapter 4?

What constitutional regime would keep Muslim women from being patronized or dominated by either church or state? According to the Pew Research Center, in 2012–2013, 50 of 198 countries had laws or policies regulating women's religious garb. About three-quarters had laws limiting women's ability to wear such attire, and a quarter required women to wear it. Is one policy more objectionable than another? See Pew Research Center, Restrictions on Women's Religious Attire (2016). The *turban* is a "headdress worn by men from northern African to western and southern Asia consisting of a cap around which a long cloth is wound." See John L. Esposito, The Oxford Dictionary of Islam 323 (2003). What should the rules be for men's head coverings?

Do Westerners criticize veiling requirements because they are committed to women's equality or because the issue provides a convenient means of criticizing Muslim culture? See Ahmed, supra; Ayse Kadioglu, Women's Subordination in Turkey: Is Islam Really the Villain?, 48 Middle East J. 645 (1994).

5.   *Secular, Laik, Laicité.* What does the Court mean by describing Turkey's government as secular or laik? In 2004, when France passed a law prohibiting religious symbols in elementary and secondary school classrooms, government officials defended the law on the grounds that France's constitutional tradition is based on laicité. France's secular government emerged from efforts to limit the Catholic Church's influence over the government, and therefore laicité "refer[s] to policies designed to restrict (or even eliminate) clerical and religious influence over the state." See T. Jeremy Gunn, Under God But Not the Scarf: The Founding Myths of Religious Freedom in the United States and Laicité in France, 46 J. Church & St. 7, 9 (2004); T. Jeremy Gunn, French Secularism as Utopia and Myth, 42 Hous. L. Rev. 81 (2005); T. Jeremy Gunn, Religious Freedom and Laicité: A Comparison of the United States and France, 2004 B.Y.U. L. Rev. 419 (2004).

The modern Turkish Constitution replaced a constitution based on Islamic law, or sharia. How do Turkey's and France's constitutional provisions compare with the First Amendment? Does the United States protect religion from the state instead of the state from religion? Is a secular or lay government the same thing as separation of church and state? What is the difference between the "passive secularism" of the United States and the "assertive secularism" of France and Turkey? See Ahmet T. Kuru, Secularism and State Policies toward Religion: The United States, France, and Turkey (2009).

France enacted a law prohibiting full-face veils in public. Although full-body coverings (the *burqa*) and full-face veils (the *niqab*) are prohibited, headscarves and other partial face coverings are permitted. A woman wearing a full-face veil in public may be fined 150 euros or assigned to re-education classes. More severe fines—30,000 euros or imprisonment—attach to those who coerce others to wear the full coverings. See Steven Erlanger & Elvire Camus, French Find a Middle Ground on Face Veils, Int'l Herald Trib., Sept. 3, 2012, at 3. The European Court upheld the ban in *S.A.S. v. France* (no. 43835/11). Although the court rejected France's argument that concern for gender equality and human dignity justified the ban, it found that "respect for the minimum requirements of life in society" or of "living together" did.

Do you agree the concealment of faces is incompatible with citizens' living together? Despite the law's effect on Muslim women, the court also concluded the law was acceptable because "the ban is not expressly based on the religious connotation of the clothing in question but solely on the fact that it conceals the face." In the court's opinion, this fact distinguished the case from *Ahmet Arslan*, infra note 2. What do you think of the court's argument that the state "cannot invoke gender equality in order to ban a practice that is defended by women"? How would the case come out under American law?

6. *The Purpose of Education.* "How does the government best foster a tradition of spiritual and intellectual liberty among its young citizens?" See Steven G. Gey, Free Will, Religious Liberty, and a Partial Defense of the French Approach to Religious Expression in Public Schools, 42 Hous. L. Rev. 1 (2005). Professor Gey argues that the "religion-free zones" in France and Turkey served different purposes. The French approach promotes a religion-free zone so that students may have a broad learning experience, while the Turkish system tries to minimize the influence of religious ideas on citizens. Do you agree? How should the balance be struck between religious belief and the demands of the secular government?

In her dissent in *Şahin*, Judge Tulkens argued that the European Court had struck an incorrect balance among religion, secularism, and equality. She wrote:

> More fundamentally, by accepting the applicant's exclusion from the University in the name of secularism and equality, the majority have accepted her exclusion from precisely the type of liberated environment in which the true meaning of these values

can take shape and develop. University affords practical access to knowledge that is free and independent of all authority. Experience of this kind is far more effective a means of raising awareness of the principles of secularism and equality than an obligation that is not assumed voluntarily, but imposed. A tolerance-based dialogue between religions and cultures is an education in itself, so it is ironic that young women should be deprived of that education on account of the headscarf. Advocating freedom and equality for women cannot mean depriving them of the chance to decide on their future. Bans and exclusions echo that very fundamentalism these measures are intended to combat. Here, as elsewhere, the risks are familiar: radicalisation of beliefs, silent exclusion, a return to religious schools. When rejected by the law of the land, young women are forced to take refuge in their own law. As we are all aware, intolerance breeds intolerance.

Do you agree? Would students learn more in schools that had teachers and students wearing different religious garb?

Recall Justice Stevens' concurrence from *Kiryas Joel*, in Chapter 2: "the State could have taken steps to alleviate the children's fear by teaching their schoolmates to be tolerant and respectful of Satmar customs." Can the state teach children to be tolerant by regulating religious garb?

Nigerian schools in the Osun State were founded by Muslims, Christians, and non-conformists. After the government took over the schools in 1975, it established a policy allowing Muslim students to wear the hijab in Muslim schools but not in the other schools. The hijab was not allowed to be made compulsory in any school. The Osun State High Court later ruled that Muslim students have a constitutional right to propagate their religion by wearing the hijab in all the schools. In protest of the ruling, Christian students wore church robes to school. The Christians argued that Muslim students shouldn't be allowed to wear hijabs in Christian schools and accused the local governor of having an "Islamization Agenda." Josiah Oluwole, Osun Hijab Crisis: Students Attend Schools in Church Garments, Premium Times, Jun. 14, 2016. How would you recommend that the Nigerian schools controversy be resolved?

7. *The U.S.: Constitutional Right or Government Accommodation?* In Goldman v. Weinberger, 475 U.S. 503 (1986), S. Simcha Goldman, an Orthodox Jew and ordained rabbi, challenged an Air Force regulation banning the wearing of non-uniform head coverings while indoors. He argued he had a Free Exercise right to wear the yarmulke, a dark-colored skullcap measuring approximately five-and-one-half inches in diameter. Goldman was a clinical psychologist who was originally allowed to wear the yarmulke in the hospital. In a 5–4 decision, Justice Rehnquist upheld the regulation out of deference to the government's argument that military discipline requires a uniform standard of apparel. According to the government, "while a yarmulke might not seem obtrusive to a Jew, neither does a turban to a Sikh, a saffron robe to a Satchidananda Ashram-Integral Yogi, nor dreadlocks to a Rastafarian. If the Court were to require the Air Force to permit yarmulkes, the service must also allow all of these other forms of dress and grooming." Justice Brennan's dissent observed that under the regulations, military personnel were allowed to wear "neat and conservative" religious symbols in rings and other jewelry, and, after asserting that the existing standards favored Christians, recommended that the same standard be applied to allow Goldman's yarmulke. Justice Stevens' concurrence, however, insisted on the difficulty of applying Brennan's multifactor test to different religious groups.

In response to *Goldman*, Congress accommodated religious garb in the military by passing 10 U.S.C. § 774(a)–(b), which allows members of the armed forces to wear religious apparel in uniform unless the Secretary "determines that the wearing of the item would interfere with the performance of the member's military duties; or if the Secretary determines . . . the item of apparel is not neat and conservative." Do you agree with Congress' decision to accommodate religious apparel?

An observant Jew wearing a kippa or yarmulke is seen during
an ordination ceremony in Cologne, Germany.
Courtesy Photothek via Getty Images.

8.   *Sikhs.* The Sikh faith is the fifth largest religion in the world, founded in the Punjab, an area of Northwest India, by Guru Nanak (1469–1539). "The Guru sought to combine Hindu and Muslim elements in a single religious creed. The Hindu concepts of Karma and rebirth were accepted, but the Indian caste system was rejected. Sikhs believe that God is the only reality and that spiritual release can be obtained by taming the ego through devotional singing, recitation of the divine name, meditation and service. . . . Sikhs are readily identifiable by their turbans. They take a

vow not to cut their hair as well as not to smoke or drink. When the tenth guru, Gobind Singh, founded the martial fraternity of Khalsa, a golden race of warrior saints, his followers vowed to keep five symbols of their religion known as the five k's. They are as follows: to wear long hair (Kesh); to keep a comb in their hair (kangha): a steel bracelet on the right wrist (Kalha); an undergarment (kasha); and a sword (kirpan)." People v. Singh, 135 Misc.2d 701, 516 N.Y.S.2d 412 (N.Y.City Civ.Ct., 1987). Sikh men must wear a turban in order to comply with a religious vow not to cut their hair and to keep their hair neat. See Neha Singh Gohil and Dawinder S. Sidhu, The Sikh Turban: 9–11 Challenges to this Article of Faith, 9 Rutgers J. L. & Religion 10 (2008).

President Barack Obama meets with Indian Prime Minister Manmohan Singh, who is wearing a Sikh turban in the Oval Office, Nov. 24, 2009.
Photo by Pete Souza.

An American Sikh soldier sought a religious accommodation allowing him to wear a religious head covering with his army combat helmet and protective mask. The Army required that, to receive this accommodation, the soldier submit to specialized testing at a cost of $32,000 to ensure "that his Sikh articles of faith, namely a cloth head covering and unshorn hair and beard, will not interfere with the helmet's ability 'to withstand ballistic and blunt forces' and the mask's ability 'to provide protection from toxic chemical and biological agents.'" Should the soldier be accommodated? How do you think the European court would analyze this case? Is there any mechanism for this soldier to gain his request other than to receive an accommodation from Congress? See Singh v. Carter, No. 16-399. 2016 WL 837924, *1 (D. D.C., Mar. 3, 2016) (holding that the soldier demonstrated a prima facie case under RFRA sufficient for the court to grant his TRO). Would courts be able to decide what shape and size turbans Sikhs should wear? Does RFRA allow the U.S. courts to defer to the military the way the Court did in Goldman v. Weinberger?

9. *Proposed Standard.* Based upon the practice of the European Court of Human Rights, Professor Evans identifies the following key questions to be considered in cases of religious garb:

- Is this restriction reflective of a general approach which is neutral and impartial as between all forms of religion or belief or does it seek to prioritise a particular conception of the good?

- Is this restriction discriminatory in that it bears more directly or more harshly on the followers of one religion or belief than of another?

- Is the restriction directly aimed at the protection of a "legitimate interest" as set out in the Convention, and notably the protection of the rights and freedoms of others?

- Is there a pressing reason why that interest needs to be protected?

- Are there alternatives to the restriction which would secure the realization of those interests and which would not involve a greater diminution of the freedom to manifest one's beliefs through the wearing of such religiously inspired clothing or artefacts?

- Assuming there to be no other viable alternative approach, is the restriction limited to the minimum that is necessary to realize the specific legitimate aims identified?

- Is the imposition of the restriction compatible with the principles of respect and or the need to foster tolerance and pluralism?

Malcolm D. Evans, Manual on the Wearing of Religious Symbols in Public Areas 87–88 (2009). Applying those principles, what should be the result of *Şahin*? Evans identifies three government interests that can be considered in these cases: public safety, public security, and public order. How would they affect the case of the Sikh soldier?

10. *Tolerance.* What do you think of the following exchange, which took place during a criminal trial in a federal district court, when the judge spoke to spectators who wore hats to court?

THE COURT: I note there are quite a few people here. As a matter of respect for the Court, the dignity of the Court does not allow any headdresses, so individuals wearing any type of headdresses will be asked to leave now or remove them. Also, no hats, no skull caps, nothing like that is permitted. Did you folks hear me in the back?

UNIDENTIFIED SPEAKER: This is my national headdress and also a part of my religion.

THE COURT: Ma'am, that is not allowed in this courtroom. You are welcome without it, so please leave until you can take it off.

UNIDENTIFIED SPEAKER: If Jews were to come in here—

THE COURT: Jews will not wear yarmulkes. I am Catholic and the Pope would not wear a miter. Please leave, take it off and come back in, or do not come back in, the choice is yours.

In the Court of Appeals, Judge Easterbrook noted that, although First Amendment jurisprudence does not require the judge to accommodate religious garb or entitle spectators to wear it:

> the judicial branch is free to extend spectators more than their constitutional minimum entitlement. Tolerance usually is the best course in a pluralistic nation. Accommodation of religiously inspired conduct is a token of respect for, and a beacon of welcome to, those whose beliefs differ from the majority's. The best way for the judiciary to receive the public's respect is to earn that respect by showing a wise appreciation of cultural and religious diversity. Obeisance differs from respect; to demand the former in the name of the latter is self-defeating. It is difficult for us to see any reason why a Jew may not wear his yarmulke in court, a Sikh his turban, a Muslim woman her chador, or a Moor his fez. Most spectators will continue to doff their caps as a sign of respect for the judiciary; those who keep heads covered as a sign of respect for (or obedience to) a power higher than the state should not be cast out of court or threatened with penalties.

United States v. James, 328 F.3d 953, 957–58 (7th Cir. 2003). Why is tolerance usually the best course in a religiously pluralistic nation? What is the most tolerant approach to speech critical of religion, which is the subject of the next section?

B. BLASPHEMY AND THE DEFAMATION OF RELIGION

People v. Ruggles

Supreme Court of New York, 1811.
8 Johns. 290, 5 Am.Dec. 335.

The offence charged is, that the defendant below did "wickedly, maliciously, and blasphemously utter, in the presence and hearing of divers good and christian people, these false, feigned, scandalous, malicious, wicked and blasphemous words, to wit, "*Jesus Christ* was a bastard, and his mother must be a whore;" and the single question is, whether this be a public offence by the law of the land.... The language was blasphemous not only in a popular, but in a legal sense; for blasphemy, according to the most precise definitions, consists in maliciously reviling God, or religion, and this was reviling Christianity through its author.... The free, equal, and undisturbed, enjoyment of religious opinion, whatever it may be, and free and decent discussions on any religious subject, is granted and secured; but to revile, with malicious and blasphemous contempt, the religion professed by almost the whole community, is an abuse of that right....Though the constitution has discarded religious establishments, it does not forbid judicial cognisance of those offences against religion and morality which have no reference to any such establishment, or to any particular form of government, but are punishable because they strike at the root of moral obligation, and weaken the security of the social ties.

Updegraph v. Commonweath
Supreme Court of Pennsylvania, 1824.
11 Serg. & Rawle 394, 1824 WL 2393.

This was an indictment for blasphemy, founded on an act of assembly, passed in 1700, which enacts, that whosoever shall wilfully, premeditatedly and despitefully blaspheme, and speak loosely and *profanely* of Almighty God, Christ Jesus, the Holy Spirit, or the Scripture of Truth, and is legally convicted thereof, shall forfeit and pay the sum of *ten pounds*. . . . It charges the defendant with contriving and intending to scandalize and bring into disrepute, and vilify the Christian religion, and the scriptures of truth; and that he, in the presence and hearing of several persons, unlawfully, wickedly, and premeditatedly, despitefully and blasphemously, did say, among other things, in substance, as follows: "that the Holy Scriptures were a mere fable, that they were a contradiction, and that although they contained a number of good things, yet they contained a great many lies" . . . We will first dispose of what is considered the grand objection—*the constitutionality of Christianity*—for, in effect, that is *the question.* Christianity, general Christianity, is and always has been a part of the common law of Pennsylvania.

NOTES AND QUESTIONS

1.   *Christian Law.* What do you think of the state courts' treatment of Christianity? Do you agree with the Pennsylvania court's conclusion that Christianity is part of the common law? Why did the New York court mention the religion "professed by almost the whole community"? Do the cases suggest that only criticism of Christianity would be illegal?

What do you think would have happened in the state courts if an individual had said that Buddha or Muhammad was a bastard? If someone said the Qur'an was a fable? Do you think blasphemy could or would be prosecuted in the United States today?

2.   *Muslim Law.* Twenty-two of 56 majority Muslim countries recognize some constitutional role for Islamic law, principles, or jurisprudence, including by establishing Islamic law, principles, or jurisprudence as "the basis for," "the principal source of," "a principal source of," or "the main source of" legislation. See USCIRF, The Religion-State Relationship and the Right to Freedom of Religion or Belief: A

Comparative Textual Analysis of the Constitutions of the Majority Muslim Countries and Other OIC Members (2012).

Sharia is "ideal Islamic law," which expresses "God's eternal and immutable will for humanity . . . and is binding for all believers." John L. Esposito, ed., The Oxford Dictionary of Islam 287–88 (2003). In some nations, sharia is incorporated into the civil law, and in other nations, Islamic principles influence the civil law. If sharia and Islamic law prohibit blasphemy and defamation of religion, is there any reason why Muslim countries should not prosecute it? Should free speech include speech critical of religion?

3.   *History of Blasphemy.* According to Professor Polymenopoulou:

> the question of blasphemy is not confined solely within the Islamic legal tradition, nor are monotheisms alone the source of the problem. Recently, Buddhists complained about the launch of a new Buddha bar in Jakarta, and few years ago, a radical Hindu group issued a 5 million dollar threat for the head of one of India's most acclaimed painters, Maqbool Fida Husain, for portraying Gods naked in his film *"Meenaxi: A Tale of Three Cities."* In addition, it is in the Judeo-Christian and not the Islamic tradition that the offences of blasphemy and idolatry are rooted. The relevant Biblical prohibitions—in particular the myth of the "Golden Calf" that is narrated in the first book of the Bible, the Exodus—have served throughout the centuries as an excellent basis to justify prohibitions of both idol-worshipping and art-making. Freedom of expression and artistic creation were restricted virtually in all phases of Christianity. In classical Judaism, painting was seen as a source of impurity and linked to all kinds of sinful behaviour. In the case of the Catholic Church artists had to conform to strict rules issued by Ecumenical councils—in particular, the Council of Trent, which, convened by Pope Pius in plain Quattrocento, provided thorough guidelines on the making of "sacred images"; the Holy Inquisition has prosecuted not only scientists, but also painters as famous as Veronese, and the notorious "Index of Prohibited Books" created in 1559 remained officially in power until 1966. In addition, the list of censored artworks in many Western states of the Judeo-Christian tradition is sufficiently long not to remain unnoticed.

Eleni Polymenopoulou, A Thousand Ways to Kiss the Earth: Artistic Freedom, Cultural Heritage and Islamic Extremism, 17 Rutgers J. L. & Religion 39, 43–44 (2015). How does that history affect your reaction to the following article about defamation of religion?

Robert C. Blitt, Should New Bills of Rights Address Emerging International Rights Norms? The Challenge of "Defamation of Religion"

9 Northwestern University Journal of International
Human Rights 1, 10–11, 17–25 (2010).

II. A COMPARATIVE OVERVIEW OF THE OFFENSE OF BLASPHEMY: A FOUNDATION FOR UNDERSTANDING DEFAMATION OF RELIGION

A. Blasphemy in the West

In theological terms, blasphemy is equated with "a direct criticism of God and sacred objects." The legal definition of blasphemy "developed historically to meet various, primarily political rather than religious, perceptions of a need for the law to protect institutions, originally the State itself." In other words, the challenge posed by alleged heretics and blasphemers represented nothing less than an act of state treason threatening the very foundation of a society held together with the brick and mortar of an exclusive religious conviction.[21] The state could level blasphemy-related charges against an individual to protect the social or ideological underpinnings of society, or more specifically, use such charges to "suppress the expression of religious beliefs or opinions" that the dominant group believed to be false. As U.S. Justice Felix Frankfurter famously observed, "Blasphemy was the chameleon phrase which meant the criticism of whatever the ruling authority of the moment established as orthodox religious doctrine."

In many states today, the offenses of blasphemy and heresy are viewed as antiquated tools for protecting a given ruler's religious worldview at the expense of all other differing opinions. Indeed, as religion and state gradually decoupled in the west,[24] charges of blasphemy grew more infrequent. While prosecutions for blasphemy in the United States became "no more frequent than the sightings of snarks," the common law offense persisted in England until its abolition in 2008. Prior to this, UK courts concluded that blasphemy required little in the way of intent,[27] could result in a sentence of hard labor,[28]

---

[21] For example, in recognizing blasphemy as a common law offense in 17th century England, the court held that "to say, religion is a cheat, is to dissolve all those obligations whereby the civil societies are preserved, and that Christianity is parcel of the laws of England; and therefore to reproach the Christian religion is to speak in subversion of the law." R v. Taylor, 1 Vent. 293 (1676); 86 Eng. Rep 189 (K.B.). In this brief quote, the court made plain the linkage between safeguarding the dominant faith and preserving the social and political order of the day.

[24] This trend may be linked to broader conditions of modernity leading to the secularization of society, wherein religion "becomes increasingly a private concern of the individual and thus loses much of its public relevance and influence." Riaz Hassan, Expressions of Religiosity and Blasphemy in Modern Societies, Negotiating the Sacred: Blasphemy and Sacrilege in a Multicultural Society 119 (Elizabeth Burns Coleman & Kevin White eds.) (2006).

[27] In 1979, the House of Lords affirmed a minimal threshold of intent for the offense of blasphemy, endorsing the trial judge's direction that "guilt of the offence of publishing a

and only operated to protect the Church of England and its specific doctrines rather than all religious beliefs.[29] In other states where blasphemy was not abolished outright, alleged violations were left unprosecuted or became unenforceable "either through stricter intent requirements or judicial attempts to strike a balance between conflicting rights." . . .

B.   Blasphemy in Muslim States

As noted above, blasphemy at its origin represented an ecclesiastical offense. In the Christian west, government implementation and enforcement of blasphemy laws through the common law often protected only specific iterations of the Christian faith. All other comers—including Muslims, Jews, and Hindus—had no means of bringing the wrath of the law to bear against the perceived disparagement of their respective religions.

Governments in the Muslim world similarly sought to outlaw offenses equivalent to blasphemous conduct. Authorities invoked religious or statutory law to impose a variety of penalties against blasphemy, apostasy, and other related acts. Like their western counterparts, these offenses[49] also shared a clearly identifiable connection with notions of treason or sedition against the state. This resulted in part due to the absence of any bright line separation between religion and state under the banner of Islam. As Cherif Bassiouni has remarked, Islam provides a "holistic conception of life, government, law and hereafter. There is no division of church and state; there is no division between matters temporal and religious, and between different aspects of law."

While the current trend in the West indicates a tendency to discard blasphemy offenses into the trash bin of history, there appears to be no parallel movement within Muslim states. For example, in Pakistan, a declared Islamic state, existing blasphemy laws continue to result in miscarriages of justice and "exacerbate a growing environment of dogma and intolerance—spawning a culture of extremism and

---

blasphemous libel did not depend on the accused having an intent to blaspheme, but that it was sufficient for the prosecution to prove that the publication had been intentional and that the matter published was blasphemous." R. v. Lemon (Denis), [1979] A.C. 617, 618 (also known as Whitehouse v. Lemon).

[28] William Gott, the last individual in the UK sentenced to a prison term for blasphemy, served nine months hard labor for distributing pamphlets describing Jesus Christ entering Jerusalem "like a circus clown on the back of two donkeys." [1922] 16 CR. APP. R. 87, 89.

[29] In Choudhury v. UK (1991) 12 HRLJ 172, members of Britain's Muslim community sought unsuccessfully to prosecute author Salman Rushdie for allegedly blaspheming against Islam in his novel, THE SATANIC VERSES; see also Q & A: Blasphemy law, BBC NEWS, Oct. 18, 2004, http://news.bbc.co.uk/2/hi/uk/3753408.stm.

[49] Although no exact offense parallel to the Judeo-Christian offense of blasphemy exists under Islam, insulting God, Mohammed or any other aspect of divine revelation amounts to an offense under Sharia. See Donna E. Arzt, Heroes or Heretics: Religious Dissidents Under Islamic Law, 14 Wis. Int'l L.J. 349, 351–352 (1996). The article provides a long list of examples of blasphemy-type offenses prosecuted in the Muslim world. See also Hassan, supra note 24.

violence." The United States Department of State has observed that Pakistani authorities "routinely use[ ] the blasphemy laws to harass religious minorities and vulnerable Muslims and to settle personal scores or business rivalries." Most recently, gunmen in Pakistan's Punjab province shot and killed two Christian brothers as they returned to prison after a court appearance on blasphemy charges, and several other Christians faced jail sentences for violating Pakistan's Penal Code ordinances against blasphemy. Under the Code, any individual who "directly or indirectly, defiles the sacred name of the Holy Prophet Muhammad" is subject to "death, or imprisonment for life."

In Malaysia, the federal constitution declares Islam as the official religion, but authorizes states rather than the federal government to legislate in the area of Islamic law. Within the Federal Territories (Kuala Lumpur, Putrajaya and Labuan), Part III of the *Syariah [Sharia] Criminal Offences (Federal Territories) Act 1997* enumerates "Offences Relating to the Sanctity of the Religion of Islam and its Institution," which include "[i]nsulting, or bringing into contempt . . . the religion of Islam."

This Act also proscribes "acts in contempt of religious authority" and "def[ying], disobey[ing] or disput[ing] the orders or directions [of the *Majlis Agama Islam Wilayah Persekutuan* (Federal Territory Islamic Council)] expressed or given by way of fatwa . . . " Upon conviction of either insulting Islam or defying an Islamic Council fatwa (a decision based on Islamic law), an individual is liable for a fine, prison sentence of up to two years, or both. According to the *Administration of Islamic Law (Federal Territories) Act 1993*, once a fatwa is issued by the Islamic Council and published in the official Gazette, it gains the status of enforceable law in the Federal Territories. In turn, such fatwas are binding on every Muslim resident in the Federal Territories, each of whom is obligated by a "religious duty to abide by and uphold the fatwa . . . " The *Administration of Islamic Law (Federal Territories) Act 1993* further mandates that all courts in the Federal Territories recognize gazetted fatwas "as authoritative of all matters laid down therein." Even in the event that a fatwa is not published, at least one former high-level government advisor has contended that the ruling demands respect as a religious decree.

The influence of Malaysia's various fatwa councils is far-reaching. On the federal level, the National Fatwa Council, a body intended to harmonize state-issued fatwas, has sought to prohibit Muslims from practicing yoga on the grounds that it risked "destroy[ing] a Muslim's faith," ban the "unacceptable" practice of women "dressing in the clothes men wear," and prohibit exhibitions concerning ghosts. In a similar vein, the Islamic Religious Council in the central state of

Selangor threatened to sue the Malaysian Bar Association for using the word "Allah" on its website.

In Indonesia, where the constitution is silent with regard to favoring secularism or Islam, the government actively invokes criminal ordinances to prosecute alleged blasphemy-related offenses. Under the Criminal Code, publicly "giving expression to feelings of hostility, hatred or contempt against one or more groups of the population of Indonesia," is punishable by a maximum imprisonment of four years or a fine. While the Indonesian law is admirable for its attempt to move away from protecting the majority faith exclusively, the U.S. Department of State has concluded that enforcement actions in practice "have almost always involved blasphemy and heresy against Islam." Human Rights Watch likewise has concluded, "Indonesian laws prohibiting blasphemy are primarily applied to practices perceived to deviate from mainstream Islam." Blasphemy charges have been invoked in a variety of situations, including an art exhibit containing photographic representations of fig leaf-covered Adam and Eve, and against various individuals claiming to be reincarnations of the Prophet Muhammad and the archangel Gabriel, among others. On a much broader scale, the government has severely restricted and even banned certain activities of the Ahmadi community, including public religious worship, as part of a clamp-down pattern targeting groups deemed "heretical," "deviant," or heterodox. Following Malaysia's lead, Indonesia's Ulema Council issued a similar *fatwa* prohibiting Muslims from practicing yoga for fear it might corrupt their faith.

From this brief overview—and in contrast to the present situation in most Western countries—snark sightings remain quite a common occurrence in the Muslim world. Many Muslim states continue to shield Islam from even minor criticism, and in certain instances use anti-blasphemy measures as an offensive tool to stifle the free exercise of religious belief for minority faiths and Muslim dissidents alike. As illustrated, such practices are not exclusive to religious regimes but rather may be observed across the spectrum of Muslim constitutional models—including in states that make no declaration regarding Islam as the official religion. It is from this milieu that the movement to prohibit "defamation of religion" (originally expressed in the more specific and decidedly less ecumenical slogan "defamation of Islam") emerged a decade ago to begin its journey in search of international legitimacy.

III.   DEFAMATION OF RELIGION: BLASPHEMY GOES INTERNATIONAL

A.   *Origins of Defamation of Religion at the United Nations*

The Organization of the Islamic Conference (OIC), whose fifty-seven member states represent "the collective voice of the Muslim world," is responsible for spearheading the effort to secure international condemnation of acts deemed defamatory of religion—and more precisely, defamatory of Islam. In addition to its own reporting and resolutions on the issue, the OIC—working through its individual member states—has focused for the past ten years on adding the creation of a norm prohibiting defamation of religion to the agendas of various UN bodies. The first step in this effort came in 1999 when Pakistan, acting on behalf of the OIC, submitted a draft resolution entitled "Defamation of Islam" to the now defunct Commission on Human Rights (UNCHR).[83] This proposed resolution sought to combat perceived negative international media coverage of "Islam as a religion hostile to human rights." In the view of Pakistan's UN ambassador, this negative media coverage amounted to a "defamation compaign [sic]" against the religion and its adherents to which the UNCHR had to react. The draft of the resolution sought to have the UNCHR both express "concern at the . . . spread [of] intolerance against Islam," and call upon the Special Rapporteur on religious intolerance to "continue to devote attention to attacks against Islam and attempts to defame it."

In response to Pakistan's draft, Western governments proposed amendments to de-specify Islam and approach the challenge of discrimination from a more general perspective inclusive of all religions. Subsequent Pakistani sub-amendments sought to preserve specificity relating to "defamatory attacks against [Islam]" and stressed that removing the resolution's focus on Islam "would defeat the purpose of the text, which was to bring a problem relating specifically to that religion to the attention of the international community." Following additional negotiations, a compromise resolution emerged expressing concern over the stereotyping of all religions rather than Islam alone, and which retained the term "defamation" in the resolution title only. The representative from Pakistan hailed the OIC member states' "considerable flexibility" in agreeing to a compromise resolution. At the same time, Germany's representative, speaking on behalf of the European Union (EU), stressed the EU's collective "wish to make it clear that they did not attach any legal meaning to the term 'defamation' as used in the title."

This seemingly insignificant resolution served as defamation's proverbial foot in the door at the UN for two reasons: first, it tasked two

---

[83] The first reference to defamation of Islam at the UN may be traced back to 1997. In reaction to a report addressing "Islamist and Arab Anti-Semitism" prepared by the UN Special Rapporteur on racism, Indonesia's ambassador alleged " 'defamation of our religion Islam and blasphemy against its Holy Book Qur'an.' " Rene Wadlow and David Littman, Blasphemy at the United Nations?, IV Middle East Quarterly 4, 85–86 (1997), available at http://www. meforum.org/379/blasphemy-at-the-united-nations. The UNCHR responded by adopting a consensus decision—supported by the United States and several other Western countries, which expressed "indignation and protest at the content of such an offensive reference to Islam and the Holy Qur'an . . . [a]ffirmed that that offensive reference should have been excluded from the report . . . [and] [r]equested . . . the Special Rapporteur to take corrective action in response." Commission on Human Rights Res. 1997/125, Reps. of Commission on Human Rights, 53d Sess., U.N. Doc E/CN.4/DEC/1997/125 (Apr. 18, 1997).

UN special rapporteurs with taking into account provisions of the resolution in future reports to the UNCHR; and second, it expressed the UNCHR's intent "to remain seized of the matter." Consequently, the effort to install a prohibition on defamation of religion became systematized and integrated not only into the UNCHR agenda, but also into the mandates of the Special Rapporteur on religious intolerance and the Special Rapporteur on racism, racial discrimination, xenophobia and related intolerance.

Over the relatively short time span of 10 years, the UNCHR, its successor the Human Rights Council (HRC), and even the UN General Assembly (U.N.G.A.) proceeded to pass regular resolutions dedicated to combating "Defamation of Religion."

NOTES AND QUESTIONS

1.   Professors Marshall & Shea argue that prohibitions on blasphemy or defamation of religion are inconsistent with human rights. Do you agree? See Paul Marshall & Nina Shea, Silenced: How Apostasy & Blasphemy Codes are Choking Freedom Worldwide (2011). Their book identifies and analyzes the Muslim-majority nations that have supported international campaigns to ban the defamation of religion. Should Western nations expect Muslim nations to change their culture on defamation of religion?

2.   *UN Resolutions.* In 2011, both the United Nations Human Rights Council and the General Assembly passed resolutions supportive of religious freedom that did not include bans on defamation of religion. The same resolution has been reaffirmed every year since then. The resolution was controversial because in a list of "actions to foster a domestic environment of religious tolerance, peace and respect," it calls on states to adopt "measures to criminalize incitement to imminent violence based on religion or belief." Was that resolution too restrictive of speech? Or was it a good compromise between nations that oppose defamation of religion and those that support free speech? Professor Blitt argues that the OIC continues to oppose defamation of religion and undermines the spirit of the UN resolution with its insistence that defamation of religion be combatted. See Robert C. Blitt, Defamation of Religion: Rumors of Its Death Are Greatly Exaggerated, 62 Case W. Res. L. Rev. 347 (2011).

According to Professor Jonathan Turley, the United States has been part of the defamation of religion problem. In 2009, he writes, "the Obama administration shockingly supported Muslim allies trying to establish a new international blasphemy standard. Likewise, in 2012, President Obama went to the United Nations and declared that 'the future must not belong to those who slander the prophet of Islam.'" Jonathan Turley, The Threat to French Free Speech Isn't Terrorism. It's the French, Wash. Post, Jan. 11, 2015, at B01. Do you think Turley and Blitt would be satisfied by anything but a clear statement that defamation of religion is an international human right?

3. *Blasphemy Prosecutions.* In Pakistan, a Christian woman, Asia Bibi, was told by Muslim women that she must convert to Islam because they had been defiled by her offer of a glass of water. Bibi announced her Christian faith and said she would not convert. She was sentenced to death for her crime. Salmaan Taseer, governor of Punjab province, spoke out in support of her and questioned Pakistan's blasphemy laws. His police guard, Mumtaz Qadri, then killed Taseer because Taseer had blasphemed. The Pakistan Supreme Court upheld Qadri's murder conviction. International pressure has been put on Pakistan to release Bibi from prison.

In Egypt, prosecutions for insulting Islam have increased from 3 cases in 2011 to 21 cases in 2015. Social media have made it easier to discover instances of blasphemy. In one case, a teacher filmed teenage Christian boys mimicking Muslims praying and then beheading each other like ISIS zealots do. The teenagers were sentenced to five years imprisonment. Maggie Michael, Blasphemy Cases Rise in Egypt and Christians Bear the Brunt, AP, Mar. 25, 2016. "In February, an online activist Mustafa Abdel-Nabi was sentenced to three years in absentia for postings about atheism on his Facebook page. A writer, Fatma Naoot, was sentenced to three years in prison in January over Facebook postings criticizing the slaughter of animals for Muslim holidays. A prominent TV host, Islam Behery, received a one-year prison sentence after calling for passages he said supported terrorism to be removed from books of Islamic religious interpretation." Id.

Do these prosecutions persuade you that prohibitions on blasphemy or defamation of religion are inconsistent with human rights?

4. *Cartoons.* In 2005 violent protests erupted and Danish embassies were burned after a Danish newspaper published cartoons of the Prophet Muhammad. Later Yale University Press refused to publish the cartoons in a book about the controversy. See Danish Paper Refuses to Apologize Over Muhammad Cartoons, BBC Monitoring Europe, Dec. 8, 2005; Dan Bilefsky, Danish Editor Takes an Indefinite Leave; He Defends Decision to Publish Drawings, Int'l Herald Trib., Feb. 11, 2006, at 1.

Then on January 7, 2015, gunmen attacked the Paris offices of satirical magazine *Charlie Hebdo*, killing the property's caretaker, a bodyguard, the editor, four cartoonists, three staff members, and a guest. The editor and cartoonists were asked for by name. See BBC, *Charlie Hebdo* Attack: Three Days of Terror, BBC News Europe, Jan. 14, 2015. The gunmen were heard to yell "We have avenged the Prophet Muhammad" and "God is Great" while fleeing the scene, and Al-Qaida in the Arabian Peninsula later claimed responsibility. The gunmen also held hostages in a kosher supermarket, where they killed four Jews and injured four others. The gunman later said he was part of ISIS and chose the market because it was Jewish. See Staff, Four Dead at Kosher Market After Raid, The Jerusalem Post, Jan. 9, 2015.

Charlie Hebdo had published cartoons critically depicting the prophet as well as the pope and other authority figures. Many Muslims believe Islam prohibits depictions of Muhammad. Representative cartoons are available at *The Huffington Post*. See Catherine Taibi, These are the *Charlie*

Hebdo Cartoons that Terrorists Thought Were Worth Killing Over, Huffington Post, Jan. 7, 2015, at http://www.huffingtonpost.com/2015/01/07/charlie-hebdo-cartoons-paris-french-newspaper-shooting_n_6429552.html. Millions marched in France after the shooting in support of free speech, and the slogan "Je Suis Charlie" appeared across the world as a mark of solidarity with the slain cartoonists. *Charlie Hebdo* published a cartoon with a weeping Muhammad holding a "Je Suis Charlie" sign.

In an op-ed in the USA Today, Professor Blitt complained about the mainstream Muslims who had "emboldened extremists" with their long campaign to ban defamation of religion:

> Many have taken false comfort in blaming the cold-blooded attack of *Charlie Hebdo* on the fanatical action of a small minority of Muslims. But attributing the horror perpetrated in Paris to a band of Salafist radicals alone betrays a willful blindness to a longstanding campaign by broad-based Islamic groups to silence those they consider blasphemers.
>
> The Islamic State and al-Qaeda are by no means the most powerful purveyors of the destructive idea that Islam demands unqualified protection against perceived insult. In the aftermath of the Paris attack, reputable Muslim groups around the world have denounced the violence, but important bodies such as the Organization of Islamic Cooperation (OIC) and the Arab League, as well as many of the individual states comprising these groups, must bear responsibility for nurturing an environment that breeds violence in the name of defending Islam.
>
> By building the expectation that dissent or insult merits suppression, groups such as the OIC and the Arab League have emboldened extremists to take protection of Islam to the next level. With the most authoritative Muslim voices prepared to denounce violence but not to combat the idea that Islam should be immune from criticism, a meaningful response to counteract the resulting violence continues to be glaringly absent.
>
> An OIC statement released after a 2011 *Charlie Hebdo* issue "guest-edited" by the prophet Mohammed typifies this troubling position: "Publication of the insulting cartoon ... was an outrageous act of incitement and hatred and abuse of freedom of expression. ... The publishers and editors of the Charlie Hebdo magazine must assume full responsibility for their ... incitement of religious intolerance."

Robert C. Blitt, Blasphemy as a Crime Incites Intolerance, The Californian (Salinas, CA), Jan. 14, 2015, at A2. Do you agree?

In contrast, Pope Francis criticized the cartoons, saying, "One cannot provoke, one cannot insult other people's faith, one cannot make fun of faith." And the editor of *Charlie* criticized newspapers that would not publish the cartoons: "When they refuse to publish this cartoon, when they blur it out, when they decline to publish it, they blur out democracy, secularism, freedom of religion and they insult the citizenship." Sophia Rosenbaum & Aaron Short, *Charlie Hebdo* Editor Rips Pope's Criticism of Cartoons, N.Y. Post, Jan. 19, 2015. Although the *New York Post* ran the cartoons, the *New York Times* did not run those featuring Muhammad. The famous Doonesbury cartoonist Gary Trudeau accused the cartoons of being "hate speech." When does criticism of religion turn into hate speech?

Norway repealed its blasphemy law after the attack on *Charlie Hebdo* out of fear that it "underpins a perception that religious expressions and symbols are entitled to a special protection," insisting "it is time to stand up for freedom of speech, even in religious matters." No one had been charged with blasphemy since 1933, and the last conviction was in 1912, when Norwegian journalist Arnfred Olsen was convicted for his criticism of Christianity in the magazine *Freethinkers*. See Religion is Fair Game in Norway After Blasphemy Law Repealed, Sputnik, May 8, 2015 at http://sputniknews.com/europe/20150508/1021880692.html#ixzz3fWvbDvS4.

C. CONSCIENCE

1. THE MILITARY

How does the European Court of Human Rights' opinion recognizing a right to conscientious objection compare to *Seeger, Welsh,* and *Gillette,* the Selective Service cases that you studied in Chapter 5?

Bayatyan v. Armenia

The European Court of Human Rights, Grand Chamber, 2011.
App. No. 23459/03.

THE FACTS

I.   THE CIRCUMSTANCES OF THE CASE

A.   Background to the case

The applicant is a Jehovah's Witness. From 1997 he attended various Jehovah's Witnesses religious services and he was baptised on 18 September 1999 at the age of 16.

On 16 January 2000 the applicant was registered as a person liable for military service with the Erebuni District Military Commissariat.

On 16 January 2001 the applicant, at the age of 17, was called to undergo a medical examination, following which he was declared fit for military service. The applicant became eligible for military service during the 2001 spring draft (April–June).

On 1 April 2001, at the outset of the draft, the applicant sent identical letters to the General Prosecutor of Armenia, the Military Commissioner of Armenia, and the Human Rights Commission of the National Assembly, with the following statement:

"I, Vahan Bayatyan, born in 1983, inform you that I have studied the Bible since 1996 and have trained my conscience by the Bible in harmony with the words of Isaiah 2:4, and I consciously refuse to perform military service. At the same time I inform you that I am ready to perform alternative civilian service in place of military service."

In early May a summons to appear for military service on 15 May 2001 was delivered to the applicant's home. On 14 May 2001 an official of the Erebuni Military Commissariat telephoned the applicant's home and asked his mother whether the applicant was aware that he had been called to appear at the Commissariat to commence military service the following day. That same evening the applicant temporarily moved away from his home for fear of being forcibly taken to the military.

On 15 and 16 May 2001 officials from the Commissariat telephoned the applicant's mother, demanding to know his whereabouts. They threatened to take him to the military by force if he did not come voluntarily. On 17 May 2001, early in the morning, the officials came to the applicant's home. His parents were asleep and did not open the door. On the same date the applicant's mother went to the Commissariat, where she stated that the applicant had left home and she did not know when he would come back. According to the applicant, the Commissariat made no further efforts to contact his family.

On 29 May 2001 the Commission for State and Legal Affairs of the National Assembly sent a reply to the applicant's letter of 1 April 2001, stating:

"In connection with your declaration, ... we inform you that in accordance with the legislation of the Republic of Armenia every citizen ... is obliged to serve in the Armenian army. Since no law has yet been adopted in Armenia on alternative service, you must submit to the current law and serve in the Armenian army."

In early to mid-June 2001 the applicant returned home, where he lived until his arrest in September 2002. [He was sentenced to two and a half years in prison.]

III. COMPARATIVE LAW

It follows from the material available to the Court on the legislation of the member States of the Council of Europe that almost all the member States which ever had or still have compulsory military service introduced laws at various points recognising and implementing the right to conscientious objection, some of them even before becoming members of the Council of Europe. The earliest was the United Kingdom in 1916, followed by Denmark (1917), Sweden (1920), the Netherlands (1920–1923), Norway (1922), Finland (1931), Germany

(1949), France and Luxembourg (1963), Belgium (1964), Italy (1972), Austria (1974), Portugal (1976) and Spain (1978).

A big wave of recognitions ensued in the late 1980s and the 1990s, when almost all the then or future member States which had not yet done so introduced such a right into their domestic legal systems. These include Poland (1988), the Czech Republic and Hungary (1989), Croatia (1990), Estonia, Moldova and Slovenia (1991), Cyprus, the former Federal Republic of Yugoslavia (which in 2006 divided into two member States: Serbia and Montenegro, both of which retained that right) and Ukraine (1992), Latvia (1993), the Slovak Republic and Switzerland (1995), Bosnia and Herzegovina, Lithuania and Romania (1996), Georgia and Greece (1997), and Bulgaria (1998).

From the remaining member States the Former Yugoslav Republic of Macedonia, which as early as in 1992 had provided for a possibility to perform non-armed military service, introduced a genuine alternative civilian service in 2001. Russia and Albania, which in 1993 and 1998 respectively had constitutionally recognised the right to conscientious objection, fully implemented it through laws in 2004 and 2003 respectively. Azerbaijan constitutionally recognised the right to conscientious objection in 1995 but no implementing laws have yet been introduced. Conscientious objectors are not recognised in Turkey.

In most of the member States where conscientious objection was or is recognised and fully implemented, conscientious objector status could or can be claimed on the basis not only of religious beliefs but also of a relatively broad range of personal beliefs of a non-religious nature, the only exceptions being Romania and Ukraine, where the right to claim conscientious objector status is limited to religious grounds alone. In some member States the right to claim conscientious objector status only applied or applies during peacetime, as in Poland, Belgium and Finland, while in others, like Montenegro and the Slovak Republic, the right to claim such status by definition applies only in time of mobilisation or war. Finally, some member States, like Finland, allow certain categories of conscientious objectors to be exempted also from alternative service.

THE LAW

I.   ALLEGED VIOLATION OF ARTICLE 9 OF THE CONVENTION

The applicant complained that his conviction for refusal to serve in the army had violated Article 9 of the Convention which reads as follows:

"1. Everyone has the right to freedom of thought, conscience and religion; this right includes freedom to change his religion or belief and freedom, either alone or in community with others and in public or private, to manifest his religion or belief, in worship, teaching, practice and observance.

2. Freedom to manifest one's religion or beliefs shall be subject only to such limitations as are prescribed by law and are necessary in a democratic society in the interests of public safety, for the protection of public order, health or morals, or for the protection of the rights and freedoms of others."

C. The Court's assessment

1. Applicability of Article 9

The Government contested the applicability of Article 9 to the applicant's case with reference to the Commission's case-law, while the applicant and the third-party interveners argued that this case-law was obsolete and requested that it be brought in line with present-day conditions.

(a) Recapitulation of the relevant case-law

The Court observes that the initial position of the European Commission of Human Rights was set out in the case of Grandrath v. the Federal Republic of Germany, which concerned a Jehovah's Witness who sought to be exempted not only from military but also from substitute civilian service. He alleged a violation of Article 9 of the Convention on the ground that the authorities had imposed on him a service which was contrary to his conscience and religion and had punished him for his refusal to perform such service. The Commission observed at the outset that, while Article 9 guaranteed the right to freedom of thought, conscience and religion in general, Article 4 of the Convention contained a provision which expressly dealt with the question of compulsory service exacted in the place of military service in the case of conscientious objectors. It concluded that, since Article 4 expressly recognised that civilian service might be imposed on conscientious objectors as a substitute for military service, objections of conscience did not, under the Convention, entitle a person to exemption from such service. The Commission found it superfluous to examine any questions of interpretation of the term "freedom of conscience and religion" used in Article 9 and concluded that that provision considered separately had not been violated.

Similarly, in the case of X. v. Austria, the Commission stated that, in interpreting Article 9 of the Convention, it had also taken into consideration the terms of Article 4 § 3 (b) of the Convention, which provided that forced or compulsory labour should not include "any service of a military character or, in cases of conscientious objectors, in countries where they are recognised, service exacted instead of compulsory military service". By including the words "in countries where they are recognised" in Article 4 § 3 (b), a choice was left to the High Contracting Parties whether or not to recognise conscientious objectors and, if they were so recognised, to provide some substitute service. The Commission, for this reason, found that Article 9, as qualified by Article 4 § 3 (b), did not impose on a state the obligation to recognise conscientious objectors and, consequently, to make special arrangements for the exercise of their right to freedom of conscience and religion as far as it affected their compulsory military service. It followed that these Articles did not prevent a State which had not recognised conscientious objectors from punishing those who refused to do military service.

This approach was subsequently confirmed by the Commission in the case of X. v. the Federal Republic of Germany, which concerned the applicant's conscientious objection to substitute civilian service. In the case of Conscientious objectors v. Denmark, the Commission reiterated that the right to conscientious objection was not included among the rights and freedoms guaranteed by the Convention. In the case of A. v. Switzerland, the Commission reaffirmed its position and added that neither the sentence passed on the applicant for refusing to perform military service nor the fact of its not being suspended could constitute a breach of Article 9.

(b)   Whether there is a need for a change of the case-law

While it is in the interests of legal certainty, foreseeability and equality before the law that the Court should not depart, without good reason, from precedents laid down in previous cases, a failure by the Court to maintain a dynamic and evolutive approach would risk rendering it a bar to reform or improvement. It is of crucial importance that the Convention is interpreted and applied in a manner which renders its rights practical and effective, not theoretical and illusory.

The Court notes that prior to this case it has never ruled on the question of the applicability of Article 9 to conscientious objectors, unlike the Commission, which refused to apply that Article to such persons. In doing so, the Commission drew a link between Article 9 and Article 4 § 3 (b) of the Convention, finding that the latter left the choice of recognising a right to conscientious objection to the Contracting Parties. Consequently, conscientious objectors were excluded from the scope of protection of Article 9, which could not be read as guaranteeing freedom from prosecution for refusal to serve in the army.

The Court, however, is not convinced that this interpretation of Article 4 § 3 (b) reflects the true purpose and meaning of this provision. It notes that Article 4 § 3 (b) excludes from the scope of "forced or compulsory labour" prohibited by Article 4 § 2 "any service of a military character or, in case of conscientious objectors in countries where they are recognised, service exacted instead of compulsory military service". The Court further notes in this respect the Travaux préparatoires on Article 4, whose paragraph 23 states: "In sub-paragraph [(b)], the clause relating to conscientious objectors was intended to indicate that any national service required of them by law would not fall within the scope of forced or compulsory labour. As the concept of conscientious objection was not recognised in many countries, the phrase 'in countries where conscientious objection is recognised' was inserted". In the Court's opinion, the Travaux préparatoires confirm that the sole purpose of sub-paragraph (b) of Article 4 § 3 is to provide a further elucidation of the notion "forced or compulsory labour". In itself it neither recognises nor excludes a right to conscientious objection and should therefore not have a delimiting effect on the rights guaranteed by Article 9.

At the same time, the Court is mindful of the fact that the restrictive interpretation of Article 9 applied by the Commission was a reflection of the ideas prevailing at the material time. It considers, however, that many years have elapsed since the Commission first set out its reasoning excluding the right to conscientious objection from the scope of Article 9 in the cases of Grandrath v. the Federal Republic of Germany and X. v. Austria. Even though that reasoning was later confirmed by the Commission on several occasions, its last decision to that effect was adopted as long ago as 1995. In the meantime there have been important developments both in the domestic legal systems of Council of Europe member States and internationally.

The Court reiterates in this connection that the Convention is a living instrument which must be interpreted in the light of present-day conditions and of the ideas prevailing in democratic States today. Since it is first and foremost a system for the protection of human rights, the Court must have regard to the changing conditions in Contracting States and respond, for example, to any emerging consensus as to the standards to be achieved. Furthermore, in defining the meaning of terms and notions in the text of the Convention, the Court can and must take into account elements of international law other than the Convention and the interpretation of such elements by competent organs. The consensus emerging from specialised international instruments may constitute a relevant consideration for the Court when it interprets the provisions of the Convention in specific cases.

The Court notes that in the late 1980s and the 1990s there was an obvious trend among European countries, both existing Council of Europe member States and those which joined the organisation later, to recognise the right to conscientious objection. All in all, nineteen of those States which had not yet recognised the right to conscientious objection introduced such a right into their domestic legal systems around the time when the Commission took its last decisions on the matter. Hence, at the time when the alleged interference with the applicant's rights under Article 9 occurred, namely in 2002–2003, only four other member States, in addition to Armenia, did not provide for the possibility of claiming conscientious objector status, although three of those had already incorporated that right into their Constitutions but had not yet introduced implementing laws. Thus, already at the material time there was nearly a consensus among all Council of Europe member States, the overwhelming majority of which had already recognised in their law and practice the right to conscientious objection.

Moreover, the Court notes that, subsequent to the facts of the present case, two more member States passed laws fully implementing the right to conscientious objection, thereby leaving Azerbaijan and Turkey as the only two member States not to have done so yet. Furthermore, the Court notes that Armenia itself also recognised that right after the applicant's release from prison and the introduction of the present application.

The Court would further point out the equally important developments concerning recognition of the right to conscientious objection in various international fora. The most notable is the interpretation by the UNHRC of the provisions of the ICCPR (Articles 8 and 18), which are similar to those of the Convention (Articles 4 and 9). Initially the UNHRC adopted the same approach as the European Commission, excluding the right of conscientious objection from the scope of Article 18 of the ICCPR. However, in 1993, in its General Comment No. 22, it modified its initial approach and considered that a right to conscientious objection could be derived from Article 18 of the ICCPR inasmuch as the obligation to use lethal force might seriously conflict with the freedom of conscience and the right to manifest one's religion or belief. In 2006 the UNHRC explicitly refused to apply Article 8 of the ICCPR in two cases against South Korea concerning conscientious objectors and examined their complaints solely under Article 18 of the ICCPR, finding a violation of that provision on account of the applicants' conviction for refusal to serve in the army for reasons of conscience.

In Europe, mention should be made of the proclamation in 2000 of the Charter of Fundamental Rights of the European Union, which entered into force in 2009. While the first paragraph of Article 10 of the Charter reproduces Article 9 § 1 of the Convention almost literally, its second paragraph explicitly states that "[t]he right to conscientious objection is recognised, in accordance with the national laws governing the exercise of this right" (see paragraph 57 above). Such explicit addition is no doubt deliberate, and reflects the unanimous recognition of the right to conscientious objection by the member States of the European Union, as well as the weight attached to that right in modern European society.

Within the Council of Europe, both the PACE and the Committee of Ministers have also on several occasions called on the member States, which had not yet done so, to recognise the right to conscientious objection. Furthermore, recognition of the right to conscientious objection became a pre-condition for admission of new member States into the organisation. In 2001 the PACE, having reiterated its calls made previously, stated specifically that the right to conscientious objection was a fundamental aspect of the right to freedom of thought, conscience and religion enshrined in the Convention. In 2010 the Committee of Ministers, relying on the developments in the UNHRC case-law and the provisions of the European Union Charter of Fundamental Rights, also confirmed such interpretation of the notion of freedom of conscience and religion as enshrined in Article 9 of the Convention and recommended that the member States ensure the right of conscripts to be granted conscientious objector status.

The Court therefore concludes that since the Commission's decision in Grandrath v. the Federal Republic of Germany and its follow-up decisions the domestic law of the overwhelming majority of Council of Europe member States, along with the relevant international instruments, has evolved to the effect that at the material time there was already a virtually general consensus on the question in Europe and beyond. In the light of these developments, it cannot be said that a shift in the interpretation of Article 9 in relation to events which occurred in 2002–2003 was not foreseeable. This is all the more the case considering that Armenia itself was a party to the ICCPR and had, moreover, pledged when joining the Council of Europe to introduce a law recognising the right to conscientious objection.

In the light of the foregoing and in line with the "living instrument" approach, the Court therefore takes the view that it is not possible to confirm the case-law established by the Commission, and that Article 9 should no longer be read in conjunction with Article 4 § 3 (b). Consequently, the applicant's complaint is to be assessed solely under Article 9.

In this respect, the Court notes that Article 9 does not explicitly refer to a right to conscientious objection. However, it considers that opposition to military service, where it is motivated by a serious and insurmountable conflict between the obligation to serve in the army and a person's conscience or his deeply and genuinely held religious or other beliefs, constitutes a conviction or belief of sufficient cogency, seriousness, cohesion and importance to attract the guarantees of Article 9. Whether and to what extent objection to military service falls within the ambit of that provision must be assessed in the light of the particular circumstances of the case.

The applicant in the present case is a member of Jehovah's Witnesses, a religious group whose beliefs include the conviction that service, even unarmed, within the military is to be opposed. The Court therefore has no reason to doubt that the applicant's objection to military service was motivated by his religious beliefs, which were genuinely held and were in serious and insurmountable conflict with his obligation to perform military service. In this sense, and contrary to the Government's claim, the applicant's situation must be distinguished from a situation that concerns an obligation which has no specific conscientious implications in itself, such as a general tax obligation. Accordingly, Article 9 is applicable to the applicant's case.

2.   Compliance with Article 9

(a) Whether there was an interference

The Court considers that the applicant's failure to report for military service was a manifestation of his religious beliefs. His conviction for draft evasion therefore amounted to an interference with his freedom to manifest his religion as guaranteed by Article 9 § 1. Such interference will be contrary to Article 9 unless it is "prescribed by law", pursues one or more of the legitimate aims set out in paragraph 2 and is "necessary in a democratic society."

(b) Whether the interference was justified

(i) Prescribed by law

The Court does not find it necessary to resolve the apparent conflict between the domestic law and Armenia's international commitment. Nor does it find it necessary, in the present context, to rule on the alleged failure of the authorities to comply with the provisions of the ICCPR.

Therefore, for the purposes of the present case and in view of its findings concerning the necessity of the interference, the Court prefers to leave open the question of whether the interference was prescribed by law.

(ii) Legitimate aim

The Court considers it unnecessary to determine conclusively whether the aims referred to by the Government were legitimate within the meaning of Article 9 § 2, since, even assuming that they were, the interference was in any event incompatible with that provision for the reasons set out below.

(iii) Necessary in a democratic society

According to its settled case-law, the Court leaves to States party to the Convention a certain margin of appreciation in deciding whether and to what extent an interference is necessary. This margin of appreciation goes hand in hand with European supervision embracing both the law and the decisions applying it. The Court's task is to determine whether the measures taken at national level were justified in principle and proportionate (see Leyla Şahin, § 110).

In order to determine the scope of the margin of appreciation in the present case the Court must take into account what is at stake, namely the need to maintain true religious pluralism, which is vital to the survival of a democratic society. The Court may also have regard to any consensus and common values emerging from the practices of the States parties to the Convention.

The Court has already pointed out above that almost all the member States of the Council of Europe which ever had or still have compulsory military service have introduced alternatives to such service in order to reconcile the possible conflict between individual conscience and military obligations. Accordingly, a State which has not done so enjoys only a limited margin of appreciation and must advance convincing and compelling reasons to justify any interference. In particular, it must demonstrate that the interference corresponds to a "pressing social need."

The Court cannot overlook the fact that, in the present case, the applicant, as a member of Jehovah's Witnesses, sought to be exempted from military service not for reasons of personal benefit or convenience but on the ground of his genuinely held religious convictions. Since no alternative civilian service was available in Armenia at the material time, the applicant had no choice but to refuse to be drafted into the army if he was to stay faithful to his convictions and, by doing so, to risk criminal sanctions. Thus, the system existing at the material time imposed on citizens an obligation which had potentially serious implications for conscientious objectors while failing to allow any conscience-based exceptions and penalising those who, like the applicant, refused to perform military service. In the Court's opinion, such a system failed to strike a fair balance between the interests of society as a whole and those of the applicant. It therefore considers that the imposition of a penalty on the applicant, in circumstances where no allowances were made for the exigencies of his conscience and beliefs, could not be considered a measure necessary in a democratic society. Still less can it be seen as necessary taking into account that there existed viable and effective alternatives capable of accommodating the competing interests, as demonstrated by the experience of the overwhelming majority of the European States.

The Court admits that any system of compulsory military service imposes a heavy burden on citizens. It will be acceptable if it is shared in an equitable manner and if exemptions from this duty are based on solid and convincing grounds. The Court has already found that the applicant had solid and convincing reasons justifying his exemption from military service. It further notes that the applicant never refused to comply with his civic obligations in general. On the contrary, he explicitly requested the authorities to provide him with the opportunity to perform alternative civilian service. Thus, the applicant was prepared, for convincing reasons, to share the societal burden equally with his compatriots engaged in compulsory military service by performing alternative service. In the absence of such an opportunity, the applicant had to serve a prison sentence instead.

The Court further reiterates that pluralism, tolerance and broadmindedness are hallmarks of a "democratic society". Although individual interests must on occasion be subordinated to those of a group, democracy does not simply mean that the views of a majority must always prevail: a balance must be achieved which ensures the fair and proper treatment of people from minorities and avoids any abuse of a dominant position (see Leyla Şahin, § 108). Thus, respect on the part of the State towards the beliefs of a minority religious group like the applicant's by providing them with the opportunity to serve society as dictated by their conscience might, far from creating unjust inequalities or discrimination as claimed by the Government, rather ensure cohesive and stable pluralism and promote religious harmony and tolerance in society.

The Court would lastly point out that the applicant's prosecution and conviction happened at a time when the Armenian authorities had already officially pledged, upon accession to the Council of Europe, to introduce alternative service within a specific period. Furthermore, while the commitment not to convict conscientious objectors during that period was not explicitly stated in PACE Opinion no. 221, it can be said to have been implicit in the following phrase: " . . . in the meantime, to pardon all conscientious objectors sentenced to prison terms . . . allowing them instead . . . , when the law . . . had come into force . . . to perform . . . alternative civilian service". Such undertakings on the part of the Armenian authorities were indicative of a recognition that freedom of conscience can be expressed through opposition to military service and that it was necessary to deal with the issue by introducing alternative measures rather than penalising conscientious objectors. Hence, the applicant's conviction for conscientious objection was in direct conflict with the official policy of reform and legislative changes being implemented in Armenia at the material time in pursuance of its international commitment and cannot be said, in such circumstances, to have been prompted by a pressing social need. This is even more so, taking into account that the law on alternative service was adopted less than a year after the applicant's final conviction. The fact that the applicant was later released on parole does not affect the situation. Nor did the adoption of the new law have any impact on the applicant's case.

For all the above reasons, the Court considers that the applicant's conviction constituted an interference which was not necessary in a democratic society within the meaning of Article 9 of the Convention. Accordingly, there has been a violation of that provision.

FOR THESE REASONS, THE COURT

1.   Holds, by sixteen votes to one, that there has been a violation of Article 9 of the Convention;

2.   Holds, by sixteen votes to one,

(a) that the respondent State is to pay the applicant, within three months, the following amounts, to be converted into Armenian drams at the rate applicable at the date of settlement:

> (i)   EUR 10,000 (ten thousand euros), plus any tax that may be chargeable, in respect of non-pecuniary damage;

> (ii) EUR 10,000 (ten thousand euros), plus any tax that may be chargeable to the applicant, in respect of costs and expenses;

(b) that from the expiry of the above-mentioned three months until settlement simple interest shall be payable on the above amounts at a rate equal to the marginal lending rate of the European Central Bank during the default period plus three percentage points;

3.   Dismisses unanimously the remainder of the applicant's claim for just satisfaction.

DISSENTING OPINION OF JUDGE GYULUMYAN

The Convention and its Protocols do not guarantee, as such, any right to conscientious objection. Article 9 of the Convention does not give conscientious objectors the right to be exempted from military or substitute civilian service. Nor does it prevent a State from imposing sanctions on those who refuse such service.

I think that the role of this Court is to protect human rights which already exist in the Convention, not to create new rights. One can argue that the evolutive approach to the Convention permits the Court to broaden the rights protected. However, this in my view is not permitted when the Convention itself leaves the recognition of particular rights to the discretion of the Contracting Parties.

NOTES AND QUESTIONS

1.   *Universal Human Right?* Do you agree "the right of conscientious objection to military service is the most startling of human rights."? Jeremy K. Kessler, The Invention of A Human Right: Conscientious Objection at the United Nations, 1947–2011, 44 Colum. Hum. Rts. L. Rev. 753 (2013). Why would this right be "startling"? See id. ("While human rights generally seek to protect individuals from state power, the right of conscientious objection radically alters the citizen-state relationship, subordinating a state's decisions about national security to the beliefs of the individual citizen.") Should the right of conscientious objection be recognized as an international human right or only as a statutory right protected by some nations in their domestic laws? What did *Bayatyan* conclude about this question?

2.   *Legal Reasoning.* What do Articles 4 and 9 of the Convention protect? Why do they appear to be in conflict in this case? How do the majority and dissent disagree about their interaction? Are you more sympathetic to the majority's argument that the Convention is a "living

instrument" that must be adapted for the times, or the dissent's statement that the court should "protect human rights which already exist in the Convention, not create new rights"? Is your answer affected by your approach to interpretation of the U.S. Constitution?

Article 18 of the International Covenant on Civil and Political Rights (ICCPR), which is a multilateral human rights treaty drafted by the United Nations, protects religious freedom in the following language:

> 1.   Everyone shall have the right to freedom of thought, conscience and religion. This right shall include freedom to have or adopt a religion or belief of his choice, and freedom, either individually or in community with others and in public or in private, to manifest his religion or belief in worship, observance, practice and teaching.
>
> 2.   No one shall be subject to coercion that would impair his freedom to have or adopt a religion or belief of his choice.
>
> 3.   Freedom to manifest one's religion or belief may be subject only to such limitations as are prescribed by law and are necessary to protect public safety, order, health or morals or the fundamental rights and freedoms of others.
>
> 4.   The State parties to the present Covenant undertake to have respect for the liberty of parents and, when applicable, legal guardians to ensure the religious and moral education of their children in conformity with their own convictions.

Should this language be interpreted to protect a human right to conscientious objection? For years, C.O. advocates fought unsuccessfully to have C.O. protection explicitly incorporated into international agreements. Then in 2006, the U.N's Human Rights Committee (HRC) ruled that Korea had violated the Article 18 rights of two Jehovah's Witnesses by requiring military conscription with no alternative service. See Mr. Yeo-Bum Yoon and Mr. Myung-Jin Choi v. Republic of Korea, Communication Nos. 1321/2004 and 1322/2004, U.N. Doc. CCPR/C/88/D/1321-1322/2004 (2006); Jeremy K. Kessler, The Invention of A Human Right: Conscientious Objection at the United Nations, 1947–2011, 44 Colum. Hum. Rts. L. Rev. 753, 791 (2013). Should Article 18 be interpreted to protect a right to conscientious objection? How do you assess the dissenting opinion of Ms. Ruth Wedgwood, HRC member from the United States, in the *Yoon* case:

> But article 18 does not suggest that a person motivated by religious belief has a protected right to withdraw from the otherwise legitimate requirements of a shared society. For example, citizens cannot refrain from paying taxes, even where they have conscientious objections to state activities. In its present interpretation of article 18, seemingly differentiating military service from other state obligations, the Committee cites no evidence from the Covenant's negotiating history to suggest that this was contemplated.

See Yoon & Choi v. Korea, infra; Kessler at 786. Do the dissenters in *Bayatyan* and *Yoon* agree about statutory interpretation? About the status of an international human right to conscientious objection?

South Korea had argued that Article 18 allowed it to protect its own public safety, order, and health by refusing conscientious objection. Because it was "the world's sole divided nation," it was confronted with "specific security circumstances" that made its system of compulsory military service absolutely "necessary to protect public safety." Kessler at 785–86. Did Armenia make a similar argument in *Bayatyan*? Why didn't the courts accept the nations' security arguments? Are these results consistent with *Şahin*, the headscarf case from Section A?

3. *Alternative Service.* What are Bayatyan's implications for a C.O. who refuses alternative service? Does the right to conscientious objection extend to a refusal of any service to the state? What does the logic of the opinion suggest? Nations vary in the ratio of military to alternative service. It is 1 to 1 in Denmark (4 years) and Moldova (12 years) but 1 to 2.09 in Finland. 1 to 1.5 appears to be the norm. See European Bureau for Conscientious Objection, Annual Report: Conscientious Objection to Military Service in Europe 39 (2015). Is it fair to make C.O.s serve longer in the alternative service than non-C.O.s serve in the military? Would difference in service time be grounds for a lawsuit for violations of religious freedom?

4. *Shepherd: C.O./Refugee.* Andre Lawrence Shepherd was an American soldier stationed in Germany who maintained Apache helicopters for the U.S. Army. During his service in Germany, Shepherd started to question the legality of the Iraq war and, specifically, how helicopters were used in combat to indiscriminately and disproportionately harm civilians. Shepherd went absent without leave and applied for asylum in Germany because he wanted to avoid committing war crimes against Iraq. Desertion is a punishable criminal offense in the U.S. Based on your readings from Chapter 5, would Shepherd qualify as a C.O. in the United States? Should Germany grant refugee status to C.O.s? What would happen to national military forces if international refugee law granted refugee status to C.O.s? Do you agree "[f]reely offering asylum to deserters may seriously undermine the effectiveness and reliability of a nation's armed forces."? See Klaus Ferdinand Gärditz, Shepherd v. Germany. Case C-472/13. at http:// curia.europa.eu. Court of Justice of the European Union, February 26, 2015, 109 Am. J. Int'l L. 623, 628 (2015). If conscientious objection is a universal human right, should international law require nations to give refugee status to soldier C.O.s?

5. *Conscientious Objection/Conscience.* In another case from Germany, a German soldier disobeyed an order to participate in a military software project to facilitate German and NATO cooperation in the Iraq war because he believed the war was illegal. A military court found him guilty of insubordination and demoted him. The appeals court, however, held he had rights of conscience to disobey the law. How do you assess the quality of the reasoning in the following summary of the opinion?

First, the court held that soldiers in active service can rely on their basic right of freedom of conscience, which is distinct from the constitutional right to recognition as a conscientious objector. Unlike a conscientious objector, who maintains an objection to armed conflict in general, the major in the present case was opposed to the particular military operation taking place with respect to Iraq. He wanted to continue his public employment as a soldier but to make use of his basic right not to be forced to act against his moral convictions in this specific situation. The court held that, in explicitly recognizing the constitutional right of conscientious objection, the Basic Law did not intend to limit soldiers' more general right to freedom of conscience but, instead, wanted to strengthen it and to put it in concrete terms for application to the military. Although the rights of a soldier might well be limited by his military obligations, the military must respect the fundamental rights of soldiers, including the right to freedom of conscience. According to the court, freedom of conscience does not involve independence from the general subjugation to law, but in balancing the duty of obedience against the soldier's freedom of conscience, the ethical implications of an order have to be taken into account.

Ilja Baudisch, Germany v. N. Decision No. 2 Wd 12.04. at http://www. bverwg.de. Bundesverwaltungsgericht (German Federal Administrative Court), June 21, 2005, 100 Am. J. Int'l L. 911, 912 (2006).

Is it possible that soldiers enjoy fundamental rights to both conscientious objection *and* conscience? Is that a better outcome than a system that "allowed an individual to refuse military service altogether, but not to refuse to participate in specific operations or situations."? Id. at 915. What do we have in the United States? Does this mean that Shepherd, from the first German case, had both C.O. and conscience rights to refuse to maintain helicopters? Or only rights of conscience?

6. *Who Qualifies?* In Belarus, only young men with a religious objection to war—not all pacifists—enjoy a statutory right to alternative serve. Ukraine identifies ten religions whose members qualify as C.O.s. See European Bureau for Conscientious Objection, Annual Report: Conscientious Objection to Military Service in Europe 24, 33 (2015). Is there a problem with these regulations? How would a U.S. Court address them? Do you now think *Seeger*, from Chapter 1, was a good decision?

7. *C.O. to Induced Abortion.* "Of the EU member states where induced abortion is legal, invoking CO is granted by law in 21 countries. The same applies to the non-EU countries Norway and Switzerland. CO is not legally granted in the EU member states Sweden, Finland, Bulgaria and the Czech Republic. The Icelandic legislation provides no right to CO either." See A. Heino et al., Conscientious Objection and Induced Abortion in Europe, 18(4) Eur. J. Contracept. Reprod. Health Care 231 (Aug. 2013). Do you agree that conscientious objection to abortion should be protected

internationally? Does the EU law persuade you that American conscience clauses are a good idea?

Recall Wedgwood's dissent from *Yoon*: "article 18 does not suggest that a person motivated by religious belief has a protected right to withdraw from the otherwise legitimate requirements of a shared society. For example, citizens cannot refrain from paying taxes, even where they have conscientious objections to state activities." Now that you know about military conscientious objection, what do you think international law should say about the religious freedom of government officials to refuse marriage ceremonies?

2. LAW AND GOVERNMENT

Eweida and Others v. United Kingdom

The European Court of Human Rights, Fourth Section, 2013.
Apps. No. 48420/10, 59842/10, 51671/10, 36516/10.

The European Court of Human Rights (Fourth Section), sitting as a Chamber composed of:

DAVID THÓR BJÖRGVINSSON, *President,*

NICOLAS BRATZA,

LECH GARLICKI,

PÄIVI HIRVELÄ,

ZDRAVKA KALAYDJIEVA,

NEBOJŠA VUČINIĆ,

VINCENT A. DE GAETANO, *judges,*

and LAWRENCE EARLY, *Section Registrar,*

Having deliberated in private on 4 September and 11 December 2012,

Delivers the following judgment:

C. Ms Ladele

The third applicant is a Christian. She holds the view that marriage is the union of one man and one woman for life, and sincerely believes that same-sex civil partnerships are contrary to God's law.

Ms Ladele was employed by the London Borough of Islington, a local public authority, from 1992. Islington had a "Dignity for All" equality and diversity policy, which stated *inter alia*:

> "Islington is proud of its diversity and the council will challenge discrimination in all its forms. 'Dignity for all' should be the experience of Islington staff, residents and service users, regardless of the age, gender, disability, faith, race, sexuality, nationality, income or health status. . . .

The council will promote community cohesion and equality for all groups but will especially target discrimination based on age, disability, gender, race, religion and sexuality. . . .

In general, Islington will:

(a) Promote community cohesion by promoting shared community values and understanding, underpinned by equality, respect and dignity for all. . . .

It is the council's policy that everyone should be treated fairly and without discrimination. Islington aims to ensure that:

- Staff experience fairness and equity of treatment in the workplace

- Customers receive fair and equal access to council services

- Staff and customers are treated with dignity and respect

The council will actively remove discriminatory barriers that can prevent people from obtaining the employment opportunities and services to which they are entitled. The council will not tolerate processes, attitudes and behaviour that amount to discrimination, including harassment, victimisation and bullying through prejudice, ignorance, thoughtlessness and stereotyping. . . .

All employees are expected to promote these values at all times and to work within the policy. Employees found to be in breach of this policy may face disciplinary action."

In 2002 Ms Ladele became a registrar of births, deaths and marriages. Although she was paid by the local authority and had a duty to abide by its policies, she was not employed by it but instead held office under the aegis of the Registrar General. The Civil Partnership Act 2004 came into force in the United Kingdom on 5 December 2005. The Act provided for the legal registration of civil partnerships between two people of the same sex, and accorded to them rights and obligations equivalent to those of a married couple. In December 2005 Islington decided to designate all existing registrars of births, deaths and marriages as civil partnership registrars. It was not required to do this; the legislation simply required it to ensure that there was a sufficient number of civil partnership registrars for the area to carry out that function. Some other United Kingdom local authorities took a different approach, and allowed registrars with a sincerely held religious objection to the formation of civil partnerships to opt out of designation as civil partnership registrars.

Initially, Ms Ladele was permitted to make informal arrangements with colleagues to exchange work so that she did not have to conduct civil partnership ceremonies. In March 2006, however, two colleagues complained that her refusal to carry out such duties was discriminatory. In a letter dated 1 April 2006 Ms Ladele was informed that, in the view of the local authority, refusing to conduct civil partnerships could put her in breach of the Code of Conduct and the equality policy. She was requested to confirm in writing that she would henceforth officiate at civil partnership ceremonies. The third applicant refused to agree, and requested that the local authority make arrangements to accommodate her beliefs. By May 2007 the atmosphere in the office had deteriorated. Ms Ladele's refusal to carry out civil partnerships was causing rota difficulties and putting a burden on others and there had been complaints from homosexual colleagues that they felt victimised. In May 2007 the local authority commenced a preliminary investigation, which concluded in July 2007 with a recommendation that a formal disciplinary complaint be brought against Ms Ladele that, by refusing to carry out civil partnerships on the ground of the sexual orientation of the parties, she had failed to comply with the local authority's Code of Conduct and equality and diversity policy. A disciplinary hearing took place on 16 August 2007. Following the hearing, Ms Ladele was asked to sign a new job description requiring her to carry out straightforward signings of the civil partnership register and administrative work in connection with civil partnerships, but with no requirement to conduct ceremonies.

Ms Ladele made an application to the Employment Tribunal, complaining of direct and indirect discrimination on grounds of religion or belief and harassment. On 1 December 2007 the Statistics and Registration Act 2007 came into force and, instead of remaining an office holder employed by the Registrar General, Ms Ladele became an employee of the local authority, which now had the power to dismiss her. It was advanced before the Employment Tribunal that if the applicant lost the proceedings, it was likely that she would be dismissed.

On 3 July 2008, the Tribunal upheld the complaints of direct and indirect religious discrimination, and harassment, holding that the local authority had "placed a greater value on the rights of the lesbian, gay, bisexual and transsexual community than it placed on the rights of [Ms Ladele] as one holding an orthodox Christian belief". The local authority appealed to the Employment Appeal Tribunal, which on 19 December 2008 reversed the decision of the Employment Tribunal. It held that the local authority's treatment of Ms Ladele had been a proportionate means of achieving a legitimate aim, namely providing the registrar service on a non-discriminatory basis.

The decision of the Employment Appeal Tribunal was appealed to the Court of Appeal, which on 15 December 2009, upheld the Employment Appeal Tribunal's conclusions. It stated, at paragraph 52:

"... the fact that Ms Ladele's refusal to perform civil partnerships was based on her religious view of marriage could not justify the conclusion that Islington should not be allowed to implement its aim to the full, namely that all registrars should perform civil partnerships as part of its Dignity for All policy. Ms Ladele was employed in a public job and was working for a public authority; she was being required to perform a purely secular task, which was being treated as part of her job; Ms Ladele's refusal to perform that task involved discriminating against gay people in the course of that job; she was being asked to perform the task because of Islington's Dignity for All policy, whose laudable aim was to avoid, or at least minimise, discrimination both among Islington's employees, and as between Islington (and its employees) and those in the community they served; Ms Ladele's refusal was causing offence to at least two of her gay colleagues; Ms Ladele's objection was based on her view of marriage, which was not a core part of her religion; and Islington's requirement in no way prevented her from worshipping as she wished."

The Court of Appeal concluded that Article 9 of the Convention and the Court's case-law supported the view that Ms Ladele's desire to have her religious views respected should not be allowed "...to override Islington's concern to ensure that all its registrars manifest equal respect for the homosexual community as for the heterosexual community." It further noted that from the time the 2007 Regulations came into force, once Ms Ladele was designated a Civil Partnership Registrar, Islington was not merely entitled, but obliged, to require her to perform civil partnerships.

The applicant's application for leave to appeal to the Supreme Court was refused on 4 March 2010.

THE LAW

II. ADMISSIBILITY

The third applicant complained of a breach of Articles 14 and 9 taken together.

Article 9 provides:

"1. Everyone has the right to freedom of thought, conscience and religion; this right includes freedom to change his religion or belief and freedom, either alone or in community with others and in public or private, to manifest his religion or belief, in worship, teaching, practice and observance.

2. Freedom to manifest one's religion or beliefs shall be subject only to such limitations as are prescribed by law and are necessary in a democratic society in the interests of public safety, for the protection of public order, health or morals, or for the protection of the rights and freedoms of others."

Article 14 provides:

"The enjoyment of the rights and freedoms set forth in [the] Convention shall be secured without discrimination on any ground such as sex, race, colour, language, religion, political or other opinion, national or social origin, association with a national minority, property, birth or other status."

The third applicant complained under Article 14 taken in conjunction with Article 9, rather than under Article 9 taken alone, because she considered that she had been discriminated against on grounds of religion. She submitted that her acts, for which she was disciplined, were a manifestation of her religion and that the claim certainly reached the lower threshold required for applicability of Article 14, namely that it fell within the ambit of Article 9. She further contended that, in failing to treat her differently from those staff who did not have a conscientious objection to registering civil partnerships, the local authority indirectly discriminated against her. The local authority could reasonably have accommodated her religious beliefs, and its refusal to adopt less restrictive means was disproportionate under Articles 14 and 9.

The third applicant contended that the Court should require "very weighty reasons" in order to justify discrimination on grounds of religion. As with suspect categories so far identified by the Court as requiring "very weighty reasons" (such as sex, sexual orientation, ethnic origin and nationality) religious faith constituted a core aspect of an individual's identity. Moreover, race, ethnicity and religion were often inter-connected and had been linked by the Court.

The third applicant accepted that the aims pursued by the local authority were legitimate, namely to provide access to services, irrespective of sexual orientation and to communicate a clear commitment to non-discrimination. However, she did not consider that the Government had demonstrated that there was a reasonable relationship of proportionality between these aims and the means employed. She emphasised that she was employed as a marriage registrar prior to the change in legislation permitting civil partnerships to be established, and that the basis on which she was employed was fundamentally altered. The local authority had had a discretion not to designate her as a registrar of civil partnerships and could still have provided an efficient civil partnership service while accommodating the applicant's conscientious objection. That objection was to participating in the creation of a legal status based on an institution that she considered to be a marriage in all but name; the applicant did not manifest any prejudice against homosexuals. In any event, it could not be assumed that, had the local authority accommodated the applicant, it would have been seen as approving of her beliefs. For example, when the State permitted doctors whom it employed to opt out of performing abortions, the State was not necessarily seen as approving of the doctors' views; instead it was a sign of tolerance on the part of the State. In this case, however, the local authority did not adequately take into account its duty of neutrality. It failed to strike a balance between delivering the service in a way which would not discriminate on grounds of sexual orientation, while avoiding discriminating against its own employees on grounds of religion.

B.   The Court's assessment

c.   The third applicant

The Court notes that the third applicant is a Christian, who holds the orthodox Christian view that marriage is the union of one man and one woman for life. She believed that same-sex unions are contrary to God's will and that it would be wrong for her to participate in the creation of an institution equivalent to marriage between a same-sex couple. Because of her refusal to agree to be designated as a registrar of civil partnerships, disciplinary proceedings were brought, culminating in the loss of her job.

The third applicant did not complain under Article 9 taken alone, but instead complained that she had suffered discrimination as a result of her Christian beliefs, in breach of Article 14 taken in conjunction with Article 9. For the Court, it is clear that the applicant's objection to participating in the creation of same-sex civil partnerships was directly motivated by her religious beliefs. The events in question fell within the ambit of Article 9 and Article 14 is applicable.

The Court considers that the relevant comparator in this case is a registrar with no religious objection to same-sex unions. It agrees with the applicant's contention that the local authority's requirement that all registrars of births, marriages and deaths be designated also as civil partnership registrars had a particularly detrimental impact on her because of her religious beliefs. In order to determine whether the local authority's decision not to make an exception for the applicant and others in her situation amounted to indirect discrimination in breach of Article 14, the Court must consider whether the policy pursued a legitimate aim and was proportionate.

The Court of Appeal held in this case that the aim pursued by the local authority was to provide a service which was not merely effective in terms of practicality and efficiency, but also one which complied with the overarching policy of being "an employer and a public authority wholly committed to the promotion of equal opportunities and to requiring all its employees to act in a way which does not discriminate against others". The Court recalls that in its case-law under Article 14 it has held that differences in treatment based on sexual orientation require particularly serious reasons by way of justification. It has also held that same-sex couples are in a relevantly similar situation to different-sex couples as regards their need for legal recognition and protection of their relationship, although since practice in this regard is still evolving across Europe, the Contracting States enjoy a wide margin of appreciation as to the way in which this is achieved within the domestic legal order. Against this background, it is evident that the aim pursued by the local authority was legitimate.

It remains to be determined whether the means used to pursue this aim were proportionate. The Court takes into account that the consequences for the applicant were serious: given the strength of her religious conviction, she considered that she had no choice but to face disciplinary action rather than be designated a civil partnership registrar and, ultimately, she lost her job. Furthermore, it cannot be said that, when she entered into her contract of employment, the applicant specifically waived her right to manifest her religious belief by objecting to participating in the creation of civil partnerships, since this requirement was introduced by her employer at a later date. On the other hand, however, the local authority's policy aimed to secure the rights of others which are also protected under the Convention. The Court generally allows the national authorities a wide margin of appreciation when it comes to striking a balance between competing Convention rights. In all the circumstances, the Court does not consider that the national authorities, that is the local authority employer which brought the disciplinary proceedings and also the domestic courts which rejected the applicant's discrimination claim, exceeded the margin of appreciation available to them. It cannot, therefore, be said that there has been a violation of Article 14 taken in conjunction with Article 9 in respect of the third applicant.

FOR THESE REASONS, THE COURT

Holds by five votes to two that there has been no violation of Article 14 taken in conjunction with Article 9 in respect of the third applicant;

JOINT PARTLY DISSENTING OPINION OF JUDGES VUČINIĆ AND DE GAETANO

We are unable to share the majority's opinion that there has been no violation of the Convention in respect of the third applicant (Ms Ladele).

The third applicant's case is not so much one of freedom of religious belief as one of freedom of conscience—that is, that no one should be forced to act against one's conscience or be penalised for refusing to act against one's conscience. Although freedom of religion and freedom of conscience are dealt with under the same Article of the Convention, there is a fundamental difference between the two which, in our view, has not been adequately made out in the judgment. Even Article 9 hints at this fundamental difference: whereas the word "conscience" features in 9 § 1, it is conspicuously absent in 9 § 2. Conscience—by which is meant moral conscience—is what enjoins a person at the appropriate moment to do good and to avoid evil. In essence it is a judgment of reason whereby a physical person recognises the moral quality of a concrete act that he is going to perform, is in the process of performing, or has already completed. This rational judgment on what is good and what is evil, although it may be nurtured by religious beliefs, is not necessarily so, and people with no particular religious beliefs or affiliations make such judgments constantly in their daily lives. The pre-eminence (and the ontological roots) of conscience is underscored by the words of a nineteenth century writer who noted that " . . . Conscience may come into collision with the word of a Pope, and is to be followed in spite of that word."

As one of the third party intervenors in this case—the European Centre for Law and Justice (ECLJ)—quite pointedly put it: "[J]ust as there is a difference in nature between conscience and religion, there is also a difference between the prescriptions of conscience and religious prescriptions." The latter type of prescriptions—not to eat certain food (or certain food on certain days); the wearing of the turban or the veil, or the display of religious symbols; attendance at religious services on certain days—may be subject to limitations in the manner and subject to the conditions laid down in Article 9 § 2. But can the same be said with regard to prescriptions of conscience? We are of the view that once that a *genuine* and *serious* case of conscientious objection is established, the State is obliged to respect the individual's freedom of conscience both positively (by taking reasonable and appropriate measures to protect the rights of the conscientious objector) and negatively (by refraining from actions which punish the objector or discriminate against him or her). Freedom of conscience has in the past all too often been paid for in acts of heroism, whether at the hands of the Spanish Inquisition or of a Nazi firing squad. As the ECLJ observes, "It is in order to avoid that obeying one's conscience must still require payment in heroism that the law now guarantees freedom of conscience."

The respondent Government accepted that the third applicant's objection to officiating at same-sex civil partnership ceremonies was a genuine and serious one, based as it was on her conviction that such partnerships are against God's law. In this sense her conscientious objection was *also* a manifestation of her deep religious conviction and beliefs. The majority decision does not dispute this—indeed, by acknowledging that "[t]he events in question fall within the ambit of Article 9 and Article 14 is applicable", the majority decision implicitly acknowledges that the third applicant's conscientious objection attained a level of cogency, seriousness, cohesion and importance worthy of protection.

It is at this point pertinent to observe that when the third applicant joined the public service (as an employee of the London Borough of Islington) in 1992, and when she became a registrar of births, deaths and marriages in 2002, her job did not include officiating at same-sex partnership ceremonies. There is nothing to suggest, and nor has it been suggested by anyone, that it was to be expected (perhaps by 2002) that marriage registrars would have to officiate at these ceremonies in the future. If anything, both the law (the Civil Partnership Act 2004) and the practice of other local authorities allowed for the possibility of compromises which would not force registrars to act against their consciences. In the third applicant's case, however, a combination of back-stabbing by her colleagues and the blinkered political correctness of the Borough of Islington (which clearly favoured "gay rights" over fundamental human rights) eventually led to her dismissal.

As the majority judgment correctly notes, the third applicant did not complain of a violation of Article 9 taken alone, but rather that "she had suffered discrimination as a result of her Christian beliefs, in breach of Article 14 taken in conjunction with Article 9" (§ 103). We also agree that for the purposes of Article 14 the relevant comparator in the third applicant's case is a registrar with no religious objection—we would rather say, no conscientious objection—to officiating at same-sex unions. It is from here that we part company with the majority. First of all, the reasoning and arguments are at best irrelevant and at worst a case of inverted logic: the issue in Ms Ladele's case is not one of discrimination by an employer, a public authority or a public official *vis-à-vis a service user* of the Borough of Islington because of the said service user's sexual orientation. Indeed, no service user or prospective service user of the Borough seems to have ever complained (unlike some of her homosexual colleagues) about the third applicant. The complainant is not a party or prospective party to a same-sex civil partnership. The aim of the Borough of Islington to provide equal opportunities and services to all without discrimination, and the legitimacy of this aim, is not, and was never, in issue. No balancing exercise can, therefore, be carried out between the third applicant's concrete right to conscientious objection, which is one of the most fundamental rights inherent in the human person—a right which is not given by the Convention but is recognised and protected by it—and a legitimate State or public authority policy which seeks to protect rights in the abstract. As a consequence, the Court was not called upon to determine whether "the means used to pursue this aim were proportionate".

What *is* in issue is the *discriminatory treatment of the third applicant* at the hands of the Borough, in respect of which treatment she did not obtain redress at domestic level. Given the cogency, seriousness, cohesion and importance of her conscientious objection (which, as noted earlier, was *also* a manifestation of her deep religious convictions) it was incumbent upon the local authority *to treat her differently* from those registrars who had no conscientious objection to officiating at same-sex unions—something which clearly could have been achieved without detriment to the overall services provided by the Borough including those services provided by registrars, as evidenced by the experience of other local authorities. Instead of practising the tolerance and the "dignity for all" it preached, the Borough of Islington pursued the doctrinaire line, the road of obsessive political correctness. It effectively sought to force the applicant to act against her conscience or face the extreme penalty of dismissal—something which, even assuming that the limitations of Article 9 § 2 apply to prescriptions of conscience, cannot be deemed necessary in a democratic society. Ms Ladele did not fail in her duty of discretion: she did not publicly express her beliefs to service users. Her beliefs had no impact on the content of her job, but only on its extent. She never attempted to impose her beliefs on others, nor was she in any way engaged, openly or surreptitiously, in subverting the rights of others. Thus, even if one were to undertake the proportionality exercise referred to in § 106 with reference to whatever legitimate aim the Borough had in view, it follows that the means used were totally disproportionate.

For the above reasons, our conclusion is that there was a violation of Article 14 taken in conjunction with Article 9 in respect of the third applicant.

NOTES AND QUESTIONS

1. *Davis.* How does Ladele compare to Kim Davis, the Kentucky clerk from Chapter 5 who refused to perform same-sex marriages? Are there any differences between their claims of conscience? Do their facts differ? Are American law and European law different in these circumstances?

2. *Religious Discrimination.* Ladele argued that the Borough discriminated against her on the basis of religion, thus grounding her lawsuit on Article 14 as well as Article 9. What is the difference between the two articles? Under Article 14, did the Court conclude the local government's policy "pursued a legitimate aim and was proportionate"? Why did the Tribunal and the dissent conclude Ladele should win her case of religious discrimination?

Recall what we learned about Title VII religious discrimination lawsuits in Chapter 6. Would Ladele be able to bring a successful Title VII lawsuit in the United States? What do you think the dissenting justices in *Obergefell* would conclude about this case?

3. *Balancing.* How did the Tribunal, the majority, and the dissent assess the balance between religious freedom rights and LGBT rights? Do you agree with the Tribunal that the local authority "placed a greater value on the rights of the lesbian, gay, bisexual and transsexual community than it placed on the rights of [Ms Ladele] as one holding an orthodox Christian belief"? With the dissent, which thought the majority "clearly favored 'gay rights' over fundamental human rights"? Should religious freedom be viewed as more fundamental than LGBT rights across the world? In the United States?

4. *Coworkers.* According to the dissent, the complaint against Ladele was from her employer and coworkers. The dissent wrote Ladele was dismissed due to "a combination of back-stabbing by her colleagues and the blinkered political correctness of the Borough of Islington." Does this distinguish Ladele from Kim Davis? Did the presence of same-sex couples in the Davis litigation strengthen the case against her? Should it matter that "no service user or prospective service user of the Borough seems to have ever complained (unlike some of her homosexual colleagues)" about Ladele?

5. *Accommodation.* Could Ladele have been accommodated? Should Ladele have been accommodated? What would the accommodation look like?

6. *Religion or Conscience?* How do you assess the dissent's distinction between religion and conscience? What are the differences between prescriptions of conscience and prescriptions of religion? If Ladele had a prescription of conscience not to register marriages and Şahin (from Section A) had a prescription of religion to wear a hijab, should the two women's claims be valued differently? Is the dissent saying the right to conscience is absolute?

7. *LGBT Rights.* On July 21, 2015, the ECHR ruled that Italy must offer some kind of protected legal relationship to same-sex couples. Although the court ruled there is no right to marriage for same-sex couples, the couples were entitled to some kind of legal protection of their private relationships. See Case of Oliari and Others v. Italy, Apps. Nos. 18766/11 and 36030/11 (July 21, 2015). What kind of accommodations and exemptions do you expect EU countries to make for same-sex unions? For other religious commitments? What do you think of the way the Supreme Court of Victoria (Australia) handled the following case about exemptions?

3. RELIGIOUS EXEMPTIONS

Christian Youth Camps LTD v. Cobaw Community Health Services LTD

Supreme Court of Victoria (Australia), Victorian Court of Appeal, 2014.
308 A.L.R. 615.

■ MAXWELL P:

Freedom from discrimination is a fundamental human right. So too is freedom of religion. The present appeal arises under the *Equal Opportunity Act 1995* (Vic) (the 'EO Act'), which gives legislative force to the first of these rights. One of the objectives of the EO Act is:

[T]o eliminate, as far as possible, discrimination against people by prohibiting discrimination on the basis of various attributes.

The EO Act recognises, however, that compliance with the obligation to act in a non-discriminatory way may, in certain circumstances, conflict with the enjoyment of the right to religious freedom. That is, a requirement that a person do, or refrain from doing, a particular thing in order to avoid prohibited discrimination may conflict with the religious doctrines to which the person subscribes.

The present case is said to involve just such a collision of these rights. At issue is the refusal by the applicants, Christian Youth Camps Ltd and Mark Rowe (to be referred to as 'CYC' and 'Mr Rowe' respectively), to allow the first respondent ('Cobaw') to hire a camping resort owned and operated by CYC, for the purposes of a weekend camp to be attended by same sex attracted young people ('SSAYP').

Cobaw is an organisation concerned with youth suicide prevention. It focuses particularly on SSAYP, aiming 'to raise awareness about their needs and the effects of homophobia and discrimination on young people and rural communities generally'. CYC was established by the trustees of the Christian Brethren Trust, itself established for purposes connected with the Christian Brethren Church. Mr Rowe was the resort manager. CYC and Mr Rowe are opposed to homosexual sexual activity, as they consider it to be contrary to God's teaching as set out in the Bible.

Before the Tribunal, CYC contended that if, contrary to their principal submission, the refusal would otherwise have constituted unlawful discrimination, the exemption provisions in the EO Act concerning religious freedom were applicable, such that there had been no contravention. As will appear, these exemptions apply to conduct 'by a body established for religious purposes' and to discrimination by a person which is necessary for that person 'to comply with the person's genuine religious beliefs or principles'.

The Tribunal held that neither exemption was applicable.

For reasons which follow, I have concluded that there was no error of law in the Tribunal's conclusion that:

(a) there was discrimination on the basis of sexual orientation; and

(b) neither of the exemptions directed at preserving religious freedom applied in the circumstances of the case.

[Part 3 of the EO Act prohibits sexual orientation discrimination by "refusing to provide goods or services to the other person.] The first relevant exception to Part 3 is to be found in s 75, which provides as follows:

75   Religious bodies

(2) Nothing in Part 3 applies to anything done by a body established for religious purposes that—

(a)   conforms with the doctrines of the religion; or

(b) is necessary to avoid injury to the religious sensitivities of people of the religion.

(3) Without limiting the generality of its application, subsection (2) includes anything done in relation to the employment of people in any educational institution under the direction, control or administration of a body established for religious purposes.

The second relevant exception is in s 77, which provides as follows:

77   Religious beliefs or principles

Nothing in Part 3 applies to discrimination by a person against another person if the discrimination is necessary for the first person to comply with the person's genuine religious beliefs or principles.

The Tribunal concluded that CYC was not 'a body established for religious purposes' [because its provision of "camping activities" at an "adventure resort" was secular]. The Tribunal held that CYC, as well as Mr Rowe, was 'a person' for the purposes of s 77 and could invoke its protection. As will appear, I do not consider that Parliament intended the s 77 exemption to be available to a corporation.

In view of my earlier conclusion that it was CYC, not Mr Rowe, which committed the act of discrimination, the first question for consideration is whether CYC can avail itself of the exemption under s 77. This is, once again, a question of statutory interpretation.

In my opinion, it is clear from the language of s 77, and from the relationship between the exemption provisions in ss 75–77, that Parliament did not intend a corporation to be able to invoke the exemption under s 77. My reasons may be summarised shortly as follows:

(a) insofar as Parliament intended to exempt conduct engaged in by religious bodies (including corporations), such exemption was intended to be available to—and only to—bodies 'established for religious purposes' within the meaning of s 75(2) and (3);

(b) s 77 would only be capable of applying to a corporation if Parliament had intended to establish a rule of attribution under which, by a legal fiction, a corporation could be said to hold religious beliefs;

(c) there being no such rule of attribution in the EO Act, the only basis for the attribution of a religious belief to a corporation would be as a matter of necessary implication, that is, if it could be shown that Parliament must have intended that there be such attribution in order for the exemption provisions to operate effectively; and

(d) particularly in view of the exemption already available to religious institutions under s 75(2), there is no basis for imputing to Parliament an intention either:

(i) to create the legislative fiction of a corporation having a religious belief; or

(ii) to make the exemption under s 77 available to a corporation without its having to establish—as a body does under s 75(2)—that it was established for religious purposes.

Read together, the exemption provisions directed at preserving religious freedom—ss 75–77—draw what seem to be perfectly sensible distinctions between bodies and individuals. Thus, s 75(2) and (3) are concerned with bodies established for religious purposes; s 76 is expressed to apply both to 'a person' and to a 'body (other than a body established for religious purposes)'; and s 77 is expressed to apply to discrimination by 'a person', the exemption being defined by reference to that person's 'genuine religious beliefs or principles'.

The scheme is structurally coherent. The provisions are complementary of each other. Clearly, the legislature wished to ensure that the protection of religious freedom extended to the activities of both bodies and individuals. The protection afforded to bodies was limited in the ways already discussed in relation to s 75(2), namely, that the body must be established for religious purposes and that the conduct in question must either conform with doctrine or be necessary to avoid injury to religious sensitivities.

Ordinarily, of course, the word 'person' includes a body corporate. So much is accepted for the purposes of the application of the substantive discrimination provisions. But the use in s 76 of the phrase 'a person or body' suggests that, at least in this part of the Act, the word 'person' was used to connote a natural person. For the reasons already given, the distinction between a natural person and a body was a necessary and appropriate one to draw for the purpose of defining the categories of conduct which would be exempted. Nor is it surprising that Parliament has sought to express in different terms the respective protections conferred on bodies and individuals.

Had s 77 been intended to apply to bodies as well as to natural persons, it must be assumed that language similar to that used in s 76(1) would have been used. That is, s 77 would have been expressed to apply to a 'body (other than a body established for religious purposes)'. Couching the provision in those terms would at least have ensured that ss 75 and 77 did not have overlapping coverage, although it would still have produced the seemingly absurd result of providing a broader exemption for a non-religious body (under s 77) than for a body established for religious purposes (under s 75(2)).

Section 77 does not, of course, contain any such qualification. According to the submission advanced by the applicants, and by the Attorney-General, s 77 was intended to be available to any body corporate, whether established for religious purposes or not. As the Commission pointed out, such a reading of s 77 would effectively render both ss 75 and 76 redundant. In particular, it would mean that conduct of a body established for religious purposes which did not satisfy the exemption conditions specified in s 75(2) would nevertheless be exempted by s 77, provided only that the conduct was necessary to comply with the 'genuine religious beliefs or principles' of the body.

The submission is unsustainable. Having carefully defined the conditions of exemption for religious bodies in s 75(2), it is hardly likely that Parliament intended to enable the conduct of such bodies to be exempted under a different provision, free of such conditions. Moreover, since this reading of s 77 would rob s 75(2) of practical utility, it offends the cardinal principle of statutory interpretation that Parliament is taken to have intended every provision in a statute to have its own work to do.

In my opinion, Parliament's intention is clear. Sections 75 and 76 were intended to define the scope—and limits—of the religious freedom exemptions available to bodies (including corporations). Those sections provide appropriately targeted protection for activities of relevant kinds engaged in by bodies corporate. As I have said, there is no policy rationale which would explain an intention to confer on such bodies a separate, broader, protection, without limit as to the types of activities engaged in.

Finally, for a body corporate to avail itself of the protection under s 77, it would have to demonstrate that it had 'genuine religious beliefs or principles' and that the relevant conduct was 'necessary ... to comply with' those beliefs or principles. A corporation, of course, has 'neither soul nor body'. The state of mind of a corporation being a legal fiction, it would be necessary—for the provision to operate intelligibly—

for the Court to identify a rule of attribution for the purposes of s 77. This would only be justified if the express provisions of the statutory scheme required for their effective operation the attribution to a corporation of a particular state of mind—in this case, the holding of genuine religious beliefs or principles.

As senior counsel for the applicants pointed out, where the legislature wishes to attribute a belief to a corporation, it typically does so by enacting a special rule of attribution appropriate to the purpose. In such a case, the statute itself identifies the officers or employees of the corporation whose beliefs are to be attributed to the corporation for this purpose. The EO Act contains no such provision.

Nothing in this legislative scheme, or in the framework of religious freedom exemptions in ss 75–77, depends for its effectiveness on the creation of such a rule of attribution in s 77. As I have said, statutory protection is already provided for the activities of bodies corporate, provided that they are established for religious purposes (s 75(2)) or are engaged in relevant educational activities within the scope of s 76. Nor is there anything intrinsic to the notion of religious freedom which would suggest that Parliament must—as a matter of necessary implication—have intended to confer on bodies corporate, by s 77, a protection which went beyond the scope of ss 75 and 76.

On the contrary, it seems to me, Parliament intended the words of s 77 to mean what they say. After all, as the Commission pointed out, the right to religious freedom recognised by the Covenant, and by the Charter, is the right of an *individual* to believe as he or she chooses to do. The Attorney-General used similar language in 1995 to explain the purpose of s 77. As the European Court of Human Rights observed in *Hasan v Bulgaria*:

> While religious freedom is primarily a matter of individual conscience, it also implies, *inter alia*, freedom to manifest one's religion, alone and in private, or in community with others, in public and within the circle of those whose faith one shares.

It has never been suggested that corporations can meaningfully be said to have religious beliefs, let alone that they should be entitled to enjoy a freedom of religious belief. The Attorney-General drew attention to the statement of Latham CJ, that it was 'obvious that a company cannot exercise a religion', but submitted that the 'generality' of this statement could no longer be regarded as correct in the light of a series of decisions of the European Commission of Human Rights concerning art 9 of the European Convention. Those decisions, which cover the period 1979–1996, hold that:

> (a) when a church body makes a complaint of discrimination under the Convention, 'it does so in reality, on behalf of its members'; and

(b) it should therefore be accepted that a church body is capable of possessing and exercising the Convention rights of religious freedom 'in its own capacity as a representative of its members'.

With respect, it seems to me that what the Commission has decided is entirely cogent. These propositions are properly reflective of the unique function of 'church bodies' as institutions in which, and through which, individuals exercise their freedom of religion. But—precisely because of the special character of such bodies—these decisions have no bearing on the present question. Indeed, as the Minister properly pointed out, the Commission has been quite clear in saying that 'a profit-making corporate body ... can neither enjoy nor rely on the [Convention] rights'. And the Supreme Court of Canada has been equally clear in saying that 'a business corporation cannot possess religious beliefs'.

■ NEAVE, JA: (concurrence)

In my view, s 77 does not apply to corporations. Like other human rights, the right to freedom of religious belief can only be enjoyed by natural persons. Because a corporation is not a natural person and has 'neither soul nor body', it cannot have a conscious state of mind amounting to a religious belief or principle. It follows that applying the s 77 exception to a corporation would require the adoption of a legal fiction which attributes the beliefs of a person or persons to the corporation.

In *News Corporation Limited v National Companies and Securities Commission* the Full Court of the Federal Court considered whether s 12(2)(a) of the *Freedom of Information Act 1982* (Cth), which gave people extended access to documents relating to their 'personal affairs', was applicable to a corporation. The Court held that a corporation did not have 'personal affairs' within the meaning of the section, noting the absence of any explicit provision to this effect. St John J remarked that although the use of the word 'person' in legislation included a corporation, '[t]his does not mean that the adjective "personal" can be likewise translated'. A corporation, like a natural person could have business affairs, but in addition—

real persons could have affairs relating to family and marital relationships, health or ill health, relationships with and emotional ties with other real people.

Like 'personal affairs' religious beliefs are personal matters, involving individual judgment on questions of faith and ethics.

In *ABC v Lenah Game Meats Pty Ltd* Gleeson CJ discussed whether a corporation could have a right of privacy. Whilst recognising that 'some forms of corporate activity may be private' for example in the sense that shareholders may be excluded from attending directors' meetings, Gleeson CJ said that the foundation of rights of privacy is, to a large extent 'human dignity' and that this concept 'may be incongruous when applied to a corporation'. Attributing a religious belief to a corporation is equally incongruous.

There are numerous legislative provisions which impose criminal or civil liability on a corporation and attribute the intention or belief of an agent of the corporation to it, for the purposes of proving the corporation has the required intention or other state of mind, or has a defence to liability. The existence of these provisions does not require the conclusion that a corporation is to be deemed to hold beliefs on matters such as the existence of a deity or deities, the presence of an afterlife, or in the case of Christianity, the centrality of the death and resurrection of Jesus Christ, in the absence of a specific legislative provision which requires such 'deeming' to occur.

An individual can give evidence on their religious beliefs and a court can make a factual decision as to whether those beliefs are genuinely held. But there would be practical difficulties in attributing a particular religious belief or principle to a corporation. The memorandum and articles of a company may show that it was established for religious purposes, but even if such documents contain statements of purposes or 'principles' they are unlikely to set out the 'beliefs' of the corporation. There are difficulties in attributing the religious beliefs of members of the board to a corporation, because board members may not have the same beliefs, or their beliefs may change over time. In *Khaira & Ors v Shergill & Ors* the United Kingdom Court of Appeal held that because religious beliefs are 'subjective inward matters' they were incapable of proof and not justiciable as a legal question:

> If s 77 applied to corporations a court could be required to decide which, among a number of competing beliefs or practices, were to be regarded as the 'genuine religious belief' of the corporation. In the absence of clear legislation requiring this to be done, s 77 should not be interpreted to require a court to adjudicate on the particular belief (among possibly competing claims) held by a corporation.

For these reasons I agree with Maxwell P that a corporation cannot rely on the s 77 exception.

■ REDLICH JA: (dissent)

It is necessary to first address the argument of Cobaw that the Tribunal erred in concluding that it was open to CYC, a corporation, to rely upon the exemption in s 77. It found that CYC was a 'person' within the meaning of s 77. The Tribunal having resolved this issue in favour of CYC, the parties were invited to provide supplementary submissions on this question. Cobaw contended that 'person' in s 77 did not include a corporation. For the reasons that follow the Tribunal was correct, in my view, in reaching the conclusion that a corporation could seek to rely upon that exemption.

Although a corporation is a distinct legal entity with legal rights, obligations, powers and privileges different from those of the natural persons who created it, own it, or whom it employs, there is ample legal basis to impute to it the religious beliefs of its directors and others who the law may regard as its mind or will. The Tribunal observed that subjective intentions may be attributed to corporations, including the necessary mental element for a crime. The corporation may make and express moral, ethical, environmental or other judgments in the discourse of the public square and participate in the defining of social norms. As this case shows, it will not necessarily be difficult to identify the corporation's state of mind. There is no principled reason for treating a corporation as capable of forming and acting upon its views in any of these areas but incapable of forming and acting upon religious ones.

Cobaw contends that there is no belief or principle to be found in the constitutive documents of CYC that would have made it necessary for CYC to engage in the discriminatory conduct. The Tribunal found that there was a consistent uniform expression of belief by all of the members of the Christian Brethren who testified before the Tribunal, including those who occupied positions within CYC, which permitted the conclusion that their beliefs were those of CYC. The conclusion of the Tribunal that the beliefs of the corporation's directors, all of whom were required to be members of the Christian Brethren and to subscribe to a declaration of faith, were properly to be characterized as the beliefs of CYC itself, has not been challenged.

Corporations have a long history of association with religious activity. Blackstone, in his *Commentaries on the Law of England,* lists 'advancement of religion' first in the list of purposes that corporations might pursue. Religious institutions have long been organised as corporations at common law and under the King's charter. It has been repeatedly held by European courts, applying art 9 of the *European Convention on Human Rights*, that entities and associations including corporations, unincorporated associations, institutions and societies are capable of possessing and exercising the right to freedom of religious beliefs and principles.

Section 77 has been described as a 'catch-all exception for religious bodies' as well as for natural persons. The attribution of legal personhood to CYC for these purposes is no more incongruous than the imputation of an intention to defraud to a corporation. In those circumstances, it is understood that the attribution of a belief or state of mind to a corporation derives from the state of mind or belief of a natural person so closely connected with that corporation that their belief is to be properly regarded as that of the corporation.

The fact that s 75(2) refers to a 'body' whilst s 77 does not is not indicative of any contrary intention. The two sections are directed at quite different persons and circumstances. Section 75(2) provides an exemption for a body 'established for religious purposes.' The exemption is for acts 'done' by such a body where the act is in conformity with 'doctrines' of the religion or is necessary 'to avoid injury' to the 'religious sensitivities of people of the religion'. Section 77 provides a broad exemption for acts of discrimination that are necessary for compliance with that person's 'genuine religious beliefs'. Religious 'beliefs or principles' and religious 'doctrines' are different concepts. Section 75(2)(b) is concerned with the necessity for the body established for religious purposes to do something to avoid injury to the 'people' of the religion. Section 77 is focussed upon the obligation of the person to do something because of their own religious belief or principles. The Tribunal rightly recognised that 'religious sensitivities' in s 75(2)(b) must involve something linked to but different from 'religious beliefs or principles' in s 77 or 'doctrines' if each provision is to have a meaningful operation.

It would be anomalous were s 75(2) alone to apply to corporate bodies. It would follow that wherever a corporation engages in commercial activity but the corporation was not established for religious purposes, s 77 would not enable the exemption to apply to both the corporation and those particular individuals whose acts are to be treated as those of a corporation. That interpretation would produce the unintended result that individuals who operate a business would have different levels of religious freedom, depending upon whether the business was incorporated or not. It would force individuals of faith to choose between forfeiting the benefits of incorporation or abandoning the precepts of their religion.

NOTES AND QUESTIONS

1. *Hobby Lobby?* Why has *Cobaw* been called the Australian *Hobby Lobby* (see Chapter 4)? How are the two cases similar? How are they different?

2. *Bodies and Persons.* Australian law offered two religious exemptions from the Equality Act, one (Section 75) for religious bodies and one (Section 77) for a person's religious beliefs or principles. Why didn't Section 75 apply to CYC? Why did Judge Maxwell rule CYC was neither a religious body nor a person? What did the concurrence by Judge Neave contribute to the discussion of the meaning of person in the corporate context? What about the dissent by Judge Redlich? Is Judge Redlich correct that the majority's interpretation would undermine the religious freedom of religious organizations?

Whose reasoning is closest to Justice Alito's? to Justice Ginsburg's? How many U.S. Supreme Court justices ruled that Hobby Lobby was a person under RFRA?

3. *Corporate Rights.* Do you agree with Rajanayagam and Evans that both *Hobby Lobby* and *Cobaw* "conceal—or at least attempt to minimise the importance of—the logically anterior question of whether corporations can hold and exercise human rights in any meaningful way."? Shawn Rajanayagam & Carolyn Evans, Corporations and Freedom of Religion: Australia and the United States Compared, 37 Sydney L. Rev. 329, 341 (2015). Did anyone on the Australian court address this question directly? Did anyone on the U.S. Supreme Court address this question directly in *Hobby Lobby*?

4. *Institutional or Individual Right.* Recall our discussion from Chapter 6 questioning whether religious freedom should protect individual or institutional rights. According to Rajanayagam and Evans, the ECHR cases produce two rules:

> first, that church bodies and similar entities—that is, entities which exist primarily (if not solely) for the purposes of advancing religious ends—may exercise religious rights because they exercise those rights for and on behalf of their members; and second, for-profit limited liability companies—or more precisely, companies that *may* be used for profit-making purposes—cannot exercise art 9 rights.

Id. at 348. They then argue that the first entities have rights that are derivative from the "right of individuals to manifest religion collectively." Id.

> If religious groups were not able to bring cases on behalf of their members, the courts would lose a sensible and valuable vehicle to assist with the protection of individual rights. At the extreme end of the scale, for example, if a church were forced to shut down by a hostile government, it would be possible for a large number of individuals to bring a claim that their religious rights had been breached because they are no longer able to worship and practise their religion as they once could. However, it is more efficient for the courts, and beneficial for the impacted individuals, for the church to be able to bring a case itself—even if it has taken the corporate form. However, when a corporation has been established and taken on separate legal entity status, impositions on the corporation do not directly impact individual rights in the same way. While shareholders may be bitterly opposed to a company with which they are associated having to, for example, pay for contraception, the shareholders themselves have no such obligation. While this might appear to be a fiction, it is precisely the same fiction that those shareholders willingly embrace when it comes to avoiding liability.

Id. at 349. Do you agree with this analysis? How would Justice Alito respond to this distinction between religious groups and corporations?

5. *The End of Exemptions?* The Australian Green Party proposed removing religious exemption clauses from the nation's Sex Discrimination

Act. One of the group's spokesman said "we shouldn't be giving religious organisations a get-out-of-jail-free card and the right to discriminate." The Party's proposal was based on concerns about the rights of LGBT teachers in religious schools. See Paul Karp, Greens Promise to End Religious Exemptions to Sex Discrimination Act, The Guardian, May 16, 2016.

In contrast, the Australian Christian Lobby favors new exemptions to antidiscrimination laws so religious believers can refuse services for same-sex weddings. See Paul Karp, Coalition Won't Rule Out letting Religious Objectors Discriminate Against Gay Weddings, The Guardian, Jun. 21, 2016. Finally, according to the Australian Labor Party's platform:

> Labor believes that no faith, no religion, no set of beliefs should ever be used as an instrument of division or exclusion, and condemning anyone, discriminating against anyone, vilifying anyone is a violation of the values we all share, a violation which can never be justified by anyone's faith or belief. Accordingly, Labor will review national anti-discrimination laws to ensure that exemptions do not place Australians in a position where they cannot access essential social services.

See Labor National Platform, A Smart, Modern, Fair Australia 139 (2016), https://cdn.australianlabor.com.au/documents/ALP_National_Platform.pdf. What do you think the Green Party would say about the Labor proposal? Would you support the end of religious exemptions?

6. *Accommodations.* In Switzerland, two Syrian immigrant brothers, sons of a Muslim imam, refused to shake their teachers' hands because Islam prohibits physical contact with a person of the opposite sex. "Shaking a teacher's hand before and after class is part of Switzerland's social fabric, and is considered an important sign of politeness and respect." What do you think of an exemption that allows the boys to refuse handshakes with both male and female teachers? See Dan Bilefsky, Swiss School Orders Morning Handshakes, N.Y. Times, May 27, 2016, at A6 (politicians were outraged by the exemption and decided that parents whose children refused to shake hands would be fined about $5,050). Are you surprised that the exemption was disallowed? What do you think of the argument that "the integration of foreigners and the fostering of gender equality were in the public interest and that this consideration trumped the private interest of the two students"? Id. Of the Swiss authorities' argument that "forcing the students to shake their female teacher's hand was an 'intrusion' on their religious beliefs but . . . a proportionate one since . . . 'it did not involve the central tenets of Islam' "? Id. The Islamic Central Council of Switzerland argued "rather than contributing to the integration of Muslims, the ruling would foster feelings of alienation among Swiss Muslims. It said that policing physical contact between individuals was a form of totalitarianism." Do you agree? What about the boys' argument that they were "trying to protect the dignity of women with their refusal to shake a woman's hand"?

What is the balance between religious freedom and the citizen-educating aspects of public education? We examine how the Supreme Court addressed that issue in *Wisconsin v. Yoder*, a case about Amish parents, in Chapter 11.

In the next chapter, we return to the United States for a discussion of religion and politics, which raises a broader range of issues than those associated with the relationship of church to state. As you read the next chapter, question how much "religion and politics" impacts the separation of church and state and whether religion must be banned from politics to maintain that principle.

CHAPTER 9

RELIGION AND POLITICS

According to Professor Jacob Neusner, "[b]ecause religion is comprehensive, it is fundamentally about power; it therefore cannot avoid politics." Jacob Neusner, ed., God's Rule: The Politics of World Religions 2 (2003). Religions' values frequently shape what the political system does. See id. In this chapter we examine how that shaping should occur. Section A focuses on American presidents and their interpretation of the connection between their religious beliefs and the obligations of the presidential office. We begin with Senator John F. Kennedy's famous address to the Greater Houston Ministerial Association, which identified a separationist ideal of religion and public service, and move forward to the rejection of that ideal by some later presidents, including George W. Bush and Barack Obama. Section A also asks if Supreme Court Justices must be separationist or if the separationist ideal is dead.

Although the constitutional questions about religion and politics focus on the institutions of church and state, institutions are run by individuals of diverse moral and religious commitments. Section B explores political morality, asking how persons of such different backgrounds can live together in a democracy. We focus on the theory of the philosopher John Rawls, a proponent of political liberalism, which holds that when "discussing constitutional essentials and matters of basic justice we are not to appeal to comprehensive religious and philosophical doctrines—to what we as individuals or members of associations see as the whole truth. . . . " Rawls provides a touchstone against which our presidents and other politicians can be judged, while their experiences furnish a practical challenge to his philosophical theory.

American law protects another kind of separation between church and state. Churches may lose their tax-exempt status if they "devote a substantial part of their activities to attempting to influence legislation" or "participate in, or intervene in, any political campaign on behalf of (or in opposition to) any candidate for public office." Section C examines whether this ban on church participation in politics violates constitutional norms.

In the United States, the president is the chief representative of the nation's civil religion; in Section D we determine what civil religion is by reading its classic description by Professor Robert Bellah. We also compare and contrast civil religion to ceremonial deism and constitutional faith. In Chapter 2 you read the Supreme Court's opinion in *Lee v. Weisman*, the high school graduation prayer case, in which Justice Kennedy asserted that the First Amendment does not allow the government to establish a civil religion. In this chapter we will ask if the justice's statement provided an accurate *description* of American public life.

A. PRESIDENTIAL RELIGION

We begin with John F. Kennedy's campaign for public office in 1960.

Address of Senator John F. Kennedy to the Greater Houston Ministerial Association
September 12, 1960.
Rice Hotel, Houston, Texas.

While the so-called religious issue is necessarily and properly the chief topic here tonight, I want to emphasize from the outset that I believe that we have far more critical issues in the 1960 election: the spread of Communist influence, until it now festers only ninety miles off the coast of Florida—the humiliating treatment of our President and Vice President by those who no longer respect our power—the hungry children I saw in West Virginia, the old people who cannot pay their doctor bills, the families forced to give up their farms—an America with too many slums, with too few schools, and too late to the moon and outer space.

These are the real issues which should decide this campaign. And they are not religious issues—for war and hunger and ignorance and despair know no religious barriers.

But because I am a Catholic, and no Catholic has ever been elected President, the real issues in this campaign have been obscured— perhaps deliberately, in some quarters less responsible than this. So it is apparently necessary for me to state once again—not what kind of church I believe in for that should be important only to me—but what kind of America I believe in.

I believe in an America where the separation of church and state is absolute—where no Catholic prelate would tell the President (should he be a Catholic) how to act and no Protestant minister would tell his parishioners for whom to vote—where no church or church school is granted any public funds or political preference—and where no man is denied public office merely because his religion differs from the President who might appoint him or the people who might elect him.

I believe in an America that is officially neither Catholic, Protestant nor Jewish—where no public official either requests or accepts instructions on public policy from the Pope, the National Council of Churches or any other ecclesiastical source—where no religious body seeks to impose its will directly or indirectly upon the general populace or the public acts of its officials—and where religious liberty is so indivisible that an act against one church is treated as an act against all.

For, while this year it may be a Catholic against whom the finger of suspicion is pointed, in other years it has been, and may someday be again, a Jew—or a Quaker—or a Unitarian—or a Baptist. It was Virginia's harassment of Baptist preachers, for example, that led to Jefferson's statute of religious freedom. Today, I may be the victim—but tomorrow it may be you—until the whole fabric of our harmonious society is ripped at a time of great national peril.

Finally, I believe in an America where religious intolerance will someday end—where all men and all churches are treated as equal— where every man has the same right to attend or not to attend the church of his choice—where there is no Catholic vote, no anti-Catholic vote, no bloc voting of any kind—and where Catholics, Protestants and Jews, at both the lay and the pastoral level, will refrain from those attitudes of disdain and division which have so often marred their works in the past, and promote instead the American ideal of brotherhood.

That is the kind of America in which I believe. And it represents the kind of Presidency in which I believe—a great office that must be neither humbled by making it the instrument of any religious group, nor tarnished by arbitrarily withholding its occupancy from the members of any one religious group. I believe in a President whose religious views are his own private affair, neither imposed by him upon the nation or imposed by the nation upon him as a condition to holding that office.

I would not look with favor upon a President working to subvert the First Amendment's guarantees of religious liberty. Nor would our system of checks and balances permit him to do so—and neither do I look with favor upon those who would work to subvert Article VI of the Constitution by requiring a religious test—even by indirection—for if they disagree with that safeguard, they should be out openly working to repeal it.

I want a chief executive whose public acts are responsible to all and obligated to none—who can attend any ceremony, service or dinner his office may appropriately require him to fulfill—and whose fulfillment of his Presidential office is not limited or conditioned by any religious oath, ritual or obligation.

This is the kind of America I believe in—and this is the kind of America I fought for in the South Pacific and the kind my brother died for in Europe. No one suggested then that we might have a "divided loyalty," that we did "not believe in liberty" or that we belonged to a disloyal group that threatened "the freedoms for which our forefathers died."

And in fact this is the kind of America for which our forefathers died—when they fled here to escape religious test oaths that denied office to members of less favored churches—when they fought for the Constitution, the Bill of Rights, the Virginia Statute of Religious Freedom—and when they fought at the shrine I visited today, the Alamo. For side by side with Bowie and Crockett died Fuentes and McCafferty and Bailey and Bedillio and Carey—but no one knows whether they were Catholics or not. For there was no religious test at the Alamo.

I ask you tonight to follow in that tradition, to judge me on the basis of fourteen years in the Congress—on my declared stands against an Ambassador to the Vatican, against unconstitutional aid to parochial schools, and against any boycott of the public schools (which I attended myself)—instead of judging me on the basis of these pamphlets and publications we all have seen that carefully select quotations out of context from the statements of Catholic Church leaders, usually in other countries, frequently in other centuries, and always omitting of course, the statement of the American bishops in 1948 which strongly endorsed church-state separation, and which more nearly reflects the views of almost every American Catholic.

I do not consider these other quotations binding upon my public acts—why should you? But let me say, with respect to other countries, that I am wholly opposed to the state being used by any religious group, Catholic or Protestant, to compel, prohibit or prosecute the free exercise of any other religion. And I hope that you and I condemn with equal fervor those nations which deny their Presidency to Protestants and those which deny it to Catholics. And rather than cite the misdeeds of those who differ, I would cite the record of the Catholic Church in such nations as Ireland and France—and the independence of such statesmen as Adenauer and de Gaulle.

But let me stress again that these are my views—for, contrary to common newspaper usage, I am not the Catholic candidate for President. I am the Democratic Party's candidate for President who happens also to be a Catholic. I do not speak for my church on public matters—and the church does not speak for me.

Whatever issue may come before me as President—on birth control, divorce, censorship, gambling, or any other subject—I will make my decision in accordance with these views, in accordance with what my conscience tells me to be the national interest, and without regard to outside religious pressures or dictates. And no power or threat of punishment could cause me to decide otherwise.

But if the time should ever come—and I do not concede any conflict to be even remotely possible—when my office would require me to either violate my conscience or violate the national interest, then I would resign the office; and I hope any conscientious public servant would do the same.

But I do not intend to apologize for these views to my critics of either Catholic or Protestant faith—nor do I intend to disavow either my views or my church in order to win this election.

If I should lose on the real issues, I shall return to my seat in the Senate satisfied that I had tried my best and was fairly judged. But if this election is decided on the basis that 40,000,000 Americans lost their chance of being President on the day they were baptized, then it is the whole nation that will be the loser in the eyes of Catholics and non-Catholics around the world, in the eyes of history, and in the eyes of our own people.

But if, on the other hand, I should win this election, then I shall devote every effort of mind and spirit to fulfilling the oath of the Presidency—practically identical, I might add, with the oath I have taken for fourteen years in the Congress. For, without reservation, I can, "solemnly swear that I will faithfully execute the office of President of the United States, and will to the best of my ability preserve, protect, and defend the Constitution . . . so help me God."

Senator Barack Obama, Call to Renewal: Keynote Address
June 28, 2006.
Washington, D.C.

But what I am suggesting is this—secularists are wrong when they ask believers to leave their religion at the door before entering into the public square. Frederick Douglass, Abraham Lincoln, Williams Jennings Bryant, Dorothy Day, Martin Luther King—indeed, the majority of great reformers in American history—were not only motivated by faith, but repeatedly used religious language to argue for their cause. So to say that men and women should not inject their "personal morality" into public policy debates is a practical absurdity. Our law is by definition a codification of morality, much of it grounded in the Judeo-Christian tradition.

Moreover, if we progressives shed some of these biases, we might recognize some overlapping values that both religious and secular people share when it comes to the moral and material direction of our country. We might recognize that the call to sacrifice on behalf of the next generation, the need to think in terms of "thou" and not just "I," resonates in religious congregations all across the country. And we might realize that we have the ability to reach out to the evangelical community and engage millions of religious Americans in the larger project of American renewal.

While I've already laid out some of the work that progressive leaders need to do, I want to talk a little bit about what conservative leaders need to do—some truths they need to acknowledge.

For one, they need to understand the critical role that the separation of church and state has played in preserving not only our democracy, but the robustness of our religious practice. Folks tend to forget that during our founding, it wasn't the atheists or the civil libertarians who were the most effective champions of the First Amendment. It was the persecuted minorities, it was Baptists like John Leland who didn't want the established churches to impose their views on folks who were getting happy out in the fields and teaching the scripture to slaves. It was the forbearers of the evangelicals who were the most adamant about not mingling government with religions, because they did not want state-sponsored religion hindering their ability to practice their faith as they understood it.

Moreover, given the increasing diversity of America's population, the dangers of sectarianism have never been greater. Whatever we once were, we are no longer just a Christian nation; we are also a Jewish nation, a Muslim nation, a Buddhist nation, a Hindu nation, and a nation of nonbelievers.

Remarks by President George W. Bush on a Constitutional Amendment to Protect Marriage in America

February 24, 2004.
Washington, D.C.

Eight years ago, Congress passed, and President Clinton signed, the Defense of Marriage Act, which defined marriage for purposes of federal law as the legal union between one man and one woman as husband and wife.

The act passed the House of Representatives by a vote of 342–67 and the Senate by a vote of 85–14.

Those congressional votes, and the passage of similar defense of marriage laws in 38 states, express an overwhelming consensus in our country for protecting the institution of marriage.

In recent months, however, some activist judges and local officials have made an aggressive attempt to redefine marriage. In Massachusetts, four judges on the highest court have indicated they will order the issuance of marriage licenses to applicants of the same gender in May of this year.

In San Francisco, city officials have issued thousands of marriage licenses to people of the same gender, contrary to the California Family

Code. That code, which clearly defines marriage as the union of a man and a woman, was approved overwhelmingly by the voters of California.

A county in New Mexico has also issued marriage licenses to applicants of the same gender.

And unless action is taken, we can expect more arbitrary court decisions, more litigation, more defiance of the law by local officials, all of which adds to uncertainty.

After more than two centuries of American jurisprudence and millennia of human experience, a few judges and local authorities are presuming to change the most fundamental institution of civilization.

Their actions have created confusion on an issue that requires clarity. On a matter of such importance, the voice of the people must be heard. Activist courts have left the people with one recourse.

If we're to prevent the meaning of marriage from being changed forever, our nation must enact a constitutional amendment to protect marriage in America. Decisive and democratic action is needed because attempts to redefine marriage in a single state or city could have serious consequences throughout the country. . . .

An amendment to the Constitution is never to be undertaken lightly. The amendment process has addressed many serious matters of national concern, and the preservation of marriage rises to this level of national importance.

The union of a man and woman is the most enduring human institution, honored and encouraged in all cultures and by every religious faith. Ages of experience have taught humanity that the commitment of a husband and wife to love and to serve one another promotes the welfare of children and the stability of society.

Marriage cannot be severed from its cultural, religious and natural roots without weakening the good influence of society.

Government, by recognizing and protecting marriage, serves the interests of all.

Today, I call upon the Congress to promptly pass and to send to the states for ratification an amendment to our Constitution defining and protecting marriage as a union of a man and woman as husband and wife.

The amendment should fully protect marriage, while leaving the state legislatures free to make their own choices in defining legal arrangements other than marriage.

America's a free society which limits the role of government in the lives of our citizens. This commitment of freedom, however, does not require the redefinition of one of our most basic social institutions.

Our government should respect every person and protect the institution of marriage. There is no contradiction between these responsibilities.

We should also conduct this difficult debate in a matter worthy of our country, without bitterness or anger.

In all that lies ahead, let us match strong convictions with kindness and good will and decency.

Thank you very much.

Barack Obama, The Audacity of Hope
222–224 (2007).

Before my election, I received a phone message from one of my strongest supporters. She was a small-business owner, a mother, and a thoughtful, generous person. She was also a lesbian who had lived in a monogamous relationship with her partner for the last decade.

She knew when she decided to support me that I was opposed to same-sex marriage, and she had heard me argue that, in the absence of any meaningful consensus, the heightened focus on marriage was a distraction from other, attainable measures to prevent discrimination against gays and lesbians. Her phone message in this instance had been prompted by a radio interview she had heard in which I had referenced my religious traditions in explaining my position on the issue. She told me that she had been hurt by my remarks; she felt that by bringing religion into the equation, I was suggesting that she, and others like her, were somehow bad people.

I felt bad, and told her so in a return call. As I spoke to her I was reminded that no matter how much Christians who oppose homosexuality may claim that they hate the sin but love the sinner, such a judgment inflicts pain on good people—people who are made in the image of God, and who are often truer to Christ's message than those who condemn them. And I was reminded that it is my obligation, not only as an elected official in a pluralistic society but also as a Christian, to remain open to the possibility that my unwillingness to support gay marriage is misguided, just as I cannot claim infallibility in my support of abortion rights. I must admit that I may have been infected with society's prejudices and predilections and attributed them to God; that Jesus' call to love one another might demand a different conclusion; and that in years hence I may be seen as someone who was on the wrong side of history. I don't believe such doubts make me a bad Christian. I believe they make me human, limited in my understandings of God's purpose and therefore prone to sin.

President Obama Supports Same-Sex Marriage
May 10, 2012.
The White House, Washington, D.C.

Yesterday, during an interview with ABC News, President Obama said, "I think same-sex couples should be able to get married."

It's no secret the President has gone through some soul-searching on this issue. He's talked to the First Lady about it, like so many couples do. He's heard from folks—gay and lesbian friends, staff members in long-term, loving relationships, as well as brave young servicemen and women he got to know through the fight to end Don't Ask, Don't Tell.

He's sat around his kitchen table with Sasha and Malia, who have friends whose parents are same-sex couples. As the President said during the interview, "it wouldn't dawn on them that somehow their friends' parents would be treated differently. It doesn't make sense to them. And frankly, that's the kind of thing that prompts a change of perspective—not wanting to somehow explain to your child why somebody should be treated differently when it come to eyes of the law."

In the end, the President said, he believes it's important to treat others the way you would want to be treated. "We need to recognize that people are going to having differing views on marriage and those views, even if we disagree strongly, should be respected."

Remarks by President Barack Obama on the Supreme Court Decision on Marriage
June 26, 2015.
The White House, Washington, D.C.

Good morning. Our nation was founded on a bedrock principle that we are all created equal. The project of each generation is to bridge the meaning of those founding words with the realities of changing times— a never-ending quest to ensure those words ring true for every single American.

Progress on this journey often comes in small increments, sometimes two steps forward, one step back, propelled by the persistent effort of dedicated citizens. And then sometimes, there are days like this when that slow, steady effort is rewarded with justice that arrives like a thunderbolt.

This morning, the Supreme Court recognized that the Constitution guarantees marriage equality. In doing so, they've reaffirmed that all Americans are entitled to the equal protection of the law. That all people should be treated equally, regardless of who they are or who they love.

I know change for many of our LGBT brothers and sisters must have seemed so slow for so long. But compared to so many other issues, America's shift has been so quick. I know that Americans of goodwill continue to hold a wide range of views on this issue. Opposition in some cases has been based on sincere and deeply held beliefs. All of us who welcome today's news should be mindful of that fact; recognize different viewpoints; revere our deep commitment to religious freedom.

But today should also give us hope that on the many issues with which we grapple, often painfully, real change is possible. Shifts in hearts and minds is possible. And those who have come so far on their journey to equality have a responsibility to reach back and help others join them. Because for all our differences, we are one people, stronger together than we could ever be alone. That's always been our story.

Obergefell v. Hodges

Supreme Court of the United States, 2015.
135 S.Ct. 2584, 192 L.Ed.2d 609.

■ JUSTICE KENNEDY delivered the opinion of the Court.

The right to marry is fundamental as a matter of history and tradition, but rights come not from ancient sources alone. They rise, too, from a better informed understanding of how constitutional imperatives define a liberty that remains urgent in our own era. Many who deem same-sex marriage to be wrong reach that conclusion based on decent and honorable religious or philosophical premises, and neither they nor their beliefs are disparaged here. But when that sincere, personal opposition becomes enacted law and public policy, the necessary consequence is to put the imprimatur of the State itself on an exclusion that soon demeans or stigmatizes those whose own liberty is then denied. Under the Constitution, same-sex couples seek in marriage the same legal treatment as opposite-sex couples, and it would disparage their choices and diminish their personhood to deny them this right.

Finally, it must be emphasized that religions, and those who adhere to religious doctrines, may continue to advocate with utmost, sincere conviction that, by divine precepts, same-sex marriage should not be condoned. The First Amendment ensures that religious organizations and persons are given proper protection as they seek to teach the principles that are so fulfilling and so central to their lives and faiths, and to their own deep aspirations to continue the family they have long revered. The same is true of those who oppose same-sex marriage for other reasons. In turn, those who believe allowing same-sex marriage is proper or indeed essential, whether as a matter of religious conviction or secular belief, may engage those who disagree with their view in an open and searching debate. The Constitution, however, does not permit the State to bar same-sex couples from marriage on the same terms as accorded to couples of the opposite sex.

■ CHIEF JUSTICE ROBERTS, with whom JUSTICE SCALIA and JUSTICE THOMAS join, dissenting.

Today's decision, for example, creates serious questions about religious liberty. Many good and decent people oppose same-sex marriage as a tenet of faith, and their freedom to exercise religion is— unlike the right imagined by the majority—actually spelled out in the Constitution.

Respect for sincere religious conviction has led voters and legislators in every State that has adopted same-sex marriage democratically to include accommodations for religious practice. The majority's decision imposing same-sex marriage cannot, of course, create any such accommodations. The majority graciously suggests that religious believers may continue to "advocate" and "teach" their views of marriage. The First Amendment guarantees, however, the freedom to *"exercise"* religion. Ominously, that word is not a word the majority uses.

Hard questions arise when people of faith exercise religion in ways that may be seen to conflict with the new right to same-sex marriage— when, for example, a religious college provides married student housing only to opposite-sex married couples, or a religious adoption agency declines to place children with same-sex married couples. Indeed, the Solicitor General candidly acknowledged that the tax exemptions of some religious institutions would be in question if they opposed same-sex marriage. There is little doubt that these and similar questions will soon be before this Court. Unfortunately, people of faith can take no comfort in the treatment they receive from the majority today.

Perhaps the most discouraging aspect of today's decision is the extent to which the majority feels compelled to sully those on the other side of the debate. The majority offers a cursory assurance that it does not intend to disparage people who, as a matter of conscience, cannot accept same-sex marriage. That disclaimer is hard to square with the very next sentence, in which the majority explains that "the necessary consequence" of laws codifying the traditional definition of marriage is to "demea[n] or stigmatiz[e]" same-sex couples. The majority reiterates such characterizations over and over. By the majority's account, Americans who did nothing more than follow the understanding of marriage that has existed for our entire history—in particular, the tens of millions of people who voted to reaffirm their States' enduring definition of marriage—have acted to "lock ... out," "disparage," "disrespect and subordinate," and inflict "[d]ignitary wounds" upon their gay and lesbian neighbors. These apparent assaults on the character of fairminded people will have an effect, in society and in court. Moreover, they are entirely gratuitous. It is one thing for the majority to conclude that the Constitution protects a right to same-sex marriage; it is something else to portray everyone who does not share the majority's "better informed understanding" as bigoted.

■ JUSTICE THOMAS, with whom JUSTICE SCALIA joins, dissenting.

Aside from undermining the political processes that protect our liberty, the majority's decision threatens the religious liberty our Nation has long sought to protect.

The history of religious liberty in our country is familiar: Many of the earliest immigrants to America came seeking freedom to practice their religion without restraint. When they arrived, they created their own havens for religious practice. Many of these havens were initially homogenous communities with established religions. By the 1780's, however, "America was in the wake of a great religious revival" marked by a move toward free exercise of religion. Every State save Connecticut adopted protections for religious freedom in their State Constitutions by 1789, and, of course, the First Amendment enshrined protection for the free exercise of religion in the U.S. Constitution. But that protection was far from the last word on religious liberty in this country, as the Federal Government and the States have reaffirmed their commitment to religious liberty by codifying protections for religious practice. See e.g., RFRA.

Numerous *amici*—even some not supporting the States—have cautioned the Court that its decision here will "have unavoidable and wide-ranging implications for religious liberty." In our society, marriage is not simply a governmental institution; it is a religious institution as well. Today's decision might change the former, but it cannot change the latter. It appears all but inevitable that the two will come into conflict, particularly as individuals and churches are confronted with demands to participate in and endorse civil marriages between same-sex couples.

The majority appears unmoved by that inevitability. It makes only a weak gesture toward religious liberty in a single paragraph. And even that gesture indicates a misunderstanding of religious liberty in our Nation's tradition. Religious liberty is about more than just the protection for "religious organizations and persons . . . as they seek to teach the principles that are so fulfilling and so central to their lives and faiths." Religious liberty is about freedom of action in matters of religion generally, and the scope of that liberty is directly correlated to the civil restraints placed upon religious practice.

Although our Constitution provides some protection against such governmental restrictions on religious practices, the People have long elected to afford broader protections than this Court's constitutional precedents mandate. Had the majority allowed the definition of marriage to be left to the political process—as the Constitution requires—the People could have considered the religious liberty implications of deviating from the traditional definition as part of their deliberative process. Instead, the majority's decision short-circuits that process, with potentially ruinous consequences for religious liberty.

■ JUSTICE ALITO, with whom JUSTICE SCALIA and JUSTICE THOMAS join, dissenting.

Today's decision usurps the constitutional right of the people to decide whether to keep or alter the traditional understanding of marriage. The decision will also have other important consequences.

It will be used to vilify Americans who are unwilling to assent to the new orthodoxy. In the course of its opinion, the majority compares traditional marriage laws to laws that denied equal treatment for African-Americans and women. The implications of this analogy will be exploited by those who are determined to stamp out every vestige of dissent.

Perhaps recognizing how its reasoning may be used, the majority attempts, toward the end of its opinion, to reassure those who oppose same-sex marriage that their rights of conscience will be protected. We will soon see whether this proves to be true. I assume that those who cling to old beliefs will be able to whisper their thoughts in the recesses of their homes, but if they repeat those views in public, they will risk being labeled as bigots and treated as such by governments, employers, and schools.

The system of federalism established by our Constitution provides a way for people with different beliefs to live together in a single nation. If the issue of same-sex marriage had been left to the people of the States, it is likely that some States would recognize same-sex marriage and others would not. It is also possible that some States would tie recognition to protection for conscience rights. The majority today makes that impossible. By imposing its own views on the entire country, the majority facilitates the marginalization of the many Americans who have traditional ideas. Recalling the harsh treatment of gays and lesbians in the past, some may think that turnabout is fair play. But if that sentiment prevails, the Nation will experience bitter and lasting wounds.

NOTES AND QUESTIONS

1. *JFK's Ideal: A Separationist Requirement?* Five non-Protestant Christians (four Democrats and one Republican) have run for president on a major party ticket: Catholic New York Governor Al Smith in 1928, Catholic Massachusetts Senators John F. Kennedy in 1960 and John F. Kerry in 2004, Massachusetts Governors Orthodox Christian Michael Dukakis in 1988 and Mormon Mitt Romney (the only Republican) in 2012. The first Jewish candidate on a major party ticket was Connecticut Senator Joseph Lieberman, an Orthodox Jew, who was a vice presidential candidate as Al Gore's running mate in 2000. See James Rudin, One More Barrier Shattered; Al Gore Chooses Joseph Lieberman, Nat'l Catholic Reporter,

Aug. 25, 2000, at 17. Only Kennedy was successful. In this famous address to the Houston ministers, he stated: "I believe in an America where the separation of church and state is absolute." Is a commitment to the separation of church and state necessary to hold elective office in the United States? Must the separation be absolute? Is it more important for religious minorities to express their commitment to separationism than for mainline Protestants to do so?

1976 was dubbed the "Year of the Evangelical" when the Democratic nominee, former Georgia Governor Jimmy Carter, ran against President Gerald R. Ford, and both candidates, especially Carter, appealed openly to their born-again Christian faith. Carter, who is a Southern Baptist, frequently invoked Kennedy's memory. He observed that the State of Georgia, with its large Baptist population, had voted for Kennedy in 1960, and that Catholics should feel free to support Carter because, like other Baptists including former president Harry Truman, Carter was committed to the *total* separation of church and state. Speech to National Conference of Catholic Charities, in The Presidential Campaign 1976, I–2, at 900–01.

Did President George W. Bush, who is a Methodist, violate Kennedy's and Carter's separationist ideals when he advocated a constitutional amendment to ban same-sex marriage? Did Senator Barack Obama, who is a member of the United Church of Christ, suggest violating separation of church and state as a presidential candidate when he said Christian marriage was the legal norm? Did Obama's Call to Renewal speech, delivered before he announced his campaign for the presidency, prove that the separationist era is over? Or is Obama a separationist in the Kennedy tradition? What would happen to a presidential candidate who gave Kennedy's speech today?

Did Governor Mitt Romney adopt the Kennedy model because, like Kennedy, he is a member of a minority religion? During his 2008 presidential campaign, Romney presented a high-profile speech about "Faith in America." According to Romney:

> Almost 50 years ago another candidate from Massachusetts explained that he was an American running for president, not a Catholic running for president. Like him, I am an American running for president. I do not define my candidacy by my religion. A person should not be elected because of his faith nor should he be rejected because of his faith. . . .
>
> Let me assure you that no authorities of my church, or of any other church for that matter, will ever exert influence on presidential decisions. Their authority is theirs, within the province of church affairs, and it ends where the affairs of the nation begin.
>
> As governor, I tried to do the right as best I knew it, serving the law and answering to the Constitution. I did not confuse the particular teachings of my church with the obligations of the office and of the Constitution—and of course, I would not do so as

President. I will put no doctrine of any church above the plain duties of the office and the sovereign authority of the law.

As a young man, Lincoln described what he called America's "political religion"—the commitment to defend the rule of law and the Constitution. When I place my hand on the Bible and take the oath of office, that oath becomes my highest promise to God. If I am fortunate to become your president, I will serve no one religion, no one group, no one cause, and no one interest. A President must serve only the common cause of the people of the United States.

See Mitt Romney, Faith in America, Dec. 6, 2007, at http://www.foxnews.com/story/0,2933,315541,00.html.

Romney also addressed the argument that he should tell the American people everything he believed theologically: "There are some who would have a presidential candidate describe and explain his church's distinctive doctrines. To do so would enable the very religious test the founders prohibited in the Constitution. No candidate should become a spokesman for his faith. For if he becomes President he will need the prayers of the people of all faiths." Id. Do you accept his reasoning? Do you think that requiring presidential candidates to explain their beliefs violates the prohibition against religious tests in Article VI of the Constitution?

Romney adopted the same approach to religion and politics in 2012, when he was the Republican Party's nominee for president. See Jodi Kantor, Convention Voices Hope to Add Texture to Romney's Faith, N.Y. Times, Aug. 28, 2012 ("[f]or most of his political career, Mr. Romney has said that his life in the church has nothing to do with politics, and he has offered only clipped discussions of his religious views, privately worrying about the impact of his faith on his electability."). Did the separationist model work against Romney because he could not discuss his faith?

Republican presidential candidate and former Pennsylvania Senator Rick Santorum, who is Roman Catholic, attracted a great deal of attention and controversy when he stated that when he read President Kennedy's remarks about separation of church and state, he "almost threw up." According to Senator Santorum,

to say that people of faith have no role in the public square? You bet that makes you throw up. What kind of country do we live that says only people of non-faith can come into the public square and make their case? That makes me throw up and it should make every American who is seen from the president, someone who is now trying to tell people of faith that you will do what the government says, we are going to impose our values on you, not that you can't come to the public square and argue against it, but now we're going to turn around and say we're going to impose our values from the government on people of faith, which of course is the next logical step when people of faith, at least according to John Kennedy, have no role in the public square.

ABC News, This Week Transcript: GOP Candidate Rick Santorum, Feb. 26, 2012, at http://abcnews.go.com/blogs/politics/2012/02/rick-santorum-jfks-1960-speech-made-me-want-to-throw-up/. Do you agree with Senator Santorum? Did he misinterpret Kennedy's speech or offer a valid criticism of it?

2.   *Presidential Conscience and Policy.* Should presidents allow their political positions to be influenced by their religious beliefs? See generally Robert Audi, Religious Commitment and Secular Reason (2000); Kent Greenawalt, Private Consciences and Public Reasons (1995). The separationist presidents believed that their religion should not be the basis of public policy. Although Jimmy Carter opposed abortion because he thought that Jesus would never condone it, he supported *Roe v. Wade* because of his commitment to the separation of church and state. President George W. Bush viewed abortion and other topics from the perspective of his faith. On stem cell research, for example: "he framed it as a moral dilemma. He summoned members of the clergy and ethicists, as well as scientists, to counsel him. He prayed over it." Jodi Wilgoren & Bill Keller, Kerry and Religion: Pressure Builds for Public Discussions, N.Y. Times, Oct. 7, 2004, at A30. Was it appropriate for Bush to oppose legal abortion and stem cell research because of his belief in the sanctity of human life? Which religious views should be the basis of stem cell policy? See R. Alta Charo, Case Study: The Ethics of Control, 2 Yale J. Health Pol'y L. & Ethics 143 (2001).

According to President Barack Obama, "Democracy demands that the religiously motivated translate their concerns into universal, rather than religion-specific, values. It requires that their proposals be subject to argument, and amenable to reason. I may be opposed to abortion for religious reasons, but if I seek to pass a law banning the practice, I cannot simply point to the teachings of my church or evoke God's will. I have to explain why abortion violates some principle that is accessible to people of all faiths, including those with no faith at all." Barack Obama, Call to Renewal, June 28, 2006. Do you agree? If Obama translates his religious convictions into universal language, is his decision-making in reality any different from Bush's? Is Bush's style of religious and political reasoning more transparent than Obama's?

Did Presidents Bush and Obama approach same-sex marriage differently? Do you think religion influenced those two presidents' perspectives on the law of same-sex marriage?

3.   *Religious Tests for Office.* Does the United States Constitution require the president to be committed to free exercise, no establishment, and/or separation of church and state? Or does it violate the Constitution to expect a president to take a specific position on these legal questions concerning religion? Should all public officials be held to the same standard regarding their position on religion? According to Article VI, "no religious Test shall ever be required as a Qualification to any Office or public Trust under the United States." In 1960, the same year that Kennedy ran for president, the governor of Maryland appointed Roy Torcaso as a notary

public in Montgomery County. When Torcaso went to the county clerk's office to pick up his commission, he was asked to take the following oath:

> In the presence of Almighty God, I, Roy R. Torcaso, do solemnly promise and declare that I will support the Constitution of the United States; and that I will be faithful and bear true allegiance to the State of Maryland, and support the Constitution and Laws thereof; and that I will, to the best of my skill and judgment, diligently and faithfully without partiality or prejudice execute the office of Notary Public of The State of Maryland In and For Montgomery County according to the Constitution and Laws of this State. I, Roy R. Torcaso, do declare that I believe in the existence of God.

Torcaso v. Watkins, 223 Md. 49, 162 A.2d 438, 440 (1960). Would you take such an oath? Why or why not? Would you take the oath if the last sentence were omitted? Is the last sentence more troubling to you than the first sentence?

Torcaso challenged the oath under Maryland law, the Free Exercise Clause, and Article VI. In June 1960, the Maryland Court of Appeals dismissed Torcaso's challenge, concluding that Article VI did not apply to the states and that no Free Exercise violation occurred because "[t]he petitioner is not compelled to believe or disbelieve, under threat of punishment or other compulsion. True, unless he makes the declaration of belief he cannot hold public office in Maryland, but he is not compelled to hold office." Id. at 442. The court concluded its opinion with the following sentence:

> If it be assumed, as has been suggested, that the real deterrent to false swearing, in our time, is not the belief in God but the fear of prosecution for perjury, we cannot say that the distinction between believers and non-believers is so patently inappropriate as a security for good conduct, as to make it invidious under the Fourteenth Amendment.

Id. at 444. How do you assess the Maryland court's ruling?

The United States Supreme Court took jurisdiction of Torcaso's appeal on November 7, 1960, the day before the presidential election, and in 1961 overruled the Maryland court on First Amendment grounds, stating that the fact "that a person is not compelled to hold public office cannot possibly be an excuse for barring him from office by state-imposed criteria forbidden by the Constitution." The Court did not address whether Article VI applied to the states. See Torcaso v. Watkins, 367 U.S. 488, 495–96 (1961). If *Torcaso* had been decided before Kennedy's election, would Kennedy have needed to make the Houston speech?

Professor Akhil Amar has explained the importance and originality of Article VI (which, of course, was part of the Constitution before the First Amendment) in the following manner:

> This formal openness to men of any religion or no religion ran well ahead of contemporary Anglo-American practice. Britain's Act of

Settlement required that all future English monarchs join in Anglican communion. As of 1787, eleven American states—nine in their state constitutions, no less—imposed religious qualifications on government officials, and no state constitution explicitly barred religious tests for public servants. Article VI thus broke new ground, as did early American practice under Article II. Thanks to the broad power they enjoyed under the liberal eligibility rules of the Constitution, early American electors were free to choose, and did in fact freely choose, presidents of various denominations and even some men with no explicit religious affiliation, such as Jefferson and Lincoln.

Shortly after Americans ratified the federal Constitution, the state constitutional pattern began to change. Among the original states that revised their constitutions in the decade after 1788, all but one moved toward increased religious openness. Three states eliminated all constitutional language requiring religious tests, and a fourth significantly narrowed the scope of religious exclusion. Delaware moved all the way from requiring belief in the Holy Trinity in 1776 to a flat prohibition on all religious tests in 1792. The influence of the federal Constitution was obvious on the face of the 1792 document, which tracked the Article VI religious-test clause virtually verbatim. Here, too, the federal Preamble process helped propel the state bandwagon toward modernity.

Akhil Amar, America's Constitution: A Biography 166 (2005) (footnotes omitted).

If the religious test prohibition was so influential in the eighteenth century that the states began to revise their constitutions in favor of "increased religious openness," why was the religious test still an issue for Torcaso and Kennedy in 1960? Are Americans still prejudiced against certain religious groups? Can the Constitution prevent prejudice on the basis of religion? See Noah Feldman, Not in the Heavens, The New Republic, Feb. 20, 2006, at 21 ("Those present in Philadelphia in the hot summer of 1787 ultimately decided that no Bill of Rights was necessary in their draft Constitution—the promises of religious liberty and non-establishment were still a couple of years away; but the religious test clause was understood to be so fundamental that it made it into the original core document. It represented a break from practice in several of the states. Everyone understood that it opened the door to Catholics and Jews serving in the national government. The clause could not, on its own, preclude political prejudice; but it did hold out the promise that such bias was fundamentally inconsistent with our constitutional project. In a sense, it opened the door to Justice Louis Brandeis and President John F. Kennedy—and now Justice Samuel Alito."). What exactly does the clause prohibit? See Paul Horwitz, Religious Tests in the Mirror: The Constitutional Law and Constitutional Etiquette of Religion in Judicial Nominations, 15 Wm. & Mary Bill of Rts. J. 75 (2006) ("The Clause applies to a narrow set of circumstances in which government requires a nominee to formally swear his allegiance to, or otherwise comply with, particular faiths or faith propositions, or to disavow that allegiance. It does nothing more."). Horwitz contrasts his view with more expansive interpretations of Article VI, which would prohibit senators from inquiring into nominees' religion.

In the 114th Congress, which was elected in 2014, 92% of the House and Senate were Christian, with about 57% Protestant and 31% Catholic. Although 20% of Americans describe themselves as religiously unaffiliated, only one member of that Congress (0.2%), Rep. Kyrsten Sinema, D-Ariz., did so. There were five fewer Jewish members in the 114th Congress than there were in the 113th, and 11 fewer than there were in the 112th Congress. Only one of the 301 Republicans in the 114th Congress was non-Christian, freshman Rep. Lee Zeldin of New York's 1st District, who is Jewish. Of the 234 Democrats in the 114th Congress, 104 (44%) were Protestant, 83 (35%) were Catholic, 27 (12%) Jewish, two (1%) were Mormon, two (1%) were Buddhist, two (1%) were Muslim, one (0.5%) was Hindu, and one (0.5%) did not identify with a particular religion. See Pew Research Center, Faith on the Hill: The Religious Composition of the 114th Congress, Pew Forum, Jan. 5, 2015, at http://www.pewforum.org/2015/01/05/faith-on-the-hill/. What do you expect the religious composition of the 115th Congress to be?

4. *Anti-Catholic, Anti-Semitism, Anti-Mormon, Anti-Muslim.* Religious discrimination—prejudice against immigrant Catholics—was an issue in Smith's 1928 campaign and Kennedy's 1960 election, and Lieberman's supporters feared anti-Semitism in 2000. While Kennedy was supposed to be taking orders from the pope, Lieberman was accused of putting Israel's needs above those of the United States. Lieberman "was wounded by the suggestion that he might give superior loyalty to Israel. 'My first and only loyalty is to America,' he said." See John Seigenthaler, When Religion Issue Threatened JFK, The Tennessean, Aug. 20, 2000, at 17A. Would it be wrong for a Catholic president to take orders from the pope? For a Jewish president to support Israel? For a Catholic or Jewish president to promote policies that are consistent with Catholic or Jewish teaching? See Jay Lefkowitz, The Election and the Jewish Vote, Commentary, Feb. 1, 2005, at 61 (a candidate's support for Israel is an important factor in explaining the Jewish vote).

Before former Massachusetts Republican Governor and Mormon Mitt Romney ran for the presidency in 2008, some journalists asked if Americans were ready to elect a Mormon president:

> Americans have indeed become more religiously tolerant, but the first Mormon to run for president will clearly have to change some minds. In the late 1960s, the percentage of Americans who said they would not vote for a Jewish or Catholic presidential candidate was in the double-digits; by 1999, those numbers had fallen to 6 and 4 percent, respectively (roughly the same as the percentage of voters who say they wouldn't vote for a Baptist).

Compare that to the 17 percent of Americans who currently say they would have qualms electing a Mormon to the White House. That number hasn't changed one whit since 1967, the year that Romney's father considered a presidential run.

Amy Sullivan, Mitt Romney's Evangelical Problem: Everyone Wants to Believe the Massachusetts Governor's Mormonism Won't Be a Problem if He Runs in 2008. Think Again, Wash. Monthly, Sept. 1, 2005, at 13. If the concern with Kennedy was allegiance to the Vatican and the concern with Lieberman was allegiance to Israel, what is the concern with Romney, if Mormonism has its roots in the United States?

Many commentators argued that Romney's 2012 candidacy was a win for the Church of Latter-day Saints because Romney created a positive image of Mormons. Do you agree "Mormonism has moved into a new place in American culture"? That " 'the world could see that a Mormon who runs for office isn't, by definition, a nut case' "? See Peggy Fletcher Stack, "Mormon Moment" Ends With a Loss, But Romney's Religion Still Won, Religion News Service, Nov. 7 2012, at http://www.religionnews.com/politics/election/mormon-moment-ends-with-a-loss-but-romneys-religion-still-won. Are you surprised that Romney carried the Bible Belt? Id.; see also Sheryl Gay Stolberg, For Mormons, A Cautious Step Toward Mainstream Acceptance, N.Y. Times, Nov. 7, 2012, at P4.

Vermont Senator Bernard "Bernie" Sanders sought the Democratic Party's 2016 nomination for President. In a debate in March 2016, Senator Sanders said, "I am very proud of being Jewish. Being Jewish is so much of what I am." However, Senator Sanders is not observant, in contrast to Senator Lieberman. Additionally, Senator Sanders does not speak about his religion openly, unless prompted by the media or a questioner. Some in the media have argued that because the United States has seen an African-American President, a Mormon as a candidate for President, and a Jewish vice-presidential candidate, the Jewish religion of Senator Sanders does not make nearly as much difference as in the past. Julie Zauzmer, Why Aren't Jews Backing Sanders?, Wash. Post, Mar. 12, 2016, at B02. Do you agree?

Senator Sanders made history as the first Jewish candidate to win a presidential primary when he won the State of New Hampshire. Jewish Telegraphic Agency, Bernie Sanders Wins New Hampshire Primary, Makes Jewish History, Feb. 9, 2016, http://www.jta.org/2016/02/09/news-opinion/politics/with-nh-win-sanders-becomes-first-jew-to-win-u-s-presidential-primary. Has the Jewish religion become more acceptable to voters in national elections? Does the fact that Senator Sanders does not openly discuss or practice his religion demonstrate that religion is not nearly as decisive for voters as it once was? Do voters care about the religion of a candidate or are they more concerned about whether the candidate's positions reflect their own? Does it matter to the presidency that Hillary Clinton is Methodist and Donald Trump is Presbyterian?

Do you think Muslim, Buddhist, or Hindu presidential candidates would be acceptable to the American people? In 2006, Keith Ellison of Minnesota was the first Muslim elected to Congress, and he immediately raised controversy when he said he would take the oath of office on the Qur'an. See Rachel L. Swarns, Congressman Criticizes Election of Muslim: Virginia Republican Warns of a Threat to Traditional Values, N.Y.Times, Dec. 21, 2006, at A19. How do you explain the fact that 29% of Americans and 43% of Republicans, believe President Obama is a Muslim? See Sarah Pulliam Bailey, A Startling Number of Americans Still Believe President Obama is a Muslim, Wash. Post Blogs, Sept. 14, 2015, at https://www. washingtonpost.com/news/acts-of-faith/wp/2015/09/14/a-startling-number-of-americans-still-believe-president-obama-is-a-muslim/.

President Barack Obama's running mate, Delaware Senator Joe Biden, was elected the first Catholic Vice President of the United States in 2008. Mitt Romney's choice of Representative Paul Ryan as his running mate made 2012 the first election with two Catholic vice presidential candidates. Biden won again. Did the presence of two Catholics on major party ballots prove that the discrimination faced by Kennedy has ended?

5. *Religious Criticism of Politicians.* Should members of churches or synagogues criticize their representatives on religious grounds? In 1984, after Catholic New York Governor Mario Cuomo gave a speech explaining why he supported laws allowing abortion despite his own moral and religious opposition to it, New York's Archbishop John O'Connor criticized both Cuomo and vice presidential candidate Geraldine Ferraro for misrepresenting the church's teaching about abortion. Ferraro had signed a 1982 letter stating that the Catholic position on abortion was "not monolithic." See Ari L. Goldman, New York's Controversial Archbishop, N.Y. Times, Oct. 14, 1984, at 38. In 2004, several bishops withheld communion from presidential candidate John Kerry because of his support for abortion rights. See Mark I. Pinsky, Kerry Takes Communion During Visit to Orlando, Orlando Sentinel (Florida), Nov. 3, 2000, at A14. In 2000, the head of the Anti-Defamation League (ADL) criticized Joseph Lieberman for using too much religion in his political campaign ("Appealing along religious lines or belief in God," the ADL wrote to Lieberman, "is contrary to the American ideal."), while other Jews thought that he was not religious enough. See David Gibson, Jews Switch from Kvelling to Kvetching About Lieberman, Newhouse News Service, Oct. 25, 2000. Some Jewish leaders were especially offended after Lieberman told Don Imus that "he 'skips' the traditional daily prayer, recited by the strictly Orthodox, in which a Jewish man thanks God for not being created a woman. Lieberman then compounded his trouble by fudging on whether Judaism bars intermarriage." Id. Should church leaders criticize politicians only when they disagree with the candidates' interpretation of theological teachings? Is such criticism a reason that politicians should not discuss theology publicly?

In February 2016, Pope Francis suggested Republican presidential candidate Donald Trump was "not Christian" because Trump wanted to build a wall between Mexico and the United States as a way to curb illegal immigration. See Jim Yardley, Pope Francis Suggests Donald Trump is "Not Christian," N.Y. Times, Feb. 18, 2016, at F0. Mr. Trump responded that the pope was too political and unaware of the dangers of an open border. Alan Rappeport, Donald Trump Criticizes Pope Francis as "Very Political" Over Plans to Visit Migrants in Mexico, N.Y. Times, Feb. 12, 2016, at A18. How should a candidate for public office respond when a religious leader targets criticism against him? Should religious leaders remain neutral and not speak out for or against any political candidate or politician?

Churches and synagogues may lose their tax exemptions for endorsing religious candidates; we examine whether this tax rule limits speech critical of presidents in Section C.

6. *Ministers, Clergy, and Politics.* Is it constitutional to bar ministers and rabbis from political office because of the separation of church and state? Although thirteen states originally banned clergy from office, by 1977 only Tennessee did so. The Tennessee Constitution barred ministers and priests from holding seats in the state legislature:

> Whereas ministers of the gospel are, by their profession, dedicated to God and the care of Souls, and ought not to be diverted from the great duties of their functions; therefore, no minister of the gospel, or priest of any denomination whatever, shall be eligible to a seat in either House of the legislature.

Tenn.Const., Art. VIII, § 1 (1796). Paul McDaniel was a Baptist minister who filed as a candidate for delegate to the state constitutional convention. His opponent, Selma Cash Paty, sued to remove his name from the ballot. The Tennessee Supreme Court ruled that his disqualification from office did not burden McDaniel's religious belief (free exercise) and that the Establishment Clause's concern to avoid divisiveness in politics justified his disqualification. Paty v. McDaniel, 547 S.W.2d 897, 903 (Tenn. 1977). Was the Tennessee court's ruling consistent with *Torcaso v. Watkins*, supra, note 2?

The United States Supreme Court ruled that Tennessee had encroached upon McDaniel's religious freedom by conditioning his access to public office upon his abandonment of his religious faith. The plurality concluded, however, that *Torcaso* was not controlling because *Torcaso* involved religious belief (which the state may absolutely not regulate) and *McDaniel* covered religious conduct, which the state may regulate. The Court subjected regulation of religion to strict scrutiny under *Sherbert v. Verner* and *Wisconsin v. Yoder*, and rejected Tennessee's argument that the Establishment Clause was an interest of "the highest order" that justified the restriction because ministers might promote their own religion in office; "the American experience provides no persuasive support for the fear that clergymen in public office will be less careful of anti-establishment interests or less faithful to their oaths of civil office than their unordained counterparts." McDaniel v. Paty, 435 U.S. 618, 629 (1978).

Is the distinction between belief and action persuasive in this context? See id. at 634 (Brennan J., concurring) (freedom of belief encompasses practicing religion to earn a livelihood). Is *McDaniel* really distinguishable from *Torcaso*? See id. at 634–35 ("The plurality … draws what I respectfully suggest is a sophistic distinction between that holding and Tennessee's disqualification provision. … I simply cannot fathom why the Free Exercise Clause 'categorically prohibits' hinging qualification for office on the *act* of declaring a belief in religion, but not on the act of discussing that belief with others."). Justice Brennan also concluded that the clergy provision violated the Establishment Clause. Do you agree that banning clergy from political office is an unconstitutional establishment of religion? Or do you agree with Tennessee's argument that the Establishment Clause gives reason for the state to keep ministers out of politics in order to eliminate "religious divisiveness or strife"? Id. at 646.

Justice White invalidated the provision under the Equal Protection Clause, arguing that Free Exercise did not apply because McDaniel was not compelled to abandon his ministry. Is that a better constitutional argument? Is Article VI a better basis for *Torcaso* and *McDaniel* than either the Free Exercise or the Establishment Clause?

Why would a member of the clergy want to hold political office? Should a priest, minister, rabbi, or imam fear that his or her religious work will be diminished by engaging in political activity? Or should he view the political arena as the appropriate place to fulfill a religious calling to seek justice? Would you vote for a member of the clergy to become president? Voters were given two separate opportunities in 2008 and 2016 to vote for former Arkansas Governor Mike Huckabee, an ordained Southern Baptist minister. In 2008, Gov. Huckabee won the Iowa caucuses, the first nominating contest in Presidential primary races. Michael D. Shear and Perry Bacon, Jr., Iowa Chooses Huckabee, Wash. Post, Jan. 4, 2008, at A01. In 2016, Governor Huckabee again ran for President, but dropped out of the race after losing in the Iowa caucuses. Karen Tumulty, Mike Huckabee Ends 2016 Presidential Bid, Wash. Post, Feb. 1, 2016. Did something change between 2008 and 2016 that made voting for a minister less acceptable? Was being an ordained minister a boost to Governor Huckabee in 2008 but a drag on his campaign in 2016? Or do you think voters make their decisions based on politics and not religion?

7. *Supreme Court Justices.* Does the religious composition of the courts matter? According to Professor Feldman:

> Through 1990, 91 of 104 Supreme Court Justices came from Protestant backgrounds. Eight Justices were Roman Catholic: Roger Taney (appointed in 1835), Edward D. White (1894), Joseph McKenna (1897), Pierce Butler (1922), Frank Murphy (1939), William Brennan (1956), Antonin Scalia (1986), and Anthony Kennedy (1987). Five Justices were Jewish: Louis Brandeis (1916), Benjamin Cardozo (1932), Felix Frankfurter (1939), Arthur Goldberg (1962), and Abe Fortas (1965). James F. Byrnes, who served as an Associate Justice for only the 1941–1942 term, was born into a Roman Catholic family, but converted to Episcopalianism when he married in 1906. More recently, two more Jewish Justices have been appointed: Ruth Bader Ginsburg

and Stephen G. Breyer. Clarence Thomas was born a Baptist, raised a Catholic, began attending an Episcopal Church, and most recently, returned to Catholicism. In fact, if Thomas is categorized as Catholic, then 1996 marked the first time that a majority of the Justices were not Protestant.

Stephen M. Feldman, Religious Minorities and the First Amendment: The History, the Doctrine and the Future, 6 U. Pa. J. Const. L. 222, 232 n.41 (2003).

With the confirmation of Justice Samuel Alito to the United States Supreme Court in 2006, the Court for the first time was composed of a majority of Catholics, as Alito joined Chief Justice John Roberts and Justices Antonin Scalia, Anthony Kennedy, and Clarence Thomas to form the new majority. Justice Sonia Sotomayor became the sixth Catholic on the Court in 2009 after the retirement of Justice David Souter. After Jewish Justice Elena Kagan replaced John Paul Stevens on the Court, the Court for the first time in its history did not include any Protestants.

Justice Antonin Scalia, who died on February 13, 2016, described himself as a "devout Catholic." Adam Liptak, Justice Scalia, Who Led Court's Conservative Renaissance, Dies at 79, N.Y. Times, Feb. 13, 2016, at A1. After Scalia's death, one of the most discussed potential nominees was Judge Sri Srinivasan. Judge Srinivasan, a judge on the Court of Appeals for the District of Columbia Circuit, would have become the first Hindu on the Supreme Court if confirmed. Judge Srinivasan was born in India and immigrated to the United States when he was a child. When he was confirmed to the Court of Appeals, Judge Srinivasan took his oath on the Bhagavad Gita, the Hindu holy book. Lauren Markoe, Sri Srinivasan: The First Hindu on the Supreme Court, Religion News Service, February 15, 2016. Instead, President Obama nominated Judge Merrick Garland, a Reform Jew. If confirmed, the Supreme Court would have five Catholic and four Jews, with the Jewish Justices occupying 44% of the Court, compared to the 2% Jewish population of the entire United States. Lauren Markoe, Merrick Garland is Jewish. Does it Matter? Religion News Service, March 16, 2016.

Does the composition of the Court—five Catholics and three Jews—suggest that the United States is more religiously tolerant than it was in 1960, or merely more tolerant of Catholics? Compare the appointment of Jewish Justice Louis Brandeis to the Supreme Court by President Woodrow Wilson in 1916, with its attendant charges of anti-Semitism, with those of two Jewish Justices, Ruth Bader Ginsburg and Stephen Breyer, by President Clinton in the 1990s, and Justice Elena Kagan in 2010. According to Professor White, "[a]n undercurrent of anti-Semitism ran through the opposition to Brandeis, reflected in a letter to Taft by Homer Albers, Dean of Boston University Law School, who stated that the 'difference between William H. Taft and Louis D. Brandeis' was that 'the former is distinguished in Jurisprudence and the latter in Jewish prudence!' " See G. Edward White, The Canonization of Holmes and Brandeis: Epistemology and Judicial Reputations, 70 N.Y.U. L. Rev. 576,

596 (1995); see also Philippa Strum, Louis D. Brandeis: Justice for the People 293 (1984); Edward A. Purcell, Jr., Brandeis and the Progressive Constitution: Erie, the Judicial Power, and the Politics of the Federal Courts in Twentieth-Century America 117 (2000); Henry J. Abraham, Justices and Presidents: A Political History of Appointments to the Supreme Court 182 (3rd ed. 1992); Winston E. Calvert, Judicial Selection and the Religious Test Clause, 82 Wash. U. L.Q. 1129, 1135 n.27 (2004) ("Symbolic importance" of the "growing acceptability" of religious minorities allegedly warrants denominational balance as an important goal in selecting justices.).

Do you think that the justices' votes on their cases are influenced by their religious upbringing? Compare Jay Sekulow, Witnessing Their Faith: Religious Influence on Supreme Court Justices and Their Opinions xii–xiii (2005) ("In every one of the cases discussed in this book, the opinion of the justices coincided with the official positions held by the religious denomination that had influenced them.") with Noah Feldman, Not in the Heavens, The New Republic, Feb. 20, 2006, at 21 ("And that is precisely the point: there is no demonstrable direct relationship between justices' religious background or beliefs and their jurisprudence."). Do you think the justices in *Obergefell* were influenced by their faith?

What should happen if a justice's religious views conflict with the law? Do you agree with Justice Antonin Scalia that judges who disagree with the morality of the death penalty should resign rather than vote against its imposition? See Antonin Scalia, A Call for Reckoning: Religion and the Death Penalty, University of Chicago, Jan. 25, 2002, available at http://www.pewforum.org/2002/01/25/a-call-for-reckoning-religion-and-the-death-penalty/. How does this compare to Kennedy's statement that the choice between violating his conscience and violating the national interest would end in his resignation? See also Mark C. Modak-Truran, Reenchanting the Law: The Religious Dimension of Judicial Decision Making, 53 Cath. U. L. Rev. 709 (2004); Sanford Levinson, The Confrontation of Religious Faith and Civil Religion: Catholics Becoming Justices, 39 DePaul L. Rev. 1047, 1048 (1990); Howard J. Vogel, The Judicial Oath and the American Creed: Comments on Sanford Levinson's The Confrontation of Religious Faith and Civil Religion: Catholics Becoming Justices, 39 DePaul L. Rev. 1107, 1109 (1990); Rodney K. Smith, Treating Others As Our Own: Professor Levinson, Friendship, Religion, and the Public Square, 38 Tulsa L. Rev. 731 (2003); Thomas C. Berg & William G. Ross, Some Religiously Devout Justices: Historical Notes and Comments, 81 Marq. L. Rev. 383 (1998). Asked by a group of high school students "how his religious faith influenced his work on the court," Justice Clarence Thomas responded: " 'I think that it really gives content to the oath that you took . . . You say, "So help me God." . . . There are some cases that will drive you to your knees, . . . In those moments you ask for strength and wisdom to have the right answer and the courage to stand up for it. Beyond that, it would be illegitimate, I think, and a violation of my oath to incorporate my religious beliefs into the decision-making process.' " Adam Liptak, Sidebar: Reticent Justice Opens Up to a Group of Students, N.Y. Times, Apr. 14, 2009. Do Justice Thomas's remarks confirm that the separationist attitude is the most appropriate one for a Supreme Court justice? Is the standard different for politicians and judges?

Chief Justice Roberts and Justices Kennedy, Scalia, Alito, and Thomas are all Catholic. Do you think their religion influenced their votes in *Obergefell*? Can you see any influence of the justices' Catholicism in the excerpts from the case that you just read?

Return to the discussion of *Town of Greece v. Galloway* in Chapter 2. Do you think the religious composition of the Court affected the decision about public prayer in that case? Is it significant that all three Jewish justices dissented in *Galloway*?

B. POLITICAL MORALITY AND RELIGION

We began this chapter with John Kennedy's invocation of the constitutional ideal of separation of church and state. Despite this emphasis on separation, however, the Constitution also provides extensive protection of free speech and free exercise, and many actions (especially presidential activities) that mix religion and politics are unlikely to warrant constitutional sanction. In this section we ask whether there are moral reasons for religious believers to rely on political and constitutional reasoning instead of their religious faith.

We begin with a specific question: How can religious believers like Kennedy, Bush, or Obama—as well as Americans of very different faiths—support the democratic process when it reaches conclusions that differ from their Catholic, Methodist, UCC, or other faith? Does morality demand that politicians follow their religious convictions instead of the law? Does morality require politicians to vote their religious convictions into law, even when their fellow citizens disagree with them about matters of religion? We explore these questions by examining the philosopher John Rawls's theory of political liberalism and responses to it by his critics. Rawls worded the moral question of political liberalism with these words: "How is it possible for those affirming a religious doctrine that is based on religious authority, for example, the Church or the Bible, also to hold a reasonable political conception that supports a just democratic regime?" John Rawls, Political Liberalism xxxix (paper ed. 1996). *Political Liberalism* provides one account of how diverse religious and philosophical commitments can be compatible with democracy. As you read the following materials, consider whether liberalism unfairly—or appropriately—asks religious believers to bracket their religious convictions from politics.

As background to the excerpts from Rawls's writings, which follow, keep in mind four concepts—pluralism, the political conception of justice, the overlapping consensus and public reason—that are central to his theory.

Pluralism. The "pluralism of incompatible yet reasonable comprehensive doctrines" is the starting point of *Political Liberalism,* the central problem with which Rawls wrestles. A comprehensive doctrine is a religion, a philosophy, or a worldview that provides the framework that gives guidance and meaning to an individual's entire life. Islam, Kantianism, Atheism, Christianity, and Utilitarianism, for example, are comprehensive doctrines. In earlier eras, philosophers such as Plato or Aristotle, or religious traditions such as Christianity, assumed that there was one comprehensive doctrine that all citizens could share. Such unity cannot occur in a constitutional democratic regime; there is no comprehensive doctrine of justice that all citizens can support. Pluralism is a fact of our lives together; it is normal and is not going to disappear.

Political Conception of Justice. Because pluralism means that there is not one comprehensive doctrine of justice that all citizens can support, such unity of doctrine among citizens can occur only if the state enforces it. In a constitutional democracy, however, it is not appropriate to use force to impose one's comprehensive worldview on others who do not share that commitment. Therefore a political conception of justice must be found that does not impose a comprehensive worldview on others, and that is itself not comprehensive. Political justice is instead an independent "module" that can be plugged into numerous reasonable but competing comprehensive doctrines. Rawls does not derive or deduce the political conception of justice from any comprehensive worldview. Instead, the derivation of the political conception of justice from the comprehensive doctrine of citizens occurs in the overlapping consensus.

Overlapping Consensus. In the presence of pluralism, the political conception of justice will be based on an overlapping consensus among the citizens of the democracy. The consensus is overlapping because citizens can agree on the political conception even though they possess a variety of comprehensive doctrines. Rawls insists that the overlapping consensus is not a *modus vivendi*; citizens in a *modus vivendi* compromise because they must. However, should circumstances change, they will renegotiate that compromise, usually in an attempt to improve their situation. Thus a *modus vivendi* lacks stability.

Citizens, however, require stability in their political lives, and so need a consensus that does not shift as power changes hands. Rawls argues that citizens have reasons within their own comprehensive doctrines to support the overlapping consensus, and that these reasons will persuade them to support the consensus even when their comprehensive group acquires enough votes to change the status quo. Citizens support the political conception of justice in the overlapping consensus—even when their comprehensive doctrine disagrees with the results—because the virtues of political cooperation and of stability are "very great virtues." Id. at 139.

Public Reason. Decisions in the overlapping consensus are made only on the basis of reasons that appeal to all citizens; as part of their "duty of civility," citizens in the overlapping consensus must employ "public reason." Public reason is quite demanding, especially for adherents of comprehensive doctrines. It "means that in discussing constitutional essentials and matters of basic justice we are not to appeal to comprehensive religious and philosophical doctrines—to what we as individuals or members of associations see as the whole truth. . . . " Instead, "each of us must have, and be ready to explain, a criterion of what principles and guidelines we think other citizens (who are also free and equal) may *reasonably be expected to endorse* along with us." Id. at 224–26 (emphasis added). A Muslim may understand why a Catholic politician would obey the pope, or an evangelical leader follow the Bible, but not be expected to endorse government by the pope's or the Bible's standards. Muslim, Catholic and Baptist may all endorse constitutional principles of free speech or equal protection, but for different comprehensive reasons.

Should presidents and other politicians live according to the ideal of public reason spelled out in following essay? Would you be able to vote according to its requirements?

John Rawls, The Idea of Public Reason Revisited

64 University of Chicago Law Review 765, 765–768, 773–776,
784–786, 797–799, 805–806 (1997).

INTRODUCTION

The idea of public reason, as I understand it, belongs to a conception of a well ordered constitutional democratic society. The form and content of this reason—the way it is understood by citizens and how it interprets their political relationship—is part of the idea of democracy itself. This is because a basic feature of democracy is the fact of reasonable pluralism—the fact that a plurality of conflicting reasonable comprehensive doctrines, religious, philosophical, and moral, is the normal result of its culture of free institutions. Citizens realize that they cannot reach agreement or even approach mutual understanding on the basis of their irreconcilable comprehensive doctrines. In view of this, they need to consider what kinds of reasons they may reasonably give one another when fundamental political questions are at stake. I propose that in public reason comprehensive doctrines of truth or right be replaced by an idea of the politically reasonable addressed to citizens as citizens.

Central to the idea of public reason is that it neither criticizes nor attacks any comprehensive doctrine, religious or nonreligious, except insofar as that doctrine is incompatible with the essentials of public reason and a democratic polity. The basic requirement is that a reasonable doctrine accepts a constitutional democratic regime and its companion idea of legitimate law. While democratic societies will differ in the specific doctrines that are influential and active within them—as they differ in the western democracies of Europe and the United States, Israel, and India—finding a suitable idea of public reason is a concern that faces them all.

§ 1: THE IDEA OF PUBLIC REASON

. . . It is imperative to realize that the idea of public reason does not apply to all political discussions of fundamental questions, but only to discussions of those questions in what I refer to as the public political forum. This forum may be divided into three parts: the discourse of judges in their decisions, and especially of the judges of a supreme court; the discourse of government officials, especially chief executives and legislators; and finally, the discourse of candidates for public office and their campaign managers, especially in their public oratory, party platforms, and political statements. We need this three-part division because, as I note later, the idea of public reason does not apply in the same way in these three cases and elsewhere. In discussing what I call the wide view of public political culture, we shall see that the idea of public reason applies more strictly to judges than to others, but that the requirements of public justification for that reason are always the same.

Distinct and separate from this three-part public political forum is what I call the background culture. This is the culture of civil society. In a democracy, this culture is not, of course, guided by any one central idea or principle, whether political or religious. Its many and diverse agencies and associations with their internal life reside within a framework of law that ensures the familiar liberties of thought and speech, and the right of free association. The idea of public reason does not apply to the background culture with its many forms of nonpublic reason nor to media of any kind. Sometimes those who appear to reject the idea of public reason actually mean to assert the need for full and open discussion in the background culture. With this political liberalism fully agrees. . . .

§ 2: THE CONTENT OF PUBLIC REASON

1.   A citizen engages in public reason, then, when he or she deliberates within a framework of what he or she sincerely regards as the most reasonable political conception of justice, a conception that expresses political values that others, as free and equal citizens might also reasonably be expected reasonably to endorse. . . .

2.   We must distinguish public reason from what is sometimes referred to as secular reason and secular values. These are not the same as public reason. For I define secular reason as reasoning in terms of comprehensive nonreligious doctrines. Such doctrines and values are

much too broad to serve the purposes of public reason. Political values are not moral doctrines, however available or accessible these may be to our reason and common sense reflection. Moral doctrines are on a level with religion and first philosophy. By contrast, liberal political principles and values, although intrinsically moral values, are specified by liberal political conceptions of justice and fall under the category of the political. These political conceptions have three features:

> First, their principles apply to basic political and social institutions (the basic structure of society);

> Second, they can be presented independently from comprehensive doctrines of any kind (although they may, of course, be supported by a reasonable overlapping consensus of such doctrines); and

> Finally, they can be worked out from fundamental ideas seen as implicit in the public political culture of a constitutional regime, such as the conceptions of citizens as free and equal persons, and of society as a fair system of cooperation.

Thus, the content of public reason is given by the principles and values of the family of liberal political conceptions of justice meeting these conditions. To engage in public reason is to appeal to one of these political conceptions—to their ideals and principles, standards and values—when debating fundamental political questions. This requirement still allows us to introduce into political discussion at any time our comprehensive doctrine, religious or nonreligious, provided that, in due course, we give properly public reasons to support the principles and policies our comprehensive doctrine is said to support. I refer to this requirement as *the proviso*, and consider it in detail below. . . .

§ 4: THE WIDE VIEW OF PUBLIC POLITICAL CULTURE

1.   Now we consider what I call the wide view of public political culture and discuss two aspects of it. The first is that reasonable comprehensive doctrines, religious or nonreligious, may be introduced in public political discussion at any time, provided that in due course proper political reasons—and not reasons given solely by comprehensive doctrines—are presented that are sufficient to support whatever the comprehensive doctrines introduced are said to support. This injunction to present proper political reasons I refer to as *the proviso*, and it specifies public political culture as distinct from the background culture. The second aspect I consider is that there may be positive reasons for introducing comprehensive doctrines into public political discussion. I take up these two aspects in turn.

Obviously, many questions may be raised about how to satisfy the proviso. One is: when does it need to be satisfied? On the same day or some later day? Also, on whom does the obligation to honor it fall? It is important that it be clear and established that the proviso is to be appropriately satisfied in good faith. Yet the details about how to satisfy this proviso must be worked out in practice and cannot feasibly be governed by a clear family of rules given in advance. How they work out is determined by the nature of the public political culture and calls for good sense and understanding. It is important also to observe that the introduction into public political culture of religious and secular doctrines, provided the proviso is met, does not change the nature and content of justification in public reason itself. This justification is still given in terms of a family of reasonable political conceptions of justice. However, there are no restrictions or requirements on how religious or secular doctrines are themselves to be expressed; these doctrines need not, for example, be by some standards logically correct, or open to rational appraisal, or evidentially supportable. Whether they are or not is a matter to be decided by those presenting them, and how they want what they say to be taken. They will normally have practical reasons for wanting to make their views acceptable to a broader audience.

2. Citizens' mutual knowledge of one another's religious and nonreligious doctrines expressed in the wide view of public political culture recognizes that the roots of democratic citizens' allegiance to their political conceptions lie in their respective comprehensive doctrines, both religious and nonreligious. In this way citizens' allegiance to the democratic ideal of public reason is strengthened for the right reasons. We may think of the reasonable comprehensive doctrines that support society's reasonable political conceptions as those conceptions' vital social basis, giving them enduring strength and vigor. When these doctrines accept the proviso and only then come into political debate, the commitment to constitutional democracy is publicly manifested. Made aware of this commitment, government officials and citizens are more willing to honor the duty of civility, and their following the ideal of public reason helps foster the kind of society that ideal exemplifies. These benefits of the mutual knowledge of citizens' recognizing one another's reasonable comprehensive doctrines bring out a positive ground for introducing such doctrines, which is not merely a defensive ground, as if their intrusion into public discussion were inevitable in any case.

Consider, for example, a highly contested political issue—the issue of public support for church schools. Those on different sides are likely to come to doubt one another's allegiance to basic constitutional and political values. It is wise, then, for all sides to introduce their comprehensive doctrines, whether religious or secular, so as to open the way for them to explain to one another how their views do indeed support those basic political values. Consider also the Abolitionists and those in the Civil Rights Movement.[54] The proviso was fulfilled in their cases, however much they emphasized the religious roots of their doctrines, because these doctrines supported basic constitutional values—as they themselves asserted—and so supported reasonable conceptions of political justice. . . .

§ 6: QUESTIONS ABOUT PUBLIC REASON

I now turn to various questions and doubts about the idea of public reason and try to allay them. . . .

(b) Others may think that public reason is too restrictive because it may lead to a stand-off and fail to bring about decisions on disputed issues. A stand-off in some sense may indeed happen, not only in moral and political reasoning but in all forms of reasoning, including science and common sense. Nevertheless, this is irrelevant. The relevant comparison is to those situations in which legislators enacting laws and judges deciding cases must make decisions. Here some political rule of action must be laid down and all must be able reasonably to endorse the process by which a decision is reached. Recall that public reason sees the office of citizen with its duty of civility as analogous to that of judge with its duty of deciding cases. Just as judges are to decide cases by legal grounds of precedent, recognized canons of statutory interpretation, and other relevant grounds, so citizens are to reason by public reason and to be guided by the criterion of reciprocity, whenever constitutional essentials and matters of basic justice are at stake.

Thus, when there seems to be a stand-off, that is, when legal arguments seem evenly balanced on both sides, judges cannot resolve the case simply by appealing to their own political views. To do that is for judges to violate their duty. The same holds with public reason: if, when stand-offs occur, citizens simply invoke grounding reasons of their comprehensive views, the principle of reciprocity is violated. From the point of view of public reason, citizens must vote for the ordering of political values they sincerely think the most reasonable. Otherwise they fail to exercise political power in ways that satisfy the criterion of reciprocity.

In particular, when hotly disputed questions, such as that of abortion, arise which may lead to a stand-off between different political conceptions, citizens must vote on the question according to their complete ordering of political values.[80] Indeed, this is a normal case:

---

[54] I do not know whether the Abolitionists and King thought of themselves as fulfilling the purpose of the proviso. But whether they did or not, they could have. And had they known and accepted the idea of public reason, they would have. I thank Paul Weithman for this point.

[80] Some have quite naturally read the footnote in Rawls, Political Liberalism, lecture VI, § 7.2 at 243–44, as an argument for the right to abortion in the first trimester. I do not intend it to be one. (It does express my opinion, but my opinion is not an argument.) I was in error in leaving it in doubt whether the aim of the footnote was only to illustrate and confirm the following statement in the text to which the footnote is attached: "The only comprehensive doctrines that run afoul of public reason are those that cannot support a reasonable balance [or ordering] of political values [on the issue]." To try to explain what I meant, I used three

unanimity of views is not to be expected. Reasonable political conceptions of justice do not always lead to the same conclusion; nor do citizens holding the same conception always agree on particular issues. Yet the outcome of the vote, as I said before, is to be seen as legitimate provided all government officials, supported by other reasonable citizens, of a reasonably just constitutional regime sincerely vote in accordance with the idea of public reason. This doesn't mean the outcome is true or correct, but that it is reasonable and legitimate law, binding on citizens by the majority principle.

Some may, of course, reject a legitimate decision, as Roman Catholics may reject a decision to grant a right to abortion. They may present an argument in public reason for denying it and fail to win a majority. But they need not themselves exercise the right to abortion. They can recognize the right as belonging to legitimate law enacted in accordance with legitimate political institutions and public reason, and therefore not resist it with force. Forceful resistance is unreasonable: it would mean attempting to impose by force their own comprehensive doctrine that a majority of other citizens who follow public reason, not unreasonably, do not accept. Certainly Catholics may, in line with public reason, continue to argue against the right to abortion. Reasoning is not closed once and for all in public reason any more than it is closed in any form of reasoning. Moreover, that the Catholic Church's nonpublic reason requires its members to follow its doctrine is perfectly consistent with their also honoring public reason.

I do not discuss the question of abortion in itself since my concern is not with that question but rather to stress that political liberalism does not hold that the ideal of public reason should always lead to a general agreement of views, nor is it a fault that it does not. Citizens learn and profit from debate and argument, and when their arguments follow public reason, they instruct society's political culture and deepen their understanding of one another even when agreement cannot be reached. . . .

---

political values (of course, there are more) for the troubled issue of the right to abortion to which it might seem improbable that political values could apply at all. I believe a more detailed interpretation of those values may, when properly developed in public reason, yield a reasonable argument. I don't say the most reasonable or decisive argument; I don't know what that would be, or even if it exists. (For an example of such a more detailed interpretation, see Judith Jarvis Thomson, *Abortion*, 20 Boston Rev. 11 (Summer 1995), though I would want to add several addenda to it.) Suppose now, for purposes of illustration, that there is a reasonable argument in public reason for the right to abortion but there is no equally reasonable balance, or ordering, of the political values in public reason that argues for the denial of that right. Then in this kind of case, but only in this kind of case, does a comprehensive doctrine denying the right to abortion run afoul of public reason. However, if it can satisfy the proviso of the wide public reason better, or at least as well as other views, it has made its case in public reason. Of course, a comprehensive doctrine can be unreasonable on one or several issues without being simply unreasonable.

§ 7: CONCLUSION

1. Throughout, I have been concerned with a torturing question in the contemporary world, namely: Can democracy and comprehensive doctrines, religious or nonreligious, be compatible? And if so, how? At the moment a number of conflicts between religion and democracy raise this question. To answer it political liberalism makes the distinction between a self-standing political conception of justice and a comprehensive doctrine. A religious doctrine resting on the authority of the Church or the Bible is not, of course, a liberal comprehensive doctrine: its leading religious and moral values are not those, say, of Kant or Mill. Nevertheless, it may endorse a constitutional democratic society and recognize its public reason. Here it is basic that public reason is a political idea and belongs to the category of the political. Its content is given by the family of (liberal) political conceptions of justice satisfying the criterion of reciprocity. It does not trespass upon religious beliefs and injunctions insofar as these are consistent with the essential constitutional liberties, including the freedom of religion and liberty of conscience. There is, or need be, no war between religion and democracy. In this respect political liberalism is sharply different from and rejects Enlightenment Liberalism, which historically attacked orthodox Christianity. . . .

The idea of the politically reasonable is sufficient unto itself for the purposes of public reason when basic political questions are at stake. Of course, fundamentalist religious doctrines and autocratic and dictatorial rulers will reject the ideas of public reason and deliberative democracy. They will say that democracy leads to a culture contrary to their religion, or denies the values that only autocratic or dictatorial rule can secure. They assert that the religiously true, or the philosophically true, overrides the politically reasonable. We simply say that such a doctrine is politically unreasonable. Within political liberalism nothing more need be said.

NOTES AND QUESTIONS

1. *Presidents and Justices.* Rawls argued that judges are exemplars of public reason. Do you agree? Should politicians be held to that same standard, or should they be more free to express their religious convictions than judges?

Were the Supreme Court justices exemplars of public reason in their opinions in *Obergefell* in Section A? Is there anything in their reasoning that Rawls would find objectionable?

Did the presidents and presidential candidates studied in Section A, including Kennedy, Bush, and Obama, employ public reason? Is Rawls's ideal of public reason similar to the argument of Senator Kennedy in the Houston speech?

In his campaign autobiography, Obama wrote:

> What our deliberative, pluralistic democracy does demand is that the religiously motivated translate their concerns into universal, rather than religion-specific, values. It requires that their proposals must be subject to argument and amenable to reason. If I am opposed to abortion for religious reasons and seek to pass a law banning the practice, I cannot simply point to the teachings of my church or invoke God's will and expect that argument to carry the day. If I want others to listen to me, then I have to explain why abortion violates some principle that is accessible to people of all faiths, including those with no faith at all.

Barack Obama, The Audacity of Hope: Thoughts on Reclaiming the American Dream 219 (2006). Is Obama's reasoning the same as Rawls's public reason? See Leslie C. Griffin, Political Reason, 22 St. John's J. Legal Comment. 493, 502 (2007) ("Obama's translation model does not solve the problem; it merely hides it, leaving politicians to govern according to religious beliefs as long as they discover a secular rationale (or any reason?) for governmental action. For this reason, in Rawls's work, the key words are 'public reason,' not secular reason, and 'public reason' is best interpreted as political. The goal is not for the Mormon, or Baptist, or Church of Christ candidate to figure a secular way to lead others to his faith. This approach to politics undermines political stability and demonstrates disrespect for one's fellow citizens. Instead, politicians should employ political reason as the starting point for their decision-making on matters of law and politics.").

In 2015, David Axelrod, President Obama's campaign strategist, wrote in his autobiography that Obama "misled Americans for his own political benefit when he claimed in the 2008 election to oppose same sex marriage for religious reasons." Axelrod advised Obama to hide his views for political reasons: "Opposition to gay marriage was particularly strong in the black church, and as he ran for higher office, he grudgingly accepted the counsel of more pragmatic folks like me, and modified his position to support civil unions rather than marriage, which he would term a 'sacred union.'" Although his advisers suggest Obama was "fully evolved behind closed doors," President Obama repeatedly told the public he was "evolving" on the issue. Obama finally announced his support for same-sex marriage in May 2012, after Vice President Biden told reporters that Biden supported marriage equality. Should Obama have withheld his support until after the November 2012 election if he believed support for marriage equality would jeopardize his reelection? Zeke J. Miller, Axelrod: Obama Misled Nation When He Opposed Gay Marriage in 2008, Time Magazine, Feb. 10, 2015, at http://time.com/3702584/gay-marriage-axelrod-obama/.

Did Obama act morally in concealing his position on same-sex marriage? What do you think Rawls would say about Obama's choice? Is there a lesson about political morality in Obama's actions?

2. *Comprehensive Doctrines.* What does Rawls mean by a comprehensive doctrine? Do all the individual religious believers we met in Chapter 1 subscribe to a comprehensive doctrine? Do comprehensive doctrines such as utilitarianism and Kantianism, or the world's religions, interpret politics differently? Consider the following classification of the world's religions' attitudes toward politics by Professor Jacob Neusner: "Judaism and Christianity begin without the assumption of political power. Islam, Hinduism, and Confucianism, by contrast, appear to take such power for granted. Buddhism stakes out a middle position, in which it knows it can rule but is prepared not to do so." Jacob Neusner, ed., God's Rule: The Politics of World Religions 5 (2003). How can members of religious traditions with such different attitudes toward political power share a common government?

In the third century B.C.E., Ashoka, the Buddhist Emperor of India, was "committed to making sure that public discussion could take place without animosity or violence." Accordingly he formulated the following rules for public discussion. "He demanded, for example, 'restraint in regard to speech, so that there should be no extolment of one's own sect or disparagement of other sects on inappropriate occasions, and it should be moderate even on appropriate occasions'. Even when engaged in arguing, 'other sects should be duly honoured in every way on all occasions.'" Amartya Sen, The Argumentative Indian: Writings on Indian History, Culture and Identity 15–16 (2005). Professor Sen notes that "[i]n the history of public reasoning in India, considerable credit must be given to the early Indian Buddhists, who had a great commitment to discussion as a means of social progress." Id. at 15. Does Sen's work add support to Rawls's argument that political disputes can be resolved by public reason, and that comprehensive doctrines may provide their members with good reasons to employ public reason?

3. Did the readings about the presidents persuade you that a Rawlsian approach takes too much religion out of the politics? Professor Stephen Carter has argued that American law and politics trivialize religion by excluding it from a dominant secular culture, and recommends the addition of more theological language to the public square, supporting what Rawls would call an "open view" of politics in which no religious arguments are off limits. Do you agree that politics should be open to all religious arguments? See Stephen L. Carter, The Culture of Disbelief (1993). In contrast to both Rawls and Carter, Professor Michael Perry recommended an "ecumenical political dialogue," according to which religious participants in political discussions should maintain two attitudes (fallibilism and pluralism) and two virtues (public intelligibility and public accessibility). That is, religious argument may enter politics and law, and indeed should enter politics and law, but it must be fallible, pluralistic, intelligible and accessible. Michael J. Perry, Love and Power: The Role of Religion and Morality in American Politics 43 (1993); see also Michael J. Perry, Religious Morality and Political Choice: Further Thoughts—And Second Thoughts—On Love and Power, 30 San Diego L. Rev. 703, 727 (1993). Would Perry's theory exclude some religious groups from the public square ("namely theologically conservative theists, including various Protestant Christians (evangelicals, fundamentalists, and pentecostals) and traditionalists (Roman Catholics, Anglicans, and Lutherans)") while allowing other groups to participate? See David M. Smolin, Regulating Religious and Cultural Conflict in a Postmodern America: A Response to Professor Perry, 76 Iowa L. Rev. 1067, 1076–77 (1992) (book review); Sanford Levinson, Religious Language and the Public Square, 105 Harv. L. Rev. 2061 (1992).

4. Is Rawls's theory of public reason a good idea, or does it unfairly ask religious believers to put aside or bracket their religious beliefs from their political lives? Would a person "annihilate herself" and her personal identity by following public reason? Do you agree with Professor Perry?

> If it is the case (as I believe it is) that a person—a "self"—is partly constituted by her moral convictions, then, in choosing principles of justice, the partisan cannot bracket her membership in her moral community, her particular moral convictions, for that membership, those convictions, are constitutive of her very self. To bracket them would be to bracket—indeed, to annihilate— herself.

See Michael J. Perry, Morality, Politics, and Law 72–73 (1988).

Is the division of religious and political reasoning *psychologically* harmful because it divides the individual's comprehensive doctrine from her public life? See Susan Moller Okin, Political Liberalism, 87 Am. Pol. Sci. Rev. 1010 (1993) (book review). Or does *moral* harm arise from the demand that the individual publicly support positions that violate her deepest convictions? Is *integrity* threatened by public reason? See Timothy P. Jackson, To Bedlam and Part Way Back: John Rawls and Christian Justice, 8.1 Faith and Phil. 423 (1991). Does the requirement to use public reason produce individuals who lack *sincerity* because they publicly advocate reasonable positions not based on their personal commitments to comprehensive doctrines? See Daniel J. Gifford, Interpersonal Distrust in the Modified Rawlsian Society, 48 SMU L. Rev. 217, 218 (1994). See Michael J. Perry, Morality, Politics, and Law 61 (1988) (A Rawlsian does not reason as "the *particular* person she is"; "it is, rather, for her to play the role of *someone else* reasoning towards principles of justice."). Is it even possible for individuals to distinguish their religious or philosophical commitments from their political views? Compare Gerald F. Gaus, Reason, Justification, and Consensus: Why Democracy Can't Have It All, in James Bohman & William Rehg, eds., Deliberative Democracy: Essays on Reason and Politics 209 (1997) ("As Kant said, to reason publicly is to 'think from the standpoint of everyone else.'") with Rawls, supra ("the roots of democratic citizens' allegiance to their political conceptions lie in their respective comprehensive doctrines, both religious and nonreligious").

Do you think that public reason *discriminates* against religion by allowing secular voices to dominate political discussion? See Gary C. Leedes, Rawls's Excessively Secular Political Conception, 27 U. Rich. L. Rev. 1083 (1993) (book review); Kent Greenawalt, On Public Reason, 69

Chi.–Kent L. Rev. 688 (1994). Is Rawls himself intolerant toward religious believers, indeed a "secular fundamentalist"? See Paul F. Campos, Secular Fundamentalism, 9 Colum. L. Rev. 1814, 1816, 1825 (1994) ("Despite its highly abstract endorsement of moral and religious pluralism, *Political Liberalism* is ultimately a paean to a secular creed that has within it the potential to become every bit as monistic, compulsory, and intolerant of any significant deviation from social verities as the traditional modes of belief it derided and displaced."). Does Rawls discriminate not against religion but among religions by favoring those doctrines that are willing to translate their convictions into public reason? As mentioned above, the Catholic Church upheld its ecumenical or catholic mission (i.e., as the one true religion that should be everywhere recognized as such) until Vatican II. Does this mean that, according to Rawls, prior to Vatican II, President Kennedy could be *either* a good Catholic *or* a good American, but not both? See Leslie Griffin, Good Catholics Should Be Rawlsian Liberals, 5 S. Cal. Interdisc. L.J. 217 (1997). Is it reasonable for Rawls to label all comprehensive doctrines that cannot support political liberalism "unreasonable"? Is political liberalism only persuasive to those who are already political liberals? Is that the meaning of the last sentence of the Rawls excerpt?

Do you agree with the argument that public discourse is impoverished if we remove biblical narratives, religious imagery or theological arguments from politics? Is "secular" language "chaste, sober, and thin," and therefore "unable to evoke the rich, polyvalent power of religious symbolism, a power which can command commitments of emotional depth"? See John A. Coleman, A Possible Role for Biblical Religion in Public Life, 40 Theological Stud. 700, 706 (1979); Miriam Galston, Rawlsian Dualism and the Autonomy of Political Thought, 94 Colum. L. Rev. 1842, 1844 (1994); Michael J. Sandel, Political Liberalism, 107 Harv. L. Rev. 1765, 1776 (1994) (book review). Does the Rawlsian approach take passion and commitment out of political argument? See Elizabeth H. Wolgast, The Demands of Public Reason, 94 Colum. L. Rev. 1936, 1943 (1994).

5. *Islam and Public Reason.* Is Islam a comprehensive doctrine that can adopt Rawlsian public reason? Discussions of that question begin against the background that Islam traditionally did not allow Muslims to live as minorities in non-Muslim countries. Andrew March identifies aspects of Islam that could keep Muslims from being minority citizens in a liberal democracy, and then explains what an Islamic affirmation of liberal citizenship entails. See Liberal Citizenship and the Search for an Overlapping Consensus: The Case of Muslim Minorities, 34 Phil. & Pub. Aff. 4 (Fall 2006); Islamic and Liberal Citizenship: The Search for an Overlapping Consensus (2009). March addresses the question "May I without great contradiction regard the terms of citizenship in a pluralist liberal democracy as reasonable from an Islamic standpoint?", and finds grounds in classical Islam for affirming Muslims' residence in, political obligation to, and loyalty toward a non-Muslim state. In addressing whether Islam can provide resources for Muslims to be citizens in non-Muslim liberal democracies, March concludes: "Political liberalism's public commitment to neutrality does in fact appeal to adherents of a non-liberal comprehensive doctrine." Islamic Foundations for a Social Contract in Non-Muslim Liberal Democracies, American Political Science Review, Vol. 101, No. 2 (May 2007), pp. 235–52.

Along similar lines, Mohammad Fadel concludes that, from the perspective of classical Islamic sources, public reason is an appropriate style of argumentation. See The True, the Good and the Reasonable: The Theological and Ethical Roots of Public Reason in Islamic Law, 21 Canadian J. of Law & Jurisprudence 5 (2008). Abdullahi Ahmed An-Na'im is more critical of public reason, proposing in its place "civic reason": "Muslims and other believers should be able to propose policy and legislative initiatives emanating from their religious beliefs, provided that they can support them in free and open public debate by reasons that are accessible and convincing to the generality of citizens regardless of their religious or other beliefs." Abdullahi Ahmed An-Na'im, Islam and the Secular State 29–30 (2008). Is An-Na'im's theory equivalent to Rawls's? Is it more similar to Obama than Rawls? See id. at 97–101 (expressing "general agreement with Rawls's thinking," but observing the risks of trying to transplant it to Islamic societies because it is "so specific to the United States"). Does Rawls emphasize politics too much at the expense of public and nongovernmental spaces? See id. at 100.

6. *Slavery and the Civil Rights Movement.* Does the history of the Abolitionist Movement, which fought to abolish slavery, and the American Civil Rights Movement of the 1960s, which was led by Reverend Martin Luther King, Jr., support Rawls's theory or contradict it? Recall that, according to Rawls, both the Abolitionists and King could meet the public reason proviso, which states that individuals may introduce their comprehensive discussions into political debate as long as, "in due course, we give properly public reasons to support the principles and policies our comprehensive doctrine is said to support." Or does Rawls misrepresent how religious the Civil Rights Movement was? See Paul J. Weithman, Taking Rites Seriously, 75 Pac. Phil. Q. 272, 284 (1994).

Do you think that Reverend King met the public reason proviso in the Letter from Birmingham Jail, in Chapter 5? On the third anniversary of *Brown v. Board of Education*, King said the following to discouraged supporters:

> I conclude by saying that each of us must keep faith in the future. Let us not despair. Let us realize that as we struggle for justice and freedom, we have cosmic companionship. This is the long faith of the Hebraic-Christian tradition: that God is not some Aristotelian Unmoved Mover who merely contemplates upon Himself. He is not merely a self-knowing God, but an other-loving God forever working through history for the establishment of His kingdom.
>
> And those of us who call the name of Jesus Christ find something of an event in our Christian faith that tells us this. There is something in our faith that says to us, "Never despair; never give

up; never feel that the cause of righteousness and justice is doomed." There is something in our Christian faith, at the center of it, which says to us that Good Friday may occupy the throne for a day, but ultimately it must give way to the triumphant beat of the drums of Easter. There is something in our faith that says evil may so shape events that Caesar will occupy the palace and Christ the cross, but one day that same Christ will rise up and split history into A.D. and B.C., so that even the name, the life of Caesar must be dated by his name. There is something in this universe which justifies Carlyle in saying: "No lie can live forever."

Go out with that faith today. Go back to your homes in the Southland to that faith, with that faith today. Go back to Philadelphia, to New York, to Detroit and Chicago with that faith today: that the universe is on our side in the struggle. Stand up for justice. Sometimes it gets hard, but it is always difficult to get out of Egypt, for the Red Sea always stands before you with discouraging dimensions. And even after you've crossed the Red Sea, you have to move through a wilderness with prodigious hilltops of evil and gigantic mountains of opposition. But I say to you this afternoon: Keep moving. Let nothing slow you up. Move on with dignity and honor and respectability.

Martin Luther King, Jr., Address Delivered at the Prayer Pilgrimage for Freedom in Washington, D.C.: Give Us the Ballot (May 17, 1957). Are these words an example of public reason, or civil religion, or both, or something else?

Are King's addresses proof that religious and biblical imagery are necessary to the public square because they can inspire and motivate in a way that public reason cannot? See John A. Coleman, An American Strategic Theology 193 (1982). Do King's arguments demonstrate that religion leads people to understand justice and truth in a way that public reason cannot? See Michael J. Sandel, Political Liberalism, 107 Harv. L. Rev. 1765, 1776 (1994) (book review). How do you explain the fact that many Christians opposed the Civil Rights Movement? See David A.J. Richards, Public Reason and Abolitionist Dissent, 69 Chi.–Kent L. Rev. 787, 835 (1994) (The abolitionist dissent was not successful *because* it was religious, but due to its moral independence from both religious and political leaders).

Why is Martin Luther King remembered but A. Philip Randolph, King's co-leader in the March on Washington, forgotten? Is it because Randolph was an atheist? Should the contribution of nontheists to the Civil Rights Movement be reexamined? Are nontheist African Americans "sacrificed to the myth that the achievements of the civil rights movement were the accomplishments of religious—mainly Christian—people"? See Kimberly Winston, Blacks Say Atheists Were Unseen Civil Rights Heroes, USA Today, Feb. 22, 2012, at http://www.usatoday.com/news/religion/story/2012-02-22/black-atheists-civil-rights/53211196/1.

7. *Abortion.* In the footnote to *Political Liberalism* referred to in footnote 80 of the reading, Rawls made the following argument:

> As an illustration, consider the troubled question of abortion. Suppose first that the society in question is well-ordered and that we are dealing with the normal case of mature adult women. . . . Suppose further that we consider the question in terms of these three important political values: the due respect for human life, the ordered reproduction of political society over time, including the family in some form, and finally the equality of women as equal citizens. (There are, of course, important values besides these.) Now I believe any reasonable balance of these three values will give a woman a duly qualified right to decide whether or not to end her pregnancy during the first trimester. The reason for this is that at this early stage of pregnancy the political value of the equality of women is overriding, and this right is required to give it substance and force. Other political values, if tallied in, would not, I think, affect this conclusion. A reasonable balance may allow her such a right beyond this, at least in certain circumstances. However, I do not discuss the question in general here, as I simply want to illustrate the point of the text by saying that any comprehensive doctrine that leads to a balance of political values excluding that duly qualified right in the first trimester is to that extent unreasonable; and depending on the details of its formulation, it may also be cruel and oppressive; for example, if it denied the right altogether except in the case of rape and incest. Thus, assuming that this question is either a constitutional essential or a matter of basic justice, we would go against the ideal of public reason if we voted from a comprehensive doctrine that denied this right.

John Rawls, Political Liberalism 243–44 (1993). Does Rawls sneak in assumptions of his comprehensive doctrine and therefore demonstrate that public reason does not work? See Robert P. George, Public Reason and Political Conflict: Abortion and Homosexuality, 106 Yale L.J. 2475 (1997). Many abortion activists believe that their public arguments about abortion, with their references to religion, are comparable to the arguments of the Civil Rights Movement's leaders for equality. See Thomas Frank, What's the Matter with Kansas? How Conservatives Won the Heart of America (2005). Do you agree?

In 2012, during the first campaign in which both vice presidential candidates were Roman Catholic, debate moderator Martha Raddatz asked both men how their Catholic faith affected their abortion policies:

> **Rep. Paul Ryan:** I don't see how a person can separate their public life from their private life or from their faith. Our faith informs us in everything we do. My faith informs me about how to take care of the vulnerable, about how to make sure that people have a chance in life.

Now, you want to ask basically why I'm pro-life? It's not simply because of my Catholic faith. That's a factor, of course, but it's also because of reason and science. You know, I think about 10 1/2 years ago, my wife Janna and I went to Mercy Hospital in Janesville where I was born for our seven-week ultrasound for our firstborn child, and we saw that heartbeat. Our little baby was in the shape of a bean, and to this day, we have nicknamed our firstborn child, Liza, "Bean." (Chuckles.)

Now, I believe that life begins at conception.

That's why—those are the reasons why I'm pro-life.

Now, I understand this is a difficult issue. And I respect people who don't agree with me on this. But the policy of a Romney administration will be to oppose abortion with the exceptions for rape, incest and life of the mother. . . .

V.P. Biden: My religion defines who I am. And I've been a practicing Catholic my whole life. And it has particularly informed my social doctrine. Catholic social doctrine talks about taking care of those who—who can't take care of themselves, people who need help.

With regard to—with regard to abortion, I accept my church's position on abortion as a—what we call de fide (doctrine?). Life begins at conception. That's the church's judgment. I accept it in my personal life.

But I refuse to impose it on equally devout Christians and Muslims and Jews and—I just refuse to impose that on others, unlike my friend here, the congressman.

I—I do not believe that—that we have a right to tell other people that women, they—they can't control their body. It's a decision between them and their doctor, in my view. And the Supreme Court—I'm not going to interfere with that.

NPR, Transcript and Audio: Vice Presidential Debate, Oct. 11, 2012, at http://www.npr.org/2012/10/11/162754053/transcript-biden-ryan-vice-presid ential-debate. Did the candidates employ public reason?

8.   *Same-Sex Marriage.* After the California Supreme Court recognized a state constitutional right to same-sex marriage, California voters passed Proposition 8, which banned gay marriage. See In re Marriage Cases, 43 Cal.4th 757, 76 Cal.Rptr.3d 683, 183 P.3d 384 (2008)

During the Proposition 8 campaign, several Christian groups, led by the Church of Jesus Christ of Latter-day Saints, vocally supported the proposition and contributed large amounts of money to effectuate its passage, while gay rights groups criticized the numerous faith-based attempts to influence the vote. One anti-8 group created a website to keep track of Mormon contributions to the Yes-on-8 drive and estimated that Mormons had contributed $20 million toward passage of the initiative. A pro-8 spokesman decried the website and the "despicable" ad:

"I am appalled at the level of Mormon-bashing that went on during the Proposition 8 campaign and continues to this day," he said. "If this activity were directed against any other church, if someone put up a website that targeted Jews or Catholics in a similar fashion for the mere act of participating in a political campaign, it would be widely and rightfully condemned."

The complaints of Mormon-bashing were then rebutted with arguments that the gay rights supporters were debating politics, not religion, and were appropriately criticizing the political activity of the Mormon church. See Jessica Garrison & Joanna Lin, Gay-rights Activists Criticize the Church for Helping to Collect Millions to Aid Passage of Ban on Gay Marriage, L.A. Times, Nov. 7, 2008, at B1.

Although the Mormon support for Proposition 8 received much of the media's attention, the Mormons were only part of a broad coalition of religious groups who joined protectmarriage.com, and Catholics and Evangelicals contributed heavily to the campaign. The Campaign for 8 was "one of the most ambitious interfaith political organizing efforts ever attempted in the state," as Catholics and evangelical Christians participated in large numbers and members of the Protect Marriage Coalition also "reach[ed] out to Jews, Muslims, Sikhs and Hindus." See Jessica Garrison, California Churches Plan a Big Push against Same-Sex Marriage, L.A. Times, Aug. 24, 2008. How would such "pan-religious, faith-based political action" differ from a group of Rawlsian liberals?

Compare the Mormon, Catholic, and Evangelical voters of California to presidents and Supreme Court justices. Should the voters have been expected to use public reason in deciding whether to support Proposition 8? Was it inappropriate to have a religious coalition leading political debate about a public policy issue?

What did the debate about same-sex marriage teach you about the appropriate role of religion in setting public policy? As you read the next section, consider whether the LDS and other churches who participated in the Prop 8 campaign should have lost their tax exemptions. Should *Obergefell* change the landscape of tax exemptions?

C. TAXES AND POLITICAL ACTIVITY

Tax law states churches should lose their tax-exempt status if they "devote a substantial part of their activities to attempting to influence legislation" or "participate in, or intervene in, any political campaign on behalf of (or in opposition to) any candidate for public office." Yet the following case is the only known example of the IRS taking action to revoke a church's tax exemptions because of its political activity. Should more churches be treated the way Branch Ministries was in the following opinion? Or do you prefer the argument that it is unconstitutional for the government to limit church activity in this way?

Branch Ministries v. Rossotti
United States Court of Appeals, District of Columbia Circuit, 2000.
211 F.3d 137.

■ BUCKLEY, SENIOR JUDGE:

Four days before the 1992 presidential election, Branch Ministries, a tax-exempt church, placed full-page advertisements in two newspapers in which it urged Christians not to vote for then-presidential candidate Bill Clinton because of his positions on certain moral issues. The Internal Revenue Service concluded that the placement of the advertisements violated the statutory restrictions on organizations exempt from taxation and, for the first time in its history, it revoked a bona fide church's tax-exempt status because of its involvement in politics. Branch Ministries and its pastor, Dan Little, challenge the revocation on the grounds that (1) the Service acted beyond its statutory authority, (2) the revocation violated its right to the free exercise of religion guaranteed by the First Amendment and the Religious Freedom Restoration Act, and (3) it was the victim of selective prosecution in violation of the Fifth Amendment. Because these objections are without merit, we affirm the district court's grant of summary judgment to the Service.

I. BACKGROUND

A.   Taxation of Churches

The Internal Revenue Code ("Code") exempts certain organizations from taxation, including those organized and operated for religious purposes, provided that they do not engage in certain activities, including involvement in "any political campaign on behalf of (or in opposition to) any candidate for public office." 26 U.S.C. § 501(a), (c)(3) (1994). Contributions to such organizations are also deductible from the donating taxpayer's taxable income. *Id.* § 170(a). Although most organizations seeking tax-exempt status are required to apply to the Internal Revenue Service ("IRS" or "Service") for an advance determination that they meet the requirements of section 501(c)(3), *id.* § 508(a), a church may simply hold itself out as tax exempt and receive the benefits of that status without applying for advance recognition from the IRS. *Id.* § 508(c)(1)(A).

The IRS maintains a periodically updated "Publication No. 78," in which it lists all organizations that have received a ruling or determination letter confirming the deductibility of contributions made to them. Thus, a listing in that publication will provide donors with advance assurance that their contributions will be deductible under section 170(a). If a listed organization has subsequently had its tax-exempt status revoked, contributions that are made to it by a donor who is unaware of the change in status will generally be treated as deductible if made on or before the date that the revocation is publicly announced. Donors to a church that has not received an advance determination of its tax-exempt status may also deduct their contributions; but in the event of an audit, the taxpayer will bear the burden of establishing that the church meets the requirements of section 501(c)(3).

The unique treatment churches receive in the Internal Revenue Code is further reflected in special restrictions on the IRS's ability to investigate the tax status of a church. The Church Audit Procedures Act ("CAPA") sets out the circumstances under which the IRS may initiate an investigation of a church and the procedures it is required to follow in such an investigation. 26 U.S.C. § 7611. Upon a "reasonable belief" by a high-level Treasury official that a church may not be exempt from taxation under section 501, the IRS may begin a "church tax inquiry." *Id.* § 7611(a). A church tax inquiry is defined, rather circularly, as

> any inquiry to a church (other than an examination) to serve as a basis for determining whether a church—
>
> (A) is exempt from tax under section 501(a) by reason of its status as a church, or
>
> (B) is . . . engaged in activities which may be subject to taxation.

Id. § 7611(h)(2). If the IRS is not able to resolve its concerns through a church tax inquiry, it may proceed to the second level of investigation: a "church tax examination." In such an examination, the IRS may obtain and review the church's records or examine its activities "to determine whether [the] organization claiming to be a church is a church for any period." *Id.* § 7611(b)(1)(A), (B).

B.   Factual and Procedural History

Branch Ministries, Inc. operates the Church at Pierce Creek ("Church"), a Christian church located in Binghamton, New York. In 1983, the Church requested and received a letter from the IRS recognizing its tax-exempt status. On October 30, 1992, four days before the presidential election, the Church placed full-page advertisements in *USA Today* and the *Washington Times.* Each bore the headline "Christians Beware" and asserted that then-Governor Clinton's positions concerning abortion, homosexuality, and the distribution of condoms to teenagers in schools violated Biblical precepts. The following appeared at the bottom of each advertisement:

> This advertisement was co-sponsored by the Church at Pierce Creek, Daniel J. Little, Senior Pastor, and by churches and concerned Christians nationwide. Tax-deductible donations for this advertisement gladly accepted. Make donations to: The Church at Pierce Creek. [mailing address].

The advertisements did not go unnoticed. They produced hundreds of contributions to the Church from across the country and were mentioned in a *New York Times* article and an Anthony Lewis column which stated that the sponsors of the advertisement had almost certainly violated the Internal Revenue Code. Peter Applebome, *Religious Right Intensifies Campaign for Bush,* N.Y. Times, Oct. 31, 1992, at A1; Anthony Lewis, *Tax Exempt Politics?,* N.Y. Times, Dec. 1, 1992, at A15.

The advertisements also came to the attention of the Regional Commissioner of the IRS, who notified the Church on November 20, 1992 that he had authorized a church tax inquiry based on "a reasonable belief . . . that you may not be tax-exempt or that you may be liable for tax" due to political activities and expenditures. The Church denied that it had engaged in any prohibited political activity and declined to provide the IRS with certain information the Service had requested. On February 11, 1993, the IRS informed the Church that it was beginning a church tax examination. Following two unproductive meetings between the parties, the IRS revoked the Church's section 501(c)(3) tax-exempt status on January 19, 1995, citing the newspaper advertisements as prohibited intervention in a political campaign.

The Church and Pastor Little (collectively, "Church") commenced this lawsuit soon thereafter. This had the effect of suspending the revocation of the Church's tax exemption until the district court entered its judgment in this case. *See* 26 U.S.C. § 7428(c). The Church challenged the revocation of its tax-exempt status, alleging that the IRS had no authority to revoke its tax exemption, that the revocation violated its right to free speech and to freely exercise its religion under the First Amendment and the Religious Freedom Restoration Act of 1993, 42 U.S.C. § 2000bb ("RFRA"), and that the IRS engaged in selective prosecution in violation of the Equal Protection Clause of the Fifth Amendment. After allowing discovery on the Church's selective prosecution claim, *Branch Ministries, Inc. v. Richardson,* 970 F.Supp. 11 (D.D.C.1997), the district court granted summary judgment in favor of the IRS. *Branch Ministries v. Rossotti,* 40 F.Supp.2d 15 (D.D.C.1999).

II. ANALYSIS

The Church advances a number of arguments in support of its challenges to the revocation. We examine only those that warrant analysis.

A. The Statutory Authority of the IRS

[The court concluded the IRS had the statutory authority to revoke the Church's tax-exempt status.]

B. First Amendment Claims and the RFRA

The Church claims that the revocation of its exemption violated its right to freely exercise its religion under both the First Amendment and the RFRA. To sustain its claim under either the Constitution or the statute, the Church must first establish that its free exercise right has been substantially burdened. . . . We conclude that the Church has failed to meet this test.

The Church asserts, first, that a revocation would threaten its existence. See Affidavit of Dan Little dated July 31, 1995 at ¶ 22, reprinted in App. at Tab 8 ("The Church at Pierce Creek will have to close due to the revocation of its tax exempt status, and the inability of congregants to deduct their contributions from their taxes."). The Church maintains that a loss of its tax-exempt status will not only make its members reluctant to contribute the funds essential to its survival, but may obligate the Church itself to pay taxes.

The Church appears to assume that the withdrawal of a conditional privilege for failure to meet the condition is in itself an unconstitutional burden on its free exercise right. This is true, however, only if the receipt of the privilege (in this case the tax exemption) is conditioned

> upon conduct proscribed by a religious faith, or . . . denie[d] . . . because of conduct mandated by religious belief, thereby putting substantial pressure on an adherent to modify his behavior and to violate his beliefs.

Jimmy Swaggart Ministries, 493 U.S. at 391–92, 110 S.Ct. 688 (internal quotation marks and citation omitted). Although its advertisements reflected its religious convictions on certain questions of morality, the Church does not maintain that a withdrawal from electoral politics would violate its beliefs. The sole effect of the loss of the tax exemption will be to decrease the amount of money available to the Church for its religious practices. The Supreme Court has declared, however, that such a burden "is not constitutionally significant." *Id.* at 391, 110 S.Ct. 688; *see also Hernandez v. Commissioner,* 490 U.S. 680, 700, 109 S.Ct. 2136, 104 L.Ed.2d 766 (1989) (the "contention that an incrementally larger tax burden interferes with [ ] religious activities . . . knows no limitation").

In actual fact, even this burden is overstated. Because of the unique treatment churches receive under the Internal Revenue Code, the impact of the revocation is likely to be more symbolic than substantial. As the IRS confirmed at oral argument, if the Church does not intervene in future political campaigns, it may hold itself out as a 501(c)(3) organization and receive all the benefits of that status. All that will have been lost, in that event, is the advance assurance of deductibility in the event a donor should be audited. See 26 U.S.C. § 508(c)(1)(A); Rev. Proc. 82–39 § 2.03. Contributions will remain tax deductible as long as donors are able to establish that the Church meets the requirements of section 501(c)(3).

Nor does the revocation necessarily make the Church liable for the payment of taxes. As the IRS explicitly represented in its brief and reiterated at oral argument, the revocation of the exemption does not convert bona fide donations into income taxable to the Church. *See* 26 U.S.C. § 102 ("Gross income does not include the value of property acquired by gift. . . . "). Furthermore, we know of no authority, and counsel provided none, to prevent the Church from reapplying for a prospective determination of its tax-exempt status and regaining the advance assurance of deductibility—provided, of course, that it renounces future involvement in political campaigns.

We also reject the Church's argument that it is substantially burdened because it has no alternate means by which to communicate its sentiments about candidates for public office. In *Regan v. Taxation With Representation,* 461 U.S. 540, 552–53, 103 S.Ct. 1997, 76 L.Ed.2d 129 (1983) (Blackmun, J., concurring), three members of the Supreme Court stated that the availability of such an alternate means of communication is essential to the constitutionality of section 501(c)(3)'s restrictions on lobbying. The Court subsequently confirmed that this was an accurate description of its holding. See *FCC v. League of Women Voters,* 468 U.S. 364, 400, 104 S.Ct. 3106, 82 L.Ed.2d 278 (1984). In *Regan,* the concurring justices noted that "TWR [Taxation with Representation] may use its present § 501(c)(3) organization for its nonlobbying activities and may create a § 501(c)(4) affiliate to pursue its charitable goals through lobbying." 461 U.S. at 552, 103 S.Ct. 1997.

The Church has such an avenue available to it. As was the case with TWR, the Church may form a related organization under section 501(c)(4) of the Code. *See* 26 U.S.C. § 501(c)(4) (tax exemption for "[c]ivic leagues or organizations not organized for profit but operated exclusively for the promotion of social welfare"). Such organizations are exempt from taxation; but unlike their section 501(c)(3) counterparts, contributions to them are not deductible. *See id.* § 170(c); *see also Regan,* 461 U.S. at 543, 552–53, 103 S.Ct. 1997. Although a section 501(c)(4) organization is also subject to the ban on intervening in political campaigns, *see* 26 C.F.R. § 1.501(c)(4)–1(a)(2)(ii) (1999), it may form a political action committee ("PAC") that would be free to participate in political campaigns. *Id.* § 1.527–6(f), (g) ("[A]n organization described in section 501(c) that is exempt from taxation under section 501(a) may, [if it is not a section 501(c)(3) organization], establish and maintain such a separate segregated fund to receive contributions and make expenditures in a political campaign.").

At oral argument, counsel for the Church doggedly maintained that there can be no "Church at Pierce Creek PAC." True, it may not itself create a PAC; but as we have pointed out, the Church can initiate a series of steps that will provide an alternate means of political communication that will satisfy the standards set by the concurring justices in *Regan.* Should the Church proceed to do so, however, it must understand that the related 501(c)(4) organization must be separately incorporated; and it must maintain records that will demonstrate that tax-deductible contributions to the Church have not been used to support the political activities conducted by the 501(c)(4) organization's political action arm. *See* 26 U.S.C. § 527(f)(3); 26 C.F.R. § 1.527–6(e), (f).

That the Church cannot use its tax-free dollars to fund such a PAC unquestionably passes constitutional muster. The Supreme Court has consistently held that, absent invidious discrimination, "Congress has not violated [an organization's] First Amendment rights by declining to subsidize its First Amendment activities." *Regan,* 461 U.S. at 548, 103 S.Ct. 1997; *see also Cammarano v. United States,* 358 U.S. 498, 513, 79 S.Ct. 524, 3 L.Ed.2d 462 (1959) ("Petitioners are not being denied a tax deduction because they engage in constitutionally protected activities, but are simply being required to pay for those activities entirely out of their own pockets, as everyone else engaging in similar activities is required to do under the provisions of the Internal Revenue Code.").

Because the Church has failed to demonstrate that its free exercise rights have been substantially burdened, we do not reach its arguments that section 501(c)(3) does not serve a compelling government interest or, if it is indeed compelling, that revocation of its tax exemption was not the least restrictive means of furthering that interest.

Nor does the Church succeed in its claim that the IRS has violated its First Amendment free speech rights by engaging in viewpoint discrimination. The restrictions imposed by section 501(c)(3) are viewpoint neutral; they prohibit intervention in favor of all candidates for public office by all tax-exempt organizations, regardless of candidate, party, or viewpoint. Cf. *Regan,* 461 U.S. at 550–51, 103 S.Ct. 1997 (upholding denial of tax deduction for lobbying activities, in spite of allowance of such deduction for veteran's groups).

C. Selective Prosecution (Fifth Amendment)

The Church alleges that the IRS violated the Equal Protection Clause of the Fifth Amendment by engaging in selective prosecution. In support of its claim, the Church has submitted several hundred pages of newspaper excerpts reporting political campaign activities in, or by the pastors of, other churches that have retained their tax-exempt status. These include reports of explicit endorsements of Democratic candidates by clergymen as well as many instances in which favored candidates have been invited to address congregations from the pulpit. The Church complains that despite this widespread and widely reported involvement by other churches in political campaigns, it is the only one to have ever had its tax-exempt status revoked for engaging in political activity. It attributes this alleged discrimination to the Service's political bias.

To establish selective prosecution, the Church must "prove that (1) [it] was singled out for prosecution from among others similarly situated and (2) that [the] prosecution was improperly motivated, i.e., based on race, religion or another arbitrary classification." *United*

States v. Washington, 705 F.2d 489, 494 (D.C.Cir.1983). This burden is a demanding one because "in the absence of clear evidence to the contrary, courts presume that [government prosecutors] have properly discharged their official duties." *United States v. Armstrong,* 517 U.S. 456, 464, 116 S.Ct. 1480, 134 L.Ed.2d 687 (1996) (internal quotation marks and citation omitted).

At oral argument, counsel for the IRS conceded that if some of the church-sponsored political activities cited by the Church were accurately reported, they were in violation of section 501(c)(3) and could have resulted in the revocation of those churches' tax-exempt status. But even if the Service could have revoked their tax exemptions, the Church has failed to establish selective prosecution because it has failed to demonstrate that it was similarly situated to any of those other churches. None of the reported activities involved the placement of advertisements in newspapers with nationwide circulations opposing a candidate and soliciting tax deductible contributions to defray their cost. As we have stated,

> "[i]f ... there was no one to whom defendant could be compared in order to resolve the question of [prosecutorial] selection, then it follows that defendant has failed to make out one of the elements of its case. Discrimination cannot exist in a vacuum; it can be found only in the unequal treatment of people in similar circumstances."

Attorney Gen. v. Irish People, Inc., 684 F.2d 928, 946 (D.C.Cir.1982); *see also United States v. Hastings,* 126 F.3d 310, 315 (4th Cir. 1997) ("[D]efendants are similarly situated when their circumstances present no distinguishable legitimate prosecutorial factors that might justify making different prosecutorial decisions with respect to them.") (internal quotation marks and citation omitted).

Because the Church has failed to establish that it was singled out for prosecution from among others who were similarly situated, we need not examine whether the IRS was improperly motivated in undertaking this prosecution.

III. CONCLUSION

For the foregoing reasons, we find that the revocation of the Church's tax-exempt status neither violated the Constitution nor exceeded the IRS's statutory authority. The judgment of the district court is therefore

Affirmed.

NOTES AND QUESTIONS

1.   *History of the Exemption.* As the opinion explains, churches and other charitable organizations qualify for exemptions from federal income tax, and contributors' contributions to them are tax-deductible. According

to the IRS, "All IRC section 501(c)(3) organizations, including churches and religious organizations, must abide by certain rules:

- their net earnings may not inure to any private shareholder or individual,

- they must not provide a substantial benefit to private interests,

- they must not devote a substantial part of their activities to attempting to influence legislation,

- they must not participate in, or intervene in, any political campaign on behalf of (or in opposition to) any candidate for public office, and

- the organization's purposes and activities may not be illegal or violate fundamental public policy."

See Internal Revenue Service, Tax Guide for Churches and Religious Organizations, Pub. 1828. at 5, available at http://www.irs.gov/pub/irs-pdf/p 1828.pdf. Violating the rules jeopardizes tax-exempt status.

Should the IRS have such rules for churches and other 501(c)(3) organizations? Are they a good idea, because they keep church and state from becoming too intertwined? Or do they intrude upon the independence of churches? See John Fritze, Political Gifts by Churches Break IRS Rules, Baltimore Sun, Feb. 26, 2006, at 1A ("Critics of the nonprofit tax code say it stifles the free speech of religious leaders and undermines the role churches play as advocates for their communities. Others argue that allowing congregations to become politically active could turn the collection plate into a vehicle for tax-free campaign finance.").

The Treasury Department has been debating how to limit charities' campaigning since 1919, when it distinguished between "educational" activities and "propaganda." The lobbying prohibition was added in 1934. See Samuel D. Brunson, Reigning in Charities: Using an Intermediate Penalty to Enforce the Campaigning Prohibition, 8 Pitt. Tax Rev. 125, 134 (2011). Texas Democratic Senator Lyndon Johnson sponsored the political activity limitation of section 501(c)(3) in 1954, reportedly because he was unhappy about opposition by tax-exempt groups to his re-election in Texas. Although the legislative history of the provision and Johnson's motives are unclear, Dean Cafardi argues that "[o]ne thing is rather clear, namely that although churches as 501(c)(3) organizations were caught in Johnson's net, churches were not his direct target." Nicholas P. Cafardi, Saving the Preachers: The Tax Code's Prohibition on Church Electioneering, 50 Duq. L. Rev. 503, 504–505 (2012). "The legislative history of the campaign prohibition thus appears to be a general unease with public charities being too involved in politics combined with particular animosity between powerful politicians and outspoken organizations that claimed tax exemptions as public charities." Brunson, supra, at 134.

Should the political activity prohibition be abolished for churches only or for all tax-exempt groups? Would allowing churches but not other tax-exempt groups to endorse political candidates violate the Establishment

Clause? See Cafardi, infra, 50 Duq. L. Rev. at 507–508 (giving preferential treatment to churches clearly violates Establishment Clause).

2. *Reasons for Prohibition of Political Activity.* Professor Johnny Rex Buckles explains the different rationales given for the prohibition of political campaigning in Not Even a Peep? The Regulation of Political Campaign Activity by Charities Through Federal Tax Law, 75 U. Cinn. L. Rev. 1071 (2007). The rationales include: *subsidy theory* (that the government sensibly gives a subsidy to charities); *private interest theory* (charities are entitled to an exemption only if they serve a public, not a private, interest); the *theory that charity is not political*; the *antithetical agency hypothesis* (government and charity should not overlap, and each agent serves the community separately from the other); and Buckles' own *community income theory* (some benefits are properly excluded from tax because they are appropriately attributed to the community and not to individuals).

Buckles also offers an alternative to the current prohibition on participation by charities in political campaigns. He argues that independently controlled charities should be allowed to participate in politics, while a charity that is not independently controlled should pay an excise tax. Buckles also provides proposed tax code language for this amendment. Id. at 1108–11.

Professor Brunson explains that supporters and opponents of the prohibition are "at an impasse." According to Brunson, supporters of the ban rely on four traditional arguments:

> First, government should not pay for or subsidize political activity. Second, allowing private charities to participate in political activity is inconsistent with pursuing the broad public interest that public charities are designed to promote. Third, partisan politics is, by definition, not charitable. Fourth, if the prohibition were lifted, political donors would take advantage of the double subsidy and funnel all of their political donations through public charities.

Brunson, supra, at 136–37. Opponents of the prohibition have three counter-arguments:

> First, they argue that there are constitutional problems with the current prohibition. Second, public charities' historic role has included "shaping major social movements with enormous political implications." Third, to protect themselves and their charitable interests from the vagaries of the political world, public charities need to have some input into their "governmental 'partners.'"

Id. at 145. Brunson concludes "[e]ven after the debate, there is not a clear justification for maintaining or repealing the prohibition. Id. at 137. Do you agree?

3. Do you agree with the D.C. Circuit's conclusion that Branch Ministries' free exercise was not burdened because the church may form a

501(c)(4) organization, which may in turn create a PAC that can participate in political campaigns? The 501(c)(4) organization is tax-exempt but contributions to it are not tax deductible. Should churches have to take these additional steps to make their political views known to the public? See Jerome Park Prather, Tax Exemption of American Churches and Other Nonprofits: One Election Cycle After Branch Ministries v. Rossotti, 94 Ky. L.J. 139, 158 (2005) ("this is really no choice at all"), and Randy Lee, When a King Speaks of God; When God Speaks to a King: Faith, Politics, Tax-Exempt Status, and the Constitution in the Clinton Administration, 63 Law & Contemp. Probs. 391, 393 (2000).

   4. *Penalties.* The IRS has two options in church electioneering cases. It can revoke the church's tax-exempt status or it can impose § 4955 excise taxes. Do you agree with Dean Cafardi that there needs to be some middle ground between the "nuclear option" of revocation and the "fly-swatter option" of an excise tax? What would be a good enforcement option that would keep churches from violating the tax laws? Nicholas P. Cafardi, Saving the Preachers: The Tax Code's Prohibition on Church Electioneering, 50 Duq. L. Rev. 503, 538 (2012). What do you think of Professor Brunson's suggestion that "[i]nstead of penalizing the public charity, the tax law should disallow a portion of the deduction taken by donors to the public charity that campaigned on behalf of or against any individual"? See Samuel D. Brunson, Reigning in Charities: Using an Intermediate Penalty to Enforce the Campaigning Prohibition, 8 Pitt. Tax Rev. 125, 159–60 (2011) ("In order to effectively deter both high-cost and low-cost campaigning, each donor's deduction would be reduced by the greater of (a) the percentage of the public charity's expenditures that went toward campaigning, or (b) a percentage calculated by the size of the audience toward which the political speech was directed.").

   5. What kinds of political activities may the churches undertake without running afoul of the tax code? Do you think churches may legally engage in the following conduct?

   a.   Invite all candidates for political office to address their congregation, provided there is a statement that says the views expressed are those of the candidates and that the church is not endorsing any candidate.

   b.   Distribute a list of voting records of all members of Congress on major legislative issues involving a wide range of subjects, provided the publication contains no editorial opinion and its content and structure do not imply approval or disapproval of any members or their voting records.

   c.   Sponsor a voter registration drive, provided it is done so in a neutral manner and is non-partisan.

Vaughn E. James, Reaping Where They Have Not Sowed: Have American Churches Failed to Satisfy the Requirements for the Religious Tax Exemption?, 43 Cath. Law. 29, 47 (2004) (churches may do all these things as long as they are neutral and nonpartisan). Does this list persuade you that the tax code adequately protects religious freedom?

6. *Voter Education Guides.* According to IRS rules, churches may distribute voter education guides and participate in voter registration drives. Are the following IRS illustrations about acceptable voter education guides helpful?

> Example 1: Church R distributes a voter guide prior to elections. The voter guide consists of a brief statement from the candidates on each issue made in response to a questionnaire sent to all candidates for governor of State I. The issues on the questionnaire cover a wide variety of topics and were selected by Church R based solely on their importance and interest to the electorate as a whole. Neither the questionnaire nor the voter guide, through their content or structure, indicate a bias or preference for any candidate or group of candidates. Church R is not participating or intervening in a political campaign.

> Example 2: Church S distributes a voter guide during an election campaign. The voter guide is prepared using the responses of candidates to a questionnaire sent to candidates for major public offices. Although the questionnaire covers a wide range of topics, the wording of the questions evidences a bias on certain issues. By using a questionnaire structured in this way, Church S is participating or intervening in a political campaign.

IRS, Tax Guide for Churches & Religious Organizations, Pub. 1829 (Rev. 09–2003), at 13. Would you have trouble drafting a voter guide that complies with the IRS's regulations?

7. *Ministerial Endorsements.* In Section B we discussed the different roles that ministers play in criticizing politicians and in running for office. Should clergy enjoy a First Amendment right to endorse politicians from the pulpit? What do you think of the following IRS examples for ministers under current law? Are they too restrictive of ministerial speech and free exercise?

> Example 3: Minister B is the minister of Church K and is well known in the community. Three weeks before the election, he attends a press conference at Candidate V's campaign headquarters and states that Candidate V should be reelected. Minister B does not say he is speaking on behalf of his church. His endorsement is reported on the front page of the local newspaper and he is identified in the article as the minister of Church K. Since Minister B did not make the endorsement at an official church function, in an official church publication or otherwise use the church's assets, and did not state that he was speaking as a representative of Church K, his actions did not constitute campaign intervention attributable to Church K.

> Example 4: Minister D is the minister of Church M. During regular services of Church M shortly before the election, Minister

D preached on a number of issues, including the importance of voting in the upcoming election, and concludes by stating, "It is important that you all do your duty in the election and vote for Candidate W." Since Minister D's remarks indicating support for Candidate W were made during an official church service, they constitute political campaign intervention attributable to Church M.

IRS Tax Guide, supra, at p. 8.

What should happen if Minister Z of Church Y is named in a newspaper ad, paid for by the candidate, on a list of ministers endorsing the candidate? See id. at 7 (not political endorsement because Church Y did not pay for the ad). If Minister X publishes a "My Views" column in Church W's newsletter advocating Candidate U's election? See id. at 8 (political campaign endorsement because it is published in an official church newspaper). Do you agree that the IRS's regulations are "very generous" in allowing ministers to preach? See Cafardi, infra, 50 Duq. L. Rev. at 535–37. Texas Senator Ted Cruz announced his presidential campaign at Liberty University, a church-related school. Did the announcement violate the tax code? See Americans United for Separation of Church and State, As 2016 Presidential Campaign Gets Under Way, IRS Should Act to Enforce Non-Profit "No-Politicking" Rule, Says Americans United, Mar. 26, 2015, at https://www.au.org/media/press-releases/as-2016-presidential-campaign-gets-under-way-irs-should-act-to-enforce-non. Is it significant that students were required to attend the event?

8.   *Lobbying*. According to the Code, 501(c)(3) organizations must not devote a substantial amount of their time to lobbying. Lobbying includes trying to influence legislation by Congress, state legislatures, or by public referenda and ballot initiatives, but not executive, judicial or administrative action. Churches may, however, get involved in issues of public policy in an educational manner. Is working in support of the nomination of a Supreme Court justice lobbying? See Tax Guide for Churches and Religious Organizations, Pub. 1828, at 6.

Why are such restrictions on lobbying constitutional? See Regan v. Taxation With Representation [TWR], 461 U.S. 540, 545 (1983) ("The Code does not deny TWR the right to receive deductible contributions to support its non-lobbying activity, nor does it deny TWR any independent benefit on account of its intention to lobby. Congress has merely refused to pay for the lobbying out of public monies. This Court has never held that the Court must grant a benefit such as TWR claims here to a person who wishes to exercise a constitutional right.").

After Proposition 8, banning gay marriage, passed in California, numerous Prop 8 opponents called for the revocation of the Mormons' tax-exempt status, arguing that the Church of Jesus Christ of Latter-day Saints (LDS) had lobbied for legislation in violation of the tax code. Professor Brian Galle examines the lobbying rules in connection with the LDS support for Proposition 8. Galle concludes it is uncertain that the LDS violated the lobbying rules, but that the events surrounding Proposition 8 identify a problem with the law of charities:

In particular, the Proposition 8 episode exposes a serious hole in the fabric of the federal law: the possibility that massive, multi-million dollar lobbying expenditures, large enough to swamp any opposition, may be perfectly legitimate, so long as they are undertaken by a sufficiently gigantic organization. It is hard to see a good justification for a rule that would, in effect, grant political influence only to the largest charities, but that seems to be one plausible interpretation of current law (albeit an interpretation I argue against here). Further, recent events show that the IRS so far has failed to grapple with the most important questions surrounding the rules against lobbying, such as the problem of how to value the use of mailing lists, websites, e-mail, and phone trees—tools that now are central to modern politics.

Brian D. Galle, The LDS Church, Proposition Eight, and the Federal Law of Charities, 103 Nw. U. L. Rev. Colloquy 370 (2009). Does this argument demonstrate that the lobbying prohibition needs to be abolished?

9. *Pulpit Freedom Sunday. Branch Ministries* was an unusual case because the church's tax-exempt status was revoked. Starting in 2008, preachers around the country defied the tax laws on Pulpit Freedom Sunday by intentionally endorsing candidates from the pulpit. The Alliance Defense Fund promoted the action in order to set up a constitutional challenge to the ban on endorsement of politicians by tax-exempt organizations. The pastors sent their sermons to the IRS. See Julia Duin, Churches to Defy IRS on Taxes, Wash. Times, Sept. 27, 2008. Do you agree with the following blog post's conclusions about Pulpit Sunday?

Sam Brunson, Stuck in the Middle with . . . the IRS?
The Surly Subgroup Blog, May 3, 2016.

Pity the IRS.[1] It is, right now, stuck in the middle of a battle over religion. See, churches, like other public charities, are exempt from tax under section 501(c)(3). But the exemption comes with certain limitations, including an absolute prohibition on supporting or opposing candidates for office.

This prohibition has become something of a culture wars battleground, at least with respect to churches. Some churches argue that they have a moral and religious obligation to support candidates whose actions are in line with their beliefs, or, alternatively, to oppose candidates whose actions violate their beliefs. As such, they claim this prohibition violates their Free Exercise rights, and is unconstitutional, at least as applied to churches.

The funny thing is that, as best I can tell, only one church [Branch Ministries] has ever lost its tax exemption for violating this campaigning prohibition.

---

[1] No, seriously. It's underfunded, overmandated, and underloved.

Though not for lack of trying. Over the last eight years or so, the Alliance Defending Freedom has sponsored an annual event it calls Pulpit Freedom Sunday, in which pastors preach a sermon that expressly violates the prohibition, then send a copy of their sermon to the IRS. Of the possibly thousands of churches that have participated over the years, none have lost their exemptions.

The Freedom From Religion Foundation noticed the IRS's lack of response and, in 2012, sued to compel the IRS to enforce the campaigning prohibition. In 2014, it announced that it was dismissing the case, because FFRF and the IRS had come to an agreement resolving the FFRF's concerns about the IRS's treatment of church campaigning.[2]

Not long after the FFRF suit was (at least temporarily) resolved, the ADF jumped in, filing a FOIA request for records relating to changes to its church audit procedures. The IRS (belatedly, according to ADF) produced fewer than half of the documents requested, and the requested documents were allegedly heavily redacted.[3]

I'm not interested here in opining on the constitutional validity of the campaigning prohibition, either writ large or as applied to churches. There's abundant scholarship arguing both for and against the prohibition's constitutionality. I do want to suggest, though, that the IRS has a way out of being the scapegoat-in-the-middle for these religious culture wars: it should revoke some church exemptions.

FFRF wants the IRS to enforce the provision. ADF wants to create a test case. And, frankly, I suspect a lot of churches want some kind of certainty.

I recognize that, besides being stuck in the middle, the IRS is stuck in what appears to be a no-win-situation. It has been villainized by the FFRF and its allies for not enforcing the provision. If it starts, it risks being villainized by the ADF and its allies for infringing on religious liberty. Either way, it seems to have significant downside without the possibility of upside.

All that said, by revoking the tax-exempt status of churches that violate the prohibition, it can finally put the constitutional question in front of the courts.

And, as I discuss in a recent law review article, it can do so without incurring significant enforcement costs and without being accused of

---

[2] In the original reports, it sounded like there was an actual contractual agreement between the two; I emailed the FFRF to ask if I could see it, and received a very nice email in response telling me the relevant information was here, https://ffrf.org/news/news-releases/item/16091-ffrf-sues-irs-to-enforce-church-electioneering-ban, and here,   https://ffrf.org/news/news-releases/item/21120-faq-on-ffrf-s-settlement-with-the-irs-over-electioneering-by-religious-organizations. It's interesting information (including the docket from the case!), but it doesn't lay out the terms of their agreement, if any.

[3] I said pity the IRS. And I meant it. But I didn't mean that the IRS never committed unforced errors.

being engaged in a partisan witch-hunt. And it can do so without imposing litigation costs on any church that doesn't want to bear them. How?

Over the next couple months, the IRS should announce that it will revoke the tax exemption of any church that participates in Pulpit Freedom Sunday and violates the campaigning prohibition.

The IRS should review any sermon that a church sends itself, not for content, but solely to ensure that the sermon does, in fact violate that campaigning prohibition.

The IRS should revoke the exemptions of all of the sermons it receives that do, in fact, violate the campaigning prohibition.

A little further explanation: with advance notice, any church that really doesn't want to fight this fight can avoid it by not preaching a violative sermon. Or, if it does, it can choose not to send the sermon to the IRS. And the IRS should only review sermons sent by the church itself, not sermons sent by whistleblowers. Basically, this would set up a series of test cases, and with presumably plenty of confident and willing participants, there's no need to investigate more.

This way, too, the IRS doesn't have to expend resources (initially, at least) to find churches.

It may be that the churches losing their exemptions are primarily conservative churches, supporting Ted Cruz. It could be that they're primarily liberal, supporting Bernie Sanders. But if the IRS has announced objective criteria, and only revokes the exemptions of churches that voluntarily participate, there's no good-faith way to accuse it of going after only churches with particular political ideologies.

My proposal isn't perfect, of course: even if the Supreme Court blesses the campaigning prohibition, the IRS has limited upside in revoking church exemptions: these revocations won't raise a significant amount of revenue for the government, and probably won't make the IRS more popular with the general taxpaying public.

But it will provide guidance to churches, and it will allow the IRS to focus on administering the tax law, rather than being buffeted by the religious culture wars.

NOTES AND QUESTIONS

1. *Enforce the Exemption?* About 1600 churches participated in Pulpit Freedom Sunday during 2014 alone. Is this reason to believe that Congress and the IRS should end the endorsement prohibition? Can you think of *any* reasons why the IRS should enforce the law and revoke churches' tax-exempt status? See Samuel D. Brunson, Dear IRS, It Is Time to Enforce the Campaigning Prohibition. Even Against Churches, 87 U. Colo. L. Rev. 143, 171 (2016) ("Even if the political system has remained

unaffected by church participation in politics, moreover, I argue that there are at least three compelling reasons for the enforcement of the campaigning prohibition against churches. First, the IRS should enforce the law as written. Second, Congress should be required to stand behind the law it has written. Third, enforcement would allow churches to place the constitutionality of the prohibition in front of the courts.")

What do you think the political reaction would be if the IRS started revoking churches' tax-exempt status? What do you think the Supreme Court would rule if one of these proposed cases got to the Court?

2. *Race and Religious Schools.* Like other charitable and religious organizations, private schools receive tax exemptions, and individuals obtain tax deductions for contributions to them. See 26 U.S.C. § 501(c)(3) (tax exemptions); 26 U.S.C. § 170 (tax deductions). Beginning in January 1970, the Internal Revenue Service denied exemptions and deductions to segregated schools because racial discrimination violates public policy. President Jimmy Carter's IRS enforced that policy more vigorously than his predecessors had. See Internal Revenue Service, Proposed Revenue Procedure on Private Tax-Exempt Schools, 43 Fed. Reg. 37296 (Aug. 22, 1978). Many different religious groups were furious about this new policy because of its intrusion into religious affairs.

In 1981, two religious schools challenged the 1970 policy in the Supreme Court. Bob Jones University had lost its tax-exempt status during the Ford Administration because of its ban on interracial dating. Goldsboro Christian Schools was sued for taxes during the Nixon Administration because of its racially discriminatory admissions policy. Both schools' policies were based on the Bible. In the Supreme Court, the First Amendment ruling was unanimous, with even dissenting Justice Rehnquist agreeing that the First Amendment was not infringed upon because the government's interest in preventing discrimination outweighed the schools' free exercise. The law was also "neutral" and "secular," and was not passed to prefer one religious group to another. See Bob Jones University v. United States, 461 U.S. 574 (1983).

Recall from Section A that Chief Justice John Roberts warned that *Obergefell* could lead to loss of tax exemption for religious organizations that discriminated against LGBT marriage. Would ending tax exemption for all organizations that discriminate on the basis of sexual orientation be a good use of the tax laws?

3. *The Sermons.* Some of the pastors' sermons have been posted online. See John Adkisson, Pulpit Politics: Pastors Endorse Candidates, Thumbing Noses at the IRS, U.S. News, Nov. 4, 2012, at http://usnews.nbc news.com/_news/2012/11/04/14703656-pulpit-politics-pastors-endorse-candi dates-thumbing-noses-at-the-irs. If you worked for the IRS and listened to the sermons, what would you do?

In one sermon, Wayne Gruden distinguished Party A from Party B. "Party A thinks we should apologize for America because we are primarily responsible for slavery, colonialism, and exploitation of many third-world countries. We should be ashamed of America's many faults. Party B says we should be proud of America. It's probably done more good for the world than any nation in the history of the earth. Although it has its faults, its faults are outweighed by the good it has done for the world." Id. If Rev. Gruden stopped his sermon there by talking about Parties A and B, would he be in violation of the tax code? Gruden took the next step to tell the listeners Party A was the Democratic Party and Barack Obama and Party B was the Republican Party and Mitt Romney. He then recommended "every citizen vote for Governor Romney and Republican candidates generally." Id. Should Gruden's church lose its tax-exempt status?

When Gruden spoke so positively about America, was he using the language of American civil religion, as described in Section D?

D. CIVIL RELIGION

Given the concerns about separation of church and state, religion and presidents in Section A, do you think the following addresses by the presidents make appropriate or inappropriate use of religious language?

Second Inaugural Address of Abraham Lincoln
March 4, 1865.

FELLOW-COUNTRYMEN: At this second appearing to take the oath of the Presidential office there is less occasion for an extended address than there was at the first. Then a statement, somewhat in detail, of a course to be pursued seemed fitting and proper. Now, at the expiration of four years, during which public declarations have been constantly called forth on every point and phase of the great contest which still absorbs the attention and engrosses the energies of the nation, little that is new could be presented. The progress of our arms, upon which all else chiefly depends, is as well known to the public as to myself, and it is, I trust, reasonably satisfactory and encouraging to all. With high hope for the future, no prediction in regard to it is ventured.

On the occasion corresponding to this four years ago, all thoughts were anxiously directed to an impending civil war. All dreaded it, all sought to avert it. While the inaugural address was being delivered from this place, devoted altogether to saving the Union without war, insurgent agents were in the city seeking to destroy it without war— seeking to dissolve the Union and divide effects by negotiation. Both parties deprecated war, but one of them would make war rather than let the nation survive, and the other would accept war rather than let it perish, and the war came.

One-eighth of the whole population were colored slaves, not distributed generally over the Union, but localized in the southern part of it. These slaves constituted a peculiar and powerful interest. All knew that this interest was, somehow, the cause of the war. To strengthen, perpetuate, and extend this interest was the object for which the insurgents would rend the Union even by war, while the Government claimed no right to do more than to restrict the territorial enlargement of it. Neither party expected for the war the magnitude or the duration which it has already attained. Neither anticipated that the cause of the conflict might cease with or even before the conflict itself should cease. Each looked for an easier triumph, and a result less fundamental and astounding. Both read the same Bible and pray to the same God, and each invokes His aid against the other. It may seem strange that any men should dare to ask a just God's assistance in wringing their bread from the sweat of other men's faces, but let us judge not, that we be not judged. The prayers of both could not be answered. That of neither has been answered fully. The Almighty has His own purposes. "Woe unto the world because of offenses; for it must needs be that offenses come, but woe to that man by whom the offense cometh." If we shall suppose that American slavery is one of those offenses which, in the providence of God, must needs come, but which, having continued through His appointed time, He now wills to remove, and that He gives to both North and South this terrible war as the woe due to those by whom the offense came, shall we discern therein any departure from those divine attributes which the believers in a living God always ascribe to Him? Fondly do we hope, fervently do we pray, that this mighty scourge of war may speedily pass away. Yet, if God wills that it continue until all the wealth piled by the bondsman's two hundred and fifty years of unrequited toil shall be sunk, and until every drop of blood drawn with the lash shall be paid by another drawn with the sword, as was said three thousand years ago, so still it must be said "the judgments of the Lord are true and righteous altogether."

With malice toward none, with charity for all, with firmness in the fight as God gives us to see the right, let us strive on to finish the work we are in, to bind up the nation's wounds, to care for him who shall have borne the battle and for his widow and his orphan, to do all which may achieve and cherish a just and lasting peace among ourselves and with all nations.

NOTES AND QUESTIONS

1. *President and Theologian Abraham Lincoln.* According to Professor Noah Feldman,

> It is difficult to find even a single government official of importance in the last several centuries who justified or explained his performance of public duties primarily in terms of private religious belief. That is not to deny a rich tradition of theological interpretation of America and its place in the world. Lincoln's Second Inaugural Address not only acknowledged that we must follow the right "as God gives us to see the right," it also depicted the Civil War itself as divine punishment for the original sin of

African slavery. Yet Lincoln was not suggesting that the Bible—
read, as he bravely pointed out, by both North and South—gave
him, or us, the answers to our constitutional problems. He was
saying, rather, that in preserving the Union he was acting
according to his constitutional conscience—so help him God.

Noah Feldman, Not in the Heavens, The New Republic, Feb. 20, 2006, at
21. Do you agree with Feldman's interpretation or do you think that
Lincoln was relying on theological arguments in his inaugural address?

Did Abraham Lincoln use too much religious language in this
inaugural address? Did he violate the Kennedy standard of separation of
church and state? Many scholars have debated the influence of Lincoln's
theology on his presidency. Can you tell from the Second Inaugural Address
what type of theology Lincoln adopted? Did Lincoln base his actions on the
belief that he knew the will of God and was enforcing it? Does the address
reflect "an altogether realistic faith that did not put its confidence in man's
ability, through war, to end conflict. It placed its hopes in God alone, as the
task of conversion continued"? Or was the Second Inaugural "very much
like a New England preacher's jeremiad" in which preachers scold sinners
and urge them to return to God? Did Lincoln believe that "God was capable
of bringing good out of difficult situations"? Did Lincoln think that the Civil
War was "divine punishment for the national sin of slavery"? Did he use
religious language to "move the people to their first duty of looking to God
rather than themselves in moments of crisis," or to tell them to "stop
looking to themselves and their own righteousness but rather turn to God"?
Or did he believe "God would heal the land no matter what the people did"?
See Hans Morgenthau & David Hein, in Kenneth W. Thompson, ed.,
Essays on Lincoln's Faith and Politics (1983) (reporting and refuting
different interpretations of Lincoln's theology). Are such theological debates
about Lincoln's beliefs reason that presidents should not use theological
language?

According to Morgenthau and Hein,

The grounds on which [Lincoln] concluded that slavery was
wrong, for example, were various: 1) it was a contradiction of
God's laws in that it robbed a man of what was rightfully his and
failed to treat him according to the prescriptions of Christian
charity and the Golden Rule, 2) it threatened the survival of
democracy inasmuch as governments derive their power from the
consent of the governed and slaves had given no consent to their
condition, 3) it constituted a betrayal of the principles embodied in
the Declaration of Independence: equality, liberty, the right of all
to rise and better themselves, and 4) it might spread and
eventually cover the whole country, thereby forcing white laborers
to compete with unpaid black workers.

Id. at 151. Does it matter which reason was the basis for Lincoln's
opposition to slavery? Are any of Lincoln's reasons more compelling than
others?

2. Is the following presidential language more or less acceptable than Lincoln's?

a. In response to the bombing of a government building in Oklahoma City, Oklahoma:

To all my fellow Americans beyond this hall, I say, one thing we owe those who have sacrificed is the duty to purge ourselves of the dark forces which gave rise to this evil. They are forces that threaten our common peace, our freedom, our way of life.

Let us teach our children that the God of comfort is also the God of righteousness. Those who trouble their own house will inherit the wind. Justice will prevail.

Let us let our own children know that we will stand against the forces of fear. When there is talk of hatred, let us stand up and talk against it. When there is talk of violence, let us stand up and talk against it. In the face of death, let us honor life. As St. Paul admonished us, let us not be overcome by evil, but overcome evil with good.

Yesterday Hillary and I had the privilege of speaking with some children of other federal employees—children like those who were lost here. And one little girl said something we will never forget. She said, we should all plant a tree in memory of the children. So this morning before we got on the plane to come here, at the White House, we planted a tree in honor of the children of Oklahoma.

It was a dogwood with its wonderful spring flower and its deep, enduring roots. It embodies the lesson of the Psalms—that the life of a good person is like a tree whose leaf does not wither.

My fellow Americans, a tree takes a long time to grow, and wounds take a long time to heal. But we must begin. Those who are lost now belong to God. Some day we will be with them. But until that happens, their legacy must be our lives.

Thank you all, and God bless you.

William Jefferson Clinton, President of the United States, Remarks During "A Time of Healing" Prayer Service at Oklahoma State Fair Arena, Oklahoma City, Oklahoma (Apr. 23, 1995).

b. In response to the attack on Pearl Harbor, Hawaii:

Yesterday, December 7th, 1941—a date which will live in infamy—the United States of America was suddenly and deliberately attacked by naval and air forces of the Empire of Japan. As commander in chief of the Army and Navy, I have directed that all measures be taken for our defense. But always will our whole nation remember the character of the onslaught against us. No matter how long it may take us to overcome this premeditated invasion, the American people in their righteous might will win through to absolute victory.

I believe that I interpret the will of the Congress and of the people when I assert that we will not only defend ourselves to the uttermost, but will make it very certain that this form of treachery shall never again endanger us. Hostilities exist. There is no blinking at the fact that our people, our territory, and our interests are in grave danger.

With confidence in our armed forces, with the unbounding determination of our people, we will gain the inevitable triumph—so help us God.

Franklin Delano Roosevelt, President of the United States, Pearl Harbor Address to the Nation (Dec. 8, 1941).

c.   In response to the terrorist attacks on the World Trade Center and Pentagon, September 11, 2001:

Our purpose as a nation is firm. Yet our wounds as a people are recent and unhealed, and lead us to pray. In many of our prayers this week, there is a searching, and an honesty. At St. Patrick's Cathedral in New York on Tuesday, a woman said, "I prayed to God to give us a sign that He is still here." Others have prayed for the same, searching hospital to hospital, carrying pictures of those still missing.

God's signs are not always the ones we look for. We learn in tragedy that his purposes are not always our own. Yet the prayers of private suffering, whether in our homes or in this great cathedral, are known and heard, and understood.

There are prayers that help us last through the day, or endure the night. There are prayers of friends and strangers, that give us strength for the journey. And there are prayers that yield our will to a will greater than our own.

This world He created is of moral design. Grief and tragedy and hatred are only for a time. Goodness, remembrance, and love have no end. And the Lord of life holds all who die, and all who mourn.

It is said that adversity introduces us to ourselves. This is true of a nation as well. In this trial, we have been reminded, and the world has seen, that our fellow Americans are generous and kind, resourceful and brave. We see our national character in rescuers working past exhaustion; in long lines of blood donors; in thousands of citizens who have asked to work and serve in any way possible.

In these acts, and in many others, Americans showed a deep commitment to one another, and an abiding love for our country. Today, we feel what Franklin Roosevelt called the warm courage of national unity. This is a unity of every faith, and every background.

It has joined together political parties in both houses of Congress. It is evident in services of prayer and candlelight vigils, and American flags, which are displayed in pride, and wave in defiance.

Our unity is a kinship of grief, and a steadfast resolve to prevail against our enemies. And this unity against terror is not extending across the world.

America is a nation full of good fortune, with so much to be grateful for. But we are not spared from suffering. In every generation, the world has produced enemies of human freedom. They have attacked America, because we are freedom's home and defender. And the commitment of our fathers is now the calling of our time.

George W. Bush, President of the United States, Remarks at National Day of Prayer and Remembrance, The National Cathedral, Washington, D.C. (Sept. 14, 2001).

Is it significant that President Bush gave his remarks during a prayer service at National Cathedral and that President Roosevelt's comments occurred during a radio address to the American people?

d.   At a memorial service for military personnel shot by a fellow soldier at Fort Hood, Texas:

It may be hard to comprehend the twisted logic that led to this tragedy. But this much we do know—no faith justifies these murderous and craven acts; no just and loving God looks upon them with favor. For what he has done, we know that the killer will be met with justice—in this world, and the next. . . .

We are a nation that endures because of the courage of those who defend it. We saw that valor in those who braved bullets here at Fort Hood, just as surely as we see it in those who signed up knowing that they would serve in harm's way.

We are a nation of laws whose commitment to justice is so enduring that we would treat a gunman and give him due process, just as surely as we will see that he pays for his crimes.

We're a nation that guarantees the freedom to worship as one chooses. And instead of claiming God for our side, we remember Lincoln's words, and always pray to be on the side of God.

Barack H. Obama, President of the United States, Remarks by the President at Memorial Service at Fort Hood (Nov. 10, 2009).

3.   Does it matter how frequently presidents refer to God? George W. Bush mentioned God in his major addresses more frequently than any president since Franklin Roosevelt. (Bush received the highest score (5.8) in contrast to Ronald Reagan (5.3), Franklin Roosevelt (1.8), and Lyndon Johnson (1.5).) Bush invoked God twenty-four times in the inaugural and State of the Union addresses of his first term, and eleven times in those two addresses in 2005, the first year of his second term. David Domke & Kevin Coe, Petitioner or Prophet?, Sightings, May 26, 2005.

4.   *Other Inaugural Addresses.*

a.   In matters of religion I have considered that its free exercise is placed by the Constitution independent of the powers of the General Government. I have therefore undertaken on no occasion to prescribe the religious exercises suited to it, but have left them, as the Constitution found them, under the direction and discipline of the church or state authorities acknowledged by the several religious societies.

Thomas Jefferson, President of the United States, Second Inaugural Address (Mar. 4, 1805).

b.   And let us reflect that, having banished from our land that religious intolerance under which mankind so long bled and suffered, we have yet gained little if we countenance a political intolerance as despotic, as wicked, and capable of as bitter and bloody persecutions.

Let us, then, with courage and confidence pursue our own Federal and Republican principles, our attachment to union and representative government. Kindly separated by nature and a wide ocean from the exterminating havoc of one quarter of the globe; too high-minded to endure the degradations of the others; possessing a chosen country, with room enough for our descendants to the thousandth and thousandth generation; entertaining a due sense of our equal right to the use of our own faculties, to the acquisitions of our own industry, to honor and confidence from our fellow-citizens, resulting not from birth, but from our actions and their sense of them; enlightened by a benign religion, professed, indeed, and practiced in various forms, yet all of them inculcating honesty, truth, temperance, gratitude, and the love of man; acknowledging and adoring an overruling Providence, which by all its dispensations proves that it delights in the happiness of man here and his greater happiness hereafter—with all these blessings, what more is necessary to make us a happy and a prosperous people?

Still one thing more, fellow-citizens—a wise and frugal Government, which shall restrain men from injuring one another, shall leave them otherwise free to regulate their own pursuits of industry and improvement, and shall not take from the mouth of labor the bread it has earned. This is the sum of good government, and this is necessary to close the circle of our felicities.

   And may that Infinite Power which rules the destinies of the universe lead our councils to what is best, and give them a favorable issue for your peace and prosperity.

Thomas Jefferson, President of the United States, First Inaugural Address (Mar. 4, 1801).

c.   And so, my fellow Americans, as we stand at the edge of the twenty-first century, let us begin anew with energy and hope, with faith and discipline. And let us work until our work is done. The Scripture says, "And let us not be weary in well doing: for in due season we shall reap, if we faint not." From this joyful mountaintop of celebration we hear a call to service in the valley. We have heard the trumpets. We have changed the guard. And now, each in our own way and with God's help, we must answer the call. Thank you, and God bless you all.

William Jefferson Clinton, President of the United States, First Inaugural Address (Jan. 21, 1993).

Are the preceding speeches all examples of the "civil religion" described by Professor Robert Bellah in the following article? What is the difference between civil religion and the president's religion? What is the difference between Christianity and American civil religion? Is this notion of American civil religion inclusive of the majority of faith traditions in the United States?

Robert N. Bellah, Civil Religion in America
96 Dædalus 1–21 (Winter 1967).

   While some have argued that Christianity is the national faith, and others that church and synagogue celebrate only the generalized religion of "the American Way of Life," few have realized that there actually exists alongside of and rather clearly differentiated from the churches an elaborate and well-institutionalized civil religion in America. This article argues not only that there is such a thing, but also that this religion—or perhaps better, this religious dimension—has its own seriousness and integrity and requires the same care in understanding that any other religion does.[1]

---

[1]   Why something so obvious should have escaped serious analytical attention is itself an interesting problem. Part of the reason is probably the controversial nature of the subject. From the earliest years of the nineteenth century, conservative religious and political groups have argued that Christianity is, in fact, the national religion. Some of them from time to time and as recently as the 1950s proposed constitutional amendments that would explicitly recognize the sovereignty of Christ. In defending the doctrine of separation of church and state, opponents of such groups have denied that the national polity has, intrinsically, anything to do with religion at all. The moderates on this issue have insisted that the

The Kennedy Inaugural

John F. Kennedy's inaugural address of 20 January 1961, serves as an example and a clue with which to introduce this complex subject. That address began:

> We observe today not a victory of party but a celebration of freedom—symbolizing an end as well as a beginning—signifying renewal as well as change. For I have sworn before you and Almighty God the same solemn oath our forebears prescribed nearly a century and three quarters ago.
>
> The world is very different now. For man holds in his mortal hands the power to abolish all forms of human poverty and to abolish all forms of human life. And yet the same revolutionary beliefs for which our forbears fought are still at issue around the globe—the belief that the rights of man come not from the generosity of the state but from the hand of God.

And it concluded:

> Finally, whether you are citizens of America or of the world, ask of us the same high standards of strength and sacrifice that we shall ask of you. With a good conscience our only sure reward, with history the final judge of our deeds, let us go forth to lead the land we love, asking His blessing and His help, but knowing that here on earth God's work must truly be our own.

These are the three places in this brief address in which Kennedy mentioned the name of God. If we could understand why he mentioned God, the way in which he did, and what he meant to say in those three references, we would understand much about American civil religion. But this is not a simple or obvious task, and American students of religion would probably differ widely in their interpretation of these passages.

Let us consider first the placing of the three references. They occur in the two opening paragraphs and in the closing paragraph, thus providing a sort of frame for more concrete remarks that form the middle part of the speech. Looking beyond this particular speech, we would find that similar references to God are almost invariably to be found in the pronouncements of American presidents on solemn occasions, though usually not in the working messages that the President sends to Congress on various concrete issues. How, then, are we to interpret this placing of references to God?

American state has taken a permissive and indeed supportive attitude toward religious groups (tax exemptions, et cetera), thus favoring religion but still missing the positive institutionalization with which I am concerned. But part of the reason this issue has been left in obscurity is certainly due to the peculiarly Western concept of "religion" as denoting a single type of collectivity of which an individual can be a member of one and only one at a time. The Durkheimian notion that every group has a religious dimension, which would be seen as obvious in southern or eastern Asia, is foreign to us. This obscures the recognition of such dimensions in our society.

It might be argued that the passages quoted reveal the essentially irrelevant role of religion in the very secular society that is America. The placing of the references in this speech as well as in public life generally indicates that religion "has only a ceremonial significance"; it gets only a sentimental nod that serves largely to placate the more unenlightened members of the community before a discussion of the really serious business with which religion has nothing whatever to do. A cynical observer might even say that an American President has to mention God or risk losing votes. A semblance of piety is merely one of the unwritten qualifications for the office, a bit more traditional than but not essentially different from the present-day requirement of a pleasing television personality.

But we know enough about the function of ceremonial and ritual in various societies to make us suspicious of dismissing something as unimportant because it is "only a ritual." What people say on solemn occasions need not be taken at face value, but it is often indicative of deep-seated values and commitments that are not made explicit in the course of everyday life. Following this line of argument, it is worth considering whether the very special placing of the references to God in Kennedy's address may not reveal something rather important and serious about religion in American life.

It might be countered that the very way in which Kennedy made his references reveals the essentially vestigial place of religion today. He did not refer to any religion in particular. He did not refer to Jesus Christ, or to Moses, or to the Christian church; certainly he did not refer to the Catholic Church. In fact, his only reference was to the concept of God, a word that almost all Americans can accept but that means so many different things to so many different people that it is almost an empty sign. Is this not just another indication that in America religion is considered vaguely to be a good thing, but that people care so little about it that it has lost any content whatever? Isn't Dwight Eisenhower reported to have said "Our government makes no sense unless it is founded in a deeply felt religious faith—and I don't care what it is,"[2] and isn't that a complete negation of any real religion?

These questions are worth pursuing because they raise the issue of how civil religion relates to the political society on the one hand and to private religious organization on the other. President Kennedy was a Christian, more specifically a Catholic Christian. Thus his general references to God do not mean that he lacked a specific religious commitment. But why, then, did he not include some remark to the effect that Christ is the Lord of the world or some indication of respect for the Catholic Church? He did not because these are matters of his own private religious belief and of his own particular church; they are

---

[2] Dwight D. Eisenhower, in Will Herberg, Protestant-Catholic-Jew (Garden City, N.Y.: Doubleday & Co., 1955), p. 97.

not matters relevant in any direct way to the conduct of his public office. Others with different religious views and commitments to different churches or denominations are equally qualified participants in the political process. The principle of separation of church and state guarantees the freedom of religious belief and association, but at the same time clearly segregates the religious sphere, which is considered to be essentially private, from the political one.

Considering the separation of church and state, how is a president justified in using the word *God* at all? The answer is that the separation of church and state has not denied the political realm a religious dimension. Although matters of personal religious belief, worship, and association are considered to be strictly private affairs, there are, at the same time, certain common elements of religious orientation that the great majority of Americans share. These have played a crucial role in the development of American institutions and still provide a religious dimension for the whole fabric of American life, including the political sphere. This public religious dimension is expressed in a set of beliefs, symbols, and rituals that I am calling American civil religion. The inauguration of a president is an important ceremonial event in this religion. It reaffirms, among other things, the religious legitimation of the highest political authority. . . .

. . . [Kennedy's] whole address can be understood as only the most recent statement of a theme that lies very deep in the American tradition, namely the obligation, both collective and individual, to carry out God's will on earth. This was the motivating spirit of those who founded America, and it has been present in every generation since. Just below the surface throughout Kennedy's inaugural address, it becomes explicit in the closing statement that God's work must be our own. That this very activist and noncontemplative conception of the fundamental religious obligation, which has been historically associated with the Protestant position, should be enunciated so clearly in the first major statement of the first Catholic president seems to underline how deeply established it is in the American outlook. Let us now consider the form and history of the civil religious tradition in which Kennedy was speaking.

The Idea of a Civil Religion

. . . The words and acts of the founding fathers, especially the first few presidents, shaped the form and tone of the civil religion as it has been maintained ever since. Though much is selectively derived from Christianity, this religion is clearly not itself Christianity. For one thing, neither Washington nor Adams nor Jefferson mentions Christ in his inaugural address; nor do any of the subsequent presidents, although not one of them fails to mention God.[3] The God of the civil

---

[3] God is mentioned or referred to in all inaugural addresses but Washington's second, which is a very brief (two paragraphs) and perfunctory acknowledgement. It is not without

religion is not only rather "unitarian," he is also on the austere side, much more related to order, law, and right than to salvation and love. Even though he is somewhat deist in cast, he is by no means simply a watchmaker God. He is actively interested and involved in history, with a special concern for America. Here the analogy has much less to do with natural law than with ancient Israel; the equation of America with Israel in the idea of the "American Israel" is not infrequent. What was implicit in the words of Washington already quoted becomes explicit in Jefferson's second inaugural when he said: "I shall need, too, the favor of that Being in whose hands we are, who led our fathers, as Israel of old, from their native land and planted them in a country flowing with all the necessaries and comforts of life." Europe is Egypt; America, the promised land. God has led his people to establish a new sort of social order that shall be a light unto all the nations. . . .

What we have, then, from the earliest years of the republic is a collection of beliefs, symbols, and rituals with respect to sacred things and institutionalized in a collectivity. This religion—there seems no other word for it—while not antithetical to and indeed sharing much in common with Christianity, was neither sectarian nor in any specific sense Christian. At a time when the society was overwhelmingly Christian, it seems unlikely that this lack of Christian reference was meant to spare the feelings of the tiny non-Christian minority. Rather, the civil religion expressed what those who set the precedents felt was appropriate under the circumstances. It reflected their private as well as public views. Nor was the civil religion simply "religion in general." While generality was undoubtedly seen as a virtue by some, . . . the civil religion was specific enough when it came to the topic of America. Precisely because of this specificity, the civil religion was saved from empty formalism and served as a genuine vehicle of national religious self-understanding.

But the civil religion was not, in the minds of Franklin, Washington, Jefferson, or other leaders, with the exception of a few radicals like Tom Paine, ever felt to be a substitute for Christianity. There was an implicit but quite clear division of function between the civil religion and Christianity. Under the doctrine of religious liberty, an exceptionally wide sphere of personal piety and voluntary social action was left to the churches. But the churches were neither to control

---

interest that the actual word "God" does not appear until Monroe's second inaugural, March 5, 1821. In his first inaugural, Washington refers to God as "that Almighty Being who rules the universe," "Great Author of every public and private good," "Invisible Hand," and "benign Parent of the Human Race." John Adams refers to God as "Providence," "Being who is supreme over all," "Patron of Order," "Fountain of Justice," and "Protector in all ages of the world of virtuous liberty." Jefferson speaks of "that Infinite Power which rules the destinies of the universe," and "that Being in whose hands we are." Madison speaks of "that Almighty Being whose power regulates the destiny of nations," and "Heaven." Monroe uses "Providence" and "the Almighty" in his first inaugural and finally "Almighty God" in his second. See *Inaugural Addresses of the Presidents of the United States from George Washington 1789 to Harry S. Truman 1949*, 82d Congress, 2d Session, House Document No. 540, 1952.

the state nor to be controlled by it. The national magistrate, whatever his private religious views, operates under the rubrics of the civil religion as long as he is in his official capacity, as we have already seen in the case of Kennedy. This accommodation was undoubtedly the product of a particular historical moment and of a cultural background dominated by Protestantism of several varieties and by the Enlightenment, but it has survived despite subsequent changes in the cultural and religious climate. . . .

Behind the civil religion at every point lie Biblical archetypes: Exodus, Chosen People, Promised Land, New Jerusalem, Sacrificial Death and Rebirth. But it is also genuinely American and genuinely new. It has its own prophets and its own martyrs, its own sacred events and sacred places, its own solemn rituals and symbols. It is concerned that America be a society as perfectly in accord with the will of God as men can make it, and a light to all the nations.

It has often been used and is being used today as a cloak for petty interests and ugly passions. It is in need—as is any living faith—of continual reformation, of being measured by universal standards. But it is not evident that it is incapable of growth and new insight.

It does not make any decision for us. It does not remove us from moral ambiguity, from being, in Lincoln's fine phrase, an "almost chosen people." But it is a heritage of moral and religious experience from which we still have much to learn as we formulate the decisions that lie ahead.

NOTES AND QUESTIONS

1. *Civil Religion.* How does Professor Bellah define civil religion? Would he agree with the following definitions? Civil religion is "the collection of beliefs, values, rites, ceremonies, and symbols which together give sacred meaning to the ongoing political life of the community and provide it with an overarching sense of unity above and beyond all internal conflicts and differences." Richard V. Pierard & Robert D. Linder, Civil Religion and the Presidency 20, 23 (1988). "At the core of the rich and subtle concept of civil religion is the idea that a nation tries to understand its historical experience and national purpose in religious terms." It is "an attempt by citizens to imbue their nation with a transcendent value." Kenneth D. Wald, Religion and Politics in the United States 55 (2003). Do these definitions clarify what civil religion is?

According to sociologist Will Herberg, Americans of different religious faiths find a "common faith" in the "American Way of Life," which is, *inter alia*, individualistic, dynamic and pragmatic; recognizes the supreme value and dignity of the individual; honors incessant activity, self-reliance, merit, character and "deeds not creeds"; and is humanitarian, optimistic, generous and idealistic. Will Herberg, Protestant Catholic Jew: An Essay in American Religious Sociology 75–80 (1955). Do you agree that civil religion or the "American Way of Life" allows Americans to transcend their religious differences in order to find a common faith? See Kenneth D. Wald, Religion and Politics in the United States 56 (2003). Or did it work when most Americans were monotheistic but now fails because the United States is so religiously diverse? See Andrew Koppelman, The New American Civil Religion: Lessons for Italy, 41 Geo. Wash. Int'l L. Rev. 861 (2010).

Professor Bellah later wrote that his essay "was not intended to celebrate the civil religion but to describe it and to see if it had resources for the work of national self-criticism." Robert Bellah, The Robert Bellah Reader (2006). Eventually Bellah stopped using the term because he "grew tired of arguing against those for whom civil religion means the idolatrous worship of the state, still the commonest meaning of the term." Robert Bellah, Comment, 50:2 Sociological Analysis 147 (1989). How can civil religion become a tool for criticism of the state rather than a celebration of the state?

In pre-World War II Japan, Shrine Shinto, Japan's indigenous religion, was transformed into the civil religion of State Shinto by the Japanese government. State Shinto promoted Japanese nationalism and recognized the Emperor of Japan as a deity. Shinto shrines across Japan deified Japanese soldiers and enshrined their remains. See Brent T. White, Reexamining Separation: The Construction of Separation of Religion and State in Post-War Japan, 22 UCLA Pac. Basin L.J. 29 (2004). After Japan's defeat in World War II, Japan adopted a new constitution that mandated separation of church and state. Nonetheless, the Japanese Supreme Court upheld the actions of the City of Tsu in paying priests to conduct a full Shinto ceremony at the ground-breaking of a new gymnasium. The Court also dismissed legal challenges to the attendance of Japanese governors at Daijosai, the Shinto ceremony enthroning the new emperor. Daijosai includes thanks to ancestors and gods in heaven and follows exact Shinto ritual. See Shigenori Matsui, Japan: The Supreme Court and the Separation of Church and State, 2 Int'l J. Const. L. 534 (2004). The Japanese Supreme Court relies on *Lemon* and other American Establishment Clause precedents in its rulings about church and state. Is Shinto the equivalent of American civil religion? Or is Shinto a religion? In the United States, the practice of Shinto was banned in the Japanese internment camps. See Kolleen Ostgaard et al., The Japanese-American Internment During WWII: A Discussion of Civil Liberties Then and Now 30 (2000). Was this an infringement on religious liberty, or was it acceptable because State Shinto was a civil religion?

2. *Constitutional Faith.* Is the Constitution part of American civil religion? See Sanford Levinson, Constitutional Faith 11 (1988) (" 'The Flag, the Declaration, the Constitution'—these, according to [Irving] Kristol, 'constitute the holy trinity of what Tocqueville called the American "civil religion." ' "). What does it mean to have "constitutional faith"? Is it different from religious faith? See id. at 4 (constitutional faith is "wholehearted attachment to the Constitution as the center of one's (and ultimately the nation's) political life."). Do you agree with Texas Representative Barbara Jordan, who, during the impeachment proceedings

against President Richard Nixon, stated that her "faith in the Constitution is whole. It is complete. It is total."? Id. at 15. Or is it better for citizens to have irreverence toward the Constitution instead of faith, so that it not "ossify" as traditional religion ossifies? See id. at 10. Is the Constitution, like civil religion, a source of national unity or of division? See id. at 17 ("[T]here is a double message contained within the analogy of the Constitution to a sacred text or the Supreme Court to a holy institution. The first, emphasizing unity and integration, is the one with which we tend to be most familiar. I propose here, however, to examine the alternative message, which is the potential of a written constitution to serve as the source of fragmentation and *dis*-integration."). Or is constitutional faith dangerous to American society, perhaps just as established religion is? See David E. Pozen, Constitutional Bad Faith, 129 Harv. L. Rev. 885, 943 (2016) ("The discursive demands of constitutional faith breed an absolutist rhetoric about constitutional compliance and commitment, which in turn breeds cynicism and distrust about that same rhetoric and the practice of constitutional law. The public sphere comes to be seen as a realm of posturing and sophistry; whatever constitutional scruples a politician might have must be communicated, if at all, through "private discourse.").

3.   *Ceremonial Deism.* If every religion has rituals, what are the rituals of American civil religion? See Pierard & Linder, supra ("In American political life, examples of civil religion include inaugural prayers, State of the Union addresses, and presidential proclamations of Thanksgiving, Christmas and National Days of Prayer. Moreover, Congress opens with a chaplain's prayer, 'In God We Trust' appears on coins, 'under God' is recited in the Pledge of Allegiance, and 'so help me God' concludes the presidential oath gof office, even though those four words are absent from the text of the Constitution.").

What is the difference between civil religion and "ceremonial deism"? A simple definition of ceremonial deism is "expressions of and to God in ceremonial, as opposed to theological, settings." Steven B. Epstein, Rethinking the Constitutionality of Ceremonial Deism, 96 Colum. L. Rev. 2083, 2091 (1996). Relying on Supreme Court precedents (many of which we read about in Chapter 3), however, Epstein developed a more detailed definition of ceremonial deism:

> the Supreme Court has utilized the concept of ceremonial deism to immunize a certain class of activities from Establishment Clause scrutiny. This class of activities seems to have or is perceived to have certain defining characteristics supporting a definition of ceremonial deism that would include all practices involving: 1) actual, symbolic, or ritualistic; 2) prayer, invocation, benediction, supplication, appeal, reverent reference to, or embrace of, a general or particular deity; 3) created, delivered, sponsored, or encouraged by government officials; 4) during governmental functions or ceremonies, in the form of patriotic expressions, or associated with holiday observances; 5) which, in and of themselves, are unlikely to indoctrinate or proselytize their

audience; 6) which are not specifically designed to accommodate the free religious exercise of a particular group of citizens; and 7) which, as of this date, are deeply rooted in the nation's history and traditions.

Practices which fit this definition can be divided into two categories, the first of which I label "core" ceremonial deism, and the second, "fringe" ceremonial deism. "Core" ceremonial deism includes practices which have been noncontroversial, have resulted in very little litigation, and have never been held unconstitutional by any court. . . . The bulk of the practices referred to in the Supreme Court opinions discussed above fall into this category, including: (1) legislative prayers and prayer rooms; (2) prayers at presidential inaugurations; (3) presidential addresses invoking the name of God; (4) the invocation "God save the United States and this Honorable Court" prior to judicial proceedings; (5) oaths of public officers, court witnesses, and jurors and the use of the Bible to administer such oaths; (6) the use of "in the year of our Lord" to date public documents; (7) the Thanksgiving and Christmas holidays; (8) the National Day of Prayer; (9) the addition of the words "under God" to the Pledge of Allegiance*; and (10) the national motto "In God We Trust." I classify other practices that fit this definition as "fringe" ceremonial deism. Compared to practices which constitute "core" ceremonial deism, these have been more controversial and have resulted in significantly more litigation and occasional findings of unconstitutionality. Fringe ceremonial deism [includes]: (1) commencement prayers; (2) governmental displays of nativity scenes; (3) religious symbols on government property or embedded in government seals; and (4) the public holiday of Good Friday.

Id. at 2094–96. Should any of the core or fringe ceremonial deism practices be held unconstitutional? Could civil religion be declared unconstitutional?

The Ninth Circuit relied on a 1970 circuit precedent to reject Michael Newdow's argument that the "In God We Trust" language on coins is unconstitutional. "Its use is of a patriotic or ceremonial character and bears no true resemblance to a governmental sponsorship of a religious exercise." Newdow v. Lefevre, 598 F.3d 638, 644 (9th Cir. 2010), cert. denied, 131 S.Ct. 1612 (2011).

Should the practices of ceremonial deism described in this note be ruled unconstitutional because they exclude nonbelievers from participation in American rituals? Does ceremonial deism confirm stereotypes of nonbelievers as immoral and unpatriotic? See Caroline Mala Corbin, Nonbelievers and Government Speech, 97 Iowa L. Rev. 347 (2012). Are all the practices listed in this note offensive to nonbelievers? As you learned in Chapters 2 and 3, the endorsement test finds an Establishment

---

* Ed.'s Note: After this article was published, the Ninth Circuit declared this language unconstitutional in Newdow, 328 F.3d 466 (9th Cir. 2003), but the Supreme Court ruled that Newdow did not have standing and the pledge was left intact. 542 U.S. 1, 17–18 (2004).

Clause violation if a reasonable observer would believe that the government endorsed religion. Instead of asking what a reasonable observer would conclude, what happens to ceremonial deism when viewed from the perspective of a "reasonable religious outsider"? See Caroline Mala Corbin, Ceremonial Deism and the Reasonable Religious Outsider, 57 UCLA L. Rev. 1545 (2010). Do you agree that "the argument that ceremonial deism merely recognizes the important role that God plays for the nation's people reveals the unstated norm in assuming that God is significant to all Americans"? Id. at 1590.

Do you agree with Professor Hill that courts should adopt a rebuttable presumption of continuing religious meaning in ceremonial deism cases? How would the government overcome the presumption? See B. Jessie Hill, Of Christmas Trees and Corpus Christi: Ceremonial Deism and Change in Meaning Over Time, 59 Duke L. J. 705, 755 (2010). Could the government, for example, rebut the presumption that Corpus Christi, St. Louis, San Francisco and Los Angeles are religious? See id. at 764 (yes). That "under God" and "In God We Trust" are religious? See id. at 765–66 (no). That A.D., meaning Anno Domini, "In the Year of the Lord," is religious? See id. at 767–68 (possibly).

The Texas Attorney General and Governor agreed that state police cars may display the motto "In God We Trust" and include crosses displayed on the car's back window. Is there religious meaning to the motto and the cross in these circumstances? Are these practices acceptable ceremonial deism or unacceptable endorsement of religion? See Bobby Blanchard, Gov. Greg Abbott Says Crosses are OK on Law Enforcement Patrol Vehicles, Too, Dallas Morning News Blogs, Feb. 5, 2016.

4. *Presidential Practice.* The president is the "foremost representative of civil religion in America." Richard V. Pierard & Robert D. Linder, Civil Religion and the Presidency 23 (1988). Does Bellah's theory of civil religion give you a new appreciation of the presidential speeches read in this chapter?

According to Article II of the U.S. Constitution, the president swears or affirms that "I will faithfully execute the Office of President of the United States, and will to the best of my Ability, preserve, protect and defend the Constitution of the United States." Professor Amar describes these words as "wholly secular." Akhil Amar, America's Constitution: A Biography 178 (2005). Nonetheless, at the first inauguration, George Washington added the words "so help me God" to the oath's end, and every president since Washington has sworn to preserve, protect and defend the Constitution "so help me God." Paul F. Boller, Jr., Presidential Inaugurations 153 (2001). Does the use of the "so help me God" language violate the Establishment Clause? Should future presidents be discouraged from including these four words in the oath of office? Michael Newdow filed a lawsuit seeking to enjoin the 2009 presidential inaugural benedictions and invocations, as well as Chief Justice John Roberts' administration of the oath of office if it included the words "so help me God." The challenge over the phrase "so help me God" was apparently to Roberts and not

Obama because the plaintiffs believed Obama's speech may be protected by free exercise. The district court dismissed the suit on standing grounds. See Newdow v. Roberts, Civil Action No. 08–2248 (RBW) (D.D.C. Mar. 12, 2009), available at http://www.scribd.com/doc/13241039/Newdow-v-Roberts –DDC–20090312–74–Order-of-Dismissal. Should the "so help me God" words be declared unconstitutional—because they are not in the Constitution?

President Thomas Jefferson wrote his famous "wall of separation" letter to the Danbury Baptist Association of Connecticut on New Year's Day 1802. The purpose of the letter was to explain Jefferson's opposition to presidential proclamations of days of fasting and thanksgiving. See Daniel L. Dreisbach, Thomas Jefferson and the Wall of Separation Between Church and State 1–2, 17 (2002). Presidents regularly declare National Days of Prayer and Thanksgiving and issue proclamations for Memorial Day, the Fourth of July and Christmas. Are such practices unconstitutional ceremonial deism or acceptable civil religion?

5. *War.* Civil religion is traditionally most vibrant in times of national crisis and war. See John F. Wilson, Public Religion in American Culture 50–51, 171 (1979). Does this mean that Presidents Clinton and Bush appropriately referred to Scripture after citizens were attacked in Oklahoma City and the World Trade Center?

What is "the most hallowed monument of the civil religion"? Do you agree with Professor Bellah, that it is either Gettysburg or Arlington National Cemetery (which includes the dead from many wars, the Tomb of the Unknown Soldier and the grave site of President Kennedy with its eternal flame). What are the holidays of American civil religion?

6. *Protestant, Catholic, Jew, Muslim, Hindu, Unaffiliated.* In 1955, the sociologist Will Herberg identified a "paradox" in American culture of "pervasive secularism amid mounting religiosity." Will Herberg, Protestant Catholic Jew: An Essay in American Religious Sociology 2 (1955). Herberg observed that new Americans change their nationality, language and culture, but are not expected to change their religion, which becomes the "differentiating element" among Americans. Id. at 23. Herberg argued that American religion broke down into three basic religious groups— Protestant, Catholic, and Jew—who, despite their religious differences, identified equally with the "American Way of Life." Because these religious groups identified with the American Way of Life, they did not have to change their religion.

Is it good for American religions to agree about the American Way of Life? Does such agreement risk compromising the religious identity of groups, especially minorities? Is it too narrow to identify three religious groups as representative of American religion?

Does American culture now break down into four basic religious groups? George W. Bush was the first president to include Islam in an inaugural address when he advocated aid to faith-based organizations by reminding listeners that "some needs and hurts are so deep they will only respond to a mentor's touch or a pastor's prayer. Church and charity, synagogue and *mosque* lend our communities their humanity, and they will have an honored place in our plans and in our laws." See Inaugural Proceedings, 151 Cong. Rec. S101, at S103–104 (Jan. 20, 2005) (emphasis added). The Muslims' sacred text, the Qur'an, also appeared in Bush's inaugural. Barack Obama's inaugural address referred to "a nation of Christians and Muslims, Jews and Hindus, and non-believers." See Inaugural Address, Barack Obama, Daily Comp. Pres. Docs., 2009 DCPD No. 00001, available at http://www.gpo.gov/fdsys/pkg/DCPD–200900001/pdf/DCPD–200900001.pdf (Jan. 20, 2009). Did he leave anyone out?

In *Tri-Faith America: How Catholics and Jews Held Postwar America to Its Protestant Promise*, historian Kevin M. Schultz explains how the idea of the tri-faith nation—Protestant-Catholic-Jew—displaced Protestant Christian America. Schultz traces the idea's development from World War I through World War II and the Cold War. Schultz explains how the idea fostered the growth of religious pluralism in the United States. What is the comparable idea today?

7. *Presidential Prayer*. Is prayer part of civil religion? Recall from Chapter 2, Justice Kennedy's statement in *Lee v. Weisman* that the Establishment Clause does not allow the government to establish a civil religion. *Weisman* focused on school prayer. Should there be prayers at presidential inaugurations, or should *Weisman* ban those as well? Does *Town of Greece v. Galloway*, also read in Chapter 2, suggest there is never a constitutional problem with presidential prayer?

Can there be a nondenominational or nonsectarian political prayer? Should the president pray in public? If he participates in religious ceremonies, how many faiths need to be represented in order to satisfy the First Amendment?

At George W. Bush's first inauguration, Pastor Kirbyjon Caldwell's benediction ended with the sentences, "We respectfully submit this humble prayer in the name that is above all other names, Jesus the Christ. Let all who agree say 'Amen.'" 147 Cong. Rec. S421–05 (Jan. 20, 2001). Did that prayer violate the Establishment Clause? Do you agree that the first prayer excluded too many people? See Cathy Lynn Grossman, "Some Call Inaugural Prayers to Jesus Exclusionary," USA Today, Jan. 24, 2001, at 10D. Caldwell also gave the benediction at the second Bush inaugural, asking God to "[r]ally the Republicans, the Democrats, and the Independents around Your common good so that America will truly become one nation under God, indivisible, with liberty, justice, and equal opportunity for all, including the least, the last and the lost," and concluding with a different final sentence: "Respecting persons of all faiths, I humbly submit this prayer in the name of Jesus Christ. Amen." Inaugural Proceedings, 151 Cong. Rec. S101, at S104–05 (Jan. 20, 2005). Is that an improvement over the first benediction?

Steven Waldman argues that the inaugural prayers have become less inclusive over time. All twelve prayers delivered since 1989 were given by Protestants; in the prior 48 years, fewer than half were given by

Protestants. Waldman identifies three stages of inaugural prayer: 1) the religious-diversity model (1937–1985) with clergy of different faiths praying in their own faith; 2) America's pastor model (1989, 1993), where Billy Graham used inclusive instead of Christian language, and 3) the Protestant-only model, where Billy Graham spoke with Christian language, and his son Franklin Graham in 2001 said Christ alone is Americans' savior. Obama too had only Protestant prayers from Rick Warren and Joseph Lowery. Which model best reflects the Constitution? Steven Waldman, Why The Inaugural Prayers Have Become Less Inclusive Over Time, Jan. 16, 2009, available at http://blog.beliefnet.com/stevenwaldman/ 2009/01/the-inaugural-prayers-have-bec.html. What can explain the move away from religious-diversity to Protestant prayer?

Does the idea of civil religion violate the free exercise of religion by favoring adherents of civil religion and secular philosophies over genuine religions? Is it better to have adherents of all religious faiths pray freely than to allow only government prayer that meets the requirements of civil religion? See James J. Knicely & John W. Whitehead, In God We Trust: The Judicial Establishment of American Civil Religion, 43 J. Marshall L. Rev. 869, 925–26 (2010) ("judiciary's approbation of the American Civil Religion in a time of religious and cultural diversity not only emasculates the expression of diverse values but grants to government indiscriminate tentacles of monopoly and its proclivity to the intolerance, oppression, and totalitarianism inherent in a 'religious' establishment.").

8. *Obama's Civil Religion.* Can you tell if President Obama's civil religion varies from his predecessors'? President-elect Obama attracted criticism from the religious left and from gay and lesbian activists when he named Pastor Rick Warren of the evangelical Saddleback Church in Lake Forest, California, to deliver the invocation at his first inauguration. Warren supported Proposition 8, the ban on gay marriage in California, and reportedly has compared gay relations to incest and bestiality. See Steven Waldman, Rick Warren's Controversial Comments on Gay Marriage, beliefnet.com, Dec. 17, 2008. Warren prayed in the name of Jesus:

> I humbly ask this in the name of the one who changed my life: Yeshua, Essa (ph), Jesus, Jesus, who taught us to pray, "Our Father who art in Heaven hallowed be thy name, thy kingdom come, thy will be done on Earth as it is in Heaven. Give us this day our daily bread and forgive us our trespasses as we forgive those who trespass against us, and lead us not into temptation, but deliver us from evil, for thine is the kingdom and the power and the glory forever."

Obama's first inaugural address was more inclusive; although he cited Scripture he also included Hindus and non-believers in the list of religions mentioned:

> On this day, we gather because we have chosen hope over fear, unity of purpose over conflict and discord. On this day, we come to proclaim an end to the petty grievances and false

promises, the recriminations and worn-out dogmas that for far too long have strangled our politics. We remain a young nation. But in the words of Scripture, the time has come to set aside childish things. The time has come to reaffirm our enduring spirit; to choose our better history; to carry forward that precious gift, that noble idea passed on from generation to generation: the God-given promise that all are equal, all are free, and all deserve a chance to pursue their full measure of happiness. . . .

For we know that our patchwork heritage is a strength, not a weakness. We are a nation of Christians and Muslims, Jews and Hindus, and non-believers. We are shaped by every language and culture, drawn from every end of this Earth; and because we have tasted the bitter swill of civil war and segregation, and emerged from that dark chapter stronger and more united, we cannot help but believe that the old hatreds shall someday pass; that the lines of tribe shall soon dissolve; that as the world grows smaller, our common humanity shall reveal itself; and that America must play its role in ushering in a new era of peace.

To the Muslim world, we seek a new way forward, based on mutual interest and mutual respect. To those leaders around the globe who seek to sow conflict, or blame their society's ills on the West, know that your people will judge you on what you can build, not what you destroy.

The first presidential prayer service included a Muslim, two Black ministers, two rabbis, an evangelical Christian and a Hindu. Roman Catholic, Episcopal and Greek Orthodox representatives were also present. According to *The New York Times*, the presence of a Hindu, women and African Americans "underscored the emphasis on diversity." Three rabbis represented the three major branches of Judaism. Must every prayer service be this inclusive in order to satisfy the Constitution? See Laurie Goodstein, A Diverse First Presidential Morning Prayer, N.Y. Times, Jan. 22, 2009, at A24. Or can no prayer service satisfy the Constitution? Did President Obama reach the ideal of inclusive prayer outlined by Justice Kagan's dissent in *Town of Greece v. Galloway*, Chapter 2?

President Obama also faced prayer controversy during his second inauguration by first naming the Rev. Louie Giglio to deliver the benediction. Giglio withdrew after reporters discovered he had given a sermon urging Christians "to fight the 'aggressive agenda' of the gay-rights movement." Sheryl Gay Stolberg, Minister Backs Out of Speech at Inaugural, N.Y. Times, Jan. 10, 2013, at A17. Instead, the benediction was given by the Reverend Luis Leon, an Episcopal priest at the traditional St. John's Church near the White House. Leon prayed "that we are created in your image, whether brown, black or white, male or female, first generation or immigrant American, or daughter of the American Revolution, gay or straight, rich or poor." Did he leave anyone out? See Elizabeth Tenety, Rev. Luis Leon Gives Benediction at Obama Inauguration: "Gay or Straight," in God's Image, Wash. Post, Jan. 21, 2013. Myrlie Evers-Williams, the widow of civil rights leader Medgar Evers, became the first woman and the first layperson to deliver the invocation. See Gary Younge, Obama's Inauguration to Provide Landmark Moment for Civil Rights Titan, The Guardian, Jan. 18, 2013.

The D.C. Circuit upheld the district court's dismissal of Michael Newdow's challenge to the inaugural prayers and to the "so help me God" part of the oath on the grounds that the past challenge was moot and plaintiffs lacked standing for future challenges. Newdow v. Roberts, 603 F.3d 1002, 1007 (D.C. Cir. 2010), cert. denied, 131 S. Ct. 2441 (2011).

Chapter 10 examines how schools can teach about religion and science. Ask yourself if it is possible to teach religion in public schools without violating the Establishment Clause. Do you think some science teachers treat science as a religion in their classrooms? Would you recommend a curriculum in which both religion and science are taught?

CHAPTER 10

TEACHING ABOUT RELIGION AND SCIENCE

Public and private schools have been at the center of much of the Supreme Court's case law about the Establishment Clause. As we learned in Chapter 3, *Everson*, the first modern Establishment Clause case, arose from New Jersey's decision to fund bus rides for students to private religious schools. Attempts to fund religious schools directly were the source of the Court's *Lemon* test, and funding private schools remained controversial through *Zelman*, when the Court approved a school voucher program in Cleveland, Ohio. The rulings about prayer, Bible reading, and the Pledge of Allegiance developed in cases brought by students in public schools.

In this chapter we examine two more specific topics that involve the curricula of public education. Section A examines prayer, theology, and religious studies. While the Court invalidated prayer and Bible reading in public schools, it insisted the academic study of religion is constitutional. These rulings led to an intense debate among academics about what the study of religion involves. The primary battle was between those who thought that the study of religion must be scientific, secular, and objective, and others who believed that members of a religious tradition were best equipped to teach it. Section A examines whether there is a difference between the purely secular study of religion (which is usually called religious studies) and theology (a study that presupposes some religious faith or belief).

In Section B we turn to the science curriculum by examining the subject of evolution. After Charles Darwin published *The Origin of Species* in 1859, his theory of evolution was gradually adopted in high school textbooks throughout the United States. Beginning in the 1920s, however, the teaching of evolution was opposed by Christians who preferred the Bible's story of creation to Darwinian evolution. Section B examines the attempts to ban evolution from the public school classroom, as well as efforts to balance its teaching with other instruction, first with creation science, and then with intelligent design.

These materials force us to re-examine a question that has engaged us since Chapter 1: Is it possible to define religion so that one may study it scientifically? The evolution materials force us to consider what science is, and whether it can be distinguished from religion. As you read this chapter, consider what curriculum you would set for the study of religion and science in the public schools. Would you set a different curriculum for religious schools?

603

A. PRAYER, THEOLOGY, AND RELIGIOUS STUDIES

In Engel v. Vitale, 370 U.S. 421 (1962), the Court invalidated a New York State education law that required the recitation of the Regents' Prayer in the public school classroom. The following year, in School District of Abington Township v. Schempp, 374 U.S. 203 (1963), the Court ruled that Pennsylvania regulations requiring the reading of Bible verses and the recitation of the Lord's Prayer in the public schools were also unconstitutional. The Court rejected the argument "that the Bible is here used either as an instrument for nonreligious moral inspiration or as a reference for the teaching of secular subjects." Instead, the Court identified Bible reading as a pervasively religious activity that violated the Establishment Clause.

As the Court rejected the argument that its decision established a "religion of secularism" in the schools, it observed that the Bible study involved in *Schempp* was different from the academic study of religion:

> It is insisted that unless these religious exercises are permitted a "religion of secularism" is established in the schools. We agree of course that the State may not establish a "religion of secularism" in the sense of affirmatively opposing or showing hostility to religion, thus "preferring those who believe in no religion over those who do believe." We do not agree, however, that this decision in any sense has that effect. In addition, it might well be said that one's education is not complete without a study of comparative religion or the history of religion and its relationship to the advancement of civilization. It certainly may be said that the Bible is worthy of study for its literary and historic qualities. Nothing we have said here indicates that such study of the Bible or of religion, when presented objectively as part of a secular program of education, may not be effected consistently with the First Amendment. But the exercises here do not fall into those categories. They are religious exercises, required by the States in violation of the command of the First Amendment that the Government maintain strict neutrality, neither aiding nor opposing religion.

374 U.S. at 225. While barring religious exercises from public schools, the justices repeatedly insisted that schools may include the study of religion in a secular curriculum. According to Justice William Brennan's concurrence, "[t]he holding of the Court today plainly does not foreclose teaching *about* the Holy Scriptures or *about* the differences between religious sects in classes in literature or history. Indeed, whether or not the Bible is involved, it would be impossible to teach meaningfully many subjects in the social sciences or the humanities without some mention of religion." Id. at 300–01. Justice Goldberg's concurrence added "that the Court would recognize the propriety . . . of

the teaching *about* religion, as distinguished from the teaching *of* religion, in the public schools." Id. at 306. The justices also agreed that determining how to teach religion was a matter for educational experts, not the Court. Id. at 300.

The academic experts seized the words "about" and "of" from the Goldberg concurrence. As the following reading explains, scholars of religion decided that, under *Schempp*, teaching religious studies, but not theology, in public schools is constitutional. What is the difference between theology and religious studies? Do you agree that teaching theology in public schools violates the Establishment Clause, while teaching religious studies is permitted?

Leslie C. Griffin, "We Do Not Preach. We Teach.": Religion Professors and the First Amendment

19 Quinnipiac Law Review 1, 9–26 (2000).

After World War I, religion was at times taught by church personnel who lived near state universities, not by professors in regular academic departments. At the University of Illinois in 1919, for example, "clergy representing the campus ministries of the Methodists, Disciples, and Roman Catholics" petitioned to have "university credit offered for courses taught at their campus houses." "The 'Illinois Plan' involve[d] the accreditation of courses in religion taught by approved scholars in the various denominational centers surrounding the state university campus." In the same era, the University of Iowa developed a school of religion that "employed teachers of religion paid by the different confessions (Catholic, Jewish, and Protestant)"; these faculty were *believing* Protestants, Catholics, and Jews. George Marsden reports that "[t]he original purpose of the [Iowa] school was not simply the academic study of religion. Rather the school was also explicitly *to promote religious interests, to foster sympathy for religion* among students, and to encourage students to go into religious *vocations*."

These *off-campus* denominational arrangements evolved in the state universities because of the conviction that the presence of religion departments in public institutions violates the Establishment Clause of the First Amendment. If fostering religious life is the goal of courses in religion, then public universities must avoid teaching religion for constitutional reasons. Hiring off-campus personnel who do not have regular academic appointments is supposed to solve the constitutional problem.

I.   The Religion Professors' Constitutional Standard: Religious Studies or Theology

In his seminal 1971 study, *Graduate Education in Religion*, Claude Welch stated that the legal status of the academic study of religion in state universities was settled in the 1963 *Schempp* case. Welch is representative of religion scholars, who after *Schempp* identified the difference between teaching *about* religion and teaching *of* religion as the constitutional standard. Teaching about religion in the state university is constitutional; teaching of religion is unconstitutional. When it barred *prayer* from the public *elementary* school classroom, the Supreme Court stated (in dicta of course) that public schools may offer religion as part of their curriculum. The Court mentioned that the Establishment Clause does not prohibit the "study of the Bible or of religion, when presented objectively as part of a *secular program of education*." The Court noted that "one's education is not complete without a study of *comparative religion* or the *history of religion* and its relationship to the advancement of civilization." The influential distinction came from Justice Goldberg's concurrence, which "recognize[d] the propriety . . . of the teaching *about* religion, as distinguished from the teaching *of* religion, in the public schools."

For scholars in religion, *Schempp* settled what had been until then an open question and established the constitutionality of teaching religious studies, but not theology, in state universities. To these scholars, religious studies is teaching about religion; theology is teaching of religion.

What is religious studies? It is the name often used in the United States for the academic study of religion, a term used to distinguish such study from the more traditional theology. The title is somewhat confusing because "the activity itself is not religious." For centuries in the Christian world, the study of religion was theology; theology was the core of the medieval university, the queen of the sciences. Theology was an intellectual discipline because it included a quest for knowledge; in its classic formulation, it was "*faith* seeking understanding." Although rooted in faith, theology was properly located, not in the church, but in the university. "It was the university, not the Church, that fostered the new understanding of *theologia* as *scientia*, a scholarly 'discipline' that demonstrated its conclusions." "*Sacra doctrina* is a discipline, sufficiently parallel to physics and metaphysics to be a science." All religions do not have theologies. Due to Christianity's influence on American and European universities, however, theology has become a generic term for a study of religion that includes some type of commitment, usually to a particular religious tradition.

In Europe in the nineteenth century, however, the scientific study of religion emerged to challenge theology's reign. This science is a "child of the Enlightenment," particularly the German Enlightenment, which contributed to "the separation of theology from religion." In 1870 Friedrich Max Müller's lectures at the Royal Institute of London proposed a "science of religion." Müller might not have been the first to use the term, but his influence on the developing field was profound.

Religionswissenschaft became a technical term for the study of religion, a study different in method and perspective from Christian theology.

The beginnings of *Religionswissenschaft* were difficult; the "modern discipline developed rather haphazardly out of more traditional ways of studying religion and religions." Many of the scholars committed to the new enterprise of religion had themselves been trained in Christian theology, in denominational and seminary settings. Accordingly they might be unable to change or challenge their theological presuppositions. Scholars trained in theology outnumbered the new scientists for many years. Joseph Kitagawa has demonstrated that

> this early history of religions did not win its independence easily. On the one hand, religiously committed Europeans did not readily accept an alternative method in the study of religion which compared Jewish and Christian traditions with other religions of the world on the same plane. Furthermore, the teaching of *Religionswissenschaft* was often done in the theological faculties of universities, faculties not inclined to trust the new discipline and its rationalistic and/or evolutionary thrust. On the other hand, those who were "scientifically oriented" suspected hidden religious or theological agendas behind what claimed to be an objective approach.

The new scientists pressed on despite these difficulties. By 1899, Cornelis P. Tiele described Müller's work as "more an apologetics for the young discipline of *Religionswissenschaft* than an introduction to the discipline itself." Nonetheless, Tiele argued that the discipline had developed in the years since Müller began his work. Scholars had begun to identify the distinctive methods that characterize the study of religion.

A new discipline might require a different institutional setting as well as a new method. University of Chicago Professor Jonathan Z. Smith reports that, in 1877, in Holland, "[f]or the first time in western academic history, there were established two, parallel possibilities for the study of religion: a humanistic mode within the secular academy and a theological course of study within the denominational seminary." Until then, the seminary had been the proper center for the study of religion (i.e., Christianity). With the institutional move from seminary to university came changes in the study of religion; the demands of the "secular academy" were different from those of the "denominational seminary."

Professor Smith explains that the United States did not immediately pursue the pathway taken by Holland in the 1870s. Instead it followed a "sequential pattern"; divinity degrees were usually prerequisites to doctoral degrees in religious studies. According to Professor Smith, however, it was not until *Schempp* that American public universities followed the "parallel" pattern of Holland and other European countries and that religious studies flourished.

The preeminence of religious studies in American universities was new in the 1960s, but the study of religion was not new, even in state schools. As Merrimon Cuninggim reported in his 1947 book *The College Seeks Religion*: "Religion has always been present in the colleges of America. Prior to the [twentieth] century the intimacy of this relationship was inevitably subject to ebb as well as flow." After all, early American universities were founded and staffed by Protestant clergy; one of their functions was to train ministers by teaching them theology. The earliest state universities shared many similarities with the Christian universities, e.g., in trying to produce "Christian gentlemen." Such religious and moral purposes in education help to explain why theology was often characterized as an integrating subject. If education's goal is the formation of Christian gentlemen, then theology may be the core study that integrates all learning, that links education to morality.

Throughout the nineteenth and into the twentieth century (indeed to the present day), the integrative possibility of religious/theological education is a recurring theme in American education. Professor Michaelsen explains, however, that in the second half of the nineteenth century the "curriculum of Christian humanism went into decline" when American university presidents adopted the German model of specialization. As the German model grew in influence, "theology, which had been considered important enough to be of interest to all students in the early American colleges, became a minor enterprise of little or no importance in the majority of developing American universities." The churches developed their own universities; theology moved to the seminaries and denominational schools. Although German universities had faculties of theology, "most American universities developed in an intellectual atmosphere which was quite hostile to theology." As agricultural schools and other state universities, including the land grant colleges, developed, they followed many of the patterns set by the private schools. "There was one sharp difference: they had no theological faculties." [5]

As theology declined in influence in the late nineteenth century, some short-lived attempts were made in the late nineteenth and early twentieth centuries to establish the scientific study of religion in American universities. Professor Michaelsen describes the years between 1890 and 1910 as "the 'golden age' of American scholarship in religion." Important history of religion chairs were established at Harvard and at Boston University in the nineteenth century. At the University of Pennsylvania, Morris Jastrow, influenced by his training in Europe, led the scientific movement with *The Study of Religion*.

Jastrow advocated the scientific study of religion and worked to establish it as a rigorous discipline at Penn. He warned that students would expect their religion courses to provide meaning to their lives, perhaps to fulfill an integrative function in their education. Questions about religion's integrative role (as the field that provides, e.g., the moral center or focus for all education) have been present in curricular debates since the founding of American universities; they continue to confound us in the 1990s. Jastrow urged scholars of religion to pursue their study as a science:

> There is a special reason for *emphasizing the importance of method* in the study of the various religious systems of the past and present, and of religious phenomena in general. In the study of religion, a factor that may be designated as the personal equation enters into play. So strong is this factor that it is perhaps impossible to eliminate it altogether, but it is possible, and indeed essential, to keep it in check and under safe control; and this can be done only by the determination of a proper method and by a close adherence to such a method.

Scholars of religion have spent the last century trying to identify and clarify this method. In the scientific study of religion, the subject matter is obviously religion. However, there are numerous disciplines that examine religion: history, sociology, anthropology, psychology, philosophy, linguistics, philology (as well as traditional theology). All are fields that are valuable to the study of religion. Once theologians are no longer the scholars best equipped to study religion, these practitioners of other disciplines are well qualified to offer "scientific" analyses of religion. Anthropologists, after all, study the anthropology of religion; sociologists focus on the sociology of religion. What insight can religion scholars offer to trained anthropologists, sociologists or philosophers? Scholars of religion have desired to build a science with its own method around the study of religion, but the nature of the science is not obvious. Is the study of religion a distinct subject that needs a separate department, a separate method? With the "abandonment" of theology, why not offer the history of religion, the sociology of religion, the philosophy of religion, the anthropology of religion, in courses taught by professors trained in those disciplines? Perhaps a religion department should include scholars trained in disciplines other than religion instead of a group of scientific students of religion in a distinctive discipline with its own method. . . .

By the end of World War I, Jastrow's model of scientific American departments of religion had faded as theology returned.

> After World War I, a self-conscious and largely successful effort was made to bend efforts on behalf of religion in American academia toward providing a theological ideology of higher education. Graduate training in religion largely passed

from departments (like Jastrow's), teaching the philologies and histories of the several religions impartially, to the theological seminaries, both Christian and Jewish, where existential and neo-orthodox *theology dominated the scene.*

Remember that it was in the post-World War I era that the denominational and Bible chairs system flourished. The integrative function of religious education was prominent. The public universities faced a special problem: if fostering religious life is the goal of courses in religion, then public universities might have to avoid religion for constitutional reasons. The Iowa, Illinois and comparable plans existed because state departments of religion were presumed unconstitutional.

The 1930s were a low point in American religious studies; the era favored theology and not religion. "Th[e] tendency favorable to the history of religions and comparative religion has been reversed since the middle of the 1930's, partly under the influence of the theological renaissance and partly because of the change which has taken place in cultural and educational domains." There were also practical reasons for the decline in religion study. For example, the scholars were not yet equipped to advance the scientific study of religion; there were not enough graduate students trained in the history of religions available to teach at either private or public universities.

After World War II, however, the "scientific-scholarly approach staged a gradual, by no means yet universal, comeback." Such growing interest in the study of religion did not settle the theology vs. scientific study debate. Cuninggim, for example, warned in 1947 of "the low intellectual level characteristic of much of the religious instruction now being offered, and the consequent lack of respect in which religion as a subject of study is often held by the rest of the college." "Courses in religion, as any experienced observer knows, are often 'snaps' or 'crips' "; this must change. Nonetheless Cuninggim argued that the goal of the courses was not only intellectual; the study of religion should integrate the curriculum and should nurture students' religious lives. He noted with approval that "the secularization of higher education seems to have reached its peak around the time of the first World War, and that since then the colleges have recaptured much of their lost concern for the religious development of their students and have increasingly assumed responsibility for such nurture."

As American higher education expanded after World War II, the study of religion prospered with it. In the 1940s, there were numerous American departments of religion; "[o]nly 27 percent of nationally accredited colleges had no formal offerings on religious topics." "By 1950 some 60 percent of state universities and land grant colleges were offering courses in religion, and during the next decades the field continued to grow." Departments of religion burgeoned in importance and quality in many schools in the 1940s and 1950s. In 1965, Robert

Michaelsen reported that "it appears that American universities have been giving more serious attention to the study of religion in the past two decades than they had since early in the century. *And in the case of state universities the recent interest in this area is unparalleled in American history.*" Yet the schools continued to vary in type and quality of course offerings.

> The particular arrangements vary widely from institution to institution. In some institutions the courses are listed in the regular catalogue and taught in University classrooms; and in others they are listed in separate bulletins and taught in private facilities. In some instances, credit is granted in the regular manner and in others credit is treated on a transfer basis. In some cases the program serves in effect as a Department of Religion.

The status of religion in public universities, moreover, remained uneven and uncertain. Part of the problem was the ongoing questioning of the constitutional status of teaching religion; before 1963 "[n]o case involving religion in a state university ha[d] ever come before the U.S. Supreme Court for consideration and decision." Some writers argued that public universities could offer religion courses as long as "such study be academic or educational in nature rather than devotional or indoctrinational." Others thought the state university should stay clear of religion because "the presence of religion in any form in a state institution is both illegal and inappropriate." Professor Cuninggim argued that schools should strengthen their courses in religious instruction instead of ignoring them because of worries about church/state separation. Paul Kauper wrote that the teaching of religion in state universities was constitutional as long as it met certain conditions:

> There should be, e.g., no discrimination against students on religious grounds; no religious conditions on employment or student status; no compulsory religious services or courses; and equality of opportunity (i.e., all religions should be taught) . . . [T]he distinction should be observed between the teaching of religion to promote knowledge and understanding and that type aimed deliberately at indoctrination and commitment to religious faith. The teaching of religious ideas in an objective and fair way is appropriately a state university function. To win converts and seek commitment is outside its function and violates the separation principle.

As we have seen, it was not until the 1960s that American universities followed the "parallel" pattern of Holland and other European countries.

It was not until the rise of programs in state universities, a development which followed the 1963 U.S. Supreme Court decision on the *School District of Abington Township v. Schempp*, in which Mr. Justice Goldberg observed, "it seems clear to me . . . that the Court would recognize the propriety of the teaching *about* religion as distinguished from the teaching *of* religion in the public schools," that the parallel course of religious studies in the academy, instituted a century ago in Holland, became possible in this country.

Conrad Cherry concludes in his study of American divinity schools that "[b]eginning in the late 1960s, the growth of religious studies programs in state universities would force a clear separation between teaching about religion and the ministry." Parallel, not sequential. Scholars in religion decided that "religious studies" was teaching *about* religion and theology was teaching *of* religion. From that point on, religious studies would thrive in the "secular academy" as theology remained in the seminaries. Professor Smith has called *Schempp* the "'Magna Carta' for religious studies within state universities." Religious studies flourished as well in private universities; its flowering often attributed to *Schempp*. With the growth of religious studies and ebb in theology came a decline in the perception of religion's important integrative role in the curriculum, in public as well as private schools.

After *Schempp*, religious studies became the popular nomenclature for American non-theological study of religion. There are other labels; one indication of the "conceptual confusion" surrounding the academic study of religion is the variety of names used to identify it. *Religionswissenschaft* and *la science des religions* were the early terms.

> [T]here was no unanimity in the nineteenth century about the nomenclature for the scholarly study of religion(s). *A completely satisfactory name has yet to be found.* The designation "Hierology," or a "treatise on sacred (*hieros*) things," was favored by some of the discipline's pioneers. Others preferred "Pistology," or the study of "faith" or "belief" systems. Other designations proposed and used in some quarters were "Comparative Religion," "Science of Comparative Religion," "The Comparative History of Religion," "The Comparative History of Religions," "The Comparative Science of Religion," "Comparative Theology," and "Science of Religion." . . . "History of Religions" has been adopted officially by the International Association for the History of Religions (IAHR) as the English counterpart to *Allgemeine Religionswissenschaft*.

The "history of religions" and "comparative religions" schools have been successful in having their names recognized; even the Supreme Court has advocated "comparative religion" and "history of religion" for the curriculum of public schools. In this essay, I follow Conrad Cherry's lead:

Departments and programs in the liberal arts would continue to use diverse designations such as "religion," "history and literature of religion," and "religion studies," as well as "religious studies." After the mid-1960s, however, most of the literature devoted to the nature of the study of religion in universities used the designation "religious studies," and I [Cherry] use the term to denote a field that took on a quite different appearance from the postwar study of religion that was shaped within the mold of theological studies in the divinity schools.

Schempp receives much credit for the surge in academic religious studies. Since its origins in Europe in the nineteenth century, the scientific study of religion had distinguished itself from theology. Now the Americans were ready to make their contribution; in the United States in the 1960s and 1970s the study of religion "t[ook] off," came into "full flower." Foreign scholars at times attribute the distinctive growth of religious studies in the United States to our separation of church and state. In the law, however, *Schempp* had not settled anything about university teaching of religion; it was a prayer and Bible reading case set in the elementary schools. Dicta. Moreover, even at the elementary school level one must ask what constitutional standard is provided by "about" and "of" religion? Nonetheless, armed with *Schempp*, American scholars promoted the study of religion (but not theology) in public and private universities. They founded the American Academy of Religion in 1964; from that point on the academic discipline of religion became more professionalized in the United States.

Private as well as public universities changed their focus after Schempp. John Wilson explained that public universities and private secular and private religious schools converged on religious studies until "basically similar approaches to the study of religion [existed] in all three types of setting." . . .

Why did the professors conclude that theology is unconstitutional? The literature on theology and religious studies is so vast that any answer risks oversimplification. It is difficult to see how any court or lawyer could compress the academic literature into a constitutional test, so we should not be surprised that religion scholars, but not courts, have chosen it as the constitutional standard. Nonetheless, one can identify some general features of theology that have made it constitutionally suspect to scholars in religion. Theologians are insiders, not outsiders; committed, not uncommitted; participants, not observers; normative, not descriptive; located in divinity schools, not universities; religious, not secular. Those characteristics raise the spectre of the Establishment Clause in a way that the secular detached professor of religious studies does not—at least in the eyes of the religion professors.

NOTES AND QUESTIONS

1.   *Theology or Religious Studies?* An article in *The Atlantic* argues that theology is a valuable subject of study for everyone, not only for believers. The author explains that theology's "inside" perspective enables students to "understand history from the inside out." In her words:

> If history and comparative religion alike offer us perspective on world events from the "outside," the study of theology offers us a chance to study those same events "from within": an opportunity to get inside the heads of those whose beliefs and choices shaped so much of our history, and who—in the world outside the ivory tower—still shape plenty of the world today. That such avenues of inquiry have virtually vanished from many of the institutions where they were once best explored is hardly a triumph of progress or of secularism. Instead, the absence of theology in our universities is an unfortunate example of blindness—willful or no—to the fact that engagement with the past requires more than mere objective or comparative analysis. It requires a willingness to look outside our own perspectives in order engage with the great questions—and questioners—of history on their own terms. Even [Richard] Dawkins might well agree with that.

Do you agree? Does it persuade you that teaching theology is constitutional? See Tara Isabella Burton, Study Theology Even If You Don't Believe in God, The Atlantic, Oct. 30, 2013.

The American Academy of Religion published its "Guidelines for Teaching About Religion in K–12 Public Schools in the United States":

> Proceeding from the premises that illiteracy about religion is widespread, this illiteracy fuels prejudice and antagonism, and teaching about religion in public schools using a non-devotional, religious studies approach can reduce illiteracy, the guidelines endeavor to offer a constitutionally permissible approach to education about religion. The guidelines offer suggested teacher competencies for cultural studies, historical, literary, and traditions-based approaches to including religion within public schools curricula.

Although not mentioning the *Lemon* test, the guidelines specifically reference *Engel v. Vitale* and *Abington v. Schemp* in stressing the need to avoid devotional teaching within a public school's curriculum. This foundation leads to an endorsement of six principles for separating constitutionally acceptable religious education from prohibited proselytizing:

> 1) The school's approach to religion is *academic*, not *devotional*; 2) The school strives for student *awareness* of religions, but does not press for student *acceptance* of any religion; 3) The school sponsors *study* about religion, not the *practice* of religion; 4) The school may *expose* students to a diversity of religious views, but may not *impose* any particular view; 5) The school *educates* about

all religions, it does not *promote* or *denigrate* religion; and 6) The school *informs* students about various beliefs; it does not seek to *conform* students to any particular belief. (emphasis in original).

See American Academy of Religion, Guidelines for Teaching about Religion in K–12 Public Schools in the United States (April 2010), available at https://www.aarweb.org/about/teaching-about-religion-aar-guidelines-for-k-12-public-schools. Has the American Academy of Religion offered a constitutional plan for teaching about religion?

2.   *The Economics of Religion.* As Griffin's article explains, scholars of religion have long considered anthropology, sociology, history, philosophy and other fields to be possible sources for the scientific study of religion. What about economics? Since the 1970s, the "economics of religion" has developed as a sub-specialty among economists. Professor Laurence Iannaccone identifies three possible types of study of religion and economics: first, the "economics of religion, which . . . interprets religious behavior from an economic perspective"; second, the study of the "economic consequences of religion"; and third, "religious economics," which "invoke[s] theological principles and sacred writings to promote or criticize economic policies." See Laurence R. Iannaccone, Introduction to the Economics of Religion, 36 J. Econ. Literature 1465, 1466 (September 1998); see also Michael W. McConnell & Richard A. Posner, An Economic Approach to Issues of Religious Freedom, 56 U. Chi. L. Rev. 1 (1989).

Countering claims that religious choice is nonrational or irrational, economists of religion apply rational choice theory to religious behavior by investigating, for example, whether established religions suffer the same problems as other monopolies, or how different religions compete for adherents in the religious marketplace. Are religions subject to the laws of supply and demand? Is choosing a religion like buying a car? See Joseph Weber, Economists Are Getting Religion, Bus. Wk., Dec. 6, 2004, at 136. Do you think religious believers are more attracted to religions that have a strong brand identity and that compete more effectively for their allegiance? See Robert B. Ekelund Jr., Robert F. Hebert, & Robert D. Tollison, The Marketplace of Christianity (2006). Are you surprised to learn that "demand for religion is determined by the sacrifice of both time and goods," so that people's wealth and job status influence the rate of their religious participation? Id. at 24–25.

Is there any reason why teaching the economics of religion in the public school would violate the First Amendment? Is there a constitutional difference between the first two types of study (economics of religion and economic consequences of religion) and the third (religious economics)? The third category, religious economics, includes, for example, Islamic theorists who try to develop economic policies consistent with the Qur'an and Christian writers who argue that wealth should be redistributed according to Christian principles.

Should Professor Iannaccone have labeled the third category theological economics instead of religious economics? Based on your readings, would it be possible to distinguish a field of religious economics from the study of theological economics? Would any courses in this third category be unconstitutional if taught in public schools?

3.   *Teaching the Bible in Public Schools.* In September 2009, Nampa Classical Academy, an Idaho charter school, filed a federal suit against members of the Idaho Public Charter School Commission and others challenging an order by the Commission prohibiting the use of the Bible or any other religious documents or texts in the classroom. See Plaintiffs' Verified Complaint, Nampa Classical Academy v. Goesling, 2009 WL 2923069 (D. Idaho). The commission had said that Article XI, Section 6 of the Idaho Constitution barred the use of the Bible in schools. See Idaho Const., art. IX, § 6 ("No books, papers, tracts or documents of a political, sectarian or denominational character shall be used or introduced in any schools established under the provisions of this article.") Classical Academy claimed it had developed an entire curriculum in a classical, liberal arts format, using both secular and religious primary texts. The school stated that it did not intend to use religious texts in a "devotional manner" and would not teach "religious tenets." Instead, the texts were used as part of the curriculum studying Western civilization in classes such as history, literature, art or music.

Is using the Bible as a primary source for studying Western civilization unconstitutional? Does it matter that the academy's curriculum also included other religious texts including the Qur'an, the Book of Mormon, the Epic of Gilgamesh, the Code of Hammurabi (Babylonian), and texts from Confucianism, Hinduism, ancient Egyptian religions, Assyrian religion, Roman mythology, Eastern religions, and Mesopotamian religion? By allowing only secular primary sources, did the Idaho Constitution and the actions of the commission amount to a level of hostility toward religion that would fail the second prong of the *Lemon* test because it has the primary effect of inhibiting religion? Why or why not?

An Idaho federal district court granted the state's motion to dismiss Nampa's complaint. According to the court, "[t]here simply is no law creating a First Amendment right of either teachers or students to use the Bible or any other sacred religious text as part of a public school curriculum." Instead, the state had the right to set its message in the classroom, where the Establishment Clause did not allow it to promote religion. Nampa Classical Academy v. Goesling, 714 F.Supp.2d 1079 (D.Idaho 2010). The court observed that if the plaintiffs were running a private school instead of a public charter school their arguments would be correct. Why? The Ninth Circuit affirmed the district court's ruling in Nampa Classical Academy v. Goesling, 447 Fed.Appx. 776 (9th Cir. 2011). The court ruled that the curriculum involved government speech, not the speech of teachers, parents or students, and that government speech is not subjected to free speech analysis. Do you agree with the court's ruling or believe it limited the education of the students?

In recent years the debate has shifted from *whether* the Bible should be taught in schools to *how* it should be taught. What do you think about the following guidelines that Texas set for its commissioner of education of public schools?

(a) The commissioner shall develop and make available training materials and other teacher training resources for a school district to use in assisting teachers of elective Bible courses in developing:

(1) expertise in the appropriate Bible course curriculum;

(2) understanding of applicable supreme court rulings and current constitutional law regarding how Bible courses are to be taught in public schools objectively as a part of a secular program of education;

(3) understanding of how to present the Bible in an objective, academic manner that neither promotes nor disparages religion, nor is taught from a particular sectarian point of view;

(4) proficiency in instructional approaches that present course material in a manner that respects all faiths and religious traditions, while favoring none; and

(5) expertise in how to avoid devotional content or proselytizing in the classroom.

Tex. Educ. Code Ann. § 21.459. Is Texas' legislation constitutional? Do you agree with a *Wall Street Journal* article that argues "we're not talking about religion here, and certainly not about politics. We're talking about knowledge. The foundations of knowledge of the ancient world—which informs the understanding of the modern world—are biblical in origin."? What about their argument that you can't have a government class without reading the Constitution and similarly can't have a successful education without reading the Bible? Roma Downey & Mark Burnett, Why Public Schools Should Teach the Bible, Wall St. J., Mar. 1, 2013, at A11.

4. *Teaching Islam in Public Schools.* If it is assumed that teaching the Bible in public schools is acceptable, then is it acceptable to teach Islam as well? If other religions are taught, should those religions be given the same amount of time for instruction with the same amount of depth? What if Islam is taught in more depth than other religions?

In order to help students understand Islam, a California public school history teacher asked the students to role-play being Muslim. The students used Muslim names, recited Muslim prayers, and gave up something every day as a fast during Ramadan. Christian students challenged the role-playing on the grounds that it was religious indoctrination. Do you agree with the Ninth Circuit that these classes did not violate the Establishment Clause? See Eklund v. Byron Union School Dist., 154 Fed.Appx. 648 (9th Cir. 2005), cert. denied, 549 U.S. 942, 127 S.Ct. 86 (2006).

C.W., a 16-year-old eleventh grader, was "instructed to finish 'a graded assignment to complete certain faith statements fundamental to the

Islamic belief system' " as part of an assignment in her World History class. Her parents, Melissa and John Wood, who are devout Lutheran Christians, alleged that the school unconstitutionally "required the students . . . to profess statements on the teachings and beliefs of Islam in written worksheets as graded homework assignments." Wood v. Bd. of Educ., 2016 U.S. Dist. LEXIS 136512, * 3 (D. Md. Sept. 30, 2016). In their complaint, the Woods alleged their daughter was removed from the classroom when she would not complete the assignments, was required to go to the student library during class time, and was forced to take a grade of zero on the assignments she would not complete. The Woods also alleged that the class spent two weeks studying Islam and only one day studying Christianity. See Complaint, Wood v. Charles County Public Schools et. al., No. 8:16-cv-00239-GHJ (D. Md. Jan. 27, 2016), at https://www.thomasmore.org/wp-con tent/uploads/2016/01/Thomas-More-Law-Center-Files-Lawsuit-On-Behalf-of-Marine-Dad-Banned-from-Schoo-After-He-Objected-to-Islamic-Indoctrination-Complaint-Time-Stamped.pdf. Did the school violate the Establishment Clause? See Wood v. Bd. of Educ., 2016 U.S. Dist. LEXIS 136512, * 20 (D. Md. Sept. 30, 2016) (Plaintiffs stated a claim under the Establishment Clause).

Does the Constitution require that if a school teaches *about* different religions then the school should provide equal amounts of instruction time for each religion? If a school should provide for more time to teach certain religions, does that go against what the Supreme Court said in *Lynch v. Donnelly*, that nonadherents are "outsiders" and that those who believe in a certain way are considered "insiders?" *Lynch v. Donnelly*, 465 U.S. 668, 688 (1982) (O'Connor, J., concurring). Alternatively, is the school district merely providing for a more robust instruction in a religion that is constantly in the news? Would it be better for future adults to have a more in-depth understanding of the particulars of Islam? Is it unconstitutional if the religions that receive more in-depth analysis make up a majority of the world's population as opposed to religions with small numbers of followers? If they make up a majority of the country's population?

5.   *Wide Awake at the University of Virginia. Wide Awake* was a student publication at the University of Virginia that had a "two-fold mission: 'to challenge Christians to live, in word and deed, according to the faith they proclaim and to encourage students to consider what a personal relationship with Jesus Christ means.' " Every page of the paper contained a cross. The paper ran articles on a wide range of subjects, including racism, pregnancy, prayer, C.S. Lewis, music, homosexuality and eating disorders. Because University guidelines barred funding to any religious activity (namely, "any activity that primarily promotes or manifests a particular belie[f] in or about a deity or an ultimate reality"), officials denied editor Ronald Rosenberger's request for funding. As we learned in Chapters 3, the Supreme Court ruled for Rosenberger under the Free Speech Clause of the First Amendment, concluding that the state had created a public forum and that it could not discriminate against Rosenberger's Christian *viewpoint* when it awarded funds. See Rosenberger v. Rector and Visitors of the University of Virginia, 515 U.S. 819 (1995).

The Court rejected the university's argument that the Establishment Clause justified the denial of funding.

Writing for the majority, Justice Anthony Kennedy observed:

Were the prohibition applied with much vigor at all, it would bar funding of essays by hypothetical student contributors named Plato, Spinoza, and Descartes ... [and] undergraduates named Karl Marx, Bertrand Russell, and Jean-Paul Sartre would likewise have some of their major essays excluded from student publications. . . . [I]t is indeed difficult to name renowned thinkers whose writings would be accepted, save perhaps for articles disclaiming all connection to their ultimate philosophy. Plato could contrive perhaps to submit an acceptable essay on making pasta or peanut butter cookies, provided he did not point out their (necessary) imperfections.

Id. at 836–37.

Although, according to Justice Kennedy, if one excludes Rosenberger one must exclude Plato, dissenting Justice David Souter's standard funds Plato, Spinoza and Descartes but not Rosenberger. Souter argued that if, as Justice Kennedy concedes, the government may set the *subject* but not the *viewpoint* of the public forum, then it is clear that *Wide Awake*'s "subject is not the discourse of the scholar's study or the seminar room, but of the evangelist's mission station and the pulpit. It is nothing other than the preaching of the word, which (along with the sacraments) is what most branches of Christianity offer those called to the religious life." Id. at 868. According to Souter, the Establishment Clause prohibits government funding of the subject matter of evangelism. Kennedy rejected Souter's standard, suggesting that the line between "religious speech" and "speech about religion" is too hard to draw.

Does Kennedy's opinion suggest the religious studies and theology distinction is not valid? Does *Rosenberger* suggest that the *Schempp* distinction between teaching about and of religion has been abandoned? Is the most important difference between *Schempp* and *Rosenberger* that the Establishment Clause limits government but not private speech?

Rosenberger's rights to funding were protected by the free *speech* protections of the First Amendment. Do you recall from Chapter 3 what role the Establishment Clause played in this case? What argument about the Establishment Clause did the University of Virginia make, and why was it rejected by the Court?

6. Justice Souter wrote in *Rosenberger* that there is an important constitutional line between preaching and teaching. Is that line respected in the following case about a ministry student? Is the following decision, *Locke v. Davey*, which we first saw in Chapter 3 as a case about the Establishment Clause and public funding, consistent with *Rosenberger*? Does it finally clarify the debate about the constitutionality of teaching theology in public schools?

Locke v. Davey

Supreme Court of the United States, 2004.
540 U.S. 712, 124 S.Ct. 1307, 158 L.Ed.2d 1.

■ CHIEF JUSTICE REHNQUIST delivered the opinion of the Court.

The State of Washington established the Promise Scholarship Program to assist academically gifted students with postsecondary education expenses. In accordance with the State Constitution, students may not use the scholarship at an institution where they are pursuing a degree in devotional theology. We hold that such an exclusion from an otherwise inclusive aid program does not violate the Free Exercise Clause of the First Amendment.

The Washington State Legislature found that "[s]tudents who work hard . . . and successfully complete high school with high academic marks may not have the financial ability to attend college because they cannot obtain financial aid or the financial aid is insufficient." Wash. Rev. Code Ann. § 28B.119.005 (West Supp. 2004). In 1999, to assist these high-achieving students, the legislature created the Promise Scholarship Program, which provides a scholarship, renewable for one year, to eligible students for postsecondary education expenses. Students may spend their funds on any education-related expense, including room and board. The scholarships are funded through the State's general fund, and their amount varies each year depending on the annual appropriation, which is evenly prorated among the eligible students. Wash. Admin. Code § 250–80–050(2). The scholarship was worth $1,125 for academic year 1999–2000 and $1,542 for 2000–2001.

To be eligible for the scholarship, a student must meet academic, income, and enrollment requirements. A student must graduate from a Washington public or private high school and either graduate in the top 15% of his graduating class, or attain on the first attempt a cumulative score of 1,200 or better on the Scholastic Assessment Test I or a score of 27 or better on the American College Test. The student's family income must be less than 135% of the State's median. Finally, the student must enroll "at least half time in an eligible postsecondary institution in the state of Washington," and may not pursue a degree in theology at that institution while receiving the scholarship. §§ 250–80–020(12)(f)–(g); see also Wash. Rev. Code § 28B.10.814 (1997) ("No aid shall be awarded to any student who is pursuing a degree in theology"). Private institutions, including those religiously affiliated, qualify as "eligible postsecondary institution[s]" if they are accredited by a nationally recognized accrediting body. A "degree in theology" is not defined in the statute, but, as both parties concede, the statute simply codifies the State's constitutional prohibition on providing funds to students to pursue degrees that are "devotional in nature or designed to induce religious faith."

A student who applies for the scholarship and meets the academic and income requirements is notified that he is eligible for the scholarship if he meets the enrollment requirements. Once the student enrolls at an eligible institution, the institution must certify that the student is enrolled at least half time and that the student is not pursuing a degree in devotional theology. The institution, rather than the State, determines whether the student's major is devotional. If the student meets the enrollment requirements, the scholarship funds are sent to the institution for distribution to the student to pay for tuition or other educational expenses.

Respondent, Joshua Davey, was awarded a Promise Scholarship, and chose to attend Northwest College. Northwest is a private, Christian college affiliated with the Assemblies of God denomination, and is an eligible institution under the Promise Scholarship Program. Davey had "planned for many years to attend a Bible college and to prepare [himself] through that college training for a lifetime of ministry, specifically as a church pastor." To that end, when he enrolled in Northwest College, he decided to pursue a double major in pastoral ministries and business management/administration. There is no dispute that the pastoral ministries degree is devotional and therefore excluded under the Promise Scholarship Program.

At the beginning of the 1999–2000 academic year, Davey met with Northwest's director of financial aid. He learned for the first time at this meeting that he could not use his scholarship to pursue a devotional theology degree. He was informed that to receive the funds appropriated for his use, he must certify in writing that he was not pursuing such a degree at Northwest. He refused to sign the form and did not receive any scholarship funds.

Davey then brought an action under 42 USC § 1983 against various state officials (hereinafter State) in the District Court for the Western District of Washington to enjoin the State from refusing to award the scholarship solely because a student is pursuing a devotional theology degree, and for damages. He argued the denial of his scholarship based on his decision to pursue a theology degree violated, *inter alia*, the Free Exercise, Establishment, and Free Speech Clauses of the First Amendment. The District Court rejected Davey's constitutional claims and granted summary judgment in favor of the State.

A divided panel of the United States Court of Appeals for the Ninth Circuit reversed. 299 F.3d 748 (2002). The court concluded that the State had singled out religion for unfavorable treatment and thus under our decision in *Church of the Lukumi Babalu Aye, Inc. v. City of Hialeah*, 508 U.S. 520, 124 L. Ed. 2d 472, 113 S. Ct. 2217 (1993), the State's exclusion of theology majors must be narrowly tailored to achieve a compelling state interest. Finding that the State's own antiestablishment concerns were not compelling, the court declared

Washington's Promise Scholarship Program unconstitutional. We granted certiorari, and now reverse.

These two Clauses, the Establishment Clause and the Free Exercise Clause, are frequently in tension. Yet we have long said that "there is room for play in the joints" between them. In other words, there are some state actions permitted by the Establishment Clause but not required by the Free Exercise Clause.

This case involves that "play in the joints" described above. Under our Establishment Clause precedent, the link between government funds and religious training is broken by the independent and private choice of recipients. [See *Zelman.*] As such, there is no doubt that the State could, consistent with the Federal Constitution, permit Promise Scholars to pursue a degree in devotional theology, and the State does not contend otherwise. The question before us, however, is whether Washington, pursuant to its own constitution,[2] which has been authoritatively interpreted as prohibiting even indirectly funding religious instruction that will prepare students for the ministry, can deny them such funding without violating the Free Exercise Clause.

Davey urges us to answer that question in the negative. He contends that under the rule we enunciated in *Church of the Lukumi Babalu Aye, Inc. v. City of Hialeah, supra,* the program is presumptively unconstitutional because it is not facially neutral with respect to religion. We reject his claim of presumptive unconstitutionality, however; to do otherwise would extend the *Lukumi* line of cases well beyond not only their facts but their reasoning. In *Lukumi,* the city of Hialeah made it a crime to engage in certain kinds of animal slaughter. We found that the law sought to suppress ritualistic animal sacrifices of the Santeria religion. In the present case, the State's disfavor of religion (if it can be called that) is of a far milder kind. It imposes neither criminal nor civil sanctions on any type of religious service or rite. It does not deny to ministers the right to participate in the political affairs of the community. See *McDaniel v. Paty,* 435 U.S. 618, 98 S.Ct. 1322, 55 L.Ed.2d 593 (1978). And it does not require students to choose between their religious beliefs and receiving a government benefit. See *ibid.; Hobbie v. Unemployment Appeals Comm'n of Florida.* 480 U.S. 136, 107 S.Ct. 1046, 94 L.Ed.2d 190 (1987); *Thomas v. Review Bd. of Indiana Employment Sec. Division,* 450 U.S. 707, 101 S.Ct. 1425, 67 L.Ed.2d 624 (1981); *Sherbert v. Verner,*

---

2   The relevant provision of the Washington Constitution, Art. I, § 11, states:

"Religious Freedom. Absolute freedom of conscience in all matters of religious sentiment, belief and worship, shall be guaranteed to every individual, and no one shall be molested or disturbed in person or property on account of religion; but the liberty of conscience hereby secured shall not be so construed as to excuse acts of licentiousness or justify practices inconsistent with the peace and safety of the state. No public money or property shall be appropriated for or applied to any religious worship, exercise or instruction, or the support of any religious establishment."

374 U.S. 398, 83 S.Ct. 1790, 10 L.Ed.2d 965 (1963). The State has merely chosen not to fund a distinct category of instruction.

JUSTICE SCALIA argues, however, that generally available benefits are part of the "baseline against which burdens on religion are measured." Because the Promise Scholarship Program funds training for all secular professions, JUSTICE SCALIA contends the State must also fund training for religious professions. But training for religious professions and training for secular professions are not fungible. Training someone to lead a congregation is an essentially religious endeavor. Indeed, majoring in devotional theology is akin to a religious calling as well as an academic pursuit. And the subject of religion is one in which both the United States and state constitutions embody distinct views—in favor of free exercise, but opposed to establishment—that find no counterpart with respect to other callings or professions. That a State would deal differently with religious education for the ministry than with education for other callings is a product of these views, not evidence of hostility toward religion.

Even though the differently worded Washington Constitution draws a more stringent line than that drawn by the United States Constitution, the interest it seeks to further is scarcely novel. In fact, we can think of few areas in which a State's antiestablishment interests come more into play. Since the founding of our country, there have been popular uprisings against procuring taxpayer funds to support church leaders, which was one of the hallmarks of an "established" religion.

Most States that sought to avoid an establishment of religion around the time of the founding placed in their constitutions formal prohibitions against using tax funds to support the ministry. The plain text of these constitutional provisions prohibited *any* tax dollars from supporting the clergy. We have found nothing to indicate, as Justice Scalia contends, that these provisions would not have applied so long as the State equally supported other professions or if the amount at stake was *de minimis*. That early state constitutions saw no problem in explicitly excluding *only* the ministry from receiving state dollars reinforces our conclusion that religious instruction is of a different ilk.

Far from evincing the hostility toward religion which was manifest in *Lukumi*, we believe that the entirety of the Promise Scholarship Program goes a long way toward including religion in its benefits. The program permits students to attend pervasively religious schools, so long as they are accredited. As Northwest advertises, its "concept of education is distinctly Christian in the evangelical sense." It prepares *all* of its students, "through instruction, through modeling, [and] through [its] classes, to use . . . the Bible as their guide, as the truth," no matter their chosen profession. And under the Promise Scholarship Program's current guidelines, students are still eligible to take devotional theology courses. Davey notes all students at Northwest are required to take at least four devotional courses, "Exploring the Bible," "Principles of Spiritual Development," "Evangelism in the Christian Life," and "Christian Doctrine," and some students may have additional religious requirements as part of their majors.

In short, we find neither in the history or text of Article I, § 11 of the Washington Constitution, nor in the operation of the Promise Scholarship Program, anything that suggests animus towards religion. Given the historic and substantial state interest at issue, we therefore cannot conclude that the denial of funding for vocational religious instruction alone is inherently constitutionally suspect.

Without a presumption of unconstitutionality, Davey's claim must fail. The State's interest in not funding the pursuit of devotional degrees is substantial and the exclusion of such funding places a relatively minor burden on Promise Scholars. If any room exists between the two Religion Clauses, it must be here. We need not venture further into this difficult area in order to uphold the Promise Scholarship Program as currently operated by the State of Washington.

The judgment of the Court of Appeals is therefore

Reversed.

■ JUSTICE SCALIA, with whom JUSTICE THOMAS joins, dissenting.

[According to *Everson*,] [w]hen the State makes a public benefit generally available, that benefit becomes part of the baseline against which burdens on religion are measured; and when the State withholds that benefit from some individuals solely on the basis of religion, it violates the Free Exercise Clause no less than if it had imposed a special tax.

That is precisely what the State of Washington has done here. It has created a generally available public benefit, whose receipt is conditioned only on academic performance, income, and attendance at an accredited school. It has then carved out a solitary course of study for exclusion: theology. No field of study but religion is singled out for disfavor in this fashion. Davey is not asking for a special benefit to which others are not entitled. He seeks only *equal* treatment—the right to direct his scholarship to his chosen course of study, a right every other Promise Scholar enjoys.

The Court's reference to historical "popular uprisings against procuring taxpayer funds to support church leaders" is therefore quite misplaced. That history involved not the inclusion of religious ministers in public benefits programs like the one at issue here, but laws that singled them out for financial aid. For example, the Virginia bill at which Madison's Remonstrance was directed provided: "[F]or the support of Christian teachers . . . [a] sum payable for tax on the property within this Commonwealth, is hereby assessed. . . ." A Bill Establishing a Provision for Teachers of the Christian Religion (1784), reprinted in *Everson*, supra, at 72, 91 L. Ed. 711, 67 S. Ct. 504. Laws supporting the clergy in other States operated in a similar fashion. One can concede the Framers' hostility to funding the clergy *specifically*, but that says nothing about whether the clergy had to be excluded from benefits the State made available to all. No one would seriously contend, for example, that the Framers would have barred ministers from using public roads on their way to church.

The Court does not dispute that the Free Exercise Clause places some constraints on public benefits programs, but finds none here, based on a principle of "play in the joints." I use the term "principle" loosely, for that is not so much a legal principle as a refusal to apply *any* principle when faced with competing constitutional directives. There is nothing anomalous about constitutional commands that abut. A municipality hiring public contractors may not discriminate *against* blacks or *in favor of* them; it cannot discriminate a little bit each way and then plead "play in the joints" when haled into court. If the Religion Clauses demand neutrality, we must enforce them, in hard cases as well as easy ones.

Even if "play in the joints" were a valid legal principle, surely it would apply only when it was a close call whether complying with one of the Religion Clauses would violate the other. But that is not the case here. It is not just that "the State could, consistent with the Federal Constitution, permit Promise Scholars to pursue a degree in devotional theology." The establishment question *would not even be close*, as is evident from the fact that this Court's decision in *Witters v. Washington Dept. of Services for the Blind*, 474 U.S. 481, 88 L. Ed. 2d 846, 106 S. Ct. 748 (1986), was unanimous. Perhaps some formally neutral public benefits programs are so gerrymandered and devoid of plausible secular purpose that they might raise specters of state aid to religion, but an evenhanded Promise Scholarship Program is not among them.

In any case, the State already has all the play in the joints it needs. There are any number of ways it could respect both its unusually sensitive concern for the conscience of its taxpayers *and* the Federal Free Exercise Clause. It could make the scholarships redeemable only at public universities (where it sets the curriculum), or only for select courses of study. Either option would replace a program that facially discriminates against religion with one that just happens not to subsidize it. The State could also simply abandon the scholarship program altogether. If that seems a dear price to pay for freedom of conscience, it is only because the State has defined that freedom so broadly that it would be offended by a program with such an incidental, indirect religious effect.

II

It may be that Washington's original purpose in excluding the clergy from public benefits was benign, and the same might be true of its purpose in maintaining the exclusion today. But those singled out for disfavor can be forgiven for suspecting more invidious forces at work. Let there be no doubt: This case is about discrimination against a religious minority. Most citizens of this country identify themselves as professing some religious belief, but the State's policy poses no obstacle to practitioners of only a tepid, civic version of faith. Those the statutory exclusion actually affects—those whose belief in their religion is so strong that they dedicate their study and their lives to its ministry—are a far narrower set. One need not delve too far into modern popular culture to perceive a trendy disdain for deep religious conviction. In an era when the Court is so quick to come to the aid of other disfavored groups, see, e.g., *Romer v. Evans*, 517 U.S. 620, 635, 134 L. Ed. 2d 855, 116 S. Ct. 1620 (1996), its indifference in this case, which involves a form of discrimination to which the Constitution actually speaks, is exceptional.

Today's holding is limited to training the clergy, but its logic is readily extendible, and there are plenty of directions to go. What next? Will we deny priests and nuns their prescription-drug benefits on the ground that taxpayers' freedom of conscience forbids medicating the clergy at public expense? This may seem fanciful, but recall that France has proposed banning religious attire from schools, invoking interests in secularism no less benign than those the Court embraces today. When the public's freedom of conscience is invoked to justify denial of equal treatment, benevolent motives shade into indifference and ultimately into repression. Having accepted the justification in this case, the Court is less well equipped to fend it off in the future. I respectfully dissent.

■ JUSTICE THOMAS, dissenting.

I write separately to note that, in my view, the study of theology does not necessarily implicate religious devotion or faith. The contested statute denies Promise Scholarships to students who pursue "a degree in theology." But the statute itself does not define "theology." And the usual definition of the term "theology" is not limited to devotional studies. "Theology" is defined as "[t]he study of the nature of God and religious truth" and the "rational inquiry into religious questions." American Heritage Dictionary 1794 (4th ed. 2000). See also Webster's Ninth New Collegiate Dictionary 1223 (1991) ("the study of religious faith, practice, and experience" and "the study of God and his relation to the world"). These definitions include the study of theology from a secular perspective as well as from a religious one.

Assuming that the State denies Promise Scholarships only to students who pursue a degree in devotional theology, I believe that Justice Scalia's application of our precedents is correct. Because neither party contests the validity of these precedents, I join Justice Scalia's dissent.

NOTES AND QUESTIONS

1.   What is the play in the joints principle identified by Chief Justice Rehnquist? Is it a useful principle by which to understand the interaction of free exercise and establishment, or, as the dissent states, "a refusal to apply *any* principle when faced with competing constitutional directives"?

2.   Is *Davey* inconsistent with *Lukumi*? See Douglas Laycock, The Supreme Court, 2003 Term; Theology Scholarships, The Pledge of Allegiance, and Religious Liberty: Avoiding the Extremes But Missing the Liberty, 118 Harv. L. Rev. 155, 173 (2004) (*Davey* "appeared to be a slam dunk under *Lukumi*. And yet it lost, 7–2."). How can you explain Davey's loss in the Supreme Court? See id. (*Davey* is "not surprising" as a funding case, but "remarkable" as a religious discrimination case.).

A Colorado statute made tuition assistance available to low-income college students at any public or private school except for "pervasively sectarian" institutions as defined by the statute:

> an institution is not "pervasively sectarian" if it meets six criteria: (i) the faculty and students are not exclusively of one religious persuasion; (ii) there is no required attendance at religious convocations or services; (iii) there is a strong commitment to principles of academic freedom; (iv) there are no required courses in religion or theology that tend to indoctrinate or proselytize; (v) the governing board does not reflect, nor is the membership limited to, persons of any particular religion; and (vi) funds do not come primarily or predominantly from sources advocating a particular religion.

Colorado Christian University (CCU) brought suit alleging the state's denial of its application to participate in the program violated the Free Exercise and Establishment Clauses of the First Amendment. After the district court granted summary judgment for the state because of *Davey*, the Tenth Circuit found the "exclusion unconstitutional for two reasons: the program expressly discriminates among religions without constitutional justification, and its criteria for doing so involve unconstitutionally intrusive scrutiny of religious belief and practice," and granted summary judgment for the university. Judge Michael McConnell, a prominent law and religion scholar, wrote that the state law favored sectarian institutions over pervasively sectarian ones, allowing scholarships to some Methodist and Catholic colleges while denying them to CCU. Moreover, the state was excessively entangled in determinations about the nature of the schools when it asked for syllabi and information about the school's leadership to judge whether the school was pervasively sectarian. See Colorado Christian University v. Weaver, 534 F.3d 1245 (10th Cir. 2008). Do you agree with the Tenth Circuit's analysis, or did the court misinterpret *Davey*?

3.   Is *Davey* inconsistent with *Rosenberger*? Davey argued, following *Rosenberger*, that the Promise Scholarship Program was an unconstitutional viewpoint restriction on speech. Chief Justice Rehnquist dismissed that argument, however, because the program was not a forum

for speech but rather an attempt to aid low-and middle-income students with tuition. See 540 U.S. at 720 n.1. Why can the state be required to fund Rosenberger's newspaper but not Davey's education?

4.   Recall that in Zelman v. Simmons-Harris, 536 U.S. 639 (2002), which we studied in Chapter 3, the Court ruled that the State of Ohio may distribute vouchers to parents of students in religious schools as long as the program is neutral (i.e., includes religious and non-religious schools) and fosters the individual choice of parents. According to Chief Justice Rehnquist in *Davey*, "[u]nder our Establishment Clause precedent, the link between government funds and religious training is broken by the independent and private choice of recipients." Is the link between Washington and religious training broken by the independent choice of Joshua Davey to study devotional theology? Is *Davey* consistent with *Zelman*? See Laycock, supra, note 1. Why doesn't the conclusion that a state *may* distribute funding to religious organizations without constitutional violation compel Washington to fund Davey?

5.   What is devotional theology? Is it the same thing as studying for the ministry? How is it similar to and different from theology? Does the experience of universities in Europe that we read about above suggest that divinity schools and ministerial training should have different constitutional status from other professional training?

Is Justice Thomas correct that the study of theology may be secular? Would the religion scholars think that Justice Thomas' type of theology is constitutional or unconstitutional? How could a course in theology be secular? How would a degree in religious studies be seen through the eyes of the majority and dissent?

6.   How does Chief Justice Rehnquist's argument that there is a longstanding American tradition, going back to the *Memorial and Remonstrance*, against paying taxes to support ministry, stand up to Justice Scalia's claim that there is a difference between singling ministers out for public aid and excluding them from public benefits programs?

As we learned in Chapter 3, like Washington, many states have stricter establishment prohibitions on church-state interaction than the federal constitution; many state constitutions prohibit state governments from giving any monetary support to religions, including aid to theology instruction. In Trinity Lutheran Church of Columbia, Inc. v. Pauley, 788 F.3d 779 (8th Cir. 2015), the Missouri case about the scrap tire grants, the majority cited *Locke v. Davey* as supporting Missouri's constitutional ban on funding. The dissent, however, read *Locke* to prohibit excluding the religious from generally available public benefits. If the Supreme Court overturns the Eighth Circuit, will the theology/religious studies distinction be affected?

7.   Should the states pursue the alternatives suggested by Justice Scalia and "make the scholarships redeemable only at public universities (where it sets the curriculum), or only for select courses of study"?

Are Davey's constitutional rights protected as long as he can pursue devotional theology with his own funds? What do you think of the following argument? "Technically, Davey could have taken advantage of some loopholes in the program that might have preserved his award while allowing him to study for the ministry. He could have enrolled half time at Northwest College to study Pastoral Ministries and then enrolled half time at another accredited college where he might have used his scholarship to study Business Management. Or, he could have declared only the Business Management major at Northwest College and taken the same theology courses as electives." Susanna Dokupil, Function Follows Form: *Locke v. Davey*'s Unnecessary Parsing, 2004 Cato Sup. Ct. Rev. 327, 330.

8.   Did the Washington program place an unconstitutional condition on Davey's free exercise of religion by forcing him to give up his religious choice in order to receive a government benefit? *Davey* raises a classic question about the government's relationship to constitutional rights, namely, "whether the government has an affirmative obligation to facilitate the exercise of a constitutional right, rather than restrain itself from interfering in the exercise of that right." Do you think the government has such an affirmative obligation to fund devotional theology? Does it have an affirmative obligation to fund abortion or artistic work? See Jason S. Marks, Spackle for the Wall? Public Funding for School Vouchers After *Locke v. Davey*, J. Missouri Bar, May–June 2005 ("In every situation, the Court has answered this question in the negative.").

The scholars of religion were eager to design a scientific study of religion that was distinguishable from unscientific subjects such as theology, divinity or evangelism. They believed that the scientific study of religion in public schools was constitutional, while unscientific approaches were not. In the next section, we examine how science can be taught in public schools. The debate arises from the teaching of Darwinian evolution in public school science classes. If the scientific study of evolution is permissible, may schoolteachers teach biblical creation, creation-science or intelligent design? Must schoolteachers introduce these subjects wherever evolution is taught? Are evolution, creationism, and intelligent design science, religion, or both?

B. CREATION, EVOLUTION, AND INTELLIGENT DESIGN

1. CREATION

The Book of Genesis contains two accounts of creation, which biblical scholars refer to as the Priestly and Yahwist stories, names based on the words that the different authors use for God and the style of their writing. See John J. Collins, Introduction to the Hebrew Bible 49–50 (2004). What are the differences between the two accounts of creation that follow?

The Book of Genesis

The Priestly Author, 1:1–2:3.
New Revised Standard Version Bible.

1 In the beginning when God created the heavens and the earth, **2** the earth was a formless void and darkness covered the face of the deep, while a wind from God swept over the face of the waters. **3** Then God said, "Let there be light"; and there was light. **4** And God saw that the light was good; and God separated the light from the darkness. **5** God called the light Day, and the darkness he called Night. And there was evening and there was morning, the first day.

6 And God said, "Let there be a dome in the midst of the waters, and let it separate the waters from the waters." **7** So God made the dome and separated the waters that were under the dome from the waters that were above the dome. And it was so. **8** God called the dome Sky. And there was evening and there was morning, the second day.

9 And God said, "Let the waters under the sky be gathered together into one place, and let the dry land appear." And it was so. **10** God called the dry land Earth, and the waters that were gathered together he called Seas. And God saw that it was good. **11** Then God said, "Let the earth put forth vegetation: plants yielding seed, and fruit trees of every kind on earth that bear fruit with the seed in it." And it was so. **12** The earth brought forth vegetation: plants yielding seed of every kind, and trees of every kind bearing fruit with the seed in it. And God saw that it was good. **13** And there was evening and there was morning, the third day.

14 And God said, "Let there be lights in the dome of the sky to separate the day from the night; and let them be for signs and for seasons and for days and years, **15** and let them be lights in the dome of the sky to give light upon the earth." And it was so. **16** God made the two great lights—the greater light to rule the day and the lesser light to rule the night—and the stars. **17** God set them in the dome of the sky to give light upon the earth, **18** to rule over the day and over the night, and to separate the light from the darkness. And God saw that it was good. **19** And there was evening and there was morning, the fourth day.

20 And God said, "Let the waters bring forth swarms of living creatures, and let birds fly above the earth across the dome of the sky." **21** So God created the great sea monsters and every living creature that moves, of every kind, with which the waters swarm, and every winged bird of every kind. And God saw that it was good. **22** God blessed them, saying, "Be fruitful and multiply and fill the waters in the seas, and let birds multiply on the earth." **23** And there was evening and there was morning, the fifth day.

24 And God said, "Let the earth bring forth living creatures of every kind: cattle and creeping things and wild animals of the earth of every kind." And it was so. *25* God made the wild animals of the earth of every kind, and the cattle of every kind, and everything that creeps upon the ground of every kind. And God saw that it was good.

26 Then God said, "Let us make humankind in our image, according to our likeness; and let them have dominion over the fish of the sea, and over the birds of the air, and over the cattle, and over all the wild animals of the earth, and over every creeping thing that creeps upon the earth."

27 So God created humankind in his image, in the image of God he created them; male and female he created them.

28 God blessed them, and God said to them, "Be fruitful and multiply, and fill the earth and subdue it; and have dominion over the fish of the sea and over the birds of the air and over every living thing that moves upon the earth." *29* God said, "See, I have given you every plant yielding seed that is upon the face of all the earth, and every tree with seed in its fruit; you shall have them for food. *30* And to every beast of the earth, and to every bird of the air, and to everything that creeps on the earth, everything that has the breath of life, I have given every green plant for food." And it was so. *31* God saw everything that he had made, and indeed, it was very good. And there was evening and there was morning, the sixth day.

2 Thus the heavens and the earth were finished, and all their multitude. *2* And on the seventh day God finished the work that he had done, and he rested on the seventh day from all the work that he had done. *3* So God blessed the seventh day and hallowed it, because on it God rested from all the work that he had done in creation.

The Book of Genesis
The Yahwist Author, 2:4b–2:25.
New Revised Standard Version Bible.

2 In the day that the LORD God made the earth and the heavens, *5* when no plant of the field was yet in the earth and no herb of the field had yet sprung up—for the LORD God had not caused it to rain upon the earth, and there was no one to till the ground; *6* but a stream would rise from the earth, and water the whole face of the ground—*7* then the LORD God formed man from the dust of the ground, and breathed into his nostrils the breath of life; and the man became a living being. *8* And the LORD God planted a garden in Eden, in the east; and there he put the man whom he had formed. *9* Out of the ground the LORD God made to grow every tree that is pleasant to the sight and good for food, the tree of life also in the midst of the garden, and the tree of the knowledge of good and evil.

10 A river flows out of Eden to water the garden, and from there it divides and becomes four branches. *11* The name of the first is Pishon;

it is the one that flows around the whole land of Havilah, where there is gold; *12* and the gold of that land is good; bdellium and onyx stone are there. *13* The name of the second river is Gihon; it is the one that flows around the whole land of Cush. *14* The name of the third river is Tigris, which flows east of Assyria. And the fourth river is the Euphrates.

15 The LORD God took the man and put him in the garden of Eden to till it and keep it. *16* And the LORD God commanded the man, "You may freely eat of every tree of the garden; *17* but of the tree of the knowledge of good and evil you shall not eat, for in the day that you eat of it you shall die."

18 Then the LORD God said, "It is not good that the man should be alone; I will make him a helper as his partner." *19* So out of the ground the LORD God formed every animal of the field and every bird of the air, and brought them to the man to see what he would call them; and whatever the man called every living creature, that was its name. *20* The man gave names to all cattle, and to the birds of the air, and to every animal of the field; but for the man there was not found a helper as his partner. *21* So the LORD God caused a deep sleep to fall upon the man, and he slept; then he took one of his ribs and closed up its place with flesh. *22* And the rib that the LORD God had taken from the man he made into a woman and brought her to the man. *23* Then the man said,

"This at last is bone of my bones and flesh of my flesh; this one shall be called Woman, for out of Man this one was taken."

24 Therefore a man leaves his father and his mother and clings to his wife, and they become one flesh. *25* And the man and his wife were both naked, and were not ashamed.

NOTES AND QUESTIONS

1.   *Creation Myths.* "A creation myth is a cosmogony, a narrative that describes the original ordering of the universe. . . . Like all myths, creation myths are etiological—they use symbolic narrative to explain beginnings because the culture at one point lacked the information to explain things scientifically." David Adams Leeming & Margaret Adams Leeming, A Dictionary of Creation Myths vii (1994). Are the Priestly and Yahwist accounts of creation in Genesis myths? Are they etiological or scientific? For example, did creation really take place in six days? Does each day represent a different geological era in the world's development? Or were there no days of creation at all? Are the days of creation actual and literal, or metaphorical, analogical, symbolic or poetic?

2.   *Creation* ex nihilo. According to Leeming and Leeming, "[t]he basic creation story, then, is that of the process by which chaos becomes cosmos, no-thing becomes some-thing. . . . Creation occurs primarily in one of five ways: 1) from chaos or nothingness (*ex nihilo*), 2) from a cosmic egg or primal maternal mound, 3) from world parents who are separated, 4)

from a process of earth-diving, or 5) from several stages of emergence from other worlds." Id. at viii. Which type of myth are these creation stories from Genesis? Does it matter if creation occurs out of chaos or *ex nihilo*, out of nothing? Or are chaos and nothingness the same thing? See Ernan McMullin, ed., Evolution and Creation 8 (1985) (the Jewish creation myth was distinctive in the ancient world because of God's creation of humans out of nothing instead of out of some existing material). Most Christians believe that Genesis supports a doctrine of creation *ex nihilo*. See David Kelsey, "The Doctrine of Creation from Nothing," in id. at 176. Mormons, however, believe that chaos was already present and that God's creation put order into the chaos or matter that was already there; this distinguishes them from the traditional Christian theology of creation *ex nihilo*. See Francis J. Beckwith, Carl Mosser & Paul Owen, eds., The New Mormon Challenge 99–107 (2002). According to the traditional Mormon theology, "God 'created' the world by organizing, shaping, or forming preexistent matter and was limited in what he could create by matter's inherent nature." Jim W. Adams, The God of Abraham, Isaac, and Joseph Smith?: God, Creation, and Humanity in the Old Testament and Mormonism, in id. at 180.

St. Augustine subscribed to the Priestly narrative and argued that in the beginning "was not absolute nothingness," but formlessness. See, e.g., Augustine, Confessions 247 (Henry Chadwick trans., 1991). According to Leeming and Leeming, sometimes it is hard to distinguish between creation from nothing and creation from chaos. This ambiguity is evident in, for example, ibn Rushd's (Latinate name Averroes) statement that the world is "made by God" and "did not come to be by chance or by itself." Averroes, Faith and Reason in Islam 78 (Ibrahim Y. Najjar trans., 2001). By contrast, Moses Maimonides, the author of the *Mishneh Torah* (the first attempt at a codification of Jewish law) and a major, if not the major, authority within the Jewish tradition, says unambiguously in *The Guide of the Perplexed* that "all who believe in the Law of Moses our Master" hold that God created the world *ex nihilo*. Moses Maimonides, The Guide of the Perplexed 281 (Shlomo Pines trans., 1963).

What do you think the text of Genesis says about creation out of nothing or out of something? What does this early Hindu text from the Rig-Veda say about creation *ex nihilo*? Is it consistent with Genesis?

> There was neither aught nor naught, nor air, nor sky beyond. What covered all? Where rested all? In watery gulf profound? Nor death was then, nor deathlessness, nor change of night and day. The One breathed calmly, self-sustained; nought else beyond it lay.

> Gloom, hid in gloom, existed first—one sea, eluding view. That One, a void in chaos wrapt, by inward fervour grew. Within it first arose desire, the primal germ of mind, Which nothing with existence links, as sages searching find.

> The kindling ray that shot across the dark and drear abyss—Was is beneath? or high aloft? What bard can answer this? There

fecundating powers were found, and mighty forces strove—A self-supporting mass beneath, and energy above.

Who knows, who ever told, from whence this vast creation rose? No gods had then been born—who then can e'er the truth disclose? Whence sprang this world, and whether framed by hand divine or no—Its lord in heaven alone can tell, if even he can show.

W.J. Wilkins, Hindu Mythology, Vedic and Puranic 342–43 (2d ed. 1973). See also id. (reporting that later generations then tried to shed more light on what happened at creation by developing different creation myths).

3.   *Alternative Stories of Origins.* How does Genesis compare with the following creation myths?

a.   China's "most colourful creation myth centres on the giant Coiled Antiquity (Pan Gu), the first-born, semi-divine human being. It tells how he lay dying and as his life ebbed away his breath became the winds and clouds, his voice thunder, his eyes the sun and moon, and his limbs mountains. His bodily fluids turned into rain and rivers, his flesh into the soil. His head hair became the stars, his body hair became vegetation. His teeth, bones and marrow turned into minerals. The insects on his body became human beings. This myth is made up of a series of metamorphoses in which the various parts of the body became analogous parts of the universe. It is one of many myths of the cosmological human body from around the world, and it contains the important myths of the dying god and the nurturing god, who gave his body for the benefit of humankind." Anne Birrell, Chinese Myths 19 (2000).

b.   Atrahasis is an old, pre-Genesis Babylonian myth from about 1700 B.C.E. in which "the chief gods were Anu, Enlil, and Enki. When the gods cast lots and divided the world, Anu took the sky, Enlil the earth, and Enki the waters below the earth. . . . The labor of agriculture was imposed on a class of gods called the Igigu. The first section of the myth deals with the rebellion of these worker gods, which led the high gods to concede that their workload was too heavy. Consequently, Enki and the mother-goddess created humanity 'to bear the load of the gods.' They slaughtered 'a god who had intelligence' (probably the god who had the idea for the rebellion), and Nintu mixed clay with his flesh and blood. From this mixture, she fashioned seven males and seven females." John J. Collins, Introduction to the Hebrew Bible (2004); see also Stephanie Dalley, Myths from Mesopotamia: Creation, the Flood, Gilgamesh and Others 4 (1989) (*Atrahasis* . . . "may be compared with that in the *Epic of Creation*, in which Marduk used the blood of Qingu, the evil leader of the enemy gods whom he had slain, to create mankind with the help of Ea; clay is not mentioned, and no birth-goddess takes part, but the purpose of man's creation is again to toil on the gods' behalf. Neither account mentions the creation of animals, which is an important preliminary to man's creation in Genesis (Priestly source).").

4. According to the *Jewish Study Bible*, in Genesis 2:7, "man has a lowlier origin than in the parallel in 1:26–28. He is created not in the image of God but from the dust of the earth." Adele Berlin & Marc Zvi Brettler, eds., The Jewish Study Bible 15 n.7 (2004). Does that mean that the Yahwist account is closer to evolutionary theory than the Priestly account? Is the following excerpt from Charles Darwin consistent with the Book of Genesis? Is this consistency literal or metaphorical?

2. EVOLUTION

Charles Darwin, The Origin of Species
371, 395–96 (1996), originally published 1859.

That many and serious objections may be advanced against the theory of descent with modification through natural selection, I do not deny. I have endeavored to give them their full force. Nothing at first can appear more difficult to believe than that the more complex organs and instincts should have been perfected, not by means superior to, though analogous with, human reason, but by the accumulation of innumerable slight variations, each good for the individual possessor. Nevertheless, this difficulty, though appearing to our imagination insuperably great, cannot be considered real if we admit the following propositions, namely,—that gradations in the perfection of any organ or instinct which we may consider, either do now exist or could have existed, each good of its kind,—that all organs and instincts are, in ever so slight of a degree, variable,—and, lastly, that there is a struggle for existence leading to the preservation of each profitable deviation of structure or instinct. The truth of these propositions cannot, I think, be disputed. . . .

It is interesting to contemplate an entangled bank, clothed with many plants of many kinds, with birds singing on the bushes, with various insects flitting about, and with worms crawling through the damp earth, and to reflect that these elaborately constructed forms, so different from each other, and dependent on each other in so complex a manner, have all been produced by laws acting around us. These laws, taken in the largest sense, being Growth with Reproduction; Inheritance, which is almost implied by reproduction; Variability, from the indirect and direct action of the external conditions of life, and from use and disuse; a Ratio of Increase so high as to lead to a Struggle for Life, and as a consequence to Natural Selection, entailing Divergence of Character and the Extinction of less-improved forms. Thus, from the war of nature, from famine and death, the most exalted object which we are capable of conceiving, namely, the production of the higher animals, directly follows. There is a grandeur in this view of life, with its several powers, having been originally breathed *by the Creator** into a few forms or into one; and that, whilst this planet has gone cycling on according to the fixed law of gravity, from so simple a beginning endless forms most beautiful and most wonderful have been, and are being, evolved.

NOTES AND QUESTIONS

1.   *What is evolution?* According to Eugenie Scott,

The broad definition of evolution is a cumulative change through time. Not just any change counts as evolution, however. . . . Think of evolution as a statement about history. If we were able to go back in time, we would find different galaxies and planets, and different forms of life on Earth. Galaxies, planets, and living things have changed through time. There is astronomical evolution, geological evolution, and biological evolution. Evolution, far from the mere "man evolved from monkeys," is thus integral to astronomy, geology, and biology . . . it is relevant to physics and chemistry as well. . . . In biology, evolution is the inference that living things share common ancestors and have, in Darwin's words, "descended with modification" from these ancestors. The main—but not the only—mechanism of biological evolution is natural selection. . . .

Natural selection is the term Charles Darwin gave to what he considered the most powerful force of evolutionary change, and virtually all modern evolutionary biologists agree. In fact, the thesis that evolution is primarily driven by natural selection is sometimes called Darwinism. Unfortunately, many people misapply the term to refer to the concept of descent with modification itself, which is erroneous. Natural selection is not the same as evolution . . . there is a conceptual difference between a phenomenon and the mechanisms or processes that bring it about. . . .

The principle [of natural selection] is simple: generate a variety of possible solutions, and then pick the one that works best for the problem at hand. The first solution is not necessarily the best one—in fact, natural selection rarely results in even a good solution to a problem in one pass. But repeated iterations of randomly generated solutions combined with selection of the characteristics that meet (or come close to meeting) the necessary criteria result in a series of solutions that more closely approximate a good solution. . . . What is selected for depends on what, in the organism's particular circumstances, will be conducive to its survival and reproduction.

---

*   Emphasis added. Darwin added the "by the Creator" to the second edition of his book; it was not present in the original. Darwin, supra, at xxiv.

Eugenie C. Scott, Evolution vs. Creationism: An Introduction 23–24, 35–36 (2d ed. 2009).

2. Charles Darwin added the words "by the Creator" to the second edition of his book; they were not present in the original. Darwin, supra, at xxiv. According to Edward Larson, "Despite Darwin's closing concession, *Origin of Species* dealt a body blow to traditional Western religious thought. At a superficial level, Darwin's chronology for the origin of species differed on its face from that set forth in Genesis. Species evolved from preexisting species over vast periods of time, he asserted; God did not separately create all of them in a few days." Edward J. Larson, Evolution: The Remarkable History of a Scientific Theory 88–89 (2004); see also Daniel C. Dennett, Darwin's Dangerous Idea: Evolution and the Meanings of Life 59 (1995) ("Here then is Darwin's dangerous idea: the algorithmic level *is* the level. . . . No matter how impressive the products of an algorithm, the underlying process always consists of nothing but a set of individually mindless steps succeeding each other without the help of any intelligent supervision; they are 'automatic' by definition: the workings of an automaton. They feed on each other, or on blind chance—coin flips, if you like—and on nothing else.").

Whether it dealt a "body blow" to Christian thought or not, evolution has been the subject of much controversy since the publication of *Origin of Species* in 1859. In his book *Trial and Error: The American Controversy Over Creation and Evolution*, Edward J. Larson provides a detailed history of the debate about Darwinism in the United States. Indeed his chapter titles summarize the story of that development: Evolution before 1920; Outlawing, 1920–25; Enforcing, 1925–60; Legalizing, 1961–70; Equal Time, 1970–81; Outlawing Creation, 1981–90; and Mandating Evolution, 1990s and beyond. (3rd ed. 2003). Larson reports that it took until the 1880s for Darwin's ideas to reach the basic biology textbooks as core scientific knowledge. After that, teaching Darwin was uncontroversial until the 1920s, when fundamentalist Christians initiated legislation in several southern states to ban Darwin from the schoolbooks. Most noteworthy was the State of Tennessee, which in 1925 passed legislation (sometimes called the "monkey law") making it a crime to teach evolution in the public schools. Although the Progressive former presidential candidate, William Jennings Bryan, led the campaign against evolution, even Bryan questioned the criminal penalty, preferring Florida's earlier law because no test case could be brought if there was no penalty. See Edward J. Larson, Summer for the Gods: The Scopes Trial and America's Continuing Debate Over Science and Religion 47–50 (1997). For a comprehensive history of creationism, see Ronald L. Numbers, The Creationists: The Evolution of Scientific Creationism (1992).

The test case came in Tennessee. In response to advertisements by the American Civil Liberties Union seeking plaintiffs to challenge the anti-evolution law, residents of Dayton, Tennessee, initiated a prosecution of John Scopes for teaching evolution in defiance of state law. The trial put Dayton on the map; the national media focused on the Scopes trial, where

Bryan, aiding the state, battled Scopes' famous lawyer Clarence Darrow. A jury took nine minutes to convict Scopes. Darrow did not get the appellate reversal that he desired; instead, the Supreme Court of Tennessee reversed Scopes' conviction because the judge, not the jury, had imposed the $100 fine. See Scopes v. State, 154 Tenn. 105, 289 S.W. 363 (1927). Because of this technical error, Scopes had no conviction to appeal to the United States Supreme Court, and the anti-evolution bill remained on the books until its repeal in 1967. See Epperson v. Arkansas, 393 U.S. 97, 102 (1968).

Larson reports that the anti-evolution acts had their desired effects from the 1930s to the 1960s, as publishers removed controversial evolutionary materials from the books. Larson, Trial and Error, supra, at 230–31. "By 1930, only five years after the Scopes trial, an estimated 70 percent of American classrooms omitted evolution, and the amount diminished even further thereafter." Eugenie C. Scott, Evolution vs. Creationism: An Introduction 97 (2004). So things remained until the 1960s, when teachers challenged the bans on teaching evolution and Americans became more interested in improving science education so they could compete with the Russians in sending men to the moon. In 1968, Susan Epperson won her challenge to a 1928 Arkansas law that forbade the teaching of evolution in public schools. See Epperson v. Arkansas, 393 U.S. 97 (1968). The Arkansas law made it a misdemeanor, punishable by dismissal, to teach or use a textbook stating "mankind ascended or descended from a lower order of animals." Id. at 99. Justice Abe Fortas' opinion concluded that the law violated the Establishment Clause because it proscribed teaching evolution "for the sole reason that it is deemed to conflict with a particular religious doctrine," namely, the Book of Genesis. Id. at 103.

Justice Hugo Black concurred in *Epperson* because he thought the statute was vague, but he raised the question why the state could not simply decide to take controversial subjects such as evolution out of the schools in order to avoid controversy. Id. at 113. Indeed, Bryan's original strategy had been to keep both evolution and creationism from the schools. Do you agree with efforts to keep both evolution and creationism out of the classroom in order to avoid the intense disagreements about their merits?

Instead of "neutrality by silence," in the 1960s the teaching of evolution in the classrooms accelerated and creationists demanded equal time in the classroom for creationism. In Tennessee, a 1974 statute required that *biblical* creationism must be included equally whenever evolution was taught; that law was invalidated as a violation of the Establishment Clause. See Daniel v. Waters, 515 F.2d 485 (6th Cir. 1975); Steele v. Waters, 527 S.W.2d 72 (Tenn. 1975). Then Yale law student Wendell Bird wrote a note that identified a different equal time strategy. See Freedom of Religion and Science Instruction in Public Schools, 87 Yale L.J. 515 (1977–78). Instead of requiring *biblical* creationism, Bird argued that teaching evolution alone violated the free exercise of opponents of evolution and proposed that *scientific* creationism be taught whenever evolution was. Id. at 517–18. Equal time statutes were introduced in some twenty-seven states in the 1980s but passed only in Louisiana and Arkansas. See Eugenie C. Scott, Evolution vs. Creationism: An Introduction 106 (2004). The Arkansas Balanced Treatment for Creation-Science and Evolution-Science Act was invalidated by a federal district court in the following case.

3. EVOLUTION AND CREATION-SCIENCE

McLean v. Arkansas Board of Education

United States District Court, Eastern District of Arkansas, 1982.
529 F.Supp. 1255.

MEMORANDUM OPINION

■ OVERTON, DISTRICT JUDGE.

Introduction

On March 19, 1981, the Governor of Arkansas signed into law Act 590 of 1981, entitled the "Balanced Treatment for Creation-Science and Evolution-Science Act." The Act is codified as Ark.Stat.Ann. § 80–1663, *et seq.* (1981 Supp.). Its essential mandate is stated in its first sentence: "Public schools within this State shall give balanced treatment to creation-science and to evolution-science." On May 27, 1981, this suit was filed challenging the constitutional validity of Act 590 on three distinct grounds.

First, it is contended that Act 590 constitutes an establishment of religion prohibited by the First Amendment to the Constitution, which is made applicable to the states by the Fourteenth Amendment. Second, the plaintiffs argue the Act violates a right to academic freedom which they say is guaranteed to students and teachers by the Free Speech Clause of the First Amendment. Third, plaintiffs allege the Act is impermissibly vague and thereby violates the Due Process Clause of the Fourteenth Amendment.

The individual plaintiffs include the resident Arkansas Bishops of the United Methodist, Episcopal, Roman Catholic and African Methodist Episcopal Churches, the principal official of the Presbyterian Churches in Arkansas, other United Methodist, Southern Baptist and Presbyterian clergy, as well as several persons who sue as parents and next friends of minor children attending Arkansas public schools. One plaintiff is a high school biology teacher. All are also Arkansas taxpayers. Among the organizational plaintiffs are the American Jewish Congress, the Union of American Hebrew Congregations, the American Jewish Committee, the Arkansas Education Association, the National Association of Biology Teachers and the National Coalition for Public Education and Religious Liberty, all of which sue on behalf of members living in Arkansas.

The defendants include the Arkansas Board of Education and its members, the Director of the Department of Education, and the State Textbooks and Instructional Materials Selecting Committee.

The trial commenced December 7, 1981, and continued through December 17, 1981. This Memorandum Opinion constitutes the Court's findings of fact and conclusions of law.

[The court applied the three part *Lemon* test: "First, the statute must have a secular legislative purpose; second, its principal or primary effect must be one that neither advances nor inhibits religion ...; finally, the statute must not foster 'an excessive government entanglement with religion.'" See Lemon v. Kurtzman, 403 U.S. 602, 612–13, 91 S.Ct. 2105, 2111, 29 L.Ed.2d 745 (1971).]

II.

The religious movement known as Fundamentalism began in nineteenth century America as part of evangelical Protestantism's response to social changes, new religious thought and Darwinism. Fundamentalists viewed these developments as attacks on the Bible and as responsible for a decline in traditional values.

The various manifestations of Fundamentalism have had a number of common characteristics,[4] but a central premise has always been a literal interpretation of the Bible and a belief in the inerrancy of the Scriptures. Following World War I, there was again a perceived decline in traditional morality, and Fundamentalism focused on evolution as responsible for the decline. One aspect of their efforts, particularly in the South, was the promotion of statutes prohibiting the teaching of evolution in public schools. In Arkansas, this resulted in the adoption of Initiated Act 1 of 1929.

Between the 1920's and early 1960's, anti-evolutionary sentiment had a subtle but pervasive influence on the teaching of biology in public schools. Generally, textbooks avoided the topic of evolution and did not mention the name of Darwin. Following the launch of the Sputnik satellite by the Soviet Union in 1957, the National Science Foundation funded several programs designed to modernize the teaching of science in the nation's schools. The Biological Sciences Curriculum Study (BSCS), a nonprofit organization, was among those receiving grants for curriculum study and revision. Working with scientists and teachers, BSCS developed a series of biology texts which, although emphasizing

---

[4] The authorities differ as to generalizations which may be made about Fundamentalism. For example, Dr. Geisler testified to the widely held view that there are five beliefs characteristic of all Fundamentalist movements, in addition, of course, to the inerrancy of Scripture: (1) belief in the virgin birth of Christ, (2) belief in the deity of Christ, (3) belief in the substitutional atonement of Christ, (4) belief in the second coming of Christ, and (5) belief in the physical resurrection of all departed souls. Dr. Marsden, however, testified that this generalization, which has been common in religious scholarship, is now thought to be historical error. There is no doubt, however, that all Fundamentalists take the Scriptures as inerrant and probably most take them as literally true.

different aspects of biology, incorporated the theory of evolution as a major theme. The success of the BSCS effort is shown by the fact that fifty percent of American school children currently use BSCS books directly and the curriculum is incorporated indirectly in virtually all biology texts.

In the early 1960's, there was again a resurgence of concern among Fundamentalists about the loss of traditional values and a fear of growing secularism in society. The Fundamentalist movement became more active and has steadily grown in numbers and political influence. There is an emphasis among current Fundamentalists on the literal interpretation of the Bible and the Book of Genesis as the sole source of knowledge about origins.

The term "scientific creationism" first gained currency around 1965 following publication of *The Genesis Flood* in 1961 by Whitcomb and Morris. There is undoubtedly some connection between the appearance of the BSCS texts emphasizing evolutionary thought and efforts by Fundamentalists to attack the theory.

In the 1960's and early 1970's, several Fundamentalist organizations were formed to promote the idea that the Book of Genesis was supported by scientific data. The terms "creation science" and "scientific creationism" have been adopted by these Fundamentalists as descriptive of their study of creation and the origins of man. Perhaps the leading creationist organization is the Institute for Creation Research (ICR), which is affiliated with the Christian Heritage College and supported by the Scott Memorial Baptist Church in San Diego, California. The ICR, through the Creation-Life Publishing Company, is the leading publisher of creation science material. Other creation science organizations include the Creation Science Research Center (CSRC) of San Diego and the Bible Science Association of Minneapolis, Minnesota. In 1963, the Creation Research Society (CRS) was formed from a schism in the American Scientific Affiliation (ASA). It is an organization of literal Fundamentalists who have the equivalent of a master's degree in some recognized area of science. A purpose of the organization is "to reach all people with the vital message of the scientific and historic truth about creation." Similarly, the CSRC was formed in 1970 from a split in the CRS. Its aim has been "to reach the 63 million children of the United States with the scientific teaching of Biblical creationism."

Creationists view evolution as a source of society's ills, ... Creationists have adopted the view of Fundamentalists generally that there are only two positions with respect to the origins of the earth and life: belief in the inerrancy of the Genesis story of creation and of a worldwide flood as fact, or belief in what they call evolution. ...

The creationist organizations consider the introduction of creation science into the public schools part of their ministry. The ICR has published at least two pamphlets containing suggested methods for convincing school boards, administrators and teachers that creationism should be taught in public schools. The ICR has urged its proponents to encourage school officials to voluntarily add creationism to the curriculum.

Citizens For Fairness In Education is an organization based in Anderson, South Carolina, formed by Paul Ellwanger, a respiratory therapist who is trained in neither law nor science. Mr. Ellwanger is of the opinion that evolution is the forerunner of many social ills, including Nazism, racism and abortion. About 1977, Ellwanger collected several proposed legislative acts with the idea of preparing a model state act requiring the teaching of creationism as science in opposition to evolution. One of the proposals he collected was prepared by Wendell Bird, who is now a staff attorney for ICR. From these various proposals, Ellwanger prepared a "model act" which calls for "balanced treatment" of "scientific creationism" and "evolution" in public schools. He circulated the proposed act to various people and organizations around the country.

Mr. Ellwanger's views on the nature of creation science are entitled to some weight since he personally drafted the model act which became Act 590. His evidentiary deposition with exhibits and unnumbered attachments (produced in response to a subpoena *duces tecum*) speaks to both the intent of the Act and the scientific merits of creation science. Mr. Ellwanger does not believe creation science is a science. In a letter to Pastor Robert E. Hays he states, "While neither evolution nor creation can qualify as a scientific theory, and since it is virtually impossible at this point to educate the whole world that evolution is not a true scientific theory, we have freely used these terms—the evolution theory and the theory of scientific creationism—in the bill's text." He further states in a letter to Mr. Tom Bethell, "As we examine evolution (remember, we're not making any scientific claims for creation, but we are challenging evolution's claim to be scientific). . . . "

Ellwanger's correspondence on the subject shows an awareness that Act 590 is a religious crusade, coupled with a desire to conceal this fact. In a letter to State Senator Bill Keith of Louisiana, he says, "I view this whole battle as one between God and anti-God forces, though I know there are a large number of evolutionists who believe in God." And further, " . . . it behooves Satan to do all he can to thwart our efforts and confuse the issue at every turn." Yet Ellwanger suggests to Senator Keith, "If you have a clear choice between having grassroots leaders of this statewide bill promotion effort to be ministerial or non-ministerial, be sure to opt for the non-ministerial. It does the bill effort no good to have ministers out there in the public forum and the adversary will surely pick at this point . . . Ministerial persons can accomplish a tremendous amount of work from behind the scenes, encouraging their congregations to take the organizational and P.R. initiatives. And they can lead their churches in storming Heaven with prayers for help against so tenacious an adversary."

Ellwanger shows a remarkable degree of political candor, if not finesse, in a letter to State Senator Joseph Carlucci of Florida:

"2. It would be very wise, if not actually essential, that all of us who are engaged in this legislative effort be careful not to present our position and our work in a religious framework. For example, in written communications that might somehow be shared with those other persons whom we may be trying to convince, it would be well to exclude our own personal testimony and/or witness for Christ, but rather, if we are so moved, to give that testimony on a separate attached note."

The same tenor is reflected in a letter by Ellwanger to Mary Ann Miller, a member of FLAG (Family, Life, America under God) who lobbied the Arkansas Legislature in favor of Act 590:

" . . . we'd like to suggest that you and your co-workers be very cautious about mixing creation-science with creation-religion. . . . Please urge your co-workers not to allow themselves to get sucked into the 'religion' trap of mixing the two together, for such mixing does incalculable harm to the legislative thrust. It could even bring public opinion to bear adversely upon the higher courts that will eventually have to pass judgment on the constitutionality of this new law."

. . . It was out of this milieu that Act 590 emerged. The Reverend W. A. Blount, a Biblical literalist who is pastor of a church in the Little Rock area and was, in February, 1981, chairman of the Greater Little Rock Evangelical Fellowship, was among those who received a copy of the model act from Ellwanger.[12]

At Reverend Blount's request, the Evangelical Fellowship unanimously adopted a resolution to seek introduction of Ellwanger's act in the Arkansas Legislature. A committee composed of two ministers, Curtis Thomas and W. A. Young, was appointed to implement the resolution. Thomas obtained from Ellwanger a revised copy of the model act which he transmitted to Carl Hunt, a business associate of Senator James L. Holsted, with the request that Hunt prevail upon Holsted to introduce the act.

Holsted, a self-described "born again" Christian Fundamentalist, introduced the act in the Arkansas Senate. He did not consult the State Department of Education, scientists, science educators or the Arkansas Attorney General. The Act was not referred to any Senate committee for

---

[12] The model act had been revised to insert "creation science" in lieu of creationism because Ellwanger had the impression people thought creationism was too religious a term. (Ellwanger Depo. at 79.)

hearing and was passed after only a few minutes' discussion on the Senate floor. In the House of Representatives, the bill was referred to the Education Committee which conducted a perfunctory fifteen minute hearing. No scientist testified at the hearing, nor was any representative from the State Department of Education called to testify.

Ellwanger's model act was enacted into law in Arkansas as Act 590 without amendment or modification other than minor typographical changes. The legislative "findings of fact" in Ellwanger's act and Act 590 are identical, although no meaningful fact-finding process was employed by the General Assembly.

Ellwanger's efforts in preparation of the model act and campaign for its adoption in the states were motivated by his opposition to the theory of evolution and his desire to see the Biblical version of creation taught in the public schools. There is no evidence that the pastors, Blount, Thomas, Young or The Greater Little Rock Evangelical Fellowship were motivated by anything other than their religious convictions when proposing its adoption or during their lobbying efforts in its behalf. Senator Holsted's sponsorship and lobbying efforts in behalf of the Act were motivated solely by his religious beliefs and desire to see the Biblical version of creation taught in the public schools.[14]

The State of Arkansas, like a number of states whose citizens have relatively homogeneous religious beliefs, has a long history of official opposition to evolution which is motivated by adherence to Fundamentalist beliefs in the inerrancy of the Book of Genesis. This history is documented in Justice Fortas' opinion in *Epperson v. Arkansas*, 393 U.S. 97, 89 S.Ct. 266, 21 L.Ed.2d 228 (1968), which struck down Initiated Act 1 of 1929, Ark.Stat.Ann. §§ 80–1627–1628, prohibiting the teaching of the theory of evolution. To this same tradition may be attributed Initiated Act 1 of 1930, Ark.Stat.Ann. § 80–1606 (Repl.1980), requiring "the reverent daily reading of a portion of the English Bible" in every public school classroom in the State.[15]

It is true, as defendants argue, that courts should look to legislative statements of a statute's purpose in Establishment Clause cases and accord such pronouncements great deference. Defendants also correctly state the principle that remarks by the sponsor or author of a bill are not considered controlling in analyzing legislative intent.

---

[14] Specifically, Senator Holsted testified that he holds to a literal interpretation of the Bible; that the bill was compatible with his religious beliefs; that the bill does favor the position of literalists; that his religious convictions were a factor in his sponsorship of the bill; and that he stated publicly to the *Arkansas Gazette* (although not on the floor of the Senate) contemporaneously with the legislative debate that the bill does presuppose the existence of a divine creator. There is no doubt that Senator Holsted knew he was sponsoring the teaching of a religious doctrine. His view was that the bill did not violate the First Amendment because, as he saw it, it did not favor one denomination over another.

[15] This statute is, of course, clearly unconstitutional under the Supreme Court's decision in *Abington School Dist. v. Schempp*, 374 U.S. 203, 83 S.Ct. 1560, 10 L.Ed.2d 844 (1963).

Courts are not bound, however, by legislative statements of purpose or legislative disclaimers. *Stone v. Graham*, 449 U.S. 39, 101 S.Ct. 192, 66 L.Ed.2d 199 (1980); *Abington School District v. Schempp*, 374 U.S. 203, 83 S.Ct. 1560, 10 L.Ed.2d 844 (1963). In determining the legislative purpose of a statute, courts may consider evidence of the historical context of the Act, *Epperson v. Arkansas*, 393 U.S. 97, 89 S.Ct. 266, 21 L.Ed.2d 228 (1968), the specific sequence of events leading up to passage of the Act, departures from normal procedural sequences, substantive departures from the normal, and contemporaneous statements of the legislative sponsor.

The unusual circumstances surrounding the passage of Act 590, as well as the substantive law of the First Amendment, warrant an inquiry into the stated legislative purposes. The author of the Act had publicly proclaimed the sectarian purpose of the proposal. The Arkansas residents who sought legislative sponsorship of the bill did so for a purely sectarian purpose. These circumstances alone may not be particularly persuasive, but when considered with the publicly announced motives of the legislative sponsor made contemporaneously with the legislative process; the lack of any legislative investigation, debate or consultation with any educators or scientists; the unprecedented intrusion in school curriculum; and official history of the State of Arkansas on the subject, it is obvious that the statement of purposes has little, if any, support in fact. The State failed to produce any evidence which would warrant an inference or conclusion that at any point in the process anyone considered the legitimate educational value of the Act. It was simply and purely an effort to introduce the Biblical version of creation into the public school curricula. The only inference which can be drawn from these circumstances is that the Act was passed with the specific purpose by the General Assembly of advancing religion. The Act therefore fails the first prong of the three-pronged test, that of secular legislative purpose, as articulated in *Lemon v. Kurtzman, supra,* and *Stone v. Graham, supra.*

III.

If the defendants are correct and the Court is limited to an examination of the language of the Act, the evidence is overwhelming that both the purpose and effect of Act 590 is the advancement of religion in the public schools.

Section 4 of the Act provides:

Definitions. As used in this Act:

(a) "Creation-science" means the scientific evidences for creation and inferences from those scientific evidences. Creation-science includes the scientific evidences and related inferences that indicate: (1) Sudden creation of the universe, energy, and life from nothing; (2) The insufficiency of mutation and natural selection in bringing about development of all living kinds from a single organism; (3) Changes only within fixed limits of originally created kinds of plants and animals; (4) Separate ancestry for man and apes; (5) Explanation of the earth's geology by catastrophism, including the occurrence of a worldwide flood; and (6) A relatively recent inception of the earth and living kinds.

(b) "Evolution-science" means the scientific evidences for evolution and inferences from those scientific evidences. Evolution-science includes the scientific evidences and related inferences that indicate: (1) Emergence by naturalistic processes of the universe from disordered matter and emergence of life from non-life; (2) The sufficiency of mutation and natural selection in bringing about development of present living kinds from simple earlier kinds; (3) Emergence by mutation and natural selection of present living kinds from simple earlier kinds; (4) Emergence of man from a common ancestor with apes; (5) Explanation of the earth's geology and the evolutionary sequence by uniformitarianism; and (6) An inception several billion years ago of the earth and somewhat later of life.

(c) "Public schools" mean public secondary and elementary schools.

The evidence establishes that the definition of "creation science" contained in 4(a) has as its unmentioned reference the first 11 chapters of the Book of Genesis. Among the many creation epics in human history, the account of sudden creation from nothing, or *creatio ex nihilo*, and subsequent destruction of the world by flood is unique to Genesis. The concepts of 4(a) are the literal Fundamentalists' view of Genesis. Section 4(a) is unquestionably a statement of religion, with the exception of 4(a)(2) which is a negative thrust aimed at what the creationists understand to be the theory of evolution.

Both the concepts and wording of Section 4(a) convey an inescapable religiosity. Section 4(a)(1) describes "sudden creation of the universe, energy and life from nothing." Every theologian who testified, including defense witnesses, expressed the opinion that the statement referred to a supernatural creation which was performed by God.

Defendants argue that: (1) the fact that 4(a) conveys ideas similar to the literal interpretation of Genesis does not make it conclusively a statement of religion; (2) that reference to a creation from nothing is not necessarily a religious concept since the Act only suggests a creator who has power, intelligence and a sense of design and not necessarily the attributes of love, compassion and justice;[18] and (3) that simply teaching about the concept of a creator is not a religious exercise unless the student is required to make a commitment to the concept of a creator.

The evidence fully answers these arguments. The ideas of 4(a)(1) are not merely similar to the literal interpretation of Genesis; they are identical and parallel to no other story of creation.[19]

The argument that creation from nothing in 4(a)(1) does not involve a supernatural deity has no evidentiary or rational support. To the contrary, "creation out of nothing" is a concept unique to Western religions. In traditional Western religious thought, the conception of a creator of the world is a conception of God. Indeed, creation of the world "out of nothing" is the ultimate religious statement because God is the only actor. As Dr. Langdon Gilkey noted, the Act refers to one who has the power to bring all the universe into existence from nothing. The only "one" who has this power is God.

The leading creationist writers, Morris and Gish, acknowledge that the idea of creation described in 4(a)(1) is the concept of creation by God and make no pretense to the contrary. The idea of sudden creation from nothing, or *creatio ex nihilo*, is an inherently religious concept. (Vawter, Gilkey, Geisler, Ayala, Blount, Hicks.)

The argument advanced by defendants' witness, Dr. Norman Geisler, that teaching the existence of God is not religious unless the teaching seeks a commitment, is contrary to common understanding and contradicts settled case law. *Stone v. Graham*, 449 U.S. 39, 101 S.Ct. 192, 66 L.Ed.2d 199 (1980); *Abington School District v. Schempp*, 374 U.S. 203, 83 S.Ct. 1560, 10 L.Ed.2d 844 (1963).

The facts that creation science is inspired by the Book of Genesis and that Section 4(a) is consistent with a literal interpretation of Genesis leave no doubt that a major effect of the Act is the advancement of particular religious beliefs. The legal impact of this

---

[18] Although defendants must make some effort to cast the concept of creation in non-religious terms, this effort surely causes discomfort to some of the Act's more theologically sophisticated supporters. The concept of a creator God distinct from the God of love and mercy is closely similar to the Marcion and Gnostic heresies, among the deadliest to threaten the early Christian church. These heresies had much to do with development and adoption of the Apostle's Creed as the official creedal statement of the Roman Catholic Church in the West. (Gilkey.)

[19] The parallels between Section 4(a) and Genesis are quite specific: (1) "sudden creation from nothing" is taken from Genesis, 1:1–10 (Vawter, Gilkey); (2) destruction of the world by a flood of divine origin is a notion peculiar to Judeo-Christian tradition and is based on Chapters 7 and 8 of Genesis (Vawter); (3) the term "kinds" has no fixed scientific meaning, but appears repeatedly in Genesis (all scientific witnesses); (4) "relatively recent inception" means an age of the earth from 6,000 to 10,000 years and is based on the genealogy of the Old Testament using the rather astronomical ages assigned to the patriarchs (Gilkey and several of defendants' scientific witnesses); (5) separate ancestry of man and ape focuses on the portion of the theory of evolution which Fundamentalists find most offensive, *Epperson v. Arkansas*, 393 U.S. 97, 89 S.Ct. 266, 21 L.Ed.2d 228 (1968).

conclusion will be discussed further at the conclusion of the Court's evaluation of the scientific merit of creation science.

IV.(A)

The approach to teaching "creation science" and "evolution science" found in Act 590 is identical to the two-model approach espoused by the Institute for Creation Research and is taken almost verbatim from ICR writings. It is an extension of Fundamentalists' view that one must either accept the literal interpretation of Genesis or else believe in the godless system of evolution.

The two model approach of the creationists is simply a contrived dualism[22] which has no scientific factual basis or legitimate educational purpose. It assumes only two explanations for the origins of life and existence of man, plants and animals: It was either the work of a creator or it was not. Application of these two models, according to creationists, and the defendants, dictates that all scientific evidence which fails to support the theory of evolution is necessarily scientific evidence in support of creationism and is, therefore, creation science "evidence" in support of Section 4(a).

IV.(B)

The emphasis on origins as an aspect of the theory of evolution is peculiar to creationist literature. Although the subject of origins of life is within the province of biology, the scientific community does not consider origins of life a part of evolutionary theory. The theory of evolution assumes the existence of life and is directed to an explanation of *how* life evolved. Evolution does not presuppose the absence of a creator or God and the plain inference conveyed by Section 4 is erroneous.

As a statement of the theory of evolution, Section 4(b) is simply a hodgepodge of limited assertions, many of which are factually inaccurate.

IV.(C)

In addition to the fallacious pedagogy of the two model approach, Section 4(a) lacks legitimate educational value because "creation

---

[22] Morris, the Director of ICR and one who first advocated the two model approach, insists that a true Christian cannot compromise with the theory of evolution and that the Genesis version of creation and the theory of evolution are mutually exclusive. Px 31, Morris, *Studies in the Bible & Science*, 102–103. The two model approach was the subject of Dr. Richard Bliss's doctoral dissertation. (Dx 35). It is presented in Bliss, *Origins: Two Models— Evolution, Creation* (1978). Moreover, the two model approach merely casts in educationalist language the dualism which appears in all creationist literature—creation (i.e. God) and evolution are presented as two alternative and mutually exclusive theories. See, e.g., Px 75, Morris, *Scientific Creationism* (1974) (public school edition); Px 59, Fox, *Fossils: Hard Facts from the Earth*. Particularly illustrative is Px 61, Boardman, et al., *Worlds Without End* (1971), a CSRC publication: "One group of scientists, known as creationists, believe that God, in a miraculous manner, created all matter and energy. . . .

"Scientists who insist that the universe just grew, by accident, from a mass of hot gases without the direction or help of a Creator are known as evolutionists."

science" as defined in that section is simply not science. Several witnesses suggested definitions of science. A descriptive definition was said to be that science is what is "accepted by the scientific community" and is "what scientists do." The obvious implication of this description is that, in a free society, knowledge does not require the imprimatur of legislation in order to become science.

More precisely, the essential characteristics of science are:

(1) It is guided by natural law;

(2) It has to be explanatory by reference to natural law;

(3) It is testable against the empirical world;

(4) Its conclusions are tentative, i.e., are not necessarily the final word; and

(5) It is falsifiable. (Ruse and other science witnesses).

Creation science as described in Section 4(a) fails to meet these essential characteristics. First, the section revolves around 4(a)(1) which asserts a sudden creation "from nothing." Such a concept is not science because it depends upon a supernatural intervention which is not guided by natural law. It is not explanatory by reference to natural law, is not testable and is not falsifiable.

If the unifying idea of supernatural creation by God is removed from Section 4, the remaining parts of the section explain nothing and are meaningless assertions.

Section 4(a)(2), relating to the "insufficiency of mutation and natural selection in bringing about development of all living kinds from a single organism," is an incomplete negative generalization directed at the theory of evolution.

Section 4(a)(3) which describes "changes only within fixed limits of originally created kinds of plants and animals" fails to conform to the essential characteristics of science for several reasons. First, there is no scientific definition of "kinds" and none of the witnesses was able to point to any scientific authority which recognized the term or knew how many "kinds" existed. One defense witness suggested there may be 100 to 10,000 different "kinds." Another believes there were "about 10,000, give or take a few thousand." Second, the assertion appears to be an effort to establish outer limits of changes within species. There is no scientific explanation for these limits which is guided by natural law and the limitations, whatever they are, cannot be explained by natural law.

The statement in 4(a)(4) of "separate ancestry of man and apes" is a bald assertion. It explains nothing and refers to no scientific fact or theory.

Section 4(a)(5) refers to "explanation of the earth's geology by catastrophism, including the occurrence of a worldwide flood." This assertion completely fails as science. The Act is referring to the Noachian flood described in the Book of Genesis. The creationist writers concede that any kind of Genesis Flood depends upon supernatural intervention. A worldwide flood as an explanation of the world's geology is not the product of natural law, nor can its occurrence be explained by natural law.

Section 4(a)(6) equally fails to meet the standards of science. "Relatively recent inception" has no scientific meaning. It can only be given meaning by reference to creationist writings which place the age at between 6,000 and 20,000 years because of the genealogy of the Old Testament. Such a reasoning process is not the product of natural law; not explainable by natural law; nor is it tentative.

Creation science, as defined in Section 4(a), not only fails to follow the canons defining scientific theory, it also fails to fit the more general descriptions of "what scientists think" and "what scientists do." The scientific community consists of individuals and groups, nationally and internationally, who work independently in such varied fields as biology, paleontology, geology and astronomy. Their work is published and subject to review and testing by their peers. The journals for publication are both numerous and varied. There is, however, not one recognized scientific journal which has published an article espousing the creation science theory described in Section 4(a). Some of the State's witnesses suggested that the scientific community was "close-minded" on the subject of creationism and that explained the lack of acceptance of the creation science arguments. Yet no witness produced a scientific article for which publication had been refused. Perhaps some members of the scientific community are resistant to new ideas. It is, however, inconceivable that such a loose knit group of independent thinkers in all the varied fields of science could, or would, so effectively censor new scientific thought. . . .

The methodology employed by creationists is another factor which is indicative that their work is not science. A scientific theory must be tentative and always subject to revision or abandonment in light of facts that are inconsistent with, or falsify, the theory. A theory that is by its own terms dogmatic, absolutist and never subject to revision is not a scientific theory.

The creationists' methods do not take data, weigh it against the opposing scientific data, and thereafter reach the conclusions stated in Section 4(a). Instead, they take the literal wording of the Book of Genesis and attempt to find scientific support for it. . . .

The Court would never criticize or discredit any person's testimony based on his or her religious beliefs. While anybody is free to approach a scientific inquiry in any fashion they choose, they cannot properly describe the methodology used as scientific, if they start with a conclusion and refuse to change it regardless of the evidence developed during the course of the investigation.

IV.(D)

The proof in support of creation science consisted almost entirely of efforts to discredit the theory of evolution through a rehash of data and theories which have been before the scientific community for decades. The arguments asserted by creationists are not based upon new scientific evidence or laboratory data which has been ignored by the scientific community.

The testimony of Marianne Wilson was persuasive evidence that creation science is not science. Ms. Wilson is in charge of the science curriculum for Pulaski County Special School District, the largest school district in the State of Arkansas. Prior to the passage of Act 590, Larry Fisher, a science teacher in the District, using materials from the ICR, convinced the School Board that it should voluntarily adopt creation science as part of its science curriculum. The District Superintendent assigned Ms. Wilson the job of producing a creation science curriculum guide. Ms. Wilson's testimony about the project was particularly convincing because she obviously approached the assignment with an open mind and no preconceived notions about the subject. She had not heard of creation science until about a year ago and did not know its meaning before she began her research.

Ms. Wilson worked with a committee of science teachers appointed from the District. They reviewed practically all of the creationist literature. Ms. Wilson and the committee members reached the unanimous conclusion that creationism is not science; it is religion. They so reported to the Board. The Board ignored the recommendation and insisted that a curriculum guide be prepared. . . .

It is easy to understand why Ms. Wilson and other educators find the creationists' textbook material and teaching guides unacceptable. The materials misstate the theory of evolution in the same fashion as Section 4(b) of the Act, with emphasis on the alternative mutually exclusive nature of creationism and evolution. Students are constantly encouraged to compare and make a choice between the two models, and the material is not presented in an accurate manner. . . .

The conclusion that creation science has no scientific merit or educational value as science has legal significance in light of the Court's previous conclusion that creation science has, as one major effect, the advancement of religion. The second part of the three-pronged test for establishment reaches only those statutes having as their *primary* effect the advancement of religion. Secondary effects which advance religion are not constitutionally fatal. Since creation science is not science, the conclusion is inescapable that the only real effect of Act 590 is the advancement of religion. The Act therefore fails both the first and second portions of the test in *Lemon v. Kurtzman*, 403 U.S. 602, 91 S.Ct. 2105, 29 L.Ed.2d 745 (1971).

IV.(E)

Act 590 mandates "balanced treatment" for creation science and evolution science. The Act prohibits instruction in any religious doctrine or references to religious writings. The Act is self-contradictory and compliance is impossible unless the public schools elect to forego significant portions of subjects such as biology, world history, geology, zoology, botany, psychology, anthropology, sociology, philosophy, physics and chemistry. Presently, the concepts of evolutionary theory as described in 4(b) permeate the public school textbooks. There is no way teachers can teach the Genesis account of creation in a secular manner.

The State Department of Education, through its textbook selection committee, school boards and school administrators will be required to constantly monitor materials to avoid using religious references. The school boards, administrators and teachers face an impossible task. How is the teacher to respond to questions about a creation suddenly and out of nothing? How will a teacher explain the occurrence of a worldwide flood? How will a teacher explain the concept of a relatively recent age of the earth? The answer is obvious because the only source of this information is ultimately contained in the Book of Genesis.

References to the pervasive nature of religious concepts in creation science texts amply demonstrate why State entanglement with religion is inevitable under Act 590. Involvement of the State in screening texts for impermissible religious references will require State officials to make delicate religious judgments. The need to monitor classroom discussion in order to uphold the Act's prohibition against religious instruction will necessarily involve administrators in questions concerning religion. These continuing involvements of State officials in questions and issues of religion create an excessive and prohibited entanglement with religion.

[The court dismissed the arguments that the statute was vague, that it violated academic freedom, and that teaching evolution violated Free Exercise or Establishment.]

The Court closes this opinion with a thought expressed eloquently by the great Justice Frankfurter:

> "We renew our conviction that 'we have staked the very existence of our country on the faith that complete separation between the state and religion is best for the state and best for religion.' *Everson v. Board of Education of Ewing Township*, 330 U.S. at 59 (67 S.Ct. at 532). If nowhere else, in the relation between Church and State, 'good fences make good neighbors.'" *McCollum v. Board of Education*, 333 U.S. 203, 232, 68 S.Ct. 461, 475, 92 L.Ed. 649 (1948).

An injunction will be entered permanently prohibiting enforcement of Act 590.

NOTES AND QUESTIONS

1.   Are you surprised that the plaintiffs included both Jewish and Christian members of the community who presumably respected the Book of Genesis? Were the defenders of the Act all Fundamentalists? What is a Fundamentalist? How is a Fundamentalist different from an Evangelical Christian? Do all Evangelical Christians oppose evolution? See David N. Livingstone, Darwin's Forgotten Defenders: The Encounter Between Evangelical Theology and Evolutionary Thought (1987) (explaining how many Evangelical scientists and theologians accepted Darwinism in the nineteenth century).

2.   *Secular and Sectarian Purpose.* Why is the conduct of Paul Ellwanger relevant to the court's decision? Does the court need to examine the motivations of the legislators who passed Act 590? If the court decided that the wording of the act itself was unconstitutional because it promoted a religious theory of origins, why did it need to examine the motivations of the act's sponsors? Should all legislation passed for a sectarian purpose be invalidated? Are you influenced by what you read about religion and politics in Chapter 9?

3.   *Religion or Science.* What made the court conclude that the statute's description of creation-science was religion and not science? Did you find all the features of creation-science in your readings from the Book of Genesis, supra? Is it unscientific to believe in creation *ex nihilo*? To believe that the earth's geology resulted from a worldwide flood? To believe that the earth's origin is recent? To believe in a separate ancestry for man and apes? Is Section 4(a)(2) of Act 590 in the Book of Genesis?

Hebrew Bible expert Father Bruce Vawter of DePaul University testified about Genesis at the trial. "On recross, [he] listed again the six elements of the Genesis account relevant to the case: ex nihilo, the use of the phrase 'all living kinds,' fixity of species, separate ancestry, the Noachic flood, and recent creation.

'Are these in Genesis?'

'Yes.'

'Are they in Act 590?'

'Yes.'

'Are there any other views of origins that contain these elements, or these elements together in this way?'

'No, there are none.' "

See Langdon Gilkey, Creationism On Trial: Evolution and God at Little Rock 87 (1985). Does Vawter's testimony persuade you Act 590 was unconstitutional?

4.   What is the relevance of the reference to Christian heresy in footnote 18?

5.   Do you understand what Judge Overton means by the "contrived dualism" of the creation scientists' two-model approach? The judge writes that the two-model approach "is an extension of Fundamentalists' view that one must either accept the literal interpretation of Genesis or else believe in the godless system of evolution." What are the alternatives to a two-model approach? Would a different creation story from another religious tradition provide a different model and so disprove the two-model approach? Would a belief by some Jews and Christians that *Genesis* is consistent with evolution disprove the two-model approach?

6.   *Religious Acceptance of Evolution?* How can mainline Protestant churches sponsor an "Evolution Sunday"? See Neela Banerjee & Anne Berryman, At Churches Nationwide, Good Words for Evolution, N.Y. Times, Feb. 13, 2006, at A14. As Judge Overton points out in the opinion, many Christians cannot accept evolution because it is inconsistent with their faith, yet other believers accept it. What religious alternatives are there to a fundamentalist rejection of evolution? Professor Ian Barbour contrasted traditionalist and modernist approaches to evolution with the fundamentalist. Fundamentalists, as we learn in the *McLean* decision, believe that the Bible should be interpreted literally and that the biblical stories provide the truth about creation. Traditionalists are less literal, and move beyond the biblical text by arguing that God works in nature and that God's work can be seen in human evolution. Modernists accept modern science and use it to correct biblical and theological teachings. See Ian G. Barbour, Issues in Science and Religion 99–101 (1966). Within religious traditions, fundamentalists, traditionalists and modernists dispute among themselves which is the proper reading of creation. Within Islam, for example, "[d]ebate about the theory of evolution has pitted traditional religious scholars against modernists. The theory is denounced by most Muslim scholars, even some early modernists such as Afghani, as a refutation of Quranic theories of creation." John L. Esposito, Evolution, Theory of, and Islam, The Oxford Dictionary of Islam 77 (2003) (also reporting that evolution is taught in Turkey, Egypt, Iraq, Iran and Indonesia, but forbidden in Pakistan, Saudi Arabia and Sudan).

What do you think of the argument that evolution can be accepted as true as long as there is an acknowledgment that God intervened at some point to give human beings a soul? Or the argument that Darwinian natural selection is not random, but planned?

7.   *When Religion Becomes Science and Science Becomes Religion.* Langdon Gilkey, a professor at the University of Chicago Divinity School, was an expert witness in the *McLean* case and wrote a book describing that experience. See Langdon Gilkey, Creationism On Trial: Evolution and God at Little Rock (1985). Gilkey testified about the important distinction between religious and scientific knowledge and argued that creation-science was not science, but religion, and that evolution was not religion, but science. Sometimes science makes religious claims, and sometimes religions make scientific claims, but those are mistakes; science and religion are different spheres. According to Gilkey:

> This religious penumbra surrounding much of modern science, what one might call its "naturalistic aura," means, however, neither that creationism represents a "scientific" alternative to evolution nor that "evolutionary science" is simply a religious rival to belief in creation. On the contrary, the creationist concept of creation, being essentially a *religious* concept, and the scientific interpretation of the development of the physical universe, being essentially a set of *scientific* theories, represent significantly different levels of ideas or forms of conceptuality—and it soon became clear that this was what we would have to establish in court. Perhaps the trickiest intellectual problem of the trial—far more subtle than just proving creation science wrong or even unscientific—would be to distinguish the scientific from the religious elements of *both* creationism and evolutionary science, so that while the truth of this point about the religious dimensions of much science could be admitted, the radical distinction *on the scientific level* between the two could be unequivocally asserted.

Id. at 25; see also Langdon Gilkey, Blue Twilight: Nature, Creationism, and American Religion (2001). When does a scientific theory turn into a religion? Does evolution proclaim the religion of atheism or agnosticism or secularism?

Gilkey explained the distinction between the two theories on the *scientific* level by distinguishing between theories of ultimate origins and proximate origins. Creationism is a theory of ultimate origins, which explains where everything comes from, while Darwinian evolution, as science, is more limited; it describes only how species developed from one point to another while remaining silent on questions of ultimate origins. As Gilkey explained the mistake of the creation-scientists: "No distinction is made between the question of *proximate origins* (how did something arise out of something else, e.g., the solar system out of a general gaseous state, life out of non-life, one species out of preceding forms of life?—that is scientific questions), and the question of *ultimate origins* (how did the *whole* system of the universe arise, what is its ultimate or final source, ground or principle?—that is, speculative, philosophical, or religious/theological questions of origins)." Id. at 34; see also Scott, supra, at 27 ("Although some people confuse the origin of life itself with evolution, the two are conceptually separate. Biological evolution is defined as the descent of living things from ancestors from which they differ. Life had to precede evolution! . . . We know much more about evolution than about the origin of life."). See also The Dalai Lama, The Universe in a Single Atom: The Convergence of Science and Spirituality 115 (2005) ("Regardless of how persuasive the Darwinian account of the origins of life may be, as a Buddhist, I find it leaves one crucial area unexamined. This is the origin of sentience—the evolution of conscious beings who have the capacity to experience pain and pleasure.").

Do these distinctions make sense to you? Do they persuade you that the district court was correct in its decision in *McLean*? Or were the creationists correct that evolution is a religion of atheism or secularism?

After establishing that creation-science was a religion, Gilkey argued that, within the field of religion, creationism adopted one sectarian Christian interpretation of creation that was disputed not only by non-Christians but also by other Christians with different theologies. Because creation-science was not a scientific equivalent to evolution, and was only one of an array of religious theories of origins, Gilkey concluded that it should not be taught in the science classroom as the sole alternative to evolution.

Should a legislator who listened to Gilkey's testimony conclude that she should propose a bill requiring the teaching of all Christian accounts of creation whenever evolution is taught? Would the Balanced Acts of Arkansas or Louisiana become constitutional if they included other stories of origin in addition to Genesis? Or would these stories remain unscientific? Would it be constitutional for the state to mandate that creationism, the Chinese myth of Pan Gu and the Mesopotamian myth of Atrahasis be taught?

If a professor of religious studies or theology wanted to design a course in creation, what should the students read? Should numerous stories of origins be added to the science classroom so that students get a rounded education? Or would it be better for students to learn these stories of origin in a religious studies or social science classroom because they are not scientific? See Jay D. Wexler, Darwin, Design, and Disestablishment: Teaching the Evolution Controversy in Public Schools, 56 Vand. L. Rev. 751 (2003) (recommending that origins stories be taught as religious studies or social science). How many stories should be taught in this course in "comparative origins"? See id. at 788–89 (Genesis, Gilgamesh, Hindu cycles of creation, Native American stories).

Gilkey testified that in Christian theology, creation is "even more religious than Christmas" because there are no secular or human components to it; not even Mary was present at creation, but God alone. Id. at 103. Is this a persuasive argument?

Is it a mistake for creationists and other believers to try to turn religion into science? See Steven Goldberg, Seduced by Science: How American Religion Has Lost Its Way 33 (1999) ("Creation science has not succeeded in shaping mainstream science or in winning a place in the nation's public school classrooms for the book of Genesis. What it has done instead is to further the troubling notion that American religion must adorn itself in the trappings of science in order to be taken seriously."). See also Sarah Lyall, Anglican Leader Says the Schools Shouldn't Teach Creationism, N.Y. Times, Mar. 22, 2006, at A3 (Archbishop of Canterbury "believes that portraying the Bible as just another theory devalues it.") and Tigay, supra, note 6, at 25 (arguing that literalism is a disservice to the Bible because it "forces the Bible to compete as science, and in such a competition it cannot win. . . . The religious message is precisely the realm in which science cannot compete, and those devoted to the cause of the Bible would do far better service to their cause by stressing its unique religious message.").

Historian and philosopher of science Michael Ruse also testified in Little Rock. He also distinguished science from religion by explaining that science is empirical, looks for laws that offer explanations and predictions, is subject to testability and confirmation, and is also tentative. Scientists, Ruse concluded, must be prepared to change their minds in the face of empirical evidence. In his words, "[i]n this regard, the scientists differ from both the philosophers and the theologians. Nothing in the real world would make the Kantian change his mind, and the Catholic is equally dogmatic, despite any empirical evidence about the stability of bread and wine. Such evidence is simply considered irrelevant." See Michael Ruse, Creation-Science Is Not Science, in Marcel Chotkowski La Follette, ed., Creationism, Science, and the Law: The Arkansas Case 150–53 (1983). Do Ruse's comments suggest that science is an alternative religion or that evolutionists are hostile to religion in a manner that violates *Lukumi*?

8. *Edwards v. Aguillard. McLean* was not appealed. As Arkansas debated its balanced treatment law, Louisiana considered a similar law. A first draft of the Louisiana bill required the teaching of creation *ex nihilo*; a second draft defined creation-science in the same manner as Section 4 of the Arkansas Act in *McLean*. After the *McLean* complaint was filed, however, the Louisiana Senate deleted that longer definition of creation-science from the bill. Thereafter the Louisiana statute stated:

> "[P]ublic schools within [the] state shall give balanced treatment to creation-science and to evolution-science. Balanced treatment of these two models shall be given in classroom lectures taken as a whole for each course, in textbook materials taken as a whole for each course, in library materials taken as a whole for the sciences and taken as a whole for the humanities, and in other educational programs in public schools, to the extent that such lectures, textbooks, library materials, or educational programs deal in any way with the subject of the origin of man, life, the earth, or the universe. When creation or evolution is taught, each shall be taught as a theory, rather than as proven scientific fact."

> "Balanced treatment" means "providing whatever information and instruction in both creation and evolution models the classroom teacher determines is necessary and appropriate to provide insight into both theories in view of the textbooks and other instructional materials available for use in his classroom."

> "Creation-science" is defined as "the scientific evidences for creation and inferences from those scientific evidences." "Evolution-science" means "the scientific evidences for evolution and inferences from those scientific evidences."

La.Rev.Stat.Ann. § 17:286.1 et seq. Does the new language mean that the Louisiana bill is constitutional under *McLean*? Or would the Court think that "the world is not made brand new every morning," as Justice Souter wrote in the Texas Ten Commandments case, Van Orden v. Perry, 545 U.S. 677 (2005), from Chapter 3, and find that the legislature lacked a secular purpose?

A district court dismissed the Louisiana case on summary judgment for the state, without ever holding the detailed trial conducted by Judge Overton in *McLean*. The United States Supreme Court upheld the lower court, ruling that the Louisiana law violated the Establishment Clause because it failed the secular purpose prong of the *Lemon* test. Edwards v. Aguillard, 482 U.S. 578 (1987). In finding that there was no secular purpose, the Court focused on the religious motivations of the legislators who passed the bill. Was the Court wrong to focus on the religious motivation of Senator Keith and other sponsors of the bill? Did the amendments to the Act post-*McLean* prove that the bill was secular and not religious? See id. at 604 (Powell, J., concurring) ("That the statute is limited to the scientific evidences supporting the theory does not render its purpose secular."); but see id. at 611 (Scalia, J., dissenting) (observing that without a trial record the court needed to await state court interpretations of the statute and its passage). Do you agree that by focusing on secular purpose, the Court "completely sidesteps the question of whether creation-science is really science"? Steven Goldberg, *Edwards v. Aguillard*: Evolution and Creation in the Legal Crucible, in Leslie C. Griffin, ed., Law and Religion: Cases in Context, 242 (2010).

Wendell Bird, who wrote the law review note advocating the equal treatment of evolution and creation-science, complained he had lost his day in court, and that the Louisiana case could have been litigated differently from *McLean*. He argued, "Were we to have an open-minded judge his decision would have said, 'religious views may not be taught as the statute says, scientific evidence may be taught.' . . . our exhibits and witnesses were about systematic gaps in the fossil records [and other scientific facts that contradict evolution]. Leslie C. Griffin, "The Story of *Edwards v. Aguillard*: The Genesis of Creation-Science," in M.A. Olivas & R.G. Schneider, eds., Education Law Stories, 313–14 (2007). Do you agree with Bird or with his opponents, who thought there was no science to present? If a trial had been held, would the role of evolution in public schools have been permanently resolved?

Louisiana argued that the purpose of the bill was to protect academic freedom. Is that a secular purpose that should survive Establishment Clause scrutiny? See id. at 587 (academic freedom is not fostered by narrowing the science curriculum); but see id. at 628 (dissenting argument that the legislation protects the academic freedom of students to hear competing arguments). Should a religious motivation by legislators suffice to invalidate a statute? See Stephen L. Carter, The Culture of Disbelief: How American Law and Politics Trivialize Religious Devotion 111 (1993) (arguing that the mistake in *Aguillard* was to rule that the statute was unconstitutional because of the motivations of the legislature).

Was a trial necessary to invalidate the Arkansas Act, or should the district court have done so on summary judgment?

9. *A Constitutional Right to Teach Creation-Science?* Post-*Aguillard* a high school biology teacher (John Peloza) argued that the school district violated Establishment and Free Exercise by forcing him to teach evolution when he wanted to teach students that evolution was not a valid scientific theory and that creationism was an acceptable alternative. The Ninth Circuit concluded that evolution was not a religion, rejected the claim that the district established religion by requiring that evolution be taught, and upheld restrictions on the teacher's right to discuss religious matters with his students. See Peloza v. Capistrano Unified Sch. Dist., 37 F.3d 517 (9th Cir. 1994); see also Webster v. New Lenox Sch. Dist. No. 122, 917 F.2d 1004 (7th Cir. 1990) (social studies teacher does not have a First Amendment right to teach nonevolutionary theories in the classroom).

In a continuation of *Peloza*, a student in the same Capistrano Unified School District brought suit against the school district and his history teacher asserting that his rights under the Establishment Clause had been violated by a practice and policy hostile toward religion and favoring irreligion over religion. Specifically, the student alleged that a teacher at his high school made numerous comments hostile to religion and Christianity. See C.F. v. Capistrano Unified School Dist., 615 F.Supp.2d 1137 (C.D. Cal. 2009). Of particular interest was a quotation by the teacher about Peloza, the former biology teacher, stating "I will not leave John Peloza alone to propagandize kids with this religious, superstitious nonsense," i.e., creationism. Do you agree that the statement violated the *Lemon* test? The Ninth Circuit ruled that the history teacher had qualified immunity because nothing in Establishment Clause jurisprudence would have alerted him that he could be subject to liability for being critical of religion in class lectures. C.F. v. Capistrano Unified School Dist., 654 F.3d 975 (9th Cir. 2011). Do you agree with that conclusion about the Establishment Clause?

10. *Disclaimers.* In response to the preceding cases, several states required disclaimers to be presented to students whenever evolution is taught. How do you assess the following disclaimer required by Alabama?

BIOLOGY TEXTBOOK INSERT A MESSAGE FROM THE ALABAMA STATE BOARD OF EDUCATION

The word "theory" has many meanings. Theories are defined as systematically organized knowledge, abstract reasoning, a speculative idea or plan, or a systematic statement of principles. Scientific theories are based on both observations of the natural world and assumptions about the natural world. They are always subject to change in view of new and confirmed observations.

Many scientific theories have been developed over time. The value of scientific work is not only the development of theories but also what is learned from the development process. The Alabama Course of Study: Science includes many theories and studies of scientists' work. The work of Copernicus, Newton, and Einstein, to name a few, has provided a basis of our knowledge of the world today.

The theory of evolution by natural selection is a controversial theory that is included in this textbook. It is controversial because it states that natural selection provides the basis for the modern scientific explanation for the diversity of living things. Since natural selection has been observed to play a role in influencing small changes in a population, it is assumed that it produces large changes, even though this has not been directly observed. Because of its importance and implications, students should understand the nature of evolutionary theories. They should learn to make distinctions between the multiple meanings of evolution, to distinguish between observations and assumptions used to draw conclusions, and to wrestle with the unanswered questions and unresolved problems still faced by evolutionary theory.

There are many unanswered questions about the origin of life. With the explosion of new scientific knowledge in biochemical and molecular biology and exciting new fossil discoveries, Alabama students may be among those who use their understanding and skills to contribute to knowledge and to answer many unanswered questions. Instructional material associated with controversy should be approached with an open mind, studied carefully, and critically considered.

11. *The Next Era: Intelligent Design.* Did *Aguillard* and *McLean* close the doors of the public school to creationism? In *Aguillard* the Court observed that "teaching a variety of scientific theories about the origins of humankind to schoolchildren might be validly done with the clear secular intent of enhancing the effectiveness of science instruction." 482 U.S. at 594. Did that case leave a "loophole" for proponents of creationism? See Scott, supra, at 114. According to Professor Francis Beckwith,

> Although the *Edwards* Court sounded the death-knell for creationism as part of the science curriculum in public schools, it neither prohibited public schools from teaching alternatives to evolution, nor prevented schools from offering to their students theories that may be consistent with, and lend support to, a religious perspective. Both of these qualifications, combined with other factors, suggest that ID [intelligent design] may be offered as part of a public school science curriculum or voluntarily by a teacher without violating the Establishment Clause, for, as we shall see, ID is an alternative to evolution that is consistent with, and lends support to, a number of philosophical and religious points of view. Unlike creationism, however, ID is not derived from a particular religion's special revelation, but is the result of arguments whose premises include empirical evidence, well-founded conceptual notions outside of the natural sciences, and conclusions that are supported by these premises.

Francis J. Beckwith, Science and Religion Twenty Years After *McLean v. Arkansas*: Evolution, Public Education, and the New Challenge of Intelligent Design, 26 Harv. J.L. & Pub. Pol'y 456 (2003). Is Professor Beckwith correct? Is ID a *scientific* alternative to evolution or a *philosophical* one? See also Francis J. Beckwith, Law, Darwinism, and Public Education: The Establishment Clause and the Challenge of Intelligent Design (2003). Would allowing classroom instruction about ID placate proponents of creationism or are they actually two separate theories?

4. INTELLIGENT DESIGN

Kitzmiller v. Dover Area School District

United States District Court for the Middle District of Pennsylvania, 2005.
400 F.Supp.2d 707.

MEMORANDUM OPINION

■ JONES, DISTRICT JUDGE.

INTRODUCTION:

On October 18, 2004, the Defendant Dover Area School Board of Directors passed by a 6–3 vote the following resolution:

Students will be made aware of gaps/problems in Darwin's theory and of other theories of evolution including, but not limited to, intelligent design. Note: Origins of Life is not taught.

On November 19, 2004, the Defendant Dover Area School District announced by press release that, commencing in January 2005, teachers would be required to read the following statement to students in the ninth grade biology class at Dover High School:

> The Pennsylvania Academic Standards require students to learn about Darwin's Theory of Evolution and eventually to take a standardized test of which evolution is a part.
>
> Because Darwin's Theory is a theory, it continues to be tested as new evidence is discovered. The Theory is not a fact. Gaps in the Theory exist for which there is no evidence. A theory is defined as a well-tested explanation that unifies a broad range of observations.
>
> Intelligent Design is an explanation of the origin of life that differs from Darwin's view. The reference book, Of Pandas and People, is available for students who might be interested in gaining an understanding of what Intelligent Design actually involves.
>
> With respect to any theory, students are encouraged to keep an open mind. The school leaves the discussion of the Origins of Life to individual students and their families. As a Standards-driven district, class instruction focuses upon preparing students to achieve proficiency on Standards-based assessments.

For the reasons that follow, we hold that the ID Policy is unconstitutional pursuant to the Establishment Clause of the First Amendment of the United States Constitution and Art. I, § 3 of the Pennsylvania Constitution.

[The court employed both the *Lemon* and the endorsement tests, see Chapter 2, to conclude the disclaimer violated the Establishment Clause. Reprinted here are the sections of the opinion that explain: 1) why ID is a religion and 2) why ID is not a science.]

E. *Application of the Endorsement Test to the ID Policy*

1. *An Objective Observer Would Know that ID and Teaching About "Gaps" and "Problems" in Evolutionary Theory are Creationist, Religious Strategies that Evolved from Earlier Forms of Creationism*

The concept of intelligent design (hereinafter "ID"), in its current form, came into existence after the *Edwards* case was decided in 1987. For the reasons that follow, we conclude that the religious nature of ID would be readily apparent to an objective observer, adult or child.

We initially note that John Haught, a theologian who testified as an expert witness for Plaintiffs and who has written extensively on the subject of evolution and religion, succinctly explained to the Court that the argument for ID is not a new scientific argument, but is rather an old religious argument for the existence of God. He traced this argument back to at least Thomas Aquinas in the 13th century, who framed the argument as a syllogism: Wherever complex design exists, there must have been a designer; nature is complex; therefore nature must have had an intelligent designer. Dr. Haught testified that Aquinas was explicit that this intelligent designer "everyone understands to be God." The syllogism described by Dr. Haught is essentially the same argument for ID as presented by defense expert witnesses Professors Behe and Minnich who employ the phrase "purposeful arrangement of parts."

Dr. Haught testified that this argument for the existence of God was advanced early in the 19th century by Reverend Paley and defense expert witnesses Behe and Minnich admitted that their argument for ID based on the "purposeful arrangement of parts" is the same one that Paley made for design. The only apparent difference between the argument made by Paley and the argument for ID, as expressed by defense expert witnesses Behe and Minnich, is that ID's "official position" does not acknowledge that the designer is God. However, as Dr. Haught testified, anyone familiar with Western religious thought would immediately make the association that the tactically unnamed designer is God, as the description of the designer in *Of Pandas and People* (hereinafter "*Pandas*") is a "master intellect," strongly suggesting a supernatural deity as opposed to any intelligent actor known to exist in the natural world. Moreover, it is notable that both Professors Behe and Minnich admitted their personal view is that the designer is God and Professor Minnich testified that he understands many leading advocates of ID to believe the designer to be God.

Although proponents of the IDM [Intellectual Design Movement] occasionally suggest that the designer could be a space alien or a time-traveling cell biologist, no serious alternative to God as the designer has been proposed by members of the IDM, including Defendants' expert witnesses. In fact, an explicit concession that the intelligent designer works outside the laws of nature and science and a direct reference to religion is *Pandas'* rhetorical statement, "what kind of intelligent agent was it [the designer]" and answer: "On its own science cannot answer this question. It must leave it to religion and philosophy."

A significant aspect of the IDM is that despite Defendants' protestations to the contrary, it describes ID as a religious argument. In that vein, the writings of leading ID proponents reveal that the designer postulated by their argument is the God of Christianity. Dr. Barbara Forrest, one of Plaintiffs' expert witnesses, is the author of the book *Creationism's Trojan Horse*. She has thoroughly and exhaustively chronicled the history of ID in her book and other writings for her testimony in this case. Her testimony, and the exhibits which were admitted with it, provide a wealth of statements by ID leaders that reveal ID's religious, philosophical, and cultural content. The following is a representative grouping of such statements made by prominent ID proponents.[5]

Phillip Johnson, considered to be the father of the IDM, developer of ID's "Wedge Strategy," which will be discussed below, and author of the 1991 book entitled *Darwin on Trial*, has written that "theistic realism" or "mere creation" are defining concepts of the IDM. This means "that God is objectively real as Creator and recorded in the biological evidence. . . . " In addition, Phillip Johnson states that the "Darwinian theory of evolution contradicts not just the Book of Genesis, but every word in the Bible from beginning to end. It contradicts the idea that we are here because a creator brought about our existence for a purpose." ID proponents Johnson, William Dembski, and Charles Thaxton, one of the editors of *Pandas*, situate ID in the Book of John in the New Testament of the Bible, which begins, "In the Beginning was the Word, and the Word was God." Dembski has written that ID is a "ground clearing operation" to allow Christianity to receive serious consideration, and "Christ is never an addendum to a scientific theory but always a completion." Moreover, in turning to Defendants' lead expert, Professor Behe, his testimony at trial indicated that ID is only a scientific, as opposed to a religious, project for him; however, considerable evidence was introduced to refute this claim. Consider, to illustrate, that Professor Behe remarkably and unmistakably claims that the *plausibility of the argument for ID depends upon the extent to which one believes in the existence of God.* (emphasis added). As no evidence in the record indicates that any other scientific proposition's validity rests on belief in God, nor is the Court aware of any such scientific   propositions,   Professor   Behe's   assertion   constitutes

---

[5] Defendants contend that the Court should ignore all evidence of ID's lineage and religious character because the Board members do not personally know Jon Buell, President of the Foundation for Thought and Ethics (hereinafter "FTE"), the publisher of *Pandas*, or Phillip Johnson, nor are they familiar with the Wedge Document or the drafting history of *Pandas*. Defendants' argument lacks merit legally and logically.

The evidence that Defendants are asking this Court to ignore is exactly the sort that the court in *McLean* considered and found dispositive concerning the question of whether creation science was a scientific view that could be taught in public schools, or a religious one that could not. The *McLean* court considered writings and statements by creation science advocates like Henry Morris and Duane Gish, as well as the activities and mission statements of creationist think-tanks like the Biblical Science Association, the Institution for Creation Research, and the Creation Science Research Center. *McLean*, 529 F.Supp. at 1259–60. The court did not make the relevance of such evidence conditional on whether the Arkansas Board of Education knew the information. Instead, the court treated the evidence as speaking directly to the threshold question of what creation science was. Moreover, in *Edwards*, the Supreme Court adopted *McLean's* analysis of such evidence without reservation, and without any discussion of which details about creation science the defendant school board actually knew. *Edwards*, 482 U.S. at 590 n. 9, 107 S.Ct. 2573.

substantial evidence that in his view, as is commensurate with other prominent ID leaders, ID is a religious and not a scientific proposition.

Dramatic evidence of ID's religious nature and aspirations is found in what is referred to as the "Wedge Document." The Wedge Document, developed by the Discovery Institute's Center for Renewal of Science and Culture (hereinafter "CRSC"), represents from an institutional standpoint, the IDM's goals and objectives, much as writings from the Institute for Creation Research did for the earlier creation-science movement, as discussed in *McLean*. The Wedge Document states in its "Five Year Strategic Plan Summary" that the IDM's goal is to replace science as currently practiced with "theistic and Christian science." As posited in the Wedge Document, the IDM's "Governing Goals" are to "defeat scientific materialism and its destructive moral, cultural, and political legacies" and "to replace materialistic explanations with the theistic understanding that nature and human beings are created by God." The CSRC expressly announces, in the Wedge Document, a program of Christian apologetics to promote ID. A careful review of the Wedge Document's goals and language throughout the document reveals cultural and religious goals, as opposed to scientific ones. ID aspires to change the ground rules of science to make room for religion, specifically, beliefs consonant with a particular version of Christianity.

In addition to the IDM itself describing ID as a religious argument, ID's religious nature is evident because it involves a supernatural designer. The courts in *Edwards* and *McLean* expressly found that this characteristic removed creationism from the realm of science and made it a religious proposition. *Edwards*, 482 U.S. at 591–92, 107 S.Ct. 2573; *McLean*, 529 F.Supp. at 1265–66. Prominent ID proponents have made abundantly clear that the designer is supernatural.

Defendants' expert witness ID proponents confirmed that the existence of a supernatural designer is a hallmark of ID. First, Professor Behe has written that by ID he means "not designed by the laws of nature," and that it is "implausible that the designer is a natural entity." Second, Professor Minnich testified that for ID to be considered science, the ground rules of science have to be broadened so that supernatural forces can be considered. Third, Professor Steven William Fuller testified that it is ID's project to change the ground rules of science to include the supernatural. Turning from defense expert witnesses to leading ID proponents, Johnson has concluded that science must be redefined to include the supernatural if religious challenges to evolution are to get a hearing. Additionally, Dembski agrees that science is ruled by methodological naturalism and argues that this rule must be overturned if ID is to prosper.

Further support for the proposition that ID requires supernatural creation is found in the book *Pandas*, to which students in Dover's ninth grade biology class are directed. *Pandas* indicates that there are two kinds of causes, natural and intelligent, which demonstrate that intelligent causes are beyond nature. Professor Haught, who as noted was the only theologian to testify in this case, explained that in Western intellectual tradition, non-natural causes occupy a space reserved for ultimate religious explanations. Robert Pennock, Plaintiffs' expert in the philosophy of science, concurred with Professor Haught and concluded that because its basic proposition is that the features of the natural world are produced by a transcendent, immaterial, non-natural being, ID is a religious proposition regardless of whether that religious proposition is given a recognized religious label. It is notable that not one defense expert was able to explain how the supernatural action suggested by ID could be anything other than an inherently religious proposition. Accordingly, we find that ID's religious nature would be further evident to our objective observer because it directly involves a supernatural designer.

A "hypothetical reasonable observer," adult or child, who is "aware of the history and context of the community and forum" is also presumed to know that ID is a form of creationism. The evidence at trial demonstrates that ID is nothing less than the progeny of creationism. What is likely the strongest evidence supporting the finding of ID's creationist nature is the history and historical pedigree of the book to which students in Dover's ninth grade biology class are referred, *Pandas*. *Pandas* is published by an organization called FTE, as noted, whose articles of incorporation and filings with the Internal Revenue Service describe it as a religious, Christian organization. *Pandas* was written by Dean Kenyon and Percival Davis, both acknowledged creationists, and Nancy Pearcey, a Young Earth Creationist, contributed to the work.

As Plaintiffs meticulously and effectively presented to the Court, *Pandas* went through many drafts, several of which were completed prior to and some after the Supreme Court's decision in *Edwards*, which held that the Constitution forbids teaching creationism as science. By comparing the pre and post *Edwards* drafts of *Pandas*, three astonishing points emerge: (1) the definition for creation science in early drafts is identical to the definition of ID; (2) cognates of the word creation (creationism and creationist), which appeared approximately 150 times were deliberately and systematically replaced with the phrase ID; and (3) the changes occurred shortly after the Supreme Court held that creation science is religious and cannot be taught in public school science classes in *Edwards*. This word substitution is telling, significant, and reveals that a purposeful change of *words* was effected without any corresponding change in *content*, which directly refutes FTE's argument that by merely disregarding the words "creation" and "creationism," FTE expressly rejected creationism in *Pandas*. In early pre-*Edwards* drafts of *Pandas*, the term "creation" was defined as "various forms of life that began abruptly through an intelligent agency with their distinctive features intact—fish with fins and scales, birds with feathers, beaks, and wings, etc.," the very same way in which ID is defined in the subsequent published versions. This definition was described by many witnesses for both parties, notably including defense experts Minnich and Fuller, as "special creation" of kinds of animals, an inherently religious and creationist concept. Professor Behe's assertion that this passage was merely a *description* of appearances in the fossil record is illogical and defies the weight of the evidence that the passage is a conclusion about how life began based upon an *interpretation* of the fossil record, which is reinforced by the content of drafts of *Pandas*.

The weight of the evidence clearly demonstrates, as noted, that the systemic change from "creation" to "intelligent design" occurred sometime in 1987, *after* the Supreme Court's important *Edwards* decision. This compelling evidence strongly supports Plaintiffs' assertion that ID is creationism re-labeled. Importantly, the objective observer, whether adult or child, would conclude from the fact that *Pandas* posits a master intellect that the intelligent designer is God.

Further evidence in support of the conclusion that a reasonable observer, adult or child, who is "aware of the history and context of the community and forum" is presumed to know that ID is a form of creationism concerns the fact that ID uses the same, or exceedingly similar arguments as were posited in support of creationism. One significant difference is that the words "God," "creationism," and "Genesis" have been systematically purged from ID explanations, and replaced by an unnamed "designer." Dr. Forrest testified and sponsored exhibits showing six arguments common to creationists. Demonstrative charts introduced through Dr. Forrest show parallel arguments relating to the rejection of naturalism, evolution's threat to culture and society, "abrupt appearance" implying divine creation, the exploitation of the same alleged gaps in the fossil record, the alleged inability of science to explain complex biological information like DNA, as well as the theme that proponents of each version of creationism merely aim to teach a scientific alternative to evolution to show its "strengths and weaknesses," and to alert students to a supposed "controversy" in the scientific community. In addition, creationists made the same argument that the complexity of the bacterial flagellum supported creationism as Professors Behe and Minnich now make for ID. The IDM openly welcomes adherents to creationism into its "Big Tent," urging them to postpone biblical disputes like the age of the earth. Moreover and as previously stated, there is hardly better evidence of ID's relationship with creationism than an explicit statement by defense expert Fuller that ID is a form of creationism.

Although contrary to Fuller, defense experts Professors Behe and Minnich testified that ID is not creationism, their testimony was primarily by way of bare assertion and it failed to directly rebut the creationist history of *Pandas* or other evidence presented by Plaintiffs showing the commonality between creationism and ID. The sole argument Defendants made to distinguish creationism from ID was their assertion that the term "creationism" applies only to arguments based on the Book of Genesis, a young earth, and a catastrophic Noaich flood; however, substantial evidence established that this is only one form of creationism, including the chart that was distributed to the Board Curriculum Committee, as will be described below.

[The Court then concluded an objective *student* would see the disclaimer as a "strong official endorsement of religion."] The overwhelming evidence at trial established that ID is a religious view, a mere re-labeling of creationism, and not a scientific theory. As the Fifth Circuit Court of Appeals held in *Freiler*, an educator's "reading of a disclaimer that not only disavows endorsement of educational materials but also juxtaposes that disavowal with an urging to contemplate alternative religious concepts implies School Board approval of religious principles." *Freiler*, 185 F.3d at 348. [Other features of the manner of the disclaimer's presentation to students were relevant to the court's analysis. Because some teachers refused to present the disclaimer, school administrators had to enter the classroom to present it. Moreover, the "administrators made the remarkable and awkward statement, as part of the disclaimer, that 'there will be no other discussion of the issue and your teachers will not answer questions on the issue.'" Finally, students who did not want to hear the disclaimer had to opt out of the classroom presentation.] Accordingly, we find that the classroom presentation of the disclaimer, including school administrators making a special appearance in the science classrooms to deliver the statement, the complete prohibition on discussion or questioning ID, and the "opt out" feature all convey a strong message of religious endorsement.

In summary, the disclaimer singles out the theory of evolution for special treatment, misrepresents its status in the scientific community, causes students to doubt its validity without scientific justification, presents students with a religious alternative masquerading as a scientific theory, directs them to consult a creationist text as though it were a science resource, and instructs students to forego scientific inquiry in the public school classroom and instead to seek out religious instruction elsewhere. Furthermore, as Drs. Alters and Miller testified, introducing ID necessarily invites religion into the science classroom as it sets up what will be perceived by students as a "God-friendly" science, the one that explicitly mentions an intelligent designer, and that the "other science," evolution, takes no position on religion. Dr. Miller testified that a false duality is produced: It "tells students . . . quite explicitly, choose God on the side of intelligent design or choose atheism on the side of science." Introducing such a religious conflict into the classroom is "very dangerous" because it forces students to "choose between God and science," not a choice that schools should be forcing on them.

[The court also concluded members of the community would perceive an endorsement of religion because of a School Board newsletter sent to members of the community and local news coverage.]

We have now found that both an objective student and an objective adult member of the Dover community would perceive Defendants' conduct to be a strong endorsement of religion pursuant to the endorsement test. Having so concluded, we find it incumbent upon the Court to further address an additional issue raised by Plaintiffs, which is whether ID is science. To be sure, our answer to this question can likely be predicted based upon the foregoing analysis. While answering this question compels us to revisit evidence that is entirely complex, if not obtuse, after a six week trial that spanned twenty-one days and included countless hours of detailed expert witness presentations, the Court is confident that no other tribunal in the United States is in a better position than are we to traipse into this controversial area. Finally, we will offer our conclusion on whether ID is science not just because it is essential to our holding that an Establishment Clause violation has occurred in this case, but also in the hope that it may prevent the obvious waste of judicial and other resources which would be occasioned by a subsequent trial involving the precise question which is before us.

4.   Whether ID Is Science

After a searching review of the record and applicable caselaw, we find that while ID arguments may be true, a proposition on which the Court takes no position, ID is not science. We find that ID fails on three different levels, any one of which is sufficient to preclude a determination that ID is science. They are: (1) ID violates the centuries-old ground rules of science by invoking and permitting supernatural causation; (2) the argument of irreducible complexity, central to ID, employs the same flawed and illogical contrived dualism that doomed creation science in the 1980's; and (3) ID's negative attacks on evolution have been refuted by the scientific community. As we will discuss in more detail below, it is additionally important to note that ID has failed to gain acceptance in the scientific community, it has not generated peer-reviewed publications, nor has it been the subject of testing and research.

Expert testimony reveals that since the scientific revolution of the 16th and 17th centuries, science has been limited to the search for natural causes to explain natural phenomena. (9:19–22 (Haught); 5:25–29 (Pennock); 1:62 (Miller)). This revolution entailed the rejection of the appeal to authority, and by extension, revelation, in favor of empirical evidence. (5:28 (Pennock)). Since that time period, science has been a discipline in which testability, rather than any ecclesiastical authority or philosophical coherence, has been the measure of a scientific idea's worth. (9:21–22 (Haught); 1:63 (Miller)). In deliberately omitting theological or "ultimate" explanations for the existence or characteristics of the natural world, science does not consider issues of "meaning" and "purpose" in the world. (9:21 (Haught); 1:64, 87 (Miller)). While supernatural explanations may be important and have merit, they are not part of science. (3:103 (Miller); 9:19–20 (Haught)). This self-imposed convention of science, which limits inquiry to testable, natural explanations about the natural world, is referred to by philosophers as "methodological naturalism" and is sometimes known as the scientific method. (5:23, 29–30 (Pennock)). Methodological naturalism is a "ground rule" of science today which requires scientists to seek explanations in the world around us based upon what we can observe, test, replicate, and verify. (1:59–64, 2:41–43 (Miller); 5:8, 23–30 (Pennock)).

As the National Academy of Sciences (hereinafter "NAS") was recognized by experts for both parties as the "most prestigious" scientific association in this country, we will accordingly cite to its opinion where appropriate. NAS is in agreement that science is limited to empirical, observable and ultimately testable data: "Science is a particular way of knowing about the world. In science, explanations are restricted to those that can be inferred from the confirmable data—the results obtained through observations and experiments that can be substantiated by other scientists. Anything that can be observed or measured is amenable to scientific investigation. Explanations that cannot be based upon empirical evidence are not part of science."

This rigorous attachment to "natural" explanations is an essential attribute to science by definition and by convention. We are in agreement with Plaintiffs' lead expert Dr. Miller, that from a practical perspective, attributing unsolved problems about nature to causes and forces that lie outside the natural world is a "science stopper." As Dr. Miller explained, once you attribute a cause to an untestable supernatural force, a proposition that cannot be disproven, there is no reason to continue seeking natural explanations as we have our answer.

ID is predicated on supernatural causation, as we previously explained and as various expert testimony revealed. ID takes a natural phenomenon and, instead of accepting or seeking a natural explanation, argues that the explanation is supernatural. Further support for the conclusion that ID is predicated on supernatural causation is found in the ID reference book to which ninth grade biology students are directed, *Pandas*. *Pandas* states, in pertinent part, as follows:

> Darwinists object to the view of intelligent design *because it does not give a natural cause explanation* of how the various forms of life started in the first place. Intelligent design means

that various forms of life began abruptly, through an intelligent agency, with their distinctive features already intact—fish with fins and scales, birds with feathers, beaks, and wings, etc.

Stated another way, ID posits that animals did not evolve naturally through evolutionary means but were created abruptly by a non-natural, or supernatural, designer. Defendants' own expert witnesses acknowledged this point. (21:96–100 (Behe); P–718 at 696, 700) ("implausible that the designer is a natural entity"); 28:21–22 (Fuller) (" . . . ID's rejection of naturalism and commitment to supernaturalism . . . "); 38:95–96 (Minnich) (ID does not exclude the possibility of a supernatural designer, including deities).

It is notable that defense experts' own mission, which mirrors that of the IDM itself, is to change the ground rules of science to allow supernatural causation of the natural world, which the Supreme Court in *Edwards* and the court in *McLean* correctly recognized as an inherently religious concept. *Edwards*, 482 U.S. at 591–92, 107 S.Ct. 2573; *McLean*, 529 F.Supp. at 1267. First, defense expert Professor Fuller agreed that ID aspires to "change the ground rules" of science and lead defense expert Professor Behe admitted that his broadened definition of science, which encompasses ID, would also embrace astrology. Moreover, defense expert Professor Minnich acknowledged that for ID to be considered science, the ground rules of science have to be broadened to allow consideration of supernatural forces.

Prominent IDM leaders are in agreement with the opinions expressed by defense expert witnesses that the ground rules of science must be changed for ID to take hold and prosper. William Dembski, for instance, an IDM leader, proclaims that science is ruled by methodological naturalism and argues that this rule must be overturned if ID is to prosper. ("Indeed, entire fields of inquiry, including especially in the human sciences, will need to be rethought from the ground up in terms of intelligent design.").

The Discovery Institute, the think tank promoting ID whose CRSC developed the Wedge Document, acknowledges as "Governing Goals" to "defeat scientific materialism and its destructive moral, cultural and political legacies" and "replace materialistic explanations with the theistic understanding that nature and human beings are created by God." In addition, and as previously noted, the Wedge Document states in its "Five Year Strategic Plan Summary" that the IDM's goal is to replace science as currently practiced with "theistic and Christian science." The IDM accordingly seeks nothing less than a complete scientific revolution in which ID will supplant evolutionary theory.[14]

---

[14] Further support for this proposition is found in the Wedge Strategy, which is composed of three phases: Phase I is scientific research, writing and publicity; Phase II is publicity and opinion-making; and Phase III is cultural confrontation and renewal. In the

Notably, every major scientific association that has taken a position on the issue of whether ID is science has concluded that ID is not, and cannot be considered as such. Initially, we note that NAS, the "most prestigious" scientific association in this country, views ID as follows:

> Creationism, intelligent design, and other claims of supernatural intervention in the origin of life or of species are not science because they are not testable by the methods of science. These claims subordinate observed data to statements based on authority, revelation, or religious belief. Documentation offered in support of these claims is typically limited to the special publications of their advocates. These publications do not offer hypotheses subject to change in light of new data, new interpretations, or demonstration of error. This contrasts with science, where any hypothesis or theory always remains subject to the possibility of rejection or modification in the light of new knowledge.

Additionally, the American Association for the Advancement of Science (hereinafter "AAAS"), the largest organization of scientists in this country, has taken a similar position on ID, namely, that it "has not proposed a scientific means of testing its claims" and that "the lack of scientific warrant for so-called 'intelligent design theory' makes it improper to include as part of science education...." Not a single expert witness over the course of the six week trial identified one major scientific association, society or organization that endorsed ID as science. What is more, defense experts concede that ID is not a theory as that term is defined by the NAS and admit that ID is at best "fringe science" which has achieved no acceptance in the scientific community.

It is therefore readily apparent to the Court that ID fails to meet the essential ground rules that limit science to testable, natural explanations. Science cannot be defined differently for Dover students than it is defined in the scientific community as an affirmative action program, as advocated by Professor Fuller, for a view that has been unable to gain a foothold within the scientific establishment. Although ID's failure to meet the ground rules of science is sufficient for the Court to conclude that it is not science, out of an abundance of caution

---

"Five Year Strategic Plan Summary," the Wedge Document explains that the social consequences of materialism have been "devastating" and that it is necessary to broaden the wedge with a positive scientific alternative to materialistic scientific theories, which has come to be called the theory of ID. "Design theory promises to reverse the stifling dominance of the materialist worldview, and to replace it with a science consonant with Christian and theistic convictions." Phase I of the Wedge Strategy is an essential component and directly references "scientific revolutions." Phase II explains that alongside a focus on influential opinion-makers, "we also seek to build up a popular base of support among our natural constituency, namely, Christians. We will do this primarily through apologetics seminars. We intend these to encourage and equip believers with new scientific evidence that support the faith, as well as to 'popularize' our ideas in the broader culture." Finally, Phase III includes pursuing possible legal assistance "in response to resistance to the integration of design theory into public school science curricula."

and in the exercise of completeness, we will analyze additional arguments advanced regarding the concepts of ID and science.

ID is at bottom premised upon a false dichotomy, namely, that to the extent evolutionary theory is discredited, ID is confirmed. This argument is not brought to this Court anew, and in fact, the same argument, termed "contrived dualism" in *McLean*, was employed by creationists in the 1980's to support "creation science." The court in *McLean* noted the "fallacious pedagogy of the two model approach" and that "[i]n efforts to establish 'evidence' in support of creation science, the defendants relied upon the same false premise as the two model approach ... all evidence which criticized evolutionary theory was proof in support of creation science." *McLean*, 529 F.Supp. at 1267, 1269. We do not find this false dichotomy any more availing to justify ID today than it was to justify creation science two decades ago.

ID proponents primarily argue for design through negative arguments against evolution, as illustrated by Professor Behe's argument that "irreducibly complex" systems cannot be produced through Darwinian, or any natural, mechanisms. However, we believe that arguments against evolution are not arguments for design. Expert testimony revealed that just because scientists cannot explain today how biological systems evolved does not mean that they cannot, and will not, be able to explain them tomorrow. As Dr. Padian aptly noted, "absence of evidence is not evidence of absence." To that end, expert testimony from Drs. Miller and Padian provided multiple examples where *Pandas* asserted that no natural explanations exist, and in some cases that none could exist, and yet natural explanations have been identified in the intervening years. It also bears mentioning that as Dr. Miller stated, just because scientists cannot explain every evolutionary detail does not undermine its validity as a scientific theory as no theory in science is fully understood.

As referenced, the concept of irreducible complexity is ID's alleged scientific centerpiece. Irreducible complexity is a negative argument against evolution, not proof of design, a point conceded by defense expert Professor Minnich (irreducible complexity "is not a test of intelligent design; it's a test of evolution"). Irreducible complexity additionally fails to make a positive scientific case for ID, as will be elaborated upon below.

We initially note that irreducible complexity as defined by Professor Behe in his book *Darwin's Black Box* and subsequently modified in his 2001 article entitled "Reply to My Critics," appears as follows:

> By irreducibly complex I mean a single system which is composed of several well-matched, interacting parts that contribute to the basic function, wherein the removal of any one of the parts causes the system to effectively cease

functioning. An irreducibly complex system cannot be produced directly by slight, successive modifications of a precursor system, because any precursor to an irreducibly complex system that is missing a part is by definition nonfunctional. . . . Since natural selection can only choose systems that are already working, then if a biological system cannot be produced gradually it would have to arise as an integrated unit, in one fell swoop, for natural selection to have anything to act on.

Professor Behe admitted in "Reply to My Critics" that there was a defect in his view of irreducible complexity because, while it purports to be a challenge to natural selection, it does not actually address "the task facing natural selection." Professor Behe specifically explained that "[t]he current definition puts the focus on removing a part from an already-functioning system," but "[t]he difficult task facing Darwinian evolution, however, would not be to remove parts from sophisticated pre-existing systems; it would be to bring together components to make a new system in the first place." In that article, Professor Behe wrote that he hoped to "repair this defect in future work;" however, he has failed to do so even four years after elucidating his defect.

In addition to Professor Behe's admitted failure to properly address the very phenomenon that irreducible complexity purports to place at issue, natural selection, Drs. Miller and Padian testified that Professor Behe's concept of irreducible complexity depends on ignoring ways in which evolution is known to occur. Although Professor Behe is adamant in his definition of irreducible complexity when he says a precursor "missing a part is by definition nonfunctional," what he obviously means is that it will not function in the same way the system functions when all the parts are present. For example in the case of the bacterial flagellum, removal of a part may prevent it from acting as a rotary motor. However, Professor Behe excludes, by definition, the possibility that a precursor to the bacterial flagellum functioned not as a rotary motor, but in some other way, for example as a secretory system.

As expert testimony revealed, the qualification on what is meant by "irreducible complexity" renders it meaningless as a criticism of evolution. In fact, the theory of evolution proffers exaptation as a well-recognized, well-documented explanation for how systems with multiple parts could have evolved through natural means. Exaptation means that some precursor of the subject system had a different, selectable function before experiencing the change or addition that resulted in the subject system with its present function. For instance, Dr. Padian identified the evolution of the mammalian middle ear bones from what had been jawbones as an example of this process. By defining irreducible complexity in the way that he has, Professor Behe attempts to exclude the phenomenon of exaptation by definitional fiat, ignoring as he does so abundant evidence which refutes his argument.

Notably, the NAS has rejected Professor Behe's claim for irreducible complexity by using the following cogent reasoning:

> [S]tructures and processes that are claimed to be "irreducibly" complex typically are not on closer inspection. For example, it is incorrect to assume that a complex structure or biochemical process can function only if all its components are present and functioning as we see them today. Complex biochemical systems can be built up from simpler systems through natural selection. Thus, the "history" of a protein can be traced through simpler organisms. . . . The evolution of complex molecular systems can occur in several ways. Natural selection can bring together parts of a system for one function at one time and then, at a later time, recombine those parts with other systems of components to produce a system that has a different function. Genes can be duplicated, altered, and then amplified through natural selection. The complex biochemical cascade resulting in blood clotting has been explained in this fashion.

As irreducible complexity is only a negative argument against evolution, it is refutable and accordingly testable, unlike ID, by showing that there are intermediate structures with selectable functions that could have evolved into the allegedly irreducibly complex systems. Importantly, however, the fact that the negative argument of irreducible complexity is testable does not make testable the argument for ID. Professor Behe has applied the concept of irreducible complexity to only a few select systems: (1) the bacterial flagellum; (2) the blood-clotting cascade; and (3) the immune system. Contrary to Professor Behe's assertions with respect to these few biochemical systems among the myriad existing in nature, however, Dr. Miller presented evidence, based upon peer-reviewed studies, that they are not in fact irreducibly complex.

[The court reviewed those studies.]

We find that such evidence demonstrates that the ID argument is dependent upon setting a scientifically unreasonable burden of proof for the theory of evolution. As a further example, the test for ID proposed by both Professors Behe and Minnich is to grow the bacterial flagellum in the laboratory; however, no-one inside or outside of the IDM, including those who propose the test, has conducted it. Professor Behe conceded that the proposed test could not approximate real world conditions and even if it could, Professor Minnich admitted that it would merely be a test of evolution, not design.

We therefore find that Professor Behe's claim for irreducible complexity has been refuted in peer-reviewed research papers and has been rejected by the scientific community at large. Additionally, even if irreducible complexity had not been rejected, it still does not support ID as it is merely a test for evolution, not design.

We will now consider the purportedly "positive argument" for design encompassed in the phrase used numerous times by Professors Behe and Minnich throughout their expert testimony, which is the "purposeful arrangement of parts." Professor Behe summarized the argument as follows: We infer design when we see parts that appear to be arranged for a purpose. The strength of the inference is quantitative; the more parts that are arranged, the more intricately they interact, the stronger is our confidence in design. The appearance of design in aspects of biology is overwhelming. Since nothing other than an intelligent cause has been demonstrated to be able to yield such a strong appearance of design, Darwinian claims notwithstanding, the conclusion that the design seen in life is real design is rationally justified. As previously indicated, this argument is merely a restatement of the Reverend William Paley's argument applied at the cell level. Minnich, Behe, and Paley reach the same conclusion, that complex organisms must have been designed using the same reasoning, except that Professors Behe and Minnich refuse to identify the designer, whereas Paley inferred from the presence of design that it was God. Expert testimony revealed that this inductive argument is not scientific and as admitted by Professor Behe, can never be ruled out.

Indeed, the assertion that design of biological systems can be inferred from the "purposeful arrangement of parts" is based upon an analogy to human design. Because we are able to recognize design of artifacts and objects, according to Professor Behe, that same reasoning can be employed to determine biological design. Professor Behe testified that the strength of the analogy depends upon the degree of similarity entailed in the two propositions; however, if this is the test, ID completely fails.

Unlike biological systems, human artifacts do not live and reproduce over time. They are non-replicable, they do not undergo genetic recombination, and they are not driven by natural selection. For human artifacts, we know the designer's identity, human, and the mechanism of design, as we have experience based upon empirical evidence that humans can make such things, as well as many other attributes including the designer's abilities, needs, and desires. With ID, proponents assert that they refuse to propose hypotheses on the designer's identity, do not propose a mechanism, and the designer, he/she/it/they, has never been seen. In that vein, defense expert Professor Minnich agreed that in the case of human artifacts and objects, we know the identity and capacities of the human designer, but we do not know any of those attributes for the designer of biological life. In addition, Professor Behe agreed that for the design of human artifacts, we know the designer and its attributes and we have a baseline for human design that does not exist for design of biological systems. Professor Behe's only response to these seemingly insurmountable points of disanalogy was that the inference still works in science fiction movies.

It is readily apparent to the Court that the only attribute of design that biological systems appear to share with human artifacts is their complex appearance, i.e. if it looks complex or designed, it must have been designed. This inference to design based upon the appearance of a "purposeful arrangement of parts" is a completely subjective proposition, determined in the eye of each beholder and his/her viewpoint concerning the complexity of a system. Although both Professors Behe and Minnich assert that there is a quantitative aspect to the inference, on cross-examination they admitted that there is no quantitative criteria for determining the degree of complexity or number of parts that bespeak design, rather than a natural process. As Plaintiffs aptly submit to the Court, throughout the entire trial only one piece of evidence generated by Defendants addressed the strength of the ID inference: the argument is less plausible to those for whom God's existence is in question, and is much less plausible for those who deny God's existence.

Accordingly, the purported positive argument for ID does not satisfy the ground rules of science which require testable hypotheses based upon natural explanations. ID is reliant upon forces acting outside of the natural world, forces that we cannot see, replicate, control or test, which have produced changes in this world. While we take no position on whether such forces exist, they are simply not testable by scientific means and therefore cannot qualify as part of the scientific process or as a scientific theory.

It is appropriate at this juncture to address ID's claims against evolution. ID proponents support their assertion that evolutionary theory cannot account for life's complexity by pointing to real gaps in scientific knowledge, which indisputably exist in all scientific theories, but also by misrepresenting well-established scientific propositions.

Before discussing Defendants' claims about evolution, we initially note that an overwhelming number of scientists, as reflected by every scientific association that has spoken on the matter, have rejected the ID proponents' challenge to evolution. Moreover, Plaintiffs' expert in biology, Dr. Miller, a widely-recognized biology professor at Brown University who has written university-level and high-school biology textbooks used prominently throughout the nation, provided unrebutted testimony that evolution, including common descent and natural selection, is "overwhelmingly accepted" by the scientific community and that every major scientific association agrees. As the court in *Selman* explained, "evolution is more than a *theory* of origin in the context of science. To the contrary, evolution is the dominant *scientific* theory of origin accepted by the majority of scientists." *Selman*, 390 F.Supp.2d at 1309 (emphasis in original). Despite the scientific community's overwhelming support for evolution, Defendants and ID proponents insist that evolution is unsupported by empirical evidence. Plaintiffs' science experts, Drs. Miller and Padian, clearly explained how ID proponents generally and *Pandas* specifically, distort and misrepresent scientific knowledge in making their anti-evolution argument.

In analyzing such distortion, we turn again to *Pandas*, the book to which students are expressly referred in the disclaimer. Defendants hold out *Pandas* as representative of ID and Plaintiffs' experts agree in that regard. A series of arguments against evolutionary theory found in *Pandas* involve paleontology, which studies the life of the past and the fossil record. Plaintiffs' expert Professor Padian was the only testifying expert witness with any expertise in paleontology. His testimony therefore remains unrebutted. Dr. Padian's demonstrative slides, prepared on the basis of peer-reviewing scientific literature, illustrate how *Pandas* systematically distorts and misrepresents established, important evolutionary principles.

We will provide several representative examples of this distortion. First, *Pandas* misrepresents the "dominant form of understanding relationships" between organisms, namely, the tree of life, represented by classification determined via the method of cladistics. Second, *Pandas* misrepresents "homology," the "central concept of comparative biology," that allowed scientists to evaluate comparable parts among organisms for classification purposes for hundreds of years. Third, *Pandas* fails to address the well-established biological concept of exaptation, which involves a structure changing function, such as fish fins evolving fingers and bones to become legs for weight-bearing land animals. Dr. Padian testified that ID proponents fail to address exaptation because they deny that organisms change function, which is a view necessary to support abrupt-appearance. Finally, Dr. Padian's unrebutted testimony demonstrates that *Pandas* distorts and misrepresents evidence in the fossil record about pre-Cambrian-era fossils, the evolution of fish to amphibians, the evolution of small carnivorous dinosaurs into birds, the evolution of the mammalian middle ear, and the evolution of whales from land animals.

In addition to Dr. Padian, Dr. Miller also testified that *Pandas* presents discredited science. Dr. Miller testified that *Pandas*' treatment of biochemical similarities between organisms is "inaccurate and downright false" and explained how *Pandas* misrepresents basic molecular biology concepts to advance design theory through a series of demonstrative slides. Consider, for example, that he testified as to how *Pandas* misinforms readers on the standard evolutionary relationships between different types of animals, a distortion which Professor Behe, a "critical reviewer" of *Pandas* who wrote a section within the book, affirmed. In addition, Dr. Miller refuted *Pandas'* claim that evolution cannot account for new genetic information and pointed to more than three dozen peer-reviewed scientific publications showing the origin of new genetic information by evolutionary processes. In summary, Dr. Miller testified that *Pandas* misrepresents molecular biology and genetic principles, as well as the current state of scientific knowledge in those areas in order to teach readers that common descent and natural selection are not scientifically sound.

Accordingly, the one textbook to which the Dover ID Policy directs students contains outdated concepts and badly flawed science, as recognized by even the defense experts in this case. [The court then explained ID was not supported by peer-reviewed publications.]

After this searching and careful review of ID as espoused by its proponents, as elaborated upon in submissions to the Court, and as scrutinized over a six week trial, we find that ID is not science and cannot be adjudged a valid, accepted scientific theory as it has failed to publish in peer-reviewed journals, engage in research and testing, and gain acceptance in the scientific community. ID, as noted, is grounded in theology, not science. Accepting for the sake of argument its proponents', as well as Defendants' argument that to introduce ID to students will encourage critical thinking, it still has utterly no place in a science curriculum. Moreover, ID's backers have sought to avoid the scientific scrutiny which we have now determined that it cannot withstand by advocating that the *controversy*, but not ID itself, should be taught in science class. This tactic is at best disingenuous, and at worst a canard. The goal of the IDM is not to encourage critical thought, but to foment a revolution which would supplant evolutionary theory with ID.

To conclude and reiterate, we express no opinion on the ultimate veracity of ID as a supernatural explanation. However, we commend to the attention of those who are inclined to superficially consider ID to be a true "scientific" alternative to evolution without a true understanding of the concept the foregoing detailed analysis. It is our view that a reasonable, objective observer would, after reviewing both the voluminous record in this case, and our narrative, reach the inescapable conclusion that ID is an interesting theological argument, but that it is not science.

Remarkably, the 6–3 vote at the October 18, 2004 meeting to approve the curriculum change occurred with absolutely no discussion of the concept of ID, no discussion of how presenting it to students would improve science education, and no justification was offered by any Board member for the curriculum change. Furthermore, Board members somewhat candidly conceded that they lacked sufficient background in science to evaluate ID, and several of them testified with equal frankness that they failed to understand the substance of the curriculum change adopted on October 18, 2004.

In fact, one unfortunate theme in this case is the striking ignorance concerning the concept of ID amongst Board members. Conspicuously, Board members who *voted for* the curriculum change testified at trial that they had utterly no grasp of ID.

Although Defendants attempt to persuade this Court that each Board member who voted for the biology curriculum change did so for the secular purpose of improving science education and to exercise critical thinking skills, their contentions are simply irreconcilable with the record evidence. Their asserted purposes are a sham, . . . [thereby violating the first prong of *Lemon*. The court concluded that the policy also violated the other prongs of the *Lemon* test.]

NOW, THEREFORE, IT IS ORDERED THAT:

1.   A declaratory judgment is hereby issued in favor of Plaintiffs pursuant to 28 U.S.C. §§ 2201, 2202, and 42 U.S.C. § 1983 such that Defendants' ID Policy violates the Establishment Clause of the First Amendment of the Constitution of the United States and Art. I, § 3 of the Constitution of the Commonwealth of Pennsylvania.

2.   Pursuant to Fed.R.Civ.P. 65, Defendants are permanently enjoined from maintaining the ID Policy in any school within the Dover Area School District.

3.   Because Plaintiffs seek nominal damages, Plaintiffs shall file with the Court and serve on Defendants, their claim for damages and a verified statement of any fees and/or costs to which they claim entitlement. Defendants shall have the right to object to any such fees and costs to the extent provided in the applicable statutes and court rules.

NOTES AND QUESTIONS

1.   *Secular Purpose.* As we learned in Chapters 2 and 3, the secular purpose prong of the *Lemon* test has been repeatedly challenged. In the context of evolution, Justice Scalia criticized the majority in *Edwards v. Aguillard*, supra, for focusing on the motivations of the legislators and concluding that there was no secular purpose even though no trial had been held. Does *Kitzmiller* persuade you that courts should not rely on the secular purpose test? Did the court focus too much on the purposes and motives of the Dover School Board? Does the scientific material about ID persuade you that it is good science, and therefore the motivations of the legislators were irrelevant? If you compare the Arkansas and Dover enactments, is it clear that the former is religious and the latter is secular?

Mark Hilliard suggests that teaching ID alongside evolution advances a secular purpose because it fosters an environment in which students of varying beliefs, including those who learned a theory other than evolution from their parents, feel more comfortable engaging in open-minded discussion about evolution without fear of being ostracized for their religious faiths. See Mark Hilliard, The Evolution and Misinterpretation of the Establishment Clause: Is Teaching Intelligent Design in Public Schools a Governmental Endorsement of Religion Prohibited by the First Amendment?, 32 Dayton L. Rev. 145, 165–66 (2006). Can teaching alternative theories, even unscientific ones, have the effect of improving science education by making more students feel comfortable and ready to approach the subject with open minds? Would doing so advance an important government purpose? If accommodating various religious backgrounds in this manner were both effective and permissible, is a science classroom the appropriate place to make such accommodations? Does this approach suggest that teaching creationism might also be appropriate?

Consider whether that argument is a logical extension of Justice Brennan's prediction in *Edwards*: "We do not imply that a legislature could never require that scientific critiques of prevailing scientific theories be taught. . . . [T]eaching a variety of scientific theories about the origins of humankind to schoolchildren might be validly done with the clear secular intent of enhancing the effectiveness of science instruction." 482 U.S. at 593–94. Is the thrust of Justice Brennan's statement focused on the permissibility of teaching other theories so long as they are *scientific*, or on the secular goal of enhancing the *effectiveness* of science instruction?

Louisiana was the first state to pass an Academic Freedom Act, which allows teachers to introduce *criticism* of evolution into the science classroom on the grounds that this discussion promotes academic freedom. Discussion of the scientific evidence for creationism is allowed as part of the criticism of evolution. This legislation is part of a new, "strengths and weaknesses" strategy in the evolution wars, which allows teachers to discuss the strengths and weaknesses of evolution. Is this legislation constitutional? See Amanda Gefter, Evolution, Global Warming and Cloning: Up for Grabs in Louisiana, New Scientist, July 12, 2008, at 8–10; Laura Beil, Opponents of Evolution Are Adopting New Strategy, N.Y. Times, June 12, 2008, at A13. Is the strengths and weaknesses strategy "subterfuge for bringing in creationism"? Id. Or is it a fair and neutral way of teaching the controversy? See Jeffrey M. Cohen, The Right to Learn: Intellectual Honesty and the First Amendment, 39 Hastings Const. L.Q. 659, 671 (2012) ("In short, the current trend is to offer permissive policies or legislation that allows teachers to present antievolutionary ideas, including intelligent design, without fear of punishment."). Are you surprised that eight states have introduced legislation protecting teachers who teach the controversy from being punished? See id. at 671, n. 63.

2.   *McLean*. How does the court make use of *McLean* in this opinion? Is this case any different from *McLean*, or are the facts and the courts' reasoning the same? Why does Judge Jones write that there is "contrived dualism" in *Kitzmiller* as in *McLean*? At one point, Judge Jones writes that

ID may be true, but it is not science. What does that mean? Is that the same conclusion that Judge Overton reached in *McLean*?

Should Judge Jones have stopped his opinion after the section on the endorsement test, without reaching the question whether ID is science? Did *McLean* require him to reach the question of ID's scientific status, or is the scientific part of the opinion unnecessary to the court's holding? Does the court have the expertise to decide if ID is a science or not?

Was Judge Jones correct about ID and science? According to Thomas Kuhn's famous work, *The Structure of Scientific Revolutions* (2d ed. 1970), science does not always progress incrementally, step-by-step, by deductive logic and discovery. Scientists rely heavily on theory within accepted paradigms, and there can be periods when scientists cling to current theories even in the face of problematic facts. When individual scientists confront anomalies that challenge their theories, he explains, they do not always abandon those theories. Instead, they resist change and continue to consider defenses of their theory. "Though they may begin to lose faith and then to consider alternatives, they do not renounce the paradigm that has led them into crisis. . . . [O]nce it has achieved the status of paradigm, a scientific theory is declared invalid only if an alternate candidate is available to take its place." Id. at 77. At that point, however, there are radical paradigm shifts where new theories are offered that do a better job of addressing the facts at hand and lead to a massive change in theory.

Is it possible that evolutionary biologists are stubbornly resisting the new paradigm of ID, which is a science? Or have they justifiably rejected ID, as Judge Jones did, because ID is not science? Is ID unscientific because it starts with a paradigm, the design of nature, and defends the paradigm no matter how many anomalies confront it? Is one difference between religion and science that religion's job is to defend the truth of its propositions against external criticism while scientists' task is to defend their theories until a better alternative appears? Can a religion undergo a paradigm shift, or would that entail the destruction of the religion? Recall Professor Smart's description of religion in Chapter 1. Is religion's purpose to reaffirm traditional insights in every generation without subjecting them to scientific scrutiny?

3. *Is Teaching Evolution Unconstitutional?* Casey Luskin, an attorney formerly with the Discovery Institute, offers an analysis that allows teaching both evolution and ID in public schools. See Casey Luskin, Darwin's Poisoned Tree: Atheistic Advocacy and the Constitutionality of Teaching Evolution in Public Schools, 21 Trinity L. Rev. 131 (Fall 2015). Historically, those who opposed the teaching of evolution were generally Christian fundamentalists, while those who advocated for banning ID were atheists. Some opponents of ID were anti-religious. Under the Establishment Clause, anti-religious legislation should be invalidated.

Under the *Lemon* test, government policies that either advance or inhibit religion are unconstitutional. Should teaching evolution be banned because its supporters are anti-religious, and teaching ID be banned because its supporters are religious? Luskin offers a different alternative, namely to abandon any analysis of the historical context of both evolution and ID. Id. at 233. Without historical context, would ID and evolution be acceptable subjects for public schools? See Adam Shapiro, Did Richard Hawkins Hand Creationists Their Next School Strategy? Religion Dispatches, Jun. 15, 2016 at http://religiondispatches.org/did-richard-daw kins-hand-creationists-their-next-school-strategy/ (suggesting possibility that "the inherent atheism of evolution needs to be balanced by the inclusion of intelligent design.").

4.   *Theological Sources of Intelligent Design.* How important is it to be clear on the origins of ID? The court defers to Professor Haught's tracing the lineage of ID back to Thomas Aquinas. Aquinas was a Christian Aristotelian. Aristotle taught there was a First Mover, whom he called "God." He developed this teaching within what we today would call his "natural science," his physics, and his metaphysics. Was Aristotle's teaching "scientific" or "religious"?

Some creationists base their opposition to evolution on the Bible, arguing that the Bible provides the truth about God's creation, and that it should be preferred to science. Under such a biblical theology, God's revelation occurs in Scripture. An alternative or supplement to biblical theology is natural theology, which emphasizes God's revelation in nature, where humans may experience God and also learn God's truth about creation. A seminal work in natural theology was William Paley's 1802 book *Natural Theology.* Paley (1734–1805), who was Archdeacon of Carlisle in England, had a strong influence on nineteenth-century American theologians. They relied on Paley in developing their preferred approach to proving God's existence: "the argument from design." According to a historian of American religion E. Brooks Holifield:

> Paley found evidence for design when he discovered distinct parts of a mechanism working toward a common end, and every instance of design indicated an intelligent designer. The argument was analogical. Just as the mechanical intricacy of a watch disclosed the intelligence of a human watchmaker, so the infinitely more complex contrivances of the natural world, from the marvels of the eye to the vastness of the cosmic harmony, required a benevolent intelligence beyond human capacity. By the middle of the nineteenth century, most American theologians, nurtured on Paley, agreed that "the central idea in natural theology" was that "design, apparent in the phenomena of creation, indicates an intelligent Designer."

See E. Brooks Holifield, Theology in America: Christian Thought from the Age of the Puritans to the Civil War 181, 180–86 (2003). Theologians who followed Paley's teaching believed that science "would confirm the argument from design." Why was Archdeacon Paley relevant to the court's analysis of ID? Is intelligent design just a newer version of natural theology, and thus, like creation-science, religion and not science?

Professor Haught testified at the *Kitzmiller* trial that there was even an older argument from design, propounded by the Catholic Dominican priest St. Thomas Aquinas in the thirteenth century. How did that testimony affect Judge Jones? See also John F. Haught, God After Darwin: A Theology of Evolution (2001).

Professor Tigay, supra, recounts the following conversation from the *Midrash Terumah*. Does it propose an argument from design? Is it different from ID?

> A sectarian once came to Rabbi Akiba and asked him, "Who created this world?" Rabbi Akiba replied: "The Holy One, blessed be He." So the sectarian said, "Show me a clear proof." Rabbi Akiba replied, "Come back to me tomorrow."
>
> On the next day the sectarian returned and Rabbi Akiba asked him, "What are you wearing?" The man replied, "A garment." Rabbi Akiba asked him, "Who made the garment?" The man replied, "A weaver." Rabbi Akiba replied, "I don't believe you. Show me a clear proof." The sectarian replied, "What can I show you? Don't you realize that a weaver made it?" Rabbi Akiba answered, "And don't you know that the Holy One, blessed be He, created His world?"
>
> When the sectarian left, Rabbi Akiba's students asked him, "What's the clear proof?" He answered them, "My sons, just as a house indicates that there's a builder, and a garment indicates that there's a weaver, and a door that there's a carpenter—so the world indicates that there is a creator, the Holy One, blessed be He."

Jeffrey H. Tigay, Genesis, Science, and "Scientific Creationism," 40:2 Conservative Judaism 20, 20–21 (Winter 1987–1988) (citing Midrash Temurah, J.D. Eisenstein, ed., Otzar Midrashim 2:583). The official Vatican newspaper stated that *Kitzmiller* was correct in ruling that ID is not a scientific alternative to evolution. Does that indicate that Judge Jones' ruling was correct? See Ian Fisher & Cornelia Dean, In "Design" vs. Darwinism, Darwin Wins Point in Rome, N.Y. Times, Jan. 29, 2006, at A9.

5. *Is ID Science?* What are the strongest arguments in support of the position that ID is a science? Why was Judge Jones not persuaded by them? Does the existence of ID prove that there is a dispute in the scientific community about science, or is this disagreement really about religion? Consider Father Vawter's testimony in *McLean*, that the tenets of the Arkansas Act were religious. Is it correct that the idea of an intelligent designer is always a religious idea? See Jay D. Wexler, Of Pandas, People, and the First Amendment: The Constitutionality of Teaching Intelligent Design in the Public Schools, 49 Stan. L. Rev. 439 (1996–97). How exactly would one distinguish a scientific statement from a religious one? In the philosophy of science, there are two general approaches to demarcating a "scientific" statement: the verificationist approach (a scientific statement is one that can be verified by experiment or experience), popular among the logical positivists of the Vienna Circle, and the falsifiability approach (a scientific statement is one that can be falsified), which is associated with the philosopher of science Karl Popper. See Karl R. Popper, The Logic of Scientific Discovery (1959). Does either of these approaches help you draw a line between scientific and religious statements? See generally Sahotra Sarkar & Jessica Pfeifer, eds., The Philosophy of Science: An Encyclopedia (2005).

"The Wedge Document," discussed throughout the opinion, supra, has, as one of its governing goals, "[t]o replace materialistic explanations with the theistic understanding that nature and human beings are created by God." The Discovery Institute, The Wedge, at https://ncse.com/files/pub/creationism/The_Wedge_Strategy.pdf. One of the twenty year goals is "to see design theory permeate our religious, cultural, moral, and political life." Id. Based on the above goals, does ID seem more like a religious revival that attempts to use science to back its goals than a science? Is it telling that the first part of one of the twenty year goals is to have ID "permeate our religious . . .life?" Does the use of the words "our religious" indicate that the scientists are theists first and scientists second or are they scientists first and theists second? Do their goals provide further evidence that their theory is based on religion and not science?

6. *Is Evolution Just Another Creation Myth?* University of California at Berkeley law professor Phillip E. Johnson, author of *Darwin on Trial* (2d ed. 1993), is one of the leaders of the ID movement. According to Johnson, evolution is another religion with its own myth of creation:

> The continual efforts to base a religion or ethical system upon evolution are not an aberration, and practically all the most prominent Darwinist writers have tried their hand at it. Darwinist evolution is an imaginative story about who we are and where we came from, which is to say it is a creation myth. As such it is an obvious starting point for speculation about how we ought to live and what we ought to value. A creationist appropriately starts with God's creation and God's will for man. A scientific naturalist just as appropriately starts with evolution and with man as a product of nature.
>
> In its mythological dimension, Darwinism is the story of humanity's liberation from the delusion that its destiny is controlled by a power higher than itself. Lacking scientific knowledge, humans at first attribute natural events like weather and disease to supernatural beings. As they learn to predict or control natural forces they put aside the lesser spirits, but a more highly evolved religion retains the notion of a rational Creator who rules the universe.
>
> At last the greatest scientific discovery of all is made, and modern humans learn that they are the products of a blind natural process that has no goal and cares nothing for them.

Phillip E. Johnson, Darwin on Trial 133 (2d ed. 1993). Based on your reading of Genesis and other creation myths, is Johnson accurate that evolution is a religion with its own creation myth?

Professor Johnson also observes that evolutionists share religion's desire to proselytize. Recall that at the McLean trial, Professor Gilkey argued that evolution is not a religion, but a science. He acknowledged, however, that some scientists turn evolution into a religion by seeing it as a broad theory that explains life's origins and presumes atheism. Did Judge Jones, by focusing on ID's status as a science, ignore the fact that evolution is also a religion? For additional readings about intelligent design, see Michael J. Behe, Darwin's Black Box: The Biochemical Challenge to Evolution (10th ann. ed. 2006); Richard Dawkins, The Blind Watchmaker (1986).

Kenneth Smith, a West Virginia parent, filed a lawsuit in federal court arguing that the teaching of evolution was a "propagation of religious faith," and that his daughter's rights were violated by "being taught a faith base (evolutionary ideology) that just doesn't exist and has no math to back it." The complaint also referenced "Plaintiff's accurate scientific mathematical system of genetic variations that proves evolution is a religion." Complaint, Smith v. Jefferson County Bd. of Educ., Case 3:15-cv-00057-GMG-RWT, May 12, 2015, at http://ncse.com/files/1-main.pdf. What should happen to the lawsuit?

7.   *The Status of Naturalism.* Professor Johnson also argues that the appropriate contrast is between creationism and naturalism. "All persons who affirm that 'God creates' are in an important sense creationists, even if they believe that the Genesis story is a myth and that God created gradually through evolution over billions of years. This follows from the fact that the theory of evolution in question is *naturalistic* evolution, meaning evolution that involves no intervention or guidance by a creator outside the world of nature." Darwin on Trial, supra, at 64. Although evolutionists believe that they are scientists who exclude creationist arguments because creationist arguments are not scientific, Johnson insists that naturalism is not a science, but a philosophical presupposition that "there is nothing outside of nature." Thus creationism and naturalism are two competing philosophies of life, not one religion and one science. See Phillip E. Johnson, Evolution as Dogma: The Establishment of Naturalism 59–76 in Pennock, supra. Do you find Johnson's argument persuasive? How do you think Langdon Gilkey, who testified at the McLean trial, would respond?

The Kansas State Board of Education, which in 2000 tried to abolish the teaching of evolution in public schools, promulgated a new definition of science while it was revising the state's science standards in 2005. According to the old definition, "[s]cience is the human activity of seeking natural explanations for what we observe in the world around us." According to the new definition, science is "a systematic method of continuing investigation that uses observation, hypothesis testing, measurement, experimentation, logical argument and theory building to lead to more adequate explanations of natural phenomena." See Dennis Overbye, Philosophers Notwithstanding, Kansas School Board Redefines Science, N.Y. Times, Nov. 15, 2005, at D3. Is this change in definition significant? Critics of the old definition of science argue that it "promotes materialism, secular humanism, atheism and leads to the idea that life is accidental." Will the new definition "open the door to supernatural explanations" of life? Can supernatural explanations of life be scientific?

8. *Rawlsian Evolution?* Are evolution and ID comprehensive doctrines as John Rawls identified them in Chapter 9? Recall the discussion of John Rawls's *Political Liberalism* from our discussion of political morality. According to Rawls, citizens hold a variety of comprehensive, religious and philosophical doctrines, and it is wrong to force their fellow citizens to live by those perspectives.

Philosopher Alvin Plantinga proposes a Rawlsian approach to the teaching of evolution. See Alvin Plantinga, Creation and Evolution: A Modest Proposal, in Robert T. Pennock, ed., Intelligent Design Creationism and Its Critics: Philosophical, Theological, and Scientific Perspectives 779–91 (2001). Under Rawls's theory, Plantinga argues, it would be unjust and unfair for one comprehensive doctrine to be taught as true in the public schools. Therefore, just as it is unfair to teach evangelical Christianity as the truth in public schools, it is equally unfair to teach evolution as truth.

Plantinga develops his argument in the following stages. Citizens in a democracy, under Rawls's social contract, have a basic right (BR):

(BR) Each of the citizens party to the contract has the right not to have comprehensive beliefs taught to her children that contradict her own comprehensive beliefs.

In response to this basic right, scientists will argue that science is empirical, or factual, or true and that:

(PC) The right way to answer questions of empirical fact—for example, questions about the origin of life, the age of the earth, whether human beings have evolved from earlier forms of life—is by way of science, or scientific method.

Plantinga insists, however, that (PC) is not an empirical commitment, but a *philosophical commitment*, and therefore a comprehensive doctrine. For that reason, Rawlsian scientists may not impose their comprehensive worldview on others. See id. at 781, 786. Do you agree with Professor Plantinga's analysis?

Plantinga concludes that both creationism and evolution can be taught in the public schools as long as they are taught *conditionally*. Do you agree? Should students be allowed to opt out of such classes if their religion is offended by it? See Mozert v. Hawkins County Bd. of Educ., 827 F.2d 1058 (6th Cir. 1987).

9. *Philosophy of Design.* A high school teacher in California offered a *philosophy* course on creationism, evolution and ID called "The Philosophy of Intelligent Design." According to the course description, "[t]his class will take a close look at evolution as a theory and will discuss the scientific, biological and biblical aspects that suggest why Darwin's philosophy is not rock solid." Local parents sued after *Kitzmiller* was decided. The teacher changed the name of the course to "The Philosophy of Design." Is it constitutional for the teacher to offer this course in a public school? See Laurie Goodstein, California Parents File Suit Over High School Course, N.Y. Times, Jan. 11, 2006, at A16. The school district cancelled the class because of the complaints. See School District Pulls ID Course After Suit, Christian Century, Feb. 7, 2006, at 14.

10. *Alternative Courses.* A public school teacher, following Darwin's ideas and relying on modern developments in neuroscience, added a section on neuroscience to her biology class. According to class readings, "the experience of God can be explained as nothing more than the effect of a particular state of brain organization" and the "Golden Rule ... is a product not of divine decree but of evolved instinct." The students learn that religious sensations arise from the areas of the brain that are specialized for religious emotion and thought. See Kelly Bulkeley, ed., Soul, Psyche, Brain: New Directions in the Study of Religion and Brain-Mind Science 4 (2005). Does the teacher violate the free exercise rights of her religious students by teaching the neuroscience segment of the course? May the teacher include in the course readings from neurotheology, a discipline that claims that "the human brain itself is revelatory of information about God," because God hardwired our brains to seek meaning? See Charlene P.E. Burns, Cognitive Science and Christian Theology, in id. at 176–79. Must she include readings in neurotheology? May the state legislature require the teacher to teach neurotheology in her course? See also Kelly Bulkeley, The Wondering Brain: Thinking About Religion With and Beyond Cognitive Neuroscience (2005).

Some writers argue that religions themselves undergo an evolutionary process of "supernatural selection": "The religious movements that have survived over the years tend to be the ones that promote health, mate selection, and security." See Michael S. Gazzaniga, The Ethical Brain 154 (2005); David Sloan Wilson, Darwin's Cathedral: Evolution, Religion, and the Nature of Society (2002). Where would you teach that thesis—in a science course, a religious studies course, a theology course, an economics of religion course, or not at all?

Is religion an evolutionary by-product of something else? Insects use the rays of light from the moon and the stars as compasses to guide their flight. If they treat the light of candles in the same way, they fly into the candle flames and die. Thus moths continue to fly into flames even though doing so has no direct survival value. "It is a misfiring by-product of a normally useful compass." In the same way, according to Richard Dawkins, children need to "believe, without question, whatever your grown-ups tell you," in order to stay safe and alive. The by-product is that they become gullible to ridiculous religious beliefs. See Richard Dawkins, The God Delusion 172–179 (2006). Can Dawkins' explanation be taught in the public schools? If Dawkins' explanation is taught, must creationism and ID be taught?

11. *Next Generation Science Standards.* With the goal of increasing interest in science, twenty-six states participated in the effort to draft the Next Generation Science Standards (NGSS). The goal of the project was to:

describe the major practices, crosscutting concepts, and disciplinary core ideas that all students should be familiar with by the end of high school, and it provides an outline of how these practices, concepts, and ideas should be developed across the grade levels. Engineering and technology are featured alongside the physical sciences, life sciences, and earth and space sciences for two critical reasons: to reflect the importance of understanding the human-built world and to recognize the value of better integrating the teaching and learning of science, engineering, and technology.

See A Framework for K-12 Science Education: Practices, Crosscutting Concepts, and Core Ideas 7 (2012).

NGSS advocates emphasize that every student—not just future scientists and engineers—should acquire this basic scientific knowledge. Do you think this study of science is as important as the study of the Bible to a public school education?

As you read the final chapter, think about all the concepts you have been exposed to so far. Do you think the Amish students in the next chapter should have been required to take science classes? Should today's Amish students be required to study NGSS? Or does that violate their—or their parents'—right to free exercise? Alternatively, does exempting students from science classes harm society by producing uneducated citizens?

CHAPTER 11

THE OLD AND NEW LAW
OF RELIGION

This chapter asks you to consider the development of law and religion by looking back at the past and forward to the future. Section A focuses on the Amish, a centuries-old Christian group that lives by traditional standards. Section B examines the Nones, who are the fastest-growing "religious" group in the United States. The highlight of Section A is the Court's 1972 *Yoder* case, while Section B provides the Pew Research Center's analysis of the growing influence of the Nones (i.e., the non-religiously-affiliated) in the United States.

We first read about *Yoder* in Chapter 4, when we focused on exemptions from the neutral laws of general applicability. The Court granted the Yoders an exemption for their children from the compulsory-attendance laws, an exemption not granted by the Court to the Mormons in *Reynolds*, or to the Native American users of peyote in *Smith*. Why did the Amish families receive the exemption? Do you think that the Court was mistaken in *Yoder*, or in *Smith* and *Reynolds*? Have you identified a constitutional standard that can protect Smith, Reynolds and Yoder? Do you think their exercise of religion deserves equal protection?

In *Yoder*, reprinted below, Justice Douglas wrote in dissent that the logic of Chief Justice Burger's opinion would offer an advance for Reynolds but a retreat for Henry David Thoreau, as well as Seeger and Welsh, the conscientious objectors we met in Chapter 5. Was Douglas correct? Does *Yoder* strike the proper balance between religious freedom and respect for the law? Can it be applied to other religious groups?

A. THE OLD

Wisconsin v. Yoder

Supreme Court of the United States, 1972.
406 U.S. 205, 92 S.Ct. 1526, 32 L.Ed.2d 15.

■ MR. CHIEF JUSTICE BURGER delivered the opinion of the Court.

On petition of the State of Wisconsin, we granted the writ of certiorari in this case to review a decision of the Wisconsin Supreme Court holding that respondents' convictions for violating the State's compulsory school-attendance law were invalid under the Free Exercise Clause of the First Amendment to the United States Constitution made applicable to the States by the Fourteenth Amendment. For the reasons hereafter stated we affirm the judgment of the Supreme Court of Wisconsin.

Respondents Jonas Yoder and Wallace Miller are members of the Old Order Amish religion, and respondent Adin Yutzy is a member of the Conservative Amish Mennonite Church. They and their families are residents of Green County, Wisconsin. Wisconsin's compulsory school-attendance law required them to cause their children to attend public or private school until reaching age 16 but the respondents declined to send their children, ages 14 and 15, to public school after they complete the eighth grade.[1] The children were not enrolled in any private school, or within any recognized exception to the compulsory-attendance law, and they are conceded to be subject to the Wisconsin statute.

On complaint of the school district administrator for the public schools, respondents were charged, tried, and convicted of violating the compulsory-attendance law in Green County Court and were fined the sum of $5 each.[3] Respondents defended on the ground that the application of the compulsory-attendance law violated their rights under the First and Fourteenth Amendments. The trial testimony showed that respondents believed, in accordance with the tenets of Old Order Amish communities generally, that their children's attendance at high school, public or private, was contrary to the Amish religion and way of life. They believed that by sending their children to high school, they would not only expose themselves to the danger of the censure of the church community, but, as found by the county court, also endanger their own salvation and that of their children. The State stipulated that respondents' religious beliefs were sincere.

In support of their position, respondents presented as expert witnesses scholars on religion and education whose testimony is uncontradicted. They expressed their opinions on the relationship of the Amish belief concerning school attendance to the more general tenets of their religion, and described the impact that compulsory high school attendance could have on the continued survival of Amish communities as they exist in the United States today. The history of the Amish sect was given in some detail, beginning with the Swiss Anabaptists of the

---

[1]   The children, Frieda Yoder, aged 15, Barbara Miller, aged 15, and Vernon Yutzy, aged 14, were all graduates of the eighth grade of public school.

[3]   Prior to trial, the attorney for respondents wrote the State Superintendent of Public Instruction in an effort to explore the possibilities for a compromise settlement. Among other possibilities, he suggested that perhaps the State Superintendent could administratively determine that the Amish could satisfy the compulsory-attendance law by establishing their own vocational training plan similar to one that has been established in Pennsylvania. Under the Pennsylvania plan, Amish children of high school age are required to attend an Amish vocational school for three hours a week, during which time they are taught such subjects as English, mathematics, health, and social studies by an Amish teacher. For the balance of the week, the children perform farm and household duties under parental supervision, and keep a journal of their daily activities. The major portion of the curriculum is home projects in agriculture and homemaking. [The Superintendent rejected this proposal on the ground that it would not afford Amish children "substantially equivalent education" to that offered in the schools of the area.

16th century who rejected institutionalized churches and sought to return to the early, simple, Christian life de-emphasizing material success, rejecting the competitive spirit, and seeking to insulate themselves from the modern world. As a result of their common heritage, Old Order Amish communities today are characterized by a fundamental belief that salvation requires life in a church community separate and apart from the world and worldly influence. This concept of life aloof from the world and its values is central to their faith.

A related feature of Old Order Amish communities is their devotion to a life in harmony with nature and the soil, as exemplified by the simple life of the early Christian era that continued in America during much of our early national life. Amish beliefs require members of the community to make their living by farming or closely related activities. Broadly speaking, the Old Order Amish religion pervades and determines the entire mode of life of its adherents. Their conduct is regulated in great detail by the *Ordnung*, or rules, of the church community. Adult baptism, which occurs in late adolescence, is the time at which Amish young people voluntarily undertake heavy obligations, not unlike the Bar Mitzvah of the Jews, to abide by the rules of the church community.

Amish objection to formal education beyond the eighth grade is firmly grounded in these central religious concepts. They object to the high school, and higher education generally, because the values they teach are in marked variance with Amish values and the Amish way of life; they view secondary school education as an impermissible exposure of their children to a "worldly" influence in conflict with their beliefs. The high school tends to emphasize intellectual and scientific accomplishments, self-distinction, competitiveness, worldly success, and social life with other students. Amish society emphasizes informal learning-through-doing; a life of "goodness," rather than a life of intellect; wisdom, rather than technical knowledge, community welfare, rather than competition; and separation from, rather than integration with, contemporary worldly society.

Formal high school education beyond the eighth grade is contrary to Amish beliefs, not only because it places Amish children in an environment hostile to Amish beliefs with increasing emphasis on competition in class work and sports and with pressure to conform to the styles, manners, and ways of the peer group, but also because it takes them away from their community, physically and emotionally, during the crucial and formative adolescent period of life. During this period, the children must acquire Amish attitudes favoring manual work and self-reliance and the specific skills needed to perform the adult role of an Amish farmer or housewife. They must learn to enjoy physical labor. Once a child has learned basic reading, writing, and elementary mathematics, these traits, skills, and attitudes admittedly fall within the category of those best learned through example and "doing" rather than in a classroom. And, at this time in life, the Amish child must also grow in his faith and his relationship to the Amish community if he is to be prepared to accept the heavy obligations imposed by adult baptism. In short, high school attendance with teachers who are not of the Amish faith—and may even be hostile to it—interposes a serious barrier to the integration of the Amish child into the Amish religious community. Dr. John Hostetler, one of the experts on Amish society, testified that the modern high school is not equipped, in curriculum or social environment, to impart the values promoted by Amish society.

The Amish do not object to elementary education through the first eight grades as a general proposition because they agree that their children must have basic skills in the "three R's" in order to read the Bible, to be good farmers and citizens, and to be able to deal with non-Amish people when necessary in the course of daily affairs. They view such a basic education as acceptable because it does not significantly expose their children to worldly values or interfere with their development in the Amish community during the crucial adolescent period. While Amish accept compulsory elementary education generally, wherever possible they have established their own elementary schools in many respects like the small local schools of the past. In the Amish belief higher learning tends to develop values they reject as influences that alienate man from God.

On the basis of such considerations, Dr. Hostetler testified that compulsory high school attendance could not only result in great psychological harm to Amish children, because of the conflicts it would produce, but would also, in his opinion, ultimately result in the destruction of the Old Order Amish church community as it exists in the United States today. The testimony of Dr. Donald A. Erickson, an expert witness on education, also showed that the Amish succeed in preparing their high school age children to be productive members of the Amish community. He described their system of learning through doing the skills directly relevant to their adult roles in the Amish community as "ideal" and perhaps superior to ordinary high school education. The evidence also showed that the Amish have an excellent record as law-abiding and generally self-sufficient members of society. . . .

I

Thus a State's interest in universal education, however highly we rank it, is not totally free from a balancing process when it impinges on fundamental rights and interests, such as those specifically protected by the Free Exercise Clause of the First Amendment, and the traditional interest of parents with respect to the religious upbringing of their children so long as they, in the words of *Pierce*, "prepare (them) for additional obligations."

II

We come then to the quality of the claims of the respondents concerning the alleged encroachment of Wisconsin's compulsory school-attendance statute on their rights and the rights of their children to the free exercise of the religious beliefs they and their forbears have adhered to for almost three centuries. In evaluating those claims we must be careful to determine whether the Amish religious faith and their mode of life are, as they claim, inseparable and interdependent. A way of life, however virtuous and admirable, may not be interposed as a barrier to reasonable state regulation of education if it is based on purely secular considerations; to have the protection of the Religion Clauses, the claims must be rooted in religious belief. Although a determination of what is a "religious" belief or practice entitled to constitutional protection may present a most delicate question, the very concept of ordered liberty precludes allowing every person to make his own standards on matters of conduct in which society as a whole has important interests. Thus, if the Amish asserted their claims because of their subjective evaluation and rejection of the contemporary secular values accepted by the majority, much as Thoreau rejected the social values of his time and isolated himself at Walden Pond, their claims would not rest on a religious basis. Thoreau's choice was philosophical and personal rather than religious, and such belief does not rise to the demands of the Religion Clauses.

Giving no weight to such secular considerations, however, we see that the record in this case abundantly supports the claim that the traditional way of life of the Amish is not merely a matter of personal preference, but one of deep religious conviction, shared by an organized group, and intimately related to daily living. That the Old Order Amish daily life and religious practice stem from their faith is shown by the fact that it is in response to their literal interpretation of the Biblical injunction from the Epistle of Paul to the Romans, "be not conformed to this world. . . ." This command is fundamental to the Amish faith. Moreover, for the Old Order Amish, religion is not simply a matter of theocratic belief. As the expert witnesses explained, the Old Order Amish religion pervades and determines virtually their entire way of life, regulating it with the detail of the Talmudic diet through the strictly enforced rules of the church community.

The record shows that the respondents' religious beliefs and attitude toward life, family, and home have remained constant— perhaps some would say static—in a period of unparalleled progress in human knowledge generally and great changes in education. The respondents freely concede, and indeed assert as an article of faith, that their religious beliefs and what we would today call "life style" have not altered in fundamentals for centuries. Their way of life in a church-oriented community, separated from the outside world and "worldly" influences, their attachment to nature and the soil, is a way inherently simple and uncomplicated, albeit difficult to preserve against the pressure to conform. Their rejection of telephones, automobiles, radios, and television, their mode of dress, of speech, their habits of manual work do indeed set them apart from much of contemporary society; these customs are both symbolic and practical.

As the society around the Amish has become more populous, urban, industrialized, and complex, particularly in this century, government regulation of human affairs has correspondingly become more detailed and pervasive. The Amish mode of life has thus come into conflict increasingly with requirements of contemporary society exerting a hydraulic insistence on conformity to majoritarian standards. So long as compulsory education laws were confined to eight grades of elementary basic education imparted in a nearby rural schoolhouse, with a large proportion of students of the Amish faith, the Old Order Amish had little basis to fear that school attendance would expose their children to the worldly influence they reject. But modern compulsory secondary education in rural areas is now largely carried on in a consolidated school, often remote from the student's home and alien to his daily home life. As the record so strongly shows, the values and programs of the modern secondary school are in sharp conflict with the fundamental mode of life mandated by the Amish religion; modern laws requiring compulsory secondary education have accordingly engendered great concern and conflict. The conclusion is inescapable that secondary schooling, by exposing Amish children to worldly influences in terms of attitudes, goals, and values contrary to beliefs, and by substantially interfering with the religious development of the Amish child and his integration into the way of life of the Amish faith community at the crucial adolescent stage of development, contravenes the basic religious tenets and practice of the Amish faith, both as to the parent and the child.

The impact of the compulsory-attendance law on respondents' practice of the Amish religion is not only severe, but inescapable, for the Wisconsin law affirmatively compels them, under threat of criminal sanction, to perform acts undeniably at odds with fundamental tenets of their religious beliefs. Nor is the impact of the compulsory-attendance law confined to grave interference with important Amish religious tenets from a subjective point of view. It carries with it precisely the kind of objective danger to the free exercise of religion that the First Amendment was designed to prevent. As the record shows, compulsory school attendance to age 16 for Amish children carries with it a very real threat of undermining the Amish community and religious practice as they exist today; they must either abandon belief and be assimilated into society at large, or be forced to migrate to some other and more tolerant region.[9]

In sum, the unchallenged testimony of acknowledged experts in education and religious history, almost 300 years of consistent practice, and strong evidence of a sustained faith pervading and regulating respondents' entire mode of life support the claim that enforcement of the State's requirement of compulsory formal education after the eighth grade would gravely endanger if not destroy the free exercise of respondents' religious beliefs. . . .

III

We turn, then, to the State's broader contention that its interest in its system of compulsory education is so compelling that even the established religious practices of the Amish must give way. Where fundamental claims of religious freedom are at stake, however, we cannot accept such a sweeping claim; despite its admitted validity in the generality of cases, we must searchingly examine the interests that the State seeks to promote by its requirement for compulsory education to age 16, and the impediment to those objectives that would flow from recognizing the claimed Amish exemption.

The State advances two primary arguments in support of its system of compulsory education. It notes, as Thomas Jefferson pointed out early in our history, that some degree of education is necessary to prepare citizens to participate effectively and intelligently in our open political system if we are to preserve freedom and independence. Further, education prepares individuals to be self-reliant and self-sufficient participants in society. We accept these propositions.

However, the evidence adduced by the Amish in this case is persuasively to the effect that an additional one or two years of formal high school for Amish children in place of their long-established program of informal vocational education would do little to serve those interests. Respondents' experts testified at trial, without challenge, that the value of all education must be assessed in terms of its capacity to prepare the child for life. It is one thing to say that compulsory education for a year or two beyond the eighth grade may be necessary when its goal is the preparation of the child for life in modern society as the majority live, but it is quite another if the goal of education be

---

[9] Some States have developed working arrangements with the Amish regarding high school attendance. See n. 3, supra. However, the danger to the continued existence of an ancient religious faith cannot be ignored simply because of the assumption that its adherents will continue to be able, at considerable sacrifice, to relocate in some more tolerant State or country or work out accommodations under threat of criminal prosecution. Forced migration of religious minorities was an evil that lay at the heart of the Religion Clauses. See, e.g., Everson v. Board of Education, 330 U.S. 1, 9–10, 67 S.Ct. 504, 508–509, 91 L.Ed. 711 (1947); Madison, Memorial and Remonstrance Against Religious Assessments, 2 Writings of James Madison 183 (G. Hunt ed. 1901).

viewed as the preparation of the child for life in the separated agrarian community that is the keystone of the Amish faith.

The State attacks respondents' position as one fostering "ignorance" from which the child must be protected by the State. No one can question the State's duty to protect children from ignorance but this argument does not square with the facts disclosed in the record. Whatever their idiosyncrasies as seen by the majority, this record strongly shows that the Amish community has been a highly successful social unit within our society, even if apart from the conventional "mainstream." Its members are productive and very law-abiding members of society; they reject public welfare in any of its usual modern forms. The Congress itself recognized their self-sufficiency by authorizing exemption of such groups as the Amish from the obligation to pay social security taxes.[11] . . .

We must not forget that in the Middle Ages important values of the civilization of the Western World were preserved by members of religious orders who isolated themselves from all worldly influences against great obstacles. There can be no assumption that today's majority is "right" and the Amish and others like them are "wrong." A way of life that is odd or even erratic but interferes with no rights or interests of others is not to be condemned because it is different.

The State, however, supports its interest in providing an additional one or two years of compulsory high school education to Amish children because of the possibility that some such children will choose to leave the Amish community, and that if this occurs they will be ill-equipped for life. The State argues that if Amish children leave their church they should not be in the position of making their way in the world without the education available in the one or two additional years the State requires. However, on this record, that argument is highly speculative. There is no specific evidence of the loss of Amish adherents by attrition, nor is there any showing that upon leaving the Amish community Amish children, with their practical agricultural training and habits of industry and self-reliance, would become burdens on society because of educational shortcomings. Indeed, this argument of the State appears to rest primarily on the State's mistaken assumption, already noted, that the Amish do not provide any education for their children beyond the eighth grade, but allow them to grow in "ignorance." To the

---

[11] Title 26 U.S.C. § 1402(h) authorizes the Secretary of Health, Education, and Welfare to exempt members of "a recognized religious sect" existing at all times since December 31, 1950, from the obligation to pay social security taxes if they are, by reason of the tenets of their sect, opposed to receipt of such benefits and agree to waive them, provided the Secretary finds that the sect makes reasonable provision for its dependent members. The history of the exemption shows it was enacted with the situation of the Old Order Amish specifically in view. H.R.Rep.No.213, 89th Cong., 1st Sess., 101–102 (1965).

The record in this case establishes without contradiction that the Green County Amish had never been known to commit crimes, that none had been known to receive public assistance, and that none were unemployed.

contrary, not only do the Amish accept the necessity for formal schooling through the eighth grade level, but continue to provide what has been characterized by the undisputed testimony of expert educators as an "ideal" vocational education for their children in the adolescent years.

There is nothing in this record to suggest that the Amish qualities of reliability, self-reliance, and dedication to work would fail to find ready markets in today's society. Absent some contrary evidence supporting the State's position, we are unwilling to assume that persons possessing such valuable vocational skills and habits are doomed to become burdens on society should they determine to leave the Amish faith, nor is there any basis in the record to warrant a finding that an additional one or two years of formal school education beyond the eighth grade would serve to eliminate any such problem that might exist.

Insofar as the State's claim rests on the view that a brief additional period of formal education is imperative to enable the Amish to participate effectively and intelligently in our democratic process, it must fall. The Amish alternative to formal secondary school education has enabled them to function effectively in their day-to-day life under self-imposed limitations on relations with the world, and to survive and prosper in contemporary society as a separate, sharply identifiable and highly self-sufficient community for more than 200 years in this country. In itself this is strong evidence that they are capable of fulfilling the social and political responsibilities of citizenship without compelled attendance beyond the eighth grade at the price of jeopardizing their free exercise of religious belief. When Thomas Jefferson emphasized the need for education as a bulwark of a free people against tyranny, there is nothing to indicate he had in mind compulsory education through any fixed age beyond a basic education. Indeed, the Amish communities singularly parallel and reflect many of the virtues of Jefferson's ideal of the "sturdy yeoman" who would form the basis of what he considered as the ideal of a democratic society. Even their idiosyncratic separateness exemplifies the diversity we profess to admire and encourage. . . .

IV

Contrary to the suggestion of the dissenting opinion of Mr. Justice DOUGLAS, our holding today in no degree depends on the assertion of the religious interest of the child as contrasted with that of the parents. It is the parents who are subject to prosecution here for failing to cause their children to attend school, and it is their right of free exercise, not that of their children, that must determine Wisconsin's power to impose criminal penalties on the parent. The dissent argues that a child who expresses a desire to attend public high school in conflict with the wishes of his parents should not be prevented from doing so. There is no reason for the Court to consider that point since it is not an issue in the case. The children are not parties to this litigation. The State has at no point tried this case on the theory that respondents were preventing their children from attending school against their expressed desires, and indeed the record is to the contrary. The State's position from the outset has been that it is empowered to apply its compulsory-attendance law to Amish parents in the same manner as to other parents—that is, without regard to the wishes of the child. That is the claim we reject today.

V

For the reasons stated we hold, with the Supreme Court of Wisconsin, that the First and Fourteenth Amendments prevent the State from compelling respondents to cause their children to attend formal high school to age 16.[26] Our disposition of this case, however, in no way alters our recognition of the obvious fact that courts are not school boards or legislatures, and are ill-equipped to determine the "necessity" of discrete aspects of a State's program of compulsory education. This should suggest that courts must move with great circumspection in performing the sensitive and delicate task of weighing a State's legitimate social concern when faced with religious claims for exemption from generally applicable education requirements. It cannot be overemphasized that we are not dealing with a way of life and mode of education by a group claiming to have recently discovered some "progressive" or more enlightened process for rearing children for modern life.

Aided by a history of three centuries as an identifiable religious sect and a long history as a successful and self-sufficient segment of American society, the Amish in this case have convincingly demonstrated the sincerity of their religious beliefs, the interrelationship of belief with their mode of life, the vital role that belief and daily conduct play in the continued survival of Old Order Amish communities and their religious organization, and the hazards presented by the State's enforcement of a statute generally valid as to others. Beyond this, they have carried the even more difficult burden of

---

[26] What we have said should meet the suggestion that the decision of the Wisconsin Supreme Court recognizing an exemption for the Amish from the State's system of compulsory education constituted an impermissible establishment of religion. In Walz v. Tax Commission, the Court saw the three main concerns against which the Establishment Clause sought to protect as "sponsorship, financial support, and active involvement of the sovereign in religious activity." 397 U.S. 664, 668, 90 S. Ct. 1409, 1411, 25 L. Ed. 2d 697 (1970). Accommodating the religious beliefs of the Amish can hardly be characterized as sponsorship or active involvement. The purpose and effect of such an exemption are not to support, favor, advance, or assist the Amish, but to allow their centuries-old religious society, here long before the advent of any compulsory education, to survive free from the heavy impediment compliance with the Wisconsin compulsory-education law would impose. Such an accommodation "reflects nothing more than the governmental obligation of neutrality in the face of religious differences, and does not represent that involvement of religious with secular institutions which it is the object of the Establishment Clause to forestall." Sherbert v. Verner, 374 U.S. 398, 409, 83 S. Ct. 1790, 1797, 10 L. Ed. 2d 965 (1963).

demonstrating the adequacy of their alternative mode of continuing informal vocational education in terms of precisely those overall interests that the State advances in support of its program of compulsory high school education. In light of this convincing showing, one that probably few other religious groups or sects could make, and weighing the minimal difference between what the State would require and what the Amish already accept, it was incumbent on the State to show with more particularity how its admittedly strong interest in compulsory education would be adversely affected by granting an exemption to the Amish. Sherbert v. Verner, supra.

Nothing we hold is intended to undermine the general applicability of the State's compulsory school-attendance statutes or to limit the power of the State to promulgate reasonable standards that, while not impairing the free exercise of religion, provide for continuing agricultural vocational education under parental and church guidance by the Old Order Amish or others similarly situated. The States have had a long history of amicable and effective relationships with church-sponsored schools, and there is no basis for assuming that, in this related context, reasonable standards cannot be established concerning the content of the continuing vocational education of Amish children under parental guidance, provided always that state regulations are not inconsistent with what we have said in this opinion.

Affirmed.

■ MR. JUSTICE DOUGLAS, dissenting in part.

I

I agree with the Court that the religious scruples of the Amish are opposed to the education of their children beyond the grade schools, yet I disagree with the Court's conclusion that the matter is within the dispensation of parents alone. The Court's analysis assumes that the only interests at stake in the case are those of the Amish parents on the one hand, and those of the State on the other. The difficulty with this approach is that, despite the Court's claim, the parents are seeking to vindicate not only their own free exercise claims, but also those of their high-school-age children. . . .

II

. . . On this important and vital matter of education, I think the children should be entitled to be heard. While the parents, absent dissent, normally speak for the entire family, the education of the child is a matter on which the child will often have decided views. He may want to be a pianist or an astronaut or an oceanographer. To do so he will have to break from the Amish tradition.

It is the future of the student, not the future of the parents, that is imperiled by today's decision. If a parent keeps his child out of school beyond the grade school, then the child will be forever barred from entry into the new and amazing world of diversity that we have today. The child may decide that that is the preferred course, or he may rebel. It is the student's judgment, not his parents', that is essential if we are to give full meaning to what we have said about the Bill of Rights and of the right of students to be masters of their own destiny. If he is harnessed to the Amish way of life by those in authority over him and if his education is truncated, his entire life may be stunted and deformed. The child, therefore, should be given an opportunity to be heard before the State gives the exemption which we honor today.

The views of the two children in question were not canvassed by the Wisconsin courts. The matter should be explicitly reserved so that new hearings can be held on remand of the case. . . .

III

I think the emphasis of the Court on the "law and order" record of this Amish group of people is quite irrelevant. A religion is a religion irrespective of what the misdemeanor or felony records of its members might be. I am not at all sure how the Catholics, Episcopalians, the Baptists, Jehovah's Witnesses, the Unitarians, and my own Presbyterians would make out if subjected to such a test. It is, of course, true that if a group or society was organized to perpetuate crime and if that is its motive, we would have rather startling problems akin to those that were raised when some years back a particular sect was challenged here as operating on a fraudulent basis. United States v. Ballard, 322 U.S. 78, 64 S.Ct. 822, 88 L.Ed. 1148. But no such factors are present here, and the Amish, whether with a high or low criminal record, certainly qualify by all historic standards as a religion within the meaning of the First Amendment.

The Court rightly rejects the notion that actions, even though religiously grounded, are always outside the protection of the Free Exercise Clause of the First Amendment. In so ruling, the Court departs from the teaching of Reynolds v. United States, 98 U.S. 145, 164, 25 L.Ed. 244, where it was said concerning the reach of the Free Exercise Clause of the First Amendment, "Congress was deprived of all legislative power over mere opinion, but was left free to reach actions which were in violation of social duties or subversive of good order." In that case it was conceded that polygamy was a part of the religion of the Mormons. Yet the Court said, "It matters not that his belief (in polygamy) was a part of his professed religion: it was still belief and belief only." Id.

Action, which the Court deemed to be antisocial, could be punished even though it was grounded on deeply held and sincere religious convictions. What we do today, at least in this respect, opens the way to give organized religion a broader base than it has ever enjoyed; and it even promises that in time Reynolds will be overruled.

In another way, however, the Court retreats when in reference to Henry Thoreau it says his "choice was philosophical and personal rather than religious, and such belief does not rise to the demands of the Religion Clauses." That is contrary to what we held in United States v. Seeger, 380 U.S. 163, where we were concerned with the meaning of the words "religious training and belief" in the Selective Service Act, which were the basis of many conscientious objector claims. We said:

> Within that phrase would come all sincere religious beliefs which are based upon a power or being, or upon a faith, to which all else is subordinate or upon which all else is ultimately dependent. The test might be stated in these words: A sincere and meaningful belief which occupies in the life of its possessor a place parallel to that filled by the God of those admittedly qualifying for the exemption comes within the statutory definition. This construction avoids imputing to Congress an intent to classify different religious beliefs, exempting some and excluding others, and is in accord with the well-established congressional policy of equal treatment for those whose opposition to service is grounded in their religious tenets.

Welsh v. United States, 398 U.S. 333, was in the same vein, the Court saying:

In this case, Welsh's conscientious objection to war was undeniably based in part on his perception of world politics. In a letter to his local board, he wrote:

> "I can only act according to what I am and what I see. And I see that the military complex wastes both human and material resources, that it fosters disregard for (what I consider a paramount concern) human needs and ends; I see that the means we employ to 'defend' our 'way of life' profoundly change that way of life. I see that in our failure to recognize the political, social, and economic realities of the world, we, *as a nation*, fail our responsibility as a nation."

The essence of Welsh's philosophy, on the basis of which we held he was entitled to an exemption, was in these words:

> "I believe that human life is valuable in and of itself; in its living; therefore I will not injure or kill another human being. This belief (and the corresponding 'duty' to abstain from violence toward another person) is not 'superior to those arising from any human relation.' On the contrary: it is essential to every human relation. I cannot, therefore, conscientiously comply with the Government's insistence that I assume duties which I feel are immoral and totally repugnant."

I adhere to these exalted views of "religion" and see no acceptable alternative to them now that we have become a Nation of many religions and sects, representing all of the diversities of the human race.

NOTES AND QUESTIONS

1.   *Old and New Religions.* Do you agree with the result of *Yoder*? Why or why not? Did the result depend upon the status of the Amish as an established religious tradition? Why did Chief Justice Burger point out that the Amish are not a progressive community with new educational ideas? Was he trying to prevent the First Amendment from protecting non-traditional groups?

"Native American religions are land based. There are certain geographical sites or physical formations that are held to be 'sacred' as an integral part of the religion. Religious practitioners therefore hold certain ceremonies, collect plants, or make pilgrimages to such places on recurring bases." Alex Tallchief Skibine, Towards a Balanced Approach for the Protection of Native American Sacred Sites, 17 Mich. J. Race & L. 1, 2 (2011). Although many of these sacred sites are on federal lands, courts have repeatedly rejected Native American lawsuits requesting access to sacred sites. If sacred sites are necessary to the "continuing existence of Indians as a tribal people," should the Supreme Court follow *Yoder* whenever it hears Native American cases? Id. at 5.

Did the Chief Justice have too limited a definition of religion or did he offer broad protection to religious freedom? According to Justice Douglas, the Court retreated from *Seeger* and *Welsh* and yet advanced over *Reynolds*. Indeed, Douglas anticipated that *Reynolds* would be overruled. As we learned in Chapters 1 and 4, *Reynolds* was not overruled but rather was reinforced by *Employment Division v. Smith*. Does this mean that the Court has offered more protection to the Amish than to newer religious groups such as the Mormons? If the age of a tradition is a good indication that it deserves constitutional protection, should the Native American peyote users receive more protection than anyone else?

Can the inconsistency in the Court's precedents be solved by Congress and the state legislatures? Should the Yoders, Reynolds, and Smith all receive exemptions from neutral laws from the legislature rather than the courts? What about a modern-day Thoreau?

Do you think *Yoder* should be overruled? If so, for what reason? Because the facts of Amish life have changed? Because *Yoder* is inconsistent with other First Amendment doctrine? Because keeping children from school has a negative impact on their education? See Gage Raley, Note, *Yoder* Revisited: Why the Landmark Amish Schooling Case Could—and Should—Be Overturned, 97 Va. L. Rev. 681 (2011). If most Amish no longer work on family farms, is there a good argument that Amish schoolchildren need compulsory public education in order to be prepared to earn a living? Do you agree that the American economy has changed so much since the 1970s that "[i]n today's world, . . . Amish children are not prepared to be economically productive adults without a high school education"? Id. at 695. If Amish parents now work in sawmills and woodworking plants instead of on farms, is there more reason to apply the child labor laws to the Amish? Id. at 699.

2. *Amish Cases.* In United States v. Lee, 455 U.S. 252 (1982), Edwin Lee, a farmer and carpenter, did not withhold Social Security taxes for his employees or pay the employer's share of taxes for them. The Amish believe that they should care for the members of their community rather than having the government do so through the Social Security system. The Supreme Court upheld the imposition of the taxes on Amish employers. Is this result consistent with *Yoder*? See 26 U.S.C. § 3127 (granting exemption to religious faiths opposed to Social Security).

If Amish farmers believe 1) farming is required by their religion; 2) they "are endowed by their Creator with dominion and control over all the animals on earth"; 3) they are not allowed to mark animals; 4) they are not allowed to use technology, including radio frequencies, scanners and computer programs; and 5) they are discouraged from outside contact; should they be exempt from the National Animal Identification System, which requires Premises Identification Numbers for each of their farms and radio frequency identification devices for each of their cattle? The data are stored on a large national database. See Farm-To-Consumer Legal Defense Fund v. Vilsack, 636 F.Supp.2d 116 (D.D.C. 2009).

Andy Bontrager purchased property from an owner who had been ordered by the state to install a new septic system. Bontrager did not install the system, and was charged under Ohio law with failing to obey a public health order requiring a sewage system. Bontrager did not install the system because it uses electricity, which violates his Amish religious beliefs. According to Bontrager,

> there are different "sects" (for lack of a better term) of the Amish—each has its own church and bishop based upon geography, i.e., where they reside in relation to the particular church. According to the defendant, while they all follow the same general religious beliefs, they all operate somewhat independently of each other. The defendant agreed that his particular church and bishop permit the possession of a telephone (in an outbuilding). If a member of his church is a construction contractor, that person is permitted to have a cell phone (only on the job). Members of the church are permitted to have gasoline-powered motors, which he has on his property and which operates a water pump for his drinking water, among other things. Conversely, while some sects allow the use of electricity, the defendant's church and bishop do not, and defendant testified that he would be expelled from the church if he complied with the Department of Health's regulation with regard to this particular septic system.

State v. Bontrager, 149 Ohio Misc.2d 33, 897 N.E.2d 244, 246–47 (2008). When Bontrager challenged his conviction, the state responded that it had

compelling interests in "preventing the discharge of untreated
septic/sewage from being washed downstream in the surface waters and
into the groundwater." Id. Should the court uphold Bontrager's conviction?
Should his testimony about different Amish sects be relevant to the
decision?

Kentucky law requires drivers of slow-moving vehicles to append a
fluorescent yellow-orange triangle with a dark red reflective border on their
vehicles for visibility and safety. Violation of the law is a misdemeanor with
a possible fine of $20 to $30. Members of the Old Order Swartzentruber
sect of the Amish religion, who operated horse-and-buggy vehicles with
gray reflective tape, were convicted in judge and jury trials. The Amish
believe that the bright triangle contradicts their religious obligation to be
plain and forces them to display the trinity, which is not a symbol of the
Amish faith. The Kentucky Supreme Court ruled that the Kentucky
Constitution offers the same protection to religious freedom as the federal
constitution and upheld the convictions because "the vehicles are regulated
on the public highways because they are slow, not because they are a
religious choice." Gingerich v. Kentucky, 283 S.W.3d 835, 844 (Ky. 2012).
What would have happened if *Yoder* strict scrutiny had applied? Would the
court have been forced to accept the Amish choice to use gray or silver
reflective tape?

The Iowa Supreme Court ruled that a Mitchell County ordinance
protecting county roads violated the free exercise rights of the Old Order
Groffdale Conference Mennonite Church. The Mennonites' religion
prohibits them from driving tractors unless they are equipped with steel
cleats. The steel wheel requirement was put into effect about 40 years ago
to keep Mennonites from riding tractors for pleasure. A member driving a
tractor without steel wheels is expelled from the church. The statute was
passed after the county used a new resurfacing concrete that was damaged
by the steel cleats. According to the law:

> No person shall drive over the hard surfaced roadways, including
> but not limited to cement, concrete and blacktop roads, of Mitchell
> County, or any political subdivision thereof, a tractor or vehicle
> equipped with steel or metal tires equipped with cleats, ice picks,
> studs, spikes, chains or other projections of any kind or steel or
> metal wheels equipped with cleats, ice picks, studs, spikes, chains,
> or other projections of any kind.

The Iowa court ruled that the law, although neutral, was not a law of
general applicability under *Smith*. The law contained an exception for
school buses, which are allowed to use ice grips and tire studs year round,
and did not regulate various other sources of road damage besides steel
wheels. Because the law was not of general applicability, the court applied
strict scrutiny. Without examining the government's compelling interest,
the court ruled that the statute was not narrowly tailored to protecting the
roads. According to the court, "Given the lack of evidence of the *degree* to
which the steel lugs harm the County's roads, the undisputed fact that
other events cause road damage, and the undisputed fact that the County

had tolerated steel lugs for many years before 2009, it is difficult to see that an outright ban on those lugs is necessary to serve a compelling state interest." Mitchell County v. Zimmerman, 810 N.W.2d 1, 17 (Iowa 2012). What means are more narrowly tailored? See id. (Mennonites could add money to a fund for the roads).

Although the rule against steel cleats was based on the Biblical text of Romans 12:2 ("be not conformed to this world"), the religious practice allowing Mennonites to use tractors (instead of horses and buggies) as long as they had steel cleats was only 40 years old. Should that have affected the ruling under *Yoder*? Or does *Yoder* require a win for the Mennonites? Is the reasoning of *Zimmerman* consistent with *Gingerich*, the Kentucky case about orange triangles?

Christian, non-Amish parents challenged the provisions of the Pennsylvania Home Schooling statute, which required them to submit a log of their children's education and samples of their children's homework to the state. A school district official then reviewed the materials to determine if parents met the minimum hours of instruction and course requirements and if the children were making progress. The parents believed that God had given them "sole responsibility" for their children's education and that the school district's supervision therefore violated the free exercise of their religion. See Combs v. Homer-Center School Dist., 540 F.3d 231 (3d Cir. 2008). Should the Court grant the parents an exemption under *Yoder* because their children's education was involved? Does *Yoder* identify a constitutional right to home-school? Would it violate Equal Protection for the Yoders to get an exemption but not the Combs family?

Yup'ik Eskimos in Alaska were prosecuted for fishing on the Kuskokwim River using gillnets of a prohibited mesh size. The mesh size was restricted in order to protect Chinook salmon from capture. The Yup'ik argued that subsistence fishing for Chinook salmon was part of their free exercise of religion protected by the Alaska Constitution. Testimony established "king salmon play a central role in traditional Yup'ik fish camps, which is where Yup'ik spiritual values are taught to the next generation." An Alaska appeals court rejected the claim, ruling the state had a compelling interest in preserving the viability of the Kuskokwim River king salmon. Is this consistent with *Yoder*? See Phillip v. State, 347 P.3d 128 (Alaska Ct. App. 2015).

3. *Individual and Community.* We learned in Chapter 6 that First Amendment case law struggles with the balance between institutional and individual free exercise. What reading of the religion clauses do you prefer: one that is "religious communitarian" or "secular individualist"? See Frederick Mark Gedicks, The Rhetoric of Church and State (1995). According to Professor Gedicks, religious communitarianism "understands religion to be the principal, if not the exclusive, source of certain values and practices that lie at the base of civilized society. . . . [It] presupposes a faith that relies primarily on tradition and authority, and only secondarily on reason, to articulate and defend these values and practices." In contrast, in secular individualism, "knowledge is discovered by the right application of critical reason, and never by simple appeal to religious authority or tradition." Id. at 11–12. Was Chief Justice Burger a religious communitarian and Justice Douglas a secular individualist? Which cases that you have read in this book appear to be "secular individualist" and which are "religious communitarian"? Consider *Sherbert* and *Smith*, *Everson* and *Zelman*, *Şahin* and *Yoder*. How can the courts and the legislatures strike a proper balance between the individual's right to free exercise and the protection of religious organizations?

Did *Yoder* place the community's religious freedom above the individual's, or the parents' free exercise above their children's? Was Justice Douglas correct that the Court should have paid more attention to the child's religious freedom? What should be the result if the children wanted to continue in a local public school and the parents wanted them to stay at home? How do you react to the following criticism of *Yoder*?

> There is something breathtakingly condescending, as well as inhumane, about the sacrificing of anyone, especially children, on the altar of "diversity" and the virtue of preserving a variety of religious traditions. The rest of us are happy with our cars and computers, our vaccines and antibiotics. But you quaint little people with your bonnets and breeches, your horse buggies, your archaic dialect and your earth-closet privies, you enrich our lives. Of course you must be allowed to trap your children with you in your seventeenth-century time warp, otherwise something irretrievable would be lost to us: a part of the wonderful diversity of human culture. A small part of me can see something in this. But the larger part is made to feel very queasy indeed.

Richard Dawkins, The God Delusion 331 (2006). What ruling would a judge who believed as Dawkins does make based on the facts of *Yoder*?

Do you agree courts should use strict scrutiny in cases where "plaintiffs demonstrate that indirect burdens on their religiously motivated exercises of secular constitutional rights may impose costs felt throughout their religious communities"? A theory of group harm focuses on minority vulnerability rather than individual rights. Does this theory help to explain and justify the Court's reasoning in *Yoder*? If this group harm theory became the law of free exercise, would Muslim plaintiffs have a better chance of winning lawsuits against the government for profiling in counterterrorism situations because profiling inflicts group harm on the entire Muslim community? See Tabbaa v. Chertoff, 509 F.3d 89 (2d Cir. 2007), a case that denied the free exercise claims of Muslim citizens who were detained at the border because the searches were the least restrictive means of meeting the government's compelling interest in security; Murad Hussain, Defending the Faithful: Speaking the Language of Group Harm in Free Exercise Challenges to Counterterrorism Profiling, 117 Yale L.J. 920, 956–59 (2008). What groups other than the Amish and Muslims would gain advantage by a theory of group harm?

4. *Preservation of Religious Traditions.* As the opinion stated, "Dr. Hostetler testified that compulsory high school attendance could not only result in great psychological harm to Amish children, because of the conflicts it would produce, but would also, in his opinion, ultimately result in the destruction of the Old Order Amish church community as it exists in the United States today." Should the First Amendment protect diverse religious traditions, or does democracy require that some groups learn to adjust to the modern world? Do you agree with the balance the Court struck in the following case?

Michigan required drivers of slow-moving vehicles to place a fluorescent orange-yellow triangle on their vehicles to protect traffic safety. Members of the Old Order Amish appealed the regulation because it violated their religion to place the triangles on their horse-drawn wagons. They believed that the triangle reflected confidence in man instead of God and demonstrated a lack of trust in God. The Amish were willing to use reflector tape and lanterns on their wagons, similar to an arrangement that was worked out between the State of Ohio and its Amish residents. The state court ruled that under *Yoder*, the government had not met its burden under the compelling interest test. See People v. Swartzentruber, 170 Mich.App. 682, 429 N.W.2d 225 (1988). Why shouldn't the Michigan Amish just move to Ohio? See *Yoder*, supra, at 218 n.9 ("Forced migration of religious minorities was an evil that lay at the heart of the Religion Clauses. See, e.g., Everson v. Board of Education of Ewing Township, 330 U.S. 1, 9–10, 67 S.Ct. 504, 508–509, 91 L.Ed. 711 (1947); Madison, Memorial and Remonstrance Against Religious Assessments, 2 Writings of James Madison 183 (G. Hunt ed. 1901).").

If the principles of *Smith* were applied to the facts of *Yoder*, would the Amish lose their case? Does that mean that the application of neutral laws of general applicability might destroy certain religious traditions? Or can members of those traditions count on the legislative branch to protect them from destruction? In an article examining the role of exemptions in constitutional law, Professor Kent Greenawalt writes:

> The idea underlying privilege is that religion or conscience deserves special consideration, because it is particularly valuable or important, or because many people care intensely about it.
>
> One argument based on privilege is that the state should aim to preserve a way of life that is intimately connected to the practice for which an exemption is sought. Reserving other claims of privilege for later consideration, we may dispose of the preservation argument, as far as religion is concerned. A liberal state cannot have the aim to preserve a religion, in the sense that some multiculturalists believe the state should try to preserve minority cultures.

Kent Greenawalt, Law and Morality: Constitutional Law: Moral and Religious Convictions as Categories for Special Treatment: The Exemption Strategy, 48 Wm. & Mary L. Rev. 1605, 1609 (2007). Why should a liberal state not preserve religions? Was it important for the Court to preserve the traditional culture of the Amish in *Yoder*? Should the legislatures seek to preserve other minority religions? Which ones?

Like the Amish, the Hutterite Brethren Church also began in the 16th century as part of the Anabaptist movement during the Protestant Reformation. Hutterites practice a communal lifestyle. The Big Sky Colony in Montana is a religious corporation formed for the purpose of operating "a Hutterische Church Brotherhood Community." As part of their communal agreement, the Colony's members do not receive wages for their work. Instead, the Colony provides food, shelter, clothing, and medical care to members who engage in commercial activity. The Colony does, however, engage in "commercial activities with nonmembers for remuneration," primarily farming and agricultural production. For that reason, Montana required the Colony to participate in the state's workers' compensation system.

Do you agree with the Colony's argument that forced participation in workers' comp violates free exercise and establishment? Does *Yoder* mandate an outcome for the Colony? What would happen to the Colony if it were forced to comply with labor laws even though it never provides wages to workers? Compare Big Sky Colony, Inc. v. Montana Dep't of Labor & Indus., 291 P.3d 1231, 1241 (Mont. 2012) (The Court in *Yoder* recognized " 'even when religiously based, [one's activities] are often subject to regulation by the States in the exercise of their undoubted power to promote the health, safety, and general welfare.' The workers' compensation system in Montana undoubtedly promotes the health, safety, and welfare of workers.") with id. at 1247 (Mont. 2012) (Rice, J. dissenting) (In *Yoder*, the Supreme Court stated " 'we must be careful to determine whether the Amish religious faith and their mode of life, are ... inseparable and interdependent.' As in *Yoder,* the record here supports the determination that the communal way of life of the Colony is 'one of deep religious conviction, shared by an organized group, and intimately related to daily living.' The command to live communally and without property or legal claims is fundamental to the Hutterite faith.") Does it affect your analysis if Hutterite members never associate with non-members?

5. *A Nation of Many Religions and Sects*. Justice Douglas observed that the United States had become a "[n]ation of many religions and sects," and accordingly defended the broad definition of religion in the conscientious objection cases that we studied in Chapter 5. Are the *Seeger* and *Welsh* definitions of religion broad enough to encompass the religions described in the following reading? Should these many religious groups receive the same treatment as the Amish? Does the increasing diversity of the American religious population that is described in the following article persuade you that *Yoder* should be overruled or, alternatively, that it should apply to all religious groups?

What should happen to the First Amendment now that the fastest-growing portion of the population is the religiously-unaffiliated, whom you meet in Section B?

B. THE NEW

America's Changing Religious Landscape[*]
The Pew Research Center on Religion & Public Life.
May 12, 2015.
http://www.pewforum.org/2015/05/12/americas-changing-religious-landscape/.

The Christian share of the U.S. population is declining, while the number of U.S. adults who do not identify with any organized religion is growing, according to an extensive new survey by the Pew Research Center. Moreover, these changes are taking place across the religious landscape, affecting all regions of the country and many demographic groups. While the drop in Christian affiliation is particularly pronounced among young adults, it is occurring among Americans of all ages. The same trends are seen among whites, blacks and Latinos; among both college graduates and adults with only a high school education; and among women as well as men.

To be sure, the United States remains home to more Christians than any other country in the world, and a large majority of Americans—roughly seven-in-ten—continue to identify with some branch of the Christian faith. But the major new survey of more than 35,000 Americans by the Pew Research Center finds that the percentage of adults (ages 18 and older) who describe themselves as Christians has dropped by nearly eight percentage points in just seven years, from 78.4% in an equally massive Pew Research survey in 2007 to 70.6% in 2014. Over the same period, the percentage of Americans who are religiously unaffiliated—describing themselves as atheist, agnostic or "nothing in particular"—has jumped more than six points, from 16.1% to 22.8%. And the share of Americans who identify with non-Christian faiths also has inched up, rising 1.2 percentage points, from 4.7% in 2007 to 5.9% in 2014. Growth has been especially great among Muslims and Hindus, albeit from a very low base.

The drop in the Christian share of the population has been driven mainly by declines among mainline Protestants and Catholics. Each of those large religious traditions has shrunk by approximately three percentage points since 2007. The evangelical Protestant share of the U.S. population also has dipped, but at a slower rate, falling by about one percentage point since 2007.

Even as their numbers decline, American Christians—like the U.S. population as a whole—are becoming more racially and ethnically diverse. Non-Hispanic whites now account for smaller shares of evangelical Protestants, mainline Protestants and Catholics than they did seven years earlier, while Hispanics have grown as a share of all three religious groups. Racial and ethnic minorities now make up 41%

---

[*]   Visit www.pewforum.org to view the tables and graphics that accompany this text.

of Catholics (up from 35% in 2007), 24% of evangelical Protestants (up from 19%) and 14% of mainline Protestants (up from 9%).

Religious intermarriage also appears to be on the rise: Among Americans who have gotten married since 2010, nearly four-in-ten (39%) report that they are in religiously mixed marriages, compared with 19% among those who got married before 1960. The rise in intermarriage appears to be linked with the growth of the religiously unaffiliated population. Nearly one-in-five people surveyed who got married since 2010 are either religiously unaffiliated respondents who married a Christian spouse or Christians who married an unaffiliated spouse. By contrast, just 5% of people who got married before 1960 fit this profile.

While many U.S. religious groups are aging, the unaffiliated are comparatively young—and getting *younger*, on average, over time. As a rising cohort of highly unaffiliated Millennials reaches adulthood, the median age of unaffiliated adults has dropped to 36, down from 38 in 2007 and far lower than the general (adult) population's median age of 46. By contrast, the median age of mainline Protestant adults in the new survey is 52 (up from 50 in 2007), and the median age of Catholic adults is 49 (up from 45 seven years earlier).

These are among the key findings of the Pew Research Center's second U.S. Religious Landscape Study, a follow-up to its first comprehensive study of religion in America, conducted in 2007.

Because the U.S. census does not ask Americans about their religion, there are no official government statistics on the religious composition of the U.S. public. Some Christian denominations and other religious bodies keep their own rolls, but they use widely differing criteria for membership and sometimes do not remove members who have fallen away. Surveys of the general public frequently include a few questions about religious affiliation, but they typically do not interview enough people, or ask sufficiently detailed questions, to be able to describe the country's full religious landscape.

The Religious Landscape Studies were designed to fill the gap. Comparing two virtually identical surveys, conducted seven years apart, can bring important trends into sharp relief. In addition, the very large samples in both 2007 and 2014 included hundreds of interviews with people from small religious groups that account for just 1% or 2% of the U.S. population, such as Mormons, Episcopalians and Seventh-day Adventists. This makes it possible to paint demographic and religious profiles of numerous denominations that cannot be described by smaller surveys. The most recent Religious Landscape Study also was designed to obtain a minimum of 300 interviews with respondents in each state and the District of Columbia as well as to represent the country's largest metropolitan areas, enabling an assessment of the religious composition not just of the nation as a whole, but also of individual states and localities.

The latest survey was conducted in English and Spanish among a nationally representative sample of 35,071 adults interviewed by telephone, on both cellphones and landlines, from June 4–Sept. 30, 2014. Findings based on the full sample have a margin of sampling error of plus or minus 0.6 percentage points. The survey is estimated to cover 97% of the non-institutionalized U.S. adult population; 3% of U.S. adults are not reachable by telephone or do not speak English or Spanish well enough to participate in the survey.

Even a very small margin of error, when applied to the hundreds of millions of people living in the United States, can yield a wide range of estimates for the size of particular faiths. Nevertheless, the results of the second Religious Landscape Study indicate that Christians probably have lost ground, not only in their relative share of the U.S. population, but also in absolute numbers.

In 2007, there were 227 million adults in the United States, and a little more than 78% of them—or roughly 178 million—identified as Christians. Between 2007 and 2014, the overall size of the U.S. adult population grew by about 18 million people, to nearly 245 million. But the share of adults who identify as Christians fell to just under 71%, or approximately 173 million Americans, a net decline of about 5 million.

This decline is larger than the combined margins of sampling error in the twin surveys conducted seven years apart. Using the margins of error to calculate a probable range of estimates, it appears that the number of Christian adults in the U.S. has shrunk by somewhere between 2.8 million and 7.8 million.

Of the major subgroups within American Christianity, mainline Protestantism—a tradition that includes the United Methodist Church, the American Baptist Churches USA, the Evangelical Lutheran Church in America, the Presbyterian Church (U.S.A.) and the Episcopal Church, among others—appears to have experienced the greatest drop in absolute numbers. In 2007, there were an estimated 41 million mainline Protestant adults in the United States. As of 2014, there are roughly 36 million, a decline of 5 million—although, taking into account the surveys' combined margins of error, the number of mainline Protestants may have fallen by as few as 3 million or as many as 7.3 million between 2007 and 2014.

By contrast, the size of the historically black Protestant tradition— which includes the National Baptist Convention, the Church of God in Christ, the African Methodist Episcopal Church, the Progressive Baptist Convention and others—has remained relatively stable in recent years, at nearly 16 million adults. And evangelical Protestants, while declining slightly as a percentage of the U.S. public, probably have grown in absolute numbers as the overall U.S. population has continued to expand.

The new survey indicates that churches in the evangelical Protestant tradition—including the Southern Baptist Convention, the Assemblies of God, Churches of Christ, the Lutheran Church-Missouri Synod, the Presbyterian Church in America, other evangelical denominations and many nondenominational congregations—now have a total of about 62 million adult adherents. That is an increase of roughly 2 million since 2007, though once the margins of error are taken into account, it is possible that the number of evangelicals may have risen by as many as 5 million or remained essentially unchanged.

Like mainline Protestants, Catholics appear to be declining both as a percentage of the population and in absolute numbers. The new survey indicates there are about 51 million Catholic adults in the U.S. today, roughly 3 million fewer than in 2007. But taking margins of error into account, the decline in the number of Catholic adults could be as modest as 1 million. And, unlike Protestants, who have been decreasing as a share of the U.S. public for several decades, the Catholic share of the population has been relatively stable over the long term, according to a variety of other surveys.

Meanwhile, the number of religiously unaffiliated adults has increased by roughly 19 million since 2007. There are now approximately 56 million religiously unaffiliated adults in the U.S., and this group—sometimes called religious "nones"—is more numerous than either Catholics or mainline Protestants, according to the new survey. Indeed, the unaffiliated are now second in size only to evangelical Protestants among major religious groups in the U.S.

Factors Behind the Changes in Americans' Religious Identification

One of the most important factors in the declining share of Christians and the growth of the "nones" is generational replacement. As the Millennial generation enters adulthood, its members display much lower levels of religious affiliation, including less connection with Christian churches, than older generations. Fully 36% of young Millennials (those between the ages of 18 and 24) are religiously unaffiliated, as are 34% of older Millennials (ages 25–33). And fewer than six-in-ten Millennials identify with any branch of Christianity, compared with seven-in-ten or more among older generations, including Baby Boomers and Gen-Xers. Just 16% of Millennials are Catholic, and only 11% identify with mainline Protestantism. Roughly one-in-five are evangelical Protestants.

However, generational replacement is by no means the only reason that religious "nones" are growing and Christians are declining. In addition, people in older generations are increasingly disavowing association with organized religion. About a third of older Millennials (adults currently in their late 20s and early 30s) now say they have no religion, up nine percentage points among this cohort since 2007, when the same group was between ages 18 and 26. Nearly a quarter of Generation Xers now say they have no particular religion or describe themselves as atheists or agnostics, up four points in seven years. Baby Boomers also have become slightly but noticeably more likely to identify as religious "nones" in recent years.

As the shifting religious profiles of these generational cohorts suggest, switching religion is a common occurrence in the United States. If all Protestants were treated as a single religious group, then fully 34% of American adults currently have a religious identity different from the one in which they were raised. This is up six points since 2007, when 28% of adults identified with a religion different from their childhood faith. If switching among the three Protestant traditions (e.g., from mainline Protestantism to the evangelical tradition, or from evangelicalism to a historically black Protestant denomination) is added to the total, then the share of Americans who currently have a different religion than they did in childhood rises to 42%.

By a wide margin, religious "nones" have experienced larger gains through religious switching than any other group. Nearly one-in-five U.S. adults (18%) were raised in a religious faith and now identify with no religion. Some switching also has occurred in the other direction: 9% of American adults say they were raised with no religious affiliation, and almost half of them (4.3% of all U.S. adults) now identify with some religion. But for every person who has joined a religion after having been raised unaffiliated, there are more than four people who have become religious "nones" after having been raised in some religion. This 1:4 ratio is an important factor in the growth of the unaffiliated population.

By contrast, Christianity—and especially Catholicism—has been losing more adherents through religious switching than it has been gaining. More than 85% of American adults were raised Christian, but nearly a quarter of those who were raised Christian no longer identify with Christianity. Former Christians represent 19.2% of U.S. adults overall.

Both the mainline and historically black Protestant traditions have lost more members than they have gained through religious switching, but within Christianity the greatest net losses, by far, have been experienced by Catholics. Nearly one-third of American adults (31.7%) say they were raised Catholic. Among that group, fully 41% no longer identify with Catholicism. This means that 12.9% of American adults are former Catholics, while just 2% of U.S. adults have converted to Catholicism from another religious tradition. No other religious group in the survey has such a lopsided ratio of losses to gains.

The evangelical Protestant tradition is the only major Christian group in the survey that has gained more members than it has lost through religious switching. Roughly 10% of U.S. adults now identify with evangelical Protestantism after having been raised in another tradition, which more than offsets the roughly 8% of adults who were raised as evangelicals but have left for another religious tradition or who no longer identify with any organized faith.

Other highlights in this report include:

The Christian share of the population is declining and the religiously unaffiliated share is growing in all four major geographic regions of the country. Religious "nones" now constitute 19% of the adult population in the South (up from 13% in 2007), 22% of the population in the Midwest (up from 16%), 25% of the population in the Northeast (up from 16%) and 28% of the population in the West (up from 21%). In the West, the religiously unaffiliated are more numerous than Catholics (23%), evangelicals (22%) and every other religious group.

Whites continue to be more likely than both blacks and Hispanics to identify as religiously unaffiliated; 24% of whites say they have no religion, compared with 20% of Hispanics and 18% of blacks. But the religiously unaffiliated have grown (and Christians have declined) as a share of the population within all three of these racial and ethnic groups.

The percentage of college graduates who identify with Christianity has declined by nine percentage points since 2007 (from 73% to 64%). The Christian share of the population has declined by a similar amount among those with less than a college education (from 81% to 73%). Religious "nones" now constitute 24% of all college graduates (up from 17%) and 22% of those with less than a college degree (up from 16%).

More than a quarter of men (27%) now describe themselves as religiously unaffiliated, up from 20% in 2007. Fewer women are religious "nones," but the religiously unaffiliated are growing among women at about the same rate as among men. Nearly one-in-five women (19%) now describe themselves as religiously unaffiliated, up from 13% in 2007.

Although it is low relative to other religious groups, the retention rate of the unaffiliated has increased. In the current survey, 53% of those raised as religiously unaffiliated still identify as "nones" in adulthood, up seven points since 2007. And among Millennials, "nones" actually have one of the highest retention rates of all the religious categories that are large enough to analyze in the survey.

As the ranks of the religiously unaffiliated continue to grow, they also describe themselves in increasingly secular terms. In 2007, 25% of the "nones" called themselves atheists or agnostics; 39% identified their religion as "nothing in particular" and also said that religion is "not too" or "not at all" important in their lives; and 36% identified their religion as "nothing in particular" while nevertheless saying that religion is either "very important" or "somewhat important" in their lives. The new survey finds that the atheist and agnostic share of the "nones" has grown to 31%. Those identifying as "nothing in particular" and describing religion as unimportant in their lives continue to account for 39% of all "nones." But the share identifying as "nothing in particular" while also affirming that religion is either "very" or "somewhat" important to them has fallen to 30% of all "nones."

While the mainline Protestant share of the population is significantly smaller today than it was in 2007, the evangelical Protestant share of the population has remained comparatively stable (ticking downward slightly from 26.3% to 25.4% of the population). As a result, evangelicals now constitute a clear majority (55%) of all U.S. Protestants. In 2007, roughly half of Protestants (51%) identified with evangelical churches.

Since 2007, the share of evangelical Protestants who identify with Baptist denominations has shrunk from 41% to 36%. Meanwhile, the share of evangelicals identifying with nondenominational churches has grown from 13% to 19%.

The United Methodist Church (UMC) continues to be the largest denomination within the mainline Protestant tradition. Currently, 25% of mainline Protestants identify with the UMC, down slightly from 28% in 2007.

More than six-in-ten people in the historically black Protestant tradition identify with Baptist denominations, including 22% who identify with the National Baptist Convention, the largest denomination within the historically black Protestant tradition.

The share of the public identifying with religions other than Christianity has grown from 4.7% in 2007 to 5.9% in 2014. Gains were most pronounced among Muslims (who accounted for 0.4% of respondents in the 2007 Religious Landscape Study and 0.9% in 2014) and Hindus (0.4% in 2007 vs. 0.7% in 2014).

Roughly one-in-seven participants in the new survey (15%) were born outside the U.S., and two-thirds of those immigrants are Christians, including 39% who are Catholic. More than one-in-ten immigrants identify with a non-Christian faith, such as Islam or Hinduism.

Hindus and Jews continue to be the most highly educated religious traditions. Fully 77% of Hindus are college graduates, as are 59% of Jews (compared with 27% of all U.S. adults). These groups also have above-average household incomes. Fully 44% of Jews and 36% of Hindus say their annual family income exceeds $100,000, compared with 19% of the public overall.

NOTES AND QUESTIONS

1. *The New Non-Affiliated.* What will it mean to the First Amendment if fewer Americans identify with religion? Do you think the United States will enter into a period of decline, chaos and unhappiness if Americans become less religious? Which countries in the world would you guess are the least religious? Would you expect those countries to have a lower standard of living and unhappier citizens? See Phil Zuckerman, Society Without God: What the Least Religious Nations Can Tell Us About Contentment 2 (2008) (Denmark and Sweden "are probably the least religious countries in the world, and possibly in the history of the world," and among the best countries in the world to live in. They have low crime rates, good environments, healthy democracies, low levels of corruption, excellent schools, architecture and arts; strong economies, and so forth).

How do you expect American politics to be affected by the Rise of the Nones? Exit polls showed that 12% of voters in the 2012 presidential election were Nones and they voted Democratic by 70–26%. Does this surprise you, given that we learned in Chapter 9 that President Obama intentionally appealed to religious voters and rejected President Kennedy's separationist approach to church and state? Are you surprised that before the election the Obama advisers didn't "view [secularists] as a constituency"? See Kimberly Winston, The "Nones" Say 2012 Election Proves They Are A Political Force, Religion News, Nov. 8, 2012, at http://www.religionnews.com/politics/election/the-nones-say-2012-election-proves-they-are-a-political-force.

In the 2016 presidential primaries, 57% of Republican Nones supported Donald Trump and 61% of Democratic Nones supported Bernie Sanders. See Pew Research Center, Campaign Exposes Fissures Over Issues, Values and How Life Has Changed in the U.S. (March 2016). According to religion scholar Mark Silk, it's "fair to say that, for the first time in American history, the Nones [are] making their influence felt on the presidential nominating process." Mark Silk, The Year of the Nones, ReligionNews, Apr. 1, 2016, at http://religionnews.com/2016/04/01/nones-presidential-election-trump-sanders/. Do you think the candidates will change more as the number of Nones increases? How would a candidate appeal to the Nones?

2. *The New Spirituality.* Consistent with the Pew findings, some scholars of religion describe a "new spirituality," in which many Americans claim to be spiritual rather than religious. Although the new spirituality has many definitions, "it seems to stress ideas of self-help and personal healing." See Catherine L. Albanese, America: Religions and Religion 238 (4th ed. 2007). Will the new spirituality undermine traditional group religions like the Amish? Is the new spirituality a religion for First Amendment purposes?

As the nature of the American religious population has changed, so too has its spirituality. Professor Robert Wuthnow explains that many Americans have moved from a spirituality of dwelling to one of seeking. "A spirituality of dwelling emphasizes *habitation*: God occupies a definite place in the universe and creates a sacred space in which humans too can dwell; to inhabit sacred space is to know its territory and to feel secure. A spirituality of seeking emphasizes *negotiation*: individuals search for sacred moments that reinforce their conviction that the divine exists, but these moments are fleeting; rather than knowing the territory, people explore new spiritual vistas, and they may have to negotiate among complex and confusing meanings of spirituality." Robert Wuthnow, After Heaven: Spirituality in America Since the 1950s 3–4 (1998). Do you think Chief Justice Burger would have been skeptical about offering First Amendment protection to the seekers? Can the First Amendment protect both types of spirituality? How? Does a spirituality of seeking meet any of the criteria for a religion that we studied in Chapter 1?

3. *Causes of Unaffiliation.* Earlier Pew reports examined four possible causes for the rise in numbers of the unaffiliated. First is political backlash: young Americans have rejected traditional religion because it is associated with conservative politics. Second are delays in marriage: married people are more likely to be religious than the non-married. Third is broad social disengagement: Americans today engage in fewer communal activities, including religion. Fourth is the secularization thesis, which has predicted for some time that religions diminish with economic development. See Pew Forum on Religion & Public Life, "Nones" on the Rise: One-in-Five Adults Have No Religious Affiliation, Oct. 9, 2012. Which, if any, of these explanations do you find persuasive in explaining the origins of the Nones? According to the secularization thesis, as nations' gross domestic product increases, their religiosity usually declines. The United States, however, is an exception to the thesis because it has high economic success and high religious participation. What can explain this difference in the United States?

4. *Divided by God or More Tolerant?* According to Professor Noah Feldman, the United States is "divided by God,"

> in that we cannot agree on the role religion should take in regard to government, and vice versa. For this the responsibility lies with us and with the structure of our man-made Constitution. Perhaps, too, it might be said that God has divided us, by virtue of the profound religious diversity that we have long had and that is daily expanding. Since Madison, this diversity has often been called a blessing and a source of strength or balance, yet is also remains, as it has always been, a fundamental challenge to the project of popular self-government.

Noah Feldman, Divided By God: America's Church-State Problem—And What We Should Do About It 251 (2005). A blessing and a challenge? What do you think of Justice O'Connor's assessment of the ability of the First Amendment to deal with that challenge? Recall that in the Ten Commandments cases that we studied in Chapter 3, she wrote:

> Reasonable minds can disagree about how to apply the Religion Clauses in a given case. But the goal of the Clauses is clear: to carry out the Founders' plan of preserving religious liberty to the

fullest extent possible in a pluralistic society. By enforcing the Clauses, we have kept religion a matter for the individual conscience, not for the prosecutor or bureaucrat. At a time when we see around the world the violent consequences of the assumption of religious authority by government, Americans may count themselves fortunate: Our regard for constitutional boundaries has protected us from similar travails, while allowing private religious exercise to flourish. The well-known statement that "[w]e are a religious people," *Zorach v. Clauson*, 343 U.S. 306, 313, 72 S.Ct. 679, 96 L.Ed. 954 (1952), has proved true. Americans attend their places of worship more often than do citizens of other developed nations, R. Fowler, A. Hertzke, & L. Olson, Religion and Politics in America 28–29 (2d ed. 1999), and describe religion as playing an especially important role in their lives, Pew Global Attitudes Project, Among Wealthy Nations U.S. Stands Alone in its Embrace of Religion (Dec. 19, 2002). Those who would renegotiate the boundaries between church and state must therefore answer a difficult question: Why would we trade a system that has served us so well for one that has served others so poorly?

McCreary County, Ky. v. American Civil Liberties Union of Ky., 545 U.S. 844, 882 (2005). Can the system that has served us so well continue to work in an era of new religious diversity?

In *American Grace: How Religion Divides and Unites Us* (2010), political scientists Robert D. Putnam & David E. Campbell provide a broad description and analysis of "old and new" religion in American culture. One feature that the authors emphasize is the paradox that although "Americans have become polarized along religious lines" and the "moderate religious middle" is shrinking, nonetheless Americans enjoy a high degree of peaceful religious pluralism and tolerance. Id. at 3.

Putnam and Campbell describe the years since the 1950s as characterized by three seismic phases including a shock and two aftershocks. The shock: during the long 1960s the Baby Boom generation departed from conventional religion and morality and commentators proclaimed "God is dead." The first aftershock (1970s and 1980s): the rise of religious conservatism in the Religious Right, primarily due to concerns about sexual immorality, especially an increase in premarital sex. Politicians who took advantage of this atmosphere to develop a religious politics triggered the second aftershock (1990s and 2000s): youth disaffection with organized religion because it is too political and judgmental. This period includes the growth in numbers of the Nones.

The last chapter of the book concludes that "America's grace" has been to maintain religious pluralism even with the growth of religious polarization. How have Americans accomplished this? "By creating a web of interlocking personal relationships among people of many different faiths" (550). The authors argue that Americans have now embraced religious diversity instead of merely tolerating it, and that this is due in part to the

U.S. Constitution. They also identify an "Aunt Susan principle"; if your aunt is of another religion, you are more likely to tolerate that religion. As Americans are more frequently exposed to persons of diverse religion, they become more tolerant. Do you agree?

Sociologist Mark Chaves, in *American Religion: Contemporary Trends* (2011) also mentions that, despite religious polarization in American politics, Americans' increasing daily interactions with friends and family members of diverse religious backgrounds have left them more tolerant of other religions. *American Religion* is a concise book that meets its goal of presenting "key big-picture changes in American religion since 1972" in an accessible manner. Id. at 3. According to Chaves, statistics show that "talk of increased religiosity in the United States in recent decades is baseless" and that there is a small trend toward decreased religious belief in America. Id. at 15.

5.   *The World's Religions and Global Religion.* Although Nones are on the rise in the United States, the religiously unaffiliated are projected to decline as a share of the world's population in the decades ahead because their net growth through religious switching will be more than offset by higher childbearing among the younger affiliated population. The religiously unaffiliated made up 16.4% of the world's population in 2010 and are expected to make up 13.2% of the world's population in 2050. See Conrad Hackett et al., The Future Size of Religious Affiliated and Unaffiliated Populations, 32 Demographic Research 829 (2015), at http://www.demographic-research.org/Volumes/Vol32/27/.

Another Pew Forum study expects the number of Muslims worldwide to nearly equal the number of Christians by 2050. Islam is expected to be the fastest growing religion in the world. See Pew Research Center, Number of Muslims Worldwide Expected to Nearly Equal Number of Christians by 2050; Religiously Unaffiliated Will Make Up Declining Share of World's Population, Apr. 2, 2015, at http://www.pewforum.org/2015/04/02/number-of-muslims-worldwide-expected-to-nearly-equal-number-of-christians-by-2050-religiously-unaffiliated-will-make-up-declining-share-of-worlds-population/. Because all religions (except Buddhism) are expected to grow, atheists, agnostics and Nones will become a declining share of the world's population. The projections suggest that, if current trends continue, by 2050:

In Europe, Muslims will make up 10% of the overall population.

India will retain a Hindu majority but also will have the largest Muslim population of any country in the world, surpassing Indonesia.

In the United States, Christians will decline from more than three-quarters of the population in 2010 to two-thirds in 2050, and Judaism will no longer be the largest non-Christian religion. Muslims will be more numerous in the U.S. than people who identify as Jewish on the basis of religion.

Four out of every 10 Christians in the world will live in sub-Saharan Africa.

The global Buddhist population is expected to remain fairly stable because of low fertility rates and aging populations in countries such as China, Thailand and Japan.

Jews, the smallest religious group for which separate projections were made, are expected to grow 16%, from a little less than 14 million in 2010 to 16.1 million worldwide in 2050.

Id. How do you think these trends will affect international religious freedom?

6. *Global Restrictions on Religion.* Religious terrorism increased from 2013 to 2014 while both governmental restrictions on religion and social hostilities among private parties involving religion decreased slightly world-wide. See Pew Research Center, Trends in Global Restrictions on Religion (Jun. 23, 2016). Countries with high or very high levels of governmental restrictions dropped from 28% to 24%. Id. Countries with social hostilities involving religion dropped from 27% to 23%. Id. "Among the world's 25 most populous countries, the highest overall restrictions on religion were in Egypt, Indonesia, Pakistan, Russia and Turkey, where both the government and society at large imposed numerous limits on religious beliefs and practices. China had the highest level of government restrictions in 2014, while Pakistan had the highest level of social hostilities involving religion." In contrast, Brazil, the Democratic Republic of the Congo, Japan, the Philippines, and South Africa have the lowest levels of restrictions and hostilities. Id. Christians and Muslims faced harassment in the largest number of countries, and harassment against Jews continued an 8-year rise. Religion-led terrorism led to injuries or deaths in 40 countries in 2012, 51 countries in 2013, and 60 countries in 2014.

The United States was one of three countries with the largest increase in social hostilities involving religion. This increase was due primarily to a growth in anti-Semitic activities. 58% of religious hate crimes in the U.S. were anti-Jewish and 16% were anti-Muslim. Id. What do you think explains these trends?

7. *Future and Past of Global Religion.* The early settlers came to America to escape religious persecution, see Everson v. Board of Education of Ewing Township, 330 U.S. 1, 8–9 (1947), and numerous groups have followed them here for that reason. According to Justice O'Connor, "[o]ur guiding principle has been James Madison's—that '[t]he Religion . . . of every man must be left to the conviction and conscience of every man.' Memorial and Remonstrance Against Religious Assessments, 2 Writings of James Madison 183, 184 (G. Hunt ed. 1901)." Can that guiding principle be enforced worldwide? Should it be?

Scholars of religion now discuss the implications of globalization for religion. As Professor Ninian Smart, whose description of religion you studied in Chapter 1, explained in an essay written shortly before his death:

> As any acquaintance with the history of religions will show, especially in the last four hundred years, faiths alter. There are evolutionary changes in their rituals, their societal emplacement, their doctrines, and perhaps especially their ethics and laws. One of the great myths is that religion is always the same: that an evangelical from Missouri has the same values as the Apostle Paul, for example. People dearly believe that they believe exactly as did their forefathers. They may of course get the heart of their faith essentially right—they may conform to the basic values of the great leaders and creeds of their traditions. But this does not mean that the religions have not changed. In a global world they are probably doing so more than ever.

Ninian Smart, The Global Future of Religion, in Mark Juergensmeyer, ed. The Oxford Handbook of Global Religions 625 (2006). Smart explored the irony that the same global forces of communication and technology that allow religions to learn from and interact positively with each other have also permitted "more intense consolidation" of other traditions. Id. at 628. Global religion therefore allows for both continuity and change in the world's religions.

What values could govern a world of global religion? See id. at 629 (a common ideology might include nonviolence, democracy, and "some overarching sense of order and respect."). Smart concluded:

> The threat of globalization is that it tries to get everyone doing the same thing and thinking alike. In some ways the world is becoming too compact. The idea of a global higher order has the advantage of not imposing a single ethic or ethos on the rest of the world, except for the higher order pattern of civility.

Id. at 630. Do you think the system devised by James Madison will contribute to this higher order, or will a new constitutional system be necessary?

INDEX

References are to Pages